TRATEGIC MANAGEMENT
Competitiveness & Globalization

Concepts
12e

Michael A. Hitt
Texas A&M University
and
Texas Christian University

R. Duane Ireland
Texas A&M University

Robert E. Hoskisson
Rice University

CENGAGE
Learning

Australia • Brazil • Japan • Korea • Mexico • Singapore • Spain • United Kingdom • United States

CENGAGE
Learning

Strategic Management: Competitiveness &
Globalization: Concepts, **12e**

**Michael A. Hitt, R. Duane Ireland, and
Robert E. Hoskisson**

Vice President, General Manager, Social
Science & Qualitative Business:
Erin Joyner

Product Director: Jason Fremder

Senior Product Manager: Scott Person

Content Developer: Tara Singer

Product Assistant: Brian Pierce

Marketing Director: Kristen Hurd

Marketing Manager: Emily Horowitz

Marketing Coordinator: Christopher Walz

Senior Content Project Manager: Kim
Kusnerak

Manufacturing Planner: Ron Montgomery

Production Service: Cenveo Publisher
Services

Senior Art Director: Linda May

Cover/Internal Designer: Tippy McIntosh

Cover Image: © RomanOkopny/Getty
Images

Intellectual Property

Analyst: Diane Garrity

Project Manager: Sarah Shainwald

Strategic Focus: © RomanOkopny/Getty
Images

Watercolor opener: © BerSonnE/Getty
Images

> For product information and technology assistance, contact us at
> **Cengage Learning Customer & Sales Support, 1-800-354-9706**
> For permission to use material from this text or product,
> submit all requests online at **www.cengage.com/permissions**
> Further permissions questions can be emailed to
> **permissionrequest@cengage.com**

Unless otherwise noted all items © Cengage Learning.

Library of Congress Control Number: 2015955692

ISBN: 978-1-305-50220-8

Cengage Learning
20 Channel Center Street
Boston, MA 02210
USA

Cengage Learning is a leading provider of customized learning solutions
with employees residing in nearly 40 different countries and sales in
more than 125 countries around the world. Find your local representative
at **www.cengage.com.**

Cengage Learning products are represented in Canada
by Nelson Education, Ltd.

To learn more about Cengage Learning Solutions,
visit **www.cengage.com**

Purchase any of our products at your local college store or
at our preferred online store **www.cengagebrain.com**

Printed in Canada
Print Number: 01   Print Year: 2016

STRATEGIC MANAGEMENT
Competitiveness & Globalization

Concepts

12e

To My Family:

I love each and every one of you. Thank you for all of your love and support.

— **MICHAEL, DAD, PAPA**

To Mary Ann:

"Now everyone dreams of a love lasting and true." This was my dream that you have completely fulfilled. Thank you for all of the love, support, and encouragement throughout our life together.

— **R. DUANE IRELAND**

To Kathy:

My love for you is eternal, and I hope that we can be eternally together. Thanks for all the support and love you've given me throughout my life.

— **BOB**

Brief Contents

Contents

7: Merger and Acquisition Strategies 204

Opening Case: Mergers and Acquisitions: Prominent Strategies for Firms Seeking to Enhance Their Performance 205

Part 3: Strategic Actions: Strategy Implementation 308

10: Corporate Governance 308

11: Organizational Structure and Controls 344

Preface

Our goal in writing each edition of this book is to present a new, up-to-date standard for explaining the strategic management process. To reach this goal with the 12th edition of our market-leading text, we again present you with an intellectually rich yet thoroughly practical analysis of strategic management.

With each new edition, we work hard to achieve the goal of maintaining the standard that we established for presenting strategic management knowledge in a readable style. To prepare for each new edition, we carefully study the most recent academic research to ensure that the content about strategic management that we present to you is up to date and accurate. In addition, we continuously read articles appearing in many different and widely read business publications (e.g., *Wall Street Journal, Bloomberg Businessweek, Fortune, Financial Times, Fast Company,* and *Forbes,* to name a few). We also study postings through social media (such as blogs) given their increasing use as channels of information distribution. By studying a wide array of sources, we are able to identify valuable examples of how companies are using (or not using) the strategic management process. Though many of the hundreds of companies that we discuss in the book will be quite familiar, some will likely be new to you. One reason for this is that we use examples of companies from around the world to demonstrate the globalized nature of business operations. To maximize your opportunities to learn as you read and think about how actual companies use strategic management tools, techniques, and concepts (based on the most current research), we emphasize a lively and user-friendly writing style. To facilitate learning, we use an Analysis-Strategy-Performance framework that is explained in Chapter 1 and referenced throughout the book.

Several *characteristics* of this 12th edition of our book are designed to enhance your learning experience:

- First, this book presents you with the most comprehensive and thorough coverage of strategic management that is available in the market.
- The research used in this book is drawn from the "classics" as well as the most recent contributions to the strategic management literature. The historically significant "classic" research provides the foundation for much of what is known about strategic management, while the most recent contributions reveal insights about how to effectively use strategic management in the complex, global business environment in which firms now compete. Our book also presents you with many up-to-date examples of how firms use the strategic management tools, techniques, and concepts that prominent researchers have developed. Indeed, although this book is grounded in the relevant theory and current research, it also is strongly application oriented and presents you, our readers, with a large number of examples and applications of strategic management concepts, techniques, and tools. In this edition, for example, we examine more than 600 companies to describe the use of strategic management. Collectively, no other strategic management book presents you with the *combination* of useful and insightful *research* and *applications* in a wide variety of organizations as does this text.

Company examples you will find in this edition range from large U.S.-based firms such as Apple, Amazon.com, McDonald's, Starbucks, Walmart, Walt Disney, General Electric, Intel, American Express, Coca-Cola, Google, Target, United Technologies, Kellogg, DuPont, Marriott, and Whole Foods. In addition, we examine firms based in countries other than the United States such as Sony, Aldi, Honda, Tata Consultancy, Alibaba, IKEA, Lenova, Luxottica, and Samsung. As these lists suggest, the firms examined in this book compete in a wide range of industries and produce a diverse set of goods and services.

■ We use the ideas of many prominent scholars (e.g., Ron Adner, Rajshree Agarwal, Gautam Ahuja, Raffi Amit, Africa Arino, Jay Barney, Paul Beamish, Peter Buckley, Ming-Jer Chen, Russ Coff, Rich D'Aveni, Kathy Eisenhardt, Gerry George, Javier Gimeno, Luis Gomez-Mejia, Melissa Graebner, Ranjay Gulati, Don Hambrick, Connie Helfat, Amy Hillman, Tomas Hult, Dave Ketchen, Dovev Lavie, Yadong Luo, Shige Makino, Costas Markides, Anita McGahan, Danny Miller, Will Mitchell, Margie Peteraf, Michael Porter, Nandini Rajagopalan, Jeff Reuer, Joan Ricart, Richard Rumelt, David Sirmon, Ken Smith, Steve Tallman, David Teece, Michael Tushman, Margarethe Wiersema, Oliver Williamson, Mike Wright, Anthea Zhang, and Ed Zajac) to shape the discussion of *what* strategic management is. We describe the practices of prominent executives and practitioners (e.g., Mary Barra, Jack Ma, Reed Hastings, Howard Schultz, John Mackey, Yang Yuanqing, Angela Ahrendt, Marilyn Hewson, Jeff Immelt, Ellen Kullman, Elon Musk, Paul Pullman, Li Ka-Shing, Karen Patz, and many others) to help us describe *how* strategic management is used in many types of organizations.

The authors of this book are also active scholars. We conduct research on a number of strategic management topics. Our interest in doing so is to contribute to the strategic management literature and to better understand how to effectively apply strategic management tools, techniques, and concepts to increase organizational performance. Thus, our own research is integrated in the appropriate chapters along with the research of numerous other scholars, some of whom are noted above.

In addition to our book's *characteristics,* there are some specific *features* and *revisions* that we have made in this 12th edition that we are pleased to highlight for you:

■ **New Opening Cases and Strategic Focus Segments.** We continue our tradition of providing all-new Opening Cases and Strategic Focus segments! Many deal with companies located outside North America. In addition, all of the company-specific examples included in each chapter are either new or substantially updated. Through all of these venues, we present you with a wealth of examples of how actual organizations, most of which compete internationally as well as in their home markets, use the strategic management process for the purpose of outperforming rivals and increasing their performance.

■ **New Mini-Cases** have been added that demonstrate how companies deal with major issues highlighted in the text. There are 13 of these cases, one for each chapter, although some of them can overlap with other chapter content. Students will like their conciseness, but they likewise provide rich content that can serve as a catalyst for individual or group analysis and class discussion. Each Mini-Case is followed by a set of questions to guide analysis and discussion.

■ **More than 1,200 new references** from 2014 and 2015 are included in the chapters' endnotes. We used the materials associated with these references to support new material added or current strategic management concepts that are included in this edition. In addition to demonstrating the classic and recent research from which we draw our material, the large number of references supporting the book's contents allow us to integrate cutting-edge research and thinking into a presentation of strategic management tools, techniques, and concepts.

- **New content** was added to several chapters. Examples include the strategic ecosystem such as the one used by Apple with its "ecosystem of app producers" (Chapters 1 and 4), sustainable physical environment (Chapter 3), mentoring new CEOs (Chapter 12), strategic leadership in family owned/controlled companies (Chapter 12), and acquisitions and innovation, open innovations, and managing the innovation portfolio (Chapters 4 and 13).
- **Updated information** is provided in several chapters. Examples include the stakeholder host communities (Chapter 1), all new and current demographic data (e.g., ethnic mix, geographic distribution) that describe the economic environment (Chapter 2), the general partner strategies of private equity firms (Chapter 7), information from the *World Economic Forum Competitiveness Report* regarding political risks of international investments (Chapter 8), updates about corporate governance practices being used in different countries (Chapter 10), updated data about the number of internal and external CEO selections occurring in companies today (Chapter 12), a ranking of countries by the amount of their entrepreneurial activities (Chapter 13), and a ranking of companies on their total innovation output (Chapter 13).
- **An Exceptional Balance** between current research and up-to-date applications of strategic management concepts in actual organizations located throughout the world. The content has not only the best research documentation but also the largest number of effective real-world examples to help active learners understand the different types of strategies organizations use to achieve their vision and mission and to outperform rivals.
- **Twenty Cases** are included in this edition. Offering an effective mix of organizations headquartered or based in North America and a number of other countries as well, the cases deal with contemporary and highly important topics. These cases are available in the MindTap digital learning suite. Many of the cases have full financial data (the analyses of which are in the Case Notes that are available to instructors). These timely cases present active learners with opportunities to apply the strategic management process and understand organizational conditions and contexts and to make appropriate recommendations to deal with critical concerns. Access the cases in the MindTap and customize your selection to best suit the needs of your course.

Supplements to Accompany This Text

MindTap. MindTap is the digital learning solution that helps instructors engage students and help them to become tomorrow's strategic leaders. All activities are designed to teach students to problem-solve and think like leaders. Through these activities and real-time course analytics, and an accessible reader, MindTap helps you turn cookie cutter into cutting edge, apathy into engagement, and memorizers into higher-level thinkers.

Customized to the specific needs of this course, activities are built to facilitate mastery of chapter content. We've addressed case analysis from cornerstone to capstone with a functional area diagnostic of prior knowledge, directed cases, branching activities, multimedia presentations of real-world companies facing strategic decisions, and a collaborative environment in which students can complete group case analysis projects together synchronously.

Instructor Website. Access important teaching resources on this companion website. For your convenience, you can download electronic versions of the instructor supplements from the password-protected section of the site, including Instructor's Resource

Manual, Comprehensive Case Notes, Cognero Testing, Word Test Bank files, PowerPoint® slides, and Video Segments and Guide. To access these additional course materials and companion resources, please visit www.cengagebrain.com.

▪ **Instructor's Resource Manual.** The Instructor's Resource Manual, organized around each chapter's knowledge objectives, includes teaching ideas for each chapter and how to reinforce essential principles with extra examples. This support product includes lecture outlines and detailed guides to integrating the MindTap activities into your course with instructions for using each chapter's experiential exercises, branching, and directed cases. Finally, we provide outlines and guidance to help you customize the collaborative work environment and case analysis project to incorporate your approach to case analysis, including creative ideas for using this feature throughout your course for the most powerful learning experience for your class.

▪ **Case Notes.** These notes include directed assignments, financial analyses, and thorough discussion and exposition of issues in the case. Select cases also have assessment rubrics tied to National Standards (AACSB outcomes) that can be used for grading each case. The Case Notes provide consistent and thorough support for instructors, following the method espoused by the author team for preparing an effective case analysis.

▪ **Cognero.** This program is easy-to-use test-creation software that is compatible with Microsoft Windows. Instructors can add or edit questions, instructions, and answers, and select questions by previewing them on the screen, selecting them randomly, or selecting them by number. Instructors can also create and administer quizzes online, whether over the Internet, a local area network (LAN), or a wide area network (WAN).

▪ **Test Bank.** Thoroughly revised and enhanced, test bank questions are linked to each chapter's knowledge objectives and are ranked by difficulty and question type. We provide an ample number of application questions throughout, and we have also retained scenario-based questions as a means of adding in-depth problem-solving questions. The questions are also tagged to National Standards (AACSB outcomes), Bloom's Taxonomy, and the Dierdorff/Rubin metrics.

▪ **PowerPoints®.** An all-new PowerPoint presentation, created for the 12th edition, provides support for lectures, emphasizing key concepts, key terms, and instructive graphics.

▪ **Video Segments.** A collection of 13 BBC videos has been included in the MindTap Learning Path. These new videos are short, compelling, and timely illustrations of today's management world. They are available on the DVD and Instructor website. Detailed case write-ups, including questions and suggested answers, appear in the Instructor's Resource Manual and Video Guide.

Cengage Learning Write Experience 3.0. This new technology is the first in higher education to offer students the opportunity to improve their writing and analytical skills without adding to *your* workload. Offered through an exclusive agreement with Vantage Learning, creator of the software used for GMAT essay grading, Write Experience evaluates students' answers to a select set of assignments for writing for voice, style, format, and originality. We have trained new prompts for this edition!

Micromatic Strategic Management Simulation (for bundles only). The Micromatic Business Simulation Game allows students to decide their company's mission, goals, policies, and strategies. Student teams make their decisions on a quarter-by-quarter basis, determining price, sales and promotion budgets, operations decisions, and financing requirements. Each decision round requires students to make approximately 100 decisions. Students can play in teams or play alone, compete against other players or the computer, or use Micromatic for practice, tournaments, or assessment. You can control any business simulation element you wish, leaving the rest alone if you desire. Because of the number and type of decisions the student users must make, Micromatic is classified as a medium to complex business simulation game. This helps students understand how the functional areas of a business fit together without being bogged down in needless detail and provides students with an excellent capstone experience in decision making.

Smartsims (for bundles only). MikesBikes Advanced is a premier strategy simulation providing students with the unique opportunity to evaluate, plan, and implement strategy as they manage their own company while competing online against other students within their course. Students from the management team of a bicycle manufacturing company make all the key functional decisions involving price, marketing, distribution, finance, operations, HR, and R&D. They formulate a comprehensive strategy, starting with their existing product, and then adapt the strategy as they develop new products for emerging markets. Through the Smartsims easy-to-use interface, students are taught the cross-functional disciplines of business and how the development and implementation of strategy involves these disciplines. The competitive nature of MikesBikes encourages involvement and learning in a way that no other teaching methodology can, and your students will have fun in the process!

Acknowledgments

We express our appreciation for the excellent support received from our editorial and production team at Cengage Learning. We especially wish to thank Scott Person, our Senior Product Manager, and Tara Singer, our Content Developer. We are grateful for their dedication, commitment, and outstanding contributions to the development and publication of this book and its package of support materials.

We are highly indebted to all of the reviewers of past editions. Their comments have provided a great deal of insight in the preparation of this current edition:

Jay Azriel
York College of Pennsylvania

Lana Belousova
Suffolk University

Ruben Boling
North Georgia University

Matthias Bollmus
Carroll University

Erich Brockmann
University of New Orleans

David Cadden
Quinnipiac University

Ken Chadwick
Nicholls State University

Bruce H. Charnov
Hofstra University

Jay Chok
Keck Graduate Institute, Claremont Colleges

Peter Clement
State University of New York–Delhi

Terry Coalter
Northwest Missouri University

James Cordeiro
SUNY Brockport

Deborah de Lange
Suffolk University

Irem Demirkan
Northeastern University

Dev Dutta
University of New Hampshire

Scott Elston
Iowa State University

Harold Fraser
California State University–Fullerton

Robert Goldberg
Northeastern University

Monica Gordillo
Iowa State University

George Griffin
Spring Arbor University

Susan Hansen
University of Wisconsin–Platteville

Glenn Hoetker
Arizona State University

James Hoyt
Troy University

Miriam Huddleston
Harford Community College

Carol Jacobson
Purdue University

James Katzenstein
California State University, Dominguez Hills

Robert Keidel
Drexel University

Nancy E. Landrum
University of Arkansas at Little Rock

Mina Lee
Xavier University

Patrice Luoma
Quinnipiac University

Mzamo Mangaliso
University of Massachusetts–Amherst

Michele K. Masterfano
Drexel University

James McClain
California State University–Fullerton

Jean McGuire
Louisiana State University

John McIntyre
Georgia Tech

Rick McPherson
University of Washington

Karen Middleton
Texas A&M–Corpus Christi

Raza Mir
William Paterson University

Martina Musteen
San Diego State University

Louise Nemanich
Arizona State University

Frank Novakowski
Davenport University

Consuelo M. Ramirez
University of Texas at San Antonio

Barbara Ribbens
Western Illinois University

Jason Ridge
Clemson University

William Roering
Michigan State University

Manjula S. Salimath
University of North Texas

Deepak Sethi
Old Dominion University

Manisha Singal
Virginia Tech

Warren Stone
University of Arkansas at Little Rock

Elisabeth Teal
University of N. Georgia

Jill Thomas Jorgensen
Lewis and Clark State College

Len J. Trevino
Washington State University

Edward Ward
Saint Cloud State University

Marta Szabo White
Georgia State University

Michael L. Williams
Michigan State University

Diana J. Wong-MingJi
Eastern Michigan University

Patricia A. Worsham
California State Polytechnic University, Pomona

William J. Worthington
Baylor University

Wilson Zehr
Concordia University

Michael A. Hitt
R. Duane Ireland
Robert E. Hoskisson

About the Authors

Michael A. Hitt

Michael Hitt is a University Distinguished Professor Emeritus at Texas A&M University and a Distinguished Research Fellow at Texas Christian University. Dr. Hitt received his Ph.D. from the University of Colorado. He has coauthored or coedited 27 books and authored or coauthored many journal articles. A recent article listed him as one of the 10 most cited authors in management over a 25-year period. The *Times Higher Education 2010* listed him among the top scholars in economics, finance, and management based on the number of highly cited articles he has authored. A recent article in the *Academy of Management Perspectives* lists him as one of the top two management scholars in terms of the combined impact of his work both inside (i.e., citations in scholarly journals) and outside of academia. He has served on the editorial review boards of multiple journals and is a former editor of the *Academy of Management Journal* and a former coeditor of the *Strategic Entrepreneurship Journal*. He received the 1996 Award for Outstanding Academic Contributions to Competitiveness and the 1999 Award for Outstanding Intellectual Contributions to Competitiveness Research from the American Society for Competitiveness. He is a fellow in the Academy of Management and in the Strategic Management Society, a research fellow in the Global Consortium of Entrepreneurship Centers, and received an honorary doctorate from the Universidad Carlos III de Madrid. He is a former president of both the Academy of Management and of the Strategic Management Society and a member of the Academy of Management's Journals' Hall of Fame. He received awards for the best article published in the *Academy of Management Executive* (1999), *Academy of Management Journal* (2000), *Journal of Management* (2006), and *Family Business Review* (2012). In 2001, he received the Irwin Outstanding Educator Award and the Distinguished Service Award from the Academy of Management. In 2004, Dr. Hitt was awarded the Best Paper Prize by the Strategic Management Society. In 2006, he received the Falcone Distinguished Entrepreneurship Scholar Award from Syracuse University. In 2014 and 2015, Dr. Hitt was listed as a Thomson Reuters Highly Cited Researcher (a listing of the world's most influential researchers), and he was also listed as one of The World's Most Influential Scientific Minds (a listing of the top cited researchers in science around the globe).

R. Duane Ireland

R. Duane Ireland is a University Distinguished Professor and holder of the Conn Chair in New Ventures Leadership in the Mays Business School, Texas A&M University. Dr. Ireland teaches strategic management courses at all levels. He has more than 200 publications, including approximately 25 books. His research, which focuses on diversification, innovation, corporate entrepreneurship, strategic entrepreneurship, and the informal economy, has been published in an array of journals. He has served as a member of multiple editorial review boards and is a former editor of the *Academy of Management Journal*. He has been a guest editor for 12 special issues of journals. He is a past president of the Academy of Management. Dr. Ireland is a fellow of the Academy of Management and a fellow of the Strategic Management Society. He is a research fellow in the Global Consortium of Entrepreneurship Centers and received an award in 1999 for Outstanding Intellectual Contributions to Competitiveness Research from the American Society for Competitiveness. He received the Falcone Distinguished Entrepreneurship Scholar Award from Syracuse University in 2005, the USASBE Scholar in Corporate Entrepreneurship Award from USASBE in 2004, and the Riata Distinguished Entrepreneurship Scholar award from Oklahoma State University in 2014. He received awards for the best article published in *Academy of Management Executive* (1999), the *Academy of Management Journal* (2000), and the *Journal of Applied Management and Entrepreneurship* (2010). He received an Association of Former Students Distinguished Achievement Award for Research from Texas A&M University (2012). In 2014 and 2015, Dr. Ireland was listed as a Thomson Reuters Highly Cited Researcher (a listing of the world's most influential researchers), and he was also listed as one of The World's Most Influential Scientific Minds (a listing of the top cited researchers in science around the globe).

Robert E. Hoskisson

Robert E. Hoskisson is the George R. Brown Chair of Strategic Management at the Jesse H. Jones Graduate School of Business, Rice University. Dr. Hoskisson received his Ph.D. from the University of California-Irvine. His research topics focus on corporate governance, acquisitions and divestitures, corporate and international diversification, and cooperative strategy. He teaches courses in corporate and international strategic management, cooperative strategy, and strategy consulting. He has coauthored 26 books, including recent books on business strategy and competitive advantage. Dr. Hoskisson has served on several editorial boards for such publications as the *Strategic Management Journal* (current Associate Editor), *Academy of Management Journal* (Consulting Editor), *Journal of International Business Studies* (Consulting Editor), *Journal of Management* (Associate Editor) and *Organization Science*. His research has appeared in over 130 publications, including the *Strategic Management Journal, Academy of Management Journal, Academy of Management Review, Organization Science, Journal of Management, Academy of Management Perspective, Academy of Management Executive, Journal of Management Studies, Journal of International Business Studies, Journal of Business Venturing, Entrepreneurship Theory and Practice, California Management Review,* and *Journal of World Business*. Dr. Hoskisson is a fellow of the Academy of Management and a charter member of the Academy of Management Journal's Hall of Fame. He is also a fellow of the Strategic Management Society and has received awards from the American Society for Competitiveness and the William G. Dyer Alumni award from the Marriott School of Management, Brigham Young University. He completed three years of service as a Representative-at-Large on the Board of Governors of the Academy of Management. Currently, he serves as Past President of the Strategic Management Society, and thereby serves on the Executive Committee of its Board of Directors.

1

Strategic Management and Strategic Competitiveness

Studying this chapter should provide you with the strategic management knowledge needed to:

1-1   Define strategic competitiveness, strategy, competitive advantage, above-average returns, and the strategic management process.

1-2   Describe the competitive landscape and explain how globalization and technological changes shape it.

1-3   Use the industrial organization (I/O) model to explain how firms can earn above-average returns.

1-4   Use the resource-based model to explain how firms can earn above-average returns.

1-5   Describe vision and mission and discuss their value.

1-6   Define stakeholders and describe their ability to influence organizations.

1-7   Describe the work of strategic leaders.

1-8   Explain the strategic management process.

ALIBABA: AN ONLINE COLOSSUS IN CHINA GOES GLOBAL

China now has the world's largest number of internet users and Alibaba is China's largest ecommerce company (23 percent owned by Yahoo and 36 percent owned by Japan's SoftBank). In 2014, when Alibaba completed its initial public offering (IPO) on the New York Stock Exchange, it immediately became worth more than Amazon and eBay combined and has a larger market capitalization than Walmart. Transactions of goods on Alibaba's websites account for more than 2 percent of China's GDP in 2012. Comparatively, Walmart's sales account for 0.03 percent of U.S. GDP in 2012. Alibaba's presence has turned China into the world's second largest ecommerce market after the United States. Chinese consumers purchase products on Tmall, a consumer shopping site on Alibaba analogous to a department store and similar to Amazon. Because of China's vast size and underdeveloped consumer market, it has few national mainland malls or brick and mortar department store chains.

As such, the presence of Alibaba is stimulating consumption that would not otherwise take place in China. Furthermore, Alibaba's presence changed consumer buying habits, especially in third- and fourth-tier (e.g., smaller and more geographically remote) cities because it gives consumers access to items that they could not previously obtain locally.

Alibaba Drone.PNG

BIDNESS ETC

Taobao is another website owned by Alibaba and is comparable to eBay in the United States. On Taobao, Alibaba does not stock or sell its own goods but rather provides platforms where manufacturers, resellers, and other middle-men open online storefronts. Larger consumer branded products prefer Tmall because Alibaba's policies promote this site more heavily and fraudulent brands are less likely to be found on this site. For instance, popular brands such as Prada handbags must provide evidence that they are a licensed distributor before they are allowed to sell on Tmall. Taobao is more focused on small sellers; it has 6 million registered sellers with a vast range in size.

Given these two websites, Alibaba is the easiest way for foreign retailers to enter the Chinese market because it has such reach. Online sales account for 90 percent of marketplace sales in China, compared with 24 percent for the United States in 2014. Accordingly, Alibaba provides the easiest way to enter the Chinese market for foreign retailers due the large access to consumers available through Alibaba's websites. Alibaba's websites also give smaller Chinese manufacturers the opportunity to increase domestic sales because of Alibaba's reach. For example, Weighing Apparatus Group, originally a supplier of household and industrial scales for Bed Bath & Beyond, set up a website on Taobao in 2009. In 2014, one-fifth of its domestic sales now flow through its Taobao online storefront, allowing it to move beyond being only a supplier for other firm's branded products.

Alibaba through its Alipay system is working on a joint venture with Apple to provide back-end services for the Apple Pay payment system allowing iPhone users in China to pay for goods with Apple Pay using their Alipay accounts. This approach is fostering an improved mobile online strategy for Alibaba. It also facilitates better service for online Apple iPhone users who desire to browse and purchase on Alibaba websites.

Fraudulent goods can be an important strategic issue in China because of previous product liability suits from banned or recalled goods sold to U.S. consumers.

As such, Alibaba is collaborating with the United States Consumer Product Safety Commission to improve its credibility among U.S. consumers by helping to ban sale of fake and fraudulently branded or recalled goods. This is also facilitating Alibaba's global access strategy.

Alibaba is also moving into online media content and streaming video services. In 2014, it announced its acquisition of ChinaVision Media, producers or co-producers of films including "Crouching Tiger, Hidden Dragon" and "Breaking the Silence." Just as Amazon and Netflix are producing their own media content, Alibaba is moving in this direction as well, as it competes with other service providers such as Tencent and Baidu in web communications and broadcasting in China. Getting its strategies right in the local domestic Chines market as well as internationally is key to Alibaba's success.

Sources: D. Tsuruoka, 2015, Alibaba blocks sale of unsafe goods to U.S. shoppers, *Investor's Business Daily*, www.investorsbusinessdaily.com, Jan 13; S. Cendrowski, 2014, Alibaba's Maggie Wu and Lucy Peng: The dynamic duo behind the IPO, *Fortune*, www.fortune.com, September 17; R. Flannery, 2014, China media entrepreneur's fortune soars on Alibaba investment, *Forbes*, www.forbes.com, March 12; C. Larson, 2014, In China its meet me at Tmall, *Bloomberg Businessweek*, www.bloombergbusinessweek.com, September 11.

As we see from the Opening Case, Alibaba is highly successful because its strategy in China has allowed it to have a massive impact in regard to online sales in a large emerging economy. It is now seeking to grow globally and gain widespread name/brand recognition through its 2014 IPO in New York. These attributes have enhanced its ability to compete in global online markets. Therefore, we can conclude that Alibaba has achieved *strategic competitiveness*. It clearly has been able to earn *above-average returns*, at least, domestically. Yet Alibaba has received its share of criticism because of its perceived contribution to the sale of fraudulent goods. However, it is addressing this issue through its collaboration with the United States Consumer Product Safety Commission. The top management of Alibaba has used the strategic management process (see Figure 1.1) as the foundation for the commitments, decisions, and actions they took to pursue strategic competitiveness and above-average returns. The strategic management process is fully explained in this book. We introduce you to this process in the next few paragraphs.

Strategic competitiveness is achieved when a firm successfully formulates and implements a value-creating strategy. A **strategy** is an integrated and coordinated set of commitments and actions designed to exploit core competencies and gain a competitive advantage. When choosing a strategy, firms make choices among competing alternatives as the pathway for deciding how they will pursue strategic competitiveness. In this sense, the chosen strategy indicates what the firm *will do* as well as what the firm *will not do*.

As explained in the Opening Case, Alibaba has been a leader in its industry as one of the most successful facilitators of online sales in China and is now seeking to become a successful global business. However, in doing so it must respond to its changing environment. In fact, to adapt to local environments, it sometimes makes major changes. For example, it is coordinating with Apple Pay to improve access for the high number iPhones that Apple is now selling in China.

A firm has a **competitive advantage** "when it implements a strategy that creates superior value for customers and that its competitors are unable to duplicate or find too costly to imitate."[1] An organization can be confident that its strategy has resulted in one or more useful competitive advantages only after competitors' efforts to duplicate its strategy have ceased or failed. In addition, firms must understand that no competitive advantage is permanent.[2] The speed with which competitors are able to acquire the skills

Strategic competitiveness is achieved when a firm successfully formulates and implements a value creating strategy.

A **strategy** is an integrated and coordinated set of commitments and actions designed to exploit core competencies and gain a competitive advantage.

A firm has a **competitive advantage** when it implements a strategy that creates superior value for customers and that competitors are unable to duplicate or find it too costly to try to imitate.

Figure 1.1 The Strategic Management Process

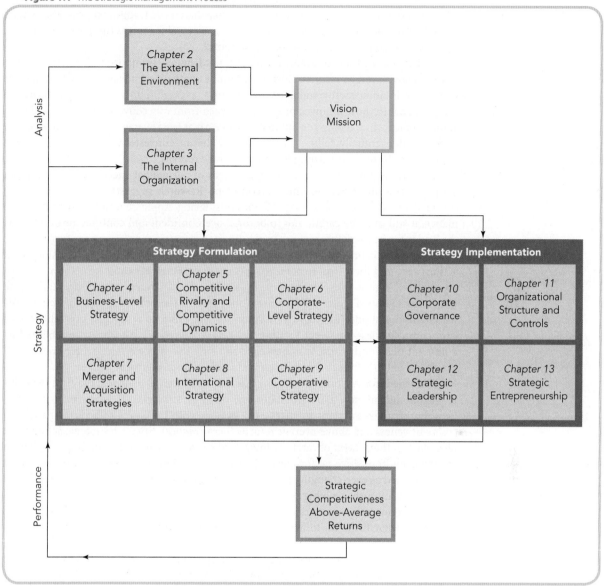

needed to duplicate the benefits of a firm's value-creating strategy determines how long the competitive advantage will last.[3]

Above-average returns are returns in excess of what an investor expects to earn from other investments with a similar amount of risk. **Risk** is an investor's uncertainty about the economic gains or losses that will result from a particular investment. The most successful companies learn how to effectively manage risk.[4] Effectively managing risks reduces investors' uncertainty about the results of their investment.[5] Returns are often measured in terms of accounting figures, such as return on assets, return on equity, or return on sales. Alternatively, returns can be measured on the basis of stock market returns, such as monthly returns (the end-of-the-period stock price minus the beginning stock price divided by the beginning stock price, yielding a percentage return).[6]

Above-average returns are returns in excess of what an investor expects to earn from other investments with a similar amount of risk

Risk is an investor's uncertainty about the economic gains or losses that will result from a particular investment.

In smaller, new venture firms, returns are sometimes measured in terms of the amount and speed of growth (e.g., in annual sales) rather than more traditional profitability measures[7] because new ventures require time to earn acceptable returns (in the form of return on assets and so forth) on investors' investments.[8]

Understanding how to exploit a competitive advantage is important for firms seeking to earn above-average returns.[9] Firms without a competitive advantage or that are not competing in an attractive industry earn, at best, average returns. **Average returns** are returns equal to those an investor expects to earn from other investments with a similar amount of risk. In the long run, an inability to earn at least average returns results first in decline and, eventually, failure.[10] Failure occurs because investors withdraw their investments from those firms earning less-than-average returns.

As previously noted, there are no guarantees of permanent success. Companies that are prospering must not become overconfident. Research suggests that overconfidence can lead to excessive risk taking.[11] Even considering Apple's excellent current performance, it still must be careful not to become overconfident and continue its quest to be the leader for its markets.

The **strategic management process** is the full set of commitments, decisions, and actions required for a firm to achieve strategic competitiveness and earn above-average returns (see Figure 1.1)[12]. The process involves analysis, strategy and performance (the A-S-P model—see Figure 1.1). The firm's first step in the process is to *analyze* its external environment and internal organization to determine its resources, capabilities, and core-competencies—on which its strategy likely will be based. Alibaba has established its dominant position because it has excelled in using this process. The *strategy* portion of the model entails strategy formulation and strategy implementation.

With the information gained from external and internal analyses, the firm develops its vision and mission and formulates one or more *strategies*. To implement its strategies, the firm takes actions to enact each strategy with the intent of achieving strategic competitiveness and above-average returns (*performance*). Effective strategic actions that take place in the context of carefully integrated strategy formulation and implementation efforts result in positive performance. This dynamic strategic management process must be maintained as ever-changing markets and competitive structures are coordinated with a firm's continuously evolving strategic inputs.[13]

In the remaining chapters of this book, we use the strategic management process to explain what firms do to achieve strategic competitiveness and earn above-average returns. We demonstrate why some firms consistently achieve competitive success while others fail to do so.[14] As you will see, the reality of global competition is a critical part of the strategic management process and significantly influences firms' performances.[15] Indeed, learning how to successfully compete in the globalized world is one of the most significant challenges for firms competing in the current century.[16]

Several topics will be discussed in this chapter. First, we describe the current competitive landscape. This challenging landscape is being created primarily by the emergence of a global economy, globalization resulting from that economy, and rapid technological changes. Next, we examine two models that firms use to gather the information and knowledge required to choose and then effectively implement their strategies. The insights gained from these models also serve as the foundation for forming the firm's vision and mission. The first model (industrial organization or I/O) suggests that the external environment is the primary determinant of a firm's strategic actions. According to this model, identifying and then operating effectively in an attractive (i.e., profitable) industry or segment of an industry are the keys to competitive success.[17] The second model (resource-based) suggests that a firm's unique resources and capabilities are the critical link to strategic competitiveness.[18] Thus, the first model is concerned primarily

Average returns are returns equal to those an investor expects to earn from other investments with a similar amount of risk.

The **strategic management process** is the full set of commitments, decisions, and actions required for a firm to achieve strategic competitiveness and earn above-average returns.

with the firm's external environment, while the second model is concerned primarily with the firm's internal organization. After discussing vision and mission, direction-setting statements that influence the choice and use of strategies, we describe the stakeholders that organizations serve. The degree to which stakeholders' needs can be met increases when firms achieve strategic competitiveness and earn above-average returns. Closing the chapter are introductions to strategic leaders and the elements of the strategic management process.

1-1 The Competitive Landscape

The fundamental nature of competition in many of the world's industries is changing. Although financial capital is no longer scarce due to the deep recession, markets are increasingly volatile.[19] Because of this, the pace of change is relentless and ever-increasing. Even determining the boundaries of an industry has become challenging. Consider, for example, how advances in interactive computer networks and telecommunications have blurred the boundaries of the entertainment industry. Today, not only do cable companies and satellite networks compete for entertainment revenue from television, but telecommunication companies are moving into the entertainment business through significant improvements in fiber-optic lines.[20] More recently, internet only streaming services have started to compete with cable, satellite, and telecommunication offerings. "Sling TV is part of a growing wave of offerings expected from tech, telecom and media companies in the coming year, posing a threat to the established television business, which takes in $170 billion a year. Meanwhile, the streaming outlets of Amazon, Hulu and Netflix continue to pour resources into developing more robust offerings. Sony, CBS, HBO and others are starting Internet-only subscription offerings."[21] Interestingly, Netflix and other streaming content providers such as Amazon are producing their own content; Netflix is producing repeat series such as "House of Cards," "Orange Is the New Black," and "Marco Polo".[22] As noted in the opening case, Alibaba intends to enter the entertainment business as Netflix and other content distributors and producers enter international markets.

Other characteristics of the current competitive landscape are noteworthy. Conventional sources of competitive advantage such as economies of scale and huge advertising budgets are not as effective as they once were (e.g., due to social media advertising) in terms of helping firms earn above-average returns. Moreover, the traditional managerial mind-set is unlikely to lead a firm to strategic competitiveness. Managers must adopt a new mind-set that values flexibility, speed, innovation, integration, and the challenges that evolve from constantly changing conditions.[23] The conditions of the competitive landscape result in a perilous business world, one in which the investments that are required to compete on a global scale are enormous and the consequences of failure are severe.[24] Effective use of the strategic management process reduces the likelihood of failure for firms as they encounter the conditions of today's competitive landscape.

Hypercompetition describes competition that is excessive such that it creates inherent instability and necessitates constant disruptive change for firms in the competitive landscape.[25] Hypercompetition results from the dynamics of strategic maneuvering among global and innovative combatants.[26] It is a condition of rapidly escalating competition based on price-quality positioning, competition to create new know-how and establish first-mover advantage, and competition to protect or invade established product or geographic markets.[27] In a hypercompetitive market, firms often aggressively challenge their competitors in the hopes of improving their competitive position and ultimately their performance.[28]

Hypercompetition describes competition that is excessive such that it creates inherent instability and necessitates constant disruptive change for firms in the competitive landscape.

Several factors create hypercompetitive environments and influence the nature of the current competitive landscape. The emergence of a global economy and technology, specifically rapid technological change, are the two primary drivers of hypercompetitive environments and the nature of today's competitive landscape.

1-1a   The Global Economy

A **global economy** is one in which goods, services, people, skills, and ideas move freely across geographic borders. Relatively unfettered by artificial constraints, such as tariffs, the global economy significantly expands and complicates a firm's competitive environment.[29]

Interesting opportunities and challenges are associated with the emergence of the global economy.[30] For example, the European Union (a group of European countries that participates in the world economy as one economic unit and operates under one official currency, the euro) has become one of the world's largest markets, with 700 million potential customers. "In the past, China was generally seen as a low-competition market and a low-cost producer. Today, China is an extremely competitive market in which local market-seeking multinational corporations (MNCs) must fiercely compete against other MNCs and against those local companies that are more cost effective and faster in product development. While China has been viewed as a country from which to source low-cost goods, lately, many MNCs such as Procter & Gamble (P&G), are actually net exporters of local management talent; they have been dispatching more Chinese abroad than bringing foreign expatriates to China."[31] China has become the second-largest economy in the world, surpassing Japan. India, the world's largest democracy, has an economy that also is growing rapidly and now ranks as the fourth largest in the world.[32] Simultaneously, many firms in these emerging economies are moving into international markets and are now regarded as MNCs. This fact is demonstrated by the case of Huawei Technologies Co. Ltd., a Chinese company that has entered the U.S. market. Barriers to entering foreign markets still exist and Huawei has encountered several, such as the inability to gain the U.S. government's approval for acquisition of U.S. firms. Essentially, Huawei must build credibility in the U.S. market, and especially build a positive relationship with stakeholders such as the U.S. government.

The nature of the global economy reflects the realities of a hypercompetitive business environment and challenges individual firms to seriously evaluate the markets in which they will compete. This is reflected in General Motor's actions and outcomes. General Motors sold 3.54 million vehicles in China while selling less in North America, 3.4 million.[33] One result of China being the largest domestic sales market is the increased competition GM now experiences in China from other competitors.

Consider the case of General Electric (GE). Although headquartered in the United States, GE expects that as much as 60 percent of its revenue growth through 2015 will be generated by competing in rapidly developing economies (e.g., China and India). The decision to count on revenue growth in emerging economies instead of in developed countries such as the United States and in Europe seems quite reasonable in the global economy. GE achieved significant growth in 2010 partly because of signing contracts for large infrastructure projects in China and Russia. GE's Chief Executive Officer (CEO), Jeffrey Immelt, argues that we have entered a new economic era in which the global economy will be more volatile and that most of the growth will come from emerging economies such as Brazil, China, and India.[34] Therefore, GE is investing significantly in these emerging economies, in order to improve its competitive position in vital geographic sources of revenue and profitability.

For example, Netflix, a subscription media streaming-video service provider, has seen its growth slow domestically. In the fourth quarter of 2014, Netflix added 1.9 million domestic U.S. streaming subscribers, which was down from 2.3 million in the fourth

A **global economy** is one in which goods, services, people, skills, and ideas move freely across geographic borders.

period a year earlier. However, Netflix was able to add 4.3 streaming customers overall because foreign markets grew faster than expected. When this was announced, its stock price increased 16 percent in after-hours trading. Netflix plans to expand to over 200 countries by 2017, up from its current 50 countries, while likewise seeking to stay profitable. Reed Hastings, Netflix's CEO, was encouraged by profitable results in Canada, Nordic countries, and Latin American countries. This group turned profitable notwithstanding the significant investment necessary to bring streaming services to these countries. In the first part of 2015, the company expects to add Australia and New Zealand and is exploring entering the Chinese market as well. Overall, Netflix added over 2.43 million

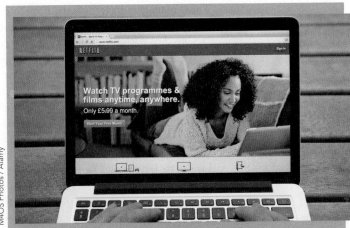

M4OS Photos / Alamy

Along with its international push, Netflix has expanded its ability to allow content to be viewed on many devices (including mobile devices) beside regular TVs, as is shown in the photo.

subscribers outside of the United States, which exceed its expectation of 2.15 million subscribers. Besides international expansion, Netflix is adding a significant number of original shows including "House of Cards," "Orange Is the New Black," and "Marco Polo." It finds that this original content costs less given viewer support compared to licensed content from major studios. This proprietary content as well as its expansion of licensing has lured customers away from cable and satellite TV providers. Its superior technology in providing precisely what consumers want and when they want it provides a domestic advantage which will carry over into its international expansion push (see Chapter 8 Opening Case for an expansion on Netflix's international strategy).[35]

The March of Globalization

Globalization is the increasing economic interdependence among countries and their organizations as reflected in the flow of goods and services, financial capital, and knowledge across country borders.[36] Globalization is a product of a large number of firms competing against one another in an increasing number of global economies.

In globalized markets and industries, financial capital might be obtained in one national market and used to buy raw materials in another. Manufacturing equipment bought from a third national market can then be used to produce products that are sold in yet a fourth market. Thus, globalization increases the range of opportunities for companies competing in the current competitive landscape.[37]

Firms engaging in globalization of their operations must make culturally sensitive decisions when using the strategic management process, as is the case in Starbucks' operations in European countries. Additionally, highly globalized firms must anticipate ever-increasing complexity in their operations as goods, services, people, and so forth move freely across geographic borders and throughout different economic markets.

Overall, it is important to note that globalization has led to higher performance standards in many competitive dimensions, including those of quality, cost, productivity, product introduction time, and operational efficiency. In addition to firms competing in the global economy, these standards affect firms competing on a domestic-only basis. The reason that customers will purchase from a global competitor rather than a domestic firm is that the global company's good or service is superior. Workers now flow rather freely among global economies, and employees are a key source of competitive advantage.[38]

Thus, managers have to learn how to operate effectively in a "multi-polar" world with many important countries having unique interests and environments.[39] Firms must learn how to deal with the reality that in the competitive landscape of the twenty-first century, only companies capable of meeting, if not exceeding, global standards typically have the capability to earn above-average returns.

Although globalization offers potential benefits to firms, it is not without risks. Collectively, the risks of participating outside of a firm's domestic markets in the global economy are labeled a "liability of foreignness."[40] One risk of entering the global market is the amount of time typically required for firms to learn how to compete in markets that are new to them. A firm's performance can suffer until this knowledge is either developed locally or transferred from the home market to the newly established global location.[41] Additionally, a firm's performance may suffer with substantial amounts of globalization. In this instance, firms may over diversify internationally beyond their ability to manage these extended operations.[42] Over diversification can have strong negative effects on a firm's overall performance.

A major factor in the global economy in recent years has been the growth in the influence of emerging economies. The important emerging economies include not only the BRIC countries (Brazil, Russia, India, and China) but also the VISTA countries (Vietnam, Indonesia, South Africa, Turkey, and Argentina). Mexico and Thailand have also become increasingly important markets.[43] Obviously, as these economies have grown, their markets have become targets for entry by large multinational firms. Emerging economy firms have also began to compete in global markets, some with increasing success.[44] For example, there are now more than 1,000 multinational firms home-based in emerging economies with more than $1 billion in annual sales.[45] In fact, the emergence of emerging-market MNCs in international markets has forced large MNCs based in developed markets to enrich their own capabilities to compete effectively in global markets.[46]

Thus, entry into international markets, even for firms with substantial experience in the global economy, requires effective use of the strategic management process. It is also important to note that even though global markets are an attractive strategic option for some companies, they are not the only source of strategic competitiveness. In fact, for most companies, even for those capable of competing successfully in global markets, it is critical to remain committed to and strategically competitive in both domestic and international markets by staying attuned to technological opportunities and potential competitive disruptions that innovations create.[47] As illustrated in the Strategic Focus, Starbucks has increased its revenue per store through an emphasis on innovation in addition to its international expansion.

1-1b Technology and Technological Changes

Technology-related trends and conditions can be placed into three categories: technology diffusion and disruptive technologies, the information age, and increasing knowledge intensity. These categories are significantly altering the nature of competition and as a result contributing to highly dynamic competitive environments.

Technology Diffusion and Disruptive Technologies

The rate of technology diffusion, which is the speed at which new technologies become available and are used, has increased substantially over the past 15 to 20 years. Consider the following rates of technology diffusion:

It took the telephone 35 years to get into 25 percent of all homes in the United States. It took TV 26 years. It took radio 22 years. It took PCs 16 years. It took the Internet 7 years.[48]

Strategic Focus

Starbucks Is "Juicing" Its Earnings per Store through Technological Innovations

An important signal for a company is who is chosen as the new CEO. Howard Schultz of Starbucks has led the company through successful strategic execution over much of its history. In 2015, Kevin Johnson, a former CEO of Juniper Networks and 16 year veteran of Microsoft took over as CEO of Starbucks, succeeding Schultz. Johnson has engaged with the company's digital operations and will supervise information technology and supply chain operations.

Many brick and mortar stores have experienced decreasing sales in the United States as online traffic has increased. Interestingly, 2014 Starbuck sales store operations have risen 5 percent in the fourth quarter; this 5 percent came from increased traffic (2 percent from growth in sales and 3 percent in increased ticket size). The driver of this increase in sales is mainly an increase in technology applications.

To facilitate this increase in sales per store, Starbucks is ramping up its digital tools such as mobile-payment platforms. Furthermore, it has ramped up online sales of gift cards as a way to drive revenue. In December 2014, it allowed customers to place online orders and pick them up in about 150 Starbucks outlets in the Portland, Oregon area. Besides leadership and a focus on technology, Starbucks receives suggestions, ideas, and experimentation from its employees. Starbucks employees, called baristas, are seen as partners who blend, steam, and brew the brand's specialty coffee in over 21,000 stores worldwide. Schultz credits the employees as a dominant force in helping it to build its revenue gains.

To further incentivize employees, Starbucks was one of the first to provide comprehensive health benefits and stock option ownership to part-time employees. Currently, employees have received more than $1 billion worth of financial gain through the stock option program. As an additional perk for U.S. employees, Schultz created a program to pay 100 percent of workers' tuition to finish their degrees through Arizona State University. To date, 1,000 workers have enrolled in this program.

Starbucks is also known for its innovations in new types of stores. For instance, it is testing smaller express stores in New York City that reduce client wait times. As noted earlier, Starbucks has emphasized online payment in its approaches which facilitates the speed of transaction. It now gives Starbucks rewards for mobile payment applications to its 12 million active users. Interestingly, this puts it ahead of iTunes and American Express Serve with its Starbucks mobile payment app in regard to number of users.

To put its innovation on display, Starbucks opened its first "Reserve Roastery and Tasting Room." This is a 15,000 square foot coffee roasting facility and also a consumer retail outlet. According to Schultz, it's a retail theater where "you can watch beans being roasted, talk to master grinders, have your drink brewed in front of you in multiple ways, lounge in a coffee library, order a selection of gourmet brews and locally prepared foods." Schultz calls this store in New York the "Willie Wonka Factory of coffee." Based on this concept, Starbucks will open small "reserve" stores inspired by this flagship roastery concept across New York in 2015.

These technology advances and different store offerings are also taking place internationally. For example, Starbucks is expanding a new store concept in India and it's debuting this new concept store in smaller towns and suburbs. These new outlets are about half the size of existing Starbuck cafes in India.

The photo illustrates the Starbuck's app that allows customers to pre-order and speed service and payment.

Sources: I. Brat & T. Stynes, 2015, Earnings: Starbucks picks a president from technology industry, *Wall Street Journal*, www.wsj.com, January 23; A. Adamczyk, 2014, The next big caffeine craze? Starbucks testing cold-brewed coffee, *Forbes*, www.forbes.com, August 18; R. Foroohr, 2014, Go inside Starbucks' wild new "Willie Wonka Factory of coffee", *Time*, www.time.com, December 8; FRPT-Retail Snapshot, 2014, Starbucks' strategy of expansion with profitability: to debut in towns and suburbs with half the size of the new stores, *FRPT-Retail Snapshot*, September 28, 9–10; L. Lorenzetti, 2014, Fortune's world most admired companies: Starbucks where innovation is always brewing, *Fortune*, www.fortune.com, October 30; P. Wahba, 2014, Starbucks to offer delivery in 2015 in some key markets, *Fortune*, www.fortune. com, November 4; V. Wong, 2014, Your boss will love the new Starbucks delivery service, *Bloomberg Businessweek*, www.businessweek.com, November 3.

The impact of technological changes on individual firms and industries has been broad and significant. For example, in the not-too-distant past, people rented movies on videotapes at retail stores. Now, movie rentals are almost entirely electronic. The publishing industry (books, journals, magazines, newspapers) is moving rapidly from hard copy to electronic format. Many firms in these industries, operating with a more traditional business model, are suffering. These changes are also affecting other industries, from trucking to mail services (public and private).

Perpetual innovation is a term used to describe how rapidly and consistently new, information-intensive technologies replace older ones. The shorter product life cycles resulting from these rapid diffusions of new technologies place a competitive premium on being able to quickly introduce new, innovative goods and services into the marketplace.[49]

In fact, when products become somewhat indistinguishable because of the widespread and rapid diffusion of technologies, speed to market with innovative products may be the primary source of competitive advantage (see Chapter 5).[50] Indeed, some argue that the global economy is increasingly driven by constant innovations. Not surprisingly, such innovations must be derived from an understanding of global standards and expectations of product functionality. Although some argue that large established firms may have trouble innovating, evidence suggests that today these firms are developing radically new technologies that transform old industries or create new ones.[51] Apple is an excellent example of a large established firm capable of radical innovation. Also, in order to diffuse the technology and enhance the value of an innovation, firms need to be innovative in their use of the new technology, building it into their products.[52]

Another indicator of rapid technology diffusion is that it now may take only 12 to 18 months for firms to gather information about their competitors' research and development (R&D) and product decisions.[53] In the global economy, competitors can sometimes imitate a firm's successful competitive actions within a few days. In this sense, the rate of technological diffusion has reduced the competitive benefits of patents.[54] Today, patents may be an effective way of protecting proprietary technology in a small number of industries such as pharmaceuticals. Indeed, many firms competing in the electronics industry often do not apply for patents to prevent competitors from gaining access to the technological knowledge included in the patent application.

Disruptive technologies—technologies that destroy the value of an existing technology and create new markets[55]—surface frequently in today's competitive markets. Think of the new markets created by the technologies underlying the development of products such as iPods, iPads, Wi-Fi, and the web browser. These types of products are thought by some to represent radical or breakthrough innovations (we discuss more about radical innovations in Chapter 13.).[56] A disruptive or radical technology can create what is essentially a new industry or can harm industry incumbents. However, some incumbents are able to adapt based on their superior resources, experience, and ability to gain access to the new technology through multiple sources (e.g., alliances, acquisitions, and ongoing internal research).[57]

Clearly, Apple has developed and introduced "disruptive technologies" such as the iPhone and iPod, and in so doing changed several industries. For example, the iPhone dramatically changed the cell phone industry, and the iPod and its complementary iTunes revolutionized how music is sold to and used by consumers. In conjunction with other complementary and competitive products (e.g., Amazon's Kindle), Apple's iPad is contributing to and speeding major changes in the publishing industry, moving from hard copies to electronic books. Apple's new technologies and products are also contributing to the new "information age." Thus, Apple provides an example of entrepreneurship through technology emergence across multiple industries.[58]

The Information Age

Dramatic changes in information technology (IT) have occurred in recent years. Personal computers, cellular phones, artificial intelligence, virtual reality, massive databases ("big data"), and multiple social networking sites are only a few examples of how information is used differently as a result of technological developments. An important outcome of these changes is that the ability to effectively and efficiently access and use information. IT has become an important source of competitive advantage in virtually all industries. The Internet and IT advances have given small firms more flexibility in competing with large firms, if the technology is used efficiently.[59]

Both the pace of change in IT and its diffusion will continue to increase. For instance, the number of personal computers in use globally is expected to surpass 2.3 billion by 2015. More than 372 million were sold globally in 2011. This number is expected to increase to about 518 million in 2015.[60] The declining costs of IT and the increased accessibility to them are also evident in the current competitive landscape. The global proliferation of relatively inexpensive computing power and its linkage on a global scale via computer networks combine to increase the speed and diffusion of IT. Thus, the competitive potential of IT is now available to companies of all sizes throughout the world, including those in emerging economies.[61]

Increasing Knowledge Intensity

Knowledge (information, intelligence, and expertise) is the basis of technology and its application. In the competitive landscape of the twenty-first century, knowledge is a critical organizational resource and an increasingly valuable source of competitive advantage.[62]

Indeed, starting in the 1980s, the basis of competition shifted from hard assets to intangible resources. For example, "Walmart transformed retailing through its proprietary approach to supply chain management and its information-rich relationships with customers and suppliers."[63] Relationships with customers and suppliers are an example of an intangible resource which needs to be managed.[64]

Knowledge is gained through experience, observation, and inference and is an intangible resource (tangible and intangible resources are fully described in Chapter 3). The value of intangible resources, including knowledge, is growing as a proportion of total shareholder value in today's competitive landscape.[65] In fact, the Brookings Institution estimates that intangible resources contribute approximately 85 percent of total shareholder value.[66] The probability of achieving strategic competitiveness is enhanced for the firm that develops the ability to capture intelligence, transform it into usable knowledge, and diffuse it rapidly throughout the company.[67] Therefore, firms must develop (e.g., through training programs) and acquire (e.g., by hiring educated and experienced employees) knowledge, integrate it into the organization to create capabilities, and then apply it to gain a competitive advantage.[68]

A strong knowledge-base is necessary to create innovations. In fact, firms lacking the appropriate internal knowledge resources are less likely to invest money in R&D.[69] Firms must continue to learn (building their knowledge-base) because knowledge spillovers to competitors are common. There are several ways in which knowledge spillovers occur, including the hiring of professional staff and managers by competitors.[70] Because of the potential for spillovers, firms must move quickly to use their knowledge in productive ways. In addition, firms must build routines that facilitate the diffusion of local knowledge throughout the organization for use everywhere that it has value.[71] Firms are better able to do these things when they have strategic flexibility.

Strategic flexibility is a set of capabilities used to respond to various demands and opportunities existing in a dynamic and uncertain competitive environment. Thus, strategic flexibility involves coping with uncertainty and its accompanying risks.[72]

Strategic flexibility is a set of capabilities used to respond to various demands and opportunities existing in a dynamic and uncertain competitive environment.

Firms should try to develop strategic flexibility in all areas of their operations. However, those working within firms to develop strategic flexibility should understand that the task is not easy, largely because of inertia that can build up over time. A firm's focus and past core competencies may actually slow change and strategic flexibility.[73]

To be strategically flexible on a continuing basis and to gain the competitive benefits of such flexibility, a firm has to develop the capacity to learn. Continuous learning provides the firm with new and up-to-date skill sets, which allow it to adapt to its environment as it encounters changes.[74] Firms capable of rapidly and broadly applying what they have learned exhibit the strategic flexibility and the capacity to change in ways that will increase the probability of successfully dealing with uncertain, hypercompetitive environments.

1-2 The I/O Model of Above-Average Returns

From the 1960s through the 1980s, the external environment was thought to be the primary determinant of strategies that firms selected to be successful.[75] The industrial organization (I/O) model of above-average returns explains the external environment's dominant influence on a firm's strategic actions. The model specifies that the industry or segment of an industry in which a company chooses to compete has a stronger influence on performance than do the choices managers make inside their organizations.[76] The firm's performance is believed to be determined primarily by a range of industry properties, including economies of scale, barriers to market entry, diversification, product differentiation, the degree of concentration of firms in the industry, and market frictions.[77] We examine these industry characteristics in Chapter 2.

Grounded in economics, the I/O model has four underlying assumptions. First, the external environment is assumed to impose pressures and constraints that determine the strategies that would result in above-average returns. Second, most firms competing within an industry or within a segment of that industry are assumed to control similar strategically relevant resources and to pursue similar strategies in light of those resources. Third, resources used to implement strategies are assumed to be highly mobile across firms, so any resource differences that might develop between firms will be short-lived. Fourth, organizational decision makers are assumed to be rational and committed to acting in the firm's best interests, as shown by their profit-maximizing behaviors.[78] The I/O model challenges firms to find the most attractive industry in which to compete. Because most firms are assumed to have similar valuable resources that are mobile across companies, their performance generally can be increased only when they operate in the industry with the highest profit potential and learn how to use their resources to implement the strategy required by the industry's structural characteristics. To do so, they must imitate each other.[79]

The five forces model of competition is an analytical tool used to help firms find the industry that is the most attractive for them. The model (explained in Chapter 2) encompasses several variables and tries to capture the complexity of competition. The five forces model suggests that an industry's profitability (i.e., its rate of return on invested capital relative to its cost of capital) is a function of interactions among five forces: suppliers, buyers, competitive rivalry among firms currently in the industry, product substitutes, and potential entrants to the industry.[80]

Firms use the five forces model to identify the attractiveness of an industry (as measured by its profitability potential) as well as the most advantageous position for the firm to take in that industry, given the industry's structural characteristics.[81]

Figure 1.2 The I/O Model of Above-Average Returns

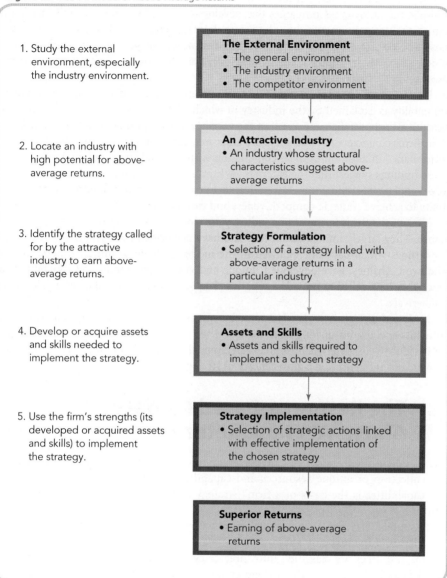

1. Study the external environment, especially the industry environment.

The External Environment
- The general environment
- The industry environment
- The competitor environment

2. Locate an industry with high potential for above-average returns.

An Attractive Industry
- An industry whose structural characteristics suggest above-average returns

3. Identify the strategy called for by the attractive industry to earn above-average returns.

Strategy Formulation
- Selection of a strategy linked with above-average returns in a particular industry

4. Develop or acquire assets and skills needed to implement the strategy.

Assets and Skills
- Assets and skills required to implement a chosen strategy

5. Use the firm's strengths (its developed or acquired assets and skills) to implement the strategy.

Strategy Implementation
- Selection of strategic actions linked with effective implementation of the chosen strategy

Superior Returns
- Earning of above-average returns

Typically, the model suggests that firms can earn above-average returns by producing either standardized goods or services at costs below those of competitors (a cost leadership strategy) or by producing differentiated goods or services for which customers are willing to pay a price premium (a differentiation strategy). The cost leadership and product differentiation strategies are discussed more fully in Chapter 4. The fact that the fast food industry faces "higher commodity costs, fiercer competition, a restaurant industry showing little to no growth, and a strapped lower-income consumer,"[82] suggests that fast food giant McDonald's is competing in a relatively unattractive industry.

As shown in Figure 1.2, the I/O model suggests that above-average returns are earned when firms are able to effectively study the external environment as the foundation for identifying an attractive industry and implementing the appropriate strategy. For example, in some industries, firms can reduce competitive rivalry and erect barriers to entry by forming joint ventures. Because of these outcomes, the joint ventures increase profit-ability in the industry.[83] Companies that develop or acquire the internal skills needed to implement strategies required by the external environment are likely to succeed, while those that do not are likely to fail.[84] Hence, this model suggests that returns are deter-mined primarily by external characteristics rather than by the firm's unique internal resources and capabilities.

Research findings support the I/O model because approximately 20 percent of a firm's profitability is explained by the industry in which it chooses to compete. However, this research also shows that 36 percent of the variance in firm profitability can be attributed to the firm's characteristics and actions.[85] Thus, managers' strategic actions affect the firm's performance in addition to or in conjunction with external environmental influences.[86] These findings suggest that the external environment and a firm's resources, capabilities, core competencies, and competitive advantages (see Chapter 3) influence the company's ability to achieve strategic competitiveness and earn above-average returns.

Most of the firms in the airline industry are similar in services offered and in perfor-mance. They largely imitate each other and have performed poorly over the years. The few airlines which have not followed in the mode of trying to imitate others, such as Southwest Airlines, have developed unique and valuable resources and capabilities on which they have relied to provide a superior product (better service at a lower price) than major rivals.

As shown in Figure 1.2, the I/O model assumes that a firm's strategy is a set of com-mitments and actions flowing from the characteristics of the industry in which the firm has decided to compete. The resource-based model, discussed next, takes a different view of the major influences on a firm's choice of strategy.

1-3 The Resource-Based Model of Above-Average Returns

The resource-based model of above-average returns assumes that each organization is a collection of unique resources and capabilities. The *uniqueness* of its resources and capabilities is the basis of a firm's strategy and its ability to earn above-average returns.[87]

Resources are inputs into a firm's production process, such as capital equipment, the skills of individual employees, patents, finances, and talented managers. In general, a firm's resources are classified into three categories: physical, human, and organiza-tional capital. Described fully in Chapter 3, resources are either tangible or intangible in nature.

Individual resources alone may not yield a competitive advantage.[88] In fact, resources have a greater likelihood of being a source of competitive advantage when they are formed into a capability. A **capability** is the capacity for a set of resources to perform a task or an activity in an integrative manner.[89] **Core competencies** are capabilities that serve as a source of competitive advantage for a firm over its rivals.[90] Core competencies are often visible in the form of organizational functions. For example, Apple's R&D function is one of its core competencies, as its ability to produce innovative new products that are per-ceived as valuable in the marketplace, is a critical reason for Apple's success.

According to the resource-based model, differences in firms' performances across time are due primarily to their unique resources and capabilities rather than the industry's structural characteristics. This model also assumes that firms acquire different resources and develop unique capabilities based on how they combine and use the resources; that resources and certainly capabilities are not highly mobile across firms; and that the

Resources are inputs into a firm's production process, such as capital equipment, the skills of individual employees, patents, finances, and talented managers.

A **capability** is the capacity for a set of resources to perform a task or an activity in an integrative manner.

Core competencies are capabilities that serve as a source of competitive advantage for a firm over its rivals.

differences in resources and capabilities are the basis of competitive advantage.[91] Through continued use, capabilities become stronger and more difficult for competitors to understand and imitate. As a source of competitive advantage, a capability must not be easily imitated but also not too complex to understand and manage.[92]

The resource-based model of superior returns is shown in Figure 1.3. This model suggests that the strategy the firm chooses should allow it to use its competitive advantages in an attractive industry (the I/O model is used to identify an attractive industry).

Not all of a firm's resources and capabilities have the potential to be the foundation for a competitive advantage. This potential is realized when resources and capabilities are valuable, rare, costly to imitate, and non-substitutable.[93] Resources are *valuable* when they allow a firm to take advantage of opportunities or neutralize threats in its external environment. They are *rare* when possessed by few, if any, current and potential competitors. Resources are *costly to imitate* when other firms either cannot obtain them or are at a

Figure 1.3 The Resource-Based Model of Above-Average Returns

1. Identify the firm's resources. Study its strengths and weaknesses compared with those of competitors.

Resources
- Inputs into a firm's production process

2. Determine the firm's capabilities. What do the capabilities allow the firm to do better than its competitors?

Capability
- Capacity of an integrated set of resources to integratively perform a task or activity

3. Determine the potential of the firm's resources and capabilities in terms of a competitive advantage.

Competitive Advantage
- Ability of a firm to outperform its rivals

4. Locate an attractive industry.

An Attractive Industry
- An industry with opportunities that can be exploited by the firm's resources and capabilities

5. Select a strategy that best allows the firm to utilize its resources and capabilities relative to opportunities in the external environment.

Strategy Formulation and Implementation
- Strategic actions taken to earn above-average returns

Superior Returns
- Earning of above-average returns

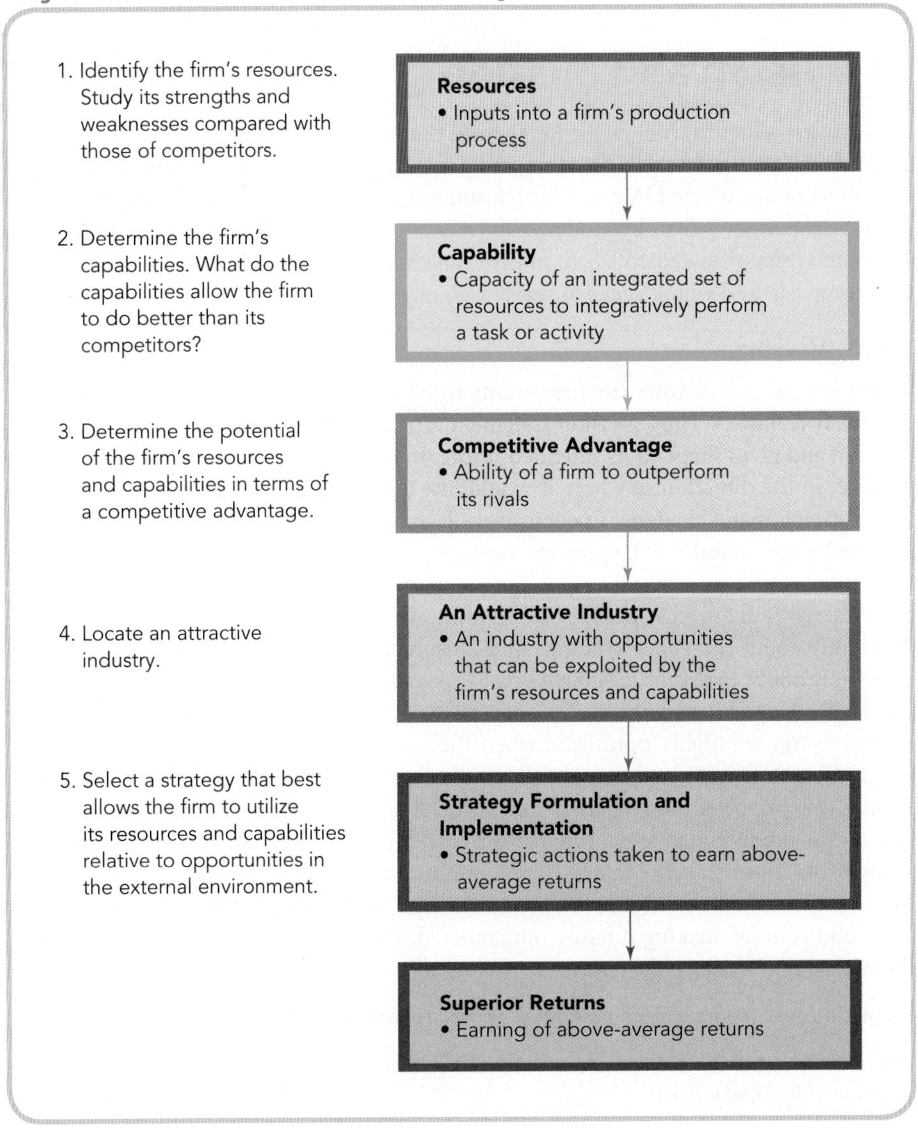

cost disadvantage in obtaining them compared with the firm that already possesses them. And they are *non-substitutable* when they have no structural equivalents. Many resources can either be imitated or substituted over time. Therefore, it is difficult to achieve and sustain a competitive advantage based on resources alone. Individual resources are often integrated to produce configurations in order to build capabilities. These capabilities are more likely to have these four attributes.[94] When these four criteria are met, however, resources and capabilities become core competencies.

As noted previously, research shows that both the industry environment and a firm's internal assets affect that firm's performance over time.[95] Thus, to form a vision and mission, and subsequently to select one or more strategies and determine how to implement them, firms use both the I/O and resource-based models.[96] In fact, these models complement each other in that one (I/O) focuses outside the firm while the other (resource-based) focuses inside the firm. Next, we discuss the formation of a firm's vision and mission—actions taken after the firm understands the realities of its external environment (Chapter 2) and internal organization (Chapter 3).

1-4   Vision and Mission

After studying the external environment and the internal organization, the firm has the information it needs to form its vision and a mission (see Figure 1.1). Stakeholders (those who affect or are affected by a firm's performance, as explained later in the chapter) learn a great deal about a firm by studying its vision and mission. Indeed, a key purpose of vision and mission statements is to inform stakeholders of what the firm is, what it seeks to accomplish, and who it seeks to serve.

1-4a   Vision

Vision is a picture of what the firm wants to be and, in broad terms, what it wants to ultimately achieve.[97] Thus, a vision statement articulates the ideal description of an organization and gives shape to its intended future. In other words, a vision statement points the firm in the direction of where it would like to be in the years to come. An effective vision stretches and challenges people as well. In her book about Steve Jobs, Apple's phenomenally successful CEO, Carmine Gallo argues that one of the reasons that Apple is so innovative was Jobs' vision for the company. She suggests that he thought bigger and differently than most people. To be innovative, she explains that one has to think differently about the firm's products and customers—"sell dreams not products"—and differently about the story to "create great expectations."[98] With Steve Jobs' death, Apple will be challenged to remain highly innovative. Interestingly, similar to Jobs, many new entrepreneurs are highly optimistic when they develop their ventures.[99] However, very few are able to develop and successfully implement a vision in the manner that Jobs did.

It is also important to recognize that vision statements reflect a firm's values and aspirations and are intended to capture the heart and mind of each employee and, hopefully, many of its other stakeholders. A firm's vision tends to be enduring while its mission can change with new environmental conditions. A vision statement tends to be relatively short and concise, making it easily remembered. Examples of vision statements include the following:

Our vision is to be the world's best quick service restaurant. (McDonald's)

To make the automobile accessible to every American. (Ford Motor Company's vision when established by Henry Ford)

Vision is a picture of what the firm wants to be and, in broad terms, what it wants to ultimately achieve.

As a firm's most important and prominent strategic leader, the CEO is responsible for working with others to form the firm's vision. Experience shows that the most effective vision statement results when the CEO involves a host of stakeholders (e.g., other top-level managers, employees working in different parts of the organization, suppliers, and customers) to develop it. In short, they need to develop a clear and shared vision for it to be successful.[100] In addition, to help the firm reach its desired future state, a vision statement should be clearly tied to the conditions in the firm's external environment and internal organization. Moreover, the decisions and actions of those involved with developing the vision, especially the CEO and the other top-level managers, must be consistent with that vision.

1-4b Mission

The vision is the foundation for the firm's mission. A **mission** specifies the businesses in which the film intends to compete and the customers it intends to serve.[101] The firm's mission is more concrete than its vision. However, similar to the vision, a mission should establish a firm's individuality and should be inspiring and relevant to all stakeholders.[102] Together, the vision and mission provide the foundation that the firm needs to choose and implement one or more strategies. The probability of forming an effective mission increases when employees have a strong sense of the ethical standards that guide their behaviors as they work to help the firm reach its vision.[103] Thus, business ethics are a vital part of the firm's discussions to decide what it wants to become (its vision) as well as who it intends to serve and how it desires to serve those individuals and groups (its mission).[104]

Even though the final responsibility for forming the firm's mission rests with the CEO, the CEO and other top-level managers often involve more people in developing the mission. The main reason for this is that the mission deals more directly with product markets and customers, and middle- and first-level managers and other employees have more direct contact with customers and the markets in which they serve. Examples of mission statements include the following:

Be the best employer for our people in each community around the world and deliver operational excellence to our customers in each of our restaurants. (McDonald's)

Our mission is to be recognized by our customers as the leader in applications engineering. We always focus on the activities customers' desire; we are highly motivated and strive to advance our technical knowledge in the areas of material, part design and fabrication technology. (LNP, a GE Plastics Company)

McDonald's mission statement flows from its vision of being the world's best quick-service restaurant. LNP's mission statement describes the business areas (material, part design, and fabrication technology) in which the firm intends to compete.

Clearly, vision and mission statements that are poorly developed do not provide the direction a firm needs to take appropriate strategic actions. Still, as shown in Figure 1.1, a firm's vision and mission are critical aspects of the *analysis* and the base required to engage in *strategic actions* that help to achieve strategic competitiveness and earn above-average returns. Therefore, firms must accept the challenge of forming effective vision and mission statements.

1-5 Stakeholders

Every organization involves a system of primary stakeholder groups with whom it establishes and manages relationships.[105] **Stakeholders** are the individuals, groups,

A **mission** specifies the businesses in which the firm intends to compete and the customers it intends to serve.

Stakeholders are the individuals, groups, and organizations that can affect the firm's vision and mission, are affected by the strategic outcomes achieved, and have enforceable claims on the firm's performance.

Strategic **Focus**

The Failure of BlackBerry to Develop an Ecosystem of Stakeholders

In 2007 the Apple iPhone was introduced as a consumer product which became known as the smartphone. At the time, the dominant player in this category was Research in Motion (RIM) and later known as BlackBerry. As late as 2010, BlackBerry held 43 percent of the commercial and government communication sectors. As consumers, including the business and government segments, found the smartphone to be superior as far as utility, BlackBerry's market share began to decrease precipitously. Although BlackBerry's technology allowed it to be a superior communication device for email and phone, the iPhone was superior as a handheld computer device, including communication and messaging, with much more versatility.

BlackBerry's demise provides an informed example of how the competitive landscape has changed in regard to successful business model implementation. Previously, having a good product or service and well run cost-effective company with sound capital structure was sufficient. With newer business models, having an effective strategy to manage the ecosystem or network of suppliers and customers has become more salient. Because BlackBerry had remarkably loyal customers and a strong product it failed to recognize the importance of Apple's ecosystem innovation, which allowed it to expand and diversify its range of applications for its handheld computer (smartphone). In particular, complementors to the industry (a concept explored in Chapter 2) were key; the innovation for Apple was its ecosystem of app developers. Apple not only focused on the value chain of making the iPhone and iPad, but it also focused on managing the ecosystem of creating valuable apps. As a result, an army of software developers were committed to producing iPhone applications, was behind the development of Apple's device for the general consumer and for business professionals. They created a network of stakeholders and facilitated a way to make it easy to install apps on the phone. App developers responded in huge numbers. When the app store launched in 2008, there were 500 apps. Within a year there were 55,000 apps and over a billion downloads. This was the significant difference between the small development community focused on BlackBerry and the massive development community that arose around applications for the iPhone. The "open" system strategy approach used by Google in fostering the Android system allowed a competitive ecosystem to develop that rivaled that of the iPhone.

Even now BlackBerry has not been able to create the type of stakeholder ecosystem comparable to those of Apple and Google.

Since 2010 BlackBerry has had two new CEOs and, although there are improvements, the firm has never recovered. Although BlackBerry has tried to focus on the business and government sectors using its classic look with physical keyboard, it still had a 34 percent drop in revenue in fourth quarter of 2014. The reviews of its latest product, the BlackBerry Classic, note that although consumers are likely to appreciate the retro feel of the device because of the perfected physical keyboard and mouse-like track pad, preloaded apps are slow and poorly designed. The app situation is problematic because BlackBerry doesn't have the number of app developers of the Apple or Google ecosystems. Many of the apps that you do find are difficult to download and often do not resize to fit the Classics' square screen well. As such you get a real physical keyboard to help with emails, manage your calendar, and browse the web, but few other good software

Both the iPhone and Android systems have more fully developed app ecosystems than Blackberry, which has limited Blackberry's success.

© Bloomua/Shutterstock.com

applications. Although this is the Classic is the best model ever released, it is expected that BlackBerry will continue to decline due to the lack of quality apps such as the ones found in its competitors' ecosystems.

Apple was able to outsource innovation to more developers than it could afford to employ thereby ensuring a steady stream of desirable new applications and content.

Transparent revenue sharing for these developers and a few early app millionaires created incentive at negligible expense. On the other hand, BlackBerry restricted its development community and could not hope to innovate fast enough to compete with the iPhone's positive feedback loop accruing value to customers, innovators, and content providers, resulting in profitable market share which drew capital market players as well.

In summary, BlackBerry's big failure was that it did not pay attention to the complementary software that became available on other ecosystems. A big lesson here is that managing supplier and stakeholder value creation also creates strong support from customers because it creates value for the all stakeholders

and likewise draws financial capital and an associated increasing stock price.

Sources: S. Cojocaru & C. Cojocaru, 2014, New trends in mobile technology leadership, *Manager*, 19(1): 79–89; M. Cording, J. S. Harrison, R. E. Hoskisson, & K. Jonsen, 2014, "Walking the talk": A multi-stakeholder exploration of organizational authenticity, employee productivity and post-merger performance, *Academy of Management Perspectives*, 28(1): 38–56; B. Dummit, 2014, BlackBerry's revenue falls 34%; decline underscores challenges smartphone maker faces, even as it cuts costs, *Wall Street Journal*, www.wsj.com, Dec 20; M. Freer, 2014, Four success strategies from failed business models, *Forbes*, www.forbes.com, Jul 21; D. Gallagher, 2014, BlackBerry's new plan could bear fruit; attempt at revival is showing signs of life, *Wall Street Journal*, www.wsj.com, Nov 16; D. Reisinger, 2014, Why BlackBerry is showing signs of stability under CEO John Chin, *eWeek*, www.eweek.com, Dec 22; M. G. Jacobides, 2013, BlackBerry forgot to manage the ecosystem, *Business Strategy Review*, 24(4), 8; B. Matichuk, 2013, BlackBerry's business model led to its failure, *Troy Media*, www.troymedia.com, Oct 1.

and organizations that can affect the firm's vision and mission, are affected by the strategic outcomes achieved, and have enforceable claims on the firm's performance.[106] Claims on a firm's performance are enforced through the stakeholders' ability to withhold participation essential to the organization's survival, competitiveness, and profitability.[107] Stakeholders continue to support an organization when its performance meets or exceeds their expectations.[108] Also, research suggests that firms that effectively manage stakeholder relationships outperform those that do not. Stakeholder relationships and the firm's overall reputation among stakeholders can therefore be a source of competitive advantage.[109] This can be illustrated through the application of a strong stakeholder strategy in the comparison between BlackBerry's and Apple's ecosystem of stakeholders in the strategic focus. BlackBerry was unable to develop a strong set of application suppliers compared to the Apple ecosystem of app supplier stakeholders.[110]

Although organizations have dependency relationships with their stakeholders, they are not equally dependent on all stakeholders at all times. As a consequence, not every stakeholder has the same level of influence.[111] The more critical and valued a stakeholder's participation, the greater a firm's dependency on it. Greater dependence, in turn, gives the stakeholder more potential influence over a firm's commitments, decisions, and actions. Managers must find ways to either accommodate or insulate the organization from the demands of stakeholders controlling critical resources.[112]

1-5a Classifications of Stakeholders

The parties involved with a firm's operations can be separated into at least three groups.[113] As shown in Figure 1.4, these groups are the capital market stakeholders (shareholders and the major suppliers of a firm's capital), the product market stakeholders (the firm's primary customers, suppliers, host communities, and unions representing the workforce), and the organizational stakeholders (all of a firm's employees, including both nonmanagerial and managerial personnel).

Each stakeholder group expects those making strategic decisions in a firm to provide the leadership through which its valued objectives will be reached.[114] The objectives of the various stakeholder groups often differ from one another, sometimes placing

Figure 1.4 The Three Stakeholder Groups

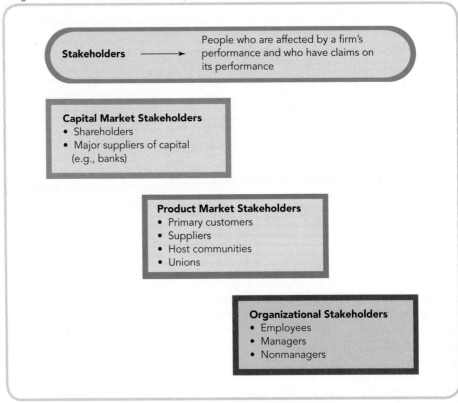

those involved with a firm's strategic management process in situations where trade-offs have to be made. The most obvious stakeholders, at least in U.S. organizations, are *shareholders*—individuals and groups who have invested capital in a firm in the expectation of earning a positive return on their investments. These stakeholders' rights are grounded in laws governing private property and private enterprise.

In contrast to shareholders, another group of stakeholders—the firm's customers—prefers that investors receive a minimum return on their investments. Customers could have their interests maximized when the quality and reliability of a firm's products are improved, but without high prices. High returns to customers, therefore, might come at the expense of lower returns for capital market stakeholders.

Because of potential conflicts, each firm must carefully manage its stakeholders. First, a firm must thoroughly identify and understand all important stakeholders. Second, it must prioritize them in case it cannot satisfy all of them. Power is the most critical criterion in prioritizing stakeholders. Other criteria might include the urgency of satisfying each particular stakeholder group and the degree of importance of each to the firm.[115]

When the firm earns above-average returns, the challenge of effectively managing stakeholder relationships is lessened substantially. With the capability and flexibility provided by above-average returns, a firm can more easily satisfy multiple stakeholders. When the firm earns only average returns, it is unable to maximize the interests of all stakeholders. The objective then becomes one of at least minimally satisfying each stakeholder.

Trade-off decisions are made in light of how important the support of each stakeholder group is to the firm. For example, environmental groups may be very important to firms in the energy industry but less important to professional service firms. A firm earning below-average returns does not have the capacity to minimally satisfy all stakeholders. The managerial challenge in this case is to make trade-offs that minimize the amount of support lost from stakeholders. Societal values also influence the general weightings allocated among the three stakeholder groups shown in Figure 1.4. Although all three groups are served by and, in turn, influence firms decisions in the major industrialized nations, the priorities in their service and influence vary because of cultural and institutional differences. Next, we present additional details about each of the three major stakeholder groups.

As a firm formulates its strategy, it must consider all of its primary stakeholders in the product and capital markets as well as organizational shareholders.

© Africa Studio/Shutterstock.com

Capital Market Stakeholders

Shareholders and lenders both expect a firm to preserve and enhance the wealth they have entrusted to it. The returns they expect are commensurate with the degree of risk they accept with those investments (i.e., lower returns are expected with low-risk investments, while higher returns are expected with high-risk investments). Dissatisfied lenders may impose stricter covenants on subsequent borrowing of capital. Dissatisfied shareholders may reflect their concerns through several means, including selling their stock. Institutional investors (e.g., pension funds, mutual funds) often are willing to sell their stock if the returns are not what they desire, or they may take actions to improve the firm's performance such as pressuring top managers and members of boards of directors to improve the strategic decisions and governance oversight.[116] Some institutions owning major shares of a firm's stock may have conflicting views of the actions needed, which can be challenging for managers. This is because some may want an increase in returns in the short-term while the others desire a focus on building long-term competitiveness.[117] Managers may have to balance their desires with those of other shareholders or prioritize the importance of the institutional owners with different goals. Clearly shareholders who hold a large share of stock (sometimes referred to as blockholders, see Chapter 10) are influential, especially in the determination of the firm's capital structure (i.e., the amount of equity versus the amount of debt used). Large shareholders often prefer that the firm minimize its use of debt because of the risk of debt, its cost, and the possibility that debt holders have first call on the firm's assets over the shareholders in case of default.[118]

When a firm is aware of potential or actual dissatisfactions among capital market stakeholders, it may respond to their concerns. The firm's response to stakeholders who are dissatisfied is affected by the nature of its dependence on them (which, as noted earlier, is also influenced by a society's values). The greater and more significant the dependency is, the more likely the firm is to provide a significant response. Sometimes firms are unable to satisfy key stakeholders such as creditors and have to file for bankruptcy.

Product Market Stakeholders

Some might think that product market stakeholders (customers, suppliers, host communities, and unions) share few common interests. However, all four groups can benefit as firms engage in competitive battles. For example, depending on product and industry characteristics, marketplace competition may result in lower product prices being charged to a firm's customers and higher prices being paid to its suppliers (the firm might be willing to pay higher supplier prices to ensure delivery of the types of goods and services that are linked with its competitive success).[119]

Customers, as stakeholders, demand reliable products at the lowest possible prices. Suppliers seek loyal customers who are willing to pay the highest sustainable prices for the goods and services they receive. Although all product market stakeholders are important, without customers, the other product market stakeholders are of little value. Therefore, the firm must try to learn about and understand current and potential customers.[120]

Host communities are represented by national (home and abroad), state/province, and local government entities with which the firm must deal. Governments want companies willing to be long-term employers and providers of tax revenue without placing excessive demands on public support services. These stakeholders also influence the firm through laws and regulations. In fact, firms must deal with laws and regulations developed and enforced at the national, state, and local levels (the influence is polycentric—multiple levels of power and influence).[121]

Union officials are interested in secure jobs, under highly desirable working conditions, for employees they represent. Thus, product market stakeholders are generally satisfied when a firm's profit margin reflects at least a balance between the returns to capital market stakeholders (i.e., the returns lenders and shareholders will accept and still retain their interests in the firm) and the returns in which they share.

Organizational Stakeholders

Employees—the firm's organizational stakeholders—expect the firm to provide a dynamic, stimulating, and rewarding work environment. Employees generally prefer to work for a company that is growing and in which the employee can develop their skills, especially those skills required to be effective team members and to meet or exceed global work standards. Workers who learn how to use new knowledge productively are critical to organizational success. In a collective sense, the education and skills of a firm's workforce are competitive weapons affecting strategy implementation and firm performance.[122] Strategic leaders are ultimately responsible for serving the needs of organizational stakeholders on a day-to-day basis. In fact, to be successful, strategic leaders must effectively use the firm's human capital.[123] The importance of human capital to their success is probably why outside directors are more likely to propose layoffs compared to inside strategic leaders, while such insiders are likely to use preventative cost-cutting measures and seek to protect incumbent employees.[124] A highly important means of building employee skills for the global competitive landscape is through international assignments. The process of managing expatriate employees and helping them build knowledge can have significant effects over time on the firm's ability to compete in global markets.[125]

1-6 Strategic Leaders

Strategic leaders are people located in different areas and levels of the firm using the strategic management process to select strategic actions that help the firm achieve its vision and fulfill its mission. Regardless of their location in the firm, successful strategic leaders are decisive, committed to nurturing those around them, and committed to helping the firm create value for all stakeholder groups.[126] In this vein, research evidence suggests that employees who perceive that their CEO is a visionary leader also believe that the CEO leads the firm to operate in ways that are consistent with the values of all stakeholder groups rather than emphasizing only maximizing profits for shareholders. In turn, visionary leadership motivates employees to expend extra effort, thereby helping to increase firm performance.

Thomas SAMSON/Getty Images

Tony Hsieh, CEO of Zappos.com, an online shoe and clothing retailer, has been helpful in shaping Zappos's entrepreneurial culture.

When identifying strategic leaders, most of us tend to think of CEOs and other top-level managers. Clearly, these people are strategic leaders. In the final analysis, CEOs are responsible for making certain their firm effectively uses the strategic management process. Indeed, the pressure on CEOs to manage strategically is stronger than ever.[127] However, many other people help choose a firm's strategy and then determine the actions for successfully implementing it.[128] The main reason is that the realities of twenty-first century competition that we discussed earlier in this chapter (e.g., the global economy, globalization, rapid technological change, and the increasing importance of knowledge and people as sources of competitive advantage) are creating a need for those "closest to the action" to be making decisions and determining the actions to be taken. In fact, all managers (as strategic leaders) must think globally and act locally.[129] Thus, the most effective CEOs and top-level managers understand how to delegate strategic responsibilities to people throughout the firm who influence the use of organizational resources. Delegation also helps to avoid too much managerial hubris at the top and the problems it causes, especially in situations allowing significant managerial discretion.[130]

Organizational culture also affects strategic leaders and their work. In turn, strategic leaders' decisions and actions shape a firm's culture. **Organizational culture** refers to the complex set of ideologies, symbols, and core values that are shared throughout the firm and that influence how the firm conducts business. It is the social energy that drives—or fails to drive—the organization.[131] For example, Southwest Airlines is known for having a unique and valuable culture. Its culture encourages employees to work hard but also to have fun while doing so. Moreover, its culture entails respect for others—employees and customers alike. The firm also places a premium on service, as suggested by its commitment to provide POS (Positively Outrageous Service) to each customer.

1-6a The Work of Effective Strategic Leaders

Perhaps not surprisingly, hard work, thorough analyses, a willingness to be brutally honest, a penchant for wanting the firm and its people to accomplish more, and tenacity are prerequisites to an individual's success as a strategic leader. The top strategic

Strategic leaders are people located in different areas and levels of the firm using the strategic management process to select strategic actions that help the firm achieve its vision and fulfill its mission.

Organizational culture refers to the complex set of ideologies, symbols, and core values that are shared throughout the firm and that influence how the firm conducts business.

leaders are chosen on the basis of their capabilities (their accumulation of human capital and skills over time). Effective top management teams (those with better human capital, management skills, and cognitive abilities) make better strategic decisions.[132] In addition, strategic leaders must have a strong strategic orientation while simultaneously embracing change in the dynamic competitive landscape we have discussed.[133] In order to deal with this change effectively, strategic leaders must be innovative thinkers and promote innovation in their organization.[134] Promoting innovation is facilitated by a diverse top management team representing different types of expertise and leveraging relationships with external parties.[135] Strategic leaders can best leverage partnerships with external parties and organizations when their organizations are ambidextrous, both innovative and good at execution.[136] In addition, strategic leaders need to have a global mind-set, or sometimes referred to as an ambicultural approach to management.[137]

Strategic leaders, regardless of their location in the organization, often work long hours, and their work is filled with ambiguous decision situations. However, the opportunities afforded by this work are appealing and offer exciting chances to dream and to act. The following words, given as advice to the late Time Warner chair and co-CEO Steven J. Ross by his father, describe the opportunities in a strategic leader's work:

There are three categories of people—the person who goes into the office, puts his feet up on his desk, and dreams for 12 hours; the person who arrives at 5 A.M. and works for 16 hours, never once stopping to dream; and the person who puts his feet up, dreams for one hour, then does something about those dreams.[138]

The operational term used for a dream that challenges and energizes a company is vision. The most effective strategic leaders provide a vision as the foundation for the firm's mission and subsequent choice and use of one or more strategies.[139]

1-7 The Strategic Management Process

As suggested by Figure 1.1, the strategic management process is a rational approach firms use to achieve strategic competitiveness and earn above-average returns. Figure 1.1 also features the topics we examine in this book to present the strategic management process.

This book is divided into three parts aligned with the A-S-P process explained in the beginning of the chapter. In Part 1, we describe the *analyses* (A) necessary for developing strategies. Specifically, we explain what firms do to analyze their external environment (Chapter 2) and internal organization (Chapter 3). These analyses are completed to identify marketplace opportunities and threats in the external environment (Chapter 2) and to decide how to use the resources, capabilities, core competencies, and competitive advantages in the firm's internal organization to pursue opportunities and overcome threats (Chapter 3). The analyses explained in Chapters 2 and 3 are the well-known SWOT analyses (strengths, weaknesses, opportunities, threats).[140] Firms use knowledge about its external environment and internal organization, then formulates its strategy taking into account its vision and mission.

The firm's analyses (see Figure 1.1) provide the foundation for choosing one or more *strategies* (S) and deciding which one(s) to implement. As suggested in Figure 1.1 by the horizontal arrow linking the two types of strategic actions, formulation and implementation must be simultaneously integrated for a successful strategic management process. Integration occurs as decision makers review implementation issues when choosing strategies and consider possible changes to the firm's strategies while implementing a current strategy.

In Part 2 of this book, we discuss the different strategies firms may choose to use. First, we examine business-level strategies (Chapter 4). A business-level strategy describes the actions a firm takes to exploit its competitive advantage over rivals. A company competing in a single product market (e.g., a locally owned grocery store operating in only one location) has but one business-level strategy, while a diversified firm competing in multiple product markets (e.g., General Electric) forms a business-level strategy for each of its businesses. In Chapter 5, we describe the actions and reactions that occur among firms in marketplace competition. Competitors typically respond to and try to anticipate each other's actions. The dynamics of competition affect the strategies firms choose as well as how they try to implement the chosen strategies.[141]

For the diversified firm, corporate-level strategy (Chapter 6) is concerned with determining the businesses in which the company intends to compete as well as how to manage its different businesses. Other topics vital to strategy formulation, particularly in the diversified company, include acquiring other businesses and, as appropriate, restructuring the firm's portfolio of businesses (Chapter 7) and selecting an international strategy (Chapter 8). With cooperative strategies (Chapter 9), firms form a partnership to share their resources and capabilities in order to develop a competitive advantage. Cooperative strategies are becoming increasingly important as firms seek ways to compete in the global economy's array of different markets.[142]

To examine actions taken to implement strategies, we consider several topics in Part 3 of the book. First, we examine the different mechanisms used to govern firms (Chapter 10). With demands for improved corporate governance being voiced by many stakeholders in the current business environment, organizations are challenged to learn how to simultaneously satisfy their stakeholders' different interests.[143] Finally, the organizational structure and actions needed to control a firm's operations (Chapter 11), the patterns of strategic leadership appropriate for today's firms and competitive environments (Chapter 12), and strategic entrepreneurship (Chapter 13) as a path to continuous innovation are addressed.

It is important to emphasize that primarily because they are related to how a firm interacts with its stakeholders, almost all strategic management process decisions have ethical dimensions.[144] Organizational ethics are revealed by an organization's culture; that is to say, a firm's decisions are a product of the core values that are shared by most or all of a company's managers and employees. Especially in the turbulent and often ambiguous competitive landscape in the global economy, those making decisions as a part of the strategic management process must understand how their decisions affect capital market, product market, and organizational stakeholders differently and regularly evaluate the ethical implications of their decisions.[145] Decision makers failing to recognize these realities accept the risk of placing their firm at a competitive disadvantage.[146]

As you will discover, the strategic management process examined in this book calls for disciplined approaches to serve as the foundation for developing a competitive advantage. Therefore, it has a major effect on the *performance* (P) of the firm.[147] Performance is reflected in the firm's ability to achieve strategic competitiveness and earn above-average returns. Mastery of this strategic management process will effectively serve you, our readers, and the organizations for which you will choose to work.

SUMMARY

- Firms use the strategic management process to achieve strategic competitiveness and earn above-average returns. Firms *analyze* the external environment and their internal organization, then formulate and implement a *strategy* to achieve a desired level of *performance* (A-S-P). Performance is reflected by the firm's level of strategic competitiveness and the extent to which it earns above-average returns. Strategic competitiveness is achieved when a firm develops and implements a value-creating strategy. Above-average returns (in excess of what investors expect to earn from other investments with similar levels of risk) provide the foundation needed to simultaneously satisfy all of a firm's stakeholders.

- The fundamental nature of competition is different in the current competitive landscape. As a result, those making strategic decisions must adopt a different mind-set, one that allows them to learn how to compete in highly turbulent and chaotic environments that produce a great deal of uncertainty. The globalization of industries and their markets along with rapid and significant technological changes are the two primary factors contributing to the turbulence of the competitive landscape.

- Firms use two major models to help develop their vision and mission when choosing one or more strategies in pursuit of strategic competitiveness and above-average returns. The core assumption of the I/O model is that the firm's external environment has a large influence on the choice of strategies more than do the firm's internal resources, capabilities, and core competencies. Thus, the I/O model is used to understand the effects an industry's characteristics can have on a firm when deciding what strategy or strategies to use in competing against rivals. The logic supporting the I/O model suggests that above-average returns are earned when the firm locates an attractive industry or part of an industry and successfully implements the strategy dictated by that industry's characteristics. The core assumption of the resource-based model is that the firm's unique resources, capabilities, and core competencies have more of an influence on selecting and using strategies than does the firm's external environment. Above-average returns are earned when the firm uses its valuable, rare, costly-to-imitate, and non-substitutable resources and capabilities to

compete against its rivals in one or more industries. Evidence indicates that both models yield insights that are linked to successfully selecting and using strategies. Thus, firms want to use their unique resources, capabilities, and core competencies as the foundation to engage in one or more strategies that allow them to effectively compete against rivals in their industry.

- Vision and mission are formed to guide the selection of strategies based on the information from the analyses of the firm's internal organization and external environment. Vision is a picture of what the firm wants to be and, in broad terms, what it wants to ultimately achieve. Flowing from the vision, the mission specifies the business or businesses in which the firm intends to compete and the customers it intends to serve. Vision and mission provide direction to the firm and signal important descriptive information to stakeholders.

- Stakeholders are those who can affect, and are affected by, a firm's performance. Because a firm is dependent on the continuing support of stakeholders (shareholders, customers, suppliers, employees, host communities, etc.), they have enforceable claims on the company's performance. When earning above-average returns, a firm generally has the resources it needs to satisfy the interests of all stakeholders. However, when earning only average returns, the firm must carefully manage its stakeholders in order to retain their support. A firm earning below-average returns must minimize the amount of support it loses from unsatisfied stakeholders.

- Strategic leaders are people located in different areas and levels of the firm using the strategic management process to help the firm achieve its vision and fulfill its mission. In general, CEOs are responsible for making certain that their firms properly use the strategic management process. The effectiveness of the strategic management process is increased when it is grounded in ethical intentions and behaviors. The strategic leader's work demands decision trade-offs, often among attractive alternatives. It is important for all strategic leaders, especially the CEO and other members of the top-management team, to conduct thorough analyses of conditions facing the firm, be brutally and consistently honest, and work jointly to select and implement the correct strategies.

KEY TERMS

above-average returns 5
average returns 6
capability 16
competitive advantage 4
core competencies 16

global economy 8
hypercompetition 7
mission 19
organizational culture 25
resources 16

REVIEW QUESTIONS

1. What are strategic competitiveness, strategy, competitive advantage, above-average returns, and the strategic management process?

2. What are the characteristics of the current competitive landscape? What two factors are the primary drivers of this landscape?

3. According to the I/O model, what should a firm do to earn above-average returns?

4. What does the resource-based model suggest a firm should do to earn above-average returns?

5. What are vision and mission? What is their value for the strategic management process?

6. What are stakeholders? How do the three primary stakeholder groups influence organizations?

7. How would you describe the work of strategic leaders?

8. What are the elements of the strategic management process? How are they interrelated?

Mini-Case

Competition in the Airlines Industry

For many years, the airline industry was highly regulated which resulted in most airlines acting like each other by definition. However, the similarities among the large airline companies remained after the industry was partially deregulated more than 30 years ago. These similarities–in services, routes, and performance–have persisted even to the present time. For example, airlines often offer a new service (e.g., Wi-Fi availability on flights), but these services are easily imitated, therefore, any differentiation in offerings is only temporary.

In recent times, consolidation has occurred in both European and U.S. airline industries. In particular, poor performance led U.S. Air and America West to merge. Additionally, much for the same reasons, Northwest Airlines and Delta Airlines merged. Likewise United Airlines and Continental merged to create the largest airline in the industry. More recently, American Airlines and U.S. Air have been approved to merge. Much of the consolidation was approved because several of the airlines went through bankruptcy proceedings (e.g., Continental and United both went through bankruptcy before their merger). All of these mergers, however, have not created highly differentiated services (or prices). All of airlines largely provide the same type of services, and prices do not differ greatly among the large "full-service" carriers.

In fact, it seems that the primary competition is in trying to make fewer mistakes. In fact, industry statistics that report positive accounts, announce such outcomes as a reduction in lost bags, fewer cancellations of flights, and fewer delays. What this suggests is that all of these areas still likely represent major problem areas. It seems pretty bad when the most positive statement one can make is that fewer bags have been lost in recent times. Although profits have been up more recently, this is primarily due to lower fuel costs and stronger demand because the economy is growing, something that is not controlled by those in charge of the strategy.

Obviously, there are differences between airlines across time. United, the largest airline, merged with Continental to create more financial efficiencies and to offer greater travel options to customers.

However, it has had significant problems making the merger of the two systems work effectively. In fact, it announced a major net loss for 2012 because of its problems. For example, in November 2012, a computer malfunction (software problem) caused the delay of 250 of United's flights globally for almost two hours. Its reservation system failed twice during 2012, which shut down its website, stranding passengers as flights were then delayed or cancelled. United's on time performance suffered and was once of the worst in the industry for 2012. The number of customer complaints for United was much higher than in the past. In short, it is relatively easy to determine why the airline suffered a serious net loss in 2012. Yet, Delta, which performed very poorly a few years earlier, performed better in 2014. It made a net profit for the third year in a row. Its on-time performance was about 10 percentage points higher than United's. And, while United is eliminating flights and furloughing employees to cuts costs (trying to make a profit), in 2012 Delta purchased a 49 percent share of Virgin Atlantic to gain access to the highly valuable New York–London routes and gates in both locations. Delta was also one of the first airlines to introduce Wi-Fi to passengers during flights, although most other airlines have duplicated this service. Interestingly, the one program most airlines have used to establish some differentiation is their loyalty programs. However, benefits of these loyalty programs have been decreasing over time with less availability and more miles deducted.

Furthermore, research shows that airlines attrack brand switching customers who tend to move to the brand with the most perks for them at the time.

Certainly, some reduced-service airlines have fared much better in most of the categories noted above (e.g., profits, on-time flights, customer complaints). Among these is Southwest Airlines. Interestingly, while it started as a low-price airline (and has maintained this feature), it also has generally offered superior service compared to the full-service airlines. The large airlines tried, but were unable, to imitate Southwest. In effect, Southwest developed its resources and capabilities which over time allowed it to provide service much more effectively and at a lower price than its full-service rivals. However, JetBlue has duplicated much of Southwest's strategy, although it is focused on business travelers.

Sources: E. Glusac, 2015, What price loyalty?, *Entrepreneur*, May, 16; S. Sharf, 2015, American Airlines reports lower revenue, higher profit, *Forbes*, www.forbes.com, April 24; S. Schaefer, 2015, Cleared for takeoff. *Forbes Asia*, May, 18; C. M. Voorhees, R. C. White, M. McCall, & P. Randhawa, 2015, Fool's gold? Assessing the impact of the value of airline loyalty programs on brand equity perceptions and share of wallet, *Cornell Hospitality Quarterly*, 56(2): 202–212; 2013, Anatomy of 99.5%, Delta Airlines Website, blog.delta.com, February 15; S. McCartney, 2013, Believe it or not, flying is improving, *Wall Street Journal*, www.wsj.com, January 9; J. Freed, 2012, Delta grabs bigger share of key NY–London route, *Bloomberg Businessweek*, www.businessweek.com, December 11; D. Benoit, 2012, Delta lands London space with Virgin joint venture, *Wall Street Journal*, blogs.wsj.com/deals, December 11; J. Mouawad, 2012, For United, big problems at biggest airline, *New York Times*, www.nytimes.com, November 28; C. Negroni, 2012, Good airlines news: Losing fewer bags, *New York Times*, www.nytimes.com, August 6.

Case Discussion Questions

1. How important is the environment to the performance of airlines in the airline industry? What does this suggest regarding the industrial organization (I/O) model to explain how firms can earn above-average returns?

2. Why is there a lot of imitation in the airlines industry, and how does this affect firm performance?

3. How important is the resource-based model to explain how well firms perform in the airlines industry?

4. How can strategic leaders be successful in an industry like the airlines industry?

NOTES

1. D. J. Teece, 2014, The foundations of enterprise performance: Dynamic and ordinary capabilities in an (economic) theory of firms. *Academy of Management Perspectives*, 28: 328–352; D. G. Sirmon, M. A. Hitt, R. D. Ireland, & B. A. Gilbert, 2011, Resource orchestration to create competitive advantage: Breadth, depth and life cycle effects, *Journal of Management*,

37: 1390–1412; D. G. Sirmon, M. A. Hitt, & R. D. Ireland, 2007, Managing firm resources in dynamic environments to create value: Looking inside the black box, *Academy of Management Review*, 32: 273–292.

2. J. Denrell, C. Fang, & Z. Zhao, 2013, Inferring superior capabilities from sustained superior performance: A Bayesian analysis, *Strategic Management*

Journal, 34: 182–196; R. D'Aveni, G. B. Dagnino, & K. G. Smith, 2010, The age of temporary advantage, *Strategic Management Journal*, 31: 1371–1385; R. D. Ireland & J. W. Webb, 2009, Crossing the great divide of strategic entrepreneurship: Transitioning between exploration and exploitation, *Business Horizons*, 52: 469–479.

3.   G. Pacheco-de-Almeida, A. Hawk, & B. Yeung, 2015, The right speed and its value, *Strategic Management Journal*, 36: 159–176; G. Pacheco-de-Almeida & P. Zemsky, 2007, The timing of resource development and sustainable competitive advantage, *Management Science*, 53: 651–666.

4.   D. Gaddis Ross, 2014, Taking a chance: A formal model of how firms use risk in strategic interaction with other firms, *Academy of Management Review*, 39: 202–226.

5.   A. Nair, E. Rustambekov, M. McShane, & S. Fainshmidt, 2014, Enterprise risk management as a dynamic capability: A test of its effectiveness during a crisis, *Managerial & Decision Economics*, 35: 555–566; K. D. Miller, 2007, Risk and rationality in entrepreneurial processes, *Strategic Entrepreneurship Journal*, 1: 57–74.

6.   C. C. Miller, N. T. Washburn, & W. H. Glick, 2013, The myth of firm performance, *Organization Science*, 24: 948–964.

7.   P. Steffens, P. Davidsson, & J. Fitzsimmons, 2009, Performance configurations over time: Implications for growth- and profit-oriented strategies, *Entrepreneurship Theory and Practice*, 33: 125–148.

8.   E. Karniouchina, S. J. Carson, J. C. Short, & D. J. Ketchen, 2013, Extending the firm vs. industry debate: Does industry life cycle stage matter? *Strategic Management Journal*, 34: 1010–1018; J. C. Short, A. McKelvie, D. J. Ketchen, Jr., & G. N. Chandler, 2009, Firm and industry effects on firm performance: A generalization and extension for new ventures, *Strategic Entrepreneurship Journal*, 3: 47–65.

9.   R. Mudambi & T. Swift, 2014, Knowing when to leap: Transitioning between exploitative and explorative R&D, *Strategic Management Journal*, 35: 126–145; D. G. Sirmon, M. A. Hitt, J.-L. Arregle, & J. T. Campbell, 2010, The dynamic interplay of capability strengths and weaknesses: Investigating the bases of temporary competitive advantage, *Strategic Management Journal*, 31: 1386–1409.

10. D. Ucbasaran, D. A. Shepherd, A. Lockett, & S. J. Lyon, 2013, Life after business failure: The process and consequences of business failure for entrepreneurs, *Journal of Management*, 39: 163–202.

11. P. M. Picone, G. B. Dagnino, G., & A. Minà, 2014, The origin of failure: A multidisciplinary appraisal of the hubris hypothesis and proposed research agenda, *Academy of Management Perspectives*, 28: 447–468.

12. J. Hansen, R. McDonald, & R. Mitchell, 2013, Competence resource specialization, causal ambiguity, and the creation and decay of competitiveness: The role of marketing strategy in new product performance and shareholder value, *Journal of the Academy of Marketing Science*, 41: 300–319; Y. Zhang & J. Gimeno, 2010, Earnings pressure and competitive behavior: Evidence from the U.S. electronics industry, *Academy of Management Journal*, 53: 743–768.

13. J. Garcia-Sanchez, L. F. Mesquita, & R. S. Vassolo, 2014, What doesn't kill you makes you stronger: The evolution of competition and entry-order advantages in economically turbulent contexts, *Strategic Management Journal*, 35: 1972–1992; J. Bock, T. Opsahl, G. George, & D. M. Gann, 2012, The effects of culture and structure on strategic flexibility during business model innovation, *Journal of Management Studies*, 49: 275–305.

14. Garcia-Sanchez, Mesquita, & Vassolo, What doesn't kill you makes you stronger; J. T. Li, 2008, Asymmetric interactions between foreign and domestic banks: Effects on market entry, *Strategic Management Journal*, 29: 873–893.

15. N. Hashai & P. J. Buckley, 2014, Is competitive advantage a necessary condition for the emergence of the multinational enterprise?. *Global Strategy Journal*, 4: 35–48; R. G. Bell, I. Filatotchev, & A. A. Rasheed, 2012, The liability of foreignness in capital markets: Sources and remedies, *Journal of International Business Studies*, 43: 107–122.

16. A. Kuznetsova & O. Kuznetsova, 2014, Building professional discourse in emerging markets: Language, context and the challenge of sensemaking, *Journal of International Business Studies*, 45: 583–599; J. H. Fisch, 2012, Information costs and internationalization performance, *Global Strategy Journal*, 2: 296–312.

17. R. Makadok & D. G. Ross, 2013, Taking industry structuring seriously: A strategic perspective on product differentiation, *Strategic Management Journal*, 34: 509–532; Karniouchina, Carson, Short, & Ketchen, Extending the firm vs. industry debate; M. A. Delmas, & M. W. Toffel, 2008, Organizational responses to environmental demands: Opening the black box, *Strategic Management Journal*, 29: 1027–1055.

18. A. V. Sakhartov & T. B. Folta, 2014, Resource relatedness, redeployability, and firm value, *Strategic Management Journal*, 35: 1781–1797; J. Barney, D. J. Ketchen, & M. Wright, 2011, The future of resource-based theory: Revitalization or decline? *Journal of Management*, 37: 37: 1299–1315.

19. R. Scaggs, 2014, Markets take wild ride on ruble, oil, *Wall Street Journal*, www.wsj.com, December 17; M. Statman, 2011, Calm investment behavior in turbulent investment times, in *What's Next 2011*, New York: McGraw-Hill Professional, E-Book; E. Thornton, 2009, The new rules, *Businessweek*, January 19, 30–34; T. Friedman, 2005, *The World Is Flat: A Brief History of the 21st Century*, New York: Farrar, Strauss and Giroux.

20. D. Searcey, 2006, Beyond cable. Beyond DSL. *Wall Street Journal*, July 24, R9.

21. E. Steel, 2015, Dish Network unveils Sling TV, a streaming service to rival cable (and it has ESPN), *New York Times*, www.nytimes.com, January 5.

22. V. Luckerson, 2014, Netflix wants new original content every three weeks, *Time*, www.time.com, December 9.

23. B. Agypt & B. A. Rubin, 2012, Time in the new economy: The impact of the interaction of individual and structural temporalities and job satisfaction, *Journal of Management*, 49: 403–428; J. A. Lamberg, H. Tikkanen, T. Nokelainen, & H. Suur-Inkeroinen, 2009, Competitive dynamics, strategic consistency, and organizational survival, *Strategic Management Journal*, 30: 45–60.

24. A. Hawk, G. Pacheco-De-Almeida, & B. Yeung, 2013, Fast-mover advantages: Speed capabilities and entry into the emerging submarket of Atlantic basin LNG, *Strategic Management Journal*, 34: 1531–1550; J. Hagel, III, J. S. Brown, & L. Davison, 2008, Shaping strategy in a world of constant disruption, *Harvard Business Review*, 86(10): 81–89.

25. B. L. King, 2013, Succeeding in a hypercompetitive world: VC advice for smaller companies *Journal of Business Strategy*, 34(4): 22–30; D'Aveni, Dagnino, & Smith, The age of temporary advantage; A. V. Izosimov, 2008, Managing hypergrowth, *Harvard Business Review*, 86(4): 121–127; J. W. Selsky, J. Goes, & O. N. Babüroglu, 2007, Contrasting perspectives of strategy making: Applications in "Hyper" environments, *Organization Studies*, 28: 71–94.

26. S. Greengard, 2015, Disruption Is the New Normal. *CIO Insight*, January 5, 2; D'Aveni, Dagnino, & Smith, The age of temporary advantage.

27. D'Aveni, Dagnino, & Smith, The age of temporary advantage.

28. A. Kriz, R. Voola, & U. Yuksel, 2014, The dynamic capability of ambidexterity in hypercompetition: Qualitative insights, *Journal of Strategic Marketing*, 22: 287–299; D. J. Bryce & J. H. Dyer, 2007, Strategies to crack well-guarded markets, *Harvard Business Review* 85(5): 84–92.

29. P. Regnér & U. Zander, 2014, International strategy and knowledge creation: The advantage of foreignness and liability of concentration, *British Journal of Management*, 25: 551–569; S. H. Lee & M. Makhija, 2009, Flexibility in internationalization: Is it valuable during an economic crisis? *Strategic Management Journal*, 30: 537–555.

30. K. E. Meyer & Y. S. Su, 2015, Integration and responsiveness in subsidiaries in emerging economies. *Journal of World Business*, 50: 149–158; Y. Luo & S. L. Wang, 2012, foreign direct investment strategies by developing country multinationals: A diagnostic model for home country effects, *Global Strategy Journal*, 2: 244–261.

31. Y. Luo, 2007, From foreign investors to strategic insiders: Shifting parameters, prescriptions and paradigms for MNCs in China, *Journal of World Business*, 42: 14–34.

32. S. Awate, M. M. Larsen, & R. Mudambi, 2015, Accessing vs sourcing knowledge: A comparative study of R&D internationalization between emerging and advanced economy firms, *Journal of International Business Studies*, 46: 63–86; M. A. Hitt & X. He, 2008, Firm strategies in a changing global competitive landscape, *Business Horizons*, 51: 363–369.

33. M. Rhodan, 2015, GM sold a record number of vehicles in 2014. *Time*, www.time.com, January 16.

34. A. Ritesh, 2014, Jeffrey Immelt on General Electric's exposure in Russia, growth in emerging markets, *Benzinga*, www.benzinga.com, December 17; J.-F. Hennart, 2012, Emerging market multinationals and the theory of the multinational enterprise, *Global Strategy Journal*, 2: 168–187; S. Malone, 2011, GE's Immelt sees new economic era for globe, *Financial Post*, www.financialpost.com, March 13.

35. S. Ramachandran & T. Stynes, 2015, Netflix steps up foreign expansion: Subscriber editions top streaming service's forecast, helped by growth in markets abroad, *Wall Street Journal*, www.wsj.com, January 21.

36. R. M. Holmes, T. Miller, M. A. Hitt, & M. P. Salmador, 2013, The interrelationships among informal institutions, formal institutions, and inward foreign direct investment, *Journal of Management*, 39: 531–566; K. D. Brouthers, 2013, A retrospective on: Institutions, cultural and transaction cost influences on entry mode choice and performance, *Journal of International Business Studies*, 44: 14–22.

37. U. Andersson, P. J. Buckley, & H. Dellestrand, 2015. In the right place at the right time!: The influence of knowledge governance tools on knowledge transfer and utilization in MNEs, *Global Strategy Journal*, 5: 27–47; H. Kirca, G. T. Hult, S. Deligonul, M. Z. Perry, & S. T. Cavusgil, 2012, A multilevel examination of the drivers of firm multinationality: A meta-analysis, *Journal of Management*, 38: 502–530.

38. D. G. Collings, 2014. Integrating global mobility and global talent management: Exploring the challenges and strategic opportunities, *Journal of World Business*, 49: 253–261; Y.-Y. Chang, Y. Gong, & M. W. Peng, 2012, Expatriate knowledge transfer, subsidiary absorptive capacity, and subsidiary performance, *Academy of Management Journal*, 55: 927–948.

39. J. P. Quinlan, 2011, Speeding towards a messy, multi-polar world, in *What's Next 2011*, New York: McGraw-Hill Professional, E-Book.

40. H. Kim & M. Jensen, 2014, Audience heterogeneity and the effectiveness of market signals: How to overcome liabilities of foreignness in film exports? *Academy of Management Journal*, 57: 1360–1384; B. Elango, 2009, Minimizing effects of "liability of foreignness": Response strategies of foreign firms in the United States, *Journal of World Business*, 44: 51–62.

41. F. Jiang, L. Liu, & B W. Stening, 2014, Do foreign firms in China incur a liability of foreignness? The local Chinese firms' perspective, *Thunderbird International Business Review*, 56: 501–518; J. Mata & E. Freitas, 2012, Foreignness and exit over the life cycle of firms, *Journal of International Business Studies*, 43: 615–630.

42. T. Chi & Z. J. Zhao, 2014, Equity Structure of MNE affiliates and scope of their activities: distinguishing the incentive and control effects of ownership, *Global Strategy Journal*, 4: 257–279; M. A. Hitt, R. E. Hoskisson, & H. Kim, 1997, International diversification: Effects on innovation and firm performance in product-diversified firms, *Academy of Management Journal*, 40: 767–798.

43. S. Keukeleire & B. Hooijmaaijers, 2014, The BRICS and other emerging power alliances and multilateral organizations in the Asia- Pacific and the Global South: Challenges for the European Union and its view on multilateralism, *Journal of Common Market Studies*, 52: 582–599.

44. K. Kalasin, P. Dussauge, & M. Rivera-Santos, 2014, The expansion of emerging economy firms into advanced markets: The influence of intentional path-breaking change, *Global Strategy Journal*, 4: 75–103; R. Ramamurti, 2012, What is really different about emerging market multinationals? *Global Strategy Journal*, 2: 41–47.

45. M. Naim, 2013, Power outage, *Bloomberg Businessweek*, March 3: 4–5.

46. H. Kim, R. E. Hoskisson, & S.-H. Lee, 2015. Why strategic factor markets matter: 'New' multinationals' geographic diversification and firm profitability, *Strategic Management Journal*, Forthcoming; G. McDermott, R. Mudambi, & R. Parente, 2013, Strategic modularity and the architecture of the multinational firm, *Global Strategy Journal*, 3: 1–7.

47. R. D. Ireland & J. W. Webb, 2007, Strategic entrepreneurship: Creating competitive advantage through streams of innovation, *Business Horizons*, 50(1): 49–59; G. Hamel, 2001, Revolution vs. evolution: You need both, *Harvard Business Review*, 79(5): 150–156.

48. K. H. Hammonds, 2001, What is the state of the new economy? *Fast Company*, September, 101–104.

49. M. E. Schramm & M. Y. Hu, 2013, Perspective: The evolution of R&D conduct in the pharmaceutical industry, *Journal of Product Innovation Management*, 30: 203–213; S. W. Bradley, J. S. McMullen, K. W. Artz, & E. M. Simiyu, 2012, Capital is not enough: Innovation in developing economies, *Journal of Management Studies*, 49: 684–717; D. Dunlap-Hinkler, M. Kotabe, & R. Mudambi, 2010, A story of breakthrough versus incremental innovation: Corporate entrepreneurship in the global pharmaceutical industry, *Strategic Entrepreneurship Journal*, 4: 106–127.

50. G. Pacheco-de-Almeida, A. Hawk, & B. Yeung, B. 2015, The right speed and its value, *Strategic Management Journal*, 36: 159–176; A. Hawk, G. Pacheco-De-Almeida, & B. Yeung, B. 2013, Fast-mover advantages: Speed capabilities and entry into the emerging submarket of Atlantic basin LNG, *Strategic Management Journal*, 34: 1531–1550.

51. P. C. Patel, S. A. Fernhaber, P. P. McDougall-Covin, & R. P. van der Have, 2014, Beating competitors to international markets: The value of geographically balanced networks for innovation, *Strategic Management Journal*, 35: 691–711; N. Furr, F. Cavarretta, & S. Garg, 2012, Who changes course? The role of domain knowledge and novel framing in making technological changes, *Strategic Entrepreneurship Journal*, 6: 236–256; L. Jiang, J. Tan, & M. Thursby, 2011, Incumbent firm invention in emerging fields: Evidence from the semiconductor industry, *Strategic Management Journal*, 32: 55–75.

52. M. G. Jacobides, 2013, BlackBerry forgot to manage the ecosystem, *Business Strategy Review*, 24(4): 8; R. Adner & R. Kapoor, 2010, Value creation in innovation ecosystems: How the structure of technological interdependence affects firm performance in new technology generations, *Strategic Management Journal*, 31: 306–333.

53. C. M. Christensen, 1997, *The Innovator's Dilemma*, Boston: Harvard Business School Press.

54. K Bilir, 2014, Patent laws, product life-cycle lengths, and multinational activity, 2014, *American Economic Review*, 104: 1979–2013.

55. C. Christensen, 2015, Disruptive innovation is a strategy, not just the technology, *Business Today*, 23(26): 150–158; A. Kaul, 2012, Technology and corporate scope: Firm and rival innovation as antecedents of corporate transactions, *Strategic Management Journal*, 33: 347–367.

56. J. Henkel, T. Rønde, & M. Wagner, 2015, And the winner is—acquired. Entrepreneurship as a contest yielding radical innovations. *Research Policy*, 44: 295–310; C M. Christensen, 2006, The ongoing process of building a theory of disruption, *Journal of Product Innovation Management*, 23: 39–55.

57. U. Stettner & D. Lavie, 2014, Ambidexterity under scrutiny: Exploration and exploitation via internal organization,

alliances, and acquisitions, *Strategic Management Journal*, 35: 1903–1929; L. Capron & O. Bertrand, 2014, Going abroad in search of higher productivity at home, *Harvard Business Review*, 92(6): 26; L Capron, 2013, Cisco's corporate development portfolio: A blend of building, borrowing and buying, *Strategy & Leadership*, 41: 27–30.

58. R. Kapoor & J. M. Lee, 2013, Coordinating and competing in ecosystems: How organizational forms shape new technology investments, *Strategic Management Journal*, 34: 274–296; J. Woolley, 2010, Technology emergence through entrepreneurship across multiple industries, *Strategic Entrepreneurship Journal*, 4: 1–21.

59. P. Chen & S. Wu, 2013, The impact and implications of on-demand services on market structure, *Information Systems Research*, 24: 750–767; K. Celuch, G. B. Murphy, & S. K. Callaway, 2007, More bang for your buck: Small firms and the importance of aligned information technology capabilities and strategic flexibility, *Journal of High Technology Management Research*, 17: 187–197.

60. 2013, Worldwide PC Market, eTForecasts, www.etforecasts.com, accessed on March 10, 2013.

61. F. De Beule, S. Elia, & L. Piscitello, 2014, Entry and access to competencies abroad: Emerging market firms versus advanced market firms. *Journal of International Management*, 20: 137–152; M. S. Giarratana & S. Torrisi, 2010, Foreign entry and survival in a knowledge-intensive market: Emerging economy countries' international linkages, technology competences and firm experience, *Strategic Entrepreneurship Journal*, 4: 85–104.

62. C. Phelps, R. Heidl, & A., Wadhwa, 2012, Knowledge, networks, and knowledge networks: A review and research agenda, *Journal of Management*, 38: 1115–1166; R. Agarwal, D. Audretsch, & M. B. Sarkar, 2010, Knowledge spillovers and strategic entrepreneurship, *Strategic Entrepreneurship Journal*, 4: 271–283.

63. M. Gottfredson, R. Puryear, & S. Phillips, 2005, Strategic sourcing: From periphery to the core, *Harvard Business Review*, 83(2): 132–139.

64. R.-J. Jean, R. R. Sinkovics, & T. P. Hiebaum, 2014, The effects of supplier involvement and knowledge protection on product innovation in customer-supplier relationships: A study of global automotive suppliers in China. *Journal of Product Innovation Management*, 31: 98–113.

65. M. J. Donate & J. D. Sánchez de Pablo, 2015, The role of knowledge-oriented leadership in knowledge management practices and innovation, *Journal of Business Research*, 68: 360–370;

66. E. Sherman, 2010, Climbing the corporate ladder, *Continental Magazine*, November, 54–56.

67. K. Srikanth & P. Puranam, 2014, The Firm as a coordination system: Evidence from software services offshoring, *Organization Science*, 25: 1253–1271; K. Z. Zhou & C. B. Li, 2012, How knowledge affects radical innovation: Knowledge base, market knowledge acquisition, and internal knowledge sharing, *Strategic Management Journal*, 33: 1090–1102.

68. D. Laureiro-Martínez, S. Brusoni, N. Canessa, & M. Zollo, 2015, Understanding the exploration-exploitation dilemma: An fMRI study of attention control and decision-making performance, *Strategic Management Journal*, 36, 319–338; C. A. Siren, M. Kohtamaki, & A. Kuckertz, 2012, Exploration and exploitation strategies, profit performance and the mediating role of strategic learning: Escaping the exploitation trap, *Strategic Entrepreneurship Journal*, 6: 18–41.

69. A. Cuervo-Cazurra & C. A. Un, 2010, Why some firms never invest in formal R&D, *Strategic Management Journal*, 31: 759–779.

70. S. Carnahan & D. Somaya, 2013, Alumni effects and relational advantage: The impact on outsourcing when a buyer hires employees from a supplier's competitors, *Academy of Management Journal*, 56: 1578–1600; H. Yang, C. Phelps, & H. K. Steensma, 2010, Learning from what others have learned from you: The effects of knowledge spillovers on originating firms, *Academy of Management Journal*, 53: 371–389.

71. R. Aalbers, W. Dolfsma, & O. Koppius, 2014, Rich ties and innovative knowledge transfer within a firm, *British Journal of Management*, 25: 833–848; A. Jain, 2013, Learning by doing and the locus of innovative capability in biotechnology research, *Organization Science*, 24: 1683–1700.

72. D. Herhausen, R. E. Morgan, & H. W. Volberda, 2014, A meta analysis of the antecedents and consequences of strategic flexibility, *Academy of Management Annual Meeting Proceedings*, 1051–1057; S. Kortmann, C. Gelhard, C. Zimmermann, & F. T. Piller, 2014, Linking strategic flexibility and operational efficiency: The mediating role of ambidextrous operational capabilities, *Journal of Operations Management*, 32(7/8): 475–490.

73. Garcia-Sanchez, Mesquita, & Vassolo, What doesn't kill you makes you; R. G. McGrath, 2013, *The end of competitive advantage*, Boston: Harvard Business School Press.

74. E. G. Anderson Jr. & K. Lewis, 2014, A dynamic model of individual and collective learning amid disruption, *Organization Science*, 25: 356–376; M. L. Santos-Vijande, J. A. Lopez-Sanchez, & J. A. Trespalacios, 2011, How organizational learning affects a firm's flexibility, competitive strategy and performance, *Journal of Business Research*, 65: 1079–1089; A. C. Edmondson, 2008, The competitive imperative of learning, *Harvard Business Review*, 86(7/8): 60–67.

75. R. E. Hoskisson, M. A. Hitt, W. P. Wan, & D. Yiu, 1999, Swings of a pendulum: Theory and research in strategic management, *Journal of Management*, 25: 417–456.

76. Karniouchina, Carson, Short, & Ketchen, Extending the firm vs. industry debate: Does industry life cycle stage matter; E. H. Bowman & C. E. Helfat, 2001, Does corporate strategy matter? *Strategic Management Journal*, 22: 1–23.

77. S. F. Karabag & C. Berggren, 2014, Antecedents of firm performance in emerging economies: Business groups, strategy, industry structure, and state support, *Journal of Business Research*, 67: 2212–2223; J. T. Mahoney & L. Qian, 2013, Market frictions as building blocks of an organizational economics approach to strategic management, *Strategic Management Journal*, 34: 1019–1041.

78. Schramm & Hu, Perspective: The evolution of R&D conduct in the pharmaceutical; J. Galbreath & P. Galvin, 2008, Firm factors, industry structure and performance variation: New empirical evidence to a classic debate, *Journal of Business Research*, 61: 109–117.

79. R. Casadesus-Masanell & F. Zhu, 2013, Business model innovation and competitive imitation: The case of sponsor-based business models, *Strategic Management Journal*, 34: 464–482; H. E. Posen, J. Lee, & S. Yi, 2013, The power of imperfect imitation, *Strategic Management Journal*, 34: 149–164; M. B. Lieberman & S. Asaba, 2006, Why do firms imitate each other? *Academy of Management Journal*, 31: 366–385.

80. M. E. Porter, 1985, *Competitive Advantage*, New York: Free Press; M. E. Porter, 1980, *Competitive Strategy*, New York: Free Press.

81. F. J. Mas-Ruiz, F. J., Ruiz-Moreno, & A. Ladrón de Guevara Martínez, 2014, Asymmetric rivalry within and between strategic groups, *Strategic Management Journal*, 35: 419–439; J. C. Short, D. J. Ketchen, Jr., T. B. Palmer, & G. T. M. Hult, 2007, Firm, strategic group, and industry influences on performance, *Strategic Management Journal*, 28: 147–167.

82. B. Kowitt, 2014, Fallen arches, *Fortune*, December 1, 106–116.

83. S. D. Pathak, Z. Wu, & D. Johnston, D. 2014, Toward a structural view of co-opetition in supply networks, *Journal of Operations Management*, 32: 254–267; T. W. Tong &

J. J. Reuer, 2010, Competitive consequences of interfirm collaboration: How joint ventures shape industry profitability, *Journal of International Business Studies*, 41: 1056–1073.

84. P. Brody & V. Pureswaran, 2015, The next digital gold rush: How the internet of things will create liquid, transparent markets, *Strategy & Leadership*, 43(1): 36–41; C. Moschieri, 2011, The implementation and structuring of divestitures: The unit's perspective, *Strategic Management Journal*, 32: 368–401.

85. A. M. McGahan & M. E. Porter, 2003, The emergence and sustainability of abnormal profits, *Strategic Organization*, 1: 79–108; M. McGahan, 1999, Competition, strategy and business performance, *California Management Review*, 41(3): 74–101.

86. N. J. Foss & P. G. Klein, 2014, Why managers still matter, *MIT Sloan Management Review*, 56(1): 73–80; J. W. Upson, D. J. Ketchen, B. L. Connelly, & A. L. Ranft, 2012, Competitor analysis and foothold moves, *Academy of Management Journal*, 55: 93–110; A. Zavyalova, M. D. Pfarrer, R. K. Reger, & D. K. Shapiro, 2012, Managing the message: The effects of firm actions and industry spillovers on media coverage following wrongdoing, *Academy of Management Journal*, 55: 1079–1101.

87. L. A., Costa, K. Cool, & I. Dierickx, 2013, The competitive implications of the deployment of unique resources, *Strategic Management Journal*, 34: 445–463; M. G. Jacobides, S. G. Winter, & S. M. Kassberger, 2012, The dynamics of wealth, profit and sustainable advantage, *Strategic Management Journal*, 33: 1384–1410; J. Kraaijenbrink, J.-C. Spender, & A. J. Groen, 2010, The resource-based view: A review and assessment of its critiques, *Journal of Management*, 38: 349–372.

88. M. Naor, J. S. Jones, E. S. Bernardes, S. M. Goldstein, & R. Schroeder, 2014, The culture-effectiveness link in a manufacturing context: A resource-based perspective, *Journal of World Business*, 49, 321–331; A. Arora & A. Nandkumar, 2012, Insecure advantage? Markets for technology and the value of resources for entrepreneurial ventures, *Strategic Management Journal*, 33: 231–251.

89. O. Schilke, 2014, On the contingent value of dynamic capabilities for competitive advantage: The nonlinear moderating effect of environmental dynamism, *Strategic Management Journal*, 35: 179–203; Teece, The foundations of enterprise performance: Dynamic and ordinary capabilities in an (economic) theory of firms.

90. P. J. Holahan, Z. Z. Sullivan, & S. K. Markham, 2014, Product development as core competence: How formal product development practices differ for radical, more innovative, and incremental product innovations, *Journal of Product Innovation Management*, 31: 329–345.

91. J. R. Lecuona & M. Reitzig, 2014, Knowledge worth having in 'excess': The value of tacit and firm-specific human resource slack, *Strategic Management Journal*, 35: 954–973; H. Wang & K. F. E. Wong, 2012, The effect of managerial bias on employees' specific human capital investments, *Journal of Management Studies*, 49: 1435–1458.

92. Y. Lin & L. Wu, 2014, Exploring the role of dynamic capabilities in firm performance under the resource-based view framework, *Journal of Business Research*, 67: 407–413; C. Weigelt, 2013, Leveraging supplier capabilities: The role of locus of capability development, *Strategic Management Journal*, 34: 1–21; S. L. Newbert, 2007, Empirical research on the resource-based view of the firm: An assessment and suggestions for future research, *Strategic Management Journal*, 28: 121–146.

93. R. Nag & D. A. Gioia, 2012, From common to uncommon knowledge: Foundations of firm-specific use of knowledge as a resource, *Academy of Management Journal*, 55: 421–455; D. M. DeCarolis, 2003, Competencies and imitability in the pharmaceutical industry: An analysis of their relationship with firm performance, *Journal of Management*, 29: 27–50.

94. Y. Y. Kor & A. Mesko, 2013, Dynamic managerial capabilities: Configuration and orchestration of top executives' capabilities and the firm's dominant logic, *Strategic Management Journal*, 34: 233–244; M. Gruber, F. Heinemann, & M. Brettel, 2010, Configurations of resources and capabilities and their performance implications: An exploratory study on technology ventures, *Strategic Management Journal*, 31: 1337–1356.

95. R. Kapoor & N. R. Furr, 2015, Complementarities and competition: Unpacking the drivers of entrants' technology choices in the solar photovoltaic industry, *Strategic Management Journal*, 36: 416–436; E. Levitas & H. A. Ndofor, 2006, What to do with the resource-based view: A few suggestions for what ails the RBV that supporters and opponents might accept, *Journal of Management Inquiry*, 15: 135–144.

96. B. Larrañeta, S. A. Zahra, & J. L. Galán González, 2014, Strategic repertoire variety and new venture growth: The moderating effects of origin and industry dynamism, *Strategic Management Journal*, 35: 761–772; M. Makhija, 2003, Comparing the source-based and market-based views of the firm: Empirical evidence from Czech privatization, *Strategic Management Journal*, 24: 433–451.

97. S. E. Reid & U. Brentani, 2015, Building a measurement model for market visioning competence and its proposed antecedents: organizational encouragement of divergent thinking, divergent thinking attitudes, and ideational behavior, *Journal of Product Innovation Management*, 32: 243–262.

98. C. Gallo, 2010, *The Innovation Secrets of Steve Jobs*, NY: McGraw-Hill.

99. G. Christ, 2014, Leadership & strategy: Life after Steve Jobs: CEO succession. *Industry Week*, April, 28.

100. A. M. Carton, C. Murphy, & J. R. Clark, 2014, A (blurry) vision of the future: How leader rhetoric about ultimate goals influences performance, *Academy of Management Journal*, 57: 1544–1570; Foss & Klein, Why managers still matter.

101. P. Bolton, M. K. Brunnermeier, & L Veldkamp, L. 2013, Leadership, coordination, and corporate culture, *Review of Economic Studies*, 80: 512–537; R. D. Ireland & M. A. Hitt, 1992, Mission statements: Importance, challenge, and recommendations for development, *Business Horizons*, 35: 34–42.

102. B. E. Perrott, 2015, Building the sustainable organization: An integrated approach, *Journal of Business Strategy*, 36(1): 41–51; S. Khalifa, 2012, Mission, purpose, and ambition: Redefining the mission statement, *Journal of Business and Strategy*, 5: 236–251.

103. R. Srinivasan, 2014, Visioning: The method and process, *OD Practitioner*, 46(1): 34–41; J. H. Davis, J. A. Ruhe, M. Lee, & U. Rajadhyaksha, 2007, Mission possible: Do school mission statements work? *Journal of Business Ethics*, 70: 99–110.

104. A. Ebrahim & V. K. Rangan, V. K. 2014, What Impact?, *California Management Review*, 56(3): 118–141; L. W. Fry & J. W. Slocum, Jr., 2008, Maximizing the triple bottom line through spiritual leadership, *Organizational Dynamics*, 37: 86–96; A. J. Ward, M. J. Lankau, A. C. Amason, J. A. Sonnenfeld, & B. A. Agle, 2007, Improving the performance of top management teams, *MIT Sloan Management Review*, 48(3): 85–90.

105. M. Cording, J. S. Harrison, R. E. Hoskisson, & K. Jonsen, 2014, "Walking the talk": A multi-stakeholder exploration of organizational authenticity, employee productivity and post-merger performance, *Academy of Management Perspectives*, 28: 38–56; K. Basu & G. Palazzo, 2008, Corporate social responsibility: A process model of sensemaking, *Academy of Management Review*, 33: 122–136.

106. R. Garcia-Castro & R. Aguilera, 2015, Incremental value creation and appropriation in a world with multiple stakeholders, *Strategic Management Journal*, forthcoming; G. Kenny, 2012, From a stakeholder viewpoint: Designing measurable objectives, *Journal of Business Strategy*, 33(6): 40–46;

D. A. Bosse, R. A. Phillips, & J. S. Harrison, 2009, Stakeholders, reciprocity, and firm performance, *Strategic Management Journal*, 30: 447–456.

107. N. Darnell, I. Henrique, & P. Sadorsky, 2010, Adopting proactive environmental strategy: The influence of stakeholders and firm size, *Journal of Management Studies*, 47: 1072–1122; G. Donaldson & J. W. Lorsch, 1983, *Decision Making at the Top: The Shaping of Strategic Direction*, New York: Basic Books, 37–40.

108. S. Sharma & I. Henriques, 2005, Stakeholder influences on sustainability practices in the Canadian forest products industry, *Strategic Management Journal*, 26: 159–180.

109. Y. Mishina, E. S. Block, & M. J. Mannor, 2015, The path dependence of organizational reputation: How social judgment influences assessments of capability and character, *Strategic Management Journal*, forthcoming; D. Crilly & P. Sloan, 2012, Enterprise logic: Explaining corporate attention to stakeholders from the 'inside-out', *Strategic Management Journal*, 33: 1174–1193.

110. Jacobides, BlackBerry forgot to manage the ecosystem.

111. K. Chang, I. Kim, & Y. Li, 2014, The heterogeneous impact of corporate social responsibility activities that target different stakeholders, *Journal of Business Ethics*, 125: 211–234.

112. J. Wolf, J. 2014, The relationship between sustainable supply chain management, stakeholder pressure and corporate sustainability performance, *Journal of Business Ethics*, 119: 317–328; A. Soleimani, W. D. Schneper, & W. Newbury, 2014, The impact of stakeholder power on corporate reputation: A cross-country corporate governance perspective, *Organization Science*, 25: 991–1008; G. Pandher & R. Currie, 2013, CEO compensation: A resource advantage and stakeholder-bargaining perspective, *Strategic Management Journal*, 34: 22–41.

113. A. H. Reilly & K. A. Hynan, 2014, Corporate communication, sustainability, and social media: It's not easy (really) being green, *Business Horizons*, 57: 747–758; D. Bush & B. D. Gelb, 2012, Antitrust enforcement: An inflection point? *Journal of Business Strategy*, 33(6): 15–21; J. L. Murrillo-Luna, C. Garces-Ayerbe, & P. Rivera-Torres, 2008, Why do patterns of environmental response differ? A stakeholders' pressure approach, *Strategic Management Journal*, 29: 1225–1240.

114. J. P. Doh & N. R. Quigley, 2014, Responsible leadership and stakeholder management: Influence pathways and organizational outcomes, *Academy of Management Perspectives*, 28: 255–274; R. Boutilier, 2009, *Stakeholder Politics: Social Capital, Sustainable Development, and the*

Corporation, Sheffield, U.K.: Greenleaf Publishing.

115. W. J. Henisz, S. Dorobantu, & L. J. Nartey, 2014, Spinning gold: The financial returns to stakeholder engagement, *Strategic Management Journal*, 35: 1727–1748; F. G. A. de Bakker & F. den Hond, 2008, Introducing the politics of stakeholder influence, *Business & Society*, 47: 8–20.

116. M. Goranova & L. V. Ryan, 2014, Shareholder activism: A multidisciplinary review, *Journal of Management*, 40: 1230–1268.

117. I. Filatotchev & O. Dotsenko, 2015, Shareholder activism in the UK: Types of activists, forms of activism, and their impact on a target's performance, *Journal of Management & Governance*, 19: 5–24; B. L. Connelly, L. Tihanyi, S. T. Certo, & M. A. Hitt, 2010, Marching to the beat of different drummers: The influence of institutional owners on competitive actions, *Academy of Management Journal*, 53: 723–742.

118. L. Jiang & Y. Zhu, 2014, Effects of foreign institutional ownership on foreign bank lending: Some evidence for emerging markets, *International Review of Finance*, 14: 263–293.

119. S. Wilkins & J. Huisman, 2014, Corporate images' impact on consumers' product choices: The case of multinational foreign subsidiaries, *Journal of Business Research*, 67: 2224–2230; L. Pierce, 2009, Big losses in ecosystems niches: How core firm decisions drive complementary product shakeouts, *Strategic Management Journal*, 30: 323–347.

120. M. Bertini & O. Koenigsberg, 2014, When customers help set prices, *MIT Sloan Management Review*, 55(4): 57–64; O. D. Fjeldstad & A. Sasson, 2010, Membership matters: On the value of being embedded in customer networks, *Journal of Management Studies*, 47: 944–966.

121. B. Batjargal, M. A. Hitt, A. S. Tsui, J.-L. Arregle, J. Webb, & T. Miller, 2013, Institutional polycentrism, entrepreneurs' social networks and new venture growth, *Academy of Management Journal*, in press.

122. H. Su, 2014, Business ethics and the development of intellectual capital, *Journal of Business Ethics*, 119: 87–98; D. A. Ready, L. A. Hill, & J. A. Conger, 2008, Winning the race for talent in emerging markets, *Harvard Business* Review, 86(11): 62–70.

123. S. E. Jackson, R. S. Schuler, & K. Jiang, 2014, An aspirational framework for strategic human resource management, *Academy of Management Annals*, 8: 1–56; T. R. Crook, S. Y. Todd, J. G. Combs, D. J. Woehr, & D. J. Ketchen, 2011, Does human capital matter? A meta-analysis of the relationship between human capital and firm performance, *Journal of Applied Psychology*, 96: 443–456.

124. R. Eckardt, B. C. Skaggs, & M. Youndt, 2014, Turnover and knowledge loss: An examination of the differential impact of production manager and worker turnover in service and manufacturing firm, *Journal of Management Studies*, 51: 1025–1057; J. I. Hancock, D. G. Allen, F. A. Bosco, K. R. McDaniel, & C. A. Pierce, 2013, Meta-analytic review of employee turnover as a predictor of firm performance, *Journal of Management*, 39: 573–603.

125. W. A. Schiemann, 2014, From talent management to talent optimization, *Journal of World Business*, 49: 281–288; R. Takeuchi, 2010, A critical review of expatriate adjustment research through a multiple stakeholder view: Progress, emerging trends and prospects, *Journal of Management*, 36: 1040–1064.

126. S. E. Reid & U. Brentani, 2015, Building a measurement model for market visioning competence and its proposed antecedents: organizational encouragement of divergent thinking, divergent thinking attitudes, and ideational behavior, *Journal of Product Innovation Management*, 32: 243–262; M. A. Hitt, K. T. Haynes, & R. Serpa, 2010, Strategic leadership for the 21st century, *Business Horizons*, 53: 437–444.

127. S. Gunz & L. Thorne, 2015, Introduction to the special issue on tone at the top, *Journal of Business Ethics*, 126: 1–2; C. Crossland, J. Zyung, N. Hiller, & D. Hambrick, 2014. CEO career variety: Effects on firm–level strategic and social novelty. *Academy of Management Journal*, 57: 652–674; D. C. Hambrick, 2007, Upper echelons theory: An update, *Academy of Management Review*, 32: 334–339.

128. G. Bhalla, 2014, How to plan and manage a project to co-create value with stakeholders, *Strategy & Leadership*, 42: 19–25; J. C. Camillus, 2008, Strategy as a wicked problem, *Harvard Business Review* 86(5): 99–106; A. Priestland & T. R. Hanig, 2005, Developing first-level managers, *Harvard Business Review*, 83(6): 113–120.

129. M. Voronov, D. De Clercq, & C. R. Hinings, 2013, Conformity and distinctiveness in a global institutional framework: The legitimation of Ontario fine wine, *Journal of Management Studies*, 50: 607–645; B. Gutierrez, S. M. Spencer, & G. Zhu, 2012, Thinking globally, leading locally: Chinese, Indian, and Western leadership, *Cross Cultural Management*, 19: 67–89.

130. D. B. Wangrow, D. J. Schepker, & V. L. Barker, 2014, Managerial discretion: An empirical review and focus on future research directions, *Journal of Management*, 41: 99–135; J. Li & Y. Tang, 2010, CEO hubris and firm risk taking in China: The moderating role of managerial discretion, *Academy of Management Journal*, 53: 45–68.

131. C. A. O'Reilly, D. F. Caldwell, J. A. Chatman, & B. Doerr, B. 2014, The promise and

problems of organizational culture: CEO personality, culture, and firm performance, *Group & Organization Management*, 39: 595–625.

132. D. C. Hambrick, S. E. Humphrey, & A. Gupta, 2015, Structural interdependence within top management teams: A key moderator of upper echelons predictions, *Strategic Management Journal*, 36: 449–461; K. D. Clark & P. G. Maggitti, 2012, TMT potency and strategic decision making in high technology firms, *Journal of Management Studies*, 49: 1168–1193.

133. M. M. Heyden, S. van Doorn, M. Reimer, F. J. Van Den Bosch, & H. W. Volberda, 2013, Perceived environmental dynamism, relative competitive performance, and top management team heterogeneity: Examining correlates of upper echelons' advice-seeking, *Organization Studies:* 34: 1327–1356; R. Shambaugh, 2011, Leading in today's economy: The transformational leadership model, in *What's Next 2011*, NY: McGraw-Hill.

134. S. Khavul & G. D. Bruton, 2013, Harnessing innovation for change: Sustainability and poverty in developing countries, *Journal of Management Studies*, 50: 285–306; A. Leiponen & C. E. Helfat, 2010, Innovation objectives, knowledge sources and the benefits of breadth, *Strategic Management Journal*, 31: 224–236.

135. L Wei & L. Wu, 2013, What a diverse top management team means: Testing an integrated model, *Journal of Management Studies*, 50: 389–412; T. Buyl, C. Boone, W. Hendriks, & P. Matthyssens, 2011, Top management team functional diversity and firm performance: The moderating role of CEO characteristics, *Journal of Management Studies*, 48: 151–177.

136. Stettner & Lavie, Ambidexterity under scrutiny: Exploration and exploitation via internal organization, alliances, and acquisitions; Q. Cao, Z. Simsek, & H. Zhang, 2010, Modelling the joint impact of the CEO and the TMT on organizational

ambidexterity, *Journal of Management Studies*, 47: 1272–1296.

137. N. Gaffney, D. Cooper, B. Kedia, & J. Clampit, 2014, Institutional transitions, global mindset, and EMNE internationalization, *European Management Journal*, 32: 383–391; M.-J. Chen & D. Miller, 2010, West meets east: Toward an ambicultural approach to management, *Academy of Management Perspectives*, 24: 17–37.

138. M. Loeb, 1993, Steven J. Ross, 1927–1992, *Fortune*, January 25, 4.

139. F. Jing, G. Avery, & H. Bergsteiner, 2014, Enhancing performance in small professional firms through vision communication and sharing, *Asia Pacific Journal of Management*, 31: 599–620.

140. R. F. Everett, 2014, A crack in the foundation: Why SWOT might be less than effective in market sensing analysis, *Journal of Marketing & Management*, 1: 58–78; M. M. Helms & J. Nixon, 2010, Exploring SWOT analysis—where are we now? A review of the academic research from the last decade, *Journal of Strategy and Management*, 3: 215–251.

141. T. Keil, T. Laamanen, & R. G. McGrath, 2013, Is a counterattack the best defense? Competitive dynamics through acquisitions, *Long Range Planning*, 46: 195–215; T. Yu, M. Subramaniam, & A. A. Cannella, Jr., 2009, Rivalry deterrence in international markets: Contingencies governing the mutual forbearance hypothesis, *Academy of Management Journal*, 52: 127–147.

142. O. Schilke & K. S. Cook, 2015, Sources of alliance partner trustworthiness: Integrating calculative and relational perspectives, *Strategic Management Journal*, 36: 276–297; K. H. Heimeriks, C. B. Bingham, & T. Laamanen, 2015, Unveiling the temporally contingent role of codification in alliance success, *Strategic Management Journal*, 36: 462–473.

143. L. A. Cunningham, 2015, The secret sauce of corporate leadership, *Wall Street Journal*, www.wsj.com, January 26; S. D. Julian, J. C. Ofori-Dankwa, & R. T. Justis, 2008, Understanding strategic responses to interest group pressures, *Strategic Management Journal*, 29: 963–984; C. Eesley & M. J. Lenox, 2006, Firm responses to secondary stakeholder action, *Strategic Management Journal*, 27: 765–781.

144. Y. Luo, Y. Liu, Q. Yang, V. Maksimov, & J. Hou, 2015, Improving performance and reducing cost in buyer–supplier relationships: The role of justice in curtailing opportunism, *Journal of Business Research*, 68: 607–615; Y. Luo, 2008, Procedural fairness and interfirm cooperation in strategic alliances, *Strategic Management Journal*, 29: 27–46.

145. H. S. James, D. Ng, & P. J. Klein, 2015, Complexity, novelty, and ethical judgment by entrepreneurs, *International Journal of Entrepreneurial Venturing*, forthcoming; B. A. Scott, A. S. Garza, D. E. Conlon, & K. You Jin, 2014, Why do managers act fairly in the first place? A daily investigation of "hot" and "cold" motives and discretion, *Academy of Management Journal*, 57: 1571–1591.

146. M. Sharif & T. Scandura, T. 2014, Do perceptions of ethical conduct matter during organizational change? Ethical leadership and employee involvement, *Journal of Business Ethics*, 124: 185–196; B. W. Heineman Jr., 2007, Avoiding integrity land mines, *Harvard Business Review*, 85(4): 100–108.

147. D. C. Hambrick & T. J. Quigley, 2014, Toward more accurate contextualization of the CEO effect on firm performance, *Strategic Management Journal*, 35: 473–491; P. Klarner & S. Raisch, 2013, Move to the beat—Rhythms of change and firm performance, *Academy of Management Journal*, 56: 160–184.

2

The External Environment: Opportunities, Threats, Industry Competition, and Competitor Analysis

Studying this chapter should provide you with the strategic management knowledge needed to:

2-1   Explain the importance of analyzing and understanding the firm's external environment.

2-2   Define and describe the general environment and the industry environment.

2-3   Discuss the four parts of the external environmental analysis process.

2-4   Name and describe the general environment's seven segments.

2-5   Identify the five competitive forces and explain how they determine an industry's profitability potential.

2-6   Define strategic groups and describe their influence on firms.

2-7   Describe what firms need to know about their competitors and different methods (including ethical standards) used to collect intelligence about them.

ARE THERE CRACKS IN THE GOLDEN ARCHES?

McDonald's is the largest restaurant chain in the world. It has 14,350 restaurants in the United States, with the largest market share of any such chain (7.3 percent). In total, it has more than 36,000 restaurants worldwide. Over the years, McDonald's was a leader, not only in market share, but also with the introduction of new menu items to the fast food market. For example, it first introduced breakfast items to this market, and its breakfast menu now accounts for about 25 percent of its sales. It successfully introduced Chicken McNuggets to this market, and currently, McDonald's is the single largest restaurant customer of Tyson Foods, the largest distributor of chicken products. In more recent years, McDonald's successfully introduced gourmet coffee products and began to compete against Starbucks. With all of this success, what is the problem?

The problems revolve around competition and changing consumer tastes. Consumers have become more health-conscious, and competitors have been more attuned to customer desires. As a result, McDonald's suffered a decline in its total sales revenue of 2.4 percent and a drop in net income of 15 percent in 2014. This was the first decline in both figures in 33 years. It seems that McDonald's did a poor job of analyzing its environment and especially its customers and competitors. During this same time, some of McDonald's competitors flourished. For example, Sonic enjoyed a 7 percent increase in its sales, and Chipotle recorded a large

Ruaridh Stewart/ZUMA Press/Newscom

20 percent increase. Other specialty burger restaurants, such as Smashburger, have stolen business from McDonald's even though their burgers are priced a little higher than McDonald's burgers. The quality of these competitors' products is perceived to be higher and many are "made to order" and thus customized to the customer's desires. And, partly because the volume and complexity of the McDonald's menu items have grown, the time required for service has also increased. This change has been most evident in the drive-through lanes in which the wait time has grown by approximately 20 percent in recent years.

Because of the lack of understanding the changing market and competitive landscape, McDonald's was unable to be proactive and now is in a reactive mode. For example, in 2013, it decided to add chicken wings to its menu. Wings were sold successfully at McDonald's in Hong Kong, and it imported its "cayenne-and-chili-pepper coating" used there. The market test for the wings in Atlanta was successful, so the firm implemented a major campaign to sell them at its restaurants throughout the United States. The eight-week campaign was a miserable failure (some referred to it as the "mighty wings debacle"). Perhaps they were too spicy for the broad market, but some believe that they were also too expensive at $1.00 per wing, with a box of five wings costing $1.00 more than a similar number at KFC. Because of these problems, McDonald's hired a new CEO in 2015, hoping to overcome its woes.

The new CEO must act quickly. McDonald's has recently announced that it is changing to use only chickens raised without antibiotics to be sensitive to human health concerns. It has also market tested custom hamburgers in Australia with success. In fact, Australia is one of

McDonald's bright spots around the world. Sales have increased in Australia when they have fallen in the United States, Europe, and Asia. Making major changes to the McDonald's menu is challenging partly because of its scale and supply chain. It orders hundreds of millions of pounds of chicken each year, so it will take a few years to fully implement the change to antibiotic-free chicken. Changing vegetables in Happy Meals (e.g., adding baby carrots) and implementing new wraps which require additional (new) vegetables (such as cucumbers) will take time because they require obtaining large scale suppliers that can provide the necessary quantity and quality at the right price and in the right location(s).

McDonald's was once a leader, and now it is fighting from behind, trying to stem its downturn. It has to respond quickly and effectively to its external environment, especially its customers and competitors.

Sources: A. Gasparro, 2015, For McDonald's, a minor menu change takes planning, MSN, www.msn.com/en-us/money, March 5; A. Gasparro, 2015, McDonald's new chief plots counter attack, *Wall Street Journal*, www.wsj.com, March 1; M. Hefferman, 2015, It's still a happy meal in Australia for McDonald's, *Sidney Times Herald*, www.smh.com.au, March 10; J. Kell, 2015, McDonald's sales still down as a new CEO takes the helm, *Fortune*, www.Fortune.com, March 9; D. Shanker, 2015, Dear McDonald's new CEO: Happy first day. Here's some (unsolicited) advice, *Fortune*, www.Fortune.com, March 2; S. Strom, 2015, McDonald's seeks its fast-food soul, *New York Times*, www.nytimes.com, March 7; S. Strom, 2015, McDonald's tests custom burgers and other new concepts as sales drop, *New York Times*, www.nytimes.com, January 23; B. Kowitt, 2014, Fallen Arches, *Fortune*, December, 106–116.

As suggested in the Opening Case and by research, the external environment (which includes the industry in which a firm competes as well as those against whom it competes) affects the competitive actions and responses firms take to outperform competitors and earn above-average returns.[1] For example, McDonald's has been experiencing a reduction in returns in recent times because of changing consumer tastes and enhanced competition. McDonald's is attempting to respond to the threats from its environment by changing its menu and types of supplies purchased. The sociocultural segment of the general environment (discussed in this chapter) is the source of some of the changing values in society placing a great emphasis on healthy food choices. The Opening Case also describes some of the ways McDonald's is responding to the specific concerns for health by purchasing only chicken that has not received antibiotics.

As noted in Chapter 1, the characteristics of today's external environment differ from historical conditions. For example, technological changes and the continuing growth of information gathering and processing capabilities increase the need for firms to develop effective competitive actions and responses on a timely basis.[2] (We fully discuss competitive actions and responses in Chapter 5.) Additionally, the rapid sociological changes occurring in many countries affect labor practices and the nature of products that increasingly diverse consumers demand. Governmental policies and laws also affect where and how firms choose to compete.[3] And, changes to a number of nations' financial regulatory systems that have been enacted since 2010 are expected to increase the complexity of organizations' financial transactions.[4]

Firms understand the external environment by acquiring information about competitors, customers, and other stakeholders to build their own base of knowledge and capabilities.[5] On the basis of the new information, firms take actions, such as building new capabilities and core competencies, in hopes of buffering themselves from any negative environmental effects and to pursue opportunities as the basis for better serving their stakeholders' needs.[6]

In summary, a firm's competitive actions and responses are influenced by the conditions in the three parts (the general, industry, and competitor) of its external environment (see Figure 2.1) and its understanding of those conditions. Next, we fully describe each part of the firm's external environment.

Figure 2.1 The External Environment

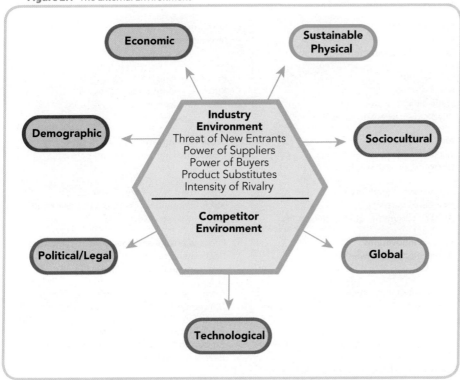

2-1 The General, Industry, and Competitor Environments

The **general environment** is composed of dimensions in the broader society that influence an industry and the firms within it.[7] We group these dimensions into seven environmental *segments:* demographic, economic, political/legal, sociocultural, technological, global, and sustainable physical. Examples of *elements* analyzed in each of these segments are shown in Table 2.1.

Firms cannot directly control the general environment's segments. Accordingly, what a company seeks to do is recognize trends in each segment of the general environment and then *predict* each trend's effect on it. For example, it has been predicted that over the next 10 to 20 years, millions of people living in emerging market countries will join the middle class. In fact, by 2030, it is predicted that two-thirds of the global middle class, about 525 million people, will live in the Asia-Pacific region of the world. Of course no firm, including large multinationals, is able to control where growth in potential customers may take place in the next decade or two. Nonetheless, firms must study this anticipated trend as a foundation for predicting its effects on their ability to identify strategies to use that will allow them to remain successful as market conditions change.[8]

The **industry environment** is the set of factors that directly influences a firm and its competitive actions and responses: the threat of new entrants, the power of suppliers, the power of buyers, the threat of product substitutes, and the intensity of rivalry among competing firms.[9] In total, the interactions among these five factors

The **general environment** is composed of dimensions in the broader society that influence an industry and the firms within it.

The **industry environment** is the set of factors that directly influences a firm and its competitive actions and responses: the threat of new entrants, the power of suppliers, the power of buyers, the threat of product substitutes, and the intensity of rivalry among competing firms.

Table 2.1 The General Environment: Segments and Elements

Demographic segment	• Population size • Age structure • Geographic distribution	• Ethnic mix • Income distribution
Economic segment	• Inflation rates • Interest rates • Trade deficits or surpluses • Budget deficits or surpluses	• Personal savings rate • Business savings rates • Gross domestic product
Political/Legal segment	• Antitrust laws • Taxation laws • Deregulation philosophies	• Labor training laws • Educational philosophies and policies
Sociocultural segment	• Women in the workforce • Workforce diversity • Attitudes about the quality of work life	• Shifts in work and career preferences • Shifts in preferences regarding product and service characteristics
Technological segment	• Product innovations • Applications of knowledge	• Focus of private and government-supported R&D expenditures • New communication technologies
Global segment	• Important political events • Critical global markets	• Newly industrialized countries • Different cultural and institutional attributes
Sustainable physical environment segment	• Energy consumption • Practices used to develop energy sources • Renewable energy efforts • Minimizing a firm's environmental footprint	• Availability of water as a resource • Producing environmentally friendly products • Reacting to natural or man-made disasters

determine an industry's profitability potential; in turn, the industry's profitability potential influences the choices each firm makes about its competitive actions and responses. The challenge for a firm is to locate a position within an industry where it can favorably influence the five factors or where it can successfully defend itself against their influence. The greater a firm's capacity to favorably influence its industry environment, the greater the likelihood it will earn above-average returns.

How companies gather and interpret information about their competitors is called **competitor analysis**. Understanding the firm's competitor environment complements the insights provided by studying the general and industry environments.[10] This means, for example, that McDonald's needs to do a better job of analyzing and understanding its general and industry environments.

An analysis of the general environment focuses on environmental trends and their implications, an analysis of the industry environment focuses on the factors and conditions influencing an industry's profitability potential, and an analysis of competitors is focused on predicting competitors' actions, responses, and intentions. In combination, the results of these three analyses influence the firm's vision, mission, choice of strategies, and the competitive actions and responses it will take to implement those strategies. Although we discuss each analysis separately, the firm can develop and implement a more effective strategy when it effectively integrates the insights provided by analyses of the general environment, the industry environment, and the competitor environment.

How companies gather and interpret information about their competitors is called **competitor analysis**.

2-2   **External Environmental Analysis**

Most firms face external environments that are turbulent, complex, and global—conditions that make interpreting those environments difficult.[11] To cope with often ambiguous and incomplete environmental data and to increase understanding of the general environment, firms complete an *external environmental analysis*. This analysis has four parts: scanning, monitoring, forecasting, and assessing (see Table 2.2).

Identifying opportunities and threats is an important objective of studying the general environment. An **opportunity** is a condition in the general environment that, if exploited effectively, helps a company reach strategic competitiveness. Most companies—and certainly large ones—continuously encounter multiple opportunities as well as threats.

In terms of possible opportunities, a combination of cultural, political, and economic factors is resulting in rapid retail growth in parts of Africa, Asia, and Latin America. Accordingly, Walmart, the world's largest retailer, and the next three largest global giants (France's Carrefour, U.K.–based Tesco, and Germany's Metro) are expanding in these regions. Walmart is expanding its number of retail units in Chile (404 units), India (20 units), and South Africa (360 units). Interestingly, Carrefour exited India after four years and in the same year (2014) that Tesco opened stores in India. While Metro closed its operations in Egypt, it has stores in China, Russia, Japan, Vietnam, and India in addition to many eastern European countries.[12]

A **threat** is a condition in the general environment that may hinder a company's efforts to achieve strategic competitiveness.[13] Finnish-based Nokia Corp. is dealing with threats including one regarding its intellectual property rights. In mid-2013, the company filed two complaints against competitor HTC Corp. alleging that the Taiwanese smartphone manufacturer had infringed on nine of Nokia's patents. However, the patent dispute ended in 2014 when the two companies signed a collaboration agreement.[14] This threat obviously deals with the political/legal segment.

Firms use multiple sources to analyze the general environment through scanning, monitoring, forecasting, and assessing. Examples of these sources include a wide variety of printed materials (such as trade publications, newspapers, business publications, and the results of academic research and public polls), trade shows, and suppliers, customers, and employees of public-sector organizations. Of course, the information available from Internet sources is of increasing importance to a firm's efforts to study the general environment.

2-2a   Scanning

Scanning entails the study of all segments in the general environment. Although challenging, scanning is critically important to the firms' efforts to understand trends in the general environment and to predict their implications. This is particularly the case for companies competing in highly volatile environments.[15]

Table 2.2 Parts of the External Environment Analysis

Scanning	• Identifying early signals of environmental changes and trends
Monitoring	• Detecting meaning through ongoing observations of environmental changes and trends
Forecasting	• Developing projections of anticipated outcomes based on monitored changes and trends
Assessing	• Determining the timing and importance of environmental changes and trends for firms' strategies and their management

An **opportunity** is a condition in the general environment that, if exploited effectively, helps a company reach strategic competitiveness.

A **threat** is a condition in the general environment that may hinder a company's efforts to achieve strategic competitiveness.

Through scanning, firms identify early signals of potential changes in the general environment and detect changes that are already under way.[16] Scanning activities must be aligned with the organizational context; a scanning system designed for a volatile environment is inappropriate for a firm in a stable environment.[17] Scanning often reveals ambiguous, incomplete, or unconnected data and information that require careful analysis.

Many firms use special software to help them identify events that are taking place in the environment and that are announced in public sources. For example, news event detection uses information-based systems to categorize text and reduce the trade-off between an important missed event and false alarm rates. Increasingly, these systems are used to study social media outlets as sources of information.[18]

Broadly speaking, the Internet provides a wealth of opportunities for scanning. Amazon.com, for example, records information about individuals visiting its website, particularly if a purchase is made. Amazon then welcomes these customers by name when they visit the website again. The firm sends messages to customers about specials and new products similar to those they purchased in previous visits. A number of other companies, such as Netflix, also collect demographic data about their customers in an attempt to identify their unique preferences (demographics is one of the segments in the general environment). More than 2.4 billion people use the Internet in some way including about 78.6 percent of the population in North America and 63.2 percent in Europe. So the Internet represents a healthy opportunity to gather information on users.[19]

2-2b   Monitoring

When *monitoring*, analysts observe environmental changes to see if an important trend is emerging from among those spotted through scanning.[20] Critical to successful monitoring is the firm's ability to detect meaning in environmental events and trends. For example, those monitoring retirement trends in the United States learned in 2013 that 57 percent of U.S. workers surveyed reported that excluding the value of their home, they have only $25,000 or less in savings and investments set aside for their retirement. This particular survey also discovered "that 28 percent of Americans have no confidence they will have enough money to retire comfortably—the highest level in the (survey's) 23-year history."[21] Partly because of the major economic recessions and low wage growth, 67 percent of respondents to a more recent survey suggested that they had savings that would cover only six months or less of their expenses. And, approximately 28 percent of the respondents said that they had no savings.[22] Firms seeking to serve retirees' financial needs will continue monitoring this change in workers' savings and investment patterns to see if a trend is developing. Once they identify that saving less for retirement (or other needs) is indeed a trend, these firms will seek to understand its competitive implications.

Effective monitoring requires the firm to identify important stakeholders and understand its reputation among these stakeholders as the foundation for serving their unique needs.[23] (Stakeholders' unique needs are described in Chapter 1.) One means of monitoring major stakeholders is by using directors that serve on other boards of directors (referred to as interlocking directorates). They facilitate information and knowledge transfer from external sources.[24] Scanning and monitoring are particularly important when a firm competes in an industry with high technological uncertainty.[25] Scanning and monitoring can provide the firm with information. These activities also serve as a means of importing knowledge about markets and about how to successfully commercialize the new technologies the firm has developed.[26]

2-2c   Forecasting

Scanning and monitoring are concerned with events and trends in the general environment at a point in time. When *forecasting*, analysts develop feasible projections of what might happen, and how quickly, as a result of the events and trends detected through scanning and monitoring.[27] For example, analysts might forecast the time that will be required for a new technology to reach the marketplace, the length of time before different corporate training procedures are required to deal with anticipated changes in the composition of the workforce, or how much time will elapse before changes in governmental taxation policies affect consumers' purchasing patterns.

Forecasting events and outcomes accurately is challenging. Forecasting demand for new technological products is difficult because technology trends are continually driving product life cycles shorter. This is particularly difficult for a firm such as Intel, whose products go into many customers' technological products, which are consistently updated. Increasing the difficulty, each new wafer fabrication or silicon chip technology production plant in which Intel invests becomes significantly more expensive for each generation of chip products. In this instance, having access to tools that allow better forecasting of electronic product demand is of value to Intel as the firm studies conditions in its external environment.[28]

2-2d   Assessing

When *assessing*, the objective is to determine the timing and significance of the effects of environmental changes and trends that have been identified.[29] Through scanning, monitoring, and forecasting, analysts are able to understand the general environment. Additionally, the intent of assessment is to specify the implications of that understanding. Without assessment, the firm has data that may be interesting but of unknown competitive relevance. Even if formal assessment is inadequate, the appropriate interpretation of that information is important.

Accurately assessing the trends expected to take place in the segments of a firm's general environment is important. However, accurately interpreting the meaning of those trends is even more important. In slightly different words, although gathering and organizing information is important, appropriately interpreting the intelligence the collected information provides to determine if an identified trend in the general environment is an opportunity or threat is critical.[30]

2-3   Segments of the General Environment

The general environment is composed of segments that are external to the firm (see Table 2.1). Although the degree of impact varies, these environmental segments affect all industries and the firms competing in them. The challenge to each firm is to scan, monitor, forecast, and assess the elements in each segment to predict their effects on it. Effective scanning, monitoring, forecasting, and assessing are vital to the firm's efforts to recognize and evaluate opportunities and threats.

2-3a   The Demographic Segment

The **demographic segment** is concerned with a population's size, age structure, geographic distribution, ethnic mix, and income distribution.[31] Demographic segments are commonly analyzed on a global basis because of their potential effects across countries' borders and because many firms compete in global markets.

Population Size

The world's population doubled (from 3 billion to 6 billion) between 1959 and 1999. Current projections suggest that population growth will continue in the twenty-first century, but at a slower pace. In 2015, the world's population was 7.3 billion, and it is projected to be 9 billion by 2042 and roughly 9.25 billion by 2050.[32] In 2015, China was the world's

The **demographic segment** is concerned with a population's size, age structure, geographic distribution, ethnic mix, and income distribution.

largest country by population with approximately 1.4 billion people. By 2050, however, India is expected to be the most populous nation in the world (approximately 1.69 billion). China (1.4 billion), the United States (439 million), Indonesia (313 million), and Pakistan (276 million) are expected to be the next four most populous countries in 2050.[33] Firms seeking to find growing markets in which to sell their goods and services want to recognize the market potential that may exist for them in these five nations.

Firms also want to study changes occurring within the populations of different nations and regions of the world to assess their strategic implications. For example, 23 percent of Japan's citizens are 65 or older, while the United States and China will not reach this level until 2036.[34] Aging populations are a significant problem for countries because of the need for workers and the burden of supporting retirement programs. In Japan and some other countries, employees are urged to work longer to overcome these problems.

Age Structure

The most noteworthy aspect of this element of the demographic segment is that the world's population is rapidly aging. For example, predictions are that "by 2050, over one-fifth of the U.S. population will be 65 or older up from the current figure (in 2012) of one-seventh. The number of centenarians worldwide will double by 2023 and double again by 2035. Projections suggest life expectancy will surpass 100 in some industrialized countries by the second half of this century—roughly triple the lifespan that prevailed worldwide throughout most of human history."[35] In China, the 65 and over population is expected to reach roughly 330 million by 2050, which will be close to one-fourth of the nation's total population.[36] In the 1950s, Japan's population was one of the youngest in the world. However, 45 is now the median age in Japan, with the projection that it will be 55 by 2040. With a fertility rate that is below replacement value, another prediction is that by 2040 there will be almost as many Japanese people 100 years old or older as there are newborns.[37] By 2050, almost 25 percent of the world's population will be aged 65 or older. These changes in the age of the population have significant implications for availability of qualified labor, healthcare retirement policies, and business opportunities among others.[38]

In Japan, an expectation that the working age population will shrink from 81 million to about 57 million by 2040 threatens companies with an inadequate workforce. On the other hand, there may be an opportunity for Japanese firms to increase the productivity of their workers and/or to establish additional operations in other nations. A potential opportunity is represented by delayed retirements of baby boomers (those born between 1947 and 1965) expected in the United States (and perhaps other countries). Delayed retirements may help companies "avoid or defer the baby-boomer brain drain that has been looming for so long." In this sense, "organizations now have a fresh opportunity to address the talent gap created by a shortage of critical skills in the marketplace as well as the experience gap created by multiple waves of downsizing over the past decade."[39] Firms can also use their older more experienced workers to transfer their knowledge to younger employees, helping them to quickly gain valuable skills. There is also an opportunity for firms to more effectively use the talent available in the workforce. For example, moving women into higher level professional and managerial jobs could offset the challenges created by decline in overall talent availability. And, based on research, it may even enhance overall outcomes.[40]

Geographic Distribution

How a population is distributed within countries and regions is subject to change over time. For example, over the last few decades the U.S. population has shifted from states in the Northeast and Great Lakes region to states in the west (California), south (Florida), and southwest (Texas). California's population has grown by approximately 5 million since 2000, while Texas's population has grown by 6.1 million, and Florida's by 3.9 million in the same time period.[41] These changes are characterized as moving from the "Frost Belt" to the "Sun Belt." Outcomes from these shifts include the facts that the gross domestic product (GDP) of California in 2011 was just under $2 trillion, an amount that makes California the ninth-largest economy in the world. In this same year, at a value of $1.3 trillion, Texas' GDP was second to that of California.[42]

The least popular states, based on people leaving in recent years, are Illinois, New Jersey New York, Michigan, Maine, Connecticut, and Wisconsin. In a shift in the pattern witnessed for the first decade-plus of the twenty-first century, Washington, D.C., has become one of the most popular destination for relocation along with Oregon. Washington, D.C., seemed to be popular because of its somewhat recession-proof economic opportunities generated by a maturing high-tech sector and federal government jobs. Additionally, the city of Portland, Oregon, is attractive for its mix of economic growth, effective urban planning, and scenic landscapes.[43]

Firms want to carefully study the patterns of population distributions in countries and regions to identify opportunities and threats. Thus, in the United States, current patterns suggest the possibility of opportunities in Washington, D.C., as well as in states on the West Coast, including Oregon, and those in the South and Southwest. In contrast, firms competing in the Northeast and Great Lakes areas may concentrate on identifying threats to their ability to operate profitably in those areas.

Of course, geographic distribution patterns differ throughout the world. For example, in China, the majority of the population still lives in rural areas; however, growth patterns are shifting to urban communities such as Shanghai and Beijing.[44] Recent shifts in Europe show small population gains for countries such as France, Germany, and the United Kingdom, while Greece experienced a small population decline. Overall, the geographic distribution patterns in Europe have been reasonably stable.[45]

Ethnic Mix

The ethnic mix of countries' populations continues to change, creating opportunities and threats for many companies as a result. For example, Hispanics have become the largest ethnic minority in the United States.[46] In fact, the U.S. Hispanic market is the third largest "Latin American" economy behind Brazil and Mexico. Spanish is now the dominant language in parts of the United States such as in Texas, California, Florida, and New Mexico. Given these facts, some firms might want to assess how their goods or services could be adapted to serve the unique needs of Hispanic consumers. Interestingly, by 2020, more than 50 percent of children in the United States will be a member of a minority ethnic group, and the population in the United States is projected to have a majority of minority ethnic members by 2044.[47] The ethnic diversity of the population is important not only because of consumer needs but also because of the labor force composition. Interestingly, research has shown that firms with greater ethnic diversity in their managerial team are likely to enjoy higher performance.[48]

Additional evidence is of interest to firms when examining this segment. For example, African countries are the most ethnically diverse in the world, with Uganda having the highest ethnic diversity rating and Liberia having the second highest. In contrast, Japan and the Koreas are the least ethnically diversified in their populations. European countries are largely ethnically homogeneous while the Americas are more diverse. "From the United States through Central America down to Brazil, the 'new world' countries, maybe in part because of their histories of relatively open immigration (and, in some cases, intermingling between natives and new arrivals) tend to be pretty diverse."[49]

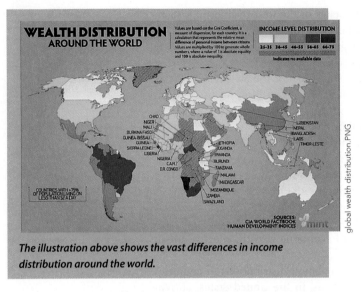

The illustration above shows the vast differences in income distribution around the world.

Income Distribution

Understanding how income is distributed within and across populations informs firms of different groups' purchasing power and discretionary income. Of particular interest to firms are the average incomes of households and individuals. For instance, the increase in dual-career couples has had a notable effect on average incomes. Although real income has been declining in general in some nations, the household income of dual-career couples has increased, especially in the United States. These figures yield strategically relevant information for firms. For instance, research indicates that whether an employee is part of a dual-career couple can strongly influence the willingness of the employee to accept an international assignment. However, because of recent global economic conditions, many companies were still pursuing international assignments but changing them to avoid some of the additional costs of funding expatriates abroad.[50]

The growth of the economy in China has drawn many firms, not only for the low-cost production, but also because of the large potential demand for products, given its large population base. However, in recent times, the amount of China's gross domestic product that makes up domestic consumption is the lowest of any major economy at less than one-third. In comparison, India's domestic consumption of consumer goods accounts for two-thirds of its economy, or twice China's level. As such, many western multinationals are interested in India as a consumption market as its middle class grows extensively. Although India has poor infrastructure, its consumers are in a better position to spend. Because of situations such as this, paying attention to the differences between markets based on income distribution can be very important.[51] These differences across nations suggest it is important for most firms to identify the economic systems that are most likely to produce the most income growth and market opportunities.[52] Thus, the economic segment is a critically important focus of firms' environmental analysis.

2-3b   The Economic Segment

The **economic environment** refers to the nature and direction of the economy in which a firm competes or may compete.[53] In general, firms seek to compete in relatively stable economies with strong growth potential. Because nations are interconnected as a result of the global economy, firms must scan, monitor, forecast, and assess the health of their host nation as well as the health of the economies outside it.

It is challenging for firms studying the economic environment to predict economic trends that may occur and their effects on them. There are at least two reasons for this. First, the global recession of 2008 and 2009 created numerous problems for companies throughout the world, including problems of reduced consumer demand, increases in firms' inventory levels, development of additional governmental regulations, and a tightening of access to financial resources. Second, the global recovery from the economic shock in 2008 and 2009 continues to be persistently slow and relatively weak compared to previous recoveries. Firms have to adjust not only to the economic shock and try to recover from it, they have to respond to what appears to be an unpredictable recovery.

The **economic environment** refers to the nature and direction of the economy in which a firm competes or may compete.

For example, the economies in a number of European countries are still suffering from the major recession (e.g., Greece, Spain). Of likely concern to firms is the fact that historically, high degrees of economic uncertainty coincide with periods of lower growth. And again, according to some research, "it is clear that (economic) uncertainty has increased in recent times."[54] This current degree of economic uncertainty suggests the possibility of slower growth for the foreseeable future.

When facing economic uncertainty, firms want to be certain to study the economic environment in multiple regions and countries throughout the world. Although economic growth remains relatively weak and economic uncertainty has been strong in Europe, the economic growth has been better in the United States in recent times. For example, the projected average annual economic growth in Europe for 2015–2017 is 1.4 percent and in the United States it is 2.9 percent. Alternatively, the projected average annual economic growth for 2015–2017 is 7.0 percent in China, 6.8 percent in India, 2.6 percent in Brazil, and 3.6 percent in Mexico. These estimates highlight the anticipation of the continuing development of emerging economies.[55] Ideally, firms will be able to pursue growth opportunities in regions and nations where they exist while avoiding the threats of slow growth periods in other settings.

Christopher Polk/ACMA2010/Getty Images

To date, most legalized gambling has been provided in resorts such as MGM Resorts. However, recent changes in regulations within the state of Nevada in the United States allows online gambling which is now being evaluated as an opportunity for these resorts.

2-3c   The Political/Legal Segment

The **political/legal segment** is the arena in which organizations and interest groups compete for attention, resources, and a voice in overseeing the body of laws and regulations guiding interactions among nations as well as between firms and various local governmental agencies.[56] Essentially, this segment is concerned with how organizations try to influence governments and how they try to understand the influences (current and projected) of those governments on their competitive actions and responses. Commonly, firms develop a political strategy to specify how they will study the political/legal segment as well as approaches they might take (such as lobbying efforts) in order to successfully deal with opportunities and threats that surface within this segment at different points in time.[57]

Regulations formed in response to new national, regional, state, and/or local laws that are legislated often influence a firm's competitive actions and responses.[58] For example, the state of Nevada in the United States recently legalized the business of online poker/gambling. New Jersey and Delaware quickly took the same action. In response to Nevada's regulatory change, firms such as MGM Resorts International were trying to decide the degree to which these decisions represented a viable opportunity. According to a MGM official, the immediate concern with respect to Nevada is that "the state may be too small to provide a lucrative online market on a stand-alone basis."[59]

At a regional level, changes in the laws regarding the appropriate regulation of European banks are still being actively debated.[60] For interactive, technology-based firms

The **political/legal segment** is the arena in which organizations and interest groups compete for attention, resources, and a voice in overseeing the body of laws and regulations guiding interactions among nations as well as between firms and various local governmental agencies.

such as Facebook, Google, and Amazon, among others, "the effort in Europe to adopt the world's strongest data protection law has drawn the attention of dozens of lobbyists from U.S. technology and advertising companies."[61] Highly restrictive laws about consumer privacy could threaten how these firms conduct business in the European Union. Finally, in a comprehensive sense, recent transformations from state-owned to private firms occurring in multiple nations have substantial implications for the competitive landscapes in a number of countries and across multiple industries.[62]

2-3d   The Sociocultural Segment

The **sociocultural segment** is concerned with a society's attitudes and cultural values. Because attitudes and values form the cornerstone of a society, they often drive demographic, economic, political/legal, and technological conditions and changes.

Individual societies' attitudes and cultural orientations are anything but stable, meaning that firms must carefully scan, monitor, forecast, and assess them to recognize and study associated opportunities and threats. Successful firms must also have an awareness of changes taking place in the societies and their associated cultures in which they are competing. Indeed, societal and culture changes challenge firms to find ways to "adapt to stay ahead of their competitors and stay relevant in the minds of their consumers."[63] Research has shown that sociocultural factors influence the entry into new markets and the development of new firms in a country.[64]

Attitudes about and approaches to health care are being evaluated in nations and regions throughout the world. For Europe, the European Commission has developed a health care strategy for all of Europe that is oriented to preventing diseases while tackling lifestyle factors influencing health such as nutrition, working conditions, and physical activity. This Commission argues that promoting attitudes to take care of one's health is especially important in the context of an aging Europe as shown by the projection that the proportion of people over 65 living in Europe will increase from 17 percent in 2010 to almost 30 percent by 2060.[65] At issue for business firms is that attitudes and values about health care can affect them; accordingly, they must carefully examine trends regarding health care in order to anticipate the effects on their operations.

The **sociocultural segment** is concerned with a society's attitudes and cultural values.

As the U.S. labor force has grown in size, it has become more diverse, with significantly more women and minorities from a variety of cultures entering the workplace. In 1993, the total U.S. workforce was slightly less than 130 million; in 2005, it was slightly greater than 148 million. It is predicted to grow to more than 192 million by 2050.

However, the rate of growth in the U.S. labor force has declined over the past two decades largely as a result of slower growth of the nation's population and because of a downward trend in the labor force participation rate. More specifically, data show that "after nearly five decades of steady growth, the overall participation rate—defined as the proportion of the civilian non-institutional population in the labor force—peaked at an annual average of 67.1 percent for each year from 1997 to 2000.

© Alexander Raths/Shutterstock.com

Healthcare is becoming increasingly important as the proportion of people older than 65 is growing larger in many nations throughout the world.

By September 2012, the rate had dropped to 63.6 percent"[66] and is expected to fall to 58.5 percent by 2050. Other changes in the U.S. labor force between 2010 and 2050 are expected. During this time period, the growth in Asian members of the labor force is projected to more than double in size, while the growth in Caucasian members of the labor force is predicted to be much slower compared to other racial groups. In contrast, people of Hispanic origin are expected to account for roughly 80 percent of the total growth in the labor force. Finally, "it is projected that the higher growth rate of the female labor force relative to that of men will end by 2020, and the growth rates for men and women will be similar for the 2020–2050 period."[67]

Greater diversity in the workforce creates challenges and opportunities, including combining the best of both men's and women's traditional leadership styles. Although diversity in the workforce has the potential to improve performance, research indicates that diversity initiatives must be successfully managed in order to reap these organizational benefits.

Although the lifestyle and workforce changes referenced previously reflect the attitudes and values of the U.S. population, each country is unique with respect to these sociocultural indicators. National cultural values affect behavior in organizations and thus also influence organizational outcomes such as differences in CEO compensation.[68] Likewise, the national culture influences to a large extent the internationalization strategy that firms pursue relative to one's home country.[69] Knowledge sharing is important for dispersing new knowledge in organizations and increasing the speed in implementing innovations. Personal relationships are especially important in China as *guanxi* (personal relationships or good connections) has become a way of doing business within the country and for individuals to advance their careers in what is becoming a more open market society. Understanding the importance of guanxi is critical for foreign firms doing business in China.[70]

2-3e   The Technological Segment

Pervasive and diversified in scope, technological changes affect many parts of societies. These effects occur primarily through new products, processes, and materials. The **technological segment** includes the institutions and activities involved in creating new knowledge and translating that knowledge into new outputs, products, processes, and materials.

Given the rapid pace of technological change and risk of disruption, it is vital for firms to thoroughly study the technological segment.[71] The importance of these efforts is suggested by the finding that early adopters of new technology often achieve higher market shares and earn higher returns. Thus, both large and small firms should continuously scan the general environment to identify potential substitutes for technologies that are in current use, as well as to identify newly emerging technologies from which their firm could derive competitive advantage.[72]

As a significant technological development, the Internet offers firms a remarkable capability in terms of their efforts to scan, monitor, forecast, and assess conditions in their general environment. Companies continue to study the Internet's capabilities to anticipate how it allows them to create more value for customers and to anticipate future trends.

Additionally, the Internet generates a significant number of opportunities and threats for firms across the world. Predictions about Internet usage in the years to come are one reason for this. By 2016, the estimate is that there will be 3 billion Internet users globally. Overall, firms can expect that in the future the Internet "will have more users (especially in developing markets), more mobile users, more users accessing it with various devices

The **technological segment** includes the institutions and activities involved in creating new knowledge and translating that knowledge into new outputs, products, processes, and materials.

throughout the day, and many more people engaged in an increasingly participatory medium."[73] Considering that about 144 billion e-mails are currently sent each day, and there has been an explosive growth in the demand for mobile Internet access, the effect of this increase in users has significant implications for businesses.[74]

In spite of the Internet's far-reaching effects and the opportunities and threats associated with its potential, wireless communication technology is becoming a significant technological opportunity for companies to pursue. Handheld devices and other wireless communications equipment are used to access a variety of network-based services. The use of handheld computers with wireless network connectivity, Web-enabled mobile phone handsets, and other emerging platforms (e.g., consumer Internet-access devices such as the iPhone, iPad, Apple Watch, and Kindle) has increased substantially and may soon become the dominant form of communication and commerce. In fact, with each new version of these products, additional functionalities and software applications are generating multiple opportunities—and potential threats—for companies of all types.

2-3f   The Global Segment

The **global segment** includes relevant new global markets, existing markets that are changing, important international political events, and critical cultural and institutional characteristics of global markets.[75] For example, firms competing in the automobile industry must study the global segment. The fact that consumers in multiple nations are willing to buy cars and trucks "from whatever area of the world"[76] supports this position.

When studying the global segment, firms should recognize that globalization of business markets may create opportunities to enter new markets as well as threats that new competitors from other economies may also enter their market.[77] In terms of an opportunity for automobile manufacturers, the possibility for these firms to sell their products outside of their home market would seem attractive. But what markets might firms choose to enter? Currently, automobile and truck sales are expected to increase in Brazil, Russia, India, China, and to a lesser extent, Indonesia, and Malaysia. In contrast, sales are expected to decline, at least in the near term, in Europe and Japan. These markets, then, are the most and least attractive ones for automobile manufacturers desiring to sell outside their domestic market. At the same time, from the perspective of a threat, Japan, Germany, Korea, Spain, France, and the United States appear to have excess production capacity in the automobile manufacturing industry. In turn, overcapacity signals the possibility that companies based in markets where this is the case will simultaneously attempt to increase their exports as well as sales in their domestic market.[78] Thus, global automobile manufacturers should carefully examine the global segment in order to precisely identify all opportunities and threats.

In light of threats associated with participating in international markets, some firms choose to take a more cautious approach to globalization. For example, family business firms, even the larger ones, often take a conservative approach to entering international markets. These firms participate in what some refer to as *globalfocusing*. Globalfocusing often is used by firms with moderate levels of international operations who increase their internationalization by focusing on global niche markets.[79] This approach allows firms to build on to and use their core competencies while limiting their risks within the niche market. Another way in which firms limit their risks in international markets is to focus their operations and sales in one region of the world.[80] Success with these efforts finds a firm building relationships in and knowledge of its markets. As the firm builds these strengths, rivals find it more difficult to enter its markets and compete successfully.

The **global segment** includes relevant new global markets, existing markets that are changing, important international political events, and critical cultural and institutional characteristics of global markets.

Firms competing in global markets should recognize each market's sociocultural and institutional attributes. For example, Korean ideology emphasizes communitarianism, a characteristic of many Asian countries. Alternatively, the ideology in China calls for an emphasis on *guanxi*—personal connections—while in Japan, the focus is on *wa*—group harmony and social cohesion.[81] The institutional context of China suggests a major emphasis on centralized planning by the government. The Chinese government provides incentives to firms to develop alliances with foreign firms having sophisticated technology in hopes of building knowledge and introducing new technologies to the Chinese markets over time.[82] As such, it is important to analyze the strategic intent of foreign firms when pursuing alliances and joint ventures abroad, especially where the local partners are receiving technology which may in the long run reduce the foreign firms' advantages.[83]

Increasingly, the *informal economy* as it exists throughout the world is another aspect of the global segment requiring analysis. Growing in size, this economy has implications for firms' competitive actions and responses in that increasingly firms competing in the formal economy will find that they are competing against informal economy companies as well.

2-3g The Sustainable Physical Environment Segment

The **sustainable physical environment segment** refers to potential and actual changes in the physical environment and business practices that are intended to positively respond to those changes with the intent of creating a sustainable environment.[84] Concerned with trends oriented to sustaining the world's physical environment, firms recognize that ecological, social, and economic systems interactively influence what happens in this particular segment and that they are part of an interconnected global society.[85]

Companies across the globe are concerned about the physical environment, and many record the actions they are taking in reports with names such as "Sustainability" and "Corporate Social Responsibility." Moreover and in a comprehensive sense, an increasing number of companies are interested in sustainable development, which is "the development that meets the needs of the present without compromising the ability of future generations to meet their own needs."[86]

There are many parts or attributes of the physical environment that firms consider as they try to identify trends in the physical environment segment.[87] Because of the importance to firms of becoming sustainable, certification programs have been developed to help them understand how to be sustainable organizations.[88] As the world's largest retailer, Walmart's environmental footprint is huge, meaning that trends in the physical environment can significantly affect this firm and how it chooses to operate. Perhaps in light of trends occurring in the physical environment, Walmart has announced that its goal is to produce zero waste and to use 100 percent renewable energy to power its operations.[89]

As our discussion of the general environment shows, identifying anticipated changes and trends among segments and their elements is a key objective of analyzing this environment. With a focus on the future, the analysis of the general environment allows firms to identify opportunities and threats. It is necessary to have a top management team with the experience, knowledge, and sensitivity required to effectively analyze the conditions in a firm's general environment and other parts such as the industry environment and competitors.[90] In fact, it seems that the prior CEO of Target may not have been committed to analyzing the environment in depth (See Strategic Focus on Target). But the new CEO, Brian Cornell, demonstrated his commitment by locating his office close to the center of the data collection unit and checking in with the staff in this unit each morning to gain the latest information.

The **sustainable physical environment segment** refers to potential and actual changes in the physical environment and business practices that are intended to positively respond to those changes with the intent of creating a sustainable environment.

Target Lost Its Sway Because Tar-zhey No Longer Drew the Customers

Target became known by consumers as Tar-zhey, the retailer of cheaper but 'chic' products. The firm offered a step up in quality goods at a slightly higher price than discount retailers such as Walmart, but was targeted below major, first line retailers such Macy's and Nordstrom. Additionally, it promoted its stores to offer one-stop shopping with clothing, toys, health products, and food goods, among other products. For many years, Tar-zhey "hit the bullseye" and performed well serving this large niche in the market. But the company took its eye off the target and began losing market share (along with other poor strategic actions).

The first major crack in the ship appeared with the announcement of a massive cyberattack on Target's computer system that netted customers' personal information. The attack exposed customers (data on 70 million customers) to potentially substantial losses due to credit card fraud. Not only was this a public relations disaster, it drew a focus on Target that identified other problems. The "light" on Target showed that the strategic decision to enter the Canadian market in a major way (133 stores across multiple geographic areas) was failing. Finally, the careful analysis showed that Target was losing customers to established competitors and new rivals, especially Internet retailers (e.g., Amazon.com).

Target's marketing chief stated that "it's not that we became insular. We were insular." This suggests that the firm was not analyzing its environment. By allowing rivals, and especially newer Internet competitors, to woo the company's customers, it lost sales, market share, and profits. It obviously did not predict and prepare for the significant competition from Internet rivals. Competitors were offering better value to customers (perhaps more variety and convenience through online sales). When combined with the loss of consumer confidence because of the massive hack of personal customer data, Target's reputation and market share were simultaneously harmed.

The unparalleled failure of the Canadian operations within a very short time (two years) also showed a lack of market understanding likely stemming from the failure to analyze the market. It is probable that all of the problems Target was experiencing were transferred to its Canadian operations as well. In addition, it failed to attract customers from its major Canadian retailers, such as Loblaw Companies, Canada's largest grocer that recently introduced low-cost clothing boutiques. Costco and Walmart were also well-established in the Canadian market. Target was unable to differentiate the value it provided from the established retailers in Canada. It also experienced problems in its Canadian supply chain suggesting again that it did not fully understand the business markets in Canada before entering the market.

Because of all of the problems experienced, Target's CEO resigned in May 2014. A new CEO, Brian Cornell, was hired three months later. He was a top executive at PepsiCo and had experience heading Sam's Warehouse for Walmart as well. Cornell is the first CEO to be hired from outside the company, and most of his experience is from outside the industry as well. Since arriving on the job in August of 2014, Cornell has started making changes. For example, he is trying to regain Target's "chic" image by focusing on fashion, infant's, children's, and health departments to increase customer traffic and sales. The focus in foods is more upscale, more organic food, specialty granola, coffee and tea, wine, and beer. Sales exceeded the forecast in the fourth quarter of 2014 with the highest growth in three years. In January 2015, Cornell also closed all Canadian stores and thereby laid off 17,600 employees, a painful but necessary move. Finally, he announced another layoff of close to 2,000 employees in March 2015. Most of these employees will come from the main office with the intent to make Target more nimble and agile.

Lily Pulitzer has been providing bold fashions for resort wear for more than 50 years.

Interestingly, Cornell did not take the large corner suite accorded to the former CEOs but instead chose a smaller office near the company's market data collection site. There a staff of ten employees gather information from social media sites such as Pinterest, Facebook, and Twitter and from television news from nine large TV screens. The CEO stops by every morning to learn the latest information. These actions alone suggest the importance he places on gathering and analyzing data on the market and competitors' actions.

Sources: 2015, What your new CEO is reading: Smell ya later; targets new CEO, *CIO Journal/Wall Street Journal*, www.wsj.com/cio, March 6; I. Austen & H. Tabuchi, 2015, Target's red ink runs out in Canada, *New York Times*, www.ntimes.com, January 15; H. Tabuchi, 2015, Target plans to cut jobs to help save $2 billion, *New York Times*, www.ntimes.com, March 3; P. Ziobro & C. Delaney, 2015, Target sales grow at fastest rate in three years, *Wall Street Journal*, www.wsj.com, February 25; J. Reingold, 2014, Can Target's new CEO get the struggling retailer back on target? *Fortune*, www.fortune.com, July 31; G. Smith, 2014, Target turns to PepsiCo's Brian Cornell to restore its fortunes, *Fortune*, www.fortune.com, July 31; P. Ziobro, M. Langley, & J. S. Lublin, 2014, Target's problem: Tar-zhey isn't working. *Wall Street Journal*, www.wsj.com, May 5.

As described in the Strategic Focus, Target failed to maintain a good understanding of its industry; hence, the loss of market share to new Internet company rivals and other more established competitors. It did not understand its markets, competitors, and suppliers in Canada, and thus its entry into the Canadian market failed miserably. We conclude that critical to a firm's choices of strategies and their associated competitive actions and responses is an understanding of its industry environment and its competitors. And, the country's general environment influences the industry and competitive environments.[91] Next, we discuss the analyses firms complete to gain such an understanding.

2-4 Industry Environment Analysis

An **industry** is a group of firms producing products that are close substitutes. In the course of competition, these firms influence one another. Typically, companies use a rich mix of different competitive strategies to pursue above-average returns when competing in a particular industry. An industry's structural characteristics influence a firm's choice of strategies.[92]

Compared with the general environment, the industry environment (measured primarily in the form of its characteristics) has a more direct effect on the competitive actions and responses a firm takes to succeed.[93] To study an industry, the firm examines five forces that affect the ability of all firms to operate profitably within a given industry. Shown in Figure 2.2, the five forces are: the threats posed by new entrants, the power of suppliers, the power of buyers, product substitutes, and the intensity of rivalry among competitors.

The five forces of competition model depicted in Figure 2.2 expands the scope of a firm's competitive analysis. Historically, when studying the competitive environment, firms concentrated on companies with which they directly competed. However, firms must search more broadly to recognize current and potential competitors by identifying

Figure 2.2 The Five Forces of Competition Model

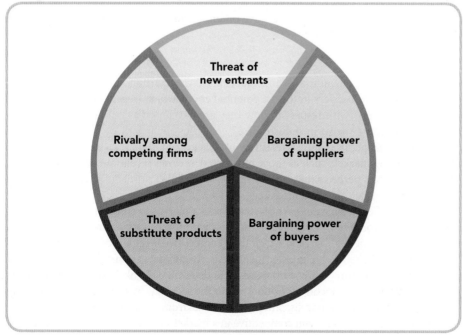

An **industry** is a group of firms producing products that are close substitutes.

potential customers as well as the firms serving them. For example, the communications industry is now broadly defined as encompassing media companies, telecoms, entertainment companies, and companies producing devices such as smartphones.[94] In such an environment, firms must study many other industries to identify companies with capabilities (especially technology-based capabilities) that might be the foundation for producing a good or a service that can compete against what they are producing.

When studying the industry environment, firms must also recognize that suppliers can become a firm's competitors (by integrating forward) as can buyers (by integrating backward). For example, several firms have integrated forward in the pharmaceutical industry by acquiring distributors or wholesalers. In addition, firms choosing to enter a new market and those producing products that are adequate substitutes for existing products can become a company's competitors.

Next, we examine the five forces the firm needs to analyze in order to understand the profitability potential within an industry (or a segment of an industry) in which it competes or may choose to compete.

2-4a Threat of New Entrants

Identifying new entrants is important because they can threaten the market share of existing competitors.[95] One reason new entrants pose such a threat is that they bring additional production capacity. Unless the demand for a good or service is increasing, additional capacity holds consumers' costs down, resulting in less revenue and lower returns for competing firms. Often, new entrants have a keen interest in gaining a large market share. As a result, new competitors may force existing firms to be more efficient and to learn how to compete in new dimensions (e.g., using an Internet-based distribution channel).

The likelihood that firms will enter an industry is a function of two factors: barriers to entry and the retaliation expected from current industry participants. Entry barriers make it difficult for new firms to enter an industry and often place them at a competitive disadvantage even when they are able to enter. As such, high entry barriers tend to increase the returns for existing firms in the industry and may allow some firms to dominate the industry.[96] Thus, firms competing successfully in an industry want to maintain high entry barriers in order to discourage potential competitors from deciding to enter the industry.

Barriers to Entry

Firms competing in an industry (and especially those earning above-average returns) try to develop entry barriers to thwart potential competitors. In general, more is known about entry barriers (with respect to how they are developed as well as paths firms can pursue to overcome them) in industrialized countries such as those in North America and Western Europe. In contrast, relatively little is known about barriers to entry in the rapidly emerging markets such as those in China. However, recent research suggests that Chinese executives perceive that advertising effects are the most significant of seven barriers to China, while capital requirements are viewed as the least important.[97]

There are different kinds of barriers to entering a market to consider when examining an industry environment. Companies competing within a particular industry study these barriers to determine the degree to which their competitive position reduces the likelihood of new competitors being able to enter the industry to compete against them. Firms considering entering an industry study entry barriers to determine the likelihood of being able to identify an attractive competitive position within the industry. Next, we discuss several significant entry barriers that may discourage competitors from entering a market and that may facilitate a firm's ability to remain competitive in a market in which it currently competes.

Economies of Scale   *Economies of scale* are derived from incremental efficiency improvements through experience as a firm grows larger. Therefore, the cost of producing each unit declines as the quantity of a product produced during a given period increases. A new entrant is unlikely to quickly generate the level of demand for its product that in turn would allow it to develop economies of scale.

Economies of scale can be developed in most business functions, such as marketing, manufacturing, research and development, and purchasing.[98] Firms sometimes form strategic alliances or joint ventures to gain scale economies. This is the case for Mitsubishi Heavy Industries Ltd. and Hitachi Ltd., as these companies "merged their operations for fossil-fuel-based power systems into a joint venture aimed at gaining scale to compete against global rivals."[99]

Becoming more flexible in terms of being able to meet shifts in customer demand is another benefit for an industry incumbent and a possible entry barrier for the firms considering entering the industry. For example, a firm may choose to reduce its price with the intention of capturing a larger share of the market. Alternatively, it may keep its price constant to increase profits. In so doing, it likely will increase its free cash flow, which is very helpful during financially challenging times.

Some competitive conditions reduce the ability of economies of scale to create an entry barrier such as the use of scale free resources.[100] Also, many companies now customize their products for large numbers of small customer groups. In these cases, customized products are not manufactured in the volumes necessary to achieve economies of scale. Customization is made possible by several factors including flexible manufacturing systems. In fact, the new manufacturing technology facilitated by advanced information systems has allowed the development of mass customization in an increasing number of industries. Online ordering has enhanced customers' ability to buy customized products. Companies manufacturing customized products can respond quickly to customers' needs in lieu of developing scale economies.

Product Differentiation   Over time, customers may come to believe that a firm's product is unique. This belief can result from the firm's service to the customer, effective advertising campaigns, or being the first to market a good or service.[101] Greater levels of perceived product uniqueness create customers who consistently purchase a firm's products. To combat the perception of uniqueness, new entrants frequently offer products at lower prices. This decision, however, may result in lower profits or even losses.

The Coca-Cola Company and PepsiCo have established strong brands in the markets in which they compete, and these companies compete against each other in countries throughout the world. Because each of these competitors has allocated a significant amount of resources over many decades to build its brands, customer loyalty is strong for each firm. When considering entry into the soft drink market, a potential entrant would be well advised to pause to determine actions it would take for the purpose of trying to overcome the brand image and consumer loyalty each of these giants possess.

Capital Requirements   Competing in a new industry requires a firm to have resources to invest. In addition to physical facilities, capital is needed for inventories, marketing activities, and other critical business functions. Even when a new industry is attractive, the capital required for successful market entry may not be available to pursue the market opportunity.[102] For example, defense industries are difficult to enter because of the substantial resource investments required to be competitive. In addition, because of the high knowledge requirements of the defense industry, a firm might acquire an existing company as a means of entering this industry, but it must have access to the capital necessary to do this.

Switching Costs   *Switching costs* are the one-time costs customers incur when they buy from a different supplier. The costs of buying new ancillary equipment and of retraining employees, and even the psychological costs of ending a relationship, may be incurred in switching to a new supplier. In some cases, switching costs are low, such as when the consumer switches to a different brand of soft drink. Switching costs can vary as a function of time, as shown by the fact that in terms of credit hours toward graduation, the cost to a student to transfer from one university to another as a freshman is much lower than it is when the student is entering the senior year.

Occasionally, a decision made by manufacturers to produce a new, innovative product creates high switching costs for customers. Customer loyalty programs, such as airlines' frequent flyer miles, are intended to increase the customer's switching costs. If switching costs are high, a new entrant must offer either a substantially lower price or a much better product to attract buyers. Usually, the more established the relationships between parties, the greater the switching costs.

Access to Distribution Channels   Over time, industry participants commonly learn how to effectively distribute their products. After building a relationship with its distributors, a firm will nurture it, thus creating switching costs for the distributors. Access to distribution channels can be a strong entry barrier for new entrants, particularly in consumer nondurable goods industries (e.g., in grocery stores where shelf space is limited) and in international markets.[103] New entrants have to persuade distributors to carry their products, either in addition to or in place of those currently distributed. Price breaks and cooperative advertising allowances may be used for this purpose; however, those practices reduce the new entrant's profit potential. Interestingly, access to distribution is less of a barrier for products that can be sold on the Internet.

Cost Disadvantages Independent of Scale   Sometimes, established competitors have cost advantages that new entrants cannot duplicate. Proprietary product technology, favorable access to raw materials, desirable locations, and government subsidies are examples. Successful competition requires new entrants to reduce the strategic relevance of these factors. For example, delivering purchases directly to the buyer can counter the advantage of a desirable location; new food establishments in an undesirable location often follow this practice. Zara is owned by Inditex, the largest fashion clothing retailer in the world.[104] From the time of its launching, Spanish clothing company Zara relied on classy, well-tailored, and relatively inexpensive items that were produced and sold by adhering to ethical practices to successfully enter the highly competitive global clothing market and overcome that market's entry barriers.[105]

Government Policy   Through their decisions about issues such as the granting of licenses and permits, governments can also control entry into an industry. Liquor retailing, radio and TV broadcasting, banking, and trucking are examples of industries in which government decisions and actions affect entry possibilities. Also, governments often restrict entry into some industries because of the need to provide quality service or the desire to protect jobs. Alternatively, deregulating industries, such as the airline and utilities industries in the United States, generally results in additional firms choosing to enter and compete within an industry.[106] It is not uncommon for governments to attempt to regulate the entry of foreign firms, especially in industries considered critical to the country's economy or important markets within it.[107] Governmental decisions and policies regarding antitrust issues also affect entry barriers. For example, in the United States, the Antitrust Division of the Justice Department or the Federal Trade Commission will sometimes disallow a proposed merger because officials conclude that approving it would create a firm that is too dominant in an industry and would thus create unfair competition.[108] Such a negative ruling would obviously be an entry barrier for an acquiring firm.

Expected Retaliation

Companies seeking to enter an industry also anticipate the reactions of firms in the industry. An expectation of swift and vigorous competitive responses reduces the likelihood of entry. Vigorous retaliation can be expected when the existing firm has a major stake in the industry (e.g., it has fixed assets with few, if any, alternative uses), when it has substantial resources, and when industry growth is slow or constrained.[109] For example, any firm attempting to enter the airline industry can expect significant retaliation from existing competitors due to overcapacity.

Locating market niches not being served by incumbents allows the new entrant to avoid entry barriers. Small entrepreneurial firms are generally best suited for identifying and serving neglected market segments. When Honda first entered the U.S. motorcycle market, it concentrated on small-engine motorcycles, a market that firms such as Harley-Davidson ignored. By targeting this neglected niche, Honda initially avoided a significant amount of head-to-head competition with well-established competitors. After consolidating its position, Honda used its strength to attack rivals by introducing larger motorcycles and competing in the broader market.

2-4b Bargaining Power of Suppliers

Increasing prices and reducing the quality of their products are potential means suppliers use to exert power over firms competing within an industry. If a firm is unable to recover cost increases by its suppliers through its own pricing structure, its profitability is reduced by its suppliers' actions.[110] A supplier group is powerful when:

© Hadrian/Shutterstock.com

Apple's Watch was a highly anticipated entry into the smartwatch market. However, Google has formed a partnership with TAG Heuer and Intel to develop a smartwatch to respond to Apple.

- It is dominated by a few large companies and is more concentrated than the industry to which it sells.
- Satisfactory substitute products are not available to industry firms.
- Industry firms are not a significant customer for the supplier group.
- Suppliers' goods are critical to buyers' marketplace success.
- The effectiveness of suppliers' products has created high switching costs for industry firms.
- It poses a credible threat to integrate forward into the buyers' industry. Credibility is enhanced when suppliers have substantial resources and provide a highly differentiated product.[111]

Some buyers attempt to manage or reduce suppliers' power by developing a long-term relationship with them. Although long-term arrangements reduce buyer power, they also increase the suppliers' incentive to be helpful and cooperative in appreciation of the longer-term relationship (guaranteed sales). This is especially true when the partners develop trust in one another.[112]

The airline industry is one in which suppliers' bargaining power is changing. Though the number of suppliers is low, the demand for major aircraft is also relatively low. Boeing and Airbus aggressively compete for orders of major aircraft, creating more power for buyers in the process. When a large airline signals that it might place a "significant" order for wide-body airliners that either Airbus or Boeing might produce, both companies are likely to battle for the business and include a financing arrangement, highlighting the buyer's power in the potential transaction. And, with China's expected entry into the large commercial airliner industry, buyer power is likely to increase in the future.

2-4c   Bargaining Power of Buyers

Firms seek to maximize the return on their invested capital. Alternatively, buyers (customers of an industry or a firm) want to buy products at the lowest possible price— the point at which the industry earns the lowest acceptable rate of return on its invested capital. To reduce their costs, buyers bargain for higher quality, greater levels of service, and lower prices.[113] These outcomes are achieved by encouraging competitive battles among the industry's firms. Customers (buyer groups) are powerful when:

- They purchase a large portion of an industry's total output.
- The sales of the product being purchased account for a significant portion of the seller's annual revenues.
- They could switch to another product at little, if any, cost.
- The industry's products are undifferentiated or standardized, and the buyers pose a credible threat if they were to integrate backward into the sellers' industry.

Consumers armed with greater amounts of information about the manufacturer's costs and the power of the Internet as a shopping and distribution alternative have increased bargaining power in many industries.

2-4d   Threat of Substitute Products

Substitute products are goods or services from outside a given industry that perform similar or the same functions as a product that the industry produces. For example, as a sugar substitute, NutraSweet (and other sugar substitutes) places an upper limit on sugar manufacturers' prices—NutraSweet and sugar perform the same function, though with different characteristics. Other product substitutes include e-mail and fax machines instead of overnight deliveries, plastic containers rather than glass jars, and tea instead of coffee.

Newspaper firms have experienced significant circulation declines over the past 15 years. The declines are a result of the ready availability of substitute outlets for news including Internet sources, cable television news channels, along with e-mail and cell phone alerts. Likewise, satellite TV and cable and telecommunication companies provide substitute services for basic media services such as television, Internet, and phone. Tablets such as the iPad are reducing the number of PCs sold as suggested by the fact that worldwide shipments of PCs been declining each year since 2010.[114]

In general, product substitutes present a strong threat to a firm when customers face few if any switching costs and when the substitute product's price is lower or its quality and performance capabilities are equal to or greater than those of the competing product. Differentiating a product along dimensions that are valuable to customers (such as quality, service after the sale, and location) reduces a substitute's attractiveness.

2-4e   Intensity of Rivalry among Competitors

Because an industry's firms are mutually dependent, actions taken by one company usually invite responses. Competitive rivalry intensifies when a firm is challenged by a competitor's actions or when a company recognizes an opportunity to improve its market position.[115]

Firms within industries are rarely homogeneous; they differ in resources and capabilities and seek to differentiate themselves from competitors. Typically, firms seek to differentiate their products from competitors' offerings in ways that customers value and in which the firms have a competitive advantage. Common dimensions on which rivalry is based include price, service after the sale, and innovation. More recently, firms have begun to act quickly (speed a new product to the market) in order to gain a competitive advantage.[116]

Next, we discuss the most prominent factors that experience shows affect the intensity of rivalries among firms.

Boring
Average
Ordinary
Corporate & Uptight

Trendy
Youthful
Creative
Unique
Casual & Easy-Going

I'am a PC   I'am a Mac.

Apple Commercial.PNG

Firms making PCs try to differentiate their products in order to gain a competitive advantage. For example, Apple visually shows and verbally explains the differences between its Mac and the typical PC.

Numerous or Equally Balanced Competitors

Intense rivalries are common in industries with many companies. With multiple competitors, it is common for a few firms to believe they can act without eliciting a response. However, evidence suggests that other firms generally are aware of competitors' actions, often choosing to respond to them. At the other extreme, industries with only a few firms of equivalent size and power also tend to have strong rivalries. The large and often similar-sized resource bases of these firms permit vigorous actions and responses. The competitive battles between Airbus and Boeing and between Coca-Cola and PepsiCo exemplify intense rivalry between relatively equal competitors.

Slow Industry Growth

When a market is growing, firms try to effectively use resources to serve an expanding customer base. Markets increasing in size reduce the pressure to take customers from competitors. However, rivalry in no-growth or slow-growth markets becomes more intense as firms battle to increase their market shares by attracting competitors' customers. Certainly, this has been the case in the fast-food industry as explained in the Opening Case about McDonald's. McDonald's, Wendy's, and Burger King use their resources, capabilities, and core competencies to try to win each other's customers. The instability in the market that results from these competitive engagements may reduce the profitability for all firms engaging in such battles. As noted in the Opening Case, McDonald's has suffered from this competitive rivalry.

High Fixed Costs or High Storage Costs

When fixed costs account for a large part of total costs, companies try to maximize the use of their productive capacity. Doing so allows the firm to spread costs across a larger volume of output. However, when many firms attempt to maximize their productive capacity, excess capacity is created on an industry-wide basis. To then reduce inventories, individual companies typically cut the price of their product and offer rebates and other special discounts to customers. However, doing this often intensifies competition. The pattern of excess capacity at the industry level followed by intense rivalry at the firm level is frequently observed in industries with high storage costs. Perishable products, for example, lose their value rapidly with the passage of time.

As their inventories grow, producers of perishable goods often use pricing strategies to sell products quickly.

Lack of Differentiation or Low Switching Costs

When buyers find a differentiated product that satisfies their needs, they frequently purchase the product loyally over time. Industries with many companies that have successfully differentiated their products have less rivalry, resulting in lower competition for individual firms. Firms that develop and sustain a differentiated product that cannot be easily imitated by competitors often earn higher returns. However, when buyers view products as commodities (i.e., as products with few differentiated features or capabilities), rivalry intensifies. In these instances, buyers' purchasing decisions are based primarily on price and, to a lesser degree, service. Personal computers are a commodity product and the cost to switch from a computer manufactured by one firm to another is low. Thus, the rivalry among Dell, Hewlett-Packard, Lenovo, and other computer manufacturers is strong as these companies consistently seek to find ways to differentiate their offerings.

High Strategic Stakes

Competitive rivalry is likely to be high when it is important for several of the competitors to perform well in the market. Competing in diverse businesses (such as semiconductors, petrochemicals, fashion, medicine, and skyscraper and plant construction, among others), Samsung is a formidable foe for Apple in the global smartphone market. Samsung has committed a significant amount of resources to develop innovative products as the foundation for its efforts to try to outperform Apple in selling this particular product. Only a few years ago, Samsung held a sizable lead in market share (33 percent to 18 percent), but in the fourth quarter of 2014, the two firms' market share was virtually equal. It seems that apple received a significant boost with the release of the iPhone 6.[117] However, this market is extremely important to both firms, suggesting that the smartphone rivalry between them (and others) will remain quite intense.

High strategic stakes can also exist in terms of geographic locations. For example, a number of automobile manufacturers have established manufacturing facilities in China, which has been the world's largest car market since 2009.[118] Because of the high stakes involved in China for General Motors and other firms (including domestic Chinese automobile manufacturers) producing luxury cars (including Audi, BMW, and Mercedes-Benz), rivalry among them in this market is quite intense.

High Exit Barriers

Sometimes companies continue competing in an industry even though the returns on their invested capital are low or even negative. Firms making this choice likely face high exit barriers, which include economic, strategic, and emotional factors causing them to remain in an industry when the profitability of doing so is questionable.

Exit barriers are especially high in the airline industry. Profitability in this industry has been very difficult to achieve in recent years partly because of the latest global financial crisis. However, profits in the airline industry increased in 2013 and 2014. Industry consolidation and efficiency enhancements to how airline alliances integrate their activities helped reduce airline companies' costs while improving economic conditions in a number of countries. This resulted in a greater demand for travel. These are positive signs, at least in the short run, for these firms given that they do indeed face very high barriers if they were to contemplate leaving the airline travel industry.[119] Common exit barriers that firms face include the following:

- Specialized assets (assets with values linked to a particular business or location)
- Fixed costs of exit (such as labor agreements)

- Strategic interrelationships (relationships of mutual dependence, such as those between one business and other parts of a company's operations, including shared facilities and access to financial markets)
- Emotional barriers (aversion to economically justified business decisions because of fear for one's own career, loyalty to employees, and so forth)
- Government and social restrictions (often based on government concerns for job losses and regional economic effects; more common outside the United States)

2-5   Interpreting Industry Analyses

Effective industry analyses are products of careful study and interpretation of data and information from multiple sources. A wealth of industry-specific data is available for firms to analyze for the purpose of better understanding an industry's competitive realities. Because of globalization, international markets and rivalries must be included in the firm's analyses. And, because of the development of global markets, a country's borders no longer restrict industry structures. In fact, in general, entering international markets enhances the chances of success for new ventures as well as more established firms.[120]

Analysis of the five forces within a given industry allows the firm to determine the industry's attractiveness in terms of the potential to earn average or above-average returns. In general, the stronger the competitive forces, the lower the potential for firms to generate profits by implementing their strategies. An unattractive industry has low entry barriers, suppliers and buyers with strong bargaining positions, strong competitive threats from product substitutes, and intense rivalry among competitors. These industry characteristics make it difficult for firms to achieve strategic competitiveness and earn above-average returns. Alternatively, an attractive industry has high entry barriers, suppliers and buyers with little bargaining power, few competitive threats from product substitutes, and relatively moderate rivalry.[121] Next, we explain strategic groups as an aspect of industry competition.

2-6   Strategic Groups

A set of firms emphasizing similar strategic dimensions and using a similar strategy is called a **strategic group**.[122] The competition between firms within a strategic group is greater than the competition between a member of a strategic group and companies outside that strategic group. Therefore, intra-strategic group competition is more intense than is inter-strategic group competition. In fact, more heterogeneity is evident in the performance of firms within strategic groups than across the groups. The performance leaders within groups are able to follow strategies similar to those of other firms in the group and yet maintain strategic distinctiveness as a foundation for earning above-average returns.[123]

The extent of technological leadership, product quality, pricing policies, distribution channels, and customer service are examples of strategic dimensions that firms in a strategic group may treat similarly. Thus, membership in a particular strategic group defines the essential characteristics of the firm's strategy.

The notion of strategic groups can be useful for analyzing an industry's competitive structure. Such analyses can be helpful in diagnosing competition, positioning, and the profitability of firms competing within an industry. High mobility barriers, high rivalry, and low resources among the firms within an industry limit the formation of strategic groups.[124] However, after strategic groups are formed, their membership remains

A **strategic group** is a set of firms emphasizing similar strategic dimensions and using a similar strategy.

Strategic **Focus**

Watch Out All Retailers, Here Comes Amazon; Watch Out Amazon, Here Comes Jet.com

Amazon's sales in 2014 were $88.99 billion, an increase of 19.4 percent over 2013. In fact, its sales in 2014 were a whopping 160 percent more than its sales in 2010, only four years prior. Amazon has been able to achieve remarkable gains in sales by providing high quality, rapid, and relatively inexpensive (relative to competitors) service. Amazon has taken on such formidable competitors as Walmart, Google, and Barnes & Noble, among others and has come out of it as a winner, particularly in the last 4–5 years.

Walmart has been making progress in its online sales. In 2014, it grew its online sales by about $3 billion, for a 30 percent increase. That is, until one compares it to Amazon's sales increase in 2014 of about $14.5 billion. Much opportunity remains for both to improve as total 2014 online sales were $300 billion.

Google is clearly the giant search engine with 88 percent of the information search market. However, when consumers are shopping to purchase goods, Amazon is the leader. In the third quarter of 2014, 39 percent of online shoppers in the United States began their search on Amazon, compared to 11 percent for Google. Interestingly, in 2009 the figures were 18 percent for Amazon and 24 percent for Google. So, Amazon appears to be winning this competitive battle with Google.

Barnes & Noble lost out to Google before by ignoring it as a threat. Today, B&N has re-established itself in market niches trying not to compete with Google. For example, its college division largely sells through college bookstores, which have a 'monopoly' location granted by the university. However, Amazon is now targeting the college market by developing agreements with universities to operate co-branded websites to sell textbooks, university t-shirts, etc. Most of the students already shop on Amazon, making the promotion easier to market to universities and to sell to students.

A few years ago, Amazon was referred to as the Walmart of the Internet. But, Amazon has diversified its product/service line much further than Walmart. For example, Amazon now competes against Netflix and other services providing video entertainment. In fact, Amazon won two Golden Globe Awards in 2015 for programs it produced. Amazon recently began to market high fashion clothing for men and women. Founder and CEO of Amazon, Jeff Bezos, stated that Amazon's goal is to become a $200 billion company, and to do that, the firm must learn how to sell clothes and food.

It appears that Amazon is beating all competitors, even formidable ones such as Google and Walmart. But, Amazon still needs to carefully watch its competition. A new company, Jet.com, is targeting Amazon. Jet.com was founded by Marc Lore, who founded the highly successful Diaper.com and a former competitor of Amazon, Quidsi. Amazon hurt Quidsi in a major price war and eventually acquired the company for $550 million. Lore worked for Amazon for two years thereafter but eventually quit to found Jet.com. Jet.com plans to market 10 million products and guarantee the lowest price. Its annual membership will be $50 compared to Amazon Prime's cost of $99. Competing with Amazon represents a major challenge. However, Jet.com has raised about $240 million in venture funding with capital from such players as Bain Capital Ventures, Google Ventures, Goldman Sachs, and Norwest Venture partners. Its current market value is estimated to be $600 million. The future competition between the two companies should be interesting.

Sources: G. Bensiger, 2015, Amazon makes a push on college campuses, *Wall Street Journal*, www.wsj.com, February 1; K. Bhasin & L. Sherman, 2015, Amazon Coutre: Jeff Bezos wants to sell fancy clothes, *Bloomberg*, www.bloomberg.com, February 18; L. Dormehl, 2015, Amazon and Netflix score big at the Golden Globe, *Fast Company*, www.fastcomany.com, January 12; S. Soper, 2015, Amazon.com rival Jet.com raises $140 million in new funding, *Bloomberg*, www.bloomberg.com, February 11; B. Stone, 2015, Amazon bought this man's company. Now he is coming for him, *Bloomberg*, www.bloomberg.com, January 7; M. Kwatinetz, 2014, In online sales, could Walmart ever top Amazon? *Fortune*, www.fortune.com, October 23; R. Winkler & A. Barr, 2014, Google shopping to counter Amazon, *Wall Street Journal*, www.wsj.com, December 15.

relatively stable over time. Using strategic groups to understand an industry's competitive structure requires the firm to plot companies' competitive actions and responses along strategic dimensions such as pricing decisions, product quality, distribution channels, and so forth. This type of analysis shows the firm how certain companies are competing similarly in terms of how they use similar strategic dimensions.

Strategic groups have several implications. First, because firms within a group offer similar products to the same customers, the competitive rivalry among them can be intense. The more intense the rivalry, the greater the threat to each firm's profitability. Second, the strengths of the five forces differ across strategic groups. Third, the closer the strategic groups are in terms of their strategies, the greater is the likelihood of rivalry between the groups.

As explained in the Strategic Focus, Amazon appears to be winning competitive battles against formidable rivals such as Google and Walmart. It must be diligent, however, because a new competitor, Jet.com, is coming after Amazon's market. Thus, even such successful firms as Amazon must continuously analyze and understand their competitors if they are to maintain their current market leading positions.

2-7 Competitor Analysis

The competitor environment is the final part of the external environment requiring study. Competitor analysis focuses on each company against which a firm competes directly. The Coca-Cola Company and PepsiCo, Home Depot and Lowe's, Carrefour SA and Tesco PLC, and Amazon and Google are examples of competitors that are keenly interested in understanding each other's objectives, strategies, assumptions, and capabilities. Indeed, intense rivalry creates a strong need to understand competitors.[125] In a competitor analysis, the firm seeks to understand the following:

- What drives the competitor, as shown by its *future objectives*.
- What the competitor is doing and can do, as revealed by its *current strategy*.
- What the competitor believes about the industry, as shown by its *assumptions*.
- What the competitor's capabilities are, as shown by its *strengths* and *weaknesses*.[126]

Knowledge about these four dimensions helps the firm prepare an anticipated response profile for each competitor (see Figure 2.3). The results of an effective competitor analysis help a firm understand, interpret, and predict its competitors' actions and responses. Understanding competitors' actions and responses clearly contributes to the firm's ability to compete successfully within the industry.[127] Interestingly, research suggests that executives often fail to analyze competitors' possible reactions to competitive actions their firm takes,[128] placing their firm at a potential competitive disadvantage as a result.

Critical to an effective competitor analysis is gathering data and information that can help the firm understand its competitors' intentions and the strategic implications resulting from them.[129] Useful data and information combine to form **competitor intelligence** which is the set of data and information the firm gathers to better understand and anticipate competitors' objectives, strategies, assumptions, and capabilities. In competitor analysis, the firm gathers intelligence not only about its competitors, but also regarding public policies in countries around the world. Such intelligence facilitates an understanding of the strategic posture of foreign competitors. Through effective competitive and public policy intelligence, the firm gains the insights needed to make effective strategic decisions regarding how to compete against rivals.

When asked to describe competitive intelligence, phrases such as "competitive spying" and "corporate espionage" come to my mind for some. These phrases denote the fact that competitive intelligence is an activity that appears to involve trade-offs.[130] The reason for this is that "what is ethical in one country is different from what is ethical in other countries." This position implies that the rules of engagement to follow when gathering competitive intelligence change in different contexts.[131] However, firms avoid the possibility of legal entanglements and ethical quandaries only when their competitive intelligence

Competitor intelligence is the set of data and information the firm gathers to better understand and anticipate competitors' objectives, strategies, assumptions, and capabilities.

Figure 2.3 Competitor Analysis Components

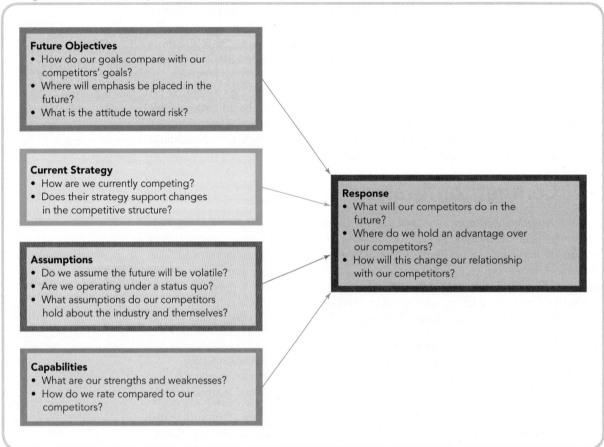

gathering methods are governed by a strict set of legal and ethical guidelines.[132] This means that ethical behavior and actions, as well as the mandates of relevant laws and regulations, should be the foundation on which a firm's competitive intelligence-gathering process is formed.

When gathering competitive intelligence, firms must also pay attention to the complementors of its products and strategy.[133] **Complementors** are companies or networks of companies that sell complementary goods or services that are compatible with the focal firm's good or service. When a complementor's good or service contributes to the functionality of a focal firm's good or service, it in turn creates additional value for that firm.

There are many examples of firms whose good or service complements other companies' offerings. For example, firms manufacturing affordable home photo printers complement other companies' efforts to sell digital cameras. Intel and Microsoft are perhaps the most widely recognized complementors. The Microsoft slogan "Intel Inside" demonstrates the relationship between two firms that do not directly buy from or sell to each other but their products are highly complementary.

Alliances among airline companies such as Oneworld and Star find member companies sharing their route structures and customer loyalty programs as a means of complementing each other's operations. (Alliances and other cooperative strategies are described

Complementors are companies or networks of companies that sell complementary goods or services that are compatible with the focal firm's good or service.

in Chapter 9.) In the example we are considering here, each of the two alliances is a network of complementors. American Airlines, British Airways, Finnair, Japan Airlines, and Royal Jordanian are among the airlines forming the Oneworld alliance. Air Canada, Brussels Airlines, Croatia Airlines, Lufthansa, and United Airlines are five of the members forming the Star alliance. Both of these alliances constantly adjust their members and services offered to better meet customers' needs.

As our discussion shows, complementors expand the set of competitors that firms must evaluate when completing a competitor analysis. In this sense, American Airlines and United Airlines examine each other both as direct competitors on multiple routes but also as complementors that are members of different alliances (Oneworld for American and Star for United). In all cases though, ethical commitments and actions should be the foundation on which competitor analyses are developed.

2-8 Ethical Considerations

Firms must follow relevant laws and regulations as well as carefully articulated ethical guidelines when gathering competitor intelligence. Industry associations often develop lists of these practices that firms can adopt. Practices considered both legal and ethical include:

1. Obtaining publicly available information (e.g., court records, competitors' help-wanted advertisements, annual reports, financial reports of publicly held corporations, and Uniform Commercial Code filings)
2. Attending trade fairs and shows to obtain competitors' brochures, view their exhibits, and listen to discussions about their products.

In contrast, certain practices (including blackmail, trespassing, eavesdropping, and stealing drawings, samples, or documents) are widely viewed as unethical and often are illegal as well.

Some competitive intelligence practices may be legal, but a firm must decide whether they are also ethical, given the image it desires as a corporate citizen. Especially with electronic transmissions, the line between legal and ethical practices can be difficult to determine. For example, a firm may develop website addresses that are similar to those of its competitors and thus occasionally receive e-mail transmissions that were intended for those competitors. The practice is an example of the challenges companies face in deciding how to gather intelligence about competitors while simultaneously determining how to prevent competitors from learning too much about them. To deal with these challenges, firms should establish principles and take actions that are consistent with them.

Professional associations are available to firms as sources of information regarding competitive intelligence practices. For example, while pursuing its mission to help firms make "better decisions through competitive intelligence," the Strategy and Competitive Intelligence Professionals association offers codes of professional practice and ethics to firms for their possible use when deciding how to gather competitive intelligence.[134]

Open discussions of intelligence-gathering techniques can help a firm ensure that employees, customers, suppliers, and even potential competitors understand its convictions to follow ethical practices when gathering intelligence about its competitors. An appropriate guideline for competitor intelligence practices is to respect the principles of common morality and the right of competitors not to reveal certain information about their products, operations, and intentions.

SUMMARY

- The firm's external environment is challenging and complex. Because of its effect on performance, the firm must develop the skills required to identify opportunities and threats that are a part of its external environment.

- The external environment has three major parts:

  1. The general environment (segments and elements in the broader society that affect industries and the firms competing in them)

  2. The industry environment (factors that influence a firm, its competitive actions and responses, and the industry's profitability potential)

  3. The competitor environment (in which the firm analyzes each major competitor's future objectives, current strategies, assumptions, and capabilities).

- Scanning, monitoring, forecasting, and assessing are the four parts of the external environmental analysis process. Effectively using this process helps the firm in its efforts to identify opportunities and threats.

- The general environment has seven segments: demographic, economic, political/legal, sociocultural, technological, global, and sustainable physical. For each segment, the firm has to determine the strategic relevance of environmental changes and trends.

- Compared with the general environment, the industry environment has a more direct effect on the firm's competitive actions and responses. The five forces model of competition includes the threat of entry, the power of suppliers, the power of buyers, product substitutes, and the intensity of rivalry among competitors. By studying these forces, the firm finds a position in an industry where it can influence the forces in its favor or where it can buffer itself from the power of the forces to achieve strategic competitiveness and earn above-average returns.

- Industries are populated with different strategic groups. A strategic group is a collection of firms following similar strategies along similar dimensions. Competitive rivalry is greater within a strategic group than between strategic groups.

- Competitor analysis informs the firm about the future objectives, current strategies, assumptions, and capabilities of the companies with which it competes directly. A thorough competitor analysis examines complementors that support forming and implementing rivals' strategies.

- Different techniques are used to create competitor intelligence: the set of data, information, and knowledge that allow the firm to better understand its competitors and thereby predict their likely competitive actions and responses. Firms absolutely should use only legal and ethical practices to gather intelligence. The Internet enhances firms' ability to gather insights about competitors and their strategic intentions.

KEY TERMS

competitor analysis   42
competitor intelligence   65
complementors   66
demographic segment   45
economic environment   48
general environment   41
global segment   52
industry environment   41

industry   55
opportunity   43
political/legal segment   49
sociocultural segment   50
sustainable physical environment segment   53
strategic group   63
threat   43
technological segment   51

REVIEW QUESTIONS

1. Why is it important for a firm to study and understand the external environment?

2. What are the differences between the general environment and the industry environment? Why are these differences important?

3. What is the external environmental analysis process (four parts)? What does the firm want to learn when using this process?

4. What are the seven segments of the general environment? Explain the differences among them.

5. How do the five forces of competition in an industry affect its profitability potential? Explain.

6. What is a strategic group? Of what value is knowledge of the firm's strategic group in formulating that firm's strategy?

7. What is the importance of collecting and interpreting data and information about competitors? What practices should a firm use to gather competitor intelligence and why?

Mini-Case

The Informal Economy: What It Is and Why It Is Important?

The informal economy refers to commercial activities that occur at least partly outside a governing body's observation, taxation, and regulation. In slightly different words, sociologists Manuel Castells and Alejandro Portes suggest that the "informal economy is characterized by one central feature: it is unregulated by the institutions of society in a legal and social environment in which similar activities are regulated." Firms located in the informal economy are typically thought of as businesses that are unregistered but that are producing and selling *legal* products (that is, they sell many of the same products you might buy in legal businesses but perhaps cheaper because they do not pay government fees and taxes). In contrast to the informal economy, the formal economy is comprised of commercial activities that a governing body taxes and monitors for society's benefit and whose outputs are included in a country's gross domestic product.

For some, working in the informal economy is a choice, such as is the case when individuals decide to supplement the income they are earning through employment in the formal economy with a second job in the informal economy. However, for most people working in the informal economy is a necessity rather than a choice—a reality that contributes to the informal economy's size and significance. Although generalizing about the quality of informal employment is difficult, evidence suggests that it typically means poor employment conditions and greater poverty for workers.

Estimates of the informal economy's size across countries and regions vary. In developing countries, the informal economy accounts for as much as three-quarters of all nonagricultural employment, and perhaps as much as 90 percent in some countries in South Asia and sub-Saharan Africa. But the informal economy is also prominent in developed countries such as Finland, Germany, and France (where the informal economy is estimated to account for 18.3 percent, 16.3 percent, and 15.3 percent, respectively, of these nations' total economic activity). In the United States, recent estimates are that the informal economy is now generating as much as $2 trillion in economic activity on an annual basis. This is double the size of the U.S. informal economy in 2009. In terms of the number of people working in an informal economy, it is suggested that "India's informal economy … (includes) hundreds of millions of shopkeepers, farmers, construction workers, taxi drivers, street vendors, rag pickers, tailors, repairmen, middlemen, black marketers, and more."

There are various causes of the informal economy's growth, including an inability of a nation's economic environment to create a significant number of jobs relative to available workers. This has been a particularly acute problem during the recent global recession. In the words of a person living in Spain: "Without the underground (informal) economy, we would be in a situation of probably violent social unrest." Governments' inability to facilitate growth efforts in their nation's economic environment is another issue. In this regard, another Spanish citizen suggests that "what the government should focus on is reforming the formal economy to make it more efficient and competitive."

In a general sense, the informal economy yields threats and opportunities for formal economy firms. One threat is that informal businesses may have a cost advantage when competing against formal economy firms because they do not pay taxes or incur the costs of regulations. But the informal economy surfaces opportunities as well. For example, formal-economy firms can try to understand the needs of customers that informal-economy firms are satisfying and then find ways to better meet their needs. Another valuable opportunity is to attract some of the informal economy's talented human capital to accept positions of employment in formal economy firms.

Sources: A. Picchi, 2013, A shadow economy may be keeping the U.S. afloat, *MSN Money*, www.msn.com, May 3; 2013, Meeting on informal economy statistics: Country experience, international recommendations, and application, *United Nations Economic Commission for Africa*, www.uneca.org, April; 2013, About the informal economy, Women in informal employment: Globalizing and organizing, www.wiego.org, May;

G. Bruton, R. D. Ireland, & D. J. Ketchen, Jr., 2012, Toward a research agenda on the informal economy, *Academy of Management Perspectives*, 26(3): 1–11; R. D. Ireland, 2012, 2012 program theme: The informal economy, *Academy of Management*, www.meeting.aomonline.org, March; R. Minder, 2012, In Spain, jobless find a refuge off the books, *New York Times*, www.nytimes.com, May 18.

Case Discussion Questions

1. What are the implications of the informal economy for firms that operate only in the formal economy?

2. When firms consider analyzing their competition, should they include firms in the informal economy? Please explain why or why not.

3. What opportunities does the informal economy present to firms operating in the formal economy?

4. What threats does the informal economy present to firms operating in the formal economy?

5. How do firms operating in the formal economy identify and analyze the parts of the informal economy relevant to their strategies?

NOTES

1. R. Krause, M. Semadeni & A. A. Cannella, 2013, External COO/presidents as expert directors: A new look at the service of role of boards, *Strategic Management Journal*, 34: 1628–1641; Y. Y. Kor & A. Mesko, 2013, Dynamic managerial capabilities: Configuration and orchestration of top executives' capabilities and the firm's dominant logic, *Strategic Management Journal*, 34: 233–234.

2. K.-Y. Hsieh, W. Tsai, & M.-J. Chen, 2015, If they can do it, why not us? Competitors as reference points for justifying escalation of commitment, *Academy of Management Journal*, 58: 38–58; R. Kapoor & J. M. Lee, 2013, Coordinating and competing in ecosystems: How organizational forms shape new technology investments, *Strategic Management Journal*, 34: 274–296.

3. C. E. Stevens, E. Xie, & M. W. Peng, 2015, Toward a legitimacy-based view of political risk: The case of Google and Yahoo in China, *Strategic Management Journal*, 36: in press; E.-H. Kim, 2013, Deregulation and differentiation: Incumbent investment in green technologies, *Strategic Management Journal*, 34: 1162–1185.

4. R. J. Sawant, 2012, Asset specificity and corporate political activity in regulated industries, *Academy of Management Review*, 37: 194–210; S. Hanson, A. Kashyap, & J. Stein, 2011, A macroprudential approach to financial regulation. *Journal of Economic Perspectives*, 25: 3–28.

5. S. Garg, 2013, Venture boards: Distinctive monitoring and implications for firm performance, *Academy of Management*

Review, 38: 90–108; J. Harrison, D. Bosse, & R. Phillips, 2010, Managing for stakeholders, stakeholder utility functions, and competitive advantage, *Strategic Management Journal*, 31: 58–74.

6. S. C. Schleimer & T. Pedersen, 2013, The driving forces of subsidiary absorptive capacity, *Journal of Management Studies*, 50: 646–672; M. T. Lucas & O. M. Kirillova, 2011, Reconciling the resource-based and competitive positioning perspectives on manufacturing flexibility, *Journal of Manufacturing Technology Management*, 22: 189–203.

7. M. Taissig & A. Delios, 2015, Unbundling the effects of institutions on firm resources: The contingent value of being local in emerging economy private equity, *Strategic Management Journal*, 36: in press; C. Qian, Q. Cao, & R. Takeuchi, 2013, Top management team functional diversity and organizational innovation in China: The moderating effects of environment, *Strategic Management Journal*, 34: 110–120.

8. EY, 2015, Middle class growth in emerging markets entering the global middle class, www.ey.com, March 6; EY, 2015 Middle class growth in emerging markets hitting the sweet spot, www.ey.com, March 6.

9. E. V. Karniouchina, S. J. Carson, J. C. Short, & D. J. Ketchen, 2013, Extending the firm vs. industry debate: Does industry life cycle stage matter? *Strategic Management Journal*, 34: 1010–1018.

10. R. B. MacKay & R. Chia, 2013, Choice, chance, and unintended consequences in strategic change: A process understanding of

the rise and fall of NorthCo Automotive, *Academy of Management Journal*, 56: 208–230; J. P. Murmann, 2013, The coevolution of industries and important features of their environments, *Organization Science*, 24: 58–78; G. J. Kilduff, H. A. Elfenbein, & B. M. Staw, 2010, The psychology of rivalry: A relationally dependent analysis of competition, *Academy of Management Journal*, 53: 943–969.

11. R. E. Hoskisson, M. Wright, I. Filatotchev, & M. W. Peng, 2013, Emerging multinationals from mid-range economies: The influence of institutions and factor markets, *Journal of Management Studies*, 50: 127–153; A. Hecker & A. Ganter, 2013, The influence of product market competition on technological and management innovation: Firm-level evidence from a large-scale survey, *European Management Review*, 10: 17–33.

12. Walmart, 2015, Our locations. www.corporate.walmart.com, March 6; Metro Cash and Carry, 2015, International Operations, en.wikipedia.org, February 1; BBC news, 2014, Carrefour to exit India business, www.bbc.com, July 8; BBC news, 2014, Tesco signs deal to enter India's supermarket sector, www.bbc.com, March 21.

13. F. Bridoux & J. W. Stoelhorst, 2014, Microfoundations for stakeholder theory: Managing stakeholders with heterogeneous motives, *Strategic Management Journal*, 35: 107–125; B. Gilad, 2011, The power of blindspots. What companies don't know, surprises them. What they don't want to know, kills them, *Strategic Direction*, 27(4): 3–4.

14. B. Bradlee, 2014, Patent battle between Nokia and HTC ends with the signing of a patent and technology collaboration agreement, Capital Technologies, www.captees.com, February 9; A. Poon & J. Rossi, 2013, Patent battle between Nokia, HTC heats up, *Wall Street Journal*, www.wsj.com, May 24.

15. D. Li, 2013, Multilateral R&D alliances by new ventures, *Journal of Business Venturing*, 28: 241–260; A. Graefe, S. Luckner, & C. Weinhardt, 2010, Prediction markets for foresight, *Futures*, 42: 394–404.

16. J. Tang, K. M. Kacmar, & L. Busenitz, 2012, Entrepreneurial alertness in the pursuit of new opportunities, *Journal of Business Venturing*, 27: 77–94; D. Chrusciel, 2011, Environmental scan: Influence on strategic direction, *Journal of Facilities Management*, 9(1): 7–15.

17. D. E. Hughes, J. Le Bon, & A. Rapp, 2013, Gaining and leveraging customer-based competitive intelligence: The pivotal role of social capital and salesperson adaptive selling skills, *Journal of the Academy of Marketing Science*, 41: 91–110; J. R. Hough & M. A. White, 2004, Scanning actions and environmental dynamism: Gathering information for strategic decision making, *Management Decision*, 42: 781–793; V. K. Garg, B. A. Walters, & R. L. Priem, 2003, Chief executive scanning emphases, environmental dynamism, and manufacturing firm performance, *Strategic Management Journal*, 24: 725–744.

18. C.-H. Lee & T.-F. Chien, 2013, Leveraging microblogging big data with a modified density-based clustering approach for event awareness and topic ranking, *Journal of Information Science*, 39: 523–543.

19. The Culturist, 2013, More than 2 billion people use the Internet, here's what they're up to, www.theculturist.com, May 9.

20. S. Garg, 2013, Venture boards: Distinctive monitoring and implications for firm performance, *Academy of Management Review*, 38: 90–108; L. Fahey, 1999, *Competitors*, New York: John Wiley & Sons, 71–73.

21. K. Greene & V. Monga, 2013, Workers saving too little to retire, *Wall Street Journal*, www.wsj.com, March 19.

22. M. Hadley, 2014, Americans still don't have enough savings, *USA Today*, www.usatoday.com, June 23.

23. B. L. Connelly & E. J. Van Slyke, 2012, The power and peril of board interlocks, *Business Horizons*, 55: 403–408; C. Dellarocas, 2010, Online reputation systems: How to design one that does what you need, *MIT Sloan Management Review*, 51: 33–37.

24. G. Martin, R. Gozubuyuk, & M. Becerra, 2015, Interlocks and firm performance: The role of uncertainty in the directorate interlock-performance relationship, *Strategic Management Journal*, 36: 235–253.

25. K. L. Turner & M. V. Makhija, 2012, The role of individuals in the information processing perspective, *Strategic Management Journal*, 33: 661–680; X. Zhang, S. Majid, & S. Foo, 2010, Environmental scanning: An application of information literacy skills at the workplace, *Journal of Information Science*, 36: 719–732.

26. L. Sleuwaegen, 2013, Scanning for profitable (international) growth, *Journal of Strategy and Management*, 6: 96–110; J. Calof & J. Smith, 2010, The integrative domain of foresight and competitive intelligence and its impact on R&D management, *R & D Management*, 40(1): 31–39.

27. S. Phandis, C. Caplice, Y. Sheffi, & M. Singh, 2015, Effect of scenario planning on field experts judgment of long-range investment decisions, *Strategic Management Journal*, in press; A. Chwolka & M. G. Raith, 2012, The value of business planning before start-up—A decision-theoretical perspective, *Journal of Business Venturing*, 27: 385–399.

28. S. D. Wu, K. G. Kempf, M. O. Atan, B. Aytac, S. A. Shirodkar, & A. Mishra, 2010, Improving new-product forecasting at Intel Corporation, *Interfaces*, 40: 385–396.

29. K. D. Miller & S.-J. Lin, 2015, Analogical reasoning for diagnosing strategic issues in dynamic and complex environments, *Strategic Management Journal*, in press; R. Klingebiel, 2012, Options in the implementation plan of entrepreneurial initiatives: Examining firms' attainment of flexibility benefit, *Strategic Entrepreneurship Journal*, 6: 307–334; T. Sueyoshi & M. Goto, 2011, Methodological comparison between two unified (operational and environmental) efficiency measurements for environmental assessment, *European Journal of Operational Research*, 210: 684–693.

30. P. Jarzabkowski & S. Kaplan, 2015, Strategy tools-in-use: A framework for understanding "technologies of rationality" in practice, *Strategic Management Journal*, 36: 537–558; N. J. Foss, J. Lyngsie, & S. A. Zahra, 2013, The role of external knowledge sources and organizational design in the process of opportunity exploitation, *Strategic Management Journal*, 34: 1453–1471.

31. D. Grewal, A. Roggeveen, & R. C. Runyan, 2013, Retailing in a connected world, *Journal of Marketing Management*, 29: 263–270; R. King, 2010, Consumer demographics: Use demographic resources to target specific audiences, *Journal of Financial Planning*, 23(12): S4–S6.

32. 2015, World, population clock: 7 billion people (2015), www.worldometers.info/world-population, March 6; 2013, U.S. Census Bureau, International Programs World Population, www.census.gov/population/international/data/worldpop/, May 21.

33. World population clock; 2013, The world population and the top ten countries with the highest population, *Internet World Stats*, www.internetworldstats.com, May 21.

34. T. Kambayashi, 2011, Brief: Aging Japan sees slowest population growth yet, *McClatchy-Tribune Business News*, www.mcclatchy.com, February 25; S. Moffett, 2005, Fast-aging Japan keeps its elders on the job longer, *Wall Street Journal*, June 15, A1, A8.

35. D. Bloom & D. Canning, 2012, How companies must adapt for an aging workforce, *HBR Blog Network*, www.hbr.org, December 3.

36. 2012, Humanity's aging, *National Institute on Aging*, www.nia.nih.gov, March 27.

37. M. B. Dougherty, 2012, Stunning facts about Japan's demographic implosion, *Business Insider*, www.businessinsider.com, April 24.

38. M. Chand & R. L. Tung, 2014, The aging of the world's population and its effects on global business, *Academy of Management Perspectives*, 28: 409–429.

39. 2013, The aging workforce: Finding the silver lining in the talent gap, *Deloitte*, www.deloitte.com, February.

40. D. Cumming, T. Leung, & O. Rui, 2015, Gender diversity and securities fraud, *Academy of Management Journal*, in press; A. Joshi, J. Son, & H. Roh, 2015, When can women close the gap? A meta-analytic test of sex differences in performance and rewards, *Academy of Management Journal*, in press.

41. 2015, List of U.S. states and territories by population, *Wikipedia*, en.wikipedia.org, March 9.

42. 2013, 2013 Cal Facts, Legislative Analysts' Office, www.lao.ca.gov, January 2.

43. J. Goudreau, 2013, The states people are fleeing in 2013, *Forbes*, www.forbes.com, February 7.

44. R. Dobbs, S. Smit, J. Remes, J. Manyika, C. Roxburgh & A. Restrepo, 2011, *Urban world: Mapping the economic power of cities*, Chicago: McKinsey Global Institute, March.

45. 2012, Population and population change statistics, *European Commission*, www.epp.eurostat.ec.europa.eu, October.

46. S. Reddy, 2011, U.S. News: Latinos fuel growth in decade, *Wall Street Journal*, March 25, A2.

47. 2015, New census bureau report analyzes U.S. population projects, www.census.gov, March 3.

48. G. Andrrevski, O. C. Richard, J.D. Shaw, & W. J. Ferrier, 2014, Racial diversity and firm performance: The mediating role of competitive intensity, *Journal of Management*, 40: 820–844.

49. M. Fisher, 2013, A revealing map of the world's most and least ethnically diverse countries, *The Washington Post*, www.washingtonpost.com, May 16.

50. A. Hain-Cole, 2010, Companies juggle cost cutting with competitive benefits for international assignments, *Benefits & Compensation International: A Magazine for Global Companies*, 40: 26.

51. J. Lee, 2010, Don't underestimate India's consumers, *Bloomberg Businessweek*, www.businessweek.com, January 21.

52. W. Q. Judge, A. Fainschmidt, & J. L. Brown, 2014, Which model of capitalism best delivers both wealth and equality? *Journal of International Business Studies*, 45: 363–386.

53. G. A. Shinkle & B. T. McCann, 2013, New product deployment: The moderating influence of economic institutional context, *Strategic Management Journal*, 35: 1090–1101; L. Fahey & V. K. Narayanan, 1986, *Macroenvironmental Analysis for Strategic Management (The West Series in Strategic Management)*, St. Paul, Minnesota: West Publishing Company, 105.

54. A. Chakrabarti, 2015, Organizational adaptation in an economic shock: The role of growth reconfiguration, *Strategic Management Journal*, in press; N. Bloom, M. A. Kose, & M. E. Terrones, 2013, Held back by uncertainty, *Finance & Development*, 50: 38–41, March.

55. 2015, Global economic prospects: Having physical space and using it, The World bank, www.worldbank.org, January.

56. J. K. Ault & A. Spicer, 2014, The institutional context of poverty: State fragility as a predictor of cross-national variation in commercial microfinance lending, *Strategic Management Journal*, 36; R. J. Sawant, 2012, Asset specificity and corporate political activity in regulated industries, *Academy of Management Review*, 37: 194–210.

57. T. A. Khoury, M. Junkunc, & S. Mingo, 2015, Navigating political hazard risks and legal system quality: Venture capital investments in Latin America, *Journal of Management*, 41: 808–840; M. R. King, 2015, Political bargaining and multinational bailouts, *Journal of International Business Studies*, 46: 206–222; N. Jia, 2014, Are collective political actions and private political actions substitutes or complements? Empirical evidence from China's private sector, *Strategic Management Journal*, 35: 292–315.

58. S. G. Lazzarini, 2015, Strategizing by the government: Can industrial policy create firm-level competitive advantage, *Strategic Management Journal*, 36: 97–112.

59. S. Zeidler, 2013, MGM assessing costs of operating online poker in Nevada, *Reuters*, www.mobile,reuters.com, May 2.

60. R. Ayadi, E. Arbak, W. P. de Goren, & D. T. Llewellyn, 2013, *Regulation of European Banks and Business Models: Towards a New Paradigm?* Brookings Institution Press, Washington, D.C.

61. K. J. O'Brien, 2013, Firms brace for new European data privacy law, *New York Times*, www.nytimes.com, May 13.

62. C. Jiang, S. Yao, & G. Feng, 2013, Bank ownership, privatization, and performance: Evidence from a transition country, *Journal of Banking & Finance*, 37: 3364–3372; N. Boubakri & L. Bouslimi, 2010, Analysts following of privatized firms around the world: The role of institutions and ownership structure, *International Journal of Accounting*, 45: 413–442.

63. L. Richards, 2013, The effects of socio-culture on business, *The Houston Chronicle*, www.chron.com, May 26.

64. J. G. York & M. J. Lennox, 2014, Exploring the sociocultural determinants of de novo and de alio entry into emerging industries, *Strategic Management Journal*, 35: 1930–1951.

65. 2013, Health strategy, *European Commission Public Health*, www.europa.eu, May 23.

66. M. Toosi, 2012, Projections of the labor force to 2050: A visual essay, *Monthly Labor Review*, October.

67. Ibid., 13.

68. T. Grenness, 2011, The impact of national culture on CEO compensation and salary gaps between CEOs and manufacturing workers, *Compensation & Benefits Review*, 43: 100–108.

69. G. Lucke, T. Kostova, & K. Roth, 2014, Multiculturalism from a cognitive perspective: Patterns and implications, *Journal of International Business Studies*, 45:169–190; Y. Zeng, O. Shenkar, S.-H. Lee, & S. Song, 2013, Cultural differences, MNE learning abilities, and the effect of experience on subsidiary mortality in a dissimilar culture: Evidence from Korean MNEs, *Journal of International Business Studies*, 44: 42–65.

70. J. Liu, C. Hui, C. Lee, & Z. X. Chen, 2013, Why do I feel valued and why do I contribute? A relational approach to employee's organization-based self-esteem and job performance, *Journal of Management Studies*, 50: 1018–1040; C. M. Chan, S. Makino, & T. Isobe, 2010, Does subnational region matter? Foreign affiliate performance in the United States and China, *Strategic Management Journal*, 31: 1226–1243; P. J. Buckley, J. Clegg, & H. Tan, 2006, Cultural awareness in knowledge transfer to China—The role of guanxi and mianzi, *Journal of World Business*, 41: 275–288.

71. S. Grodal, 2015, The co-evolution of technologies and categories during industry emergence, *Academy of Management Review*, in press; N. R. Furr & D. C. Snow, Intergenerational hybrids: Spillbacks, spillforwards and adapting to technological discontinuities, *Organization Science*, in press; J. P. Eggers, 2014, Competing technologies and industry evolution: The benefits of making mistakes in the flat panel display industry, *Strategic Management Journal*, 35: 159–178.

72. L. Fuentelsaz, E. Garrido, & J. P. Maicas, 2015, Incumbents, technological change and institutions: How the value of complementary resources varies across markets, *Strategic Management Journal*, in press; A. Furlan, A. Cabigiosu, & A. Camuffo, 2014, When the mirror gets misted up: Modularity and technological change, *Strategic Management Journal*, 35; 789–807.

73. 2013, Consumers (everywhere) know a good deal when they see it, *bcg.perspectives*, www.bcgperspectives.com, January 11.

74. W. Bock, D. Field, P. Zwillenberg, & K. Rogers, 2015, The growth of the global mobile Internet economy, *bcg.perspectives, www.bcgperspectives.com*; The Culturist, 2013.

75. P. Buckley & R. Strange, 2015, The governance of the global factory: Location and control of world economic activity, *Academy of Management Perspectives*, in press; J.-E. Vahlne & I. Ivarsson, 2014, The globalization of Swedish MNEs: Empirical evidence and theoretical explanations, *Journal of International Business Studies*, 45: 227–247; E. R. Banalieva & C. Dhanaraj, 2013, Home-region orientation in international expansion strategies, *Journal of International Business Studies*, 44: 89–116.

76. K. Kyung-Tae, R. Seung-Kyu, & O. Joongsan, 2011, The strategic role evolution of foreign automotive parts subsidiaries in China, *International Journal of Operations & Production Management*, 31: 31–55.

77. S. T. Cavusgil & G. Knight, 2015, The born global firm: An entrepreneurial and capabilities perspective on early and rapid internationalization, *Journal of International Business Studies*, 46: 3–16; S. Sui & M. Baum, 2014, Internationalization strategy, firm resources and the survival of SMEs in the export market, *Journal of International Business Studies*, 45: 821–841.

78. 2013, Growth and globalization: Keeping a lid on capacity, KPMG, Automotive executive survey, www.kpmb.com, January 15.

79. T.J. Pukall & A. Calabro, 2014, The internationalization of family firms: A critical review and integrative model, *Family Business Review*, 27: 103–125; K. E. Meyer, 2006, Globalfocusing: From domestic conglomerates to global specialists, *Journal of Management Studies*, 43: 1110–1144.

80. R. G. Flores, R. V. Aguilera, A. Mahdian, & P. M. Vaaler, 2013, How well do supra-national regional grouping schemes fit international business research models? *Journal of International Business Studies*, 44: 451–474; Hoskisson, Wright, Filatotchev, & Peng, Emerging multinationals.

81. F. J. Froese, 2013, Work values of the next generation of business leaders in Shanghai, Tokyo, and Seoul, *Asia Pacific Journal of Management*, 30: 297–315; M. Muethel & M. H. Bond, 2013, National context and individual employees' trust of the out-group: The role of societal trust, *Journal of International Business Studies*, 4: 312–333; M. A. Hitt, M. T. Dacin, B. B. Tyler, & D. Park, 1997, Understanding the differences in Korean and U.S. executives' strategic orientations, *Strategic Management Journal*, 18: 159–167.

82. D. Ahlstrom, E. Levitas, M. A. Hitt, T. Dacin, & H. Zhu, 2014, The three faces of China: Strategic alliance partner selection in three Chinese economies," *Journal of World Business*, 49: 572–585; X. Li, 2012, Behind the recent surge of Chinese patenting: An institutional view, *Research Policy*, 41: 236–249.

83. T. Yu, M. Subramaniam, & A. A. Cannella, Jr., 2013, Competing globally, allying locally: Alliances between global rivals and host-country factors, *Journal of International Business Studies*, 44: 117–137; T. K. Das & R. Kumar, 2011, Regulatory focus and opportunism in the alliance development process, *Journal of Management*, 37: 682–708.

84. B. Perrott, 2014, The sustainable organization: Blueprint for an integrated model, *Journal of Business Strategy*, 35: 26–37; A. G. Scherer, G. Palazzo, & D. Seidl, 2013, Managing legitimacy in complex and heterogeneous environments: Sustainable development in a globalized world, *Journal of Management Studies*, 50: 259–284; J. Harris, 2011, Going green to stay in the black: Transnational capitalism and renewable energy, *Perspectives on Global Development & Technology*, 10: 41–59.

85. B. W. Lewis, J. L. Walls, & G. W. S. Dowell, 2014, Difference in degrees: CEO characteristics and firm environmental disclosure, *Strategic Management Journal*, 35: 712–722; P. Berrone, A. Fosfuri, L. Gelabert, & L. R. Gomez-Mejia, 2013, Necessity as the mother of 'green' inventions: Institutional pressures and environmental innovations, *Strategic Management Journal*, 34: 891–909; M. Delmas, V. H. Hoffmann, & M. Kuss, 2011, Under the tip of the iceberg: Absorptive capacity, environmental strategy, and competitive advantage, *Business & Society*, 50: 116–154.

86. 2013, What is sustainable development? International institute for sustainable development, www.iisd.org, May 5.

87. J. K. Hall, G. A. Daneke, & M. J. Lenox, 2010, Sustainable development and entrepreneurship: Past contributions and future directions, *Journal of Business Venturing*, 25: 439–448.

88. M. A. Delmas & O. Gergaud, 2014, Sustainable certification for future generations: The case of family firms, *Family Business Review*, 27: 228–243.

89. D. Ferris, 2012, Will economic growth destroy the environment—or save it? *Forbes*, www.forbes.com, October 17.

90. S. M. Ben-Menahern, Z. Kwee, H. W. Volberda, & F. A. J. Van Den Bosch, 2013, Strategic renewal over time: The enabling role of potential absorptive capacity in aligning internal and external rates of change, *Long Range Planning*, 46: 216–235; V. Souitaris & B. Maestro, 2010, Polychronicity in top management teams: The impact on strategic decision processes and performance of new technology ventures, *Strategic Management Journal*, 31: 652–678.

91. S.-J. Chang & B. Wu, 2014, Institutional barriers and industry dynamics, *Strategic Management Journal*, 35: 1103–1121.

92. M. Schimmer & M. Brauer, 2012, Firm performance and aspiration levels as determinants of a firm's strategic repositioning within strategic group structures, *Strategic Organization*, 10: 406–435; J. Galbreath & P. Galvin, 2008, Firm factors, industry structure and performance variation: New empirical evidence to a classic debate, *Journal of Business Research*, 61: 109–117.

93. J. J. Tarzijan & C. C. Ramirez, 2011, Firm, industry and corporation effects revisited: A mixed multilevel analysis for Chilean companies, *Applied Economics Letters*, 18: 95–100; V. F. Misangyi, H. Elms, T. Greckhamer, & J. A. Lepine, 2006, A new perspective on a fundamental debate: A multilevel approach to industry, corporate, and business unit effects, *Strategic Management Journal*, 27: 571–590.

94. E. T. Fukui, A. B. Hammer, & L. Z. Jones, 2013, Are U.S. exports influenced by stronger IPR protection measures in recipient markets? *Business Horizons*, 56: 179–188; D. Sullivan & J. Yuening, 2010, Media convergence and the impact of the Internet on the M&A activity of large media companies, *Journal of Media Business Studies*, 7(4): 21–40.

95. G. D. Markman & T. L. Waldron, 2014, Small entrants and large incumbents: A framework of micro entry, *Academy of Management Perspectives*, 28: 179–197; K. Muller, K. Huschelrath, & V. Bilotkach, 2012, The construction of a low-cost airline network—facing competition and exploring new markets, *Managerial and Decision Economics*, 33: 485–499.

96. F. Karakaya & S. Parayitam, 2013, Barriers to entry and firm performance: A proposed model and curvilinear relationships, *Journal of Strategic Marketing*, 21: 25–47; B. F. Schivardi & E. Viviano, 2011, Entry barriers in retail trade, *Economic Journal*, 121: 145–170; A. V. Mainkar, M. Lubatkin, & W. S. Schulze, 2006, Toward a product-proliferation theory of entry barriers, *Academy of Management Review*, 31: 1062–1075.

97. V. Niu, L. C. Dong, & R. Chen, 2012, Market entry barriers in China, *Journal of Business Research*, 65: 68–76.

98. R. Vandaie & A. Zaheer, 2014, Surviving bear hugs: Firm capability, large partner alliances and growth, *Strategic Management Journal*, 35: 566–577; V. K. Garg, R. L. Priem, & A. A. Rasheed, 2013, A theoretical explanation of the cost advantages of multi-unit franchising, *Journal of Marketing Channels*, 20: 52–72.

99. P. Jackson & M. Iwata, 2012, Global deal: Mitsubishi Heavy, Hitachi to merge businesses, *Wall Street Journal*, www.wsj.com, November 30.

100. C. G. Asmussen, 2015, Strategic factor markets, scale free resources and economic performance: The impact of product market rivalry, *Strategic Management Journal*, in press.

101. G. A. Shinkle & B. T. McCann, 2014, New produce deployment: The moderating influence of economic institutional context, *Strategic Management Journal*, 35: 1090–1101.

102. J. J. Ebbers & N. M. Wijnberg, 2013, Nascent ventures competing for start-up capital: Matching reputations and investors, *Journal of Business Venturing*, 27: 372–384; T. Rice & P. E. Strahan, 2010, Does credit competition affect small-firm finance? *Journal of Finance*, 65: 861–889.

103. Z. Khan, Y. K. Lew, & R. R. Sinkovics, 2015, International joint ventures as boundary spanners: Technological knowledge transfer in an emerging economy, *Global Strategy Journal*, 5: 48–68.

104. 2013, Zara-owned Inditex's profits rise by 22%, *BBC News Business*, www.bbc.co.uk, March 13.

105. M. Hume, 2011, The secrets of Zara's success, *Telegraph.co.uk*, www.telegraph.co.uk, June 22.

106. Y. Pan, L. Teng, A. B. Supapol, X. Lu, D. Huang, & Z. Wang, 2014, Firms; FDI ownership: The influence of government ownership and legislative connections, *Journal of International Business*, 45: 1029–1043; 2011, Airline deregulation, revisited, *Bloomberg Businessweek*, www.businessweek.com, January 21.

107. S. H. Ang, M. H. Benischke, & J. P. Doh, 2015, The interactions of institutions on foreign market entry mode, *Strategic Management Journal*, in press.

108. J. Jaeger, 2010, Anti-trust reviews: Suddenly, they're a worry, *Compliance Week*, 7(80): 48–59.

109. N. Argyes, L. Bigelow, & J. A. Nickerson, 2015, Dominant designs, innovation shocks and the follower's dilemma, *Strategic Management Journal*, 36: 216–234.

110. J. B. Heide, A. Kumar, & K. H. Wathne, 2014, Concurrent sourcing, governance mechanisms and performance outcomes in industrial value chains, *Strategic Management Journal*, 35: 1164–1185; L. Poppo & K. Z. Zhou, 2014, Managing contracts for fairness in buyer-supplier exchanges, *Strategic Management Journal*, 35: 1508–1527.

111. M. J. Mol & C. Brewster, 2014, The outsourcing strategy of local and multinational firms: A supply base perspective, *Global Strategy Journal*, 4: 20–34.

112. J. Roloff, M. S. ABländer, & D. Z. Nayir, 2015, The supplier perspective: Forging strong partnerships with buyers; *Journal of Business Strategy*, 36(1): 25–32; L. Poppo, K. Z. Zhou, & J. J. Li, 2015, When can you trust "trust?" Calculative trust, relational trust and supplier performance, *Strategic Management Journal*, in press.

113. F. H. Liu, 2014, OEM supplier impact on buyer competence development, *Journal of Strategy and Management*, 7: 2–18; S. Bhattacharyya & A. Nain, 2011, Horizontal acquisitions and buying power: A product market analysis, *Journal of Financial Economics*, 99: 97–115.

114. 2015, Computer sales statistics, *Statistic Brain*, www.statisticbrain.com, January 14; I. Sherr & S. Ovide, 2013, Computer sales in free fall, *Wall Street Journal*, www.wsj.com, April 11.

115. C. Giachetti & G. B. Dagnino, 2014, Detecting the relationship between competitive intensity and firm product line length: Evidence from the worldwide mobile phone industry, *Strategic Management Journal*, 35: 138–1409.

116. G. Pacheco-de-Almeida, A. Hawk, & B. Yeung, 2015, The right speed and its value, *Strategic Management Journal*, 36: 159–176.

117. M.-J. Lee & J. Cheng, 2015, Samsung vs. Apple: who was no. 1? *Wall Street Journal Digits*, blog.wsj.com, January 29; P. Cohan, 2013, Samsung trouncing Apple, *Forbes*, www.forbes.com, April 26.

118. K. Bradsher, 2014, China's embrace of foreign cars, *New York Times*, www.nytimes.com, April 8; K. Bradsher, 2013, Chinese auto buyers grow hungry for larger cars, *New York Times*, www.nytimes.com, April 21.

119. H. Martin, 2014, Global airline industry expects record profits in 2014, *Los Angeles Times*, articles.latimes.com, February 9; R. Wall, 2013, Airline profits to top $10 billion on improving sales outlook, *Bloomberg*, www.bloomberg.com, March 20.

120. M. A. Hitt, D. Li, & K Xu, 2015, International Strategy: From local to global and beyond, *Journal of World Business*, in press; A. Goerzen, C. G. Asmussen, & B. B. Nielsen, 2013, Global cities and multinational enterprise location strategy, *Journal of International Business Studies*, 44: 427–450.

121. M. E. Porter, 1980, *Competitive Strategy*, New York: Free Press.

122. F. J. Mas-Ruiz, F. Ruiz-Moreno, & A. L. de Guevara Martinez, 2013, Asymmetric rivalry within and between strategic groups, *Strategic Management Journal*, in press; M. S. Hunt, 1972, Competition in the major home appliance industry, 1960–1970 (doctoral dissertation, Harvard University); Porter, *Competitive Strategy*, 129.

123. D. Miller, I. Le Breton-Miller, & R. H. Lester, 2013, Family firm governance, strategic conformity, and performance: Institutional vs. strategic perspectives, *Organization Science*, 24: 189–209; S. Cheng & H. Chang, 2009, Performance implications of cognitive complexity: An empirical study of cognitive strategic groups in semiconductor industry, *Journal of Business Research*, 62: 1311–1320; G. McNamara, D. L. Deephouse, & R. A. Luce, 2003, Competitive positioning within and across a strategic group structure: The performance of core, secondary, and solitary firms, *Strategic Management Journal*, 24: 161–181.

124. B. P. S. Murthi, A. A. Rasheed, & I. Goll, 2013, An empirical analysis of strategic groups in the airline industry using latent class regressions, *Managerial and Decision Economics*, 34(2): 59–73; J. Lee, K. Lee, & S. Rho, 2002, An evolutionary perspective on strategic group emergence: A genetic algorithm-based model, *Strategic Management Journal*, 23: 727–746.

125. K.-Y. Hsieh, W. Tsai, & M.-J. Chen, 2015, If they can do it, why not us? Competitors as reference points in justifying escalation of commitment, *Academy of management Journal, 58: 38–58;* T. Keil, T. Laarmanen, & R. G. McGrath, 2013, Is a counterattack the best defense? Competitive dynamics through acquisitions, *Long Range Planning*, 46: 195–215.

126. Porter, *Competitive Strategy*, 49.

127. R. L. Priem, S. Li, & J. C. Carr, 2012, Insights and new directions from demand-side approaches to technology innovation, entrepreneurship, and strategic management research, *Journal of Management*, 38: 346–374; J. E. Prescott & R. Herko, 2010, TOWS: The role of competitive intelligence, *Competitive Intelligence Magazine*, 13(3): 8–17.

128. D. E. Hughes, J. Le Bon, & A. Rapp, 2013. Gaining and leveraging customer-based competitive intelligence: The pivotal role of social capital and salesperson adaptive selling skills, *Journal of the Academy of Marketing Science*, 41: 91–110; D. B. Montgomery, M. C. Moore, & J. E. Urbany, 2005, Reasoning about competitive reactions: Evidence from executives, *Marketing Science*, 24: 138–149.

129. H. Akbar & N. Tzokas, 2012, An exploration of new product development's front-end knowledge conceptualization process in discontinuous innovations, *British Journal of Management*, 24: 245–263; K. Xu, S. Liao, J. Li, & Y. Song, 2011, Mining comparative opinions from customer reviews for competitive intelligence, *Decision Support Systems*, 50: 743–754; S. Jain, 2008, Digital piracy: A competitive analysis, *Marketing Science*, 27: 610–626.

130. S. Wright, 2013, Converting input to insight: Organising for intelligence-based competitive advantage. In S. Wright (ed.), *Competitive Intelligence, Analysis and Strategy: Creating Organisational Agility*. Abingdon: Routledge, 1–35; J. G. York, 2009, Pragmatic sustainability: Translating environmental ethics into competitive advantage, *Journal of Business Ethics*, 85: 97–109.

131. R. Huggins, 2010, Regional competitive intelligence: Benchmarking and policy-making. *Regional Studies*, 44: 639–658.

132. L. T. Tuan, 2013, Leading to learning and competitive intelligence, *The Learning Organization*, 20: 216–239; K. A. Sawka, 2008, The ethics of competitive intelligence, *Kiplinger Business Resource Center Online*, www.kiplinger.com, March.

133. R. B. Bouncken & S. Kraus, 2013, Innovation in knowledge-intensive industries: The double-edged sword of coopetition, *Journal of Business Research*, 66: 2060–2070; T. Mazzarol & S. Reboud, 2008, The role of complementary actors in the development of innovation in small firms, *International Journal of Innovation Management*, 12: 223–253; A. Brandenburger & B. Nalebuff, 1996, *Co-opetition*, New York: Currency Doubleday.

134. 2015, SCIP Code of ethics for CI professionals, www.scip.org, March 25.

3

The Internal Organization: Resources, Capabilities, Core Competencies, and Competitive Advantages

Studying this chapter should provide you with the strategic management knowledge needed to:

3-1   Explain why firms need to study and understand their internal organization.

3-2   Define value and discuss its importance.

3-3   Describe the differences between tangible and intangible resources.

3-4   Define capabilities and discuss their development.

3-5   Describe four criteria used to determine if resources and capabilities are core competencies.

3-6   Explain how firms analyze their value chain for the purpose of determining where they are able to create value when using their resources, capabilities, and core competencies.

3-7   Define outsourcing and discuss reasons for its use.

3-8   Discuss the importance of identifying internal strengths and weaknesses.

3-9   Discuss the importance of avoiding core rigidities.

DATA ANALYTICS, LARGE PHARMACEUTICAL COMPANIES, AND CORE COMPETENCIES: A BRAVE NEW WORLD

To date, and perhaps surprisingly, the idea of using data strategically remains somewhat novel in some organizations. However, the reality of "big data" and "big data analytics" (which is "the process of examining big data to uncover hidden patterns, unknown correlations, and other useful information that can be used to make better decisions") is quickly changing this situation. Indeed, some suggest that, today, an organization wishing to be innovative will, at a minimum, commit to quickly learning how to comprehensively use big data analytics (BDA) across all customer channels (mobile, Web, e-mail and physical stores) as well as throughout its supply chain.

This is the situation for large pharmaceutical companies (these firms are often called "big pharma") in that many are considering the possibility of developing a core competence in terms of BDA. (We define and discuss core competencies in this chapter.) But why are these firms evaluating this possibility? There are several reasons. In addition to the vast increases in the amounts of data that must be studied and interpreted for competitive purposes, "health care reform and the changing landscape of health care delivery" systems throughout the world are influencing these firms to think about developing BDA as a core competence.

© Creativa Images/Shutterstock.com

Many benefits can accrue to big pharma firms capable of forming BDA as a core competence. For example, having BDA as a core competence is expected to help a firm quickly identify trial candidates and accelerate their recruitment, develop improved inclusion and exclusion criteria to use in clinical trials, and uncover unintended uses and indications for products. In terms of customer functionality, superior products can be provided at a faster pace as a foundation for helping patients live better and healthy lives.

Big pharma firms could try to develop BDA as a core competence themselves or collaborate with companies specializing in helping others do so. Currently, venture capitalists are funding an increasing number of entrepreneurial start-ups that specialize in the data analytics field. Regardless of the approach used, changes to an organization's culture often are required if the BDA process is to be appropriately supported. This is the case at Ford Motor Company where the firm is using BDA to establish the view that it is a mobility company rather than an automotive company. This perspective finds Ford using BDA and research on autonomous vehicles and mobile technologies to support its work on a number of functionalities for customers including, for example, being able to use their Ford product to "communicate with home thermostats so a person's heat might be automatically lowered as he or she drives away from the house."

As we discuss in this chapter, capabilities are the foundation for developing core competencies. There are several capabilities big pharma companies could form and emphasize in order for BDA to be a core competence. Supportive architecture, the proper mix of data scientists, and "technology that integrates and manages new types and sources of data flexibly and scalably while maintaining the highest standards of data governance, data quality, and data security" are examples of capabilities that big pharma firms may seek to possess if they wish to develop BDA as a core competence.

As with most companies, big pharma firms may encounter difficulty in the short run when seeking to develop BDA as a core competence. A recent survey suggests that insufficient skills by senior-level managers to permit a full operational understanding of the BDA process, the difficulty associated with determining the data that are the most strategically relevant, and an inability to consistently and quickly gain access to complete and fully accurate data are challenges requiring attention. Of course, not all big pharma firms will be successful in their efforts to develop the BDA process as a core competence.

Sources: Big data analytics: What it is & why it matters, 2015, SAS, www.sas.com, April 2; Big data for the pharmaceutical industry, *Informatica*, www.informatica.com, March 17; B. Atkins, 2015, Big data and the board, *Wall Street Journal Online*, www.wsj.com, April 16; D. Gage, 2015, Zetta Venture Partners closes $60M fund to back data-analytics startups, *Wall Street Journal Online*, www.wsj.com, February 11; R. King, 2015, Ford wants to sharpen big data skills at its Silicon Valley innovation center, *Wall Street Journal Online*, www.wsj.com, January 22; Are you prepared to make the decisions that matter most? *PcW's Global Data & Analytics Survey 2014*, www.pwc.com, November 12; S. F. DeAngelis, 2014, Pharmaceutical big data analytics promises a healthier future, *Enterrasolutions.com*, www.enterrasolutions.com, June 5; T. Wolfram, 2014, Data analytics has big pharma rethinking its core competencies, *Forbes Online*, www.forbes.com, December 22.

As discussed in the first two chapters, several factors in the global economy, including the rapid development of the Internet's capabilities and globalization in general, are making it difficult for firms to find ways to develop competitive advantages.[1] Increasingly, innovation appears to be a vital path to efforts to develop competitive advantages, particularly sustainable ones.[2] Fashion retailer Zara's ability to produce new clothing designs quickly is a core competence and also a competitive advantage for the firm. This ability is a product of innovations the firm established in terms of sophisticated information technologies that are used to track inventories and relying on groups of creative designers rather than individuals to quickly develop new fashions. The continual appearance of fresh designs the firm consistently produces through its innovations results in 17 visits per customer per year in its stores compared to the average of three visits per year in competitors stores.[3] You will learn more about Zara given that this firm is the subject of the Mini-Case appearing at the end of this chapter. Innovative actions will be required by big pharma companies seeking to develop capabilities that can be the foundation on which the process of big data analytics can become a core competence (see the Opening Case).

As is the case for Zara and big pharma companies, innovation is critical to firm success. This means that many firms seek to develop innovation as a core competence. We define and discuss core competencies in this chapter and explain how firms use their resources and capabilities to form them. As a core competence, innovation has long been critical to Boeing's success, too. Today however, the firm is focusing on incremental innovations as well as developing new technologies that are linked to major innovations and the projects they spawn, such as the 787 Dreamliner. The incremental innovations are ones Boeing believes enable the firm to more quickly deliver reliable products to customers at a lower cost.[4] Innovation is also becoming more vital to U.S. medical schools. Efforts are underway for the purpose of identifying methods to use to produce "young doctors who are better prepared to meet the demands of the nation's changing health-care system."[5] As we discuss in this chapter, firms and organizations such as those we mention here, achieve strategic competitiveness and earn above-average returns by acquiring, bundling, and leveraging their resources for the purpose of taking advantage of opportunities in the external environment in ways that create value for customers.[6]

Even if the firm develops and manages resources in ways that create core competencies and competitive advantages, competitors will eventually learn how to duplicate the benefits of any firm's value-creating strategy; thus, all competitive advantages have a limited life.[7] Because of this, the question of duplication of a competitive advantage is not if it will happen, but when. In general, a competitive advantage's sustainability is a function of three factors:

1. The rate of core competence obsolescence because of environmental changes.
2. The availability of substitutes for the core competence.
3. The imitability of the core competence.[8]

For all firms, the challenge is to effectively manage current core competencies while simultaneously developing new ones.[9] Only when firms are able to do this can they expect to achieve strategic competitiveness, earn above-average returns, and remain ahead of competitors in both the short and long term.

We studied the general, industry, and competitor environments in Chapter 2. Armed with knowledge about the realities and conditions of their external environment, firms have a better understanding of marketplace opportunities and the characteristics of the competitive environment in which those opportunities exist. In this chapter, we focus on the firm itself. By analyzing its internal organization, a firm determines what it can do. Matching what a firm *can do* (a function of its resources, capabilities, and core competencies in the internal organization) with what it *might do* (a function of opportunities and threats in the external environment) is a process that yields insights that the firm requires to select strategies from among those we discuss in Chapters 4 through 9.

We begin this chapter by briefly describing conditions associated with analyzing the firm's internal organization. We then discuss the roles of resources and capabilities in developing core competencies, which are the sources of the firm's competitive advantages. Included in this discussion are the techniques firms use to identify and evaluate resources and capabilities and the criteria for identifying core competencies from among them. Resources by themselves typically are not competitive advantages. In fact, resources create value when the firm uses them to form capabilities, some of which become core competencies, and hopefully competitive advantages. Because of the relationship among resources, capabilities, and core competencies, we also discuss the value chain and examine four criteria that firms use to determine if their capabilities are core competencies and, as such, sources of competitive advantage.[10] The chapter closes with comments about outsourcing as well as the need for firms to prevent their core competencies from becoming core rigidities. The existence of core rigidities indicates that the firm is too anchored to its past, a situation that prevents it from continuously developing new capabilities and core competencies.

3-1 Analyzing the Internal Organization

3-1a The Context of Internal Analysis

One of the conditions associated with analyzing a firm's internal organization is the reality that in today's global economy, some of the resources that were traditionally critical to firms' efforts to produce, sell, and distribute their goods or services, such as labor costs, access to financial resources and raw materials, and protected or regulated markets, although still important, are now less likely to be the source of competitive advantages.[11] An important reason for this is that an increasing number of firms are using their resources to form core competencies through which they successfully implement an international strategy (discussed in Chapter 8) as a means of overcoming the advantages created by these more traditional resources.

Upscale retailer Neiman Marcus Group, for example, is taking actions to enable it to cater to wealthy shoppers across the world. These actions demonstrate CEO Karen Katz's international ambitions for Neiman Marcus, a retailer that historically has operated store fronts in the United States only. To quickly gain access to international markets, one of the actions the firm is taking is to acquire e-commerce sites located outside the United States.

Munich-based Mytheresa.com is a recent and significant acquisition and provides Neiman Marcus with a strong foothold in Europe and a developing foothold in Asia. Establishing effective distribution channels is critical to Neiman Marcus' efforts to develop new competencies as a foundation for serving affluent customers throughout the world.[12]

Given the increasing importance of the global economy, those analyzing their firm's internal organization should use a global mind-set to do so. A **global mind-set** is the ability to analyze, understand, and manage an internal organization in ways that are not dependent on the assumptions of a single country, culture, or context.[13] Because they are able to span artificial boundaries, those with a global mind-set recognize that their firms must possess resources and capabilities that allow understanding of and appropriate responses to competitive situations that are influenced by country-specific factors and unique cultures. Using a global mind-set to analyze the internal organization has the potential to significantly help the firm in its efforts to outperform rivals.[14] A global mind-set is influencing Neiman Marcus' decisions to find ways to serve wealthy customers in countries throughout the world rather than in the United States only.

Finally, analyzing the firm's internal organization requires that evaluators examine the firm's entire portfolio of resources and capabilities. This perspective suggests that individual firms possess at least some resources and capabilities that other companies do not—at least not in the same combination. Resources are the source of capabilities, some of which lead to the development of core competencies; in turn, some core competencies may lead to a competitive advantage for the firm.[15] Understanding how to leverage the firm's unique bundle of resources and capabilities is a key outcome decision makers seek when analyzing the internal organization.[16] Figure 3.1 illustrates the relationships among resources, capabilities, core competencies, and competitive advantages and shows how their integrated use can lead to strategic competitiveness. As we discuss next, firms use the resources in their internal organization to create value for customers.

A **global mind-set** is the ability to analyze, understand, and manage an internal organization in ways that are not dependent on the assumptions of a single country, culture, or context.

Figure 3.1 Components of an Internal Analysis

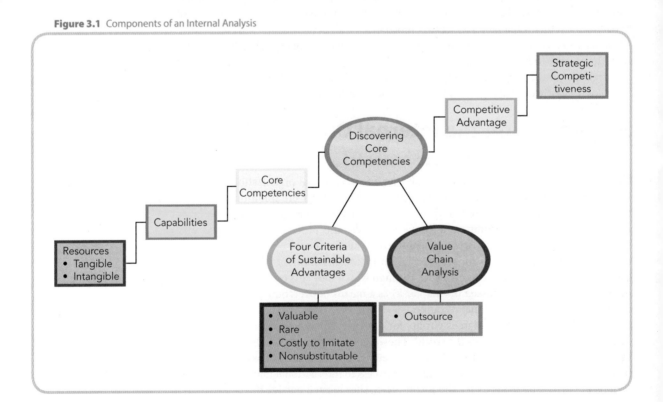

3-1b Creating Value

Firms use their resources as the foundation for producing goods or services that will create value for customers.[17] **Value** is measured by a product's performance characteristics and by its attributes for which customers are willing to pay. Firms create value by innovatively bundling and leveraging their resources to form capabilities and core competencies.[18] Firms with a competitive advantage create more value for customers than do competitors.[19] Walmart uses its "every day low price" approach to doing business (an approach that is grounded in the firm's core competencies, such as information technology and distribution channels) to create value for those seeking to buy products at a low price compared to competitors' prices for those products. The stronger these firms' core competencies, the greater the amount of value they're able to create for their customers.[20]

Ultimately, creating value for customers is the source of above-average returns for a firm. What the firm intends regarding value creation affects its choice of business-level strategy (see Chapter 4) and its organizational structure (see Chapter 11).[21] In Chapter 4's discussion of business-level strategies, we note that value is created by a product's low cost, by its highly differentiated features, or by a combination of low cost and high differentiation compared to competitors' offerings. A business-level strategy is effective only when it is grounded in exploiting the firm's capabilities and core competencies. Thus, the successful firm continuously examines the effectiveness of current capabilities and core competencies while thinking about the capabilities and competencies it will require for future success.[22]

At one time, firms' efforts to create value were largely oriented toward understanding the characteristics of their industry in which they competed and, in light of those characteristics, determining how they should be positioned relative to competitors. This emphasis on industry characteristics and competitive strategy underestimated the role of the firm's resources and capabilities in developing core competencies as the source of competitive advantages. In fact, core competencies, in combination with product-market positions, are the firm's most important sources of competitive advantage.[23] A firm's core competencies, integrated with an understanding of the results of studying the conditions in the external environment, should drive the selection of strategies.[24] As Clayton Christensen noted, "successful strategists need to cultivate a deep understanding of the processes of competition and progress and of the factors that undergird each advantage. Only thus will they be able to see when old advantages are poised to disappear and how new advantages can be built in their stead."[25] By emphasizing core competencies when selecting and implementing strategies, companies learn to compete primarily on the basis of firm-specific differences. However, while doing so they must be simultaneously aware of changes in the firm's external environment.[26]

3-1c The Challenge of Analyzing the Internal Organization

The strategic decisions managers make about the internal organization are nonroutine,[27] have ethical implications,[28] and significantly influence the firm's ability to earn above-average returns.[29] These decisions involve choices about the resources the firm needs to collect and how to best manage and leverage them.

Making decisions involving the firm's assets—identifying, developing, deploying, and protecting resources, capabilities, and core competencies—may appear to be relatively easy. However, this task is as challenging and difficult as any other with which managers are involved; moreover, the task is increasingly internationalized.[30] Some believe that the pressure on managers to pursue only decisions that help the firm meet anticipated quarterly earnings makes it difficult to accurately examine the firm's internal organization.[31]

Value is measured by a product's performance characteristics and by its attributes for which customers are willing to pay.

At one time, Polaroid's cameras created a significant amount of value for customers. Poor decisions may have contributed to the firm's subsequent inability to create value and its initial filing for bankruptcy in 2001.

Gene Blevins/Polaris/Newscom

The challenge and difficulty of making effective decisions are implied by preliminary evidence suggesting that one-half of organizational decisions fail.[32] Sometimes, mistakes are made as the firm analyzes conditions in its internal organization.[33] Managers might, for example, think a capability is a core competence when it is not. This may have been the case at Polaroid Corporation as decision makers continued to believe that the capabilities it used to build its instant film cameras were highly relevant at the time its competitors were developing and using the capabilities required to introduce digital cameras. In this instance, Polaroid's decision makers may have concluded that superior manufacturing was a core competence, as was the firm's ability to innovate in terms of creating value-adding features for its instant cameras. If a mistake is made when analyzing and managing a firm's resources, such as appears to have been the case some years ago at Polaroid, decision makers must have the confidence to admit it and take corrective actions.[34]

A firm can improve by studying its mistakes; in fact, the learning generated by making and correcting mistakes can be important to efforts to create new capabilities and core competencies.[35] One capability that can be learned from failure is when to quit. Polaroid should have obviously changed its strategy earlier than it did, and by doing so it may have been able to avoid more serious failure. Another potential example concerns News Corp.'s Amplify unit. As of mid-2015, the firm had invested over $1 billion in the unit that makes tablets, sells online curricula, and offers testing services. In 2014, Amplify generated a $193 million dollar loss as it seeks to change the way children are taught. Facing competition from well-established textbook publishers that are enhancing their ability to sell digital products such as those Amplify sells, News Corp. may want to carefully evaluate its previous decisions to see if mistakes were made and if so, how future decisions might be error free.[36]

As we discuss next, three conditions—uncertainty, complexity, and intraorganizational conflict—affect managers as they analyze the internal organization and make decisions about resources (see Figure 3.2).

Figure 3.2 Conditions Affecting Managerial Decisions about Resources, Capabilities, and Core Competencies

Conditions	**Uncertainty**	Uncertainty exists about the characteristics of the firm's general and industry environments and customers' needs.
	Complexity	Complexity results from the interrelationships among conditions shaping a firm.
	Intraorganizational Conflicts	Intraorganizational conflicts may exist among managers making decisions as well as among those affected by the decisions.

When studying the internal organization, managers face uncertainty because of a number of issues, including those of new proprietary technologies, rapidly changing economic and political trends, transformations in societal values, and shifts in customers' demands.[37] Environmental uncertainty increases the complexity and range of issues to examine when studying the internal environment.[38] Consider how uncertainty affects how to use resources at coal companies such as Peabody Energy Corp. and Murray Energy Corp.

Peabody is the world's largest private coal sector producer. The firm's coal products fuel approximately 10 percent of all U.S. electricity generation and 2 percent of worldwide electricity. But this firm and others competing in its industry face a great deal of uncertainty, particularly political uncertainty. As a result, there are questions about how Peabody and its competitors might best allocate their resources *today* to prepare for success *tomorrow*. Viewing coal as a "dirty fuel" and its production as environmental unfriendly, the U.S. Environmental Protection Agency (EPA) announced in 2014 and described in greater detail in 2015 new regulations. Focusing on carbon emissions, the EPA's carbon regulations "call for a 30 percent cut in power-plant carbon emissions by 2030 based on emissions levels in 2005." Coal producers such as Peabody, Arch Coal, and Murray Energy to name only a few, believe that the regulations are too strict and that moreover, the EPA misinterpreted the Clean Air Act when developing them. Time is required for the parties to sort through all of these issues, some of which will be decided by various courts given lawsuits filed by states (such as West Virginia) and firms (such as Murray Energy Corp.).[39] The issue though is that the decision makers in these energy firms face a great deal of uncertainty as they examine the resources, capabilities, and core competencies that form their firms' internal organization.[40]

Biases regarding how to cope with uncertainty affect decisions made about how to manage the firm's resources and capabilities to form core competencies.[41] Additionally, intraorganizational conflict may surface when decisions are made about the core competencies a firm should develop and nurture. Conflict might surface in the energy companies mentioned above about the degree to which resources and capabilities should be used to form new core competencies to support newer "clean technologies."

In making decisions affected by these three conditions, judgment is required. *Judgment* is the capability of making successful decisions when no obviously correct model or rule is available or when relevant data are unreliable or incomplete. In such situations, decision makers must be aware of possible cognitive biases, such as overconfidence. Individuals who are too confident in the decisions they make about how to use the firm's resources may fail to fully evaluate contingencies that could affect those decisions.[42]

When exercising judgment, decision makers often take intelligent risks. In the current competitive landscape, executive judgment can become a valuable capability. One reason is that, over time, effective judgment that decision makers demonstrate allows a firm to build a strong reputation and retain the loyalty of stakeholders whose support is linked to above-average returns.[43]

Finding individuals who can make the most successful decisions about using the organization's resources is challenging. Being able to do this is important because the quality of leaders' decisions regarding resources and their management affect a firm's ability to achieve strategic competitiveness. Individuals holding these key decision-making positions are called *strategic leaders*. Discussed fully in Chapter 12, for our purposes in this chapter we can think of strategic leaders as individuals with an ability to make effective decisions when examining the firm's resources, capabilities, and core competencies for the purpose of making choices about their use.

Next, we consider the relationships among a firm's resources, capabilities, and core competencies. While reading these sections, keep in mind that organizations have more resources than capabilities and more capabilities than core competencies.

3-2 Resources, Capabilities, and Core Competencies

Resources, capabilities, and core competencies are the foundation of competitive advantage. Resources are bundled to create organizational capabilities. In turn, capabilities are the source of a firm's core competencies, which are the basis of establishing competitive advantages.[44] We show these relationships in Figure 3.1 and discuss them next.

3-2a Resources

Broad in scope, resources cover a spectrum of individual, social, and organizational phenomena. By themselves, resources do not allow firms to create value for customers as the foundation for earning above-average returns. Indeed, resources are combined to form capabilities.[45] For example, Subway links its fresh ingredients with several other resources including the continuous training it provides to those running the firm's fast food restaurants as the foundation for customer service as a capability; customer service is also a core competence for Subway.

As its sole distribution channel, the Internet is a resource for Amazon.com. The firm uses the Internet to sell goods at prices that typically are lower than those offered by competitors selling the same goods through more costly brick-and-mortar storefronts. By combining other resources (such as access to a wide product inventory), Amazon has developed a reputation for excellent customer service. Amazon's capability in terms of customer service is a core competence as well in that the firm creates unique value for customers through the services it provides to them. Amazon also uses its technological core competence to offer AWS (Amazon Web Services), services through which businesses can rent computing power from Amazon at a cost of pennies per hour. Much smaller than AWS, Rackspace seeks to leverage its core competence of "economies of expertise" as it competes against its larger rival.[46]

Some of a firm's resources (defined in Chapter 1 as inputs to the firm's production process) are tangible while others are intangible. **Tangible resources** are assets that can be observed and quantified. Production equipment, manufacturing facilities, distribution centers, and formal reporting structures are examples of tangible resources. Its stock of oil and gas pipelines is a key tangible resource for energy giant Kinder Morgan. **Intangible resources** are assets that are rooted deeply in the firm's history, accumulate over time, and are relatively difficult for competitors to analyze and imitate. Because they are embedded in unique patterns of routines, intangible resources are difficult for competitors to analyze and imitate. Knowledge, trust between managers and employees, managerial capabilities, organizational routines (the unique ways people work together), scientific capabilities, the capacity for innovation, brand name, the firm's reputation for its goods or services and how it interacts with people (such as employees, customers, and suppliers), and organizational culture are intangible resources.[47]

Intangible resources require nurturing to maintain their ability to help firms engage in competitive battles. This is the case for brand as an intangible. Brand has long been a valuable intangible resource for Coca-Cola Company. The same is true for "logo-laden British brand Superdry." Recently though, SuperGroup PLC, the owner of Superdry, has encountered problems in efforts to maintain and hopefully enhance the value of the Superdry brand. We discuss these issues in the Strategic Focus.

Tangible resources are assets that can be observed and quantified.

Intangible resources are assets that are rooted deeply in the firm's history, accumulate over time, and are relatively difficult for competitors to analyze and imitate.

Strategic **Focus**

Strengthening the Superdry Brand as a Foundation to Strategic Success

British-based SuperGroup, owner of Superdry and its carefully banded product lines, is taking actions to deal with recent performance problems. These problems manifested themselves in various ways, including the need for the firm to issue three profit warnings in one six-month period and a 34 percent decline in the price of its stock in 2014 compared to 2013.

Founded in 1985, the firm is recognized as a distinctive, branded fashion retailer selling quality clothing and accessories. In fact, the firm says that "the Superdry brand is at the heart of the business." The brand is targeted to discerning customers who seek to purchase "stylish clothing that is uniquely designed and well made." In this sense, the company believes that its men's and women's products have "wide appeal, capturing elements of 'urban' and 'streetwear' designs with subtle combinations of vintage Americana, Japanese imagery, and British tailoring, all with strong attention to detail." Thus, the firm's brand is critical to the image it conveys with its historical target customer—teens and those in their early twenties. Those leading SuperGroup believe that customers love the Superdry products as well as the "theatre and personality" of the stores in which they are sold. These outcomes are important given the company's intention of providing customers with "personalized shopping experiences that enhance the brand rather than just selling clothes."

As noted above, problems have affected the firm's performance. What the firm wants to do, of course, is correct the problems before the Superdry brand is damaged. Management turmoil is one of the firm's problems. In January of 2015, the CEO abruptly left. Almost simultaneously, the CFO was suspended for filing for personal bankruptcy, and the Chief Operating Officer left to explore other options. Some analysts believe that the firm's growth had been ill-conceived, signaling the possibility of ineffective strategic decisions on the part of the firm's upper-level leaders. As one analyst said: "The issue with SuperGroup is that they've expanded too quickly, without the supporting infrastructure."

Efforts are now underway to address these problems. In particular, those now leading SuperGroup intend to better control the firm as a means of protecting the value of its brand. A new CEO has been appointed who believes that "the business is very much more in control" today than has been the case recently. A well-regarded interim CFO has been appointed, and the firm's board has been strengthened by added experienced individuals. Commenting about these changes, an observer

Products are displayed in this Superdry store in ways that will personalize customers' shopping experiences.

Bloomberg/Getty Images

said that SuperGroup has "moved from an owner-entrepreneurial style of management to a more professional and experienced type of management. The key thing is, it is much better now than it was."

Direct actions are also being taken to enhance the Superdry brand. The appointment of Idris Elba, *The Wire* actor, is seen as a major attempt to reignite the brand's image. In fact, SuperGroup says that Elba epitomizes what the Superdry brand is—British, grounded, and cool. The thinking here, too, is that Elba, who at the time of his selection was 42, would appeal to the customer who was "growing up" with the Superdry brand. For these customers, who are 25 and older, SuperGroup is developing Superdry products with less dramatic presentations of the brand's well-known large logos. Additional lines of clothing, for skiing and rugby for example, are being developed for the more mature Superdry customer. After correcting the recently encountered problems, SuperGroup intends to expand into additional markets, including China. In every instance though, the firm will protect the brand when entering new competitive arenas and will rely on it as the foundation for intended success.

Sources: About SuperGroup, 2015, SuperGroupPLC.com, www.supergroup.co.uk, April 5; S. Chaudhuri, 2015, Superdry brand works to iron out problems, *Wall Street Journal Online*, www.wsj.com, April 15; S. Chaudhuri, 2015, Superdry looks to U.S. to drive growth, *Wall Street Journal Online*, www.wsj.com, March 26; H. Mann, 2015, SuperGroup strategy oozes Hollywood glamour, *Interactive Investor*, www.iii.co.uk, March 26; A. Monaghan & S. Butler, 2015, Superdry signs up Idris Elba, *The Guardian Online*, www.theguardian.com, March 26; A. Petroff, 2015, Is this the worst CFO ever? *CNNMoney*, www.money.cnn.com, February 25.

For each analysis, tangible and intangible are grouped into categories. The four primary categories of tangible resources are financial, organizational, physical, and technological (see Table 3.1). The three primary categories of intangible resources are human, innovation, and reputational (see Table 3.2).

Table 3.1 Tangible Resources

Financial Resources	• The firm's capacity to borrow • The firm's ability to generate funds through internal operations
Organizational Resources	• Formal reporting structures
Physical Resources	• The sophistication of a firm's plant and equipment and the attractiveness of its location • Distribution facilities • Product inventory
Technological Resources	• Availability of technology-related resources such as copyrights, patents, trademarks, and trade secrets

Sources: Adapted from J. B. Barney, 1991, Firm resources and sustained competitive advantage, *Journal of Management*, 17: 101; R. M. Grant, 1991, *Contemporary Strategy Analysis*, Cambridge: U.K.: Blackwell Business, 100–102.

Table 3.2 Intangible Resources

Human Resources	• Knowledge • Trust • Skills • Abilities to collaborate with others
Innovation Resources	• Ideas • Scientific capabilities • Capacity to innovate
Reputational Resources	• Brand name • Perceptions of product quality, durability, and reliability • Positive reputation with stakeholders such as suppliers and customers

Sources: Adapted from R. Hall, 1992, The strategic analysis of intangible resources, *Strategic Management Journal*, 13: 136–139: R. M. Grant, 1991, *Contemporary Strategy Analysis*, Cambridge: U.K.: Blackwell Business, 101–104.

Tangible Resources

As tangible resources, a firm's borrowing capacity and the status of its physical facilities are visible. The value of many tangible resources can be established through financial statements, but these statements do not account for the value of all of the firm's assets because they disregard some intangible resources.[48] The value of tangible resources is also constrained because they are hard to leverage—it is difficult to derive additional business or value from a tangible resource. For example, an airplane is a tangible resource, but "you can't use the same airplane on five different routes at the same time. You can't put the same crew on five different routes at the same time. And the same goes for the financial investment you've made in the airplane."[49]

Although production assets are tangible, many of the processes necessary to use them are intangible. Thus, the learning and potential proprietary processes associated with a tangible resource, such as manufacturing facilities, can have unique intangible attributes, such as quality control processes, unique manufacturing processes, and technologies that develop over time.[50]

Intangible Resources

Compared to tangible resources, intangible resources are a superior source of capabilities and subsequently, core competencies.[51] In fact, in the global economy, a firm's intellectual capital often plays a more critical role in corporate success than do physical assets.[52] Because of this, being able to effectively manage intellectual capital is an increasingly important skill for today's leaders to develop.[53]

Because intangible resources are less visible and more difficult for competitors to understand, purchase, imitate, or substitute for, firms prefer to rely on them rather than on tangible resources as the foundation for their capabilities. In fact, the more unobservable (i.e., intangible) a resource is, the more valuable that resource is to create capabilities.[54] Another benefit of intangible resources is that, unlike most tangible resources, their use can be leveraged. For instance, sharing knowledge among employees does not diminish its value for any one person. To the contrary, two people sharing their individualized knowledge sets often can be leveraged to create additional knowledge that, although new to each individual, contributes potentially to performance improvements for the firm.

Reputational resources (see Table 3.2) are important sources of a firm's capabilities and core competencies. Indeed, some argue that a positive reputation can even be a source of competitive advantage.[55] Earned through the firm's actions as well as its words, a value-creating reputation is a product of years of superior marketplace competence as perceived by stakeholders.[56] A reputation indicates the level of awareness a firm has been able to develop among stakeholders and the degree to which they hold the firm in high esteem.[57]

A well-known and highly valued brand name is a specific reputational resource.[58] A continuing commitment to innovation and aggressive advertising facilitates firms' efforts to take advantage of the reputation associated with their brands.[59] Harley-Davidson has a reputation for producing and servicing high-quality motorcycles with unique designs. Because of the desirability of its reputation, the company also produces a wide range of accessory items that it sells on the basis of its reputation for offering unique products with high quality. Sunglasses, jewelry, belts, wallets, shirts, slacks, belts, and hats are just a few of the large variety of accessories customers can purchase from a Harley-Davidson dealer or from its online store.[60]

Taking advantage of today's technologies, some firms are using social media as a means of influencing their reputation. Comcast for example is "adding more social media representatives as it tries to work on its reputation for inefficient, unresponsive or just plain rude customer service."[61] Similarly, General Motors is using social media to respond to customer concerns about product recalls the firm has experienced over the past few years. A key purpose of GM's efforts with its social media campaign is to "fundamentally redefine (itself) as an open, transparent, listening organization."[62] Recognizing that thousands of conversations occur daily throughout the world and that what is being said can affect its reputation,

©iStockPhoto.com/Courtney Keating

Developing capabilities in specific functional areas can give companies a competitive edge. The effective use of social media to direct advertising to specific market segments has given some firms an advantage over their rivals.

Coca-Cola company encourages its employees to be a part of these social-media based discussion as a means of positively influencing the company's reputation. Driving the nature of these conversations is a set of social media "commitments" that Coca-Cola employees use as a foundation for how they will engage with various social media. Being transparent and protecting consumers' privacy are examples of the commitments the firm established.[63]

3-2b Capabilities

The firm combines individual tangible and intangible resources to create capabilities. In turn, capabilities are used to complete the organizational tasks required to produce, distribute, and service the goods or services the firm provides to customers for the purpose of creating value for them. As a foundation for building core competencies and hopefully competitive advantages, capabilities are often based on developing, carrying, and exchanging information and knowledge through the firm's human capital.[64] Hence, the value of human capital in developing and using capabilities and, ultimately, core competencies cannot be overstated.[65] In fact, it seems to be "well known that human capital makes or breaks companies."[66] At pizza-maker Domino's, human capital is critical to the firm's efforts to change how it competes. Describing this, CEO Patrick Doyle says that, in many ways, Domino's is becoming "a technology company … that has adapted the art of pizza-making to the digital age."[67]

As illustrated in Table 3.3, capabilities are often developed in specific functional areas (such as manufacturing, R&D, and marketing) or in a part of a functional area (e.g., advertising). Table 3.3 shows a grouping of organizational functions and the capabilities that some companies are thought to possess in terms of all or parts of those functions.

Table 3.3 Example of Firms' Capabilities

Functional Areas	Capabilities	Examples of Firms
Distribution	• Effective use of logistics management techniques	• Walmart
Human Resources	• Motivating, empowering, and retaining employees	• Microsoft
Management Information Systems	• Effective and efficient control of inventories through point-of-purchase data collection methods	• Walmart
Marketing	• Effective promotion of brand-name products • Effective customer service • Innovative merchandising	• Procter & Gamble • Ralph Lauren Corp. • McKinsey & Co. • Nordstrom Inc. • Crate & Barrel
Management	• Ability to envision the future of clothing	• Hugo Boss • Zara
Manufacturing	• Design and production skills yielding reliable products • Product and design quality • Miniaturization of components and products	• Komatsu • Witt Gas Technology • Sony
Research & Development	• Innovative technology • Development of sophisticated elevator control solutions • Rapid transformation of technology into new products and processes • Digital technology	• Caterpillar • Otis Elevator Co. • Chaparral Steel • Thomson Consumer Electronics

3-2c   Core Competencies

Defined in Chapter 1, core competencies are capabilities that serve as a source of competitive advantage for a firm over its rivals. Core competencies distinguish a company competitively and reflect its personality. Core competencies emerge over time through an organizational process of accumulating and learning how to deploy different resources and capabilities.[68] As the capacity to take action, core competencies are the "crown jewels of a company," the activities the company performs especially well compared to competitors and through which the firm adds unique value to the goods or services it sells to customers.[69] Thus, if a big pharma company (such as Pfizer) developed big data analytics as a core competence, one could conclude that the firm had formed capabilities through which it was able to analyze and effectively use huge amounts of data in a competitively-superior manner.

Innovation is thought to be a core competence at Apple. As a capability, R&D activities are the source of this core competence. More specifically, the way Apple has combined some of its tangible (e.g., financial resources and research laboratories) and intangible (e.g., scientists and engineers and organizational routines) resources to complete research and development tasks creates a capability in R&D. By emphasizing its R&D capability, Apple is able to innovate in ways that create unique value for customers in the form of the products it sells, such as the iWatch, suggesting that innovation is a core competence for Apple.

Excellent customer service in its retail stores is another of Apple's core competencies. In this instance, unique and contemporary store designs (a tangible resource) are combined with knowledgeable and skilled employees (an intangible resource) to provide superior service to customers. A number of carefully developed training and development procedures are capabilities on which Apple's core competence of excellent customer service is based. The procedures that are capabilities include specification of how employees are to interact with customers, carefully written training manuals to describe on-site tech support that is to be provided to customers, and deep thinking about every aspect of the store's design including music that is played.[70]

3-3   Building Core Competencies

Two tools help firms identify their core competencies. The first consists of four specific criteria of sustainable competitive advantage that can be used to determine which capabilities are core competencies. Because the capabilities shown in Table 3.3 have satisfied these four criteria, they are core competencies. The second tool is the value chain analysis. Firms use this tool to select the value-creating competencies that should be maintained, upgraded, or developed and those that should be outsourced.

3-3a   The Four Criteria of Sustainable Competitive Advantage

Capabilities that are valuable, rare, costly to imitate, and nonsubstitutable are core competencies (see Table 3.4). In turn, core competencies can lead to competitive advantages for the firm over its rivals. Capabilities failing to satisfy the four criteria are not core competencies, meaning that although every core competence is a capability, not every capability is a core competence. In slightly different words, for a capability to be a core competence, it must be valuable and unique from a customer's point of view. For a core competence to be a potential source of competitive advantage, it must be inimitable and nonsubstitutable by competitors.[71]

Table 3.4 The Four Criteria of Sustainable Competitive Advantage

Valuable Capabilities	• Help a firm neutralize threats or exploit opportunities
Rare Capabilities	• Are not possessed by many others
Costly-to-Imitate Capabilities	• Historical: A unique and a valuable organizational culture or brand name • Ambiguous cause: The causes and uses of a competence are unclear • Social complexity: Interpersonal relationships, trust, and friendship among managers, suppliers, and customers
Nonsubstitutable Capabilities	• No strategic equivalent

A sustainable competitive advantage exists only when competitors are unable to duplicate the benefits of a firm's strategy or when they lack the resources to attempt imitation. For some period of time, the firm may have a core competence by using capabilities that are valuable and rare, but imitable. For example, some firms are trying to develop a core competence and potentially a competitive advantage by out-greening their competitors.[72] (Interestingly, developing a "green" core competence can contribute to the firm's efforts to earn above-average returns while benefitting the broader society.) For many years, Walmart has been committed to using its resources in ways that support environmental sustainability while pursuing a competitive advantage in the process. To facilitate these efforts, Walmart recently labeled over 10,000 products on its e-commerce site as products that are "Made by a Sustainability Leader." Initially, these items were batched into roughly 80 product categories. In addition to seeking a competitive advantage through these actions, Walmart hoped to make it easier for customers to make "sustainable choices" when purchasing products. Walmart is also working to supply 100 percent of its needs from renewable energy sources, to create zero waste from its operations, and to lead the industry in deploying clean technologies as a means of reducing fuel consumption and air pollution.[73] Of course, Walmart competitors such as Target are engaging in similar actions. Time will reveal the degree to which Walmart's green practices can be imitated.

The length of time a firm can expect to create value by using its core competencies is a function of how quickly competitors can successfully imitate a good, service, or process. Value-creating core competencies may last for a relatively long period of time only when all four of the criteria we discuss next are satisfied. Thus, Walmart would know that it has a core competence and possibly a competitive advantage in terms of green practices if the ways the firm uses its resources to complete these practices satisfy the four criteria.

Valuable

Valuable capabilities allow the firm to exploit opportunities or neutralize threats in its external environment. By effectively using capabilities to exploit opportunities or neutralize threats, a firm creates value for customers.[74] For example, Groupon created the "daily deal" marketing space; the firm reached $1 billion in revenue faster than any other company in history. In essence, the opportunity Groupon's founders pursued when launching the firm in 2008 was to create a marketplace through which businesses could introduce their goods or services to customers who would be able to experience them at a discounted price. Restaurants, hair and nail salons, and hotels are examples of the types of companies making frequent use of Groupon's services.

Valuable capabilities allow the firm to exploit opportunities or neutralize threats in its external environment.

Young, urban professionals desiring to affordably experience the cities in which they live are the firm's target customers.[75] However, competing daily-deal websites such as LivingSocial and Blackboard Eats quickly surfaced and are offering similar and often less expensive deals. Groupon may succeed but shorter development cycles, especially for such online firms, makes it harder for successful startups to create enduring competitive advantage. "In other words, they are increasingly vulnerable to the same capital-market pressures that plague big companies—but before they've developed lasting corporate assets."[76]

Rare

Rare capabilities are capabilities that few, if any, competitors possess. A key question to be answered when evaluating this criterion is "how many rival firms possess these valuable capabilities?" Capabilities possessed by many rivals are unlikely to become core competencies for any of the involved firms. Instead, valuable but common (i.e., not rare) capabilities are sources of competitive parity.[77] Competitive advantage results only when firms develop and exploit valuable capabilities that become core competencies and that differ from those shared with competitors. The central problem for Groupon is that its capabilities to produce the "daily deal" reached competitive parity quickly. Similarly, Walmart has developed valuable capabilities that it uses to engage in green practices; but, as mentioned previously, Target seeks to develop sustainability capabilities[78] through which it can duplicate Walmart's green practices. Target's success in doing so, if this happens, would suggest that Walmart's green practices are valuable but not rare.

Costly to Imitate

Costly-to-imitate capabilities are capabilities that other firms cannot easily develop. Capabilities that are costly to imitate are created because of one reason or a combination of three reasons (see Table 3.4). First, a firm sometimes is able to develop capabilities because of *unique historical conditions*. As firms evolve, they often acquire or develop capabilities that are unique to them.[79]

A firm with a unique and valuable *organizational culture* that emerged in the early stages of the company's history "may have an imperfectly imitable advantage over firms founded in another historical period;"[80] one in which less valuable or less competitively useful values and beliefs strongly influenced the development of the firm's culture. Briefly discussed in Chapter 1, organizational culture is a set of values that are shared by members in the organization. An organizational culture is a source of advantage when employees are held together tightly by their belief in it and the leaders who helped to create it.[81] Historically, emphasizing cleanliness, consistency, and service and the training that reinforces the value of these characteristics created a culture at McDonald's that some thought was a core competence and a competitive advantage for the firm. However, as explained in Chapter 2's Opening Case, McDonald's recent performance is worrying investors. One of the actions the firm is taking to address this matter is to change its organizational structure in its U.S. operations, largely for the purpose of giving "leaders in its 22 U.S. regions more autonomy in making local menu and marketing decisions."[82] Hopefully, a different organizational structure will facilitate McDonald's efforts to reinvigorate its historically unique culture as a core competence.

A second condition of being costly to imitate occurs when the link between the firm's core competencies and its competitive advantage is *causally ambiguous*.[83] In these instances, competitors aren't able to clearly understand how a firm uses its capabilities that are core competencies as the foundation for competitive advantage. As a result, firms are uncertain about the capabilities they should develop to duplicate the benefits of a

Rare capabilities are capabilities that few, if any, competitors possess.

Costly-to-imitate capabilities are capabilities that other firms cannot easily develop.

Although it has close to 150 stores and over 22,000 employees, CarMax has developed a small-company culture that is difficult for competitors to imitate.

competitor's value-creating strategy. For years, firms tried to imitate Southwest Airlines' low-cost strategy, but most have been unable to do so, primarily because they can't duplicate this firm's unique culture.

Social complexity is the third reason that capabilities can be costly to imitate. Social complexity means that at least some, and frequently many, of the firm's capabilities are the product of complex social phenomena. Interpersonal relationships, trust, friendships among managers and between managers and employees, and a firm's reputation with suppliers and customers are examples of socially complex capabilities. Southwest Airlines is careful to hire people who fit with its culture. This complex interrelationship between the culture and human capital adds value in ways that other airlines cannot, such as jokes on flights by the flight attendants or the cooperation between gate personnel and pilots.

Nonsubstitutable

Nonsubstitutable capabilities are capabilities that do not have strategic equivalents. This final criterion "is that there must be no strategically equivalent valuable resources that are themselves either not rare or imitable. Two valuable firm resources (or two bundles of firm resources) are strategically equivalent when they each can be separately exploited to implement the same strategies."[84] In general, the strategic value of capabilities increases as they become more difficult to substitute. The more intangible, and hence invisible, capabilities are, the more difficult it is for firms to find substitutes and the greater the challenge is to competitors trying to imitate a firm's value-creating strategy. Firm-specific knowledge and trust-based working relationships between managers and nonmanagerial personnel, such as has existed for years at Southwest Airlines, are examples of capabilities that are difficult to identify and for which finding a substitute is challenging. However, causal ambiguity may make it difficult for the firm to learn and may stifle progress because the firm may not know how to improve processes that are not easily codified and thus are ambiguous.[85]

In summary, only using valuable, rare, costly-to-imitate, and nonsubstitutable capabilities has the potential for the firm to create sustainable competitive advantages. Table 3.5 shows the competitive consequences and performance implications resulting from combinations of the four criteria of sustainability. The analysis suggested by the table helps managers determine the strategic value of a firm's capabilities. The firm should not emphasize capabilities that fit the criteria described in the first row in the table (i.e., resources and capabilities that are neither valuable nor rare and that are imitable and for which strategic substitutes exist). Capabilities yielding competitive parity and either temporary or sustainable competitive advantage, however, should be supported. Some competitors such as Coca-Cola and PepsiCo and Boeing and Airbus may have capabilities that result in competitive parity. In such cases, the firms will nurture these capabilities while simultaneously trying to develop capabilities that can yield either a temporary or sustainable competitive advantage.

Nonsubstitutable capabilities are capabilities that do not have strategic equivalents.

Table 3.5 Outcomes from Combinations of the Criteria for Sustainable Competitive Advantage

Is the Capability Valuable?	Is the Capability Rare?	Is the Capability Costly to Imitate?	Is the Capability Nonsubstitutable?	Competitive Consequences	Performance Implications
No	No	No	No	• Competitive disadvantage	• Below-average returns
Yes	No	No	Yes/no	• Competitive parity	• Average returns
Yes	Yes	No	Yes/no	• Temporary competitive advantage	• Average returns to above-average returns
Yes	Yes	Yes	Yes/no	• Sustainable competitive advantage	• Above-average returns

3-3b Value Chain Analysis

Value chain analysis allows the firm to understand the parts of its operations that create value and those that do not.[86] Understanding these issues is important because the firm earns above-average returns only when the value it creates is greater than the costs incurred to create that value.[87]

The value chain is a template that firms use to analyze their cost position and to identify the multiple means that can be used to facilitate implementation of a chosen strategy.[88] Today's competitive landscape demands that firms examine their value chains in a global rather than a domestic-only context.[89] In particular, activities associated with supply chains should be studied within a global context.[90]

We show a model of the value chain in Figure 3.3. As depicted in the model, a firm's value chain is segmented into value chain activities and support functions. **Value chain activities** are activities or tasks the firm completes in order to produce products and

Value chain activities are activities or tasks the firm completes in order to produce products and then sell, distribute, and service those products in ways that create value for customers.

Figure 3.3 A Model of the Value Chain

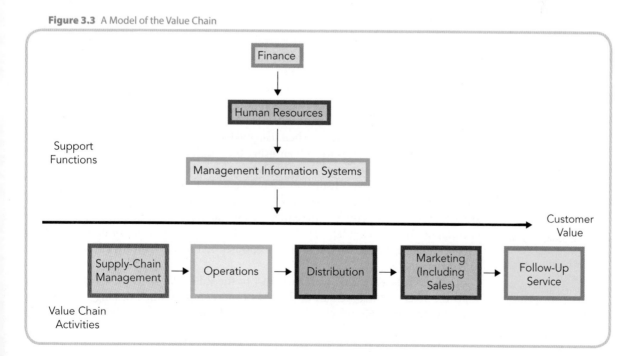

Figure 3.4 Creating Value through Value Chain Activities

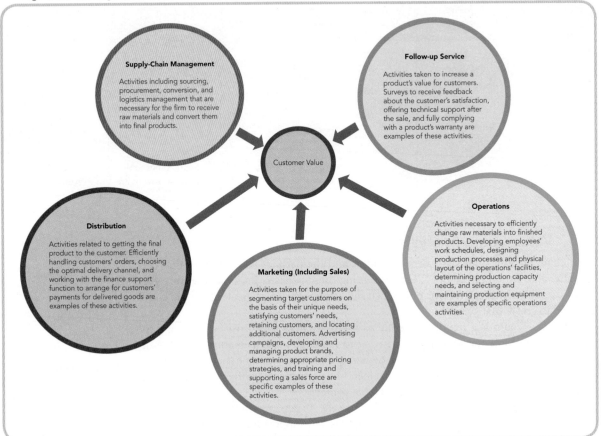

then sell, distribute, and service those products in ways that create value for customers. **Support functions** include the activities or tasks the firm completes in order to support the work being done to produce, sell, distribute, and service the products the firm is producing. A firm can develop a capability and/or a core competence in any of the value chain activities and in any of the support functions. When it does so, it has established an ability to create value for customers. In fact, as shown in Figure 3.3, customers are the ones firms seek to serve when using value chain analysis to identify their capabilities and core competencies. When using their unique core competencies to create unique value for customers that competitors cannot duplicate, firms have established one or more competitive advantages. Deutsche Bank believes that its application development and information security technologies are proprietary core competencies that are a source of competitive differentiation for the firm.[91] As explained in a Strategic Focus about outsourcing later in the chapter, Deutsche Bank will not outsource these two technologies given that the firm concentrates on them as a means of creating value for customers.

The activities associated with each part of the value chain are shown in Figure 3.4, while the activities that are part of the tasks firms complete when dealing with support functions appear in Figure 3.5. All items in both figures should be evaluated relative to

Support functions include the activities or tasks the firm completes in order to support the work being done to produce, sell, distribute, and service the products the firm is producing.

Figure 3.5 Creating Value through Support Functions

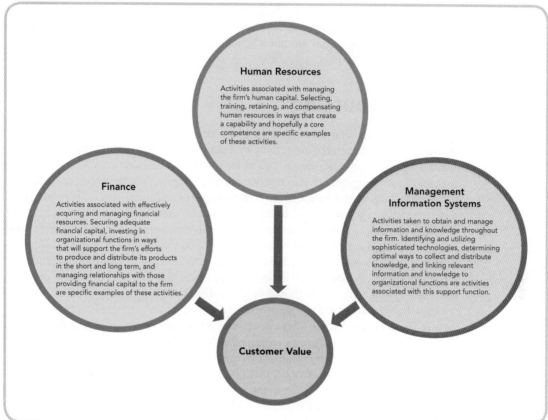

competitors' capabilities and core competencies. To become a core competence and a source of competitive advantage, a capability must allow the firm to either

1. Perform an activity in a manner that provides value superior to that provided by competitors.
2. Perform a value-creating activity that competitors cannot perform.

Only under these conditions does a firm create value for customers and have opportunities to capture that value.

Creating value for customers by completing activities that are part of the value chain often requires building effective alliances with suppliers (and sometimes others to which the firm outsources activities, as discussed in the next section) and developing strong positive relationships with customers. When firms have strong positive relationships with suppliers and customers, they are said to have social capital.[92] The relationships themselves have value because they lead to transfers of knowledge as well as to access to resources that a firm many not hold internally.[93] To build social capital whereby resources such as knowledge are transferred across organizations requires trust between partners. Indeed, partners must trust each other in order to allow their resources to be used in such a way that both parties will benefit over time while neither party will take advantage of the other.[94]

Evaluating a firm's capability to execute its value chain activities and support functions is challenging. Earlier in the chapter, we noted that identifying and assessing the value of a firm's resources and capabilities requires judgment. Judgment is equally necessary when using value chain analysis because no obviously correct model or rule is universally available to help in the process.

What should a firm do about value chain activities and support functions in which its resources and capabilities are not a source of core competence? Outsourcing is one solution to consider.

3-4 Outsourcing

Concerned with how components, finished goods, or services will be obtained, **outsourcing** is the purchase of a value-creating activity or a support function activity from an external supplier. Not-for-profit agencies as well as for-profit organizations actively engage in outsourcing.[95] Firms engaging in effective outsourcing increase their flexibility, mitigate risks, and reduce their capital investments.[96] In multiple global industries, the trend toward outsourcing continues at a rapid pace.[97] Moreover, in some industries virtually all firms seek the value that can be captured through effective outsourcing. However, as is the case with other strategic management process decisions, careful analysis is required before the firm decides to outsource.[98] And if outsourcing is to be used, firms must recognize that only activities where they cannot create value or where they are at a substantial disadvantage compared to competitors should be outsourced.[99] Experience suggests that virtually any activity associated with the value chain functions or the support functions may fall into this category. We discuss different activities that some firms outsource in the Strategic Focus. We also consider core competencies that firms to whom others outsource activities may try to develop to satisfy customers' future outsourcing needs.

Outsourcing can be effective because few, if any, organizations possess the resources and capabilities required to achieve competitive superiority in each value chain activity and support function. For example, research suggests that few companies can afford to internally develop all the technologies that might lead to competitive advantage.[100] By nurturing a smaller number of capabilities, a firm increases the probability of developing core competencies and achieving a competitive advantage because it does not become overextended. In addition, by outsourcing activities in which it lacks competence, the firm can fully concentrate on those areas in which it has the potential to create value.

There are concerns associated with outsourcing.[101] Two significant ones are the potential loss in a firm's ability to innovate and the loss of jobs within the focal firm. When evaluating the possibility of outsourcing, firms should anticipate possible effects on their ability to innovate in the future as well as the impact of losing some of their human capital. On the other hand, firms are sometimes able to enhance their own innovation capabilities by studying how the companies to which they've outsourced complete those activities.[102] Because a focal firm likely knows less about a foreign company to which it chooses to outsource, concerns about potential negative outsourcing effects in these cases may be particularly acute, requiring careful study and analysis as a result.[103] Deciding to outsource to a foreign supplier is commonly called *offshoring*.

3-5 Competencies, Strengths, Weaknesses, and Strategic Decisions

By analyzing the internal organization, firms identify their strengths and weaknesses as reflected by their resources, capabilities, and core competencies. If a firm has weak capabilities or does not have core competencies in areas required to achieve a competitive advantage, it must acquire those resources and build the needed capabilities and competencies.

Outsourcing is the purchase of a value-creating activity or a support function activity from an external supplier.

Strategic **Focus**

"We're Outsourcing that Activity but Not That One? I'm Surprised!"

Clearly, firms do not want to outsource activities through which they are able to create value. Moreover, they want to concentrate on those activities in the value chain functions and the support functions where they are able to create the greatest amount of value. Recognizing the activities in these two categories is a critical responsibility of those studying a firm's internal organization.

As we discussed in the Opening Case, big pharma companies are considering the possibility that they may use some of their resources and capabilities to try to develop "big data analytics" as a core competence given the increasing value that is thought to accrue to companies in this industry that are able to do so. In contrast, these same firms are outsourcing drug safety processes and procedures to firms, many of which are located in India or have offices located there. In fact, monitoring drug safety is "one of outsourcing's newest frontiers and the now $2 billion business is booming as regulators require closer tracking of rare side effects and interactions between medicines." Accenture, Cognizant, and Tata Consultancy Services Ltd. are some of the firms to which big pharma companies AstraZeneca PLC, Novartis AG, and Bristol-Myers Squibb Co. are outsourcing the monitoring of drug safety. Thus, the big pharma firms have decided that data analytics processes are an activity in which they can capture value while monitoring drug safety is not.

Similar examples exist within firms competing in other industries. As mentioned above, Deutsche Bank has outsourced some data center services to Hewlett-Packard; however, it is retaining control over certain technology application areas it believes are proprietary and, as such, are core competencies through which the firm creates value. United Airlines is outsourcing U.S. airport jobs that employ "workers in areas including check-in, baggage-handling, and customer service." This outsourcing decision suggests that United believes that it cannot create value by completing these tasks in house or that it is too expensive to attempt to do so.

Based in India, Wipro and Infosys are two companies that have historically been successful as firms to whom others outsource activities. However, this success has been largely a product of being able to employ relatively inexpensive programmers to complete tasks lacking significant amounts of complexity. This is no longer the case today as customers are asking outsourcing firms to help them analyze large amounts of data and engage the cloud for computing purposes. Stated more directly, some believe that "Bangalore's outsourcing industry—which grew at breakneck speeds for years and changed the way the world of IT works—has matured. While it will continue to find ways to peddle the talents of India's inexpensive programmers and engineers, it needs to find new businesses if it wants to thrive."

These individuals are working in a firm to which other companies have outsourced certain activities for completion.

This reality means that these outsourcing firms must find ways to produce their own software that can be used to create different types of value for customers rather than remaining focused on their initial core competencies in terms of integrating and maintaining their customers' software. It seems that firms such as Wipro and Infosys are challenged to develop competencies in terms of their own software niches and to learn how to competitively price their new products to compete against the likes of SAP. To do this, these outsourcing firms are hiring specialized code writers, data scientists, and statisticians for the purpose of creating their own proprietary software through which they can generate value by how they uniquely scrub and crunch customers' data.

Sources: Deutsche Bank, H-P divide IT responsibility in cloud deal, *Wall Street Journal Online*, www.wsj.com, February 25; D. A. Thoppil, 2015, Indian outsourcers struggle to evolve as growth slows, *Wall Street Journal Online*, www.wsj.com, February 22; S McLain, 2015, Big Pharma farms out drug safety to India, *Wall Street Journal Online*, www.wsj.com, February 2; S. McLain, 2015, New outsourcing frontier in India: Monitoring drug safety, *Wall Street Journal Online*, www.wsj.com, February 1; D. A. Thoppil, 2015, Wipro profit rises 8.8%, *Wall Street Journal Online*, www.wsj.com, January 16; S. Carey, 2015, United studies outsourcing up to 2,000 airport jobs, *Wall Street Journal Online*, www.wsj.com, January 13; D. A. Thoppil, 2015, Infosys profit rises 13%, *Wall Street Journal Online*, www.wsj.com, January 9.

Stuart Forster/Alamy

Alternatively, the firm could decide to outsource a function or activity where it is weak in order to improve its ability to use its remaining resources to create value.[104]

In considering the results of examining the firm's internal organization, managers should understand that having a significant quantity of resources is not the same as having the "right" resources. The "right" resources are those with the potential to be formed into core competencies as the foundation for creating value for customers and developing competitive advantages as a result of doing so. Interestingly, decision makers sometimes become more focused and productive when seeking to find the right resources when the firm's total set of resources is constrained.[105]

Tools such as outsourcing help the firm focus on its core competencies as the source of its competitive advantages. However, evidence shows that the value-creating ability of core competencies should never be taken for granted. Moreover, the ability of a core competence to be a permanent competitive advantage can't be assumed. The reason for these cautions is that all core competencies have the potential to become *core rigidities*.[106] Typically, events occurring in the firm's external environment create conditions through which core competencies can become core rigidities, generate inertia, and stifle innovation. "Often the flip side, the dark side, of core capabilities is revealed due to external events when new competitors figure out a better way to serve the firm's customers, when new technologies emerge, or when political or social events shift the ground underneath."[107]

Historically, Borders Group Inc. relied on its large storefronts that were conveniently located for customers to visit and browse through books and magazines in a pleasant atmosphere as sources of its competitive success. Over the past two decades or so, though, digital technologies (part of the firm's external environment) rapidly changed customers' shopping patterns for reading materials. Amazon.com's use of the Internet significantly changed the competitive landscape for Borders and similar competitors such as Barnes & Noble. It is possible that Borders' core competencies of store locations and a desirable physical environment for customers became core rigidities for this firm, eventually leading to its filing of bankruptcy in early 2011 and subsequent liquidation.[108] Managers studying the firm's internal organization are responsible for making certain that core competencies do not become core rigidities.

After studying its external environment to determine what it *might choose to do* (as explained in Chapter 2) and its internal organization to understand what it *can do* (as explained in this chapter), the firm has the information required to select a business-level strategy that it will use to compete against rivals. We describe different business-level strategies in the next chapter.

SUMMARY

- In the current competitive landscape, the most effective organizations recognize that strategic competitiveness and above-average returns result only when core competencies (identified by studying the firm's internal organization) are matched with opportunities (determined by studying the firm's external environment).

- No competitive advantage lasts forever. Over time, rivals use their own unique resources, capabilities, and core competencies to form different value-creating propositions that duplicate the focal firm's ability to create value for customers.

Because competitive advantages are not permanently sustainable, firms must exploit their current advantages while simultaneously using their resources and capabilities to form new advantages that can lead to future competitive success.

- Effectively managing core competencies requires careful analysis of the firm's resources (inputs to the production process) and capabilities (resources that have been purposely integrated to achieve a specific task or set of tasks). The knowledge the firm's human capital possesses is among the most significant of an organization's capabilities and ultimately provides the base for most competitive advantages. The firm must create an organizational culture that allows people to integrate their individual knowledge with that held by others so that, collectively, the firm has a significant amount of value-creating organizational knowledge.

- Capabilities are a more likely source of core competence and subsequently of competitive advantages than are individual resources. How a firm nurtures and supports its capabilities so they can become core competencies is less visible to rivals, making efforts to understand and imitate the focal firm's capabilities difficult.

- Only when a capability is valuable, rare, costly to imitate, and nonsubstitutable is it a core competence and a source of competitive advantage. Over time, core competencies must be supported, but they cannot be allowed to become core rigidities. Core competencies are a source of competitive advantage only when they allow the firm to create value by exploiting opportunities in its external environment. When this is no

longer possible, the company shifts its attention to forming other capabilities that satisfy the four criteria of sustainable competitive advantage.

- Value chain analysis is used to identify and evaluate the competitive potential of resources and capabilities. By studying their skills relative to those associated with value chain activities and support functions, firms can understand their cost structure and identify the activities through which they are able to create value.

- When the firm cannot create value in either a value chain activity or a support function, outsourcing is considered. Used commonly in the global economy, outsourcing is the purchase of a value-creating activity from an external supplier. The firm should outsource only to companies possessing a competitive advantage in terms of the particular value chain activity or support function under consideration. In addition, the firm must continuously verify that it is not outsourcing activities through which it could create value.

KEY TERMS

costly-to-imitate capabilities 91
global mind-set 80
intangible resources 84
nonsubstitutable capabilities 92
outsourcing 96
rare capabilities 91

support functions 94
tangible resources 84
value 81
valuable capabilities 90
value chain activities 93

REVIEW QUESTIONS

1. Why is it important for a firm to study and understand its internal organization?

2. What is value? Why is it critical for the firm to create value? How does it do so?

3. What are the differences between tangible and intangible resources? Why is it important for decision makers to understand these differences? Are tangible resources more valuable for creating capabilities than are intangible resources, or is the reverse true? Why?

4. What are capabilities? How do firms create capabilities?

5. What four criteria must capabilities satisfy for them to become core competencies? Why is it important for firms to

use these criteria to evaluate their capabilities' value-creating potential?

6. What is value chain analysis? What does the firm gain by successfully using this tool?

7. What is outsourcing? Why do firms outsource? Will outsourcing's importance grow in the future? If so, why?

8. How do firms identify internal strengths and weaknesses? Why is it vital that managers have a clear understanding of their firm's strengths and weaknesses?

9. What are core rigidities? What does it mean to say that each core competence could become a core rigidity?

Mini-Case

Zara: The Capabilities behind the Spanish "Fast Fashion" Retail Giant

Amancio Ortega built the world's largest fashion empire through his Zara branded products and company-owned stores. Through his management approach, Ortega became quite wealthy. In fact, in 2015 he was the fourth wealthiest person in the world (with a worth of $64.5 billion). This placed him behind only Bill Gates (the wealthiest of all), Carlos "Slim" Helu and family, and Warren Buffett.

Headquartered in La Coruña, in Spain's Galicia region, Ortega founded the Inditex Group with Zara as its flagship brand. Despite Spain's 24 percent unemployment rate and crippling debt, in 2012 Zara increased its revenue 17 percent. Also in 2012, Zara averaged a new store opening every day, including its six thousandth store launched on London's Oxford Street. Although the influence of the economic environment (an influence from the external environment that we examined in Chapter 2) affects Zara's success, the way Zara uses its resources and capabilities as the foundation for core competencies (core competencies are capabilities that serve as a potential source of competitive advantage for a firm over its rivals) demonstrates the value of understanding a firm's internal organization.

Ortega built this successful business based on two critical goals: Give customers what they want, and get it to them faster than anyone else. To do "fast fashion," as it is called, there are several critical capabilities that must be in place. The first critical capability is the ability to design quickly; the design pace at Zara has been described as "frantic." The designers create about three items of new clothing a day, and pattern makers cut one sample for each. The second critical capability is the commercial sales specialists from each region where Zara has stores. They provide input on customers' tastes and buying habits which are reported through store managers. Each specialist is trained to keep an eye on what people are wearing, which Ortega, as well, does personally since founding Zara. As such, Zara has a team approach to match quick and creative design with information coming in from the sales staff through regional specialists and sector specialists to operationalize new fashion ideas.

Zara's supply chain is also managed much more efficiently than those of other companies. The logistics department is the essence of the company. Rather than waiting for cloth to come in after designing, Zara already has a large supply of basic cloth and owns its own dyeing operation to maintain control and speed. Zara's objective is to deliver customized orders to every store in its empire with a 24-hour turnaround for Europe, the Mideast, and much of the United States, and a 48 hour turnaround for Asia and Latin America. The frequent shipments keep product inventories fresh but also scarce since they send out very few items in each shipment. This approach compels customers to visit stores frequently in search of what they want and, because of the scarcity, creates an incentive for them to buy on the spot because it will likely not be in stock tomorrow. Accordingly, Zara's global store average of 17 visits per customer per year is considerably higher than the average of three visits per year for its competitors.

Until 2010 Zara did not have an online strategy. Unlike most retailers it has used very little advertising because it has focused on a rather cheap but fashionable approach. The fashion draws the interest of customers and, thereby, created a huge following on Facebook, with approximately 10 million followers. This compares favorably to other competitors such as Gap. The rarity of the individual pieces of clothing gives customers a sense of individuality. This creates a stronger potential for Zara to pursue an online strategy relative to its competitors.

Most Zara stores are owned by the parent company, and many of its suppliers, although not owned by the company, are considered long-time, relationship-oriented partners. As such, these partners identify with the company and, therefore, are loyal. This approach also sets Zara apart and makes its strategy difficult to duplicate because all of the various facets and capabilities of the company fit together through a unified culture. As noted above, Zara also operates its own dyeing plant for cloth, giving it significant control over its products. Likewise, it sews many of these garments in its own factories and, thus, maintains a high level of quality control and an ability to make quick changes. Overall, the company has a unique set of capabilities that fit together well as it manages activities to produce "fast fashion," which creates demand from their customers and loyalty from their partner suppliers.

Sources: E. Carlyle, 2013, The year's biggest winner: Zara billionaire Amancio Ortega, *Forbes*, www.forbes.com, March 4; R. Dudley, A. Devnath, & M. Townsend, 2013, The hidden cost of fast fashion, *Bloomberg Businessweek*, February 11, 15–17; V. Walt, 2013, Meet the third-richest man in the world, *Fortune*, January 14, 74–79; 2012, Inditex, Asos post double-digit sales gains, *Women's Wear Daily*, September 20, 6; B. Borzykowski, 2012, Zara eludes the pain in Spain, *Canadian Business*, September 17, 67; K. Willems, W. Janssens, G. Swinnen, M. Brengman, S. Streukens, & N. Vancauteren, 2012, From Armani to Zara: Impression formation based on fashion store patronage, *Journal of Business Research*, 65: 1487–1494.

Case Discussion Questions

1. What influences from the external environment over the next several years do you think might affect the way Zara competes?

2. How easy or difficult do you think it would be for competitors to imitate Zara's supply chain as a capability?

3. Is getting products to customers as quickly as possible an outcome that you believe would create value in industries in addition to clothing? If so, which industries and why?

4. What value does Zara create for its customers?

5. As you study how Zara competes and the capabilities it uses to do so, are there areas of the firm's operations you believe might be candidates for outsourcing? If so, what areas and why might those be outsourced in the future?

NOTES

1. A. Gambardella, C. Panico, & G. Valentini, 2015, Strategic incentives to human capital, *Strategic Management Journal*, 36: 37–52; C. Gilbert, M. Eyring, & R. N. Foster, 2012, Two routes to resilience. *Harvard Business Review*, 90(12): 65–73; H. A. Ndofor, D. G. Sirmon, & X. He, 2011, Firm resources, competitive actions and performance: Investigating a mediated model with evidence from the in-vitro diagnostics industry, *Strategic Management Journal*, 32: 640–657.

2. R. Khanna, I. Guler, & A. Nerkar, 2015, Fail often, fail big, and fail fast: Learning from small failures and R&D performance in the pharmaceutical industry, *Academy of Management Journal*, in press; C. Engel & M. Kleine, 2015, Who is afraid of pirates? An experiment on the deterrence of innovation by imitation, *Research Policy*, 44: 20–33; K. Wilson & Y. L. Doz, 2012, 10 rules for managing global innovation, *Harvard Business Review*, 90(10): 84–90.

3. S. Denning, 2015, How Agile and Zara are transforming the U.S. fashion industry, *Forbes Online*, www.forbes.com, March 13; M. Schoultz, 2015, Is Zara the most innovative fashion retailer? *Digital Spark Marketing*, www.digitalsparkmarketing.com, April 10.

4. J. Ostrower, 2015, At Boeing, innovation means small steps, not giant leaps, *Wall Street Journal Online*, www.wsj.com, April 2.

5. M. Beck, 2015, Innovation is sweeping through U.S. medical schools, *Wall Street Journal Online*, www.wsj.com, February 16.

6. M. Keyhani, M. Levesque, & A. Madhok, 2015, Toward a theory of entrepreneurial rents: A simulation of the market process, *Strategic Management Journal*, 36: 76–96; L. Ngo & A. O'Cass, 2012, In search of innovation and customer-related performance superiority: The role of market orientation, marketing capability, and innovation capability interactions, *Journal of Product Innovation Management*, 29: 861–877; D. G. Sirmon, M. A. Hitt, & R. D. Ireland, 2007, Managing firm resources in dynamic markets to create value: Looking inside the black box, *Academy of Management Review*, 32: 273–292.

7. M.-J. Chen & D. Miller, 2015, Reconceptualizing competitive dynamics: A multidimensional framework, *Strategic Management Journal*, 36: 758–775; F. Polidoro, Jr. & P. K. Toh, 2011, Letting rivals come close or warding them off? The effects of substitution threat on imitation deterrence, *Academy of Management Journal*, 54: 369–392; A. W. King, 2007, Disentangling interfirm and intrafirm causal ambiguity: A conceptual model of causal ambiguity and sustainable competitive advantage, *Academy of Management Review*, 32: 156–178.

8. I. Le Breton-Miller & D. Miller, 2015, The paradox of resource vulnerability: Considerations for organizational curatorship, *Strategic Management Journal*, 36: 397–415; M. Semadeni & B. S. Anderson, 2010, The follower's dilemma: Innovation and imitation in the professional services industry, *Academy of Management Journal*, 53: 1175–1193.

9. U. Stettner & D. Lavie, 2014, Ambidexterity under scrutiny: Exploration and exploitation via internal organization, alliances, and acquisitions, *Strategic Management Journal*, 35: 1903–1929; M. G. Jacobides, S. G. Winter, & S. M. Kassberger, 2012, The dynamics of wealth, profit, and sustainable advantage, *Strategic Management Journal*, 33: 1384–1410.

10. S. Nadkarni, T. Chen, & J. Chen, 2015, The clock is ticking: Executive temporal depth, industry velocity and competitive aggressiveness, *Strategic Management Journal*, in press; L. A. Costa, K. Cool, & I. Dierickx, 2013, The competitive implications of the deployment of unique resources, *Strategic Management Journal*, 34: 445–463; M. A. Peteraf & J. B. Barney, 2003, Unraveling the resource-based tangle, *Managerial and Decision Economics*, 24: 309–323; J. B. Barney, 2001, Is the resource-based "view" a useful perspective for strategic management research? Yes, *Academy of Management Review*, 26: 41–56.

11. R. Roy & M. B. Sarkar, 2015, Knowledge, firm boundaries, and innovation: Mitigating the incumbent's curse during radical technological change, *Strategic Management Journal*: in press; G. Zied & J. McGuire, 2011, Multimarket competition, mobility barriers, and firm performance, *Journal of Management Studies*, 48: 857–890.

12. P. Wahba, 2014, Neiman Marcus goes after international luxury with e-commerce deal, *Fortune Online*, www.fortune.com, September 15.

13. D. Piaskowska & G. Trojanowski, 2014, Twice as smart: The importance of managers' formative-years' international experience for their international orientation and foreign acquisition decisions, *British Journal of Management*, 25: 40–57; M. Javidan, R. M. Steers, & M. A. Hitt (eds.), 2007, *The Global Mindset*: Amsterdam: Elsevier Ltd.

14. H. Liang, B. Ren, & S. Li Sun, 2015, An anatomy of state control in the globalization of state-owned enterprises, *Journal of International Business Studies*, 46: 223–240; A. Diaz, M. Magni, & F. Poh, 2012, From oxcart to Wal-Mart: Four keys to reaching emerging-market consumers, *McKinsey Quarterly*, October, 58–67; O. Levy, S. Taylor, & N. A. Boyacigiller, 2010, On the rocky road to strong global culture, *MIT Sloan Management Review*, 51: 20–22.

15. J. J. Ebbers, 2014, Networking behavior and contracting relationships among entrepreneurs in business incubators, *Entrepreneurship Theory and Practice*, 38: 1159–1181; R. A. D'Aveni, G. B. Dagnino, & K. G. Smith, 2010, The age of temporary advantage, *Strategic Management Journal*, 31: 1371–1385; E. Danneels, 2008, Organizational antecedents of second-order competences, *Strategic Management Journal*, 29: 519–543.

16. R. Vandaie & A. Zaheer, 2015, Alliance partners and firm capability: Evidence from the motion picture industry, *Organization Science*, in press; S. A. Zahra & S. Nambisan, 2012, Entrepreneurship and strategic thinking in business ecosystems, *Business Horizons*, 55: 219–229.

17. A. Waeraas & H. L. Sataoen, 2015, Being all things to all customers: Building reputation in an institutionalized field, *British Journal of Management*, 26: 310–326; D. G. Sirmon, M. A. Hitt, R. D. Ireland, & B. A. Gilbert, 2011, Resource orchestration to create competitive advantage: Breadth, depth, and life cycle effects, *Journal of Management*, 37: 1390–1412; R. Adner & R. Kapoor, 2010, Value creation in innovation ecosystems: How the structure of technological interdependence affects firm performance in new technology generations, *Strategic Management Journal*, 31: 306–333.

18. C. Grimpe & K. Hussinger, 2014, Resource complementarity and value capture in firm acquisitions: The role of intellectual property rights, *Strategic Management Journal*, 35: 1762–1780; M. A. Hitt, R. D. Ireland, D. G. Sirmon, & C. A. Trahms, 2011, Strategic entrepreneurship: Creating value for individuals, organizations, and society, *Academy of Management Perspectives*, 25: 57–75; D. G. Sirmon, S. Gove, & M. A. Hitt, 2008, Resource management in dyadic competitive rivalry: The effects of resource bundling and deployment, *Academy of Management Journal*, 51: 919–935.

19. B. Clarysse, M. Wright, J. Bruneel, & A. Mahajan, 2014, Creating value in ecosystems: Crossing the chasm between knowledge and business ecosystems, *Research Policy*, 43: 1164–1176; J. S. Harrison, D. A. Bosse, & R. A. Phillips, 2010, Managing for stakeholders, stakeholder utility functions, and competitive advantage, *Strategic Management Journal*, 31: 58–74; J. L. Morrow, Jr., D. G. Sirmon, M. A. Hitt, & T. R. Holcomb, 2007, Creating value in the face of declining performance: Firm strategies and organizational recovery, *Strategic Management Journal*, 28: 271–283.

20. P. Bromiley & D. Rau, 2014, Towards a practice-based view of strategy, *Strategic Management Journal*, 35: 1249–1256; V. Rindova, W. J. Ferrier, & R. Wiltbank, 2010, Value from gestalt: How sequences of competitive actions create advantage for firms in nascent markets, *Strategic Management Journal*, 31: 1474–1497.

21. C. Tantalo & R. L. Priem, 2015, Value creation through stakeholder synergy, *Strategic Management Journal*, in press; E. R. Brenes, D. Montoya, & L. Ciravegna, 2014, Differentiation strategies in emerging markets: The case of Latin American agribusinesses, *Journal of Business Research*, 67: 847–855; D. G. Sirmon, M. A. Hitt, J.-L. Arregle, & J. T. Campbell, 2010, The dynamic interplay of capability strengths and weaknesses: Investigating the bases of temporary competitive advantage, *Strategic Management Journal*, 31: 1386–1409.

22. S. Nadkarni & J. Chen, 2015, Bridging yesterday, today, and tomorrow: CEO temporal focus, environmental dynamism, and rate of new product introduction, *Academy of Management Journal*, in press; S. Nadkarni, T. Chen, & J. Chen, 2014, The clock is ticking: Executive temporal depth, industry velocity, and competitive aggressiveness, *Strategic Management Journal*, in press; F. Aime, S. Johnson, J. W. Ridge, & A. D. Hill, 2010, The routine may be stable but the advantage is not: Competitive implications of key employee mobility, *Strategic Management Journal*, 31: 75–87.

23. M. Arrfelt, R. M. Wiseman, G. McNamara, & G. T. M. Hult, 2015, Examining a key corporate role: The influence of capital allocation competency on business unit performance, *Strategic Management Journal*, in press; D. Li & J. Liu, 2014, Dynamic capabilities, environmental dynamism, and competitive advantage: Evidence from China, *Journal of Business Research*, 67: 2793–2799; D. J. Teece, 2012, Dynamic capabilities: Routines versus entrepreneurial action, *Journal of Management Studies*, 49: 1395–1401.

24. A. M. Kleinbaum & T. E. Stuart, 2015, Network responsiveness: The social structural microfoundations of dynamic capabilities, *Academy of Management Perspectives*, in press; M. H. Kunc & J. D. W. Morecroft, 2010, Managerial decision making and firm performance under a resource-based paradigm, *Strategic Management Journal*, 31: 1164–1182.

25. C. M. Christensen, 2001, The past and future of competitive advantage, *Sloan Management Review*, 42(2): 105–109.

26. J. Gomez, R. Orcos, & S. Palomas, 2015, Competitors' strategic heterogeneity and firm performance, *Long Range Planning*, in press; S. K. Parker & C. G. Collins, 2010, Taking stock: Integrating and differentiating multiple proactive behaviors, *Journal of Management*, 36: 633–662.

27. M. G. Butler & C. M. Callahan, 2014, Human resource outsourcing: Market and operating performance effects of administrative HR functions, *Journal of Business Research*, 67: 218–224; Y. Y. Kor & A. Mesko, 2013, Dynamic managerial capabilities: Configuration and orchestration of top executives' capabilities and the firm's dominant logic, *Strategic Management Journal*, 34: 233–244; D. P. Forbes, 2007, Reconsidering the strategic implications of decision comprehensiveness, *Academy of Management Review*, 32: 361–376.

28. E. Maitland & A. Sammartino, 2015, Decision making and uncertainty: The role of heuristics and experience in assessing a politically hazardous environment, *Strategic Management Journal*, in press; L. B. Mulder, J. Jordan, & F. Rink, 2015, The effect of specific and general rules on ethical decisions, *Organizational Behavior and Human Decision Processes*, 126: 115–129; T. M. Jones, W. Felps, & G. A. Bigley, 2007, Ethical theory and stakeholder-related decisions: The role of stakeholder culture, *Academy of Management Review*, 32: 137–155.

29. D. C. Hambrick & T. J. Quigley, 2014, Toward a more accurate contextualization of the CEO effect on firm performance, *Strategic Management Journal*, 35: 473–491; M. S. Gary & R. E. Wood, 2011, Mental models, decision rules, and performance heterogeneity, *Strategic Management Journal*, 32: 569–594.

30. T. W. Tong, J. J. Reuer, B. B. Tyler, & S. Zhang, 2015, Host country executives' assessments of international joint ventures and divestitures: An experimental approach, *Strategic Management Journal*, 36: 254–275; A. Arrighetti, F. Landini, & A. Lasagni, 2014, Intangible assets and firm heterogeneity: Evidence from Italy, *Research Policy*, 43: 202–213; C. B. Bingham & K. M. Eisenhardt, 2011, Rational heuristics: The 'simple rules' that strategists learn from process experience, *Strategic Management Journal*, 32: 1437–1464.

31. R. Mudambi & T. Swift, 2014, Knowing when to leap: Transitioning between exploitative and explorative R&D, *Strategic Management Journal*, 35: 126–145; Y. Zhang & J. Gimeno, 2010, Earnings pressure and

competitive behavior: Evidence from the U.S. electricity industry, *Academy of Management Journal*, 53: 743–768; L. M. Lodish & C. F. Mela, 2007, If brands are built over years, why are they managed over quarters? *Harvard Business Review*, 85(7/8): 104–112.

32. M. Jenkins, 2014, Innovate or imitate? The role of collective beliefs in competences in competing firms, *Long Range Planning*, 47: 173–185; P. Madsen & V. Desai, 2010, Failing to learn? The effects of failure and success on organizational learning in the global orbital launch vehicle industry, *Academy of Management Journal*, 53: 451–476; P. C. Nutt, 2002, *Why Decisions Fail*, San Francisco, Barrett-Koehler Publishers.

33. A. O. Laplume & P. Dass, 2015, Outstreaming for ambidexterity: Evolving a firm's core business from components to systems by serving internal and external customers, *Long Range Planning*, in press; D. Maslach, 2015, Change and persistence with failed technological innovation, *Strategic Management Journal*, in press; J. P. Eggers, 2012, All experience is not created equal: Learning, adapting and focusing in product portfolio management, *Strategic Management Journal*, 33: 315–335.

34. S. Singh, P. D. Corner, & K. Pavlovich, 2015, Failed, not finished: A narrative approach to understanding venture failure stigmatization, *Journal of Business Venturing*, 30: 150–166; S. Mousavi & G. Gigerenzer, 2014, Risk, uncertainty, and heuristics, *Journal of Business Research*, 67: 1671–1678; J. D. Ford & L. W. Ford, 2010, Stop blaming resistance to change and start using it, *Organizational Dynamics*, 39: 24–36.

35. V. Desai, 2015, Learning through the distribution of failures within an organization: Evidence from heart bypass surgery performance, *Academy of Management Journal*, in press; J. P. Eggers & L. Song, 2015, Dealing with failure: Serial entrepreneurs and the costs of changing industries between ventures, *Academy of Management Journal*, in press; K. Muehlfeld, P. Rao Sahib, & A. Van Witteloostuijn, 2012, A contextual theory of organizational learning from failures and successes: A study of acquisition completion in the global newspaper industry, 1981–2008, *Strategic Management Journal*, 33: 938–964.

36. L. Colby, 2015, News Corp.'s $1 billion plan to overhaul education is riddled with failures, *Bloomberg Online*, www.bloomberg.com, April 7.

37. W. Smith, 2015, Dynamic decision making: A model of senior leaders managing strategic paradoxes, *Academy of Management Journal*, in press; 2013, Strategy in a world of "biblical change": Our era of uncertainty calls for business leaders with vision, foresight and a global perspective, *Strategic Direction*, 29(3): 19–22; G. S. Dowell, M. B. Shackell & N. V. Stuart, 2011, Boards, CEOs, and surviving a financial crisis: Evidence from the internet shakeout, *Strategic Management Journal*, 32: 1025–1045.

38. S. R. Hiatt & W. D. Sine, 2014, Clear and present danger: Planning and new venture survival amid political and civil violence, *Strategic Management Journal*, 35: 773–785; A. Arora & A. Nandkumar, 2012, Insecure advantage? Markets for technology and the value of resources for entrepreneurial ventures, *Strategic Management Journal*, 33: 231–251; S. S. K. Lam & J. C. K. Young, 2010, Staff localization and environmental uncertainty on firm performance in China, *Asia Pacific Journal of Management*, 27: 677–695.

39. B. Kendall & A. Harder, 2015, Litigation awaits new EPA emissions rules, *Wall Street Journal Online*, www.wsj.com, March 22.

40. C. Dulaney, 2015, Peabody Energy names new CEO, *Wall Street Journal Online*, www.wsj.com, January 22.

41. J. Winkler, C. P. Jian-Wej Kuklinski, & R. Moser, 2015, Decision making in emerging markets: The Delphi approach's contribution to coping with uncertainty and equivocality, *Journal of Business Research*, 68: 1118–1126; O. H. Azar, 2014, The default heuristic in strategic decision making: When is it optimal to choose the default without investing in information search? *Journal of Business Research*, 67: 1744–1748.

42. D. M. Cain, D. A. Moore, & U. Haran, 2015, Making sense of overconfidence in market entry, *Strategic Management Journal*, 36: 1–18; M. Gary, R. E. Wood, & T. Pillinger, 2012, Enhancing mental models, analogical transfer, and performance in strategic decision making, *Strategic Management Journal*, 33: 1229–1246; J. R. Mitchell, D. A. Shepherd, & M. P. Sharfman, 2011, Erratic strategic decisions: When and why managers are inconsistent in strategic decision making, *Strategic Management Journal*, 32: 683–704.

43. D. Laureiro-Martinez, 2014, Cognitive control capabilities, routinization propensity, and decision-making performance, *Organization Science*, 25: 1111–1133; P. D. Windschitl, A. M. Scherer, A. R. Smith, & J. P. Rose, 2013, Why so confident? The influence of outcome desirability on selective exposure and likelihood judgment, *Organizational Behavior & Human Decision Processes*, 120: 73–86.

44. D. Albert, M. Kreutzer, & C. Lechner, 2015, Resolving the paradox of interdependency and strategic renewal in activity systems, *Academy of Management Review*, 40: 210–234; L. Alexander & D. van Knippenberg, 2014, Teams in pursuit of radical innovation: A goal orientation perspective, *Academy of Management Review*, 39: 423–438; C. Weigelt, 2013, Leveraging supplier capabilities: The role of locus of capability deployment, *Strategic Management Journal*, 34: 1–21.

45. A. Lipparini, G. Lorenzoni, & S. Ferriani, 2014, From core to periphery and back: A study on the deliberate shaping of knowledge flows in interfirm dyads and networks, *Strategic Management Journal*, 35: 578–595; J. M. Shaver, 2011, The benefits of geographic sales diversification: How exporting facilitates capital investment, *Strategic Management Journal*, 32: 1046–1060.

46. J. Bloomberg, 2015, Is Rackspace the Nordstrom of cloud? *Forbes Online*, www.forbes.com, January 21.

47. S. Raithel & M. Schwaiger, 2015, The effects of corporate reputation perceptions of the general public on shareholder value, *Strategic Management Journal*: in press; B. S. Anderson & Y. Eshima, 2013, The influence of firm age and intangible resources on the relationship between entrepreneurial orientation and firm growth among Japanese SMEs, *Journal of Business Venturing*, 28: 413–429.

48. A. Vomberg, C. Homburg, & T. Bornemann, 2015, Talented people and strong brands: The contribution of human capital and brand equity to firm value, *Strategic Management Journal*, 36: in press; J. Choi, G. W. Hecht, & W. B. Tayler, 2012, Lost in translation: The effects of incentive compensation on strategy surrogation, *Accounting Review*, 87: 1135–1163.

49. A. M. Webber, 2000, New math for a new economy, *Fast Company*, January/February, 214–224.

50. R. Sydler, S. Haefliger, & R. Pruksa, 2014, Measuring intellectual capital with financial figures: Can we predict firm profitability? *European Management Journal*, 32: 244–259; F. Neffke & M. Henning, 2013, Skill relatedness and firm diversification, *Strategic Management Journal*, 34: 297–316; E. Danneels, 2011, Trying to become a different type of company: Dynamic capability at Smith Corona, *Strategic Management Journal*, 32: 1–31.

51. F. Honore, F. Munari, & B. van Pottelsberghe de La Potterie, 2015, corporate governance practices and companies' R&D intensity: Evidence from European countries, *Research Policy*, 44: 533–543; J. Gómez & P. Vargas, 2012, Intangible resources and technology adoption in manufacturing firms, *Research Policy*, 41: 1607–1619; K. E. Meyer, R. Mudambi, & R. Narula, 2011, Multinational enterprises and local contexts: The opportunities and challenges of multiple embeddedness, *Journal of Management Studies*, 48: 235–252.

52. J.-Y. Lee, D. G. Bachrach, & D. M. Rousseau, 2015, Internal labor markets, firm-specific human capital, and heterogeneity antecedents of employee idiosyncratic deal requests, *Organization Science*, in press.

53. J. Raffiee & R. Coff, 2015, Micro-foundations of firm-specific human capital: When do employees perceive their skills to be firm-specific? *Academy of Management Journal*, in press.

54. A. Jain & R.-A. Thietart, 2014, Capabilities as shift parameters for the outsourcing decision, *Strategic Management Journal*, 35: 1881–1890; R. E. Ployhart, C. H. Van Iddekinge, & W. I. MacKenzie, Jr., 2011, Acquiring and developing human capital in service contexts: The interconnectedness of human capital resources, *Academy of Management Journal*, 54: 353–368.

55. S. Raithel & M. Schwaiger, 2015, The effects of corporate reputation perceptions of the general public on shareholder value, *Strategic Management Journal*, in press; K. Kim, B. Jeon, H. Jung, W. Lu, & J. Jones, 2012, Effective employment brand equity through sustainable competitive advantage, marketing strategy, and corporate image, *Journal of Business Research*, 65: 1612–1617; L. Diestre & N. Rajagopalan, 2011, An environmental perspective on diversification: The effects of chemical relatedness and regulatory sanctions, *Academy of Management Journal*, 54: 97–115.

56. W.-Y. Hun, H. Kim, & J. Woo, 2014, How CSR leads to corporate brand equity: Mediating mechanisms of corporate brand credibility and reputation, *Journal of Business Ethics*, 125: 75–86; G. Dowling & P. Moran, 2012, Corporate reputations: Built in or bolted on? *California Management Review*, 54(2): 25–42; M. D. Pfarrer, T. G. Pollock, & V. P. Rindova, 2010, A tale of two assets: The effects of firm reputation and celebrity on earnings surprises and investors' reactions, *Academy of Management Journal*, 53: 1131–1152; T. G. Pollock, G. Chen, & E. M. Jackson, 2010, How much prestige is enough? Assessing the value of multiple types of high-status affiliates for young firms, *Journal of Business Venturing*, 25: 6–23.

57. A. P. Petkova, A. Wadhwa, X. Yao, & S. Jain, 2014, Reputation and decision making under ambiguity: A study of U.S. venture capital firms' investments in the emerging clean energy sector, *Academy of Management Journal*, 57: 422–448; Y. Wang, G. Berens, & C. van Riel, 2012, Competing in the capital market with a good reputation, *Corporate Reputation Review*, 15: 198–221; J. J. Ebbers & N. M. Wijnberg, 2012, Nascent ventures competing for start-up capital: Matching reputations and investors, *Journal of Business Venturing*, 27: 372–384.

58. P. Foroudi, T.C. Melewar, & S. Gupta, 2014, Linking corporate logo, corporate image, and reputation: An examination of consumer perceptions in the financial setting, *Journal of Business Research*, 67: 2269–2281; S. Tischer & L. Hildebrandt, 2014, Linking corporate reputation and shareholder value using the publication of reputation rankings, *Journal of Business Research*, 67: 1007–1017.

59. C. A. Roster, 2014, Cultural influences on global firms' decisions to cut the strategic brand ties that bind: A commentary essay, *Journal of Business Research*, 67: 486–488; N. Rosenbusch & J. Brinckmann, 2011, Is innovation always beneficial? A meta-analysis of the relationship between innovation and performance in SMEs, *Journal of Business Venturing*, 26: 441–457.

60. 2015, Harley-Davidson Motor Apparel, www.harley-davidson.com, April 5.

61. T. Arbel, 2015, Comcast gets social to shake bad customer-service reputation, Yahoo.com, www.yahoo.com, March 24.

62. V. Goel, 2014, G.M. uses social media to manage customers and its reputation, *New York Times Online*, www.nytimes.com, March 23.

63. Social media principles, 2015, Coca-Cola Company Home page, www.coca-colacompany.com, April 6.

64. Y. Lin & L.-Y. Wu, 2014, Exploring the role of dynamic capabilities in firm performance under the resource-based view framework, *Journal of Business Research*, 67: 407–413; R. W. Coff, 2010, The coevolution of rent appropriation and capability development, *Strategic Management Journal*, 31: 711–733; J. Bitar & T. Hafsi, 2007, Strategizing through the capability lens: Sources and outcomes of integration, *Management Decision*, 45: 403–419.

65. S. Chowdhury, E. Schulz, M. Milner, & D. Van De Voort, 2014, Core employee based human capital and revenue productivity in small firms: An empirical investigation, *Journal of Business Research*, 67: 2473–2479; A. M. Subramanian, 2012, A longitudinal study of the influence of intellectual human capital on firm exploratory innovation, *IEEE Transactions on Engineering Management*, 59: 540–550; T. Dalziel, R. J. Gentry, & M. Bowerman, 2011, An integrated agency-resource dependence view of the influence of directors' human and relational capital on firms' R&D spending, *Journal of Management Studies*, 48: 1217–1242.

66. K. Freeman, 2015, CEOs must prioritize human capital, *Wall Street Journal Online*, www.wsj.com, February 27.

67. S. Moore, 2015, How pizza became a growth stock, *Wall Street Journal Online*, www.wsj.com, March 13.

68. D. J. Teece, 2014, The foundations of enterprise performance: Dynamic and ordinary capabilities in an (economic) theory of firms, *Academy of Management Perspectives*, 28: 328–352; K. M. Heimeriks, M. Schijven, & S. Gates, 2012, Manifestations of higher-order routines: The underlying mechanisms of deliberate learning in the context of postacquisition integration, *Academy of Management Journal*, 55: 703–726; C. Zott, 2003, Dynamic capabilities and the emergence of intraindustry differential firm performance: Insights from a simulation study, *Strategic Management Journal*, 24: 97–125.

69. Y. Zhao, E. Cavusgil, & S. T. Cavusgil, 2014, An investigation of the black-box supplier integration in new product development, *Journal of Business Research*, 67: 1058–1064; H. R. Greve, 2009, Bigger and safer: The diffusion of competitive advantage, *Strategic Management Journal*, 30: 1–23; C. K. Prahalad & G. Hamel, 1990, The core competence of the corporation, *Harvard Business Review*, 68(3): 79–93.

70. D. Reisinger, 2015, Apple's genius bar to get smarter with 'concierge'—report, *CNET*.com, www.cnet.com, February 24; Y. I. Kane & I. Sherr, 2011, Secrets from Apple's genius bar: Full loyalty, no negativity, *Wall Street Journal*, www.wsj.com, June 15.

71. J. Schmidt, R. Makadok, & T. Keil, 2015, Customer-specific synergies and market convergence, *Strategic Management Journal*, in press; M. Makri, M. A. Hitt, & P. J. Lane, 2010, Complementary technologies, knowledge relatedness, and invention outcomes in high technology mergers and acquisitions, *Strategic Management Journal*, 31: 602–628; S. Newbert, 2008, Value, rareness, competitive advantage, and performance: A conceptual-level empirical investigation of the resource-based view of the firm, *Strategic Management Journal*, 29: 745–768.

72. J. Boynton, 2015, Walmart unveils virtual sustainability shop, *Triple Pundit.com*, www.triplepundit.com, February 24.

73. Walmart environmental sustainability, 2015, *Wall-Mart Homepage*, www.walmart.com, March 30; A. Winston, 2015, Can Walmart get us to buy sustainable products? *Harvard Business Review blog*, www.hbr.org, February 24.

74. A. Kaul & Z (Brian) Wu, 2015, A capabilities-based perspective on target selection in acquisitions, *Strategic Management Journal*: in press; D. S. K. Lim, N. Celly, E. A. Morse, & W. G. Rowe, 2013, Rethinking the effectiveness of asset and cost retrenchment: The contingency effects of a firm's rent creation mechanism, *Strategic Management Journal*, 34: 42–61.

75. D. Roos, 2011, How does Groupon work? *Howstuffworks.com*, www.howstuffworks.com, June 12.

76. S. D. Anthony, 2012, The new corporate garage, *Harvard Business Review*, 90(9): 44–53.

77. H. A. Ndofor, D. G. Sirmon, & X. He, 2015, Utilizing the firm's resources: How TMT heterogeneity and resulting faultlines affect TMT tasks, *Strategic Management Journal*: in press; Q. Gu & J. W. Lu, 2011, Effects of inward investment on outward investment: The venture capital industry worldwide—1985–2007, *Journal of International Business Studies*, 42: 263–284.

78. Sustainability, 2015, Target Home Page, www.target.com, April 10.

79. S. G. Lazzarini, 2015, Strategizing by the government: Can industrial policy create firm-level competitive advantage? *Strategic Management Journal*, 36: 97–112; H. Rahmandad, 2012, Impact of growth opportunities and competition on firm-level capability development trade-offs, *Organization Science*, 23: 138–154; C. A. Coen & C. A. Maritan, 2011, Investing in capabilities: The dynamics of resource allocation, *Organization Science*, 22: 199–217.

80. J. B. Barney, 1991, Firm resources and sustained competitive advantage, *Journal of Management*, 17: 99–120.

81. M. E. B. Herrera, 2015, Creating competitive advantage by institutionalizing corporate social innovation, *Journal of Business Research*: in press; C. M. Wilderom, P. T. van den Berg, & U. J. Wiersma, 2012, A longitudinal study of the effects of charismatic leadership and organizational culture on objective and perceived corporate performance, *Leadership Quarterly*, 23: 835–848; C. C. Maurer, P. Bansal, & M. M. Crossan, 2011, Creating economic value through social values: Introducing a culturally informed resource-based view, *Organization Science*, 22: 432–448.

82. J. Jargon, 2014, McDonald's plans to change U.S. structure, *Wall Street Journal Online*, www.wsj.com, October 30.

83. T. Alnuaimi & G. George, 2015, Appropriability and the retrieval of knowledge after spillovers, *Strategic Management Journal*: in press; L. Mulotte, P. Dussauge, & W. Mitchell, 2013, Does pre-entry licensing undermine the performance of subsequent independent activities? Evidence from the global aerospace industry, 1944–2000, *Strategic Management Journal*, 34: 358–372; A. W. King & C. P. Zeithaml, 2001, Competencies and firm performance: Examining the causal ambiguity paradox, *Strategic Management Journal*, 22: 75–99.

84. Barney, Firm resources, 111.

85. Z. Erden, D. Klang, R. Sydler, & G. von Krogh, 2014, Knowledge-flows and firm performance, *Journal of Business Research*, 67: 2777–2785; E. Beleska-Spasova & K. W. Glaister, 2013, Intrafirm causal ambiguity in an international context, *International Business Review*, 22: 32–46; K. Srikanth & P. Puranam, 2011, Integrating distributed work: Comparing task design, communication, and tacit coordination mechanisms, *Strategic Management Journal*, 32: 849–875.

86. M. G. Jacobides & C. J. Tae, 2015, Kingpins, bottlenecks, and value dynamics along a sector, *Organization Science:* in press; J. B. Heide, A. Kumar, & K. H. Wathne, 2014, Concurrent sourcing, governance mechanisms, and performance outcomes in industrial value chains, *Strategic Management Journal*, 35: 1164–1185; G. K. Acharyulu & B. Shekhar, 2012, Role of value chain strategy in healthcare supply chain management: An empirical study in India, *International Journal of Management*, 29: 91–97.

87. M. E. Porter, 1985, *Competitive Advantage*, New York: Free Press, 33–61.

88. P. Frow, S. Nenonen, A. Payne, & K. Storbacka, 2015, Managing co-creation design: A strategic approach to innovation, *British Journal of Management*: in press; R. Garcia-Castro & C. Francoeur, 2015, When more is not better: Complementarities, costs and contingencies in stakeholder management, *Strategic Management Journal*, in press; J. Alcacer, 2006, Location choices across the value chain: How activity and capability influence co-location, *Management Science*, 52: 1457–1471.

89. Y. M. Zhou, 2015, Supervising across borders: The case of multinational hierarchies, *Organization Science*, in press; S. T. Cavusgil & G. Knight, 2014, The born global firm: An entrepreneurial and capabilities perspective on early and rapid internationalization, *Journal of International Business Studies*, 46: 3–16; N. Haworth, 2013, Compressed development: Global value chains, multinational enterprises and human resource development in 21st century Asia, *Journal of World Business*, 48: 251–259.

90. R. Garcia-Castro & R. V. Aguilera, 2015, Incremental value creation and appropriation in a world with multiple stakeholders, *Strategic Management Journal*, 36: 137–147; S. Manning, M. M. Larsen, & P. Bharati, 2015, Global delivery models: The role of talent, speed and time zones in the global outsourcing industry, *Journal of International Business Studies*, in press; A. Jara & H. Escaith, 2012, Global value chains, international trade statistics and policymaking in a flattening world, *World Economics*, 13(4): 5–18.

91. C. Boulton & S. Norton, 2015, Deutsche Bank, H-P divide IT responsibility in cloud deal, *Wall Street Journal Online*, www.wsj.com, February 26.

92. R. Lungeanu & E. Zajac, 2015, Venture capital ownership as a contingent resource: How owner/firm fit influences IPO outcomes, *Academy of Management Journal*, in press; J.-Y. Lee, D. G. Bachrach, & K. Lewis, 2014, Social network ties, transactive memory, and performance in groups, *Organization Science*, 25: 951–967.

93. S. G. Lazzarini, 2015, Strategizing by the government: Can industrial policy create firm-level competitive advantage? *Strategic Management Journal*, 36: 97–112; H. Yang, Y. Zheng, & X. Zhao, 2014, Exploration or exploitation: Small firms' alliance strategies with large firms, *Strategic Management Journal*, 35: 146–157.

94. C. Lioukas & J. Reuer, 2015, Isolating trust outcomes from exchange relationships: Social exchange and learning benefits of prior ties in alliances, *Academy of Management Journal*, in press; J. Song, 2014, Subsidiary absorptive capacity and knowledge transfer within multinational corporations, *Journal of International Business Studies*, 45: 73–84.

95. G. E. Mitchell, 2014, Collaborative propensities among transnational NGOs registered in the United States, *The American Review of Public Administration*, 44: 575–599.

96. S. M. Handley & C. M. Angst, 2015, The impact of culture on the relationship between governance and opportunism in outsourcing relationships, *Strategic Management Journal*, in press; D. J. Teece, 2014, A dynamic capabilities-based entrepreneurial theory of the multinational enterprise, *Journal of International Business Studies*, 45: 8–37.

97. C. Peeters, C. Dehon, & P. Garcia-Prieto, 2015, The attention stimulus of cultural differences in global services sourcing, *Journal of International Business Studies*, 46: 241–251; D. O. Kazmer, 2014, Manufacturing outsourcing, onshoring, and global equilibrium, *Business Horizons*, 57: 463–472; A. J. Mauri & J. Neiva de Figueiredo, 2012, Strategic patterns of internationalization and performance variability: Effects of US-based MNC cross-border dispersion, integration, and outsourcing, *Journal of International Management*, 18: 38–51.

98. A. Gunasekaran, Z. Irani, K.-L. Choy, L. Filippi, & T. Papadopoulos, 2015, Performance measures and metrics in outsourcing decisions: A review for research and applications, *International Journal of Production Economics*, 161: 153–166; W. L. Tate, L. M. Ellram, T. Schoenherr, & K. J. Petersen, 2014, Global competitive conditions driving the manufacturing location decision, *Business Horizons*, 57: 381–390; C. Weigelt & M. B. Sarkar, 2012, Performance implications of outsourcing for technological innovations: Managing the efficiency and adaptability trade-off, *Strategic Management Journal*, 33: 189–216.

99. A. Jain & R.-A. Thietart, 2014, Capabilities as shift parameters for the outsourcing decision, *Strategic Management Journal*, 35: 1881–1890; J. Li, 2012, The alignment between organizational control mechanisms and outsourcing strategies: A commentary essay, *Journal of Business Research*, 65: 1384–1386.

100. R. Kapoor & N. R. Furr, 2015, Complementarities and competition: Unpacking the drivers of entrants' technology choices in the solar photovoltaic industry, *Strategic Management Journal*, 36: 416–436; N. Raassens, S. Wuyts, & I. Geyskens, 2012, The market valuation of outsourcing new product development, *Journal of Marketing Research*, 49: 682–695.

101. S. Holloway & A. Parmigiani, 2015, Friends and profits don't mix: The performance implications of repeated partnerships, *Academy of Management Journal*, in press; A. Arino, J. J. Reuer, K. J. Mayer, & J. Jane, 2014, Contracts, negotiation, and learning: An examination of termination provisions, *Journal of Management Studies*, 51: 379–405; A. Martinez-Noya, E. Garcia-Canal, & M. F. Guillen, 2013, R&D outsourcing and the effectiveness of intangible investments: Is proprietary core knowledge walking out of the door? *Journal of Management Studies*, 50: 67–91.

102. J. Alcacer & J. Oxley, 2014, Learning by supplying, *Strategic Management Journal*, 35: 204–223; S. Sonenshein, 2013, How organizations foster the creative use of resources, *Academy of*

Management Journal, 57: 814–848; C. Grimpe & U. Kaiser, 2010, Balancing internal and external knowledge acquisition: The gains and pains from R&D outsourcing, *Journal of Management Studies*, 47: 1483–1509.

103. T. Obloj & P. Zemsky, 2015, Value creation and value capture under moral hazard: Exploring the micro-foundations of buyer-supplier relationships, *Strategic Management Journal*, in press; S. M. Handley, 2012, The perilous effects of capability loss on outsourcing management and performance, *Journal of Operations Management*, 30: 152–165; P. D. O. Jensen & T. Pederson, 2011, The economic geography of offshoring: The fit between activities and local context, *Journal of Management Studies*, 48: 352–372.

104. S. M. Handley & C. M. Angst, 2015, The impact of culture on the relationship between governance and opportunism in outsourcing relationships, *Strategic Management Journal*, in press; M. Kang, X. Wu, P. Hong, & Y. Park, 2012, Aligning organizational control practices with competitive outsourcing performance, *Journal of Business Research*, 65: 1195–1201.

105. M. Taussig & A. Delios, 2015, Unbundling the effects of institutions on firm resources: The contingent value of being local in emerging economy private equity, *Strategic Management Journal*, in press; O. Baumann & N. Stieglitz, 2014, Rewarding value-creating ideas in organizations: The power of low-powered incentives, *Strategic Management Journal*, 35: 358–375.

106. U. Stettner & D. Lavie, 2014, Ambidexterity under scrutiny: Exploration and exploitation via internal organization, alliances, and acquisitions, *Strategic Management Journal*, 35: 1903–1929; E. Rawley, 2010, Diversification, coordination costs, and organizational rigidity: Evidence from microdata, *Strategic Management Journal*, 31: 873–891.

107. D. L. Barton, 1995, *Wellsprings of Knowledge: Building and Sustaining the Sources of Innovation*, Boston: Harvard Business School Press, 30–31.

108. J. Linkner, 2014, Book highlight—Disrupt or be disrupted, *Global Business and Organizational Excellence*, 34: 78–87; J. Milliot, 2013, As e-books grow, so does Amazon, *Publishers Weekly*, February 11, 4.

4

Business-Level Strategy

Studying this chapter should provide you with the strategic management knowledge needed to:

4-1   Define business-level strategy.

4-2   Discuss the relationship between customers and business-level strategies in terms of *who, what,* and *how*.

4-3   Explain the differences among business-level strategies.

4-4   Use the five forces of competition model to explain how above-average returns can be earned through each business-level strategy.

4-5   Describe the risks of using each of the business-level strategies.

HAIN CELESTIAL GROUP: A FIRM FOCUSED ON "ORGANIC" DIFFERENTIATION

This chapter is about a firm's business-level strategy, and what it takes to be successful in creating a strategy that allows a firm to compete successfully in a particular industry or industry segment. Hain Celestial Group is an example of a differentiation strategy at the business level. Differentiation is a business-level strategy that will be defined more clearly in this chapter. Briefly, it allows a firm to be differentiated from its competitors and allows it to build a loyal following of customers. As indicated in Chapter 2, consumers often follow social trends. Hain Celestial Group has built strong capabilities in producing natural and organic foods, and it has built its strategy to take advantage of this changing consumer trend in the food business across a number of related industries: consumer food producers, grocery stores, and restaurants.

Hain Celestial's CEO, Irwin Simon, founded the company in 1983 and it went public in 1993. The company grew through a series of acquisitions of small organic and natural foods producers.

These acquisitions, as Simon's puts it, are "not GE or Heinz or Campbells' …. Growth is coming from companies like Ell's and BluePrint—entrepreneurial start-ups." The largest acquisition to date was Celestial Seasonings which is a supplier of teas and juices. The effect of these acquisitions has allowed Hain Celestial to become the largest supplier to natural food retailer Whole Foods Markets. BluePrint, the company noted above, is focused on natural juices marketed to consumers to 'clean' their bodies. Brands like Terra vegetable chips, Dream nondairy milk, and Celestial Seasonings tea are household names for the health-oriented shopper and these brands have made Hain Celestial the largest natural foods company in the world.

The natural food trend has allowed Hain Celestial to sell their branded products to traditional grocery store chains, which account for about 60 percent of its U.S. sales. Its brands are also having an impact on sales outside of the United States, representing approximately 40 percent of total revenues in 2014. Their successful acquisition strategy has focused on "buying brands started by someone else" and then "figure out how to grow them from there."

Meanwhile, large branded food firms that have not focused as intensely on this natural segment have experienced earning "indigestion." Branded packaged food producers such as Kellogg's Company (maker of breakfast cereals and foods including Frosted Flakes and Pop-Tarts), Kraft Foods Group (maker of Oscar Meyer deli meats, Maxwell House coffee, and Velveeta cheese), Campbell Soup Company (Campbell's Soup, Pepperidge Farm, and Goldfish snacks), ConAgra Foods, Inc. (maker of Chef Boyardee ravioli, Hunt's ketchup, Marie Callender's pies and snacks, Orville Redenbacher's popcorn, PAM nonstick cooking spray, and Peter Pan peanut butter), J.M. Smucker Company (makers of Smucker's jams and jellies, Pillsbury baking mixes, Crisco shortening, Jif peanut butter, and Folgers coffee), and Mondelēz International, Inc. (maker of Oreo cookies and Cadbury chocolate) only have a peripheral focus on this segment. Their earnings have stalled in part because their brands are not focused on the natural and organic trend desired by consumers as much as Hain Celestial, whose earnings and stock price has climbed much higher on a relative basis. Of course, U.S. main-line brand firms such as those mentioned above have experienced a downturn in earning from the increased value of the dollar, but Hain Celestial also has substantial foreign exposure, as noted above.

Bob Kreisel/Alamy

To deal with the slump, different strategic approaches have been taken. Smucker's, for example, has moved into pet food through its acquisition of Big Heart Pet Foods (maker of Milk-Bone dog treats and Meow Mix cat food). Others, such as Nestlé (maker of Crunch and Butterfinger candy bars and other chocolates), are removing artificial ingredients such as colors and dyes from candy and chocolate. Hershey Company and Mars, Incorporated, who make up 65 percent of the global markets share in packaged candy, are reducing high fructose corn syrup and increasing the sugar content. Mondelēz is seeking to reduce saturated fats and sodium in its snacks by 10 percent. However, these changes do not allow these firms to overcome the problem of rapidly changing consumer tastes toward nature food.

Grocery stores are also seeking to enter in this natural segment. To compete with Trader Joe's, Whole Foods, and the trend among other supermarkets (such as Kroger and Safeway) who are moving into in this segment, Walmart is introducing a line of low-priced organic foods. Walmart is joining Wild Oats Marketplace (an independent producer in the natural food segment) "to place about 100 organic products into its store" and the "Wild Oats line will be priced 25 percent lower than competing national organic brands." However, Hain Celestial has the more direct strategy and image to take advantage of this trend and sell to those outlets seeking to distribute more natural and organic food products.

This same trend is occurring in restaurants. Chipotle Mexican Grill, Inc. has successfully taken advantage of the trend towards natural foods, while McDonald's is struggling to take advantage of the same trend.

Sources: J. Bacon, 2015, Brands capitalise on health-driven resolutions, *Marketing Week*, www.marketingweek.com, January 29; A. Chen & A. Gasparro, 2015, Smucker's latest food firm hurt by changing tastes, *Wall Street Journal*, February 14–15, B4; A. Gasparro, 2015, Indigestion hits food giants, *Wall Street Journal*, February 13, B1; A. Gasparro, 2015, Nestlé bars artificial color, flavors, *Wall Street Journal*, February 18, B6; M. Esterl, 2015, PepsiCo earnings, revenue drop on foreign-exchange impact. *Wall Street Journal*, www.wsj.com, February 12; L. Light, 2015, How to revive McDonald's, *Wall Street Journal*, www.wsj.com, February 11; M. Alva, 2014, Organic growth comes naturally to Hain Celestial Group, *Investor's Business Daily*, July 24, A5; A. Kingston, 2014, Juice junkies, *Maclean's*, June 30, 64–66; SCTWeek, 2014, Walmart to sell low-price organic food, 2014, *SCTWeek*, April 11, 4.

Increasingly important to firm success, strategy is concerned with making choices among two or more alternatives.[1] As noted in Chapter 1, when choosing a strategy, the firm decides to pursue one course of action instead of others. The choices are influenced by opportunities and threats in the firm's external environment[2] (see Chapter 2) as well as the nature and quality of the resources, capabilities, and core competencies in its internal organization[3] (see Chapter 3). As shown in the Opening Case, Hain Celestial Group has the right capabilities (strong producer of natural and organic food products) matched to an opportunity in the industry environment (strong consumer demand for natural and organic food products) which has made it a formidable competitor producing above-average returns. However, other branded food producers have struggled to meet changing consumer tastes and have realized poorer performance as a result.[4]

In previous chapters, analysis of the external environment and of internal firm resources and capabilities, which is the first step in the strategic management process, was discussed. This chapter is the first on strategy, which is the second part of the strategic management process explained in Chapter 1. The fundamental objective of using any type of strategy (see Figure 1.1) is to gain strategic competitiveness and earn above-average returns.[5] Strategies are purposeful, precede the taking of actions to which they apply, and demonstrate a shared understanding of the firm's vision and mission.[6] An effectively formulated strategy marshals, integrates, and allocates the firm's resources, capabilities, and competencies so that it will be properly aligned with its external environment.[7] A properly developed strategy also rationalizes the firm's vision and mission along with the actions taken to achieve them. Information about a host of variables including markets, customers, technology, worldwide finance, and the changing world economy must be collected and analyzed to properly form and use strategies. In the final analysis, sound strategic choices that reduce uncertainty regarding outcomes are the foundation for building successful strategies.[8]

Business-level strategy, this chapter's focus, indicates the choices the firm has made about how it intends to compete in individual product markets. **Business-level strategy** is an integrated and coordinated set of commitments and actions the firm uses to gain a competitive advantage by exploiting core competencies in specific product markets.[9] The choices are important because long-term performance is linked to a firm's strategies. Given the complexity of successfully competing in the global economy, the choices about how the firm will compete can be difficult.[10] For example, King Digital Entertainment, a video game developer, has done well recently through its "Candy Crush" franchise. The simple concepts of this game series has made it popular among players not typically drawn to traditional video games. It has focused on casual game players rather than on a more dedicated base of gamers. Electronic Arts, Inc. (EA) has focused on the more dedicated game consumers and has developed franchises such as "Call of Duty" and "Madden NFL" and not only has developed this digitally but also into mobile devices. However, Zynga focused on the casual game market and has faced severe declines of its Facebook-based games "FarmVille" and "CityVille." These games also focused on the casual market, and these consumers, as Zynga has discovered, can be fickle. As such, King Digital Entertainment has been seeking to expand beyond the casual game segment for mobile devices and create stronger franchises across many platforms. However, it may be difficult to break into and maintain the loyalty of more dedicated customers as EA has done through its ever more graphic and sophisticated game software.[11]

Every firm must develop and implement a business-level strategy. However, some firms may not use all the strategies—corporate-level, merger and acquisition, international, and cooperative—we examine in Chapters 6 through 9. A firm competing in a single-product market in a single geographic location does not need a corporate-level strategy regarding product diversity or an international strategy to deal with geographic diversity. In contrast, a diversified firm will use one of the corporate-level strategies as well as a separate business-level strategy for each product market in which it competes. Every firm—ranging from the local dry cleaner to the multinational corporation—must develop and use at least one business-level strategy. Thus business-level strategy is the *core* strategy—the strategy that the firm forms to describe how it intends to compete in a product market.[12]

We discuss several topics to examine business-level strategies. Because customers are the foundation of successful business-level strategies and should never be taken for granted,[13] we present information about customers that is relevant to business-level strategies. In terms of customers, when selecting a business-level strategy the firm determines

1. *who* will be served,
2. *what* needs those target customers have that it will satisfy, and
3. *how* those needs will be satisfied.

Selecting customers and deciding which of their needs the firm will try to satisfy, as well as how it will do so, are challenging tasks. Global competition has created many attractive options for customers, thus making it difficult to determine the strategy to best serve them.[14] Effective global competitors have become adept at identifying the needs of customers in different cultures and geographic regions as well as learning how to quickly and successfully adapt the functionality of a firm's good or service to meet those needs.

A **business-level strategy** is an integrated and coordinated set of commitments and actions the firm uses to gain a competitive advantage by exploiting core competencies in specific product markets.

Descriptions of the purpose of business-level strategies—and of the five business-level strategies—follow the discussion of customers. The five strategies we examine are called *generic* because they can be used in any organization competing in any industry.[15] Our analysis describes how effective use of each strategy allows the firm to favorably position itself relative to the five competitive forces in the industry (see Chapter 2). In addition, we use the value chain (see Chapter 3) to show examples of the primary and support activities necessary to implement specific business-level strategies. Because no strategy is risk-free,[16] we also describe the different risks the firm may encounter when using these strategies. In Chapter 11, we explain the organizational structures and controls linked with the successful use of each business-level strategy.

4-1 Customers: Their Relationship with Business-Level Strategies

Strategic competitiveness results only when the firm satisfies a group of customers by using its competitive advantages as the basis for competing in individual product markets.[17] A key reason firms must satisfy customers with their business-level strategy is that returns earned from relationships with customers are the lifeblood of all organizations.[18]

The most successful companies try to find new ways to satisfy current customers and/or to meet the needs of new customers. Being able to do this can be even more difficult when firms and consumers face challenging economic conditions. During such times, firms may decide to reduce their workforce to control costs. This can lead to problems, however, because having fewer employees makes it more difficult for companies to meet individual customers' needs and expectations. In these instances, firms can follow several possible courses of action, including paying extra attention to their best customers and developing a flexible workforce by cross-training employees so they can undertake a variety of responsibilities on their jobs.

4-1a Effectively Managing Relationships with Customers

The firm's relationships with its customers are strengthened when it delivers superior value to them. Strong interactive relationships with customers often provide the foundation for the firm's efforts to profitably serve customers' unique needs.

Importantly, delivering superior value often results in increased customer satisfaction. In turn, customer satisfaction has a positive relationship with profitability because satisfied customers are most likely to be repeat customers. However, more choices and easily accessible information about the functionality of the firms' products are creating increasingly sophisticated and knowledgeable customers, making it difficult to earn their loyalty. As such, many firms are working with customers to co-create value through working closely together to ensure customer satisfaction.[19]

A number of companies have become skilled at the art of *managing* all aspects of their relationship with their customers.[20] For example, Amazon.com, Inc. is widely

Customers standing in a grocery store checkout line. Successful business strategies satisfy customers' needs.

Rubberball/Mike Kemp/Getty Images

recognized for the quality of information it maintains about its customers, the services it renders, and its ability to anticipate customers' needs. Using the information it has, Amazon tries to serve what it believes are the unique needs of each customer; and it has a strong reputation for being able to do this successfully.[21]

As we discuss next, firms' relationships with customers are characterized by three dimensions. Companies such as Acer Inc. and Amazon understand these dimensions and manage their relationships with customers in light of them.

4-1b Reach, Richness, and Affiliation

The *reach* dimension of relationships with customers is concerned with the firm's access and connection to customers. In general, firms seek to extend their reach, adding customers in the process of doing so.

Reach is an especially critical dimension for social networking sites such as Facebook and MySpace in that the value these firms create for users is to connect them with others. Traffic to MySpace has been declining in recent years; at the same time, the number of Facebook users has been dramatically increasing in the United States and abroad. Reach is also important to Netflix, Inc. Although its user base is still growing in the United States, its growth rate has slowed. However, streaming video customers in foreign markets grew faster than expected. When this was announced, their stock price increased 16 percent in after-hours trading. Netflix plans to expand to over 200 countries by 2017, up from its 50 in 2014.[22]

Richness, the second dimension of firms' relationships with customers, is concerned with the depth and detail of the two-way flow of information between the firm and the customer. The potential of the richness dimension to help the firm establish a competitive advantage in its relationship with customers leads many firms to offer online services in order to better manage information exchanges with their customers. Broader and deeper information-based exchanges allow firms to better understand their customers and their needs. Such exchanges also enable customers to become more knowledgeable about how the firm can satisfy them. Internet technology and e-commerce transactions have substantially reduced the costs of meaningful information exchanges with current and potential customers. As we have noted, Amazon is a leader in using the Internet to build relationships with customers. In fact, it bills itself as the most "customer-centric company" on earth. Amazon and other firms use rich information from customers to help them develop innovative new products that better satisfy customers' needs.[23]

Affiliation, the third dimension, is concerned with facilitating useful interactions with customers. Viewing the world through the customer's eyes and constantly seeking ways to create more value for the customer have positive effects in terms of affiliation.[24] This approach enhances customer satisfaction and produces fewer customer complaints. In fact, for services, customers often do not complain when dissatisfied; instead they simply go to competitors for their service needs, although a firm's strong brand can mitigate the switching.[25] Tesco, the largest retail grocer in the United Kingdom, as well as other firms have changed the title of its lead marketing officer to "Chief Customer Officer." This suggests the importance of the customer to most businesses, especially those focused on consumers. Likewise, because of data available through digitization, firms have a tremendous amount of individual customer data, and this data-gathering trend is growing, allowing firms to customize their products and services.[26]

As we discuss next, effectively managing customer relationships (along the dimensions of reach, richness, and affiliation) helps the firm answer questions related to the issues of *who, what*, and *how*.

4-1c   Who: Determining the Customers to Serve

Deciding *who* the target customer is that the firm intends to serve with its business-level strategy is an important decision.[27] Companies divide customers into groups based on differences in the customers' needs (needs are discussed further in the next section) to make this decision. Dividing customers into groups based on their needs is called **market segmentation**. Market segmentation is a process used to cluster people with similar needs into individual and identifiable groups.[28] In the animal food products business, for example, the food-product needs of owners of companion pets (e.g., dogs and cats) differ from the needs for food and health-related products of those owning production animals (e.g., livestock). A subsidiary of Colgate-Palmolive Company, Hill's Pet Nutrition, sells food products for pets. In fact, the company's mission is "to help enrich and lengthen the special relationship between people and their pets."[29] Thus, Hill's Pet Nutrition targets the needs of different segments of customers with the food products it sells for animals.

Almost any identifiable human or organizational characteristic can be used to subdivide a market into segments that differ from one another on a given characteristic. Common characteristics on which customers' needs vary are illustrated in Table 4.1.

4-1d   What: Determining Which Customer Needs to Satisfy

After the firm decides *who* it will serve, it must identify the targeted customer group's needs that its goods or services can satisfy. In a general sense, *needs (what)* are related to a product's benefits and features. Successful firms learn how to deliver to customers what they want, when they want it. Having close and frequent interactions with both current and potential customers helps the firm identify those individuals' and groups' current and future needs. Target, a retail store and online marketer, has been successful with analyzing its many sources of data and customizing its information for in store and online "guests." It has available data, through online sources, of many customer demographics (age, marital status, income category, etc.) as well as shopping frequency, products purchased, and geographic distance from local stores. It utilizes this information to develop is promotion and marketing strategies.[30]

From a strategic perspective, a basic need of all customers is to buy products that create value for them. The generalized forms of value that goods or services provide are either low cost with acceptable features or highly differentiated features with acceptable cost. The most effective firms continuously strive to anticipate changes in customers' needs. The firm that fails to anticipate and certainly to recognize changes in its customers' needs

Market segmentation
is a process used to cluster people with similar needs into individual and identifiable groups.

Table 4.1 Basis for Customer Segmentation

Consumer Markets
1. Demographic factors (age, income, sex, etc.)
2. Socioeconomic factors (social class, stage in the family life cycle)
3. Geographic factors (cultural, regional, and national differences)
4. Psychological factors (lifestyle, personality traits)
5. Consumption patterns (heavy, moderate, and light users)
6. Perceptual factors (benefit segmentation, perceptual mapping)

Industrial Markets
1. End-use segments (identified by Standard Industrial Classification [SIC] code)
2. Product segments (based on technological differences or production economics)
3. Geographic segments (defined by boundaries between countries or by regional differences within them)
4. Common buying factor segments (cut across product market and geographic segments)
5. Customer size segments

Source: Based on information in S. C. Jain, 2009, *Marketing Planning and Strategy*, Mason, OH: South-Western Cengage Custom Publishing.

may lose its customers to competitors whose products can provide more value to the focal firm's customers. It is also recognized that consumer needs and desires have been changing in recent years. For example, more consumers desire to have an experience rather than to simply purchase a good or service. As a result, one of Starbucks' goals has been to provide an experience, not just a cup of coffee. Customers also prefer to receive customized goods and services. Again, Starbucks has been doing this for some time, allowing customers to design their own drinks, within their menus (which have become rather extensive over time).

Customers also demand fast service. Chipotle Mexican Grill, as noted in the Opening Case, is a leader in the fast-casual dining segment catering to the millennial generation. This fast-casual segment, including Chipotle, Panera Bread, Five Guys Burgers and Fries, Panda Express, and others, has been increasing their presence, as well as growth per outlet, compared to McDonald's who has had a difficult time maintaining a level playing field against the fast-casual service speed and per outlet growth. Also, one observer noted: "A decade ago, there were 9,000 fast-casual restaurants in the U.S., versus nearly 14,000 McDonald's. Now, fast-casual restaurants number more than 21,000 ... while McDonald's U.S. restaurant count has risen only slightly."[31] Unhappy consumers lead to lost sales—both theirs and those of others who learn of their dissatisfaction. Therefore, it is important to maintain customer satisfaction by meeting and satisfying their needs.[32]

4-1e How: Determining Core Competencies Necessary to Satisfy Customer Needs

After deciding *who* the firm will serve and the specific *needs* of those customers, the firm is prepared to determine how to use its capabilities and competencies to develop products that can satisfy the needs of its target customers. As explained in Chapters 1 and 3, *core competencies* are resources and capabilities that serve as a source of competitive advantage for the firm over its rivals. Firms use core competencies (*how*) to implement value-creating strategies, thereby satisfying customers' needs. Only those firms with the capacity to continuously improve, innovate, and upgrade their competencies can expect to meet and hopefully exceed customers' expectations across time.[33] Firms must continuously upgrade their capabilities to ensure that they maintain the advantage over their rivals by providing customers with a superior product.[34] Often these capabilities are difficult for competitors to imitate, partly because they are constantly being upgraded, but also because they are integrated and used as configurations of capabilities to perform an important activity (e.g., R&D).[35]

Companies draw from a wide range of core competencies to produce goods or services that can satisfy customers' needs. For example, Merck & Co., Inc. is a large pharmaceutical firm well-known for its research and development (R&D) capabilities. In recent times, Merck has been building on these capabilities by investing heavily in R&D. The new drugs Merck intends to produce are directed at meeting the needs of consumers and to sustain Merck's competitive advantage in the industry.[36]

SAS Institute Inc. is the world's largest, privately owned software company and is the leader in business intelligence and analytics. Customers use SAS programs for data warehousing, data mining, and decision support purposes. SAS serves 60,000 sites in 139 countries and serves 93 percent of the top *Fortune* 100 firms. Allocating approximately 23 percent of revenues to R&D in 2014, a percentage exceeding those allocated by its competitors, SAS relies on its core competence in R&D to satisfy the data-related needs of such customers as the U.S. Census Bureau and a host of consumer goods firms (e.g., hotels, banks, and catalog companies).[37]

Many types of firms now emphasize innovation, not only those in high technology industries. This innovation appears to be driven by customers, along with providing a product or service that satisfies their customers' needs in a manner superior to that of rivals' products or services to gain or sustain a competitive advantage. For example, L'Oréal has gained competitive advantages due to their innovations in cosmetic and beauty products. The Executive Vice President of L'Oréal in the United States, Frédéric Rozé, noted: "At the end of the day, our success comes from our capacity to transform ourselves, to metamorphose ourselves."[38]

Our discussion about customers shows that all organizations must use their capabilities and core competencies (the *how*) to satisfy the needs (the *what*) of the target group of customers (the *who*) the firm has chosen to serve. Next, we describe the different business-level strategies that are available to firms to use to satisfy customers as the foundation for earning above-average returns.

4-2　The Purpose of a Business-Level Strategy

The purpose of a business-level strategy is to create differences between the firm's position and those of its competitors.[39] To position itself differently from competitors, a firm must decide whether it intends to *perform activities differently* or to *perform different activities*. Strategy defines the path which provides the direction of actions to be taken by leaders of the organization.[40] In fact, "choosing to perform activities differently or to perform different activities than rivals" is the essence of business-level strategy.[41] Thus, the firm's business-level strategy is a deliberate choice about how it will perform the value chain's primary and support activities to create unique value. Indeed, in the current complex competitive landscape, successful use of a business-level strategy results from the firm learning how to integrate the activities it performs in ways that create superior value for customers.

The manner in which Southwest Airlines Co. has integrated its activities is the foundation for the successful use of its primary cost leadership strategy (this strategy is discussed later in the chapter) but also includes differentiation through the unique services provided to customers. The tight integration among Southwest's activities is a key source of the firm's ability, historically, to operate more profitably than its competitors.

Southwest Airlines has configured the activities it performs into six areas of strategic intent—limited passenger service; frequent, reliable departures; lean, highly productive ground and gate crews; high aircraft utilization with few aircraft models; very low ticket prices; and short-haul, point-to-point routes between mid-sized cities and secondary airports. Individual clusters of tightly linked activities make it possible to achieve its strategic intent. For example, no meals, no seat assignments, and no baggage transfers form a cluster of individual activities that support the strategic intent to offer limited passenger service.

Southwest's tightly integrated activities make it difficult for competitors to imitate the firm's cost leadership strategy. The firm's unique culture and customer service are sources of competitive advantage that rivals have been unable to imitate, although some have tried and largely failed (e.g., US Airways' MetroJet subsidiary, United Airlines' Shuttle by United, Delta's Song, and Continental Airlines' Continental Lite). Hindsight shows that these competitors offered low prices to customers, but weren't able to operate at costs close to those of Southwest or to provide customers with any notable sources of differentiation, such as a unique experience while in the air. The key to Southwest's success has been its ability to continuously maintain low costs while providing customers with *acceptable* levels of differentiation such as an engaging culture. Firms using the cost leadership strategy must understand that in terms of sources of differentiation accompanying the cost leader's product, the customer defines *acceptable*. Fit among activities is a key to the sustainability of competitive advantage for all firms, including Southwest Airlines. Strategic fit among the many activities is critical for competitive advantage. It is more difficult for a competitor to match a configuration of integrated activities than to imitate a particular activity such as sales promotion, or a process technology.[42]

4-3 Types of Business-Level Strategies

Firms choose between five business-level strategies to establish and defend their desired strategic position against competitors: *cost leadership, differentiation, focused cost leadership, focused differentiation*, and *integrated cost leadership/differentiation* (see Figure 4.1). Each business-level strategy can help the firm to establish and exploit a particular *competitive advantage* within a particular *competitive scope*. How firms integrate the activities they perform within each different business-level strategy demonstrates how they differ from one another.[43] For example, firms have different activity maps, and thus, a Southwest Airlines activity map differs from those of competitors JetBlue, United Airlines, American Airlines, and so forth. Superior integration of activities increases the likelihood of being able to gain an advantage over competitors and to earn above-average returns.

When selecting a business-level strategy, firms evaluate two types of potential competitive advantages: "lower cost than rivals or the ability to differentiate and command a premium price that exceeds the extra cost of doing so."[44] Having lower costs results from the firm's ability to perform activities differently than rivals; being able to differentiate indicates the firm's capacity to perform different (and valuable) activities. Thus, based on the nature and quality of its internal resources, capabilities, and core competencies, a firm seeks to form either a cost competitive advantage or a distinctiveness competitive advantage as the basis for implementing its business-level strategy.[45]

Figure 4.1 Five Business-Level Strategies

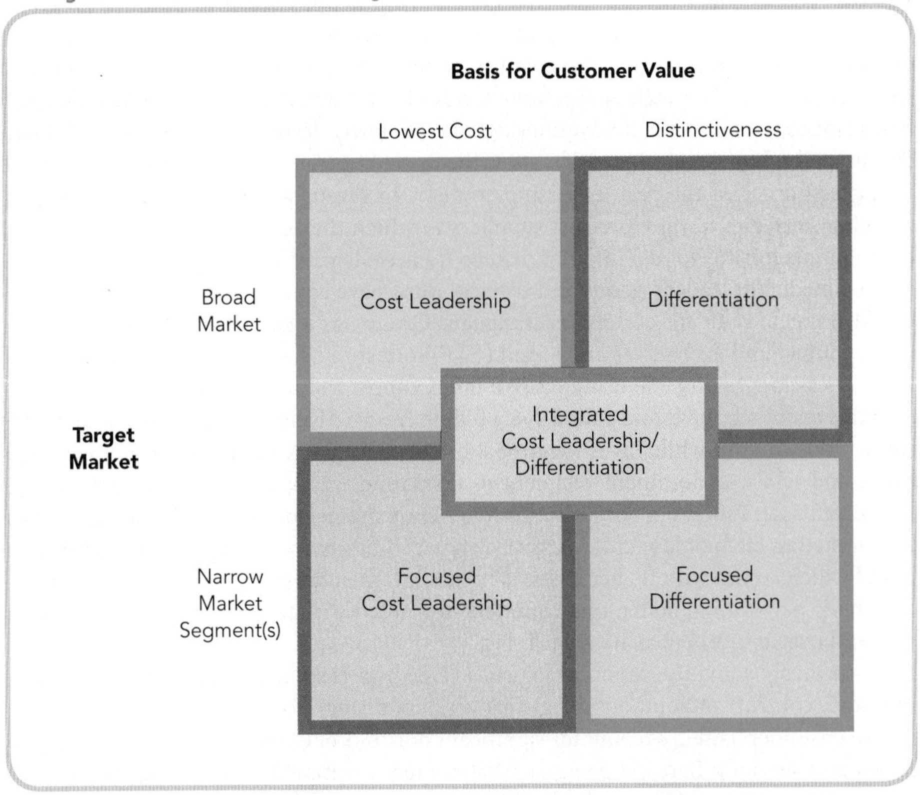

Source: Based on M. E. Porter, 1998, *Competitive Advantage: Creating and Sustaining Superior Performance*, New York: The Free Press; D. G. Sirmon, M. A. Hitt, & R. D. Ireland, 2007, Managing firm resources in dynamic environments to create value: Looking inside the black box, *Academy of Management Review*, 32: 273–292; D. G. Sirmon, M. A. Hitt, R. D. Ireland, & B. A. Gilbert, 2011, Resource orchestration to create competitive advantage: Breadth, depth and life cycles effects, *Journal of Management*, 37: 1390–1412.

Two types of target markets are broad market and narrow market segment(s) (see Figure 4.1). Firms serving a broad market seek to use their capabilities to create value for customers on an industry-wide basis. A narrow market segment means that the firm intends to serve the needs of a narrow customer group. With focus strategies, the firm "selects a segment or group of segments in the industry and tailors its strategy to serving them to the exclusion of others."[46] Buyers with special needs and buyers located in specific geographic regions are examples of narrow customer groups. As shown in Figure 4.1, a firm could also strive to develop a combined low cost/distinctiveness value creation approach as the foundation for serving a target customer group that is larger than a narrow market segment but not as comprehensive as a broad (or industry-wide) customer group. In this instance, the firm uses the integrated cost leadership/differentiation strategy.

None of the five business-level strategies shown in Figure 4.1 is inherently or universally superior to the others.[47] The effectiveness of each strategy is contingent both on the opportunities and threats in a firm's external environment and on the strengths and weaknesses derived from the firm's resource portfolio. It is critical, therefore, for the firm to select a business-level strategy that represents an effective match between the opportunities and threats in its external environment and the strengths of its internal organization based on its core competencies.[48] After the firm chooses its strategy, it should consistently emphasize actions that are required to successfully use it.

4-3a   Cost Leadership Strategy

The **cost leadership strategy** is an integrated set of actions taken to produce goods or services with features that are acceptable to customers at the lowest cost, relative to that of competitors.[49] Firms using the cost leadership strategy commonly sell standardized goods or services, but with competitive levels of differentiation, to the industry's most typical customers. Process innovations, which are newly designed production and distribution methods and techniques that allow the firm to operate more efficiently, are critical to successful use of the cost leadership strategy. In recent years, firms have developed sourcing strategies to find low-cost suppliers to which they outsource various functions (e.g., manufacturing goods) in order to keep their costs very low.[50]

As noted, cost leaders' goods and services must have competitive levels of differentiation that create value for customers. Vanguard Group has established a low-cost strategy in the mutual and exchange traded fund (ETF) industry. Its approach is to drive costs to investors as low as possible using passive index funds, and it is winning over customers with this approach. Investors pulled $98.4 billion from actively-managed mutual and ETF stock funds in 2014 while investing $166.8 billion into passively-managed index mutual funds and ETFs. A dominant recipient of this trend was Vanguard Group which saw significant asset inflows in 2014. One commentator suggested, "it is hard to argue against the marketing pitch of low-cost." Actively-managed funds are more focused on trust in a brand which comes with higher costs. Whereas low-cost passively-managed index funds have been performing better, one commentator noted, "when you're fighting the power of brand over performance, it's a hard slog."[51]

As primary activities, inbound logistics (e.g., materials handling, warehousing, and inventory control) and outbound logistics (e.g., collecting, storing, and distributing products to customers) often account for significant portions of the total cost to produce some goods and services. Research suggests that having a competitive advantage in logistics creates more value with a cost leadership strategy than with a differentiation strategy.[52] Thus, cost leaders seeking competitively valuable ways to reduce costs may want to concentrate on the primary activities of inbound logistics and outbound logistics. In so doing, many firms choose to outsource their manufacturing operations to low-cost firms with

The **cost leadership strategy** is an integrated set of actions taken to produce goods or services with features that are acceptable to customers at the lowest cost, relative to that of competitors.

low-wage employees (e.g., China).[53] However, care must be taken because outsourcing also makes the firm more dependent on supplier firms over which they have little control. Outsourcing creates interdependencies between the outsourcing firm and the suppliers. If dependencies become too great, it gives the supplier more power with which the supplier may increase prices of the goods and services provided. Such actions could harm the firm's ability to maintain a low-cost competitive advantage.[54]

Cost leaders also carefully examine all support activities to find additional potential cost reductions. Developing new systems for finding the optimal combination of low cost and acceptable levels of differentiation in the raw materials required to produce the firm's goods or services is an example of how the procurement support activity can facilitate successful use of the cost leadership strategy.

Big Lots, Inc. uses the cost leadership strategy. With its vision of being "The World's Best Bargain Place," Big Lots is the largest closeout retailer in the United States with annual sales approaching $5 billion from more than 1,400 stores. For Big Lots, closeout goods are brand-name products from 3,000 manufacturers provided for sale at substantially lower prices than sold by other retailers.[55]

As described in Chapter 3, firms use value-chain analysis to identify the parts of the company's operations that create value and those that do not. Figure 4.2 demonstrates

Figure 4.2 Examples of Value-Creating Activities Associated with the Cost Leadership Strategy

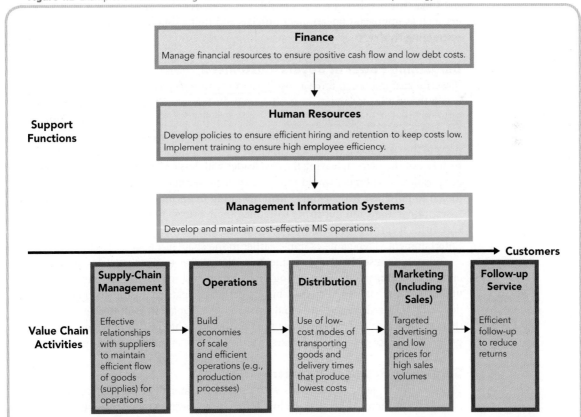

Source: Based on M. E. Porter, 1998, *Competitive Advantage: Creating and Sustaining Superior Performance*, New York: The Free Press; D. G. Sirmon, M. A. Hitt, & R. D. Ireland, 2007, Managing firm resources in dynamic environments to create value: Looking inside the black box, *Academy of Management Review*, 32: 273–292; D. G. Sirmon, M. A. Hitt, R. D. Ireland, & B. A. Gilbert, 2011, Resource orchestration to create competitive advantage: Breadth, depth and life cycles effects, *Journal of Management*, 37: 1390–1412.

the value-chain activities and support functions that allow a firm to create value through the cost leadership strategy. Companies unable to effectively integrate the activities and functions shown in this figure typically lack the core competencies needed to successfully use the cost leadership strategy.

Effective use of the cost leadership strategy allows a firm to earn above-average returns in spite of the presence of strong competitive forces (see Chapter 2). The next sections (one for each of the five forces) explain how firms implement a cost leadership strategy.

Rivalry with Existing Competitors

Having the low-cost position is valuable when dealing with rivals. Because of the cost leader's advantageous position, rivals hesitate to compete on the basis of price, especially before evaluating the potential outcomes of such competition.[56] The changes Walmart made to attract upscale customers created vulnerability in its low-cost position to rivals. Amazon, Family Dollar, and others took advantage of the opportunity. Amazon appears to have become a low-cost leader, and the Family Dollar stores provide low costs and easy access for customers. Both of these rivals have siphoned off some of Walmart's customers.

The degree of rivalry present is based on a number of different factors such as size and resources of rivals, their dependence on the particular market, and location and prior competitive interactions, among others.[57] Firms may also take actions to reduce the amount of rivalry that they face. For example, firms sometimes form joint ventures to reduce rivalry and increase the amount of profitability enjoyed by firms in the industry.[58] In China, firms build strong relationships, often referred to as guanxi, with key stakeholders such as important government officials and units, suppliers, and customers, thereby restraining rivalry.[59]

Bargaining Power of Buyers (Customers)

Powerful customers can force a cost leader to reduce its prices, but not below the level at which the cost leader's next-most-efficient industry competitor can earn average returns. Although powerful customers might be able to force the cost leader to reduce prices even below this level, they probably would choose not to do so. Prices that are low enough to prevent the next-most-efficient competitor from earning average returns would force that firm to exit the market, leaving the cost leader with less competition and in an even stronger position. Customers would thus lose their power and pay higher prices if they were forced to purchase from a single firm operating in an industry without rivals. In some cases, rather than forcing firms to reduce their prices, powerful customers may pressure firms to provide innovative products and services as explained in the King Digital Entertainment video game example earlier in the chapter.

Buyers can also develop a counterbalancing power to the customers' power by thoroughly analyzing and understanding each of their customers. To obtain information and understand the customers' needs, buyers can participate in customers' networks. In so doing, they share information, build trust, and participate in joint problem solving with their customers.[60] In turn, they use the information obtained to provide a product that provides superior value to customers by most effectively satisfying their needs.

Bargaining Power of Suppliers

The cost leader generally operates with margins greater than those of competitors and often tries to increase its margins by driving costs lower. Among other benefits, higher gross margins relative to those of competitors make it possible for the cost leader to absorb its suppliers' price increases. When an industry faces substantial increases in the cost of its supplies, only the cost leader may be able to pay the higher prices and continue to earn either average or above-average returns. Alternatively, a powerful cost leader may be able to force its suppliers to hold down their prices, which would reduce the suppliers' margins in the process. Walmart lost its way in this regard. By reducing the number and type of products sold in Walmart stores, it reduced its bargaining power with several suppliers. In so doing, it was unable to gain the best (lowest) prices on goods relative to its competitors. Thus, Amazon and the Dollar Stores began winning market share from Walmart by offering lower prices.

The fact remains that Walmart is the largest retailer in North America, thus giving the firm a great deal of power with its suppliers. Walmart is the largest supermarket operator in the United States, and its Sam's Club division is the second largest warehouse club in the United States. Collectively, its sales volume of approximately $485.7 billion in fiscal 2014 and the market penetration (more than 200 million people visit one of Walmart's 11,000 stores each week) still allow Walmart to obtain low prices from its suppliers.[61]

Some firms create dependencies on suppliers by outsourcing whole functions. They do so to reduce their overall costs.[62] They may outsource these activities to reduce their costs because of earnings pressures from stakeholders (e.g., institutional investors who own a major stock holding in the company) in the industry.[63] However, "outsourcing can create new costs, as suppliers and partners demand a larger share of the value created."[64] Often when there is such earnings pressure, the firm may see foreign suppliers whose costs are also lower, providing them the capability to offer the goods at lower prices.[65] Yet, when firms outsource, particularly to a foreign supplier, they also need to invest time and effort into building a good relationship, hopefully developing trust between the firms. Such efforts facilitate the integration of the supplier into the firm's value chain.[66]

Potential Entrants

Through continuous efforts to reduce costs to levels that are lower than competitors, a cost leader becomes highly efficient. Because increasing levels of efficiency (e.g., economies of scale) enhance profit margins, they serve as a significant entry barrier to potential competitors.[67] New entrants must be willing to accept less than average returns until they gain the experience required to approach the cost leader's efficiency. To earn even average returns, new entrants must have the competencies required to match the cost levels of competitors other than the cost leader. The low profit margins (relative to margins earned by firms implementing the differentiation strategy) make it necessary for the cost leader to sell large volumes of its product to earn above-average returns. However, firms striving to be the cost leader must avoid pricing their products so low that they cannot operate profitably, even though volume increases.

Product Substitutes

Compared with its industry rivals, the cost leader also holds an attractive position relative to product substitutes. A product substitute becomes a concern for the cost leader when its features and characteristics, in terms of cost and differentiation, are potentially attractive to the firm's customers. When faced with possible substitutes, the cost leader has more flexibility than its competitors. To retain customers, it often can reduce the price of its good or service. With still lower prices and competitive levels of differentiation, the cost leader increases the probability that customers prefer its product rather than a substitute.

Competitive Risks of the Cost Leadership Strategy

The cost leadership strategy is not risk free. One risk is that the processes used by the cost leader to produce and distribute its good or service could become obsolete because of competitors' innovations.[68] These innovations may allow rivals to produce goods or services at costs lower than those of the original cost leader, or to provide additional differentiated features without increasing the product's price to customers.

A second risk is that too much focus by the cost leader on cost reductions may occur at the expense of trying to understand customers' perceptions of "competitive levels of differentiation." Walmart, for example, has been criticized for having too few salespeople available to help customers and too few individuals at checkout registers. These complaints suggest that there might be a discrepancy between how Walmart's customers define "minimal acceptable levels of service" and the firm's attempts to drive its costs increasingly lower.

Imitation is a final risk of the cost leadership strategy. Using their own core competencies, competitors sometimes learn how to successfully imitate the cost leader's strategy. When this happens, the cost leader must increase the value its good or service provides to customers. Commonly, value is increased by selling the current product at an even lower price or by adding differentiated features that create value for customers while maintaining price.

4-3b   Differentiation Strategy

The **differentiation strategy** is an integrated set of actions taken to produce goods or services (at an acceptable cost) that customers perceive as being different in ways that are important to them.[69] While cost leaders serve a typical customer in an industry, differentiators target customers for whom value is created by the manner in which the firm's products differ from those produced and marketed by competitors. Product innovation, which is "the result of bringing to life a new way to solve the customer's problem—through a new product or service development—that benefits both the customer and the sponsoring company,"[70] is critical to successful use of the differentiation strategy.[71]

Firms must be able to produce differentiated products at competitive costs to reduce upward pressure on the price that customers pay. When a product's differentiated features are produced at noncompetitive costs, the price for the product may exceed what the firm's target customers are willing to pay. If the firm has a thorough understanding of what its target customers value, the relative importance they attach to the satisfaction of different needs and for what they are willing to pay a premium, the differentiation strategy can be effective in helping it earn above-average returns. Of course, to achieve these returns, the firm must apply its knowledge capital (knowledge held by its employees and managers) to provide customers with a differentiated product that provides them with superior value.[72]

Through the differentiation strategy, the firm produces distinctive products for customers who value differentiated features more than they value low cost. For example, superior product reliability, durability and high-performance sound systems are among the differentiated features of Toyota Motor Corporation's Lexus products. However, Lexus offers its vehicles to customers at a competitive purchase price relative to other luxury automobiles. As with Lexus products, a product's unique attributes, rather than its purchase price, provide the value for which customers are willing to pay.

To maintain success with the differentiation strategy results, the firm must consistently upgrade differentiated features that customers value and/or create new valuable features (i.e., innovate) without significant cost increases.[73] This approach requires firms to constantly change their product lines.[74] These firms may also offer a portfolio of products that complement each other, thereby enriching the differentiation for the customer and perhaps satisfying a portfolio of consumer needs.[75] Because a differentiated product satisfies customers' unique needs, firms following the differentiation strategy are able to charge premium prices. The ability to sell a good or service at a price that substantially exceeds the cost of creating its differentiated features allows the firm to outperform rivals and earn above-average returns. Rather than costs, a firm using the differentiation strategy primarily concentrates on investing in and developing features that differentiate a product in ways that create

The **differentiation strategy** is an integrated set of actions taken to produce goods or services (at an acceptable cost) that customers perceive as being different in ways that are important to them.

value for customers.[76] Overall, a firm using the differentiation strategy seeks to be different from its competitors on as many dimensions as possible. The less similarity between a firm's goods or services and those of its competitors, the more buffered it is from rivals' actions. Commonly recognized differentiated goods include Toyota's Lexus, Ralph Lauren's wide array of product lines, Caterpillar's heavy-duty earth-moving equipment, and McKinsey & Co.'s differentiated consulting services.

Bernhard Lang/fortune.com

Under Armour, a company in fitness apparel, has specialized in the strong knowledge of its base customer. To re-enforce this focus it has been purchasing fitness apps such as MyFitnessPal.

Under Armour, Inc. is a fitness apparel company which concentrates on high-tech exercise gear for both on consumer and professional markets. It recently surpassed Adidas to become the number two sportswear apparel brand in the United States by retail sales. Although it remains far behind Nike, which has long held the lead, Under Armour has continued its strong growth by pursuing a differentiation strategy. It has built an even stronger knowledge of its consumer base by purchasing the nutrition and exercise tracking platforms MyFitnessPal and Endomondo. MyFitnessPal has 120 million users (mostly in the United States), while Endomondo has 80 million users (mostly in Europe). In the 2015 Consumer Electronics Show in Las Vegas, Under Armour unveiled UA Record, "a dashboard under which it hopes to unite its digital resources." Although the acquisitions will continue to be operated separately, they will help Under Armour in "developing a digital ecosystem which provides unparalleled data" on potential customers. Through this information, it can further customize products for those who are drawn to its brand.[77]

A good or service can be differentiated in many ways. Unusual features, responsive customer service, rapid product innovations and technological leadership, perceived prestige and status, different tastes, and engineering design and performance are examples of approaches to differentiation.[78] While the number of ways to reduce costs may be finite, virtually anything a firm can do to create real or perceived value is a basis for differentiation. Consider product design as a case in point. Because it can create a positive experience for customers, design is an important source of differentiation (even for cost leaders seeking to find ways to add functionalities to their low-cost products as a way of differentiating their products from competitors) and, hopefully, for firms emphasizing it, of competitive advantage.[79] Apple is often cited as the firm that sets the standard in design, with the iPod, iPhone, and iPad demonstrating Apple's product design capabilities. Apple's extremely successful new product launches and market share captured with them has invited competition, the most significant of which is Samsung. As described in Chapter 3, Samsung has some strong capabilities and thus has become a formidable competitor. Although it largely imitates Apple's products, it also improves on them by adding features attractive to customers (i.e., imperfect imitation).[80] Therefore, Samsung is partially differentiating from Apple's unique (differentiated) products.

The value chain can be analyzed to determine if a firm is able to link the activities required to create value by using the differentiation strategy. Examples of value chain activities and support functions that are commonly used to differentiate a good or service are shown in Figure 4.3. Companies without the skills needed to link these activities

Figure 4.3 Examples of Value-Creating Activities Associated with the Differentiation Strategy

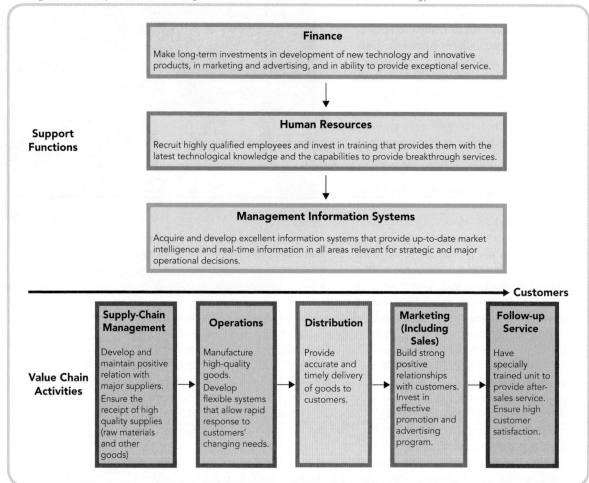

Source: Based on information from M. E. Porter, 1998, *Competitive Advantage: Creating and Sustaining Superior Performance*, New York: The Free Press; D. G. Sirmon, M. A. Hitt, & R. D. Ireland, 2007, Managing firm resources in dynamic environments to create value: Looking inside the black box, *Academy of Management Review*, 32: 273–292; D. G. Sirmon, M. A. Hitt, R. D. Ireland, & B. A. Gilbert, 2011, Resource orchestration to create competitive advantage: Breadth, depth and life cycles effects, *Journal of Management*, 37: 1390–1412.

cannot expect to successfully use the differentiation strategy. Next, we explain how firms using the differentiation strategy can successfully position themselves in terms of the five forces of competition (see Chapter 2) to earn above-average returns.

Rivalry with Existing Competitors

Customers tend to be loyal purchasers of products differentiated in ways that are meaningful to them. As their loyalty to a brand increases, customers' sensitivity to price increases is reduced. The relationship between brand loyalty and price sensitivity insulates a firm from competitive rivalry. Thus, reputations can sustain the competitive advantage of firms following a differentiation strategy.[81] Alternatively, when highly capable rivals such as Samsung practice imperfect imitation by imitating and improving on products, companies such as Apple must pay attention. Thus, Apple must try to incrementally improve its iPhone and iPad products to exploit its investments. However, it must also invest in exploring highly novel and valuable products to establish new markets to remain ahead of Samsung.[82]

Bargaining Power of Buyers (Customers)

The distinctiveness of differentiated goods or services reduces customers' sensitivity to price increases. Customers are willing to accept a price increase when a product still satisfies their unique needs better than a competitor's offering. Thus, the golfer whose needs are specifically satisfied by Callaway golf clubs will likely continue buying those products even if the price increases. Purchasers of brand-name food items (e.g., Heinz ketchup and Kleenex tissues) accept price increases in those products as long as they continue to perceive that the product satisfies their distinctive needs at an acceptable cost. In all of these instances the customers are relatively insensitive to price increases because they do not think an acceptable product alternative exists.

Bargaining Power of Suppliers

Because the firm using the differentiation strategy charges a premium price for its products, suppliers must provide high-quality components, driving up the firm's costs. However, the high margins the firm earns in these cases partially insulate it from the influence of suppliers in that higher supplier costs can be paid through these margins.[83] Alternatively, because of buyers' relative insensitivity to price increases, the differentiated firm might choose to pass the additional cost of supplies on to the customer by increasing the price of its unique product. However, when buyer firms outsource the total function or large portions of it to a supplier, especially R&D for a firm following a differentiation strategy, they can become dependent on and thus vulnerable to that supplier.[84]

Potential Entrants

Customer loyalty and the need to overcome the uniqueness of a differentiated product create substantial barriers to potential entrants. Entering an industry under these conditions typically demands significant investments of resources and patience while seeking customers' loyalty. In these cases, some potential entrants decide to make smaller investments to see if they can gain a "foothold" in the market. If it does not work they will not lose major resources, but if it works they can then invest greater resources to enhance their competitive position.[85]

Product Substitutes

Firms selling brand-name goods and services to loyal customers are positioned effectively against product substitutes. In contrast, companies without brand loyalty face a higher probability of their customers switching either to products which offer differentiated features that serve the same function (particularly if the substitute has a lower price) or to products that offer more features and perform more attractive functions. As such, they may be vulnerable to innovations from outside the industry that better satisfy customers' needs (e.g., Apple's iPod in the music industry).[86]

Competitive Risks of the Differentiation Strategy

One risk of the differentiation strategy is that customers might decide that the price differential between the differentiator's product and the cost leader's product is too large. In this instance, a firm may be offering differentiated features that exceed target customers' needs. The firm then becomes vulnerable to competitors that are able to offer customers a combination of features and price that is more consistent with their needs.

Another risk of the differentiation strategy is that a firm's means of differentiation may cease to provide value for which customers are willing to pay. A differentiated product becomes less valuable if imitation by rivals causes customers to perceive that competitors offer essentially the same goods or services, but at a lower price. This is the case, as illustrated

Apple vs. Samsung: Apple Differentiates and Samsung Imperfectly Imitates

In recent history Apple has been a product innovator and dominates the tech industry by creating new markets through first-mover advantage. This has been done with new concept products such the iPod, iPhone, and iPad products. Almost none of its high-tech rivals, such as Samsung, Nokia, BlackBerry, Google, Dell, and now Lenovo, have created whole new mobile product categories. However, more recently, Samsung has been a successful challenger of Apple's products. In fact, it has been so successful that Apple took Samsung to court with a lawsuit for patent infringement. Apple won the lawsuit with a nearly $1 billion judgment against Samsung. Samsung with its Android (created by Google) operating system appears to be a quick follower or imitator of Apple's differentiation strategy. Although Samsung's Galaxy S4 smartphone with a larger screen was a great success, the Galaxy S5 fell flat and allowed Apple iPhone 6 products to overtake the market share lead from Samsung.

However, Samsung itself has been challenged by low-end imitators of the smartphone product. One of these competitors is Xiaomi Inc., a privately owned smartphone producer in Beijing, China. Xiaomi's smartphone product has been wildly successful and popular in China because of its "fan base" network and online approach for selling low-end smartphones. A competitor of Xiaomi is Lenovo which recently purchased the Motorola mobility assets from Google. Xiaomi has been more successful than Lenovo. Lenovo CEO, Yang Yuanqing, has suggested, "the online model is disrupting the traditional model … we definitely need to address this." Xiaomi's fan club approach and online distribution channel has resulted in lower overhead and a pricing edge compared to traditional retail vendors. Although Apple outsold Xiaomi in the fourth quarter of 2014, Xiaomi was not too far behind. While Apple is seen as a differentiated "luxury product," there is enough quality in the Xiaomi product to challenge the market share of Apple. However, because the Galaxy S5 product was relatively less well received by consumers, Xiaomi has surpassed the sales of Samsung. Similarly, Micromax, a low-end smartphone producer in India, has overtaken Samsung in India by following Xiaomi's "copycat" strategy. As such, these low-end producers have provided relatively high quality products often sold through nontraditional channels (e.g., Xiaomi's fan club and online sales channel). They are also rapid second followers of Apple and have created a dilemma for Samsung.

In response to the very significant success of iPhone 6, as well as the significant success of low-end phones in large emerging economies, Samsung has recently introduced its Galaxy S6 products. Given the competition, Samsung Galaxy S6

phones have copied many of the features of the iPhone 6: high grade aluminum back and glass screen (Galaxy S5 had a plastic back) with smooth curved edges, embedded battery, and better finger print scanning. Samsung also focused on high quality apps, even reducing some of their own proprietary apps that were perceived to be of lower quality. They have also tried to

©D8nn/Shutterstock.com

The Xiaomi Note smartphone device picture here has help the company challenge Apple and Samsung products in China and other emerging markets due to its quality at a low price.

improve on the battery life compared to the iPhone 6 and have added wireless charging as an upgrade. The initial showing of these products suggests a strong upgrade and a fast response to the iPhone 6 success. It remains to be seen whether these products will allow it to regain its preeminence in the luxury market behind Apple. Samsung obviously has a lot riding on the success of these new products.

Additionally, it has also has come out with the Samsung Pay system similar to Apple Pay. However it has upped the ante on Apple Pay by being compatible with the equipment currently used by most stores. Apple Pay has been slow to be adopted by retailers because they need to pay switching costs for new equipment to process transactions through Apple Pay. It remains to be seen whether Samsung will be able to maintain its differentiation relative to Apple's luxury branded products and the challengers on the low end such as Xiaomi, Lenovo, and Micromax.

Sources: J. Cheng, 2015, Samsung unveils Galaxy S6 to answer iPhone 6, *Wall Street Journal*, www.wsj.com, March 1; E. Dou, 2015, Lenovo's smartphone challenge: Battling Apple, Xiaomi in China with Motorola, *Wall Street Journal*, www.wsj.com, February 4; A. Fitzpatrick, 2015, Apple might finally be beating Samsung

in smartphone sales, *Time*, www.time.com, February 3; R. Flannery, 2015, China's smartphone sensation Xiaomi says sells triple in '14: Eyes int'l growth, *Forbes*, www.forbes.com, January 3; V. Govindarajan & G. Bagla, 2015, Can Indians innovate in India?, *Business Today*, 24(4): 120–121; S. Grobart, 2015, Samsung's fancy new Galaxy S6 Edge phones, *Bloomberg BusinessWeek*, www.bloomberg.com, March 1; S. Y. Lee & H. T. Wolde, 2015, Samsung unveils sleek new Galaxy phones to battle Apple, *Reuters*, www.reuters.com, March 2; P. Olson, 2015, Apple's U.S. iPhone sells surpass Android for first time in years, *Forbes*, www.forbes.com, February 4; M. Reardon, 2015, Samsung answers Apple with curvy Galaxy S6 phones, Samsung Pay, *CNET*, www.cnet.com, March 1; T. Bajarin, 2014, How tiny tech firms are disrupting the giants, *PC Magazine*, December, 36–38. B. Einhorn, B. Shrivastava, & J. Lee, 2014, Samsung's China problems come to India, *Bloomberg BusinessWeek*, October 27, 44–45; D. Reisinger, 2014, Xiaomi sours while Samsung sinks in Gartner smartphone market study, *eWeek*, www.eweek.com, December 16.

in the Strategic Focus, where low-end smartphone producers, Xiaomi and Micromax in China and India, respectively, are having success competing against Samsung smartphones.[87] A third risk of the differentiation strategy is that experience can narrow customers' perceptions of the value of a product's differentiated features. For example, customers having positive experiences with generic tissues may decide that the differentiated features of the Kleenex product are not worth the extra cost. To counter this risk, firms must continue to meaningfully differentiate their product (e.g., through innovation) for customers at a price they are willing to pay.[88]

Counterfeiting is the differentiation strategy's fourth risk. Counterfeits are products which are labeled with a trademark or logo that is identical to or indistinguishable from a legal logo owned by another party, thus infringing the rights of the legal owner. When a consumer purchases such a product and discovers the deception, regret creates distrust of the branded product and reduces differentiation.[89] Companies such as Dell must take actions to deal with the problems counterfeit goods create for them when their rights are infringed upon.

4-3c Focus Strategies

The **focus strategy** is an integrated set of actions taken to produce goods or services that serve the needs of a particular competitive segment. Thus, firms use a focus strategy when they utilize their core competencies to serve the needs of a particular industry segment or niche to the exclusion of others. Examples of specific market segments that can be targeted by a focus strategy include

1. a particular buyer group (e.g., youths or senior citizens),
2. a different segment of a product line (e.g., products for professional painters or the do-it-yourself group), or
3. a different geographic market (e.g., northern or southern Italy by using a foreign subsidiary).[90]

There are many specific customer needs firms can serve by using a focus strategy. For example, Goya Foods, Inc. is the largest Hispanic-owned food company in the United States. Segmenting the Hispanic market into unique groups, Goya offers more than 2,200 products to consumers. The firm is a leading authority on Hispanic food and seeks "to be the premier source for authentic Latin cuisine."[91] By successfully using a focus strategy, firms such as Goya gain a competitive advantage in specific market niches or segments, even though they do not possess an industry-wide competitive advantage.

The **focus strategy** is an integrated set of actions taken to produce goods or services that serve the needs of a particular competitive segment.

Although the breadth of a target is clearly a matter of degree, the essence of the focus strategy "is the exploitation of a narrow target's differences from the balance of the industry."[92] Firms using the focus strategy intend to serve a particular segment of an industry more effectively than can industry-wide competitors. In fact, entrepreneurial firms commonly serve a specific market niche or segment, partly because they do not have the knowledge or resources to serve the broader market. In fact, they generally prefer to operate "below the radar" of larger and more resource rich firms that serve the broader market. They succeed when they effectively serve a segment whose unique needs are so specialized that broad-based competitors choose not to serve that segment or when they satisfy the needs of a segment being served poorly by industry-wide competitors.

Firms can create value for customers in specific and unique market segments by using the focused cost leadership strategy or the focused differentiation strategy.

Focused Cost Leadership Strategy

Based in Sweden, IKEA, a global furniture retailer with locations in 35 countries and territories and sales revenue of 28.7 billion euros in 2014, uses the focused cost leadership strategy. Young buyers desiring style at a low cost are IKEA's target customers.[93] For these customers, the firm offers home furnishings that combine good design, function, and acceptable quality with low prices. According to the firm, it seeks "to offer a wide range of well-designed, functional home furnishing products at prices so low that as many people as possible will be able to afford them."[94]

IKEA emphasizes several activities to keep its costs low. For example, instead of relying primarily on third-party manufacturers, the firm's engineers design low-cost, modular furniture ready for assembly by customers. To eliminate the need for sales associates or decorators, IKEA positions the products in its stores so that customers can view different living combinations (complete with sofas, chairs, tables, etc.) in a single room-like setting, which helps the customer imagine how furniture will look in their home. A third practice that helps keep IKEA's costs low traditionally has been to require customers to transport their own purchases rather than providing delivery service. However, for competitive reason, they have recently started to offer a low cost delivery service as an option.

Although it is a cost leader, IKEA also offers some differentiated features that appeal to its target customers, including its unique furniture designs, in-store playrooms for children, wheelchairs for customer use, and extended hours. Thus, IKEA's focused cost leadership strategy also includes some differentiated features with its low-cost products.

Focused Differentiation Strategy

Other firms implement the focused differentiation strategy. As noted earlier, there are many dimensions on which firms can differentiate their goods or services. For example, the new generation of food trucks populating cities such as Los Angeles use the focused differentiation strategy. They serve organic food crafted by highly trained chefs and well-known restaurateurs who own and operate many of these trucks. In fact, the Green Truck, headquartered in Los Angeles, demonstrates these characteristics. Moreover, the owners of these trucks often use Twitter and Facebook to inform customers of their locations as they move from point to point in their focal city.[95]

With a focus strategy, firms must be able to complete various primary value-chain activities and support functions in a competitively superior manner to develop and sustain a competitive advantage and earn above-average returns. The activities required to use the focused cost leadership strategy are virtually identical to those of the industry-wide cost leadership strategy (see Figure 4.2), and activities required to use the focused differentiation strategy are largely identical to those of the industry-wide differentiation strategy (see Figure 4.3). Similarly, the manner in which each of the two focus strategies allows a firm to deal successfully with the five competitive forces parallels those of the two broad strategies. The only difference is in the firm's competitive scope; the firm focuses on a narrow industry segment. Thus, Figures 4.2 and 4.3 and the text describing the five competitive forces also explain the relationship between each of the two focus strategies and competitive advantage. However, the competitive forces in a given industry often favor either a cost leadership or a differentiation strategy.[96]

Competitive Risks of Focus Strategies

With either focus strategy, the firm faces the same general risks as does the company using the cost leadership or the differentiation strategy on an industry-wide basis. However, focus strategies have three additional risks.

First, a competitor may be able to focus on a more narrowly defined competitive segment and thereby "out-focus" the focuser. This would happen to IKEA if another firm found a way to offer IKEA's customers (young buyers interested in stylish furniture at a low cost) additional sources of differentiation while charging the same price or to provide the same service with the same sources of differentiation at a lower price. Second, a company competing on an industry-wide basis may decide that the market segment served by the firm using a focus strategy is attractive and worthy of competitive pursuit.[97] For example, as noted in the Opening Case, Krogers, Safeway, and Walmart are seeking to compete with focused organic grocers Whole Foods and Trader Joe's. As a result, Whole Food's has lowered its prices on many items, increased its advertising, introduced more private brands, and is testing a loyalty program in order to compete more effectively. Co-CEO and founder, John Mackey, said, "Whole Foods Market is a very competitive company, and when we are challenged, when competition rears its head, we respond."[98] Its strategy has resulted in more customers coming to its stores, although in earlier stages of its response, it profit margins were eroding.

The third risk involved with a focus strategy is that the needs of customers within a narrow competitive segment may become more similar to those of industry-wide customers as a whole over time. As a result, the advantages of a focus strategy are either reduced or eliminated. As illustrated in the example in the Strategic Focus, the unique demand of do-it-yourself electronic dabblers that RadioShack traditionally focused on dissipated over time. RadioShack executives struggled over many years to find the right focus and made too many strategic changes over time, which ultimately lead to bankruptcy.

4-3d   Integrated Cost Leadership/Differentiation Strategy

Most consumers have high expectations when purchasing goods or services. In general, it seems that most consumers want to pay a low price for products with somewhat highly differentiated features. Because of these customer expectations, a number of firms engage in primary value-chain activities and support functions that allow them to simultaneously pursue low cost and differentiation.[99] Firms seeking to do this use the **integrated cost leadership/differentiation strategy** which involves engaging in primary value-chain activities and support functions that allow a firm to simultaneously pursue low cost and differentiation. The objective of using this strategy is to efficiently produce products with some differentiated features. Efficient production is the source of maintaining low costs, while differentiation is the source of creating unique value. Firms that successfully use the integrated cost leadership/differentiation strategy usually adapt quickly to new technologies and rapid changes in their external environments. Simultaneously concentrating on developing two sources of competitive advantage (cost and differentiation) increases the number of primary value-chain activities and support functions in which the firm must become competent. Such firms often have strong networks with external parties that perform some of the value-chain activities and/or support functions.[100] In turn, having skills in a larger number of activities and functions makes a firm more flexible.

The **integrated cost leadership/differentiation strategy** involves engaging in primary value-chain activities and support functions that allow a firm to simultaneously pursue low cost and differentiation.

Strategic **Focus**

RadioShack's Failed Focus Strategy: Strategic Flip-Flopping

RadioShack filed for bankruptcy in February 2015 after nearly a century of being a mainstay in American malls and on "Main Street" throughout the United States. Of course, one reason is that the business of selling electronic components products has been degraded by online sellers such as Amazon. RadioShack tried to avert bankruptcy by closing stores, but its finances deteriorated faster than expected. Because of the financial distress, it had turned to private equity for capital as it tried to turn around its poor performance, but the demands by these creditors increased the decline.

The real strategy difficulties, however, pertain to its efforts to pursue many different trends without a consistent underlying strategic approach. RadioShack was founded in Boston in 1921, 94 years prior to its bankruptcy. It flourished in the 1970s and 1980s by focusing on "electronic gadgetry." At first their strategy focused on ham radio enthusiasts. When Charles Tandy took over as CEO in 1963, the chain had been well established for decades with a focus on hobbyist and do-it-yourselfers. At the time, RadioShack eschewed national brands and sold private RadioShack brands including accessories, batteries, and a wide range of transistors and capacitors. All of these items could be heavily marked up. One could describe this as a focus differentiation strategy with an emphasis on electronic gadgets that the customers could improve through modifications and accessorizing. "The target audience was people who needed one piece of equipment every week," focusing on technologically oriented people with enthusiasm for RadioShack's products.

They also had a 100+ page catalogs filled with stuff like stylus', tape head demagnetizers, Realistic (RadioShack private brand) receivers and speakers, intercoms, and boomboxes. CB radios became another trend the RadioShack consumers followed, which became popular during the oil crisis in the early 1970s. When this trend slowed, they focused on personal computers. The TRS 80, one of the first mass-market personal computers, helped to replace the CB radio boom. This computer, with 16K of memory, used software designed by a "little known start-up named Microsoft." However as the computer business became commoditized and profit-margins decreased, RadioShack needed a new "anchor" product. They found it in cell phones.

In the 1990s, Radio-Shack opened a number of big box electronic stores, including Incredible Universe, Famous Brand Electronics, and Computer City. These were essentially "anti-RadioShacks." These RadioShack-owned brands were ultimately pillaged by large online sellers of electronic products and became an albatross for RadioShack even though the large volume of products sold allowed them to reach the peak revenue in 1996 ($6.3B). RadioShack was a specialty store. These large stores failed because, as CEO Leonard Roberts looking back lamented, "I don't think we knew how to operate those stores."

However, RadioShack was good at selling cell phones when they became popular. Their customers were intrigued but intimidated with this new product, and the salespeople could spend time helping them to pick the right product. However, signing someone up for a mobile phone contract took 45 minutes, and many stores were staffed for long stretches by a single employee. Their regular customers in search of the right small electronic component or accessory often left in frustration because they couldn't get the help needed because RadioShack employees were focused on selling cell phones. Likewise, RadioShack lost in e-commerce. They tried a ship-to-store model with RadioShack Unlimited, but RadioShack's executives never truly committed to e-commerce. In essence, because its differentiation focus

Paul Hawthorne/WireImage/Getty Images

It it early stages (this photo is from 2003), Radio Shack was very successful but it lost its focus as it tried too many different strategic approaches.

strategy on the hobbyist and electronic enthusiast was compromised by trying to focus on different trends and achieve growth, seemingly required by capital markets, RadioShack was never able to recover its focus and apply a consistent strategic approach.

Ultimately its technologically-oriented mainstay customers were offended and found other sources for their product purchases, mostly through online sources. In the end, RadioShack just wasn't getting the traffic needed to drive revenues, and its differentiation strategy failed.

Sources: J. Brustein, 2015, Inside RadioShack's collapse: How did the electronics retailer go broke? Gradually, then all at once, *Bloomberg Business*

Week, Feb 9–15, 54–59; L. Chen, 2015, Next RadioShack? Here are the most troubled retail stores. *Forbes*, February 10, 13; D. Fitzgerald & M. Jarzemsky, 2015, Beseiged RadioShack spirals into bankruptcy, *Wall Street Journal*, Feb 6, A1–A2; S. Grossman, 2015, John Oliver wants you to remember that one day we'll all be like RadioShack, *Time*, www.time.com, February 12; C. Mims, 2015, RadioShack suffers as free time evaporated, *Wall Street Journal*, Feb 9, B1, B6; P. Wahba, 2015, RadioShack pulls the plug and files for bankruptcy, *Fortune*, www.fortune.com, February 9.

Concentrating on the needs of its core customer group (e.g., higher-income, fashion-conscious discount shoppers), Target stores uses an integrated cost leadership/differentiation strategy as shown by its "Expect More. Pay Less." brand promise in its mission statement. It does this by seeking to provide convenience by a faster checkout, increased savings for quality products, and a dedicated team providing more personalized service.[101]

Often firms are "caught in the middle" because they do not differentiate effectively or provide the lowest-cost goods. JCPenney is a prime example of this failure. It attempted to integrate low cost (reducing pricing on most goods in the store) with differentiation (creating specialized stores for name-brand goods within each store). This strategy is very difficult to implement effectively. It could not compete with the low-cost leaders such as Walmart and Family Dollar stores, nor could it compete effectively with the more upscale and differentiated department stores, such as Target and Macy's. RadioShack (see the Strategic Focus) provides another example of a firm "caught in the middle" between maintain differentiation on electronic dabblers and seeking new growth trends such as selling cellphones to achieve low cost through volume.

Interestingly, most emerging market firms have competed using the cost leadership strategy. Their labor and other supply costs tend to be considerably lower than multinational firms based in developed countries. However, in recent years some of the emerging market firms are building their capabilities to produce innovation. Coupled with their capabilities to produce lower cost goods, they may be able to gain an advantage on large multinational firms. As such, some of the emerging market firms are beginning to use an integrated low cost and differentiation strategy.[102]

Flexibility is required for firms to complete primary value-chain activities and support functions in ways that allow them to use the integrated cost leadership/differentiation strategy in order to produce somewhat differentiated products at relatively low costs. Chinese auto manufacturers have developed a means of product design that provides a flexible architecture that allows low-cost manufacturing but also car designs that are differentiated from competitors.[103] Flexible manufacturing systems, information networks, and total quality management systems are three sources of flexibility that are particularly useful for firms trying to balance the objectives of continuous cost reductions and continuous enhancements to sources of differentiation as called for by the integrated strategy.

Flexible Manufacturing Systems

Using a flexible manufacturing system (FMS), the firm integrates human, physical, and information resources to create relatively differentiated products at relatively low costs. A significant technological advance, the FMS is a computer-controlled process used to produce a variety of products in moderate, flexible quantities with a minimum of manual intervention.[104] Automobile manufacturing in the Ford-Changan alliance in Chongqing

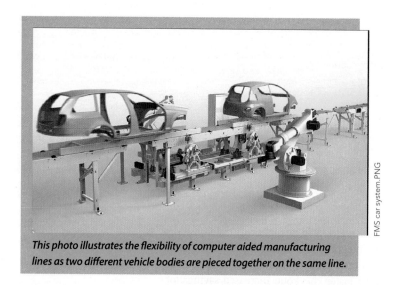

This photo illustrates the flexibility of computer aided manufacturing lines as two different vehicle bodies are pieced together on the same line.

shows the clear benefits of flexible production. As Yuan Fleng Xin, manufacturing engineering manager for the Changan Ford partnership, notes: "We can introduce new models within hours, simply by configuring the line for production of the next model, while still being able to produce the existing models during the introduction of new models ... This allows the phasing-in of new models, and the phasing-out of old models, directly driven by market demand and not by production capacity, lead time nor a need to wait for infrastructure build-up."[105] Often the flexibility is derived from modularization of the manufacturing process (and sometimes other value-chain activities as well).[106]

The goal of a FMS is to eliminate the "low cost versus product variety" trade-off that is inherent in traditional manufacturing technologies. Firms use a FMS to change quickly and easily from making one product to making another. Used properly, a FMS allows the firm to respond more effectively to changes in its customers' needs, while retaining low-cost advantages and consistent product quality. Because a FMS also enables the firm to reduce the lot size needed to manufacture a product efficiently, the firm's capacity to serve the unique needs of a narrow competitive scope is higher. In industries of all types, effective combinations of the firm's tangible assets (e.g., machines) and intangible assets (e.g., employee skills) facilitate implementation of complex competitive strategies, especially the integrated cost leadership/differentiation strategy.

Information Networks

By linking companies with their suppliers, distributors, and customers information networks provide another source of flexibility. These networks, when used effectively, help the firm satisfy customer expectations in terms of product quality and delivery speed.[107]

Earlier, we discussed the importance of managing the firm's relationships with its customers in order to understand their needs. Customer relationship management (CRM) is one form of an information-based network process that firms use for this purpose.[108] An effective CRM system provides a 360-degree view of the company's relationship with customers, encompassing all contact points, business processes, and communication media and sales channels. Salesforce.com is the largest provider of online customer relationship management, and it is moving to the cloud, allowing large database storage and access from multiple devices including smartphones.[109] The firm can use this information to determine the trade-offs its customers are willing to make between differentiated features and low cost—an assessment that is vital for companies using the integrated cost leadership/differentiation strategy. Managing supply chains through sophisticated information networks is also prominent in today's information-based society.[110] Such systems help firms to monitor their markets and stakeholders and allow them to better predict future scenarios. This capability helps firms to adjust their strategies to be better prepared for the future. Thus, to make comprehensive strategic decisions with effective knowledge of the organization's context, good information flow is essential. Better quality managerial decisions require accurate information on the firm's environment.

Total Quality Management Systems

Total quality management (TQM) is a managerial process that emphasizes an organization's commitment to the customer and to continuous improvement of all processes through problem-solving approaches based on empowerment of employees.[111] Firms develop and use TQM systems to

1. increase customer satisfaction,
2. cut costs, and
3. reduce the amount of time required to introduce innovative products to the marketplace.[112]

Firms able to simultaneously reduce costs while enhancing their ability to develop innovative products increase their flexibility, an outcome that is particularly helpful to firms implementing the integrated cost leadership/differentiation strategy. Exceeding customers' expectations regarding quality is a differentiating feature and eliminating process inefficiencies to cut costs allows the firm to offer that quality to customers at a relatively low price. Thus, an effective TQM system helps the firm develop the flexibility needed to identify opportunities to simultaneously increase differentiation and reduce costs. Research has found that TQM systems facilitate cost leadership strategies more effectively than they do differentiating strategies when the strategy is implemented alone.[113] However, it facilitates the potential synergy between the two strategies when they are integrated into one. TQM systems are available to all competitors so they may help firms maintain competitive parity, but alone they rarely lead to a competitive advantage.[114]

Competitive Risks of the Integrated Cost Leadership/Differentiation Strategy

The potential to earn above-average returns by successfully using the integrated cost leadership/differentiation strategy is appealing. However, it is a risky strategy because firms find it difficult to perform primary value-chain activities and support functions in ways that allow them to produce relatively inexpensive products with levels of differentiation that create value for the target customer. Moreover, to properly use this strategy across time, firms must be able to simultaneously reduce costs incurred to produce products (as required by the cost leadership strategy) while increasing product differentiation (as required by the differentiation strategy).

Firms that fail to perform the value-chain activities and support functions in an optimum manner become "stuck in the middle."[115] Being stuck in the middle means that the firm's cost structure is not low enough to allow it to attractively price its products and that its products are not sufficiently differentiated to create value for the target customer. This appears to be the problem experienced by JCPenney, at least as perceived by the customers. Its prices were not low enough and the differentiation not great enough to attract the customers needed. In fact, its declining sales suggest that it lost many of its current customers without attracting others to offset the loss. These firms will not earn above-average returns and will earn average returns only when the structure of the industry in which it competes is highly favorable.[116] Thus, companies implementing the integrated cost leadership/differentiation strategy must be able to produce (or offer) products that provide the target customer some differentiated features at a relatively low cost/price.

Firms can also become stuck in the middle when they fail to successfully implement *either* the cost leadership *or* the differentiation strategy. In other words, industry-wide competitors too can become stuck in the middle. Trying to use the integrated strategy is costly in that firms must pursue both low costs and differentiation.

Firms may need to form alliances with other companies to achieve differentiation, yet alliance partners may extract prices for the use of their resources that make it difficult

Total quality management (TQM) is a managerial process that emphasizes an organization's commitment to the customer and to continuous improvement of all processes through problem-solving approaches based on empowerment of employees.

to meaningfully reduce costs.[117] Firms may be motivated to make acquisitions to maintain their differentiation through innovation or to add products to their portfolio not offered by competitors.[118] Research suggests that firms using "pure strategies," either cost leadership or differentiation, often outperform firms attempting to use a "hybrid strategy" (i.e., integrated cost leadership/differentiation strategy). This research suggests the risky nature of using an integrated strategy.[119] However, the integrated strategy is becoming more common and perhaps necessary in many industries because of technological advances and global competition. This strategy often necessitates a long-term perspective to make it work effectively, and therefore requires dedicated owners that allow the implementation of a long-term strategy that can require several years to produce positive returns.[120]

SUMMARY

- A business-level strategy is an integrated and coordinated set of commitments and actions the firm uses to gain a competitive advantage by exploiting core competencies in specific product markets. Five business-level strategies (cost leadership, differentiation, focused cost leadership, focused differentiation, and integrated cost leadership/differentiation) are examined in the chapter.

- Customers are the foundation of successful business-level strategies. When considering customers, a firm simultaneously examines three issues: *who*, *what*, and *how*. These issues, respectively, refer to the customer groups to be served, the needs those customers have that the firm seeks to satisfy, and the core competencies the firm will use to satisfy customers' needs. Increasing segmentation of markets throughout the global economy creates opportunities for firms to identify more distinctive customer needs that they can serve with one of the business-level strategies.

- Firms seeking competitive advantage through the cost leadership strategy produce no-frills, standardized products for an industry's typical customer. However, these low-cost products must be offered with competitive levels of differentiation. Above-average returns are earned when firms continuously emphasize efficiency such that their costs are lower than those of their competitors, while providing customers with products that have acceptable levels of differentiated features.

- Competitive risks associated with the cost leadership strategy include (1) a loss of competitive advantage to newer technologies, (2) a failure to detect changes in customers' needs, and (3) the ability of competitors to imitate the cost leader's competitive advantage through their own distinct strategic actions.

- Through the differentiation strategy, firms provide customers with products that have different (and valued) features. Differentiated products must be sold at a cost that customers believe is competitive relative to the product's features as compared to the cost/feature combinations available from competitors' goods. Because of their distinctiveness,

differentiated goods or services are sold at a premium price. Products can be differentiated on any dimension that some customer group values. Firms using this strategy seek to differentiate their products from competitors' goods or services on as many dimensions as possible. The less similarity to competitors' products, the more buffered a firm is from competition with its rivals.

- Risks associated with the differentiation strategy include (1) a customer group's decision that the unique features provided by the differentiated product over the cost leader's goods or services are no longer worth a premium price, (2) the inability of a differentiated product to create the type of value for which customers are willing to pay a premium price, (3) the ability of competitors to provide customers with products that have features similar to those of the differentiated product, but at a lower cost, and (4) the threat of counterfeiting, whereby firms produce a cheap imitation of a differentiated good or service.

- Through the cost leadership and the differentiated focus strategies, firms serve the needs of a narrow market segment (e.g., a buyer group, product segment, or geographic area). This strategy is successful when firms have the core competencies required to provide value to a specialized market segment that exceeds the value available from firms serving customers across the total market (industry).

- The competitive risks of focus strategies include (1) a competitor's ability to use its core competencies to "out focus" the focuser by serving an even more narrowly defined market segment, (2) decisions by industry-wide competitors to focus on a customer group's specialized needs, and (3) a reduction in differences of the needs between customers in a narrow market segment and the industry-wide market.

- Firms using the integrated cost leadership/differentiation strategy strive to provide customers with relatively low-cost products that also have valued differentiated features. Flexibility is required for firms to learn how to use primary value-chain activities and support functions in ways that allow them to produce differentiated products at relatively low costs. This flexibility is facilitated by flexible manufacturing systems and improvements and interconnectedness in information systems within and between firms (buyers and suppliers). The primary risk of this strategy is that a firm might produce products that do not offer sufficient value in terms of either low cost or differentiation. In such cases, the company becomes "stuck in the middle." Firms stuck in the middle compete at a disadvantage and are unable to earn more than average returns.

KEY TERMS

business-level strategy 111
cost leadership strategy 118
differentiation strategy 122
focus strategy 127

integrated cost leadership/differentiation strategy 129
market segmentation 114
total quality management (TQM) 133

REVIEW QUESTIONS

1. What is a business-level strategy?

2. What is the relationship between a firm's customers and its business-level strategy in terms of *who, what,* and *how*? Why is this relationship important?

3. What are the differences among the cost leadership, differentiation, focused cost leadership, focused differentiation, and integrated cost leadership/differentiation business-level strategies?

4. How can each of the business-level strategies be used to position the firm relative to the five forces of competition in a way that helps the firm earn above-average returns?

5. What are the specific risks associated with using each business-level strategy?

Mini-Case

Is JCPenney Killing Itself with a Failed Strategy?

A few years ago, JCPenney was a traditional, low-end department store that appeared to be in a slow decline. Bill Ackman of Pershing Square Capital Management, a hedge fund investor, bought a large stake in the company and pushed to hire a new CEO, Ron Johnson. Johnson, who had successfully created the Apple retail store concept, was tasked with turning around the company's fortunes.

In January 2012, Johnson announced the new strategy for the company and rebranding of JCPenny. The strategy announced by Johnson entailed a remake of the JCPenny retail stores to create shops focused on specific brands such as Levi's, IZOD, and Liz Claiborne and types of goods such as home goods featuring Martha Stewart products within each store. Simultaneously, Johnson announced a new pricing system.

The old approach of offering special discounts throughout the year was eliminated in favor of a new customer-value pricing approach that reduced prices on goods across the board by as much as 40 percent. So, the price listed was the price to be paid without further discounts. The intent was to offer customers a "better deal" on all products as opposed to providing special, high discounts on selected products.

The intent was to build JCPenny into a higher-end (a little more upscale) retailer that provided good prices on branded merchandise (mostly clothes and home goods). These changes overlooked the firm's current customers; JCPenny began competing for customers who normally shopped at Target, Macy's, and Nordstrom, to name a few of its competitors. Unfortunately, the first year of this new strategy appeared it to be a failure. Total sales in 2012 were \$4.28 billion less than in 2011, and the firm's stock price declined by 55 percent. Interestingly, its Internet sales declined by 34 percent compared to an increase of 48 percent for its new rival, Macy's. All of this translated into a net loss for the year of slightly less than \$1 billion for JCPenny.

It seems that the new executive team at JCPenny thought that they could retain their current customer base (perhaps with the value pricing across the board), while attracting new customers with the new "store-within-a-store" concept. According to Roger Martin, a former executive, strategy expert, and current Dean at the University of Toronto, "… the new JCPenney is competing against and absolutely slaughtering an important competitor, and it's called the old J.C. Penney." Only about one-third of the stores had been converted to the new approach when the company began to heavily promote the concept. Its new store sales produced increases in sales per square foot, but the old stores' sales per square foot markedly declined. It appears that Penney was not attracting customers from its rivals but rather cannibalizing customers from its old stores. According to Martin the new CEO likely understands a lot about capital markets but does not know how to satisfy customers and gain a competitive advantage. Additionally, the former CEO of JCPenney, Allen Questrom, described Johnson as having several capabilities (e.g., intelligent, strong communicator) but believes that he and his executive team made a major strategic error and was especially insensitive to the JCPenny customer base.

The question now is whether the company can survive such a major decline in sales and stock price. In 2013, it announced the layoff of approximately 2,200 employees to reduce costs. In addition, CEO Johnson announced that he was reinstituting selected discounts in pricing and offering comparative pricing on products (relative prices with rivals). The good news is that transformed stores are obtaining sales of \$269 per square foot, whereas the older stores are producing \$134 per square foot. Will Johnson's strategy survive long enough for all of the stores to be converted and save the company? The answer is probably not, because Johnson was fired by the JCPenny board of directors on April 8, 2013, about 1.5 years after he assumed the CEO position.

Sources: P. Wahba, 2015, J.C. Penney still blaming Ron Johnson-era for slow profit growth *Fortune*, www.fortune.com, March; N. Tichy, 2014, J.C. Penney and the terrible costs of hiring an outsider CEO, *Fortune*, www.fortune.com, November 13; J. Reingold, A. Sloan, & D. Burke, 2013, When Wall Street wears the pants, *Fortune*, April 8, 74–81; S. Schaefer, 2013, Ron Johnson out as JCPenney chief, *Forbes*, www.forbes.com, April 8; M. Nisen, 2013, Former JC Penney CEO says Ron Johnson is 'a very nice man' who will probably fail, *Yahoo! Finance*, finance.yahoo.com, accessed April 6; B. Byrnes, 2013, How J.C. Penney is killing itself, *The Motley Fool*, www.fool.com, March 31; B. Jopson, 2013, JC Penney cuts 2,200 jobs as retailer struggles, *Financial Times*, www.ft.com, March 8; J. Macke, 2013, J.C. Penney's last shot at survival, *Yahoo! Finance*, finance. yahoo.com, accessed March 1; S. Clifford, 2013, Chief talks of mistakes and big loss at JC Penney, *New York Times*, www.nytimes.com, February 27; M. Halkias, 2013, J.C. Penney CEO Ron Johnson says changes will return retailer to growth, *Dallas Morning news*, www.dallasnews.com, February 9; They're back: JCPenney adds sales, 2013, *USA Today*, www. usatoday.com, January 28; A. R. Sorkin, 2012, A dose of realism for the chief of J.C. Penney, *New York Times DealB%k*, dealbook.nytimes.com, November 12.

Case Discussion Questions

1. What strategy was the new CEO at JCPenney seeking to implement given the generic strategies found in Chapter 4?

2. What was the result of change in strategy implemented?

3. Why was this strategy a disaster for JCPenney?

4. What does it mean to be "stuck in the middle" between two strategies (i.e., between low cost and differentiation strategies)?

NOTES

1. J. Garcia-Sanchez, L. F. Mesquita, & R. S. Vassolo, 2014, What doesn't kill you makes you stronger: The evolution of competition and entry-order advantages in economically turbulent contexts, *Strategic Management Journal*, 35: 1972–1992; H. Greve, 2009, Bigger and safer: The diffusion of competitive advantage, *Strategic Management Journal*, 30: 1–23.

2. O. Schilke, 2014, On the contingent value of dynamic capabilities for competitive advantage: The nonlinear moderating effect of environmental dynamism, *Strategic Management Journal*, 35: 179–203; M. A. Delmas & M. W. Toffel, 2008, Organizational responses to environmental demands: Opening the black box, *Strategic Management Journal*, 29: 1027–1055.

3. M. E. Porter & J. E. Heppelmann, 2014, How smart, connected products are transforming competition, *Harvard Business Review*, 92(11): 64–88; M. G. Jacobides, S. G. Winter, & S. M. Kassberger, 2012, The dynamics of wealth, profit, and sustainable advantage, *Strategic Management Journal*, 33: 1384–1410.

4. A. Gasparro, 2015, Indigestion hits food giants, *Wall Street Journal*, February 13, B1.

5. F. F. Suarez, S. Grodal, & A. Gotsopoulos, 2015, Perfect timing? Dominant category, dominant design, and the window of opportunity for firm entry, *Strategic Management Journal*, 36: 437–448; J. Schmidt & T. Keil, 2013, What makes a resource valuable? Identifying the drivers of firm-idiosyncratic resource value, *Academy of Management Review*, 38: 208–228; C. Zott & R. Amit, 2008, The fit between product market strategy and business model: Implications for firm performance, *Strategic Management Journal*, 29: 1–26.

6. S. E. Reid & U. Brentani, 2015, Building a measurement model for market visioning competence and its proposed antecedents: Organizational encouragement of divergent thinking, divergent thinking attitudes, and ideational behavior, *Journal of Product Innovation Management*, 32: 243–262; S. Kaplan, 2008, Framing contests: Strategy making under uncertainty, *Organization Science*, 19: 729–752.

7. J. R. Lecuona & M. Reitzig, 2014, Knowledge worth having in 'excess': The value of tacit and firm-specific human resource slack. *Strategic Management Journal*, 35: 954–973; L. A. Costa, K. Cool, & I. Dierickx, 2013, The competitive implications of the deployment of unique resources, *Strategic Management Journal*, 34: 445–463; K. Shimizu & M. A. Hitt, 2004, Strategic flexibility: Organizational preparedness to reverse ineffective strategic decisions, *Academy of Management Executive*, 18: 44–59.

8. C. Eesley, D. H. Hsu, & E. B. Roberts, 2014, The contingent effects of top management teams on venture performance: Aligning founding team composition with innovation strategy and commercialization environment, *Strategic Management Journal*, 35: 1798–1817; J. A. Lamberg, H. Tikkanen, T. Nokelainen, & H. Suur-Inkeroinen, 2009, Competitive dynamics, strategic consistency, and organizational survival, *Strategic Management Journal*, 30: 45–60.

9. R. Kapoor & N. R. Furr, 2015, Complementarities and competition: Unpacking the drivers of entrants' technology choices in the solar photovoltaic industry, *Strategic Management Journal*, 36: 416–436; I. Goll, N. B. Johnson, & A. A. Rasheed, 2008, Top management team demographic characteristics, business strategy, and firm performance in the U.S. airline industry: The role of managerial discretion, *Management Decision*, 46: 201–222.

10. S. L. Fourné, J. P. Jansen, & T. M. Mom, 2014, Strategic agility in MNEs: Managing tensions to capture opportunities across emerging and established markets, *California Management Review*, 56(3): 13–38; J. W. Spencer, 2008, The impact of multinational enterprise strategy on indigenous enterprises: Horizontal spillovers and crowding out in developing countries, *Academy of Management Review*, 33: 341–361.

11. D. Gallagher, 2015, King not yet fit to wear a crown, *Wall Street Journal*, Feb 14–15, B14.

12. R. E. Hoskisson, M. A. Hitt, R. D. Ireland, & J. S. Harrison, 2013, *Competing for Advantage*, Mason, OH: Cengage Learning.

13. M. Subramony & S. D. Pugh, 2015, Services management research: Review, integration, and future directions, *Journal of Management*, 41: 349–373; R. J. Harrington & A. K. Tjan, 2008, Transforming strategy one customer at a time, *Harvard Business Review*, 86(3): 62–72.

14. M. J. Mol & C. Brewster, 2014, The outsourcing strategy of local and multinational firms: A supply base perspective, *Global Strategy Journal*, 4: 20–34; K. R. Fabrizio & L. G. Thomas, 2012, The impact of local demand on innovation in a global industry, *Strategic Management Journal*, 33: 42–64.

15. M. E. Porter, 1980, *Competitive Strategy*, New York: Free Press.

16. J. Calandro Jr., 2015, A leader's guide to strategic risk management, *Strategy & Leadership*, 43: 26–35; M. Baghai, S. Smit, & P. Viguerie, 2009, Is your growth strategy flying blind?, *Harvard Business Review*, 87(5): 86–96.

17. I. Le Breton-Miller & D. Miller, 2015, The paradox of resource vulnerability: Considerations for organizational curatorship, *Strategic Management Journal*, 36(3): 397–415; D. G. Sirmon, S. Gove, & M. A. Hitt, 2008, Resource management in dyadic competitive rivalry: The effects of resource bundling and deployment, *Academy of Management Journal*, 51: 919–935.

18. L. A. Bettencourt, R. F. Lusch, & S. L. Vargo, 2014, A service lens on value creation: Marketing's role in achieving strategic advantage, *California Management Review*, 57(1): 44–66.

19. F. J. Gouillart, 2014, The race to implement co-creation of value with stakeholders: Five approaches to competitive advantage, *Strategy & Leadership*, 42: 2–8.

20. L. A. Bettencourt, C. P. Blocker, M. B. Houston, & D. J. Flint, 2015, Rethinking customer relationships, *Business Horizons*, 58: 99–108; P. E. Frown & A. F. Payne, 2009, Customer relationship management: A strategic perspective, *Journal of Business Market Management*, 3: 7–27.

21. M. Ritson, 2014, Amazon has seen the future of predictability, *Marketing Week*, January 23, 10; H. Green, 2009, How Amazon aims to keep you clicking, *BusinessWeek*, March 2: 34–35.

22. S. Ramachandran & T. Stynes, 2015, Netflix steps up foreign expansion: Subscriber editions top streaming service's forecast, helped by growth in markets abroad, *Wall Street Journal*, www.wsj.com, January 21.

23. R. Parmar, I. Mackenzie, D. Cohn, & D. Gann, 2014, The new patterns of innovation, *Harvard Business Review*, 92(1/2): 86–95; M. Bogers, A. Afuah, & B. Bastian, 2010, Users as innovators: A review, critique and future research directions, *Journal of Management*, 36: 857–875.

24. D. Yagil & H. Medler-Liraz, 2013, Moments of truth: Examining transient authenticity and identity in service encounters. *Academy of Management Journal*, 56: 473–497.

25. A. S. Balaji & B. C. Krishnan, 2015, How customers cope with service failure? A study of brand reputation and customer satisfaction, *Journal of Business Research*, 68: 665–674; L-Y Jin, 2010, Determinants of customers' complaint intention, *Nankai Business Review International*, 1: 87–99.

26. R. Mortimer, 2014, The creation of a chief customer officer role at Tesco signals a quiet revolution in marketing thinking, *Marketing Week*, June 6, 3.

27. P. Skålén, J. Gummerus, C. Koskull, & P. Magnusson, 2015, Exploring value propositions and service innovation: A service-dominant logic study, *Journal of the Academy of Marketing Science*, 43: 137–158; M. Dixon, E. V. Karniouchina, B. D. Rhee, R. Verma, & L. Victorino, 2014, The role of coordinated marketing-operations strategy in services: Implications for managerial decisions and execution, *Journal of Service Management*, 25: 275–294; S. F. Slater, E. M. Olson, & G. T. Hult, 2010, Worried about strategy implementation? Don't overlook marketing's role, *Business Horizons*, 53: 469–479.

28. S. Han, Y. Ye, X. Fu, & Z. Chen, 2014, Category role aided market segmentation approach to convenience store chain category management, *Decision Support Systems*, 57: 296–308; P. Riefler, A. Diamantopoulos, & J. A. Siguaw, 2012, Cosmopolitan consumers as a target group for segmentation, *Journal of International Business Studies*, 43: 285–305.

29. 2015, About Hill's pet nutrition, Hill's Pet Nutrition, www.hillspet.com, February 23.

30. H. B. Corrigan, G. Craciun, & A. M. Powell, 2014, How does Target know so much about its customers? Utilizing customer analytics to make marketing decisions, *Marketing Education Review*, 24(2): 159–166.

31. J. Jargon, 2014, Millennials lose taste for McDonald's, *Wall Street Journal*, August 25, B1.

32. A. S. Sengupta, M. Balaji, & B. C. Krishnan, 2015, How customers cope with service failure? A study of brand reputation and customer satisfaction, *Journal of Business Research*, 68: 665–674; C. A. Funk, J. D. Arthurs, L. J. Trevino, & J. Joireman, 2010, Consumer animosity in the global value chain: The effect of international shifts on willingness to purchase hybrid products. *Journal of International Business Studies*, 41: 639–651.

33. Schilke, On the contingent value of dynamic capabilities for competitive advantage; P. J. Holahan, Z. Z. Sullivan, & S. K. Markham, 2014, Product development as core competence: How formal product

development practices differ for radical, more innovative, and incremental product innovations, *Journal of Product Innovation Management*, 31: 329–345.

34. D. J. Teece, 2014, The foundations of enterprise performance: Dynamic and ordinary capabilities in an (economic) theory of firms, *Academy of Management Perspectives*, 28: 328–352; D. J. Teece, 2012, Dynamic capabilities: Routines versus entrepreneurial action, *Journal of Management Studies*, 49: 1395–1401; P. L. Drnevich & A. P. Kriauciunas, 2011, Clarifying the conditions and limits of the contributions of ordinary and dynamic capabilities to relative firm performance, *Strategic Management Journal*, 32: 254–279.

35. R. Mudambi & T. Swift, 2014, Knowing when to leap: Transitioning between exploitative and explorative R&D, *Strategic Management Journal*, 35: 126–145; M. Gruber, F. Heinimann, M. Brietel, & S. Hungeling, 2010, Configurations of resources and capabilities and their performance implications: An exploratory study on technology ventures, *Strategic Management Journal*, 31: 1337–1356.

36. J. Haas, 2014, Focus on the core: Merck claims R&D restructuring poised to produce results, *In Vivo*, 32: 6–8.

37. 2015, About SAS, www.sas.com, February 24.

38. WWD: Women's Wear Daily, 2014, Change agents set the agenda, *WWD: Women's Wear Daily*, May 23, 8–10.

39. M. E. Porter, 1985, *Competitive Advantage*, New York: Free Press, 26.

40. R. Rumelt, 2011, *Good Strategy/Bad Strategy*, New York: Crown Business.

41. M. E. Porter, 1996, What is strategy?, *Harvard Business Review*, 74(6): 61–78.

42. Porter, What is strategy?

43. A. Agnihotri, 2014, The role of the upper echelon in the value chain management, *Competitiveness Review*, 24: 240–255; J. S. Srai & L. S. Alinaghian, 2013, Value chain reconfiguration in highly disaggregated industrial systems: Examining the emergence of health care diagnostics, *Global Strategy Journal*, 3: 88–108.

44. M. E. Porter, 1994, Toward a dynamic theory of strategy. In R. P. Rumelt, D. E. Schendel, & D. J. Teece (eds.), *Fundamental Issues in Strategy*. Boston: Harvard Business School Press: 423–461.

45. Porter, What is strategy?, 62.

46. Porter, *Competitive Advantage*, 15.

47. J. Block, K. Kohn, D. Miller, & K. Ullrich, 2015, Necessity entrepreneurship and competitive strategy, *Small Business Economics*, 44: 37–54; J. Gonzales-Benito & I. Suarez-Gonzalez, 2010, A study of the role played by manufacturing strategic objectives and capabilities in understanding the relationship between Porter's generic strategies and business performance, *British Journal of Management*, 21: 1027–1043.

48. Schilke, On the contingent value of dynamic capabilities for competitive advantage: The nonlinear moderating effect of environmental dynamism; Hoskisson, Ireland, Hitt, & Harrison, *Competing for Advantage*.

49. Porter, *Competitive Strategy*, 35–40.

50. B. Berman, 2015, How to compete effectively against low-cost competitors, *Business Horizons*, 58: 87–97; P. D. Orberg Jensen & B. Petersen, 2013, Global sourcing of services: Risk, process, and collaborative architecture, *Global Strategy Journal*, 3: 67–87; C. Weigelt, 2013, Leveraging supplier capabilities: The role of locus of capability deployment, *Strategic Management Journal*, 34: 1–21.

51. K. Grind, 2015, Vanguard problem riddles Fidelity, *Wall Street Journal*, Feb 13, C2.

52. J.-K. Park & Y. K. Ro, 2013, Product architectures and sourcing decisions: Their impact on performance, *Journal of Management*, 39: 814–846; M. Kotabe & R. Mudambi, 2009, Global sourcing and value creation: Opportunities and challenges, *Journal of International Management*, 15: 121–125.

53. S. Carnahan & D. Somaya, 2013, Alumni effects and relational advantage: The impact on outsourcing when a buyer hires employees from a supplier's competitors, *Academy of Management Journal*, 56: 1578–1600; R. Liu, D. J. Feils, & B. Scholnick, 2011, Why are different services outsources to different countries?, *Journal of International Business Studies*, 42: 558–571.

54. M. J. Lennox, S. F. Rockart, & A. Y. Lewin, 2010, Does interdependency affect firm and industry profitability? An empirical test, *Strategic Management Journal*, 31: 121–139.

55. 2015, Company overview, Big Lots, www.biglots.com, February 25.

56. A. Hinterhuber & S. M. Liozu, 2014, Is innovation in pricing your next source of competitive advantage?, *Business Horizons*, 57: 413–423; J. Morehouse, B. O'Mera, C. Hagen, & T. Huseby, 2008, Hitting back: Strategic responses to low-cost rivals, *Strategy & Leadership*, 36: 4–13.

57. J. Alcácer, C. L. Dezső, & M. Zhao, 2013, Firm rivalry, knowledge accumulation, and MNE location choices, *Journal of International Business Studies*, 44: 504–520; G. J. Kilduff, H. A. Elfenbein, & B. W. Staw, 2010, The psychology of rivalry: A relationally dependent analysis of competition, *Academy of Management Journal*, 53: 943–969.

58. S. D. Pathak, Z. Wu, & D, Johnston, D. 2014, Toward a structural view of co-opetition in supply networks, *Journal of Operations Management*, 32: 254–267; T. W. Tong & J. J. Reuer, 2010, Competitive consequences of interfirm collaboration: How joint ventures shape industry profitability, *Journal of International Business Studies*, 41: 1056–1073.

59. Y. Luo, Y. Huang, & S. L. Wang, 2011, Guanxi and organizational performance: A meta-analysis, *Management and Organization Review*, 8: 139–172.

60. G. Bhalla, 2014, How to plan and manage a project to co-create value with stakeholders, *Strategy & Leadership*, 42: 19–25; O. D. Fjeldstad & A. Sasson, 2010, Membership matters: On the value of being embedded in customer networks, *Journal of Management Studies*, 47: 944–966.

61. 2015, Our story, http://corporate.walmart.com, accessed February 25.

62. F. J. Contractor, V. Kumar, S. K. Kundu, & T. Pedersen, 2010, Reconceptualizing the firm in a world of outsourcing and offshoring: The organizational and geographical relocation of high-value company functions. *Journal of Management Studies*, 47: 1417–1433.

63. Y. Zhang & J. Gimeno, 2010, Earnings pressure and competitive behavior: Evidence from the U.S. electricity industry, *Academy of Management Journal*, 53: 743–768.

64. Heppelmann & Porter, How smart, connected products are transforming competition.

65. M. M. Larsen, S. Manning, & T. Pedersen, 2013, Uncovering the hidden costs of offshoring: The interplay of complexity, organizational design, and experience, *Strategic Management Journal*, 34: 533–552.

66. S. Chang & B. Wu, 2014, Institutional barriers and industry dynamics, *Strategic Management Journal*, 35: 1103–1123; Heppelmann & Porter, How smart, connected products are transforming competition; T. J. Kull, S. C. Ellis, & R. Narasimhan, 2013, Reducing behavioral constraints to supplier integration: A socio-technical systems perspective, *Journal of Supply Chain Management*, 49: 64–86; J. Dyer & W. Chu, 2011, The determinants of trust in supplier-automaker relations in the U.S., Japan and Korea: A retrospective, *Journal of International Business Studies*, 42: 28–34.

67. Heppelmann & Porter, How smart, connected products are transforming competition; O. Ormanidhi & O. Stringa, 2008, Porter's model of generic competitive strategies, *Business Economics*, 43: 55–64; J. Bercovitz & W. Mitchell, 2007, When is more better? The impact of business scale and scope on long-term business survival, while controlling for profitability, *Strategic Management Journal*, 28: 61–79.

68. Heppelmann & Porter, How smart, connected products are transforming competition; A. Kaul, 2012, Technology and corporate scope: Firm and rival innovation as antecedents of corporate transactions, *Strategic Management Journal*, 33: 347–367; K. Z. Zhou & F. Wu, 2010, Technological capability, strategic flexibility and product innovation, *Strategic Management Journal*, 31: 547–561.

69. Porter, *Competitive Strategy*, 35–40.

70. 2015, Product innovation, www.1000ventures.com, March 5.

71. H. Ryu, J. Lee, & B. Choi, 2015, Alignment between service innovation strategy and business strategy and its effect on firm performance: An empirical investigation, *IEEE Transactions on Engineering Management*, 62: 100–113; C. A. Siren, M. Kohtamaki, & A. Kuckertz, 2012, Exploration and exploitation strategies, profit performance and the mediating role of strategic learning: Escaping the exploitation trap, *Strategic Entrepreneurship Journal*, 6: 18–41.

72. M. Terpstra & F. H. Verbeeten, 2014, Customer satisfaction: Cost driver or value driver? Empirical evidence from the financial services industry, *European Management Journal*, 32: 499–508; U. Lichtenthaler & H. Ernst, 2012, Integrated knowledge exploitation: The complementarity of product development and technology licensing, *Strategic Management Journal*, 33: 513–534.

73. K. Rahman & C. S. Areni, 2014, Generic, genuine, or completely new? Branding strategies to leverage new products. *Journal of Strategic Marketing*, 22: 3–15; R. Kotha, Y. Zheng, & G. George, 2011, Entry into new niches: The effects of firm age and the expansion of technological capabilities on innovative output and impact, *Strategic Management Journal*, 32: 1011–1024.

74. M. J. Donate, & J. D. Sánchez de Pablo, 2015, The role of knowledge-oriented leadership in knowledge management practices and innovation, *Journal of Business Research*, 68: 360–370; J. T. Macher & C. Boerner, 2012, Technological development at the boundaries of the firm: A knowledge-based examination in drug development, *Strategic Management Journal*, 33: 1016–1036.

75. R. Kapoor & J. M. Lee, 2013, Coordinating and competing in ecosystems: How organizational forms shape new technology investments, *Strategic Management Journal*, 34: 274–296; F. T. Rothaermel, M. A. Hitt, & L. A. Jobe, 2006, Balancing vertical integration and strategic outsourcing: Effects on product portfolio, product success and firm performance, *Strategic Management Journal*, 27: 1033–1056.

76. Kapoor & Furr, 2015, Complementarities and competition: Unpacking the drivers of entrants' technology choices in the solar photovoltaic industry; D. Somaya, 2012, Patent strategy and management: An integrative review and research agenda, *Journal of Management*, 38: 1084–1114.

77. S. Germano, 2015, UnderArmour grows online, *Wall Street Journal*, Feb 5, B3.

78. Bettencourt, Lusch, & Vargo, A service lens on value creation; N. E. Levitas & T. Chi, 2010, A look at the value creation effects of patenting and capital investment through a real-option lens: The moderation role of uncertainty, *Strategic Entrepreneurship Journal*, 4: 212–233; L. A. Bettencourt & A. W. Ulwick, 2008, The customer-centered innovation map, *Harvard Business Review*, 86(5): 109–114.

79. R. Simons, 2014, Choosing the right customer. *Harvard Business Review*, 92(3): 48–55; M. Abbott, R. Holland, J. Giacomin, & J. Shackleton, 2009, Changing affective content in brand and product attributes, *Journal of Product & Brand Management*, 18: 17–26.

80. H. E. Posen, J. Lee, & S. Yi, 2013, The power of imperfect imitation, *Strategic Management Journal*, 34: 149–164.

81. Y. Mishina, E. S. Block, & M. J. Mannor, 2015, The path dependence of organizational reputation: How social judgment influences assessments of capability and character, *Strategic Management Journal*, forthcoming; B. K. Boyd, D. D. Bergh, & D. J. Ketchen, 2010, Reconsidering the reputation-performance relationship: A resource-based view, *Journal of Management*, 36: 588–609.

82. D. Laureiro-Martínez, S. Brusoni, N. Canessa, & M. Zollo, 2015, Understanding the exploration-exploitation dilemma: An fMRI study of attention control and decision-making performance, *Strategic Management Journal*, 36, 319–338; R. Mudambi & T. Swift, 2013, Knowing when to leap: Transitioning between exploitative and explorative R&R, *Strategic Management Journal*, in press.

83. S. Wilkins & J. Huisman, 2014, Corporate images' impact on consumers' product choices: The case of multinational foreign subsidiaries, *Journal of Business Research*, 67: 2224–2230; O. Chatain, 2011, Value creation, competition and performance in buyer-supplier relationships, *Strategic Management Journal*, 32: 76–102.

84. A. Marinez-Noya, E. Garcia-Canal, & M. F. Guillen, 2013, R&D outsourcing and the effectiveness of intangible investments: Is proprietary core knowledge walking out the door?, *Journal of Management Studies*, 5: 67–91.

85. Heppelmann & Porter, How smart, connected products are transforming competition; J. W. Upson, S. J. Ketchen, B. L. Connelly, & A. L. Ranft, 2012, Competitor analysis and foothold moves, *Academy of Management Journal*, 55: 93–110.

86. J. Harvey, P. Cohendet, L Simon, & S. Borzillo, 2015, Knowing communities in the front end of innovation, *Research Technology Management*, 58: 46–54; S. Anokhin & J. Wincent, 2012, Start-up rates and innovation: A cross-country examination, *Journal of International Business Studies*, 43: 41–60.

87. T. Bajarin, 2014, How tiny tech firms are disrupting the giants, *PC Magazine*, December, 36–38. B. Einhorn, B. Shrivastava, & J. Lee, 2014, Samsung's China problems come to India, *Bloomberg BusinessWeek*, October 27, 44–45.

88. J. West & M. Bogers, 2014, Leveraging external sources of innovation: A review of research on open innovation, *Journal of Product Innovation Management*, 31: 814–831; M. M. Crossan & M. Apaydin, 2010, A multi-dimensional framework of organizational innovation: A systematic review of the literature, *Journal of Management Studies*, 47: 1154–1180.

89. J. Chen, L. Teng, L., S. Liu, & H. Zhu, 2015, Anticipating regret and consumers' preferences for counterfeit luxury products, *Journal of Business Research*, 68: 507–515; X. Bian & L. Moutinho, 2009, An investigation of determinants of counterfeit purchase consideration, *Journal of Business Research*, 62: 368–378.

90. Porter, *Competitive Strategy*; M. Selove, 2014, How do firms become different? A dynamic model, *Management Science*, 60: 980–989.

91. 2015, About Goya foods, www.goyafoods. com, March 3.

92. Porter, *Competitive Advantage*, 15.

93. J. Mcintosh, 2015, IKEA profits flat in fiscal 2014. *Furniture/Today*, February 2, 47; K. Kling & I. Goteman, 2003, IKEA CEO Andres Dahlvig on international growth and IKEA's unique corporate culture and brand identity, *Academy of Management Executive*, 17: 31–37.

94. 2015, About IKEA, IKEA, www.ikea.com, March 3.

95. 2015, about Green Truck, www. greentruckonthego.com; March 3; A. Kadet, 2015, City news–metro money: Wheelin' and dealin' from a truck, *Wall Street Journal*, www.wsj.com, February 28. K. McLaughlin, 2009, Food truck nation, *Wall Street Journal*, www.wsj.com, June 5.

96. A. Barroso & M. S. Giarratana, 2013, Product proliferation strategies and firm performance: The moderating role of product space complexity, *Strategic Management Journal*, 34: 1435–1452.

97. C. E. Armstrong, 2012, Small retailer strategies for battling the big boxes: A "Goliath" victory?, *Journal of Strategy and Management*, 5: 41–56.

98. A. Gasparro & T. Stynes, 2015, Whole Foods benefits from increase in customers, *Wall Street Journal*, February 12, B4.

99. R. D. Banker, R. Mashruwala, & A. Tripathy, 2014, Does a differentiation strategy lead to more sustainable financial performance than a cost leadership strategy?, *Management Decision*, 56: 872–896; C. L. Hill, 1988, Differentiation versus low cost or differentiation and low cost: A contingency framework, *Academy of Management Review*, 13: 401–412.

100. C. Cennamo & J. Santalo, 2013, Platform competition: Strategic trade-offs in platform markets, *Strategic Management Journal*, 34: 1331–1350; H. A. Ndofor, D. G. Sirmon, & X. He, 2011, Firm resources, competitive actions and performance: Investigating a mediated model with evidence from the in-vitro diagnostics

industry, *Strategic Management Journal*, 32: 640–657; R. A. D'Aveni, G. B. Dagnino, & K. G. Smith, 2010, The age of temporary advantage, *Strategic Management Journal*, 31: 1371–1385.

101. 2015, Mission and Value, www.target.com, March 5.

102. S. Awate, M. M. Larsen, & R. Mudambi, 2015, Accessing vs sourcing knowledge: A comparative study of R&D internationalization between emerging and advanced economy firms, *Journal of International Business Studies*, 46: 63–86; E. R. Brenes, D. Montoya, & L. Ciravegna, 2014, Differentiation strategies in emerging markets: The case of Latin American agribusinesses, *Journal of Business Research*, 67: 847–855; G. A. Shinkle, A. P. Kriauciunas, & G. Hundley, 2013, Why pure strategies may be wrong for transition economy firms, *Strategic Management Journal*, 34: 1244–1254.

103. C. Eckel, L. Iacovone, B. Javorcik, & J. P. Neary, 2015, Multi-product firms at home and away: Cost-versus quality-based competence, *Journal of International Economics*, 95: 216–232; H. Wang & C. Kimble, 2010, Low-cost strategy through product architecture: Lessons from China, *Journal of Business Strategy*, 31(3): 12–20.

104. M. I. M. Wahab, D. Wu, and C.-G. Lee, 2008, A generic approach to measuring the machine flexibility of manufacturing systems, *European Journal of Operational Research*, 186: 137–149.

105. 2014, Rethinking car assembly, *Automotive Manufacturing Solutions*, November, 2–3.

106. A. Furlan, A. Cabigiosu, & A. Camuffo, 2014, When the mirror gets misted up: Modularity and technological change, *Strategic Management Journal*, 35, 789–807; M. Kotabe, R. Parente, & J. Y. Murray, 2007, Antecedents and outcomes of modular production in the Brazilian automobile industry: A grounded theory approach, *Journal of International Business Studies*, 38: 84–106.

107. P. Theodorou & G. Florou, 2008, Manufacturing strategies and financial performance—the effect of advanced information technology: CAD/CAM systems, *Omega*, 36: 107–121.

108. N. A. Morgan & L. L. Rego, 2009, Brand portfolio strategy and firm performance, *Journal of Marketing*, 73: 59–74.

109. P. Barlas, 2015, Salesforce.com large deals boom, fueling growth, *Investors Business Daily*, www.investors.com, February 26; D. Elmuti, H. Jia, & D. Gray, 2009, Customer relationship management strategic application and organizational effectiveness: An empirical investigation, *Journal of Strategic Marketing*, 17: 75–96.

110. D. J. Ketchen, T. R. Crook, & C. W. Craighead, 2014, From Supply chains to supply ecosystems: Implications for strategic sourcing research and practice, *Journal of Business Logistics*, 35: 165–171; B. Huo, Y. Qi, Z. Wang, & X. Zhao, 2014, The impact of supply chain integration on firm performance: The moderating role of competitive strategy, *Supply Chain Management*, 19: 369–384.

111. J. D. Westphal, R. Gulati, & S. M. Shortell, 1997, Customization or conformity: An institutional and network perspective on the content and consequences of TQM adoption, *Administrative Science Quarterly*, 42: 366–394.

112. H. Su, K. Linderman, R. G. Schroeder, & A. H. Van de Ven, 2014, A comparative case study of sustaining quality as a competitive advantage, *Journal of Operations Management*, 32: 429–445; S. Modell, 2009, Bundling management control innovations: A field study of organisational experimenting with total quality management and the balanced scorecard, *Accounting, Auditing & Accountability Journal*, 22: 59–90.

113. C. D. Zatzick, T. P. Moliterno, & T. Fang, 2012, Strategic (mis)fit: The implementation of TQM in manufacturing organizations, *Strategic Management Journal*, 33: 1321–1330.

114. J. Singh & H. Singh, 2015, Continuous improvement philosophy—literature review and directions, *Benchmarking: An International Journal*, 22: 75–119; A. Keramati & A. Albadvi, 2009, Exploring the relationship between use of information technology in total quality management and SMEs performance using canonical correlation analysis: A survey on Swedish car part supplier sector, *International Journal of Information Technology and Management*, 8: 442–462; R. J. David & S. Strang, 2006, When fashion is fleeting: Transitory collective beliefs and the dynamics of TQM consulting, *Academy of Management Journal*, 49: 215–233.

115. Porter, *Competitive Advantage*, 16.

116. Ibid., 17.

117. Y. Wang & N. Rajagopalan, 2014, Alliance capabilities: Review and research agenda, *Journal of Management*, 41: 236–260; M. A. Hitt, L. Bierman, K. Uhlenbruck, & K. Shimizu, 2006, The importance of resources in the internationalization of professional service firms: The good, the bad, and the ugly, *Academy of Management Journal*, 49: 1137–1157.

118. C. Christensen, 2015, Disruptive innovation is a strategy, not just the technology, *Business Today*, 23: 150–158; P. Puranam, H. Singh, & M. Zollo, 2006, Organizing for innovation: Managing the coordination-autonomy dilemma in technology acquisitions, *Academy of Management Journal*, 49: 263–280.

119. S. Thornhill & R. E. White, 2007, Strategic purity: A multi-industry evaluation of pure vs. hybrid business strategies, *Strategic Management Journal*, 28: 553–561.

120. A. Faelten, M. Gietzmann, & V. Vitkova, 2015, Learning from your investors: Can the geographical composition of institutional investors affect the chance of success in international M&A deals?, *Journal of Management & Governance*, 19: 47–69; B. Connelly, L. Tihanyi, S. T. Certo, & M. A. Hitt, 2010, Marching to the beat of different drummers: The influence of institutional owners on competitive actions, *Academy of Management Journal*, 53: 723–742.

5

Competitive Rivalry and Competitive Dynamics

Studying this chapter should provide you with the strategic management knowledge needed to:

5-1   Define competitors, competitive rivalry, competitive behavior, and competitive dynamics.

5-2   Describe market commonality and resource similarity as the building blocks of a competitor analysis.

5-3   Explain awareness, motivation, and ability as drivers of competitive behavior.

5-4   Discuss factors affecting the likelihood a competitor will take competitive actions.

5-5   Describe factors affecting the likelihood a competitor will respond to actions taken by its competitors.

5-6   Explain competitive dynamics in slow-cycle, in fast-cycle, and in standard-cycle markets.

DOES GOOGLE HAVE COMPETITION? DYNAMICS OF THE HIGH TECHNOLOGY MARKETS

Google is especially known for its search business. In fact, many people now say they "googled it" when explaining that they searched the Internet for information on a particular subject. Google's market share of the search markets is estimated to be about 75 percent in the United States and an even higher 90 percent in Europe. In fact, many argue that this level of market share gives Google an effective monopoly in these markets. Of course, this level of market share has given Google significant power with advertisers and customers, power which the firm can use against its competitors. For example, the Federal Trade Commission (FTC) in the United States has stated that Google has pressured sites such as Yelp, TripAdvisor, and even Amazon to allow it to obtain information on users of their sites. Additionally, the FTC argued that Google has prevented advertisers from placing advertisements on other search engines. But, the FTC also stated that Google had violated no laws. Google's two largest rivals in the search business are Bing and Yahoo, both of which have about 12+ percent of the market. Yet, with continuing changes at other Internet-based companies, firms such as Amazon and Facebook may become important search market rivals in the near future by changing the focus of online shoppers. These companies now compete for advertisers in a number of markets.

Google is much more than a search business. It has entered many markets and is doing research on and/or preparing to enter many more markets. For example, Google recently opened its first Google retail shop in London and plans to open several more. The intent is to compete, at least partially, with Apple's successful retail stores. In another service market, Google recently introduced Android Pay as a competitive response to Apple Pay and Samsung Pay (also in response to Apple's service product). Google has introduced a new flight search tool, Google Flights, that helps customers find the best (including cheapest) airplane flights. This new service competes with several such services but especially with its large rival Expedia (originally started by Microsoft) which acquired Travelocity and Orbitz (two major competitors) in 2015.

Google has also recently entered several other new markets, such as the insurance search market (e.g., for the best auto insurance), and is offering wireless connection to the Internet competing with large telecommunications providers AT&T and Verizon. It is also planning entries in the smartphone and smartwatch markets. The smartwatch product is being developed in an alliance with TAG Heuer and Intel. The Google prototype smartphone will operate with a core product and multiple components. It will be similar to a Lego product where a customer can change screens such as adding a large screen to watch a major sporting event (e.g., the Super Bowl). Of course, these smartphone and smartwatch products will compete directly with Apple products and other companies as well.

Thus, Google competes in many markets and with multiple rivals. In some markets, Google dominates such as information search. But in other markets, it is a new entrant with a small market share competing against established and major companies (e.g., airline flight search and wireless Internet services). In some markets, Google is a primary actor (e.g., search) offering major new services, and in other markets, it is a responder (e.g., Android Pay). As a result, Google's competitive actions are exceedingly complex with competitive dynamics across multiple markets and competitors.

Sources: K. Benner, 2015, Don't be afraid of the big, bad Google, *The New Zealand Herald*, www.nzherald.co.nz, March 28; S. Buckley, 2015, Google Fiber's presence pressures AT&T to adjust 1 gig pricing plans, *FierceTelecom*, www.fiercetelecom.com, April 1; A. Chowdhry, 2015, Google's new flight search tool helps you find the best price, *Forbes*, www.forbes.com, February 27; C. Dougherty, 2015, Google and Intel to team up with TAG Heuer on a luxury smartwatch, *New York Times*, bitys.blog.nytimes.com, March 19; 2015, Google high street riposte to Apple, *Yahoo*, uk.news.yahoo.com, March 11; 2015, Google opens its first retail store, *RTE News*, www.rte.ie, March 11; D. Lumb, 2015, Google answers Apple Pay with (surprise) Android Pay, *Fast Company*, www.fastcompany.com, March 2; V. Kotsev, 2015, Google shows off the smartphone of the future, and it's basically a Lego set, *Fast Company*, www.fastcompany.com, January 14; D. Lyons, 2015, Five myths about Google, *The Washington Post*, www.washingtonpost.com, March 20; 2015, Zuckerberg downplays Facebook/Google rivalry, *SeekingAlpha*, www.seekingalpha.com, March 26; 2014, Google plans to test high-speed wireless Internet, *Fortune*, fortune.com, October 15.

Competitors are firms operating in the same market, offering similar products, and targeting similar customers.

Competitive rivalry is the ongoing set of competitive actions and competitive responses that occur among firms as they maneuver for an advantageous market position.

Competitive behavior is the set of competitive actions and responses a firm takes to build or defend its competitive advantages and to improve its market position.

Multimarket competition occurs when firms compete against each other in several product or geographic markets.

Competitive dynamics refer to all competitive behaviors—that is, the total set of actions and responses taken by all firms competing within a market.

Firms operating in the same market, offering similar products, and targeting similar customers are **competitors**.[1] Google has many competitors because it competes in a number of markets. For example, Google competes against Bing and Yahoo in the general search market and against AT&T and Verizon in the wireless Internet market. Its planned entry into the smartphone market will compete against Apple and Samsung, among others. Thus, Google engages in a significant amount of competitive behavior (defined fully below, competitive behavior is essentially the set of actions and responses a firm takes as it competes against its rivals).

Firms interact with their competitors as part of the broad context within which they operate while attempting to earn above-average returns.[2] Another way to consider this is to note that no firm competes in a vacuum; rather, each firm's actions are part of a mosaic of competitive actions and responses taking place among a host of companies seeking the same objective—superior performance. And evidence shows that the decisions firms make about their interactions with competitors significantly affect their ability to earn above-average returns.[3] Because of this, firms seek to reach optimal decisions when considering how to compete against their rivals.[4]

Competitive rivalry is the ongoing set of competitive actions and competitive responses that occur among firms as they maneuver for an advantageous market position.[5] Especially in highly competitive industries, firms constantly jockey for advantage as they launch strategic actions and respond or react to rivals' moves.[6] It is important for those leading organizations to understand competitive rivalry because the reality is that some firms learn how to outperform their competitors, meaning that competitive rivalry influences an individual firm's ability to gain and sustain competitive advantages.[7] Rivalry results from firms initiating their own competitive actions and then responding to actions taken by competitors.[8]

Competitive behavior is the set of competitive actions and responses a firm takes to build or defend its competitive advantages and to improve its market position.[9] As explained in the Opening Case, Google takes many major actions to compete but also responds to rival's strategic action as exemplified by its Android Pay in response to similar services offered by Apple and Samsung. Through competitive behavior, Google seeks to successfully position itself relative to the five forces of competition (see Chapter 2) and to defend its current competitive advantages while building advantages for the future (see Chapter 3).

Increasingly, competitors engage in competitive actions and responses in more than one market which can be observed with Google and Apple and with Google and Amazon, for example.[10] Firms competing against each other in several product or geographic markets are engaged in **multimarket competition**.[11] All competitive behavior—that is, the total set of actions and responses taken by all firms competing within a market—is called **competitive dynamics**. The relationships among all of these key concepts are shown in Figure 5.1.

Figure 5.1 From Competition to Competitive Dynamics

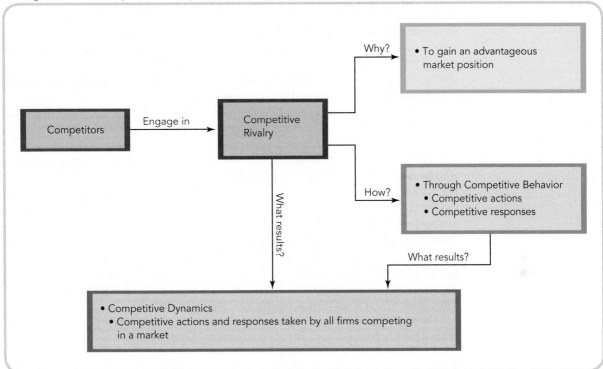

Source: Adapted from M. J. Chen, 1996, Competitor analysis and inferfirm rivalry: Toward a theoretical integration, *Academy of Management Review*, 21: 100-134.

This chapter focuses on competitive rivalry and competitive dynamics. A firm's strategies are dynamic in nature because actions taken by one firm elicit responses from competitors that, in turn, typically result in responses from the firm that took the initial action.[12] For example, in recent years, cigarette manufacturers took actions to introduce electronic cigarettes as a new product. Commonly called e-cigarettes, and with their health benefits still unknown, this product is a battery-powered device that converts heated, nicotine-laced liquid into vapor. The more prominent position in this market has been held by Lorillard, Inc., which is now merging with Reynolds American to become an even more formidable competitor in this market and other tobacco product markets. The other large tobacco product firm, Altria Group, introduced its MarkTen e-cigarette to compete with the other major firms in this market. Additional competitive actions and responses among these firms and with international cigarette manufacturers can be expected in the foreseeable future.[13]

Competitive rivalries affect a firm's strategies, as a strategy's success is determined not only by the firm's initial competitive actions but also by how well it anticipates competitors' responses to them *and* by how well the firm anticipates and responds to its competitors' initial actions (also called attacks).[14] Although competitive rivalry affects all types of strategies (e.g., corporate-level, merger and acquisition, and international), its dominant influence is on the firm's business-level strategy or strategies. Indeed, firms' actions and responses to those of their rivals are part of the basic building blocks of business-level strategies.[15]

Recall from Chapter 4 that business-level strategy is concerned with what the firm does to successfully use its core competencies in specific product markets. In the global economy, competitive rivalry is intensifying, meaning that its effect on firms' strategies is increasing. However, firms that develop and use effective business-level strategies tend to outperform competitors in individual product markets, even when experiencing intense competitive rivalry.

5-1   A Model of Competitive Rivalry

Competitive rivalry evolves from the pattern of actions and responses as one firm's competitive actions have noticeable effects on competitors, eliciting competitive responses from them.[16] This pattern suggests that firms are mutually interdependent, that they are affected by each other's actions and responses, and that marketplace success is a function of both individual strategies and the consequences of their use.[17]

Increasingly, executives recognize that competitive rivalry can have a major effect on the firm's financial performance and market position.[18] For example, research shows that intensified rivalry within an industry results in decreased average profitability for the competing firms.[19] Although Apple essentially created the smartphone market in 2007 by launching the iPhone, some believe that Google's Android has rapidly reshaped the market, as evidenced by the fact that nearly half of all smartphones shipped in 2012 ran on the Android platform. The Opening Case explains how Google is creating the smartphone of the future which, when introduced, will likely only increase its rivalry with Apple, Samsung, and other smartphone providers.

Figure 5.2 presents a straightforward model of competitive rivalry at the firm level; this type of rivalry is usually dynamic and complex. The competitive actions and responses the firm takes are the foundation for successfully building and using its capabilities and core competencies to gain an advantageous market position.[20]

The model in Figure 5.2 presents the sequence of activities commonly involved in competition between a firm and its competitors. Companies use this model to understand how to predict a competitor's behavior and reduce the uncertainty associated with it.[21] Being able to predict competitors' actions and responses has a positive effect on the firm's market position and its subsequent financial performance.[22] The total of all the individual rivalries modeled in Figure 5.2 that occur in a particular market reflect the competitive dynamics in that market.

The remainder of the chapter explains components of the model shown in Figure 5.2. We first describe market commonality and resource similarity as the building blocks of a competitor analysis. Next, we discuss the effects of three organizational characteristics— awareness, motivation, and ability—on the firm's competitive behavior. We then examine competitive rivalry between firms (interfirm rivalry). To do this, we explain the factors

Figure 5.2 A Model of Competitive Reality

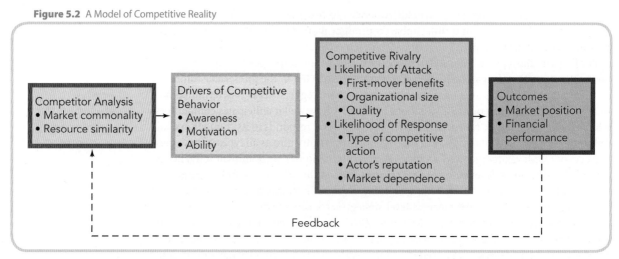

Source: Adapted from M. J. Chen, 1996, Competitor analysis and inferfirm rivalry: Toward a theoretical integration, *Academy of Management Review*, 21: 100–134.

that affect the likelihood a firm will take a competitive action and the factors that affect the likelihood a firm will respond to a competitor's action. In the chapter's final section, we turn our attention to competitive dynamics to describe how market characteristics affect competitive rivalry in slow-cycle, fast-cycle, and standard-cycle markets.

5-2 Competitor Analysis

As previously noted, a competitor analysis is the first step the firm takes to be able to predict the extent and nature of its rivalry with each competitor. Competitor analyses are especially important when entering a foreign market because firms doing so need to understand the local competition and foreign competitors currently operating in that market.[23] Without such analyses, they are less likely to be successful.

The number of markets in which firms compete against each other is called market commonality while the similarity in their resources is called resource similarity (both terms will be discussed later). These two dimensions of competition determine the extent to which firms are competitors. Firms with high market commonality and highly similar resources are direct and mutually acknowledged competitors. The drivers of competitive behavior—as well as factors influencing the likelihood that a competitor will initiate competitive actions and will respond to its competitors' actions—influence the intensity of rivalry.[24]

In Chapter 2, we discussed competitor analysis as a technique firms use to understand their competitive environment. Together, the general, industry, and competitive environments comprise the firm's external environment. We also described how competitor analysis is used to help the firm *understand* its competitors. This understanding results from studying competitors' future objectives, current strategies, assumptions, and capabilities (see Figure 2.3 in Chapter 2). In this chapter, the discussion of competitor analysis is extended to describe what firms study to be able to *predict* competitors' behavior in the form of their competitive actions and responses. The discussions of competitor analysis in Chapter 2 and in this chapter are complementary in that firms must first *understand* competitors (Chapter 2) before their competitive actions and responses can be *predicted* (this chapter).

Being able to accurately predict rivals' likely competitive actions and responses helps a firm avoid situations in which it is unaware of competitors' objectives, strategies, assumptions, and capabilities. Lacking the information needed to predict these conditions for competitors creates *competitive blind spots*. Typically, competitive blind spots find a firm being surprised by a competitor's actions, potentially resulting in negative outcomes.[25] Increasingly, members of a firm's board of directors are expected to use their knowledge and expertise about other businesses and industry environments to help a firm avoid competitive blind spots.[26]

5-2a Market Commonality

Every industry is composed of various markets. The financial services industry has markets for insurance, brokerage services, banks, and so forth. To concentrate on the needs of different, unique customer groups, markets can be further subdivided. The insurance market could be broken into market segments (such as commercial and consumer), product segments (such as health insurance and life insurance), and geographic markets (such as Southeast Asia and Western Europe). In general, the capabilities that Internet technologies generate help to shape the nature of industries' markets along with patterns of competition within those industries. For example, according to a Procter and Gamble (P&G) official: "Facebook is both a marketing and a distribution channel, as P&G has worked to develop 'f-commerce' capabilities on its fan pages, fulfilled by Amazon, which has become a top 10 retail account for Pampers," a disposable diaper product.[27]

Competitors tend to agree about the different characteristics of individual markets that form an industry. For example, in the transportation industry, the commercial air travel market differs from the ground transportation market, which is served by such firms as YRC Worldwide (one of the largest, less-than-truckload—LTL—carriers in North America and selected as Walmart's LTL Carrier of the Year) and its major competitors Arkansas Best, Con-way, Inc., and FedEx Freight.[28] Although differences exist, many industries' markets are partially related in terms of technologies used or core competencies needed to develop a competitive advantage. For example, although railroads and truck ground transport compete in a different segment and can be substitutes, different types of transportation companies need to provide reliable and timely service. Commercial air carriers such as Southwest, United, and Jet Blue must therefore develop service competencies to satisfy their passengers, while ground transport companies such as YRC, railroads, and their major competitors must develop such competencies to satisfy the needs of those using their services to ship goods.

Firms sometimes compete against each other in several markets, a condition called market commonality. More formally, **market commonality** is concerned with the number of markets with which the firm and a competitor are jointly involved and the degree of importance of the individual markets to each.[29] Firms competing against one another in several or many markets are said to be engaging in multimarket competition.[30] Coca-Cola and PepsiCo compete across a number of product markets (e.g., soft drinks, bottled water) as well as geographic markets (throughout North America and in many other countries throughout the world). Airlines, chemicals, pharmaceuticals, and consumer foods are examples of other industries with firms often competing against each other in multiple markets.

Firms competing in several of the same markets have the potential to respond to a competitor's actions not only within the market in which a given set of actions are taken, but also in other markets where they compete with the rival. This potential creates a complicated mosaic in which the competitive actions or responses a firm takes in one market may be designed to affect the outcome of its rivalry with a particular competitor in a second market.[31] This potential complicates the rivalry between competitors. In fact, research suggests that a firm with greater multimarket contact is less likely to initiate an attack, but more likely to move (respond) aggressively when attacked. For instance, research in the computer industry found that "firms respond to competitive attacks by introducing new products but do not use price as a retaliatory weapon."[32] Thus in general, multimarket competition reduces competitive rivalry, but some firms will still compete when the potential rewards (e.g., potential market share gain) are high.[33]

5-2b Resource Similarity

Resource similarity is the extent to which the firm's tangible and intangible resources are comparable to a competitor's in terms of both type and amount.[34] Firms with similar types and amounts of resources are likely to have similar strengths and weaknesses and use similar strategies on the basis of their strengths to pursue what may be similar opportunities in the external environment.

"Resource similarity" describes part of the relationship between FedEx and United Parcel Service (UPS). These companies compete in many of the same markets, and thus are also accurately described as having market commonality. For example, these firms have similar types of truck and airplane fleets, similar levels of financial capital, and rely on equally talented reservoirs of human capital along with sophisticated information

Market commonality is concerned with the number of markets with which the firm and a competitor are jointly involved and the degree of importance of the individual markets to each.

Resource similarity is the extent to which the firm's tangible and intangible resources are comparable to a competitor's in terms of both type and amount.

technology systems (resources). In addition to competing aggressively against each other in North America, the firms share many other country markets in common. Thus, the rivalry between these two firms is intense.

When performing a competitor analysis, a firm analyzes each of its competitors with respect to market commonality and resource similarity. The results of these analyses can be mapped for visual comparisons. In Figure 5.3, we show different hypothetical intersections between the firm and individual competitors in terms of market commonality and resource similarity. These intersections indicate the extent to which the firm and those with which it compares itself are competitors. For example, the firm and its competitor displayed in quadrant I have similar types and amounts of resources (i.e., the two firms have a similar portfolio of resources). The firm and its competitor in quadrant I would use their similar resource portfolios to compete against each other in many markets that are important to each. These conditions lead to the conclusion that the firms modeled in quadrant I are direct and mutually acknowledged competitors.

In contrast, the firm and its competitor shown in quadrant III share few markets and have little similarity in their resources, indicating that they aren't direct and mutually acknowledged competitors. Thus a small, local, family-owned restaurant concentrating on selling "gourmet" hamburgers does not compete directly against McDonald's. The mapping of competitive relationships is fluid as companies enter and exit markets and as rivals' resources change in type and amount, meaning that the companies with which a given firm is a direct competitor change over time.

Kellogg has held a dominant market position in cold cereal sales for a long time but its sales of cereals have begun to decline as explained in the Strategic Focus. Its major competitors are responding better to the changes in the market than Kellogg. Kellogg seems to be trying to force its products on the market rather than changing its product lines to satisfy consumer needs. General Mills' purchase of Yoplait is positioning that firm to advance in the newer breakfast food market. Kellogg's response appears to be weak and is likely to be ineffective. Without major changes, Kellogg is likely to suffer additional decline.

Figure 5.3 A Framework of Competitor Analysis

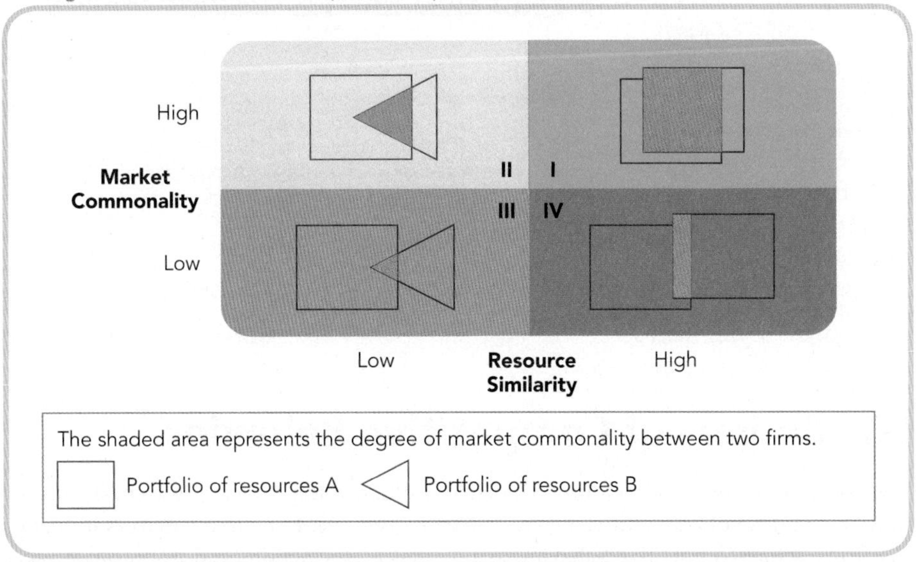

The shaded area represents the degree of market commonality between two firms.

Portfolio of resources A   Portfolio of resources B

Source: Adapted from M. J. Chen, 1996, Competitor analysis and inferfirm rivalry: Toward a theoretical integration, *Academy of Management Review*, 21: 100–134.

Strategic Focus

Does Kellogg Have the Tiger by the Tail or Is It the Reverse?

Kellogg Company has been the leading and largest cereal maker in the U.S. market for some time. It once had 45 percent of the U. S. cereal market. Thus, for a number of years, Kellogg was flying high with its "Tony the Tiger" advertisements and its leading cereals of Frosted Flakes, Frosted Mini-Wheats, and Special K cereals, among others. That is no longer the case, especially with the changes in the breakfast food market. In fact, cereal, which at one time comprised approximately 38 percent of the breakfast foods in the United States, currently accounts for about 28 percent of the breakfast food sales. United States consumers are moving away from processed foods and carbohydrates to fruit, yogurt, and protein such as eggs for breakfast meals. As a result, Kellogg's sales of its cereals are slumping, profits are slipping, and its stock price is declining. A recent survey of analysts found that 90 percent recommended selling or putting a hold on Kellogg stock, with only 10 percent recommending that investors buy it.

In 2014, sales for 19 of Kellogg's top 25 cereals declined. While other major cereal makers also struggled, General Mills' (e.g., Cheerios, Lucky Charms) sales were 50 percent better than Kellogg's. And, Post's sales in 2014 even net a two percent increase. So, Kellogg's competitors seem to be weathering the crisis better than it is able to do. To deal with the declining sales, Kellogg acquired Pringles for $2.7 billion. Yet, Pringles clearly represents processed foods which the consumer is beginning to resist. Alternatively, General Mills acquired a controlling ownership position in Yoplait, the second-largest manufacturer of yogurt in the world. This acquisition strengthened General Mill's market position with the increasing demand for yogurt. Kellogg is also trying to revive its Special K and Kashi sales by adding fruit and other items. Some believe that these actions will generate few positive returns. In addition, Kellogg invests heavily in advertising with outlays of more than $1 billion annually.

Obviously, Kellogg is losing market share to its major rivals in the cereal market, but it is also losing to other firms that are providing different breakfast foods increasingly desired by the United States consumer. Kellogg's breakfast cereal sales declined by 6 percent in 2014, and their outlook is not good. Yet, Kellogg is investing in special advertising campaigns to encourage consumers to eat more cereal for breakfast. At one time, Kellogg had an advantage because of its size; it could invest more resources in advertising and marketing in general, thereby building relations with retailers (and consumers). Today, its large size appears to be hurting the firm. Kellogg seems unable to make the major changes required to respond to the new demands in the breakfast food market. Its competitors are responding more effectively, suggesting a dark future for Kellogg.

Perhaps Kellogg would do well to promote a healthy breakfast that includes cereal (e.g., along with fruit, milk, juice and egg).

Sources: J. Kell, 2014, Decline in cereal sales bites into Kellogg's results, *Fortune*, www.fortune.com, October 30; A. A. Newman, 2014, With a night campaign, Kellogg's aims for snappier sales, *New York Times*, www.nytimes.com, December 17; S. Danshkhu and S. Neville, 2015, Food companies give frosty reception to labour sugar clamp, *Financial Times*, www.ft.com, January 15; M. Badkar, 2015, Kellogg loses ground after forecasts cut, *Financial Times*, www.ft.com, February 12; S. A. Gasparro, 2015, Kellogg posts loss, cautions on outlook, *Wall Street Journal*, www.wsj.com, February 12; S. Strom, 2015, A sharp loss for Kellogg as sales of cereal falter, *New York Times*, www.nytimes.com, February 12; 2015, Kellogg cuts long-term outlook on sluggish cereal, snack sales, *Fortune*, www.fortune.com, February 12; D. Leonard, 2015, Bad news in cereal city, *Bloomberg Business*, March 2–6, pp. 42–47.

5-3 Drivers of Competitive Behavior

Market commonality and resource similarity influence the drivers (awareness, motivation, and ability) of competitive behavior (see Figure 5.2). In turn, the drivers influence the firm's actual competitive behavior, as revealed by the actions and responses it takes while engaged in competitive rivalry.[35]

Awareness, which is a prerequisite to any competitive action or response taken by a firm, refers to the extent to which competitors recognize the degree of their mutual interdependence that results from market commonality and resource similarity.[36] Awareness affects the extent to which the firm understands the consequences of its competitive actions and responses. A lack of awareness can lead to excessive competition, resulting in a negative effect on all competitors' performance.[37]

Awareness tends to be greatest when firms have highly similar resources (in terms of types and amounts) to use while competing against each other in multiple markets. Komatsu Ltd., Japan's top construction machinery maker, and U.S.-based Caterpillar Inc. have similar resources and are aware of each other's actions given that they compete against each other in markets throughout the world. Founded in 1925, Caterpillar is the world's leading manufacturer of construction and mining equipment, diesel and natural gas engines, and industrial gas turbines, while Komatsu is the world's second largest seller of construction and mining machinery behind Caterpillar. Recently, differences in the exchange rates for the U. S. dollar and the Japanese yen have favored Komatsu. Komatsu has used this advantage to aggressively seek new customers and sales through its product pricing strategies.[38] Over the years, these firms have competed aggressively against each other for market share in multiple countries and regions.

Motivation, which concerns the firm's incentive to take action or to respond to a competitor's attack, relates to perceived gains and losses. Thus, a firm may be aware of competitors but may not be motivated to engage in rivalry with them if it perceives that its position will not improve or that its market position won't be damaged if it doesn't respond.[39] A benefit of not having the motivation to engage in rivalry at a point in time with a competitor is that the firm that lacks motivation to compete against another firm retains resources that can be used for other purposes including competing against a different rival.

Market commonality affects the firm's perceptions and resulting motivation. For example, a firm is generally more likely to attack the rival with whom it has low market commonality than the one with whom it competes in multiple markets. The primary reason for this is the high stakes involved in trying to gain a more advantageous position over a rival with whom the firm shares many markets. As mentioned earlier, multimarket competition can result in a competitor responding to the firm's action in a market different from the one in which that action was taken. Actions and responses of this type can cause both firms to lose focus on core markets and to battle each other with resources that had been allocated for other purposes. Because of the high competitive stakes under the condition of market commonality, the probability is high that the attacked firm will respond to its competitor's action in an effort to protect its position in one or more markets.[40]

In some instances, the firm may be aware of the markets it shares with a competitor and be motivated to respond to an attack by that competitor, but lack the ability to do so. *Ability* relates to each firm's resources and the flexibility they provide. Without available resources (such as financial capital and people), the firm is not able to attack a competitor or respond to its actions. For example, smaller and newer firms tend to be more innovative but generally have fewer resources to attack larger and established competitors. Likewise, foreign firms often are at a disadvantage against local firms because of the local firms' social capital (relationships) with consumers, suppliers, and government officials.[41] However, similar resources suggest similar abilities to attack and respond. When a firm faces a competitor with similar resources, careful study of a possible attack before initiating it is essential because the similarly resourced competitor is likely to respond to that action.[42]

Resource *dissimilarity* also influences competitive actions and responses between firms in that the more significant the difference between resources owned by the acting firm and those against whom it has taken action, the longer is the delay by the firm

Small competitors, such as A&T Grocery, find it difficult to respond to the competitive threat that exists with Walmart. Yet, they must find a way to respond, perhaps by offering personalized services, in order to survive such a threat.

with a resource disadvantage.[43] For example, Walmart initially used a focused cost leadership strategy to compete only in small communities (those with a population of 25,000 or less). Using sophisticated logistics systems and efficient purchasing practices, among other methods, to gain competitive advantages, Walmart created a new type of value (primarily in the form of wide selections of products at the lowest competitive prices) for customers in small retail markets. Local competitors lacked the ability to marshal needed resources at the pace required to respond to Walmart's actions quickly and effectively. However, even when facing competitors with greater resources (greater ability) or more attractive market positions, firms should eventually respond, no matter how daunting the task seems. Choosing not to respond can ultimately result in failure, as happened with at least some local retailers who didn't respond to Walmart's competitive actions. Today, with Walmart as the world's largest retailer, it is indeed difficult for smaller competitors to have the resources required to effectively respond to its competitive actions or competitive responses.[44]

5-4 Competitive Rivalry

The ongoing competitive action/response sequence between a firm and a competitor affects the performance of both firms. Because of this, it is important for companies to carefully analyze and understand the competitive rivalry present in the markets in which they compete.[45]

As we described earlier, the predictions drawn from studying competitors in terms of awareness, motivation, and ability are grounded in market commonality and resource similarity. These predictions are fairly general. The value of the final set of predictions the firm develops about each of its competitors' competitive actions and responses is enhanced by studying the "Likelihood of Attack" factors (such as first-mover benefits and organizational size) and the "Likelihood of Response" factors (such as the actor's reputation) that are shown in Figure 5.2. Evaluating and understanding these factors allow the firm to refine the predictions it makes about its competitors' actions and responses.

5-4a Strategic and Tactical Actions

Firms use both strategic and tactical actions when forming their competitive actions and competitive responses in the course of engaging in competitive rivalry.[46] A **competitive action** is a strategic or tactical action the firm takes to build or defend its competitive advantages or improve its market position. A **competitive response** is a strategic or tactical action the firm takes to counter the effects of a competitor's competitive action. A **strategic action** or a **strategic response** is a market-based move that involves a significant commitment of organizational resources and is difficult to implement and reverse. A **tactical action** or a **tactical response** is a market-based move that is taken to fine-tune

A **competitive action** is a strategic or tactical action the firm takes to build or defend its competitive advantages or improve its market position.

A **competitive response** is a strategic or tactical action the firm takes to counter the effects of a competitor's competitive action.

A **strategic action** or a **strategic response** is a market-based move that involves a significant commitment of organizational resources and is difficult to implement and reverse.

A **tactical action** or a **tactical response** is a market-based move that is taken to fine-tune a strategy; it involves fewer resources and is relatively easy to implement and reverse.

a strategy; it involves fewer resources and is relatively easy to implement and reverse. When engaging rivals in competition, firms must recognize the differences between strategic and tactical actions and responses and develop an effective balance between the two types of competitive actions and responses.

A few years ago, Nokia Corporation, implemented an important strategic action by partnering with Microsoft "to deliver an ecosystem with unrivalled global reach and scale" in its smartphone business. This relationship was, in part, a strategic response to Apple's success. However, in 2013, Microsoft acquired Nokia's cellphone business as a critical part of Microsoft's mobile device strategy.[47] This represented a strategic action by Microsoft.

Walmart prices aggressively as a means of increasing revenues and gaining market share at the expense of competitors. In this regard, the firm engages in a continuous stream of tactical actions to attack rivals by changing some of its products' prices and tactical responses to respond to price changes taken by competitors such as Costco and Target.

5-5 Likelihood of Attack

In addition to market commonality; resource similarity; and the drivers of awareness, motivation, and ability, other factors affect the likelihood a competitor will use strategic actions and tactical actions to attack its competitors. Three of these factors—first-mover benefits, organizational size, and quality—are discussed next. Second and late movers are considered as part of the discussion of first-mover benefits.

5-5a First-Mover Benefits

A **first mover** is a firm that takes an initial competitive action in order to build or defend its competitive advantages or to improve its market position. The first-mover concept has been influenced by the work of the famous economist Joseph Schumpeter, who argued that firms achieve competitive advantage by taking innovative actions[48] (innovation is defined and discussed in Chapter 13). In general, first movers emphasize research and development (R&D) as a path to develop innovative goods and services that customers will value.[49]

The benefits of being a successful first mover can be substantial.[50] This is especially true in fast-cycle markets (discussed later in the chapter) where changes occur rapidly, and where it is virtually impossible to sustain a competitive advantage for any length of time. A first mover in a fast-cycle market can experience many times the valuation and revenue of a second mover.[51] This evidence suggests that although first-mover benefits are never absolute, they are often critical to a firm's success in industries experiencing rapid technological developments and relatively short product life cycles.[52] In addition to earning above-average returns until its competitors respond to its successful competitive action, the first mover can gain

- the loyalty of customers who may become committed to the goods or services of the firm that first made them available.
- market share that can be difficult for competitors to take during future competitive rivalry[53]

The general evidence that first movers have greater survival rates than later market entrants is perhaps the culmination of first-mover benefits.[54]

The firm trying to predict its rivals' competitive actions might conclude that they will take aggressive strategic actions to gain first movers' benefits. However, even though a firm's competitors might be motivated to be first movers, they may lack the ability to do so.

A **first mover** is a firm that takes an initial competitive action in order to build or defend its competitive advantages or to improve its market position.

First movers tend to be aggressive and willing to experiment with innovation and take higher yet reasonable levels of risk, and their long-term success depends on retaining the ability to do so.[55]

To be a first mover, the firm must have the readily available resources to significantly invest in R&D as well as to rapidly and successfully produce and market a stream of innovative products.[56] Organizational slack makes it possible for firms to have the ability (as measured by available resources) to be first movers. *Slack* is the buffer or cushion provided by actual or obtainable resources that aren't currently in use and are in excess of the minimum resources needed to produce a given level of organizational output.[57] As a liquid resource, slack can quickly be allocated to support competitive actions, such as R&D investments and aggressive marketing campaigns that lead to first-mover advantages. This relationship between slack and the ability to be a first mover allows the firm to predict that a first-mover competitor likely has available slack and will probably take aggressive competitive actions to continuously introduce innovative products. Furthermore, the firm can predict that, as a first mover, a competitor will try to rapidly gain market share and customer loyalty in order to earn above-average returns until its competitors are able to effectively respond to its first move.

Firms evaluating their competitors should realize that being a first mover carries risk. For example, it is difficult to accurately estimate the returns that will be earned from introducing product innovations to the marketplace.[58] Additionally, the first mover's cost to develop a product innovation can be substantial, reducing the slack available to support further innovation. Thus, the firm should carefully study the results a competitor achieves as a first mover. Continuous success by the competitor suggests additional product innovations, while lack of product acceptance over the course of the competitor's innovations may indicate less willingness in the future to accept the risks of being a first mover.[59]

A **second mover** is a firm that responds to the first mover's competitive action, typically through imitation. More cautious than the first mover, the second mover studies customers' reactions to product innovations. In the course of doing so, the second mover also tries to find any mistakes the first mover made so that it can avoid them and the problems they created. Often, successful imitation of the first mover's innovations allows the second mover to avoid the mistakes and the major investments required of the pioneering first movers.[60]

Second movers have the time to develop processes and technologies that are more efficient than those used by the first mover or that create additional value for consumers.[61] The most successful second movers rarely act too fast (so they can fully analyze the first mover's actions) nor too slow (so they do not give the first mover time to correct its mistakes and "lock in" customer loyalty). Overall, the outcomes of the first mover's competitive actions may provide a blueprint for second and even late movers as they determine the nature and timing of their competitive responses.[62]

Determining whether a competitor is an effective second mover (based on its past actions) allows a first-mover firm to predict when or if the competitor will respond quickly to successful, innovation-based market entries. The first mover can expect a successful second-mover competitor to study its market entries and to respond with a new entry into the market within a short time period. As a second mover, the competitor will try to respond with a product that provides greater customer value than does the first mover's product. The most successful second movers are able to rapidly and meaningfully interpret market feedback to respond quickly yet successfully to the first mover's successful innovations.

Home-improvement rating site Angie's List was founded roughly two decades ago. More than two million U.S. households have been using the service to gain information about the quality of 700-plus services (plumbing, electrical work, and so forth) provided

A **second mover** is a firm that responds to the first mover's competitive action, typically through imitation.

by local companies. Angie's List members submit reviews at the rate of over 60,000 per month. Although the firm enjoyed success for several years, it suffered net losses during the of 2009–2014. And, because of this, its stock price has tumbled almost 50 percent from its highest values. The firm has suffered a number of problems in recent years, but perhaps the largest challenge has come from its competition. Its primary competitor is Consumer Reports. But, it also has suffered from competitors that offer free lists and/or search services such as Yelp, Porch.com, home improvement network, and Google Local.[63] Second movers have clearly responded to the initial success of Angie's List. Each of the second movers offers a slightly different service to customers, trying to improve on the quality, breath, and/or depth of what Angie's List offers. Thus, being successful requires substantial and continuous efforts because competitors are likely to erode or eliminate existing competitive advantages.

Daniel Acker/Bloomberg/Getty Images

The Angie's List website is displayed on a computer screen. The consumer-review website has spawned a number of second movers that attempt to improve on Angie's List features and target narrow market segments.

A **late mover** is a firm that responds to a competitive action a significant amount of time after the first mover's action and the second mover's response. Typically, a late response is better than no response at all, although any success achieved from the late competitive response tends to be considerably less than that achieved by first and second movers. However, on occasion, late movers can be successful if they develop a unique way to enter the market and compete. For firms from emerging economies, this often means a niche strategy with lower-cost production and manufacturing. It can also mean that they need to learn from the competitors or others in the market in order to market products that allow them to compete.[64]

The firm competing against a late mover can predict that the competitor will likely enter a particular market only after both the first and second movers have achieved success in that market. Moreover, on a relative basis, the firm can predict that the late mover's competitive action will allow it to earn average returns only after the considerable time required for it to understand how to create at least as much customer value as that offered by the first and second movers' products.

5-5b Organizational Size

An organization's size affects the likelihood it will take competitive actions as well as the types and timing of those actions.[65] In general, small firms are more likely than large companies to launch competitive actions and tend to do it more quickly. Smaller firms are thus perceived as nimble and flexible competitors who rely on speed and surprise to defend their competitive advantages or develop new ones while engaged in competitive rivalry, especially with large companies, to gain an advantageous market position.[66] Small firms' flexibility and nimbleness allow them to develop variety in their competitive actions; large firms tend to limit the types of competitive actions used.[67]

Large firms, however, are likely to initiate more competitive actions along with more strategic actions during a given period.[68] Thus, when studying its competitors in terms of organizational size, the firm should use a measurement such as total sales revenue or total number of employees. The competitive actions the firm likely will encounter from

A **late mover** is a firm that responds to a competitive action a significant amount of time after the first mover's action and the second mover's response.

competitors larger than it is will be different from the competitive actions it will encounter from smaller competitors.

The organizational size factor adds another layer of complexity. When engaging in competitive rivalry, firms prefer to be able to have the capabilities required to take a large number of unique competitive actions. For this to be the case, a firm needs to have the amount of slack resources that a large, successful company typically holds if it is to be able to launch a greater *number* of competitive actions. Simultaneously though, the firm needs to be flexible when considering competitive actions and responses it might take if it is to be able to launch a greater *variety* of competitive actions. Collectively then, firms are best served competitively when their size permits them to take an appropriate number of unique or diverse competitive actions and responses.

5-5c   Quality

Quality has many definitions, including well-established ones relating it to the production of goods or services with zero defects and as a cycle of continuous improvement.[69] From a strategic perspective, we consider quality to be the outcome of how a firm competes through its value chain activities and support functions (see Chapter 3). Thus, **quality** exists when the firm's goods or services meet or exceed customers' expectations. Some evidence suggests that quality may be the most critical component in satisfying the firm's customers.[70]

In the eyes of customers, quality is about doing the right things relative to performance measures that are important to them.[71] Customers may be interested in measuring the quality of a firm's goods and services against a broad range of dimensions. Sample quality dimensions in which customers commonly express an interest are shown in Table 5.1.

Table 5.1 Quality Dimensions of Products and Services

Product Quality Dimensions

1. *Performance*—Operating characteristics
2. *Features*—Important special characteristics
3. *Flexibility*—Meeting operating specifications over some period of time
4. *Durability*—Amount of use before performance deteriorates
5. *Conformance*—Match with pre-established standards
6. *Serviceability*—Ease and speed of repair
7. *Aesthetics*—How a product looks and feels
8. *Perceived quality*—Subjective assessment of characteristics (product image)

Service Quality Dimensions

1. *Timeliness*—Performed in the promised period of time
2. *Courtesy*—Performed cheerfully
3. *Consistency*—Giving all customers similar experiences each time
4. *Convenience*—Accessibility to customers
5. *Completeness*—Fully serviced, as required
6. *Accuracy*—Performed correctly each time

Source: Adapted from J. Evans, 2008, *Managing for Quality and Performance*, 7th Ed., Mason, OH: Thomson Publishing.

Quality exists when the firm's goods or services meet or exceed customers' expectations.

Quality is possible only when top-level managers support it and when its importance is institutionalized throughout the entire organization and its value chain.[72] When quality is institutionalized and valued by all, employees and managers alike become vigilant about continuously finding ways to improve it.[73]

Quality is a universal theme in the global economy and is a necessary but insufficient condition for competitive success.[74] Without quality, a firm's products lack credibility, meaning that customers don't think of them as viable options. Indeed, customers won't consider buying a product or using a service until they believe that it can satisfy at least their base-level expectations in terms of quality dimensions that are important to them.[75]

Quality affects competitive rivalry. The firm evaluating a competitor whose products suffer from poor quality can predict declines in the competitor's sales revenue until the quality issues are resolved. In addition, the firm can predict that the competitor likely won't be aggressive in its competitive actions until the quality problems are corrected in order to gain credibility with customers.[76] However, after the problems are corrected, that competitor is likely to take more aggressive competitive actions.

5-6   Likelihood of Response

The success of a firm's competitive action is affected by the likelihood that a competitor will respond to it as well as by the type (strategic or tactical) and effectiveness of that response. As noted earlier, a competitive response is a strategic or tactical action the firm takes to counter the effects of a competitor's competitive action. In general, a firm is likely to respond to a competitor's action when either

- the action leads to better use of the competitor's capabilities to develop a stronger competitive advantage or an improvement in its market position,
- the action damages the firm's ability to use its core competencies to create or maintain an advantage or
- the firm's market position becomes harder to defend.[77]

In addition to market commonality and resource similarity, and awareness, motivation, and ability, firms evaluate three other factors—type of competitive action, actor's reputation, and market dependence—to predict how a competitor is likely to respond to competitive actions (see Figure 5.2).

5-6a   Type of Competitive Action

Competitive responses to strategic actions differ from responses to tactical actions. These differences allow the firm to predict a competitor's likely response to a competitive action that has been launched against it. Strategic actions commonly receive strategic responses and tactical actions receive tactical responses. In general, strategic actions elicit fewer total competitive responses because strategic responses, such as market-based moves, involve a significant commitment of resources and are difficult to implement and reverse.[78]

Another reason that strategic actions elicit fewer responses than do tactical actions is that the time needed to implement a strategic action and to assess its effectiveness can delay the competitor's response to that action.[79] In contrast, a competitor likely will respond quickly to a tactical action, such as when an airline company almost immediately matches a competitor's tactical action of reducing prices in certain markets. Either strategic actions or tactical actions that target a large number of a rival's customers are likely to elicit strong responses.[80] In fact, if the effects of a competitor's strategic action on the focal firm are significant (e.g., loss of market share, loss of major resources such as critical employees), a response is likely to be swift and strong.[81]

The IBM brand has had a very strong positive reputation for many years.

5-6b Actor's Reputation

In the context of competitive rivalry, an *actor* is the firm taking an action or a response, while *reputation* is "the positive or negative attribute ascribed by one rival to another based on past competitive behavior."[82] A positive reputation may be a source of above-average returns, especially for consumer goods producers.[83] Thus, a positive corporate reputation is of strategic value[84] and affects competitive rivalry. To predict the likelihood of a competitor's response to a current or planned action, firms evaluate the responses that the competitor has taken previously when attacked—past behavior is assumed to be a predictor of future behavior.

Competitors are more likely to respond to strategic or tactical actions when they are taken by a market leader.[85] In particular, evidence suggests that commonly successful actions, especially strategic actions, will be quickly imitated. For example, although a second mover, IBM committed significant resources to enter the information service market. Competitors such as Hewlett-Packard (HP), Dell Inc., and others responded with strategic actions to enter this market as well.[86] IBM has invested heavily to build its capabilities in service related software as well. And, the investments appear to be paying off as IBM recently reported that a study of 800 firms using its Software-as-a-Service (SaaS) had achieved a competitive advantage in their markets.[87]

In contrast to a firm with a strong reputation, competitors are less likely to respond to actions taken by a company with a reputation for risky, complex, and unpredictable competitive behavior. For example, the firm with a reputation as a price predator (an actor that frequently reduces prices to gain or maintain market share) generates few responses to its pricing tactical actions because price predators, which typically increase prices once their market share objective is reached, lack credibility with their competitors.[88]

5-6c Market Dependence

Market dependence denotes the extent to which a firm's revenues or profits are derived from a particular market.[89] In general, competitors with high market dependence are likely to respond strongly to attacks threatening their market position.[90] Interestingly, the threatened firm in these instances may not always respond quickly, even though an effective response to an attack on the firm's position in a critical market is important.

At an annual compound growth rate of 11 percent, recent predictions are that e-commerce sales will grow more than any other segment of the retail industry through at least 2017. Obviously, this growth rate is attractive to firms of all kinds including, as it turns out, Walmart. Established in 2000 as part of the world's largest firm by sales volume (with revenue of roughly $469 billion in 2012), Walmart.com is the giant retailer's attempt to become extremely successful in the e-commerce space. Today, over 1 million products are available through Walmart.com, with additional ones being regularly added to the site. Of course, competing in e-commerce pits Walmart.com squarely in competition with Amazon.com the largest online store on the planet.[91]

Although important, Walmart currently has very little dependence for its success on the e-commerce market. Of course, Walmart is taking actions such as trying to better integrate its physical stores with its technological and logistics skills[92] and is searching for ways to deliver purchases to online buyers in a fast and efficient (e.g., low cost) manner hoping to better compete with Amazon.com.

In contrast to Walmart, Amazon.com currently derives a strong majority of its sales volume from the e-commerce market, meaning that it has a high degree of market dependence. With approximately $89 billion in revenue in 2014, the firm is substantially smaller than Walmart's sales revenue of slightly more than $476 billion, although its total e-commerce sales revenue dwarfs that of Walmart.com's.[93] Given its dominant market position in e-commerce and in light of its dependence on the e-commerce market, it is virtually guaranteed that Amazon.com will continue responding to Walmart.com's competitive actions and responses.

5-7 Competitive Dynamics

Whereas competitive rivalry concerns the ongoing actions and responses between a firm and its direct competitors for an advantageous market position, *competitive dynamics* concerns the ongoing actions and responses among *all* firms competing within a market for advantageous positions.

To explain competitive dynamics, we explore the effects of varying rates of competitive speed in different markets (called slow-cycle, fast-cycle, and standard-cycle markets) on the behavior (actions and responses) of all competitors within a given market. Competitive behaviors, as well as the reasons for taking them, are similar within each market type, but differ across types of markets. Thus, competitive dynamics differ in slow-cycle, fast-cycle, and standard-cycle markets.

As noted in Chapter 1, firms want to sustain their competitive advantages for as long as possible, although no advantage is permanently sustainable. However, as we discuss next, the sustainability of the firm's competitive advantages differs by market type. The degree of sustainability is primarily affected by how quickly competitors can imitate a rival's competitive advantages and how costly it is to do so.

5-7a Slow-Cycle Markets

Slow-cycle markets are markets in which the firm's competitive advantages are shielded from imitation, commonly for long periods of time, and where imitation is costly.[94] Thus, competitive advantages are sustainable over longer periods of time in slow-cycle markets.

Building a unique and proprietary capability produces a competitive advantage and success in a slow-cycle market. This type of advantage is difficult for competitors to understand. As discussed in Chapter 3, a difficult-to-understand and costly-to-imitate capability usually results from unique historical conditions, causal ambiguity, and/or social complexity. Copyrights and patents are examples of these types of capabilities. After a proprietary advantage is developed on the basis of using its capabilities, the competitive actions and responses a firm takes in a slow-cycle market are oriented to protecting, maintaining, and extending that advantage. Major strategic actions in these markets, such as acquisitions, usually carry less risk than in faster-cycle markets.[95] Clearly, firms that gain an advantage can grow more and earn higher returns than those who simply track with the industry, especially in mature and declining industries.[96] However, as shown by the example of Kellogg, executives must be careful not to become overconfident in their success as competitors and markets change.[97]

Slow-cycle markets are markets in which the firm's competitive advantages are shielded from imitation, commonly for long periods of time, and where imitation is costly.

The Walt Disney Company continues to extend its proprietary characters, such as Mickey Mouse, Minnie Mouse, and Goofy. These characters have a unique historical development as a result of Walt and Roy Disney's creativity and vision for entertaining people. Products based on the characters seen in Disney's animated films are sold through Disney's theme park shops as well as freestanding retail outlets called Disney Stores. Because copyrights shield it, the proprietary nature of Disney's advantage in terms of animated character trademarks protects the firm from imitation by competitors.

Consistent with another attribute of competition in a slow-cycle market, Disney protects its exclusive rights to its characters and their use. As with all firms competing in slow-cycle markets, Disney's competitive actions (such as building theme parks in France, Japan, and China) and responses (such as lawsuits to protect its right to fully control use of its animated characters) maintain and extend its proprietary competitive advantage while protecting it.

Patent laws and regulatory requirements in the United States requiring FDA (Food and Drug Administration) approval to launch new products shield pharmaceutical companies' positions. Competitors in this market try to extend patents on their drugs to maintain advantageous positions that patents provide. However, after a patent expires, the firm is no longer shielded from competition, allowing generic imitations and usually leading to a loss of sales and profits. This was the case for Pfizer when Lipitor (which is the best-selling drug in history) went off patent in the fall of 2011. The firm's profits declined 19 percent in the first quarter after that event.

The competitive dynamics generated by firms competing in slow-cycle markets are shown in Figure 5.4. In slow-cycle markets, firms launch a product (e.g., a new drug) that has been developed through a proprietary advantage (e.g., R&D) and then exploit it for as long as possible while the product is shielded from competition. Eventually, competitors respond to the action with a counterattack. In markets for drugs, this counterattack commonly occurs as patents expire or are broken through legal means, creating the need for another product launch by the firm seeking a protected market position.

Figure 5.4 Gradual Erosion of a Sustained Competitive Advantage

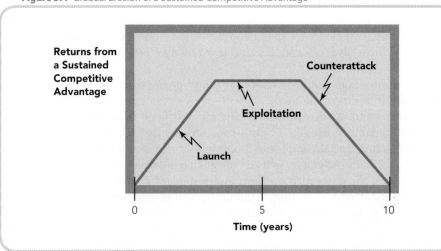

Source: Adapted from I. C. MacMillan, 1988, Controlling competitive dynamics by taking strategic initiative, *Academy of Management Executive*, II(2): 111–118.

5-7b Fast-Cycle Markets

Fast-cycle markets are markets in which the firm's capabilities that contribute to competitive advantages aren't shielded from imitation and where imitation is often rapid and inexpensive.[98] Thus, competitive advantages aren't sustainable in fast-cycle markets. Firms competing in fast-cycle markets recognize the importance of speed; these companies appreciate that "time is as precious a business resource as money or head count—and that the costs of hesitation and delay are just as steep as going over budget or missing a financial forecast."[99] Such high-velocity environments place considerable pressures on top managers to quickly make strategic decisions that are also effective. The often substantial competition and technology-based strategic focus make the strategic decision complex, increasing the need for a comprehensive approach integrated with decision speed, two often-conflicting characteristics of the strategic decision process.[100]

Reverse engineering and the rate of technology diffusion facilitate the rapid imitation that takes place in fast-cycle markets. A competitor uses reverse engineering to quickly gain the knowledge required to imitate or improve the firm's products. Technology is diffused rapidly in fast-cycle markets, making it available to competitors in a short period. The technology often used by fast-cycle competitors isn't proprietary, nor is it protected by patents as is the technology used by firms competing in slow-cycle markets. For example, only a few hundred parts, which are readily available on the open market, are required to build a PC. Patents protect only a few of these parts, such as microprocessor chips. Interestingly, research also demonstrates that showing what an incumbent firm knows and its research capability can be a deterrent to other firms to enter a market, even a fast-cycle market.[101]

Fast-cycle markets are more volatile than slow-cycle and standard-cycle markets. Indeed, the pace of competition in fast-cycle markets is almost frenzied, as companies rely on innovations as the engines of their growth. Because prices often decline quickly in these markets, companies need to profit rapidly from their product innovations.

Recognizing this reality, firms avoid "loyalty" to any of their products, preferring to cannibalize their own products before competitors learn how to do so through successful imitation. This emphasis creates competitive dynamics that differ substantially from those found in slow-cycle markets. Instead of concentrating on protecting, maintaining, and extending competitive advantages, as in slow-cycle markets, companies competing in fast-cycle markets focus on learning how to rapidly and continuously develop new competitive advantages that are superior to those they replace. They commonly search for fast and effective means of developing new products. For example, it is common in some industries with fast-cycle markets for firms to use strategic alliances to gain access to new technologies and thereby develop and introduce more new products into the market.[102] In recent years, many of these alliances have been offshore (with partners in foreign countries) in order to access appropriate skills while maintaining lower costs. However, finding the balance between sharing knowledge and skills with a foreign partner and preventing that partner from appropriating value from the focal firm's contributions to the alliance is challenging.[103]

The competitive behavior of firms competing in fast-cycle markets is shown in Figure 5.5. Competitive dynamics in this market type entail actions and responses that are oriented to rapid and continuous product introductions and the development of a stream of ever-changing competitive advantages. The firm launches a product to achieve a competitive advantage and then exploits the advantage for as long as possible. However, the firm also tries to develop another temporary competitive advantage before competitors can respond to the first one. Thus, competitive dynamics in fast-cycle markets often result in rapid product upgrades as well as quick product innovations.[104]

Fast-cycle markets are markets in which the firm's capabilities that contribute to competitive advantages aren't shielded from imitation and where imitation is often rapid and inexpensive.

Figure 5.5 Developing Temporary Advantages to Create Sustained Advantage

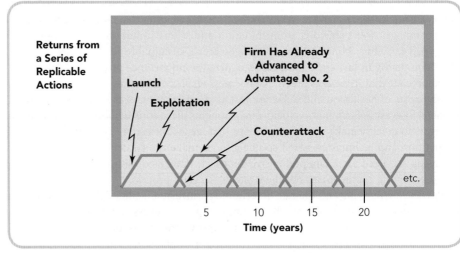

Source: Adapted from I. C. MacMillan, 1988, Controlling competitive dynamics by taking strategic initiative, *Academy of Management Executive*, II(2): 111–118.

Apple largely competes in fast-cycle markets; with the introduction of the new apple watch, Apple and its rivals are changing a typical standard cycle market to a fast-cycle market with 'smart' watches. Some analysts suggested that Apple had orders for at least a million watches before the official launch date. But, Apple's watch enters a market in which the product not only serves functional purposes but often is used as a 'fashion statement' for the owner. Apple's entry is inviting significant competition. As noted in the Opening Case, Google has partnered with TAG Heuer and Intel to develop a prestigious 'smart watch'. Apple may also experience some difficulties with its pricing for the watch. The base price for the watch is $349 with an aluminum case and elastic wrist band. The high-end price is $17,000 that comes with an 18-caret gold case, leather wrist band, and a brass buckle. Apple's watch is reported to continue its tradition of technological excellence which is difficult for competitors to match or beat. This new product market will have significantly interesting competitive dynamics.[105]

As our discussion suggests, innovation plays a critical role in the competitive dynamics in fast-cycle markets. For individual firms then, innovation is a key source of competitive advantage. Through innovation, the firm can cannibalize its own products before competitors successfully imitate them and still maintain an advantage through next-generation products.

As explained in the Strategic Focus, Aldi is having a major effect in the retail food markets across countries, especially in the United Kingdom, United States, and Australia. Aldi's extreme emphasis on low cost is hurting many of the major supermarket chains in each of those countries, and Aldi is gaining market share and expanding in all of them. The competitive rivalry is gaining strength. The retail food industry has largely operated as a standard-cycle market and sold products with small margins. With Aldi's growing power in the markets, firms are forced to operate with even smaller margins and reduced profits or cut their costs in order to compete on prices. It will be interesting to observe the winners and losers in this "war" in each country.

5-7c   Standard-Cycle Markets

Standard-cycle markets
are markets in which the firm's competitive advantages are partially shielded from imitation and imitation is moderately costly.

Standard-cycle markets are markets in which the firm's competitive advantages are partially shielded from imitation, and imitation is moderately costly. Competitive advantages are partially sustainable in standard-cycle markets, but only when the firm is able to continuously

Strategic Focus

The Ripple Effect of Supermarket Wars: Aldi Is Changing the Markets in Many Countries

Aldi was started as a small, family-owned grocery store by Mrs. Albrecht located in Essen, Germany in 1913. Two sons, Karl and Theo, took over the store in 1946 and soon began expansion. They emphasized low costs from the very beginning and thereby, provided very low prices for customers relative to competitors. Over time, Aldi expanded to other European countries, and it entered the United States market in 1976. Currently, Aldi has 8,500 stores with 1,400 of those in the United States. It operates stores in 18 countries, and it has stores in 36 states in the United States. Its annual sales revenues in the United States are approximately $70 million.

Aldi holds its costs down in a variety of ways. It largely sells its own brand-label products in "no frill" stores. The company limits the number of external brands it sells (usually one or two per product), and it has low packaging, transportation, and employee costs. The products are sold in stores similar to warehouse stores—on pallets and boxed in cut-a-way cardboard boxes. In Germany, Aldi advertises very little, but it does advertise in the United States. It produces its own ads in-house (no external agency) and advertises mostly through newspaper inserts and a few television commercials.

Aldi and another discount store, Lidl, have hurt the largest four supermarkets in the U.K. market—Tesco, Walmart's Asda, J Sainsbury, and Wm. Morrison Supermarkets. Aldi and Lidl have stolen market share from these retailers, especially Tesco and Morrison, and now have about 8.6 percent of the market. And, they are targeting growth to about 17 percent share of the market within the next five years. Tesco has controlled about 30 percent of the discount supermarket market, but it has been declining. Morrison's recent poor performance has precipitated turnover in most of the top executives at the firm. In addition, the new CEO, David Potts, has been making major changes—largely cutting costs in order to compete on prices. As a result of reduced costs, Morrison cut its prices on 130 staple items such as milk and eggs. Likewise, Tesco reduced prices of 380 of its brand products by about 25 percent. Yet, Aldi is emboldened by its gain in market share and plans to invest about $900 million to open 550 new stores in Britain by 2022.

Aldi is having similar effects on the Australian market. It has gained market share from the two largest supermarkets in Australia—Coles and Woolworths. Woolworths has signaled its plans to reduce its prices to avoid being perceived as the "expensive option." This action does not seem to concern Aldi which has announced plans for a $700 million expansion of 120–130 new stores by 2020 to add to its current number of 300 stores in Australia.

Aldi appears to be harming some competition in the United States as well. For example, a rival discount food retailer, Bottom

Dollar owned by Delhaize from Belgium, closed all of its stores (New Jersey, Pennsylvania, and Ohio) and sold the locations and leases to Aldi. Aldi does have stiffer competition in the United States from Walmart, Sam's (Walmart's warehouse stores), and Costco, among other discount food retailers. Yet, Aldi is still, not only surviving, but flourishing and growing in the U.S. market as well.

These supermarket wars caused by Aldi in the various markets are not only causing a ripple effect across country borders. The effects are also rippling to wholesalers and other suppliers. For example, wholesale prices have been declining, and some of the major supermarket chains, such as Tesco and Morrison, have been reducing the number of brands on their shelves. Interestingly, manufacturers of popular products, such as Mr. Kipling cakes and Bistro gravy, stand to gain shelf space and increase sales as a result to rivals' products being taken off the shelves. Of course, the suppliers whose products are eliminated will suffer.

The bottom line is that Aldi is having a major effect on rivals in multiple countries and on many other companies that supply products to the industry.

Aldi's low cost technique for displaying and selling goods with cutout boxes of goods stacked on pallets.

Sources: 2014, Aldi targets doubling of UK stores with 600 million pound investment, *New York Times*, www.nytimes.com, November 10; T. Hua, 2015, Tesco's overhaul points to a price war, *Wall Street Journal*, www.wsj.com, January 5; L. Northrup, 2015, Bottom dollar food to close stores, sell chain to Aldi, *Consumerist*, www.consumerist.com, January 5; 2015, Mr. Kipling Maker Premier Foods sees positives in supermarket wars, *New York Times*, www.nytimes.com, January 23; 2015, Morrisons cuts prices on 130 grocery staples like milk, eggs, *New York Times*, www.nytimes.com, February 15; 2015, British shop price decline steepens in February—BRC, *New York Times*, www.nytimes.com, March 3; K. Ross, 2015, Supermarket wars: Aldi takes on market share as Woolworths drops prices, Smart Company, www.smartcompany.com, March 9; A. Felsted, 2015, Morrison chiefs take express checkout from struggling supermarket, *Financial Times*, www.ft.com, March 24; 2015, Aldi Foods, www.grocery.com, accessed March 25.

upgrade the quality of its capabilities as a foundation for being able to stay ahead of competitors. The competitive actions and responses in standard-cycle markets are designed to seek large market shares, to gain customer loyalty through brand names, and to carefully control a firm's operations in order to consistently provide the same positive experience for customers.[106] This is how the retail food industry operated for many years. But, it is changing with discount competitors such as Aldi gaining strength in the market.

Companies competing in standard-cycle markets tend to serve many customers in what are typically highly competitive markets. Because the capabilities and core competencies on which their competitive advantages are based are less specialized, imitation is faster and less costly for standard-cycle firms than for those competing in slow-cycle markets. However, imitation is slower and more expensive in these markets than in fast-cycle markets. Thus, competitive dynamics in standard-cycle markets rest midway between the characteristics of dynamics in slow-cycle and fast-cycle markets. Imitation comes less quickly and is more expensive for standard-cycle competitors when a firm is able to develop economies of scale by combining coordinated and integrated design and manufacturing processes with a large sales volume for its products.

Because of large volumes, the size of mass markets, and the need to develop scale economies, the competition for market share is intense in standard-cycle markets. This form of competition is readily evident in the battles among consumer foods' producers, such as candy makers and major competitors Hershey Co.; Nestlé, SA; Mondelēz International, Inc. (the name for the former Kraft Foods Inc.); and Mars. (Of the firms, Hershey is far more dependent on candy sales than are the others.) Taste and the ingredients used to develop it, advertising campaigns, package designs, and availability through additional distribution channels are some of the many dimensions on which these competitors aggressively compete for the purpose of increasing their share of the candy market, as broadly defined.[107] In recent years, candy manufacturers have also had to contend with criticism from health professionals about the sugar, saturated fats, and calories their products provide, in terms of how all of these attributes can have negative effects on personal health.[108]

Innovation can also drive competitive actions and responses in standard-cycle markets, especially when rivalry is intense. Some innovations in standard-cycle markets are incremental rather than radical in nature (incremental and radical innovations are discussed in Chapter 13). For example, consumer foods producers are innovating within their lines of healthy products (as discussed in the Strategic Focus on Kellogg). Today, many firms are relying on innovation as a means of competing in standard-cycle markets and earning above-average returns.

Overall, innovation has a substantial influence on competitive dynamics as it affects the actions and responses of all companies competing within a slow-cycle, fast-cycle, or standard-cycle market. We have emphasized the importance of innovation to the firm's strategic competitiveness in earlier chapters and do so again in Chapter 13. These discussions highlight the importance of innovation for firms regardless of the type of competitive dynamics they encounter while competing.

SUMMARY

■ Competitors are firms competing in the same market, offering similar products, and targeting similar customers. Competitive rivalry is the ongoing set of competitive actions and responses occurring between competitors as they compete against each other for an advantageous market position. The outcomes of competitive rivalry influence the firm's ability to sustain its competitive advantages as well as the level (average, below average, or above average) of its financial returns.

- Competitive behavior is the set of competitive actions and responses an individual firm takes while engaged in competitive rivalry. Competitive dynamics is the set of actions and responses taken by all firms that are competitors within a particular market.

- Firms study competitive rivalry in order to predict the competitive actions and responses each of their competitors are likely to take. Competitive actions are either strategic or tactical in nature. The firm takes competitive actions to defend or build its competitive advantages or to improve its market position. Competitive responses are taken to counter the effects of a competitor's competitive action. A strategic action or a strategic response requires a significant commitment of organizational resources, is difficult to successfully implement, and is difficult to reverse. In contrast, a tactical action or a tactical response requires fewer organizational resources and is easier to implement and reverse. For example, for an airline company, entering major new markets is an example of a strategic action or a strategic response; changing its prices in a particular market is an example of a tactical action or a tactical response.

- A competitor analysis is the first step the firm takes to be able to predict its competitors' actions and responses. In Chapter 2, we discussed what firms do to *understand* competitors. This discussion was extended in this chapter to describe what the firm does to *predict* competitors' market-based actions. Thus, understanding precedes prediction. Market commonality (the number of markets with which competitors are jointly involved and their importance to each) and resource similarity (how comparable competitors' resources are in terms of type and amount) are studied to complete a competitor analysis. In general, the greater the market commonality and resource similarity, the more firms acknowledge that they are direct competitors.

- Market commonality and resource similarity shape the firm's awareness (the degree to which it and its competitors understand their mutual interdependence), motivation (the firm's incentive to attack or respond), and ability (the quality of the resources available to the firm to attack and respond). Having knowledge of these characteristics of a competitor increases the quality of the firm's predictions about that competitor's actions and responses.

- In addition to market commonality, resource similarity, awareness, motivation, and ability, three more specific factors affect the likelihood a competitor will take competitive actions. The first of these is first-mover benefits. First movers, those taking an initial competitive action, often gain loyal customers and earn above-average returns until competitors can successfully respond to their action. Not all firms can be first movers because they may lack the awareness, motivation, or ability required to engage in this type of competitive behavior. Moreover, some firms prefer to be a second mover (the firm responding to the first mover's action). One reason for this is that second movers, especially those acting quickly, often can

successfully compete against the first mover. By evaluating the first mover's product, customers' reactions to it, and the responses of other competitors to the first mover, the second mover may be able to avoid the early entrant's mistakes and find ways to improve upon the value created for customers by the first mover's goods or services. Late movers (those that respond a long time after the original action was taken) commonly are lower performers and are much less competitive.

- Organizational size tends to reduce the variety of competitive actions that large firms launch, while it increases the variety of actions undertaken by smaller competitors. Ideally, a firm prefers to initiate a large number of diverse actions when engaged in competitive rivalry. Another factor, quality, is a base denominator for competing successfully in the global economy. It is a necessary prerequisite to achieving competitive parity. However, it is a necessary but insufficient condition for establishing an advantage.

- The type of action (strategic or tactical) the firm took, the competitor's reputation for the nature of its competitor behavior, and that competitor's dependence on the market in which the action was taken are analyzed to predict a competitor's response to the firm's action. In general, the number of tactical responses taken exceeds the number of strategic responses. Competitors respond more frequently to the actions taken by the firm with a reputation for predictable and understandable competitive behavior, especially if that firm is a market leader. In general, the firm can predict that when its competitor is highly dependent on its revenue and profitability in the market in which the firm took a competitive action, that competitor is likely to launch a strong response. However, firms that are more diversified across markets are less likely to respond to a particular action that affects only one of the markets in which they compete.

- In slow-cycle markets, competitive advantages generally can be maintained for at least a period of time, and competitive dynamics often include actions and responses intended to protect, maintain, and extend the firm's proprietary advantages. In fast-cycle markets, competition is substantial as firms concentrate on developing a series of temporary competitive advantages. This emphasis is necessary because firms' advantages in fast-cycle markets aren't proprietary and, as such, are subject to rapid and relatively inexpensive imitation. Standard-cycle markets have a level of competition between that in slow-cycle and fast-cycle markets; firms often (but not always) are moderately shielded from competition in these markets as they use capabilities that produce competitive advantages that are moderately sustainable. Competitors in standard-cycle markets serve mass markets and try to develop economies of scale to enhance their profitability. Innovation is vital to competitive success in each of the three types of markets. Companies should recognize that the set of competitive actions and responses taken by all firms differs by type of market.

KEY TERMS

competitors 144
competitive rivalry 144
competitive behavior 144
competitive dynamics 144
competitive action 152
competitive response 152
first mover 153
fast-cycle markets 161
late mover 155
multimarket competition 144

market commonality 148
quality 156
resource similarity 148
strategic action 152
strategic response 152
second mover 154
slow-cycle markets 159
standard-cycle markets 162
tactical action 152
tactical response 152

REVIEW QUESTIONS

1. Who are competitors? How are competitive rivalry, competitive behavior, and competitive dynamics defined in the chapter?

2. What is market commonality? What is resource similarity? In what way are these concepts the building blocks for a competitor analysis?

3. How do awareness, motivation, and ability affect the firm's competitive behavior?

4. What factors affect the likelihood a firm will take a competitive action?

5. What factors affect the likelihood a firm will initiate a competitive response to a competitor's action(s)?

6. What competitive dynamics can be expected among firms competing in slow-cycle markets? In fast-cycle markets? In standard-cycle markets?

Mini-Case

FedEx and United Parcel Service (UPS): Maintaining Success while Competing Aggressively

Identified recently as one of the 50 greatest or most intense competitive rivalries of all time, FedEx and UPS are similar in many ways, including their resources, the markets they serve, and the competitive dimensions that they emphasize to implement similar strategies. These similarities mean that the firms are direct competitors and that they are keenly aware of each other and have the motivation and ability to respond to the competitive actions they take against each other. The two firms are the largest global courier delivery companies in what is a highly competitive industry on a global basis.

FedEx and UPS compete in many of the same product markets, including next day delivery, cheaper ground delivery, time-guaranteed delivery (both domestically and internationally), and freight services. However, the firms concentrate on different segments

in attempting to create superior stakeholder value and to avoid direct, head-to-head competition in a host of product segments and markets. In this regard, FedEx "intends to leverage and extend the FedEx brand and to provide customers with seamless access to its entire portfolio of integrated transportation services," while UPS "seeks to position itself as the primary coordinator of the flow of goods, information, and funds throughout the entire supply chain (the movement from the raw materials and parts stage through final consumption of the finished product)."

Thus, while these firms are similar, they also seek to differentiate themselves in ways that enhance the possibility of being able to gain strategic competitiveness and earn above-average returns. In broad-stroke terms, FedEx concentrates more on transportation services and international markets. (Recently, FedEx was generating 48 percent of revenue internationally, while UPS was earning 22 percent of its revenue from international markets.) Meanwhile, UPS concentrates more on the entire value chain while competing domestically. FedEx is the world's largest international air shipping firm, while UPS is the world's largest package delivery company.

There are many actions the firms have recently taken to sharpen their ability to outcompete their primary competitor. In mid-2013, FedEx learned that its contract to fly domestic mail for the U.S. Postal Service had been selected for renewal. UPS also bid on the contract, and thus it lost this competitive battle to its rival. To support its strength in logistics as part of the entire supply chain, UPS recently agreed to buy "Hungary-based pharmaceutical-logistics company Cemelog Zrt for an undisclosed amount in a deal to strengthen its health-care business in Europe, giving it access to the increasingly important markets of Central and Eastern Europe." UPS is also emphasizing trans-border European Union services as a

growth engine for the foreseeable future. To enhance its ability to compete against UPS and other rivals as well, FedEx is restructuring some of its operations to increase efficiency. Similarly, the firm is increasing its emphasis on finding ways for its independent express, ground, and freight networks to work together more synergistically.

Although the rivalry between FedEx and UPS is intense and aggressive, it is also likely that this rivalry makes each firm stronger and more agile because each has to be at its best in order to outperform the other. Thus in many ways, each of these firms is a "good competitor" for the other one.

Sources: 2013, FedEx Corp., *Standard & Poor's Stock Report*, www.standardandpoors.com, May 25; 2013; United Parcel Service, Inc., *Standard & Poor's Stock Report*, www.standardandpoors.com, May 25; L. Eaton, 2013, FedEx CEO: Truck fleets to shift to natural gas from diesel, *Wall Street Journal*, www.wsj.com, March 8; V. Mock, 2013, UPS to appeal EU's block of TNT merger, *Wall Street Journal*, www.wsj.com, April 7; B. Morris & B. Sechler, 2013, FedEx customers like slower and cheaper, *Wall Street Journal*, www.wsj.com, March 20; B. Sechler, 2013, Online shopping boosts profit for UPS, *Wall Street Journal*, www.wsj.com, April 25; B. Sechler, 2013, FedEx fends off rivals for U.S. Postal, *Wall Street Journal*, www.wsj.com, April 23.

Case Discussion Questions

1. FedEx and UPS have many similar resources and compete across many of the same markets. How are they different? Stated differently, how do they differentiate themselves?

2. What are some of the major and unique strategic actions taken by each firm? Have these actions been successful?

3. Based on information in the case and from your research, which of these firms do you predict will be the most successful in the future? Please explain your reasons.

NOTES

1. S. Carnahan & D. Somaya, 2013, Alumni effects and relational advantage: The impact of outsourcing when your buyer hires employees from your competitors, *Academy of Management Journal*, 56: 1578–1600; M.-J. Chen & D. Miller, 2012, Competitive dynamics: Themes, trends, and a prospective research platform, *Academy of Management Annals*, 6: 135–210; M.-J. Chen, 1996, Competitor analysis and interfirm rivalry: Toward a theoretical integration, *Academy of Management Review*, 21: 100–134.

2. M. G. Jacobides & C. J. Tae, 2015, Kingpins, bottlenecks, and value dynamics along a sector, *Organization Science*, in press; P. C. Patel, S. A. Fernhaber, P. P. McDougall-Covin, & R. P. van der Have, 2014, Beating competitors to international markets: The value of geographically balanced networks

for innovation, *Strategic Management Journal*, 35: 691–711.

3. S. B. Choi & C. Williams, 2014, The impact of innovation intensity, scope and spillovers on sales growth in Chinese firms, *Asia Pacific Journal of Management*, 31: 25–46; T. Zahavi & D. Lavie, 2013, Intra-industry diversification and firm performance, *Strategic Management Journal*, 34: 978–998.

4. K. M. Park, K. Jung, & K. C. Noh, 2014, Strategic actions and customer mobility: Antecedents and consequences of strategic actions in the Korean mobile telecommunications service industry, *Asia Pacific Journal of Management*, 31: 171–193; P. T. M. Ingenbleek & I. A. van der Lans, 2013, Relating price strategies and price-setting practices, *European Journal of Marketing*, 47: 27–48.

5. F. J. Mas-Ruiz, F. Ruiz-Moreno, & A. L. de Guevara Martinez, 2014, Asymmetric rivalry within and between strategic groups, *Strategic Management Journal*, 35: 419–439; P. J. Derfus, P. G. Maggitti, C. M. Grimm, & K. G. Smith, 2008, The red queen effect: Competitive actions and firm performance, *Academy of Management Journal*, 51: 61–80; C. M. Grimm, H. Lee, & K. G. Smith, 2006, *Strategy as Action: Competitive Dynamics and Competitive Advantage*, New York: Oxford University Press.

6. C. Giachetti & G. B. Dagnino, 2014, Detecting the relationship between competitive intensity and firm product line length: Evidence from the worldwide mobile phone industry, *Strategic Management Journal*, 35: 1398–1409; R. B. Mackay & R. Chia, 2012, Choice, chance,

and unintended consequences in strategic change: A process understanding of the rise and fall of NorthCo Automotive, *Academy of Management Journal*, 56: 1–13.

7. M. Srivastava, A. Frankly, & L. Martinette, 2013, Building a sustainable competitive advantage, *Journal of Technology Management & Innovation*, 8: 47–60; G. J. Kilduff, H. A. Elfenbein, & B. M. Staw, 2010, The psychology of rivalry: A relationally dependent analysis of competition, *Academy of Management Journal*, 53: 943–969; D. G. Sirmon, S. Gove, & M. A. Hitt, 2008, Resource management in dyadic competitive rivalry: The effects of resource bundling and deployment, *Academy of Management Journal*, 51: 919–935.

8. R. Kapoor & N. R. Furr, 2015, Complementarities and competition: Unpacking the drivers of entrants' technology choices in the solar photovoltaic industry, *Strategic Management Journal*, 6: 416–436; S.-J. Chang & S. H. Park, 2012, Winning strategies in China: Competitive dynamics between MNCs and local firms, *Long Range Planning*, 45: 1–15.

9. A. Nair & D. D. Selover, 2012, A study of competitive dynamics, *Journal of Business Research*, 65: 355–361; Grimm, Lee, & Smith, *Strategy as Action*.

10. R. Chellappa, V. Sambamurthy, & N. Saraf, 2010, Competing in crowded markets: Multimarket contact and the nature of competition in the enterprise systems software industry, *Information Systems Research: Special Issue on Digital Systems and Competition*, 21: 614–630.

11. T. Yu, M. Subramaniam, & A. A. Cannella, 2009, Rivalry deterrence in international markets: Contingencies governing the mutual forbearance hypothesis, *Academy of Management Journal*, 52: 127–147; K. G. Smith, W. J. Ferrier, & H. Ndofor, 2001, Competitive dynamics research: Critique and future directions. In M. A. Hitt, R. E. Freeman, & J. S. Harrison (eds.), *Handbook of Strategic Management*, Oxford, U.K.: Blackwell Publishers, 326.

12. F. Bridoux, K. G. Smith, & C. M. Grimm, 2011, The management of resources: Temporal effects of different types of actions on performance, *Journal of Management*, 33: 1281–1310; G. Young, K. G. Smith, & C. M. Grimm, 1996, "Austrian" and industrial organization perspectives on firm-level competitive activity and performance, *Organization Science*, 73: 243–254.

13. R. Duprey, 2015, Giant tobacco merger finds itself at the mercy of a tiny rival, *Motley Fool*, www.motleyfool.com, March 23; 2014, Altria set to pose a stiff challenge to existing e-cigarette leaders, *Forbes*, www.forbes.com, June 3; M. Esteri, 2013, Big tobacco is about to dive into e-cigarettes, *Wall Street Journal*, www.wsj.com, May 29.

14. R. Katila, E. L. Chen, & H. Piezunka, 2012, All the right moves: How entrepreneurial firms compete effectively, *Strategic Entrepreneurship Journal*, 6: 116–132; J. Marcel, P. Barr, & I. Duhaime, 2011, The influence of executive cognition on competitive dynamics, *Strategic Management Journal*, 32: 115–138.

15. R. Casadesus-Masanell & F. Zhu, 2013, Business model innovation and competitive imitation: The case of sponsor-based business models, *Strategic Management Journal*, 34: 464–482; M.-J. Chen & D. C. Hambrick, 1995, Speed, stealth, and selective attack: How small firms differ from large firms in competitive behavior, *Academy of Management Journal*, 38: 453–482.

16. M. A. Abebe & A. Angriawan, 2014, Organizational and competitive influences of exploration and exploitation activities in small firms, *Journal of Business Research*, 67: 339–345; V. Rindova, W. Ferrier, & R. Wiltbank, 2010, Value from gestalt: How sequences of competitive actions create advantage for firms in nascent markets, *Strategic Management Journal*, 31: 1474–1497; T. Yu & A. A. Cannella, Jr., Rivalry between multinational enterprises: An event history approach, *Academy of Management Journal*, 50: 665–686.

17. A. E. Bass & S. Chakrabarti, 2014, Resource security: Competition for global resources, strategic intent and governments as owners, *Journal of International Business Studies*, 45: 961–979; J. Villanueva, A. H. Van de Ven, & H. Sapienza, 2012, Resource mobilization in entrepreneurial firms, *Journal of Business Venturing*, 27: 19–30; Smith, Ferrier, & Ndofor, Competitive dynamics research, 319.

18. C. Boone, F. C. Wezel, & A. van Witteloostuijn, 2013, Joining the pack or going solo? A dynamic theory of new firm positioning, *Journal of Business Venturing*, 28: 511–527; H. Ndofor, D. G. Sirmon, & X. He, 2011, Firm resources, competitive actions and performance: Investigating a mediated model with evidence from the in-vitro diagnostics industry, *Strategic Management Journal*, 32: 640–657.

19. S.-J. Chang & B. Wu, 2014, Institutional barriers and industry dynamics, *Strategic Management Journal*, 35: 1103–1123; L. M. Ellram, W. L. Tate, & E. G. Feitzinger, 2013, Factor-market rivalry and competition for supply chain resources, *Journal of Supply Chain Management*, 49: 29–46; D. G. Sirmon, M. A. Hitt, J. Arregle, & J. Campbell, 2010, The dynamic interplay of capability strengths and weaknesses: Investigating the bases of temporary competitive advantage, *Strategic Management Journal*, 31: 1386–1409.

20. H. Rahmandad, 2012, Impact of growth opportunities and competition on firm-level capability development trade-offs, *Organization Science*, 34: 138–154; Y. Y. Kor & J. T. Mahoney, 2005, How dynamics, management, and governance of resource deployments influence firm-level performance, *Strategic Management Journal*, 26: 489–496.

21. Y. Zhang, Y. Li, & H. Li, 2014, FDI Spillovers over time in an emerging market: The roles of entry tenure and barriers to imitation, *Academy of Management Journal*, 57: 698–722; L. Mulotte, P. Dussauge, & W. Mitchell, 2013, Does pre-entry licensing undermine the performance of subsequent independent activities? Evidence from the global aerospace industry, 1944–2000, *Strategic Management Journal*, 34: 358–372.

22. L. K. S. Lim, 2013, Mapping competitive prediction capability: Construct conceptualization and performance payoffs, *Journal of Business Research*, 66: 1576–1586; J. C. Baum & A. Satorra, 2007, The persistence of abnormal returns at industry and firm levels: Evidence from Spain, *Strategic Management Journal*, 28: 707–722.

23. M. A. Hitt & K. Xu, 2015, The transformation of China: Effects of the institutional environment on business actions, *Long Range Planning*, in press; J.-L. Arregle, T. L. Miller, M. A. Hitt, & P. W. Beamish, 2013, Do regions matter? An integrated institutional and semiglobalization perspective on the internationalization of MNEs, *Strategic Management Journal*, 34: 910–934.

24. R. M. Holmes, H. Li, M. A. Hitt, & K. DeGetto, 2015, The effects of China's location advantages and location disadvantages on MNCs' establishment of China R&D centers, *Long Range Planning*, in press; O. Alexy, G. George, & A. Salter, 2013, Cui Bono? The selective revealing of knowledge and its implications for innovative activity, *Academy of Management Review*, 38: 270–291; Chen, Competitor analysis, 109.

25. T. Lawton, T. Rajwani, & P. Reinmoeller, 2012, Do you have a survival instinct? Leveraging genetic codes to achieve fit in hostile business environments, *Business Horizons*, 55: 81–91; 2011, The power of blindspots. What companies don't know, surprises them. What they don't want to know, kills them, *Strategic Direction*, 27(4): 3–4; D. Ng, R. Westgren, & S. Sonka, 2009, Competitive blind spots in an institutional field, *Strategic Management Journal*, 30: 349–369.

26. E. Metayer, 2013, How intelligent is your company? *Competia*, www.competia.com, March.

27. J. Neff, 2011, P&G e-commerce chief sees blurring of sales, marketing, *Advertising Age*, April 11, 8.

28. 2015, About YRC, YRC homepage, www.yrc.com, April 13.

29. J. W. Upson, D. J. Ketchen, Jr., B. L. Connelly, & A. L. Ranft, 2012, Competitor analysis and foothold moves, *Academy of Management Journal*, 55: 93–110; Chen, Competitor analysis, 106.

30. T. Yu & A. A. Cannella, Jr., 2013, A comprehensive review of multimarket competition research, *Journal of*

Management, 39: 76–109; J. Anand, L. F. Mesquita, & R. S. Vassolo, 2009, The dynamics of multimarket competition in exploration and exploitation activities, *Academy of Management Journal*, 52: 802–821.

31. S. P. L. Fourne, J. J. P. Jansen, & T. J. M. Mom, 2014, Strategic agility in MNEs: Managing tensions to capture opportunities across emerging and established markets, *California Management Review*, 56(3): 1–26.

32. W. Kang, B. Bayus, & S. Balasubramanian, 2010, The strategic effects of multimarket contact: Mutual forbearance and competitive response in the personal computer industry, *Journal of Marketing Research*, 47: 415–427.

33. V. Bilotkach, 2011, Multimarket contact and intensity of competition: Evidence from an airline merger, *Review of Industrial Organization*, 38: 95–115; H. R. Greve, 2008, Multimarket contact and sales growth: Evidence from insurance, *Strategic Management Journal*, 29: 229–249; J. Gimeno, 1999, Reciprocal threats in multimarket rivalry: Staking out "spheres of influence" in the U.S. airline industry, *Strategic Management Journal*, 20: 101–128.

34. M. Liu, 2015, Davids against goliaths? Collective identities and the market success of peripheral organizations during resource partitioning, *Organization Science*, in press; L. A. Costa, K. Cool, & I. Dierickx, 2013, The competitive implications of the deployment of unique resources, *Strategic Management Journal*, 34: 445–463; Chen, Competitor analysis, 107.

35. P. J. Patel, S. A. Fernhaber, P. P. McDougal-Covin, & R. P. Van Der Have, 2014, Beating competitors to international markets: The value of geographically balanced networks for innovation, *Strategic Management Journal*, 35: 691–711; J. Haleblian, G. McNamara, K. Kolev, & B. J. Dykes, 2012, Exploring firm characteristics that differentiate leaders from followers in industry merger waves: A competitive dynamics perspective, *Strategic Management Journal*, 33: 1037–1052; Chen, Competitor analysis, 110.

36. K.-Y. Hsieh, W. Tsai, & M.-J. Chen, 2015, If they can do it, why not us? Competitors reference points for justifying escalation of commitment, *Academy of Management Journal*, 58: 38–58; C. Flammer, 2013, Corporate social responsibility and shareholder reaction: The environmental awareness of investors, *Academy of Management Journal*, 56: 758–781.

37. B. Larraneta, S. A. Zahra, & J. L. Galan, 2014, Strategic repertoire variety and new venture growth: The moderating effects of origin and industry dynamism, *Strategic Management Journal*, 35: 761–772; J. Tang & B. S.-C. Liu, 2012, Strategic alignment and foreign entry performance: A holistic approach of the impact of entry timing, mode and location, *Business and Systems Research*, 6: 456–478; R. S. Livengood & R. K. Reger, 2010, That's our turf! Identity domains and competitive dynamics, *Academy of Management Review*, 35: 48–66.

38. S. D. Singh, 2015, Caterpillar faces 'aggressive' Komatsu fueled by yen, *Yahoo*, finance.yahoo.com, March 23; B. Tita, 2013, Caterpillar expected to cut 2013 forecasts, *Wall Street Journal*, www.wsj.com, April 21.

39. A. Compagni, V. Mele, & D. Ravasi, 2015, How early implementations influence later adoptions of innovation: Social positioning and skill reproduction in the diffusion of robotic surgery, *Academy of Management Journal*, 58: 242–278; S. H. Park & D. Zhou, 2005, Firm heterogeneity and competitive dynamics in alliance formation, *Academy of Management Review*, 30: 531–554.

40. T.-J. A. Peng, S. Pike, J. C.-H. Yang, & G. Roos, 2012, Is cooperation with competitors a good idea? An example in practice, *British Journal of Management*, 23: 532–560; Chen, Competitor analysis, 113.

41. L.-H. Lin, 2014, Subsidiary performance: The contingency of the multinational corporation's strategy, *European Management Journal*, 32: 928–937; C. Williams & S. Lee, 2011, Entrepreneurial contexts and knowledge coordination within the multinational corporation, *Journal of World Business*, 46: 253–264; M. Leiblein & T. Madsen, 2009, Unbundling competitive heterogeneity: Incentive structures and capability influences on technological innovation, *Strategic Management Journal*, 30: 711–735.

42. R. Makadok, 2010, The interaction effect of rivalry restraint and competitive advantage on profit: Why the whole is less than the sum of the parts, *Management Science*, 56: 356–372.

43. C. M. Grimm & K. G. Smith, 1997, *Strategy as Action: Industry Rivalry and Coordination*, Cincinnati: South-Western Publishing Co., 125.

44. H. Brea-Solis, R. Casadesus-Masanell, & E. Grifell-Tatje, 2015, Business model evaluation: Quantifying Walmart's sources of advantage, *Strategic Entrepreneurship Journal*, 9: 12–33.

45. M. A. Cusumano, S. J. Kahl, & F. F. Suarez, 2015, Services, industry evolution and the competitive strategies of product firms, *Strategic Management Journal*, 36: 559–575; J. Alcacer, C. L. Dezso, & M. Zhao, 2013, Firm rivalry, knowledge accumulation, and MNE location choices, *Journal of International Business Studies*, 44: 504–520.

46. G. Gavetti, 2012, Perspective—Toward a behavioral theory of strategy, *Organization Science*, 23: 267–285; B. L. Connelly, L. Tihanyi, S. T. Certo, & M. A. Hitt, 2010, Marching to the beat of different drummers: The influence of institutional owners on competitive actions, *Academy of Management Journal*, 53: 723–742.

47. T. B. Lee, 2013, Here's why Microsoft is buying Nokia's phone business, *Washington Post*, www.washingtonpost. com, September 3; 2011, Nokia and Microsoft announce plans for a broad strategic partnership to build a new global mobile ecosystem, Microsoft Home Page, www.microsoft.com, February 10.

48. J. Schumpeter, 1934, *The Theory of Economic Development*, Cambridge, MA: Harvard University Press.

49. N. Argyres, L. Bigelow, & J. A. Nickerson, 2015, Dominant designs, innovation schocks and the follower's dilemma, *Strategic Management Journal*, 36: 216–234; S. Bakker, H. van Lente, & M. T. H. Meeus, 2012, Dominance in the prototyping phase—The case of hydrogen passenger cars, *Research Policy*, 41: 871–883.

50. C. B. Bingham, N. R. Furr, & K. M. Eisenhardt, 2014, The opportunity paradox, *MIT Sloan Management Review*, 56(1): 29–39; L. Sleuwaegen & J. Onkelinx, 2014, International commitment, post-entry growth and survival of international new ventures, *Journal of Business Venturing*, 29: 106–120; F. F. Suarez & G. Lanzolla, 2007, The role of environmental dynamics in building a first mover advantage theory, *Academy of Management Review*, 32: 377–392.

51. G. M. McNamara, J. Haleblian, & B. J. Dykes, 2008, The performance implications of participating in an acquisition wave: Early mover advantages, bandwagon effects, and the moderating influence of industry characteristics and acquirer tactics, *Academy of Management Journal*, 51, 113–130.

52. R. K. Sinha & C. H. Noble, 2008, The adoption of radical manufacturing technologies and firm survival, *Strategic Management Journal*, 29: 943–962; D. P. Forbes, 2005, Managerial determinants of decision speed in new ventures, *Strategic Management Journal*, 26: 355–366.

53. H. R. Greve, 2009, Bigger and safer: The diffusion of competitive advantage, *Strategic Management Journal*, 30: 1–23; W. T. Robinson & S. Min, 2002, Is the first to market the first to fail? Empirical evidence for industrial goods businesses, *Journal of Marketing Research*, 39: 120–128.

54. J. C. Short & G. T. Payne, 2008, First-movers and performance: Timing is everything, *Academy of Management Review*, 33: 267–270.

55. E. de Oliveira & W. B. Werther, Jr., 2013, Resilience: Continuous renewal of competitive advantages, *Business Horizons*, 56: 333–342.

56. A. Hawk, G. Pacheco-De-Almeida, & B. Yeung, 2013, Fast-mover advantages: Speed capabilities and entry into the emerging submarket of Atlantic basin LNG, *Strategic Management Journal*, 34: 1531–1550; N. M. Jakopin & A. Klein, 2012, First-mover and incumbency advantages in mobile telecommunications, *Journal of Business Research*, 65: 362–370.

57. E. R. Banalieva, 2014, Embracing the second best? Synchronization of reform speeds, excess high discretion slack and performance of transition economy firms, *Global Strategy Journal*, 4: 104–126; K. Mellahi & A. Wilkinson, 2010, A study of the association between level of slack reduction following downsizing and innovation output, *Journal of Management Studies*, 47: 483–508.

58. R. Mudambi & T. Swift, 2014, Knowing when to leap: Transitioning between exploitative and explorative R&D, *Strategic Management Journal*, 35: 126–145; M. B. Lieberman & D. B. Montgomery, 1988, First-mover advantages, *Strategic Management Journal*, 9: 41–58.

59. H. R. Greve & M.-D. L. Seidel, 2015, The thin red line between success and failure: Path dependence in the diffusion of innovative production technologies, *Strategic Management Journal*, 36: 475–496; G. Pacheco-De-Almeida, 2010, Erosion, time compression, and self-displacement of leaders in hypercompetitive environments, *Strategic Management Journal*, 31: 1498–1526.

60. J. Y. Yang, J. Li, & A. Delios, 2015, Will a second mouse get the cheese? Learning from early entrant's failures in a foreign market, *Organization Science*, in press; F. Zhu & M. Iansiti, 2012, Entry into platform-based markets, *Strategic Management Journal*, 33: 88–106.

61. M. A. Stanko & J. D. Bohlmann, 2013, Demand-side inertia factors and their benefits for innovativeness, *Journal of the Academy of Marketing Science*, 41: 649–668; M. Poletti, B. Engelland, & H. Ling, 2011, An empirical study of declining lead times: Potential ramifications on the performance of early market entrants, *Journal of Marketing Theory and Practice*, 19: 27–38.

62. S. Bin, 2011, First-mover advantages: Flexible or not?, *Journal of Management & Marketing Research*, 7: 1–13; J. Gimeno, R. E. Hoskisson, B. B. Beal, & W. P. Wan, 2005, Explaining the clustering of international expansion moves: A critical test in the U.S. telecommunications industry, *Academy of Management Journal*, 48: 297–319; K. G. Smith, C. M. Grimm, & M. J. Gannon, 1992, *Dynamics of Competitive Strategy*, Newberry Park, CA: Sage Publications.

63. A. Picchi, 2014, Why Angie's list is getting a rash of bad reviews, CBS News, www. cbsnews.com, January 16.

64. N. K. Park, J. M. Mezias, J Lee, & J.-H. Han, 2014, Reverse knowledge diffusion: competitive dynamics and the knowledge seeking behavior of Korean high-tech firms, *Asia Pacific Journal of Management*, 31: 355–37; A. Fleury & M. Fleury, 2009, Understanding the strategies of late-movers in international manufacturing, *International Journal of Production Economics*, 122: 340–350; J. Li & R. K. Kozhikode, 2008, Knowledge management and innovation strategy:

The challenge for latecomers in emerging economies, *Asia Pacific Journal of Management*, 25: 429–450.

65. E. Golovko & G. Valentini, 2014, Selective learning-by-exporting: Firm size and product versus process innovation, *Global Strategy Journal*, 4: 161–180; F. Karakaya & P. Yannopoulos, 2011, Impact of market entrant characteristics on incumbent reactions to market entry, *Journal of Strategic Marketing*, 19: 171–185; S. D. Dobrev & G. R. Carroll, 2003, Size (and competition) among organizations: Modeling scale-based selection among automobile producers in four major countries, 1885–1981, *Strategic Management Journal*, 24: 541–558.

66. W. Stam, S. Arzianian, & T. Elfring, 2014, Social capital of entrepreneurs and small firm performance: A meta-analysis of contextual and methodological moderators, *Journal of Business Venturing*, 29: 152–173; L. F. Mesquita & S. G. Lazzarini, 2008, Horizontal and vertical relationships in developing economies: Implications for SMEs access to global markets, *Academy of Management Journal*, 51: 359–380.

67. G. D. Markman & T. L. Waldron, 2014, Small entrants and large incumbents: A framework of micro entry, *Academy of Management Perspectives*, 28: 178–197; C. Zhou & A. Van Witteloostuijn, 2010, Institutional constraints and ecological processes: Evolution of foreign-invested enterprises in the Chinese construction industry, 1993–2006, *Journal of International Business Studies*, 41: 539–556; M. A. Hitt, L. Bierman, & J. D. Collins, 2007, The strategic evolution of U.S. law firms, *Business Horizons*, 50: 17–28.

68. Young, Smith, & Grimm, "Austrian" and industrial organization perspectives.

69. P. B. Crosby, 1980, *Quality Is Free*, New York: Penguin; W. E. Deming, 1986, *Out of the Crisis*, Cambridge, MA: MIT Press.

70. X. Luo, V. K. Kanuri, & M. Andrews, 2014, How does CEO tenure matter? The mediating role of firm-employee and firm-customer relationships, *Strategic Management Journal*, 35: 492–511; R. C. Ford & D. R. Dickson, 2012, Enhancing customer self-efficacy in co-producing service experiences, *Business Horizons*, 55: 179–188.

71. B. G. King & E. T. Walker, 2014, Winning hearts and minds: Field theory and the three dimensions of strategy, *Strategic Organization*, 12: 134–141; L. A. Bettencourt & S. W. Brown, 2013, From goods to great: Service innovation in a product-dominated company, *Business Horizons*, 56: 277–283.

72. F. Pakdil, 2010, The effects of TQM on corporate performance. *The Business Review*, 15: 242–248; A. Azadegan, K. J. Dooley, P. L. Carter, & J. R. Carter, 2008, Supplier innovativeness and the role of interorganizational learning in enhancing manufacturing capabilities, *Journal of Supply Chain Management*, 44(4): 14–35.

73. M. Terziovski & P. Hermel, 2011, The role of quality management practice in the performance of integrated supply chains: A multiple cross-case analysis, *The Quality Management Journal*, 18(2): 10–25; K. E. Weick & K. M. Sutcliffe, 2001, *Managing the Unexpected*, San Francisco: Jossey-Bass, 81–82.

74. D. P. McIntyre, 2011, In a network industry, does product quality matter? *Journal of Product Innovation Management*, 28: 99–108; G. Macintosh, 2007, Customer orientation, relationship quality, and relational benefits to the firm, *Journal of Services Marketing*, 21: 150–159.

75. K. R. Sarangee & R. Echambadi, 2014, Firm-specific determinants of product line technology strategies in high technology markets, *Strategic Entrepreneurship Journal*, 8: 149–166; S. Thirumalai & K. K. Sinha, 2011, Product recalls in the medical device industry: An empirical exploration of the sources and financial consequences, *Management Science*, 57: 376–392.

76. M. Su & V. R. Rao, 2011, Timing decisions of new product preannouncement and launch with competition, *International Journal of Production Economics*, 129: 51–64.

77. M. L. Sosa, 2013, Decoupling market incumbency from organizational prehistory: Locating the real sources of competitive advantage in R&D for radical innovation, *Strategic Management Journal*, 34: 245–255; T. R. Crook, D. J. Ketchen, J. G. Combs, & S. Y. Todd, 2008, Strategic resources and performance: A meta-analysis, *Strategic Management Journal*, 29: 1141–1154.

78. S. W. Smith, 2014, Follow me to the innovation frontier? Leaders, laggards and the differential effects of imports and exports on technological innovation, *Journal of International Business Studies*, 45: 248–274; C. Lutz, R. Kemp, & S. Gerhard Dijkstra, 2010, Perceptions regarding strategic and structural entry barriers, *Small Business Economics*, 35: 19–33; M. J. Chen & I. C. MacMillan, 1992, Nonresponse and delayed response to competitive moves, *Academy of Management Journal*, 35: 539–570.

79. S. Awate, M. M. Larsen, & R. Mudambi, 2015, Accessing vs sourcing knowledge: A comparative study of R&D internationalization between emerging and advanced economy firms, *Journal of International Business Studies*, 46: 63–86; S. M. Ben-Menahem, Z. Kwee, H. W. Volberda, & F. A. J. Van Den Bosch, 2013, Strategic renewal over time: The enabling role of potential absorptive capacity in aligning internal and external rates of change, *Long Range Planning*, 46: 216–235; M. J. Chen, K. G. Smith, & C. M. Grimm, 1992, Action characteristics as predictors of competitive responses, *Management Science*, 38: 439–455.

80. S. Ansari & P. Krop, 2012, Incumbent performance in the face of a radical innovation: Towards a framework for incumbent challenger dynamics, *Research Policy*, 41: 1357–1374; M. J. Chen & D. Miller, 1994, Competitive attack, retaliation and performance: An expectancy-valence framework, *Strategic Management Journal*, 15: 85–102.

81. K. Muller, K. Huschelrath, & V. Bilotkach, 2012, The construction of a low-cost airline network—facing competition and exploring new markets, *Managerial and Decision Economics*, 33: 485–499; N. Huyghebaert & L. M. van de Gucht, 2004, Incumbent strategic behavior in financial markets and the exit of entrepreneurial start-ups, *Strategic Management Journal*, 25: 669–688.

82. O. Sorenson, 2014, Status and reputation: Synonyms or separate concepts? *Strategic Organization*, 12: 62–69; Smith, Ferrier, & Ndofor, Competitive dynamics research, 333.

83. E. Fauchart & R. Cowan, 2014, Weak links and the management of reputational interdependencies, *Strategic Management Journal*, 35: 532–549; V. Babic-Hodovic, M. Arlsanagic, & E. Mehic, 2013, Importance of internal marketing for service companies corporate reputation and customer satisfaction, *Journal of Business Administration Research*, 2: 49–57; T. Obloj & L. Capron, 2011, Role of resource gap and value appropriation: Effect of reputation gap on price premium in online auctions, *Strategic Management Journal*, 32: 447–456.

84. Q. Gu & X. Lu, 2014, Unraveling the mechanisms of reputation and alliance formation: A study of venture capital syndication in China, *Strategic Management Journal*, 35: 739–750; I Stern, J. M. Dukerich, & E. Zajac, 2014, Unmixed signals: How reputation and status affect alliance formation, *Strategic Management Journal*, 35: 512–531; P. W. Roberts & G. R. Dowling, 2003, Corporate reputation and sustained superior financial performance, *Strategic Management Journal*, 24: 1077–1093.

85. B. Larraneta, S. A. Zahra, & J. L. G. Gonzalez, 2014, Strategic repertoire variety and new venture growth: The moderating effects of origin and industry dynamism, *Strategic Management Journal*, 35: 761–772; W. J. Ferrier, K. G. Smith, & C. M. Grimm, 1999, The role of competitive actions in market share erosion and industry dethronement: A study of industry leaders and challengers, *Academy of Management Journal*, 42: 372–388.

86. R. Karlgaard, 2011, Transitions: Michael reinvents Dell, *Forbes*, www.forbes.com, May 9.

87. 2014, While many companies try SaaS for cost savings, top performers discover competitive advantage according to IBM study, IBM News Release, www-03.ibm.com, January 28.

88. M. Fassnacht & S. El Husseini, 2013, EDLP versus Hi-Lo pricing strategies in retailing—a state of the art article, *Journal of Business Economics*, 83: 259–289; Smith, Grimm, & Gannon, *Dynamics of Competitive Strategy*.

89. J. Xia & S. Li, 2013, The divestiture of acquired subunits: A resource dependence approach, *Strategic Management Journal*, 34: 131–148; A. Karnani & B. Wernerfelt, 1985, Multiple point competition, *Strategic Management Journal*, 6: 87–97.

90. G. Ahrne, P. Aspers, & N. Brusson, 2014, The organization of markets, *Organization Studies*, 36: 7–27; Smith, Ferrier, & Ndofor, Competitive dynamics research, 330.

91. C. O'Connor, 2013, Wal-Mart vs. Amazon: World's biggest e-commerce battle could boil down to vegetables, *Forbes*, www.forbes.com, April 23.

92. J. Wohl & A. Barr, 2013, Wal-Mart steps up its online game with help from stores, Reuters, www.reuters.com, March 26.

93. 2015, Walmart Stores, Inc., MarketWatch, www.marketwatch.com, April 15; 2015, Amazon.com's investor relations, Amazon.com, www.amazon.com, January 29.

94. C. Boone, F. C. Wezel, & A. van Witleloostuijn, 2013, Joining the pack or going solo? A dynamic theory of new firm positioning, *Journal of Business Venturing*, 28: 511–527; J. R. Williams, 1992, How sustainable is your competitive advantage? *California Management Review*, 34(3): 29–51.

95. R. A. D'Aveni, G. Dagnino, & K. G. Smith, 2010, The age of temporary advantage, *Strategic Management Journal*, 31: 1371–1385; N. Pangarkar & J. R. Lie, 2004, The impact of market cycle on the performance of Singapore acquirers, *Strategic Management Journal*, 25: 1209–1216.

96. G. N. Chandler, J. C. Broberg, & T. H. Allison, 2014, Customer value propositions in declining industries: Differences between industry representative and high-growth firms, *Strategic Entrepreneurship Journal*, 8: 234–253.

97. D. M. Cain, D. A. Moore, & U. Haran, 2015, Making sense of overconfidence in market entry, *Strategic Management Journal*, 36: 1–18.

98. M. A. Schilling, 2015, Technology shocks, technological collaboration and innovation outcomes, *Organization Science*, in press; L.-C. Hsu & C.-H. Wang, 2012, Clarifying the effect of intellectual capital on performance: The mediating role of dynamic capability, *British Journal of Management*, 23: 179–205.

99. 2003, How fast is your company? *Fast Company*, June, 18.

100. N. R. Furr & D. C. Snow, 2015, Intergenerational hybrids: Spillbacks, spillforwards and adapting to technological discontinuities, *Organization Science*, in press; R. Klingebiel & A. De Meyer, 2013, Becoming aware of the unknown: Decision making during the implementation of a strategic initiative, *Organization Science*, 24: 133–153; C. Hall & D. Lundberg, 2010, Competitive knowledge and strategy in high velocity environments, *IUP Journal of Knowledge Management*, 8(1/2): 7–17.

101. C. B. Dobni, M. Klassen, & W. T. Nelson, 2015, Innovation strategy in the U.S.: Top executives offer their views, *Journal of Business Strategy*, 36(1): 3–13; G. Clarkson & P. Toh, 2010, 'Keep out' signs: The role of deterrence in the competition for resources, *Strategic Management Journal*, 31: 1202–1225.

102. A. K. Chatterji & K. R. Fabrizio, 2014, Using users: When does external knowledge enhance corporate product innovation? *Strategic Management Journal*, 35: 1427–1445; M. Kumar, 2011, Are joint ventures positive sum games? The relative effects of cooperative and noncooperative behavior, *Strategic Management Journal*, 32: 32–54; D. Li, L. Eden, M. A. Hitt, & R. D. Ireland, 2008, Friends, acquaintances or strangers? Partner selection in R&D alliances, *Academy of Management Journal*, 51: 315–334.

103. M. M. Larsen, S. Manning, & T. Pedersen, 2013, Uncovering the hidden costs of offshoring: The interplay of complexity, organizational design, and experience, *Strategic Management Journal*, 34: 533–552; F. Zirpoli & M. C. Becker, 2011, What happens when you outsource too much?, *MIT Sloan Management Review*, 52(2): 59–64.

104. B. Wu, Z. Wan, & D. A. Levinthal, 2014, Complementary assets as pipes and prisms: Innovation incentives and trajectory choices, *Strategic Management Journal*, 35: 1257–1278; D. Desai, 2013, The competitive advantage of adaptive networks: An extension of the dynamic capability view, *International Journal of Business Environment*, 5: 379–397.

105. R. Mohammed, 2015, The Apple watch's big pricing problem, *Harvard Business Review*, hbr.org, April 10.

106. S. P. Gudergan, T. Devinney, N. F. Richter, & R. S. Ellis, 2012, Strategic implications for (non-equity) alliance performance, *Long Range Planning*, 45: 451–476; V. Kumar, F. Jones, R. Venkatesan, & R. Leone, 2011, Is market orientation a source of sustainable competitive advantage or simply the cost of competing?, *Journal of Marketing*, 75: 16–30.

107. L. Josephs, 2011, Candy lovers face bitter Easter, *Wall Street Journal*, February 18, C10.

108. M. Kulas, 2015, Why is candy bad for your health? Livestrong.com, www.livestrong.com, January 28.

6

Corporate-Level Strategy

Studying this chapter should provide you with the strategic management knowledge needed to:

6-1   Define corporate-level strategy and discuss its purpose.

6-2   Describe different levels of diversification achieved using different corporate-level strategies.

6-3   Explain three primary reasons firms diversify.

6-4   Describe how firms can create value by using a related diversification strategy.

6-5   Explain the two ways value can be created with an unrelated diversification strategy.

6-6   Discuss the incentives and resources that encourage diversification.

6-7   Describe motives that can encourage managers to over diversify a firm.

DISNEY ADDS VALUE USING A RELATED DIVERSIFICATION STRATEGY

The Walt Disney Company has pursued a related diversification strategy by using its movies to create franchises and platforms around its popular cartoon and action movie figures. It is the second largest mass media producer after Comcast. While other more focused content providers such as Discover Communications, CBS, and Viacom have seen decreasing revenues because of lower ratings and TV ad weakness, Disney was strengthened through its other businesses based on its diversification strategy. These other businesses include consumer products, interactive consumer products, interactive parks and resorts, and studio entertainment parks. It also has strong cable and TV franchises through ESPN and ABC. Although its ad revenues have decreased like other more focused content producers and distributors, its other businesses are growing and allow it to maintain higher earnings compared to other rival media producing firms.

Disney's strategy is successful because its corporate strategy, compared to its business-level strategy, adds value across its set of businesses above what the individual businesses could create individually. In the literature this is often known as synergy, or in the more academic literature it is known as economies of scope (which will be defined more formally later in the chapter). First, Disney has a related set of businesses in its studio entertainment, consumer products and interactive media, media network

outlets, parks and resorts, and studio entertainment parks. Within its studio entertainment businesses, Disney can share activities across its different production firms: Touchstone Pictures, Hollywood Pictures, Dimension Films, Pixar Films, and Marvel Entertainment (a fairly recent acquisition). By sharing activities among these semi-independent studios, it can learn faster and gain success by the knowledge sharing and efficiencies associated with each studio's expertise. The corporation also has broad and deep knowledge about its customers which is a corporate-level capability in terms advertising and marketing. This capability allows Disney to cross sell products highlighted in its movies through its media distribution outlets, parks and resorts, as well as consumer product businesses.

Recently, Disney, for example, has been moving from its historical central focus on animation in movies such as *Cinderella*, *The Jungle Book*, and *Beauty and the Beast*, into the same titles or stories using a live action approach. The recent release of *Cinderella*, a live action version of the original 1950 animated classic, stays particularly close to the "fairy tale version of the script." This approach comes from its understanding of its customers and what they prefer. Other approaches such as this can be found in *Alice in Wonderland* with Johnny Depp and *Maleficent*, which was a slight twist on the original *Sleeping Beauty*, starring Angelina Jolie as the wicked queen. The action versions of these two movies grossed $1.3 billion and $813 million globally, respectively. Although Disney has had some relatively unsuccessful pictures, *John Carter*, *The Lone Ranger*, and *The Sorcerer's Apprentice*, its action movies based on its animated fairy tales have been relatively more successful. Disney will be promoting *Cinderella* products in its stores and in other focused retail outlets and will be advertising its products along with the direct connections to *Alice*, *Maleficent*, and *Frozen*. All of these have been consumer product successes, and *Cinderella* is likely to have the same appeal. Disney is also seeking to produce action movies such as *Beauty and the Beast*, *The Jungle Book*, and others in the near future. All of these feed products into its Disney stores and Disney themed sections in department stores, such as J. C. Penney, as well as promote resort themes and thus drive interrelated revenue through cross selling.

One of the downside problems for these fairy tale themes is that the stories are in the public domain. As such, other competitors are seeking to follow Disney's successful approach. For example, Time Warner Inc.'s Warner Bros. Studio will release *Pan*, which seems to be beating Disney to the punch on its former *Peter Pan* movie success. Likewise, Time Warner will release *Jungle Book* in 2017 and has another script based on *Beauty and the Beast*. Comcast's Universal Pictures is developing the *Little Mermaid*. However, neither of these studios has the marketing power nor the franchising capability of Disney and its interrelated business and corporate skills. Although they are seeking to build these skills, they cannot duplicate Disney's corporate strategy and parent added value because they are more primarily focused on content and distribution as well as advertising. As such, Disney has a current corporate parental advantage over its more focused movie and content producing and distribution competitors. Disney's corporate strategy has put it in the list of top 10 most admired firms in *Fortune* magazine.

Sources: B. Fritz, 2015, Disney recycles fairy tales, minus cartoons, *Wall Street Journal*, March 11, B1, B6; M. Gottfried, 2015, Walt Disney has built a better mousetrap, *Wall Street Journal*, Feb 5, C8; M. Lev-Ram, 2015, Empire of tech, *Fortune*, January 1, 48–58; C. Palmeri & A. Sakoui, 2015, Disney's princesses' give a little live action, *Bloomberg BusinessWeek*, March 9, 30–31; C. Tkaczyk, 2015, The world's most admired companies, *Fortune*, March 1, 97–104; D. Leonard, 2014, The master of Marvel universe, *Bloomberg BusinessWeek*, April 7, 62–68; C. Palmeri & B. Faries, 2014, Big Mickey is watching, *Bloomberg BusinessWeek*, March 10, 22–23.

Our discussions of business-level strategies (Chapter 4) and the competitive rivalry and competitive dynamics associated with them (Chapter 5) have concentrated on firms competing in a single industry or product market.[1] In this chapter, we introduce you to corporate-level strategies, which are strategies firms use to *diversify* their operations from a single business competing in a single market into several product markets—most commonly, into several businesses. Thus, a **corporate-level strategy** specifies actions a firm takes to gain a competitive advantage by selecting and managing a group of different businesses competing in different product markets. Corporate-level strategies help companies to select new strategic positions—positions that are expected to increase the firm's value.[2] As explained in the Opening Case, Disney competes in a number of related entertainment and distribution industries.[3]

As is the case with Disney, firms use corporate-level strategies as a means to grow revenues and profits, but there can be additional strategic intents to growth. Firms can pursue defensive or offensive strategies that realize growth but have different strategic intents. Firms can also pursue market development by entering different geographic markets (this approach is discussed in Chapter 8). Firms can acquire competitors (horizontal integration) or buy a supplier or customer (vertical integration). As we see in the Opening Case, Disney has acquired Pixar and Marvel movie production studios, thereby increasing its horizontal integration in the movie product and distribution business. Such acquisition strategies are discussed in Chapter 7. The basic corporate strategy, the topic of this chapter, focuses on diversification.

The decision to pursue growth is not a risk-free choice for firms. Indeed, General Electric (GE) experienced difficulty in its media businesses, especially with NBC, which it eventually sold to Comcast. GE also suffered significant revenue declines in its financial services businesses and thus reduced its assets in that area, choosing to seek growth in other businesses such as equipment for the oil industry and equipment for industrial firms to better utilize the Internet. Effective firms carefully evaluate their growth options (including the different corporate-level strategies) before committing firm resources to any of them.

A **corporate-level strategy** specifies actions a firm takes to gain a competitive advantage by selecting and managing a group of different businesses competing in different product markets.

Because the diversified firm operates in several different and unique product markets and likely in several businesses, it forms two types of strategies: corporate-level (company-wide) and business-level (competitive).[4] Corporate-level strategy is concerned with two key issues: in what product markets and businesses the firm should compete and how corporate headquarters should manage those businesses.[5] For the diversified company, a business-level strategy (see Chapter 4) must be selected for each of the businesses in which the firm has decided to compete. In this regard, each of GE's product divisions uses different business-level strategies; while most focus on differentiation, its consumer electronics business has products that compete in market niches which include some that are intended to serve the average income consumer. Thus, cost must also be an issue along with some level of quality.

As is the case with a business-level strategy, a corporate-level strategy is expected to help the firm earn above-average returns by creating value.[6] Some suggest that few corporate-level strategies actually create value.[7] As the Opening Case indicates, realizing value through a corporate strategy can be achieved, but it is challenging to do so. In fact, Disney is one of the few large, widely diversified firms that has been successful over time.

Evidence suggests that a corporate-level strategy's value is ultimately determined by the degree to which "the businesses in the portfolio are worth more under the management of the company than they would be under any other ownership."[8] Thus, an effective corporate-level strategy creates, across all of a firm's businesses, aggregate returns that exceed what those returns would be without the strategy[9] and contributes to the firm's strategic competitiveness and its ability to earn above-average returns.[10]

Product diversification, a primary form of corporate-level strategies, concerns the scope of the markets and industries in which the firm competes as well as "how managers buy, create, and sell different businesses to match skills and strengths with opportunities presented to the firm."[11] Successful diversification is expected to reduce variability in the firm's profitability as earnings are generated from different businesses.[12] Diversification can also provide firms with the flexibility to shift their investments to markets where the greatest returns are possible rather than being dependent on only one or a few markets.[13] Because firms incur development and monitoring costs when diversifying, the ideal portfolio of businesses balances diversification's costs and benefits. CEOs and their top-management teams are responsible for determining the best portfolio for their company.[14]

We begin this chapter by examining different levels of diversification (from low to high). After describing the different reasons firms diversify their operations, we focus on two types of related diversification (related diversification signifies a moderate to high level of diversification for the firm). When properly used, these strategies help create value in the diversified firm, either through the sharing of resources (the related constrained strategy) or the transferring of core competencies across the firm's different businesses (the related linked strategy). We then examine unrelated diversification, which is another corporate-level strategy that can create value. Thereafter, the chapter shifts to the incentives and resources that can stimulate diversification which is value neutral. However, managerial motives to diversify, the final topic in the chapter, can actually destroy some of the firm's value.

6-1 Levels of Diversification

Diversified firms vary according to their level of diversification and the connections between and among their businesses. Figure 6.1 lists and defines five categories of businesses according to increasing levels of diversification. The single and dominant business categories denote no or relatively low levels of diversification; more fully diversified

Figure 6.1 Levels and Types of Diversification

Low Levels of Diversification

Single business:	95% or more of revenue comes from a single business.
Dominant business:	Between 70% and 95% of revenue comes from a single business.

Moderate to High Levels of Diversification

Related constrained:	Less than 70% of revenue comes from the dominant business, and all businesses share product, technological, and distribution linkages.
Related linked (mixed related and unrelated):	Less than 70% of revenue comes from the dominant business, and there are only limited links between businesses.

Very High Levels of Diversification

Unrelated:	Less than 70% of revenue comes from the dominant business, and there are no common links between businesses.

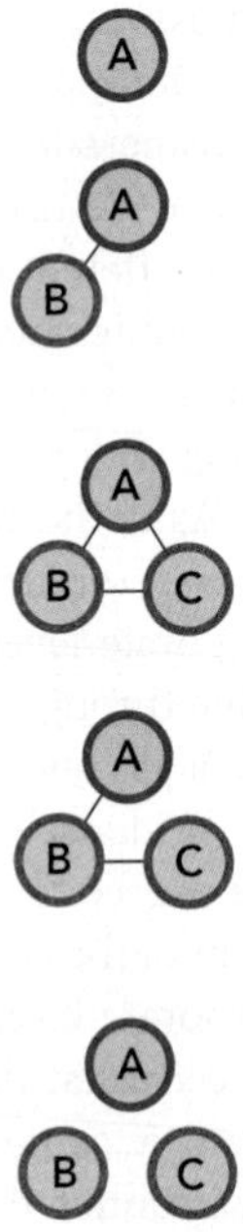

Source: Adapted from R. P. Rumelt, 1974, *Strategy, Structure and Economic Performance*, Boston: Harvard Business School.

firms are classified into related and unrelated categories. A firm is related through its diversification when its businesses share several links. For example, businesses may share product markets (goods or services), technologies, or distribution channels. The more links among businesses, the more "constrained" is the level of diversification. "Unrelated" refers to the absence of direct links between businesses.

6-1a Low Levels of Diversification

A firm pursuing a low level of diversification uses either a single- or a dominant-business, corporate-level diversification strategy. A *single-business diversification strategy* is a corporate-level strategy wherein the firm generates 95 percent or more of its sales revenue from its core business area.[15] For example, McIlhenny Company, headquartered on Avery Island in Louisiana and producer of Tabasco brand, has maintained is focus on its family's hot sauce products for seven generations. On its website, the following quote is provided about its products: "Back in 1868, Edmund McIlhenny experimented with pepper seeds from Mexico (or somewhere in Central America) to create his own style of Louisiana hot sauce—our Original Red Sauce. Since then we've continued this tradition of exploration and experimentation, and today McIlhenny Company crafts seven unique and distinct flavors of sauce, each with its own variety of deliciousness. From mild to wild, there's something for everyone!"[16] Historically McIlhenny has used a single-business strategy while operating in relatively few product markets. Recently, it has begun to partner with other firms so that the Tabasco taste can be found in jelly bean candies (Jelly Belly brand), Hot & Spicy Cheez-It snack crackers (Sunshine brand), jerky (Slim Jim brand), and even Tabasco flavored canned meat (Spam brand).

With the *dominant-business diversification strategy*, the firm generates between 70 and 95 percent of its total revenue within a single business area. United Parcel Service (UPS) uses this strategy. Recently UPS generated 61 percent of its revenue from its U.S. package delivery business and 22 percent from its international package business, with the remaining 17 percent coming from the firm's nonpackage business.[17] Though the U.S. package delivery business currently generates the largest percentage of UPS's sales revenue, the firm anticipates that in the future its other two businesses will account for the majority of revenue growth. This expectation suggests that UPS may become more diversified, both in terms of its goods and services and in the number of countries in which those goods and services are offered.

Firms that focus on one or very few businesses and markets can earn positive returns, because they develop capabilities useful for these markets and can provide superior service to their customers. Additionally, there are fewer challenges in managing one or a very small set of businesses, allowing them to gain economies of scale and efficiently use their resources.[18] Family-owned and controlled businesses, such as McIlhenny Company's Tabasco sauce business, are commonly less diversified. They prefer the narrower focus because the family's reputation is related closely to that of the business. Thus, family members prefer to provide quality goods and services which a focused strategy better allows.[19]

Sany Heavy Industry Co., Ltd is China's largest producer of heavy equipment. In fact, it is the fifth largest producer of this type of equipment globally. Sany has seven core businesses including: concrete machinery, excavators, hoisting machinery, pile driving machinery, road construction machinery, port machinery, and wind turbine.[20] While each is distinct, some similar technologies are used in the production and equipment. Furthermore, related technologies allow similarities in production processes and equipment for certain parts allowing a transfer of knowledge across these businesses. In addition, customers and markets share some similarities because most relate to some form of construction. Although Sany might be evaluated by some to be using a single-business corporate strategy because of its focus on heavy equipment manufacturing. If this is the case, it has a series of differentiated products and is likely following a product proliferation strategy. A product proliferation strategy represents a form of intra-industry diversification.[21] Yet, as noted, Sany also has seven business divisions, one for each type of heavy equipment it manufactures. Thus, it might also be considered by some to engage in moderate diversification in the form of highly related constrained diversification, which is discussed next.

6-1b Moderate and High Levels of Diversification

A firm generating more than 30 percent of its revenue outside a dominant business and whose businesses are related to each other in some manner uses a related diversification corporate-level strategy. When the links between the diversified firm's businesses are rather direct, meaning they use similar sourcing, throughput and outbound processes, it is a *related constrained diversification strategy*. Campbell Soup, Procter & Gamble, and Merck & Co. use a related constrained strategy. A firm shares resources and activities across its businesses with a related constrained strategy.

For example, the Publicis Groupe uses a related constrained strategy, deriving value from the potential synergy across its various groups (mobile and interactive online communication, television, magazines and newspapers, cinema and radio, and outdoor signage), especially the digital capabilities in its advertising business. Given its recent performance, the related constrained strategy has created value for Publicis customers and its shareholders by helping target particular audiences through appropriate media and digital strategies.[22]

The diversified company with a portfolio of businesses that have only a few links between them is called a mixed related and unrelated firm and is using the *related linked diversification strategy* (see Figure 6.1). GE uses a related-linked corporate-level diversification strategy. Compared with related constrained firms, related linked firms share fewer resources and assets between their businesses, concentrating instead on transferring knowledge and core competencies between the businesses. GE has four strategic business units (see Chapter 11 for a definition of SBUs) it calls "divisions," each composed of related businesses. There are few relationships across the strategic business units, but many among the subsidiaries or divisions within them. As with firms using each type of diversification strategy, companies implementing the related linked strategy constantly adjust the mix in their portfolio of businesses as well as make decisions about how to manage these businesses.[23] Managing a diversified firm such as GE is highly challenging, but GE appears to have been well managed over the years given its success.

A highly diversified firm that has no relationships between its businesses follows an *unrelated diversification strategy*. United Technologies Corporation, Textron, Samsung, and Hutchison Whampoa Limited (HWL) are examples of firms using this type of corporate-level strategy. Commonly, firms using this strategy are called *conglomerates*. HWL is a leading international corporation with five core businesses: ports and related services; property and hotels; retail; energy, infrastructure, investments and others; and telecommunications. These businesses are not related to each other, and the firm makes no efforts to share activities or to transfer core competencies between or among them. Each of these five businesses is quite large as exemplified by the retailing arm of the retail and manufacturing business which has more than 9,300 stores in 33 countries. Groceries, cosmetics, electronics, wine, and airline tickets are some of the product categories featured in these stores. This firm's size and diversity suggest the challenge of successfully managing the unrelated diversification strategy. However, Hutchison's past CEO and Board Chair, Li Ka-shing, has been successful at not only making smart acquisitions, but also at divesting businesses with good timing.[24] Another form of unrelated diversification strategy is pursued by private equity firms such Carlyle Group, Blackstone, and KKR.[25] They often have an unrelated set of portfolio firms.

6-2 Reasons for Diversification

A firm uses a corporate-level diversification strategy for a variety of reasons (see Table 6.1). Typically, a diversification strategy is used to increase the firm's value by improving its overall performance. Value is created either through related diversification or through unrelated diversification when the strategy allows a company's businesses to increase revenues or reduce costs while implementing their business-level strategies.[26]

Other reasons for using a diversification strategy may have nothing to do with increasing the firm's value; in fact, diversification can have neutral effects or even reduce a firm's value. Value-neutral reasons for diversification include a desire to match and thereby neutralize a competitor's market power (e.g., to neutralize another firm's advantage by acquiring a similar distribution outlet). Decisions to expand a firm's portfolio of businesses to reduce managerial risk or increase top managers pay can have a negative effect on the firm's value. Greater amounts of diversification reduce managerial risk in that if one of the businesses in a diversified firm fails, the top executive of that business does not risk total failure by the corporation. As such, this reduces the top executives' employment risk. In addition, because diversification can increase a firm's size and thus managerial compensation, managers have motives to diversify a firm to a level that reduces its value.[27] Diversification rationales that may have a neutral or negative effect on the firm's value are discussed later in the chapter.

Table 6.1 Reasons for Diversification

Value-Creating Diversification
• Economies of scope (related diversification)
• Sharing activities
• Transferring core competencies
• Market power (related diversification)
• Blocking competitors through multipoint competition
• Vertical integration
• Financial economies (unrelated diversification)
• Efficient internal capital allocation
• Business restructuring
Value-Neutral Diversification
• Antitrust regulation
• Tax laws
• Low performance
• Uncertain future cash flows
• Risk reduction for firm
• Tangible resources
• Intangible resources
Value-Reducing Diversification
• Diversifying managerial employment risk
• Increasing managerial compensation

Operational relatedness and corporate relatedness are two ways diversification strategies that can create value (see Figure 6.2). Studies of these independent relatedness dimensions show the importance of resources and key competencies.[28] The figure's vertical dimension depicts opportunities to share operational activities between businesses (operational relatedness) while the horizontal dimension suggests opportunities for transferring corporate-level core competencies (corporate relatedness). The firm with a strong capability in managing operational synergy, especially in sharing assets between its businesses, falls in the upper left quadrant, which also represents vertical sharing of assets through vertical integration. The lower right quadrant represents a highly developed corporate capability for transferring one or more core competencies across businesses.

This capability is located primarily in the corporate headquarters office. Unrelated diversification is also illustrated in Figure 6.2 in the lower left quadrant. Financial economies (discussed later), rather than either operational or corporate relatedness, are the source of value creation for firms using the unrelated diversification strategy.

6-3 Value-Creating Diversification: Related Constrained and Related Linked Diversification

With the related diversification corporate-level strategy, the firm builds upon or extends its resources and capabilities to build a competitive advantage by creating value for customers.[29] The company using the related diversification strategy wants to develop and exploit economies of scope between its businesses.[30] In fact, even nonprofit organizations have found that carefully planned and implemented related diversification can create value.[31]

Figure 6.2 Value-Creating Diversification Strategies: Operational and Corporate Relatedness

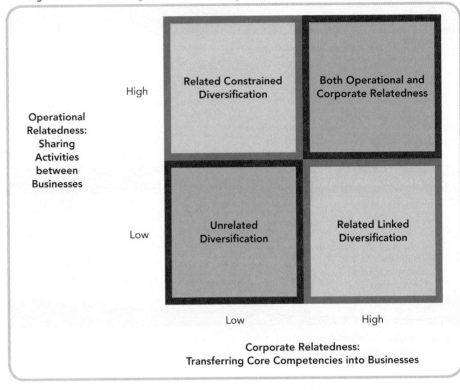

Economies of scope are cost savings a firm creates by successfully sharing resources and capabilities or transferring one or more corporate-level core competencies that were developed in one of its businesses to another of its businesses.[32]

As illustrated in Figure 6.2, firms seek to create value from economies of scope through two basic kinds of operational economies: sharing activities (operational relatedness) and transferring corporate-level core competencies (corporate relatedness). The difference between sharing activities and transferring competencies is based on how separate resources are jointly used to create economies of scope. To create economies of scope, tangible resources such as plant and equipment or other business-unit physical assets often must be shared. Less tangible resources such as manufacturing know-how and technological capabilities can also be shared.[33] However, know-how transferred between separate activities with no physical or tangible resource involved is a transfer of a corporate-level core competence, not an operational sharing of activities.[34]

6-3a   Operational Relatedness: Sharing Activities

Firms can create operational relatedness by sharing either a primary activity (e.g., inventory delivery systems) or a support activity (e.g., purchasing practices)—see Chapter 3's discussion of the value chain. Firms using the related constrained diversification strategy share activities in order to create value. Procter & Gamble uses this corporate-level strategy. Sany, described in an example above, also shares activities. For example, Sany's various businesses share marketing activities because all of their equipment is sold to firms in the construction industry. This is evidenced by the sponsorship of a NASCAR racecar in an attempt to reach executives in the construction industry. (see more on Sany in the Mini-case at the end of the Chapter)

Economies of scope are cost savings a firm creates by successfully sharing resources and capabilities or transferring one or more corporate-level core competencies that were developed in one of its businesses to another of its businesses.

Activity sharing is also risky because ties among a firm's businesses create links between outcomes. For instance, if demand for one business's product is reduced, it may not generate sufficient revenues to cover the fixed costs required to operate the shared facilities. These types of organizational difficulties can reduce activity-sharing success. Additionally, activity sharing requires careful coordination between the businesses involved. The coordination challenges must be managed effectively for the appropriate sharing of activities (see Chapter 11 for further discussion).[35]

Although activity sharing across businesses is not risk-free, research shows that it can create value. For example, studies of acquisitions of firms in the same industry (horizontal acquisitions), such as the banking and software industries, found that sharing resources and activities and thereby creating economies of scope contributed to post-acquisition increases in performance and higher returns to shareholders.[36] Additionally, firms that sold off related units in which resource sharing was a possible source of economies of scope have been found to produce lower returns than those that sold off businesses unrelated to the firm's core business.[37] Still other research discovered that firms with closely related businesses have lower risk.[38] These results suggest that gaining economies of scope by sharing activities across a firm's businesses may be important in reducing risk and in creating value. More attractive results are obtained through activity sharing when a strong corporate headquarters office facilitates it.[39]

Charles Pertwee/Corbis News/Corbis

Procter & Gamble (P&G) is a consumer products firm that shares a lot of activities among its divisions; for example, most of its products are sold through retail outlets and those sales activities can be shared among its divisions.

6-3b Corporate Relatedness: Transferring of Core Competencies

Over time, the firm's intangible resources, such as its know-how, become the foundation of core competencies. **Corporate-level core competencies** are complex sets of resources and capabilities that link different businesses, primarily through managerial and technological knowledge, experience, and expertise.[40] Firms seeking to create value through corporate relatedness use the related linked diversification strategy as exemplified by GE.

In at least two ways, the related linked diversification strategy helps firms to create value. First, because the expense of developing a core competence has already been incurred in one of the firm's businesses, transferring this competence to a second business eliminates the need for that business to allocate resources to develop it. Resource intangibility is a second source of value creation through corporate relatedness. Intangible resources are difficult for competitors to understand and imitate. Because of this difficulty, the unit receiving a transferred corporate-level competence often gains an immediate competitive advantage over its rivals.[41]

A number of firms have successfully transferred one or more corporate-level core competencies across their businesses. Virgin Group Ltd. transfers its marketing core competence across airlines, cosmetics, music, drinks, mobile phones, health clubs, and a number of other businesses.[42] Honda has developed and transferred its competence in engine design and manufacturing among its businesses making products such as motorcycles,

Corporate-level core competencies are complex sets of resources and capabilities that link different businesses, primarily through managerial and technological knowledge, experience, and expertise.

Virgin Group, known for its airline, has also transferred its brand through its marketing competence to other product areas such as cosmetics, music, drinks, mobile phones, health clubs, and a number of other businesses.

lawnmowers, and cars and trucks. Company officials state that Honda is a major manufacturer of engines focused on providing products for all forms of human mobility.[43]

One way managers facilitate the transfer of corporate-level core competencies is by moving key people into new management positions.[44] However, the manager of an older business may be reluctant to transfer key people who have accumulated knowledge and experience critical to the business's success. Thus, managers with the ability to facilitate the transfer of a core competence may come at a premium, or the key people involved may not want to transfer. Additionally, the top-level managers from the transferring business may not want the competencies transferred to a new business to fulfill the firm's diversification objectives.[45] Research suggests that the nature of the top management team can influence the success of the knowledge and skill transfer process.[46] Research also suggests too much dependence on outsourcing can lower the usefulness of core competencies thereby, reducing their useful transferability to other business units in the diversified firm.[47]

6-3c   Market Power

Firms using a related diversification strategy may gain market power when successfully using a related constrained or related linked strategy. **Market power** exists when a firm is able to sell its products above the existing competitive level or to reduce the costs of its primary and support activities below the competitive level, or both.[48] Heinz was bought by a private equity firm in Brazil called 3G Capital Partners LP that is currently approaching Kraft Foods Group to combine these two firms. This deal is supported by Warren Buffet's Berkshire Hathaway & Co. who teamed up with 3G to buy Heinz's well established ketchup and frozen food brands businesses for $23 billion. In a similar deal to build market power, 3G took private food restaurant Burger King Worldwide, Inc., and also bought Tim Hortons Inc. (a Canadian coffee and donut fast-food restaurant) through its Burger King holdings. Warren Buffet also contributed $11 million to help finance the latter deal. These deals obvious build market power for the combining firms in branded consumer foods and fast food restaurants.[49]

Ericsson has the largest share of the global market in telecommunications equipment, and for many years its leadership position has afforded the company considerable market power. That market power and its leadership position in research helped it garner major contracts in telecommunications equipment; "About 40 percent of the world's wireless calls and data move through Ericsson's network hardware."[50] As communication firms move to the "cloud" it is seeking acquisitions and contracts to maintain that market power.

In addition to efforts to gain scale as a means of increasing market power, firms can foster increased market power through multipoint competition and vertical integration. **Multipoint competition** exists when two or more diversified firms simultaneously compete in the same product areas or geographical markets.[51] Through multi-point competition, rival firms often experience pressure to diversify because other firms in their dominant industry segment have made acquisitions to compete in a different market segment.

Market power exists when a firm is able to sell its products above the existing competitive level or to reduce the costs of its primary and support activities below the competitive level, or both.

Multipoint competition exists when two or more diversified firms simultaneously compete in the same product areas or geographical markets.

RUBY WASHINGTON/The New York Tim/Redux

The actions taken by UPS and FedEx in two markets, overnight delivery and ground shipping, illustrate multipoint competition. UPS moved into overnight delivery, FedEx's stronghold; in turn, FedEx bought trucking and ground shipping assets to move into ground shipping, UPS's stronghold. Similarly, J.M. Smucker Company, a snack food producer, recently bought Big Heart Pet Brands which specializes in snacks such as Milk-Bone dog biscuits, treats and chews and has over $2.2 billion in annual revenue. Smucker's competitor, Mars, had acquired a significant portion of Proctor & Gamble's dog and cat food division in 2014. Apparently Smucker's was seeking to keep up its size and cross-industry positions relative to Mars by also diversifying into snacks for pets.[52]

When firm pursue vertical integration more information is processed at headquarters and thus more knowledge processing is needed as illustrated by these servers. External relations with suppliers are also supported by such information networks.

Some firms using a related diversification strategy engage in vertical integration to gain market power. **Vertical integration** exists when a company produces its own inputs (backward integration) or owns its own source of output distribution (forward integration). In some instances, firms partially integrate their operations, producing and selling their products by using company-owned businesses as well as outside sources.[53]

Vertical integration is commonly used in the firm's core business to gain market power over rivals. Market power is gained as the firm develops the ability to save on its operations, avoid sourcing and market costs, improve product quality, possibly protect its technology from imitation by rivals, and potentially exploit underlying capabilities in the marketplace. Vertically integrated firms are better able to improve product quality and improve or create new technologies than specialized firms because they have access to more information and knowledge that are complementary.[54] Market power also is created when firms have strong ties between their productive assets for which no market prices exist. Establishing a market price would result in high search and transaction costs, so firms seek to vertically integrate rather than remain separate businesses.[55]

Vertical integration has its limitations. For example, an outside supplier may produce the product at a lower cost. As a result, internal transactions from vertical integration may be expensive and reduce profitability relative to competitors.[56] Also, bureaucratic costs can be present with vertical integration.[57] Because vertical integration can require substantial investments in specific technologies, it may reduce the firm's flexibility, especially when technology changes quickly. Finally, changes in demand create capacity balance and coordination problems. If one business is building a part for another internal business but achieving economies of scale requires the first division to manufacture quantities that are beyond the capacity of the internal buyer to absorb, it would be necessary to sell the parts outside the firm as well as to the internal business. Thus, although vertical integration can create value, especially through market power over competitors, it is not without risks and costs.[58]

Around the turn of the twenty-first century, manufacturing firms such as Intel and Dell began to reduce vertical integration by reducing ownership of self-manufactured parts and component. This trend also occurred in some large auto companies, such

Vertical integration exists when a company produces its own inputs (backward integration) or owns its own source of output distribution (forward integration).

as Ford and General Motors, as they developed independent supplier networks.[59] Flextronics, an electronics contract manufacturer, is a large contract manufacturer that helps to support this approach to supply-chain management.[60] Such firms often manage their customers' entire product lines and offer services ranging from inventory management to delivery and after-sales service. Interestingly, however, some firms are beginning to reintegrate in order to gain better control over the quality and timing of their supplies.[61] Samsung has maintained control of its operations through a vertical integration strategy, while being a manufacturer for competitors such as Apple in consumer electronics.

6-3d Simultaneous Operational Relatedness and Corporate Relatedness

As Figure 6.2 suggests, some firms simultaneously seek operational and corporate relatedness to create economies of scope.[62] The ability to simultaneously create economies of scope by sharing activities (operational relatedness) and transferring core competencies (corporate relatedness) is difficult for competitors to understand and learn how to imitate. However, if the cost of realizing both types of relatedness is not offset by the benefits created, the result is diseconomies because the cost of organization and incentive structure is very expensive.[63]

As noted in the Opening Case, The Walt Disney Company uses a related diversification strategy to simultaneously create economies of scope through operational and corporate relatedness. Disney has five separate but related businesses: media networks, parks and resorts, studio entertainment, consumer products, and interactive media. Within the firm's Studio Entertainment business, for example, Disney can gain economies of scope by sharing activities among its different movie distribution companies, such as Touchstone Pictures, Hollywood Pictures, and Dimension Films. Broad and deep knowledge about its customers is a capability on which Disney relies to develop corporate-level core competencies in terms of advertising and marketing. With these competencies, Disney is able to create economies of scope through corporate relatedness as it cross-sells products that are highlighted in its movies through the distribution channels that are part of its parks and resorts and consumer products businesses. Thus, characters created in movies become figures that are marketed through Disney's retail stores (which are part of the consumer products business). In addition, themes established in movies become the source of new rides in the firm's theme parks, which are part of the parks and resorts business, and provide themes for clothing and other retail business products.[64]

Although The Walt Disney Company has been able to successfully use related diversification as a corporate-level strategy through which it creates economies of scope by sharing some activities and by transferring core competencies, it can be difficult for investors to identify the value created by a firm (e.g., The Walt Disney Company) as it shares activities and transfers core competencies. For this reason, the value of the assets of a firm using a diversification strategy to create economies of scope often is discounted by investors.[65]

RICHARD B. LEVINE/Newscom

Disney sells many products related to its movies in its own stores as well as more broadly through other retail outlets.

6-4 Unrelated Diversification

Firms do not seek either operational relatedness or corporate relatedness when using the unrelated diversification corporate-level strategy. An unrelated diversification strategy (see Figure 6.2) can create value through two types of financial economies. **Financial economies** are cost savings realized through improved allocations of financial resources based on investments inside or outside the firm.[66]

Efficient internal capital allocations can lead to financial economies. Efficient internal capital allocations reduce risk among the firm's businesses—for example, by leading to the development of a portfolio of businesses with different risk profiles. The second type of financial economy concerns the restructuring of acquired assets. Here, the diversified firm buys another company, restructures that company's assets in ways that allow it to operate more profitably, and then sells the company for a profit in the external market.[67] Next, we discuss the two types of financial economies in greater detail.

6-4a Efficient Internal Capital Market Allocation

In a market economy, capital markets are believed to efficiently allocate capital. Efficiency results as investors take equity positions (ownership) with high expected future cash-flow values. Capital is also allocated through debt as shareholders and debt holders try to improve the value of their investments by taking stakes in businesses with high growth and profitability prospects.

In large diversified firms, the corporate headquarters office distributes capital to its businesses to create value for the overall corporation. As exampled in the Strategic Focus, GE has used this approach to internal capital allocation among its unrelated business units. The nature of these distributions can generate gains from internal capital market allocations that exceed the gains that would accrue to shareholders as a result of capital being allocated by the external capital market.[68] Because those in a firm's corporate headquarters generally have access to detailed and accurate information regarding the actual and potential future performance of the company's portfolio of businesses, they have the best information to make capital distribution decisions.[69]

Compared with corporate office personnel, external investors have relatively limited access to internal information and can only estimate the performances of individual businesses as well as their future prospects. Moreover, although businesses seeking capital must provide information to potential suppliers (e.g., banks or insurance companies), firms with internal capital markets can have at least two informational advantages. First, information provided to capital markets through annual reports and other sources emphasize positive prospects and outcomes. External sources of capital have a limited ability to understand the operational dynamics within large organizations. Even external shareholders who have access to information are unlikely to receive full and complete disclosure.[70] Second, although a firm must disseminate information, that information also becomes simultaneously available to the firm's current and potential competitors. Competitors might attempt to duplicate a firm's value-creating strategy with insights gained by studying such information. Thus, the ability to efficiently allocate capital through an internal market helps the firm protect the competitive advantages it develops while using its corporate-level strategy as well as its various business-unit–level strategies.

If intervention from outside the firm is required to make corrections to capital allocations, only significant changes are possible because the power to make changes by outsiders is often indirect (e.g., through members of the board of directors). External parties can try to make changes by forcing the firm into bankruptcy or changing the top management team. Alternatively, in an internal capital market, the corporate headquarters office can fine-tune its corrections, such as choosing to adjust managerial incentives

Financial economies are cost savings realized through improved allocations of financial resources based on investments inside or outside the firm.

Strategic Focus

GE and United Technology Are Firms that Have Pursued Internal Capital Allocation and Restructuring Strategies

GE competes in many different industries ranging from appliances, aviation, and consumer electronics to energy, financial services, health care, oil, and wind turbines. Historically, GE has done an exceptionally good job of allocating capital across its many businesses, although it has suffered a discount to other diversified competitors of late. Even though GE is a related linked firm, it differentially allocates capital across its major strategic business units. Even though GE Capital (GE's financial services business unit) produced high returns for GE over the last few decades, it received a healthy amount of capital from internal allocations. However, GE has been balancing its financial services portfolio over the last few years.

In particular, GE committed to shrinking its financial operation because Jeff Immelt, GE's CEO, has been under pressure by investors to make GE a more focused industrial company, primarily because its stock price has stayed below $30 since the financial crisis. Ultimately, the goal is to scale back GE Capital from 42 percent of the profit in 2014 to 25 percent of GE's profit in 2016. Before the financial crisis, almost 50 percent of profits were derived from GE Capital. Regulation has forced GE to keep more capital in its financial arm, and thus it can no longer pull as much cash out "to help pay dividends, buy back shares, and help finance GE's industrial operations." It also prevents other restructuring efforts. For example, GE wanted to sell its appliance business, but had to hold on to it for several years during the crisis because the price it could get would be too low. Immelt added, "make no mistake, the ultimate size of GE Capital will be based on competitiveness, returns, and the impact of regulation on the entire company." However, since the financial crisis, GE realized the risks of have so much capital invested in GE Capital which almost toppled GE.

GE is also under pressure because it had built up its oil and gas service operations through acquisitions. However, since the drop in oil prices, this unit has come under pressure. When these assets were purchased, crude oil was selling for $100 per barrel, but crude oil has been recently selling for near $50 per barrel.

Also, United Technologies, an unrelated firm, has allocated resources internally according to their best and most efficient use. Similar to GE, it often bought, restructured, and operated the businesses until it made sense to sell them. United Technologies owns Otis Elevator, building fires and security system brands Chubb and Kidde, Pratt & Whitney jet engines, Carrier air conditioners, and Sikorsky Aircraft. Sikorsky is best known for its Black Hawk helicopters, and it is one of the largest helicopter makers in the world. United Technologies' new CEO,

Gregory J. Hayes, told analysts that it was evaluating its portfolio. The Sikorsky division has come under pressure amidst softer military spending and weakness in demand for oil services companies which utilize helicopters to fly employees to platforms offshore as well as onshore. Although Hayes had considered a tax free spinoff, he ultimately contracted to sell the Sikorsky business unit to Lockheed Martin, a big defense contractor. Interestingly, he is also hunting for a large acquisition to purchase, restructure, and include in United Technologies portfolio.

Both GE and United Technology have used internal capital allocate resources among their diversified business units efficiently. Also, both businesses have used the restructuring strategy to make their operations more efficient and, when appropriate, sold them on the open market, either through selloff to another acquirer or through spinoffs where two stock prices are created, one for the legacy business and one for the spinoff firm (the variety of restructuring strategies will be developed and compared more fully in Chapter 7).

Although GE is seeking to pare back its financial business, GE Capital, with the downturn in oil and gas commodity prices, its Oil and Gas service unit has also experienced difficulties.

Sources: D. Cameron, 2015, Lockheed Martin to buy Sikorsky for $9 billion, *Wall Street Journal*, www.wsj.com, July 21; R. Clough, 2015, A crude awakening for GE, *Bloomberg Businessweek*, March 16, 19; C. Dillow, 2015, What happens if United Technologies unloads Sikorsky?, *Fortune*, www.fortune.com, March 23; C. Grant, 2015, GE's capital control isn't a cure; selling its Asian lending unit won't be enough to revive its stock, *Wall Street Journal*, www.wsj.com, March 16; T. Mann, 2015, GE weighs deeper cuts in bank unit, *Wall Street Journal*, March 12, B1, B2; D. Mattioli & D. Cimilluca, 2015, Sikorsky spin-off considered, *Wall Street Journal*, March 12, B3; G. Smith, 2015, Siemens' long-feared slimdown isn't as drastic as feared, *Fortune*, www.fortune,com, February 23; J. Bogaisky, 2014, Is Bouygues crying uncle on Alstom?, GE said in talks for $13b acquisition. *Forbes*, April 23, 19; T. Mann, 2014, United Technologies CEO hunting for major acquisition, *Wall Street Journal*, www.wsj.com, December 12.

Simon Dawson/Bloomberg/Getty Images

or encouraging strategic changes in one of the firm's businesses.[71] Thus, capital can be allocated according to more specific criteria than is possible with external market allocations. Because it has less accurate information, the external capital market may fail to allocate resources adequately to high-potential investments. The corporate headquarters office of a diversified company can more effectively perform such tasks as disciplining underperforming management teams through resource allocations.[72]

In spite of the challenges associated with it, a number of corporations continue to use the unrelated diversification strategy, especially in Europe and in emerging markets. As an example, Siemens is a large diversified German conglomerate that engages in substantial diversification in order to balance its economic risk. In economic downturns, diversification can help some companies improve future performance.[73]

The Achilles' heel for firms using the unrelated diversification strategy in a developed economy is that competitors can imitate financial economies more easily than they can replicate the value gained from the economies of scope developed through operational relatedness and corporate relatedness. This issue is less of a problem in emerging economies, in which the absence of a "soft infrastructure" (including effective financial intermediaries, sound regulations, and contract laws) supports and encourages use of the unrelated diversification strategy.[74] In fact, in emerging economies such as those in Korea, India, and Chile, research has shown that diversification increases the performance of firms affiliated with large diversified business groups.[75]

6-4b   Restructuring of Assets

Financial economies can also be created when firms learn how to create value by buying, restructuring, and then selling the restructured companies' assets in the external market.[76] As in the real estate business, buying assets at low prices, restructuring them, and selling them at a price that exceeds their cost generates a positive return on the firm's invested capital. This is a strategy that has been taken up by private equity firms, who buy, restructure and then sell, often within a four or five year period.[77]

Unrelated diversified companies that pursue this strategy try to create financial economies by acquiring and restructuring other companies' assets, but it involves significant trade-offs. For example, United Technologies as illustrated in the Strategic Focus has used this strategy. Likewise, Danaher Corp.'s success requires a focus on mature manufacturing businesses because of the uncertainty of demand for high-technology products. It has acquired 400 businesses since 1984 and applied the Danaher Business System to reduce costs and create a lean organization.[78] In high-technology businesses, resource allocation decisions are highly complex, often creating information-processing overload on the small corporate headquarters offices that are common in unrelated diversified firms. High-technology and service businesses are often human-resource dependent; these people can leave or demand higher pay and thus appropriate or deplete the value of an acquired firm.[79]

Buying and then restructuring service-based assets so they can be profitably sold in the external market is also difficult. Thus, for both high-technology firms and service-based companies, relatively few tangible assets can be restructured to create value and sell profitably. It is difficult to restructure intangible assets such as human capital and effective relationships that have evolved over time between buyers (customers) and sellers (firm personnel). Ideally, executives will follow a strategy of buying businesses when prices are lower, such as in the midst of a recession, and selling them at late stages in an expansion.[80] Because of the increases in global economic activity, including more cross-border acquisitions, there is also a growing number of foreign divestitures and restructuring in internal markets (e.g., partial or full privatization of state-owned enterprises). Foreign divestitures are even more complex than domestic ones and must be managed carefully.[81]

6-5 Value-Neutral Diversification: Incentives and Resources

The objectives firms seek when using related diversification and unrelated diversification strategies all have the potential to help the firm create value through the corporate-level strategy. However, these strategies, as well as single- and dominant-business diversification strategies, are sometimes used with objectives that are value-neutral. Different incentives to diversify sometimes exist, and the quality of the firm's resources may permit only diversification that is value neutral rather than value creating.

6-5a Incentives to Diversify

Incentives to diversify come from both the external environment and a firm's internal environment. External incentives include antitrust regulations and tax laws. Internal incentives include low performance, uncertain future cash flows, and the pursuit of synergy, and reduction of risk for the firm.

Antitrust Regulation and Tax Laws

Government antitrust policies and tax laws provided incentives for U.S. firms to diversify in the 1960s and 1970s.[82] Antitrust laws prohibiting mergers that created increased market power (via either vertical or horizontal integration) were stringently enforced during that period.[83] Merger activity that produced conglomerate diversification was encouraged primarily by the Celler-Kefauver Antimerger Act (1950), which discouraged horizontal and vertical mergers. As a result, many of the mergers during the 1960s and 1970s were "conglomerate" in character, involving companies pursuing different lines of business. Between 1973 and 1977, 79.1 percent of all mergers were conglomerate in nature.[84]

During the 1980s, antitrust enforcement lessened, resulting in more and larger horizontal mergers (acquisitions of target firms in the same line of business, such as a merger between two oil companies).[85] In addition, investment bankers became more open to the kinds of mergers facilitated by regulation changes; as a consequence, takeovers increased to unprecedented numbers.[86] The conglomerates, or highly diversified firms, of the 1960s and 1970s became more "focused" in the 1980s and early 1990s as merger constraints were relaxed and restructuring was implemented.[87]

In the beginning of the twenty-first century, antitrust concerns emerged again with the large volume of mergers and acquisitions (see Chapter 7).[88] Mergers are now receiving more scrutiny than they did in the 1980s, 1990s, and the first decade of the 2000s.[89]

The tax effects of diversification stem not only from corporate tax changes, but also from individual tax rates. Some companies (especially mature ones) generate more cash from their operations than they can reinvest profitably. Some argue that *free cash flows* (liquid financial assets for which investments in current businesses are no longer economically viable) should be redistributed to shareholders as dividends.[90] However, in the 1960s and 1970s, dividends were taxed more heavily than were capital gains. As a result, before 1980, shareholders preferred that firms use free cash flows to buy and build companies in high-performance industries. If the firm's stock value appreciated over the long term, shareholders might receive a better return on those funds than if the funds had been redistributed as dividends because returns from stock sales would be taxed more lightly than would dividends.

Under the 1986 Tax Reform Act, however, the top individual ordinary income tax rate was reduced from 50 to 28 percent, and the special capital gains tax was changed to treat capital gains as ordinary income. These changes created an incentive for shareholders to stop encouraging firms to retain funds for purposes of diversification. These tax law changes also influenced an increase in divestitures of unrelated business units after 1984. Thus, while individual tax rates for capital gains and dividends created a shareholder incentive to increase diversification before 1986, they encouraged lower diversification after 1986, unless the diversification was funded by tax-deductible debt. Yet, there have been changes in the maximum individual tax rates since the 1980s. The top individual tax rate has varied from 31 percent in 1992 to 39.6 percent in 2013. There have also been some changes in the capital gains tax rates.

Corporate tax laws also affect diversification. Acquisitions typically increase a firm's depreciable asset allowances. Increased depreciation (a non-cash-flow expense) produces lower taxable income, thereby providing an additional incentive for acquisitions. At one time, acquisitions were an attractive means for securing tax benefits, but changes recommended by the Financial Accounting Standards Board (FASB) eliminated the "pooling of interests" method to account for the acquired firm's assets. It also eliminated the write-off for research and development in process, and thus reduced some of the incentives to make acquisitions, especially acquisitions in related high-technology industries (these changes are discussed further in Chapter 7).[91]

Thus, regulatory changes such as the ones we have described create incentives or disincentives for diversification. Interestingly, European antitrust laws have historically been stricter regarding horizontal mergers than those in the United States, but recently have become more similar.[92]

Low Performance

Some research shows that low returns are related to greater levels of diversification.[93] If high performance eliminates the need for greater diversification, then low performance may provide an incentive for diversification. In the Strategic Focus, Coca-Cola has not met its growth and profit targets in its dominant business of soft drinks in recent years. As such, it has sought to diversify into higher growth areas such as bottled water, tea, and fruit juices.

Firms such as Coca-Cola, which has an incentive to diversify, need to be careful because often there are brand risks to moving into areas that are new and where the company lacks operational expertise. There can be negative synergy (where potential synergy between acquiring and target firms is illusory) and problems between leaders and cultural fit difficulties with recent acquisitions.[94] Research evidence and the experience of a number of firms suggest that an overall curvilinear relationship, as illustrated in Figure 6.3,

Figure 6.3 The Curvilinear Relationship between Diversification and Performance

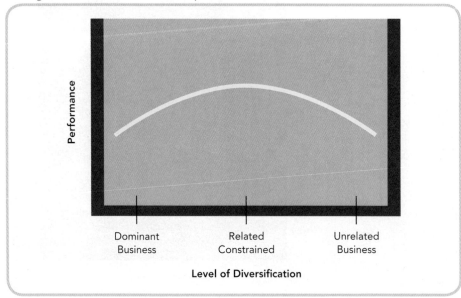

Coca-Cola's Diversification to Deal with Its Reduced Growth in Soft Drinks

Many package good and food distribution companies have been facing difficulties with the changing tastes among consumers. As indicated in an earlier chapter, McDonald's has been facing healthy fast-food competitors like Chipotle Mexican Grill. Likewise, companies such as Campbell's Soup and General Mills have also been experiencing more health conscious consumers both from millennials and baby boomers. Coca-Cola also has experienced a drop in demand for its dominant soft drink business. Coca-Cola had promised a 3–4 percent annual growth volume to investors for 2014 and that "this would be the year of execution" declared CEO Muhtar Kent. However, by 2015 Coca-Cola had fallen short of this volume goal. Its revenue slipped 2 percent to $46 billion, and profits fell 17 percent to $7.1 billion from the prior year (2013). Because consumers' tastes are changing, Coca-Cola has chosen to "polish the diamond" by improving its marketing and execution in soft drinks. However, its efforts through advertising and execution to realize its revenue and profit goals were not sufficient.

Seeing this decline over time, Coca-Cola has been diversifying, as well as trying to improve execution, to deal with depressed volumes in its dominant soft drink business. Sixty-three percent of Americans told a Gallop poll in 2014 that they were avoiding soft drinks. In fact, soft drink sales have been falling for 10 straight years and, as a result, Coca-Cola sales are slowing or shrinking around the world. In fact, supermarket firm Whole Foods will not carry the product. It seems that today's consumers want "healthier, tastier, more unique, and less mass market" products. This trend has impacted Kellogg Company, Kraft Foods Group, McDonald's, and others that have focused on general consumers. In fact, Heinz was taken private by 3G Capital Partners LP and was recently combined with Kraft Foods Group to form the Kraft Heinz Company. This deal is supported by Warren Buffet's Berkshire Hathaway & Co. because these are high cash flow businesses that fit the Berkshire Hathaway unrelated diversification approach of investing. Businesses which are still independent, such as Coca-Cola, have been pursuing diversification to deal with the future risks of consumers' changing tastes.

In 2007, Coca-Cola commissioned a study focused on nonalcoholic drink concepts. It launched its "Venture & Emerging Brands" (VEB) unit to cultivate relationships and to ultimately purchase small start-ups. Through this process, it now owns Fuze Tea, Zico coconut water, and the organic brand Honest Tea. In fact, soft drinks have decreased in consumption almost 90 percent between 2003 and 2013, while sports drinks and bottled water have increased nearly 40 percent during the same period. Coca-Cola partnered with Monster, the leader in energy drinks, which have become very popular, and in 2015 Coca-Cola took ownership of Monster's non-energy drink business. In the "water" market, Coca-Cola owns Glacéau and Fruitwater, which it launched in 2013. In "juices," it owns Odwalla, Simply, and Fuze, in addition to its long standing brand, Minute Maid. Finally, Coca-Cola is trying to adjust its marketing strategy and advertise new products along with its standard, more-healthy products such as Caffeine-free Coke, Coke Zero, and others. However, no one wants to repeat the "new Coke" marketing disaster that occurred previously, so they are very cautious about product proliferation where there could be potential for a huge mistake that damages the brand.

Coca-Cola has also tinkered with other approaches such as its Freestyle soda fountain machine "that offers more than 100 different drink choices; some, such as Orange Coke, aren't available in cans." It now has these drink machines in fast food chains such as Five Guys and Burger King. This approach has consistently raised drink sales by double-digits every year, mostly because the volume for these drink machines is higher; "the largest fountain drink is 40 ounces versus 16 ounces for a standard Coca-Cola can product."

Freestyle Soda Fountain.PNG

©DisneyFoodBlog.com

The photo illustrates a Freestyle soda machine that Coca-Cola and other firms have been using to dispense and mix their various drink products.

Even with some of these new approaches, health critics are challenging some of the advertising for "healthy products" which have a lot of sugar but are classified as "juices." Often these products have as much sugar as standard soft drinks. As such, diversification away from falling sales is not an easy approach because you have to build up growth in new areas that are more risky but also, when mistakes are made, can damage the overall company brand equity. Nonetheless, the diversification approach is often taken when there are risks and uncertainty around the future success of your main product line.

Sources: M. Chahal, 2015, Coca-Cola's strategy: Heritage with 'digital backbone', *Marketing Week*, www.marketingweek.com, March 11; D. Cimilluca, D. Mattioli, & A. Gasparro, 2015, Brazil's 3G in serious talks for Kraft, *Wall Street Journal*, www.wsj.com, March 25, A1, A6; M. Esterl, 2015; Soft drinks hit 10th year of decline, *Wall Street Journal*, www.wsj.com, March 27; M. Esterl, 2015, What is Coke CEO's solution for lost fizz? More soda: Despite changing consumer taste, Muhtar Kent pushes strategy to sell more cola, *Wall Street Journal*, www.wsj.com, March 19; B. Geier, 2015, Coke's plan to save Coke is to sell more Coke, *Fortune*, www.fortune.com, March 19; A. Brones, 2014, Americans are drinking less soda, but we're still addicted to sugar, *Care2*, www.care2.com, April 15; S. Sharf, 2014, Coca-Cola profit declines 14%, future growth plan fails to impress, *Forbes*, www.forbes.com, October 21; C. Suddath & D. Stanford, 2014, Coke confronts its big fat problem, *Bloomberg BusinessWeek*, www.bloombergbusinessweek.com, July 31.

may exist between diversification and performance.[95] Although low performance can be an incentive to diversify, firms that are more broadly diversified compared to their competitors may have overall lower performance.

Uncertain Future Cash Flows

As a firm's product line matures or is threatened, diversification may be an important defensive strategy.[96] Small firms and companies in mature or maturing industries sometimes find it necessary to diversify for long-term survival.[97]

Diversifying into other product markets or into other businesses can reduce the uncertainty about a firm's future cash flows. Alcoa, the largest U.S. aluminum producer, has been pursuing a "multi-material" diversification strategy driven by the highly competitive nature of its basic commodity business.[98] Alcoa has been diversifying into other metals beside aluminum while simultaneously moving into a variety of end product industries. In 2015, for example, it announced that it would acquire RTI International Metals, Inc., which is one of the largest titanium producers for the aerospace industry. Alcoa's CEO, Klaus Kleinfield, noted that the deal "increases our position substantially in titanium and high-tech machinery" with "almost no overlap" with Alcoa's current business.[99] In 2014, it bought Firth Rixson Limited and Germany's TITAL, which make titanium and aluminum casting for jet engines and airframes. However, 40 percent of its revenue still comes from mining and smelting raw aluminum, the price of which has suffered because of lower demand and associated excess capacity and foreign competition, especially from Chinese producers.

Synergy and Firm Risk Reduction

Diversified firms pursuing economies of scope often have investments that are too inflexible to realize synergy among business units. As a result, a number of problems may arise. **Synergy** exists when the value created by business units working together exceeds the value that those same units create working independently. However, as a firm increases its relatedness among business units, it also increases its risk of corporate failure because synergy produces joint interdependence among businesses that constrains the firm's flexibility to respond. This threat may force two basic decisions.

Synergy exists when the value created by business units working together exceeds the value that those same units create working independently.

First, the firm may reduce its level of technological change by operating in environments that are more certain. This behavior may make the firm risk averse and thus uninterested in pursuing new product lines that have potential but are not proven. Alternatively, the firm may constrain its level of activity sharing and forgo potential benefits of synergy. Either or both decisions may lead to further diversification.[100] Operating in environments that are more certain will likely lead to related diversification into industries which lack less potential[101], while constraining the level of activity sharing may produce additional, but unrelated, diversification, where the firm lacks expertise. Research suggests that a firm using a related diversification strategy is more careful in bidding for new businesses, whereas a firm pursuing an unrelated diversification strategy may be more likely to overbid because it is less likely to have full information about the firm it wants to acquire.[102] However, firms using either a related or an unrelated diversification strategy must understand the consequences of paying large premiums.[103] These problems often cause managers to become more risk averse and focus on achieving short-term returns. When this occurs, managers are less likely to be concerned about social problems and in making long-term investments (e.g., developing innovation). Alternatively, diversified firms (related and unrelated) can be innovative if the firm pursues these strategies appropriately.[104]

6-5b   Resources and Diversification

As already discussed, firms may have several value-neutral incentives as well as value-creating incentives (e.g., the ability to create economies of scope) to diversify. However, even when incentives to diversify exist, a firm must have the types and levels of resources and capabilities needed to successfully use a corporate-level diversification strategy.[105] Although both tangible and intangible resources facilitate diversification, they vary in their ability to create value. Indeed, the degree to which resources are valuable, rare, difficult to imitate, and nonsubstitutable (see Chapter 3) influences a firm's ability to create value through diversification. For instance, free cash flows are a tangible financial resource that may be used to diversify the firm. However, compared with diversification that is grounded in intangible resources, diversification based on financial resources only is more visible to competitors and thus more imitable and less likely to create value on a long-term basis.[106] Tangible resources usually include the plant and equipment necessary to produce a product and tend to be less-flexible assets. Any excess capacity often can be used only for closely related products, especially those requiring highly similar manufacturing technologies. For example, large computer makers such as Dell and Hewlett-Packard have underestimated the demand for tablet computers. Apple developed a tablet computer, the iPad, and many expect such tablets to eventually replace the personal computer (PC). In fact, Dell's and HP's sales of their PCs have been declining since the introduction of the iPad. Apple sold 42.4 million iPads in in the last quarter of 2012 and the first quarter of 2013. While Samsung and other competitors have developed tablets to rival Apple's iPad and are selling a considerable number; Dell, HP, Lenovo, and others have responded by making cheaper tablet-like laptops and iPad like tablets and have stayed in the game without having to diversify too much.[107]

Excess capacity of other tangible resources, such as a sales force, can be used to diversify more easily. Again, excess capacity in a sales force is more effective with related diversification because it may be utilized to sell products in similar markets (e.g., same customers). The sales force would be more knowledgeable about related product characteristics, customers, and distribution channels.[108] Tangible resources may create resource interrelationships in production, marketing, procurement, and technology, defined earlier as activity sharing. Interestingly, Dyson, which produces vacuum cleaners, has invested in battery technology. Dyson's CEO, James Dyson, has indicated that the company, besides producing a battery operated vacuum, "will launch 100 products in four categories that are new to the company" using the new more efficient battery technology.[109]

Intangible resources are more flexible than tangible physical assets in facilitating diversification. Although the sharing of tangible resources may induce diversification, intangible resources such as tacit knowledge could encourage even more diversification.[110] Service firms also pursue diversification strategies especially through greenfield ventures (opening a new business for the firm without acquiring a previous established brand-name business). Alvarez & Marsal, a professional service firm that has focused on helping to restructure firms that experience financial distress, has diversified into several additional service businesses. It has a reputation (an intangible asset) in New York financial circles for its ability to do interim management for firms that are experiencing financial distress and often gone into bankruptcy. Alvarez & Marsal managed the largest U.S. bankruptcy in history, the wind down of Lehman Bros. after it folded. As part of this massive wind down, it needed to manage the treasury and cash assets of the company in a way to realize the best returns possible for the remaining stakeholders and creditors who held right to debt secured assets. Through its experience over a number of bankruptcies, but in particular the Lehman Bros. bankruptcy, Alvarez & Marsal has gained a reputation and ability in investment management especially for short-term treasury deposits. These capabilities have lead the firm to open a new business to manage treasury and cash assets for other companies, but also for endowments and local and state government entities. It also serves as a consultant for private equity firms which are closely associated with firms in financial distress and restructuring strategies. From its interim management business, it has moved into performance improvement consulting. Through its reputation and skills in serving private equity clients, Alvarez and Marsal also gained knowledge about investing in private equity businesses and have likewise started a private equity fund.[111] This approach to diversification is not unfamiliar to other professional service firms such as Bain Strategy Consulting, which also started Bain Capital, a private equity fund through the support of Bain partners (owners) in their consulting business.

Sometimes, however, the benefits expected from using resources to diversify the firm for either value-creating or value-neutral reasons are not gained. Research suggests that picking the right target firm partner is critical to acquisition success.[112] For example, Sara Lee Corporation executives found that they could not realize synergy between elements of their company's diversified portfolio, and subsequently shed businesses accounting for 40 percent of company revenue to focus on food and food-related products and more readily achieve synergy. Ultimately, Sara Lee split into two companies: Hillshire Brands which focuses on meat and food products, and D.E. Master Blenders 1753, a beverage and bakery company. Incidentally, Hillshire Brands was purchased by Tyson Foods in 2014 and Sara Lee no longer exists as a separate company, although the brand is part of Tyson Foods.[113]

6-6 Value-Reducing Diversification: Managerial Motives to Diversify

Managerial motives to diversify can exist independent of value-neutral reasons (i.e., incentives and resources) and value-creating reasons (e.g., economies of scope).

The desire for increased compensation and reduced managerial risk are two motives for top-level executives to diversify their firm beyond value-creating and value-neutral levels.[114] In slightly different words, top-level executives may diversify a firm in order to spread their own employment risk, as long as profitability does not suffer excessively.[115]

Diversification provides additional benefits to top-level managers that shareholders do not enjoy. Research evidence shows that diversification and firm size are highly correlated, and as firm size increases, so does executive compensation.[116] Because large firms are complex, difficult-to-manage organizations, top-level managers commonly receive substantial levels of compensation to lead them, but the amounts vary across countries.[117] Greater levels of diversification can increase a firm's complexity, resulting in still more compensation for executives to lead an increasingly diversified organization. Governance mechanisms, such as the board of directors, monitoring by owners, executive compensation practices, and the market for corporate control, may limit managerial tendencies to over diversify.[118] These mechanisms are discussed in more detail in Chapter 10.

In some instances, though, a firm's governance mechanisms may not be strong, allowing executives to diversify the firm to the point that it fails to earn even average returns.[119] The loss of adequate internal governance may result in relatively poor performance, thereby triggering a threat of takeover. Although takeovers may improve efficiency by replacing ineffective managerial teams, managers may avoid takeovers through defensive tactics, such as "poison pills," or may reduce their own exposure with "golden parachute" agreements.[120] Therefore, an external governance threat, although restraining managers, does not flawlessly control managerial motives for diversification.[121]

Most large publicly held firms are profitable because the managers leading them are positive stewards of firm resources, and many of their strategic actions, including those related to selecting a corporate-level diversification strategy, contribute to the firm's success.[122] As mentioned, governance mechanisms should be designed to deal with exceptions to the managerial norms of making decisions and taking actions that increase the firm's ability to earn above-average returns. Thus, it is overly pessimistic to assume that managers usually act in their own self-interest as opposed to their firm's interest.[123]

Top-level executives' diversification decisions may also be held in check by concerns for their reputation. If a positive reputation facilitates development and use of managerial power, a poor reputation can reduce it. Likewise, a strong external market for managerial talent may deter managers from pursuing inappropriate diversification.[124] In addition, a diversified firm may acquire other firms that are poorly managed in order to restructure its own asset base. Knowing that their firms could be acquired if they are not managed successfully encourages executives to use value-creating diversification strategies.

As shown in Figure 6.4, the level of diversification with the greatest potential positive effect on performance is based partly on the effects of the interaction of resources, managerial motives, and incentives on the adoption of particular diversification strategies. As indicated earlier, the greater the incentives and the more flexible the resources, the higher the level of expected diversification. Financial resources (the most flexible) should have a stronger relationship to the extent of diversification than either tangible or intangible resources. Tangible resources (the most inflexible) are useful primarily for related diversification.

As discussed in this chapter, firms can create more value by effectively using diversification strategies. However, diversification must be kept in check by corporate governance

Figure 6.4 Summary Model of the Relationship between Diversification and Firm Performance

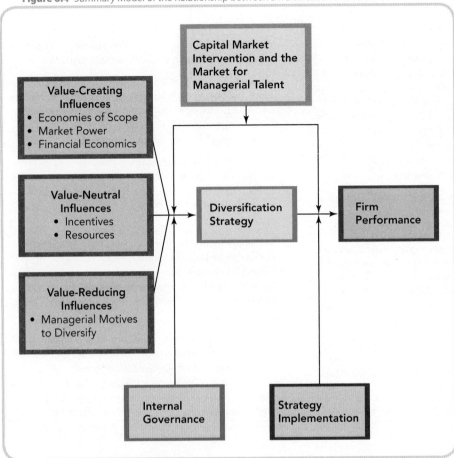

Source: Adapted from R. E. Hoskisson & M. A. Hitt, 1990, Antecedents and performace outcomes of diversification: A review and critique of theoretical perspectives, *Journal of Management*, 16: 498.

(see Chapter 10). Appropriate strategy implementation tools, such as organizational structures, are also important for the strategies to be successful (see Chapter 11).

We have described corporate-level strategies in this chapter. In the next chapter, we discuss mergers and acquisitions as prominent means for firms to diversify and to grow profitably. These trends toward more diversification through acquisitions, which have been partially reversed due to restructuring (see Chapter 7), indicate that learning has taken place regarding corporate-level diversification strategies.[125] Accordingly, firms that diversify should do so cautiously, choosing to focus on relatively few, rather than many, businesses. In fact, research suggests that although unrelated diversification has decreased, related diversification has increased, possibly due to the restructuring that continued into the 1990s through the early twenty-first century. This sequence of diversification followed by restructuring has occurred in Europe and in countries such as Korea, following actions of firms in the United States and the United Kingdom.[126] Firms can improve their strategic competitiveness when they pursue a level of diversification that is appropriate for their resources (especially financial resources) and core competencies and the opportunities and threats in their country's institutional and competitive environments.[127]

SUMMARY

- The primary reason a firm uses a corporate-level strategy to become more diversified is to create additional value. Using a single- or dominant-business corporate-level strategy may be preferable to seeking a more diversified strategy, unless a corporation can develop economies of scope or financial economies between businesses, or unless it can obtain market power through additional levels of diversification. Economies of scope and market power are the main sources of value creation when the firm uses a corporate-level strategy to achieve moderate to high levels of diversification.

- The related diversification corporate-level strategy helps the firm create value by sharing activities or transferring competencies between different businesses in the company's portfolio.

- Sharing activities usually involves sharing tangible resources between businesses. Transferring core competencies involves transferring core competencies developed in one business to another business. It also may involve transferring competencies between the corporate headquarters office and a business unit.

- Sharing activities is usually associated with the related constrained diversification corporate-level strategy. Activity sharing is costly to implement and coordinate, may create unequal benefits for the divisions involved in the sharing, and can lead to fewer managerial risk-taking behaviors.

- Transferring core competencies is often associated with related linked (or mixed related and unrelated) diversification,

although firms pursuing both sharing activities and transferring core competencies can also use the related linked strategy.

- Efficiently allocating resources or restructuring a target firm's assets and placing them under rigorous financial controls are two ways to accomplish successful unrelated diversification. Firms using the unrelated diversification strategy focus on creating financial economies to generate value.

- Diversification is sometimes pursued for value-neutral reasons. Incentives from tax and antitrust government policies, low performance, or uncertainties about future cash flow are examples of value-neutral reasons that firms choose to become more diversified.

- Managerial motives to diversify (including to increase compensation) can lead to over diversification and a subsequent reduction in a firm's ability to create value. Evidence suggests, however, that many top-level executives seek to be good stewards of the firm's assets and avoid diversifying the firm in ways that destroy value.

- Managers need to consider their firm's internal organization and its external environment when making decisions about the optimum level of diversification for their company. Of course, internal resources are important determinants of the direction that diversification should take. However, conditions in the firm's external environment may facilitate additional levels of diversification, as might unexpected threats from competitors.

KEY TERMS

corporate-level strategy 174
economies of scope 180
corporate-level core competencies 181
market power 182

multipoint competition 182
vertical integration 183
financial economies 185
synergy 191

REVIEW QUESTIONS

1. What is corporate-level strategy and why is it important?

2. What are the different levels of diversification firms can pursue by using different corporate-level strategies?

3. What are three reasons firms choose to diversify their operations?

4. How do firms create value when using a related diversification strategy?

5. What are the two ways to obtain financial economies when using an unrelated diversification strategy?

6. What incentives and resources encourage diversification?

7. What motives might encourage managers to over diversify their firm?

Mini-Case

Sany Heavy Industry Co., Ltd

The Sany Heavy Industry Co., Ltd is China's largest producer of heavy equipment. In fact, it is the fifth largest producer of this type of equipment globally. In 2014, its revenue was decreasing because of the downturn of overall GNP in China. Sany's total sales revenue in 2012 was $12.9 billion, well behind industry leader Caterpillar at $65.9 billion. However, Sany has a goal of eventually unseating Caterpillar as the industry leader. Sany plans to achieve $47 billion in annual sales within 10 years. Sany has already surpassed Caterpillar as a leader in its Chinese domestic markets.

Sany has four core businesses: (1) cranes, (2) road construction machinery, (3) port machinery, and (4) pumpover machinery. While each is distinct, some similar technologies are used in the production and equipment. Furthermore, similar technologies allow similarities in production processes and equipment for certain parts. Therefore, there is a transfer of knowledge across these businesses. In addition, customers and markets share some similarities because all relate to some form of construction. For this reason, in the United States, Sany has become a major sponsor of a Chevrolet on the NASCAR auto racing circuit. Sany America's marketing director, Joe Hanneman, said that research showed NASCAR racing events to be the primary recreation event for people in the U.S. construction industry.

Sany invests 5 percent of its annual sales in R&D to continuously improve the quality of existing products, identify new technologies, and develop new products. Through the end of 2012, Sany held 3,303 patents as a result of its R&D efforts. Indicative of its intent to be a technological leader in its industry, Sany has developed new postdoctoral research centers to attract top research scientists. In 2013, the company was awarded China's National Technology Invention Prize for its "super-length-boom" technology.

Although it has been pursuing technological innovations, Sany was recently accused of patent violations by Manitowoc, a diversified producer of equipment including large cranes. In 2014, a judgement went against Sany concluding "one Sany crane product infringed one of Manitowoc's patents and that six trade secrets of Manitowoc were both protectable as trade secrets and misappropriated." This is a negative signal for Sany as it seeks to pursue more diversified growth outside of China.

Sany continues to grow organically and through acquisitions. For example, in 2012, it acquired Putzmeister, a well-known concrete pump manufacturer. In addition, it has established subsidiaries in many countries, including the United States, Germany, and Brazil, to enhance its international equipment sales and broaden its market reach. Largely because of its major goal of internationalization, it is moving its corporate headquarters from Changsha to Beijing for enriched international connections.

Sources: 2015, Sany Heavy Industry Co. Ltd., www.sanygroup.com, accessed on June 12; 2015, www.manitowoc.com, press release, The Manitowoc Company receives favorable final determination in Sany patent infringement lawsuit, April 17; R. Flannery, 2014, Profit drops by 48% at Chinese billionaire's equipment flagship Sany Heavy, Forbes, www.forbes.com, August 31; 2015, www.manitowoc.com, 2013, Yellow Table Survey: Sany ranks no. 5 among construction machinery manufacturers in 2013, China Construction Machinery Online, www.cmbol.com, April 15; M. Barris, 2013, Sany turns to NASCAR to fuel sales, China Daily, www.chinadaily.com, April 4; 2013, Awarded National Technology Invention Prize, Get to Know Sany, 15th issue, February 15; L. Hooks, P. J. Davis, & N. Munshi, 2013, Caterpillar digs into trouble in China, Financial Times, www.ft.com, February 12; J. R. Hagerty & C. Murphy, 2013, Sany tries to gain traction in the U.S., Wall Street Journal, www.wsj.com, January 28; 2013, Sany Heavy Industry Co. Ltd: Sany Group's top 10 events in 2012, $-traders, www.4-traders.com, January 22; Z. Yangpeng & F. Zhiwei, 2012, Sany to move HQ to Beijing from Changsha, China Daily, www.usa.chinadaily.com, November 11.

Case Discussion Questions

1. What corporate diversification strategy is being pursued by Sany? What evidence do you have that supports your position?

2. How does the level of change in gross domestic product (indicator of country economic health) influence a firm like Sany?

3. Why does a firm such as Sany (in the heavy equipment industry) spend so much of its revenue on R&D and innovation?

4. Given that it is now seeking international expansion, how do you expect the judgement against it (patent and trade secret infringement case) to affect its growth prospects outside of China?

NOTES

1. M. E. Porter, 1980, *Competitive Strategy*, New York: The Free Press, xvi.

2. J. P. O'Brien, P. David, T. Yoshikawa, & A. Delios, 2014, How capital structure influences diversification performance: A transaction cost perspective, *Strategic Management Journal*, 35: 1013–1031; M. D. R. Chari, S. Devaraj, & P. David, 2008, The impact of information technology investments and diversification strategies on firm performance, *Management Science*, 54: 224–234.

3. M. Gottfried, 2015, Walt Disney has built a better mousetrap, *Wall Street Journal*, Feb 5, C8.

4. M. E. Porter, 1987, From competitive advantage to corporate strategy, *Harvard Business Review*, 65(3): 43–59.

5. P. C. Nell & B. Ambos, 2013, Parenting advantage in the MNC: An embeddedness perspective on the value added by headquarters, *Strategic Management Journal*, 34: 1086–1103; M. E. Raynor, 2007, What is corporate strategy, really? *Ivey Business Journal*, 71: 1–3.

6. Queen, P. 2015, Enlightened shareholder maximization: Is this strategy achievable?, *Journal of Business Ethics*, 127: 683–694; W. P. Wan, R. E. Hoskisson, J. C. Short, & D. W. Yiu, 2011, Resource-based theory and corporate diversification: Accomplishments and opportunities, *Journal of Management*, 37: 1335–1368.

7. C. Custódio, 2014, Mergers and acquisitions accounting and the diversification discount, *Journal of Finance*, 69: 219–240; K. Lee, M. W. Peng, & K. Lee, 2008, From diversification premium to diversification discount during institutional transitions, *Journal of World Business*, 43: 47–65.

8. Campbell, M. Goold, & M. Alexander, 1995, Corporate strategy: The question for parenting advantage, *Harvard Business Review*, 73(2): 120–132.

9. W. Su & E. W. K. Tsang, 2015, Product diversification and financial performance: The moderating role of secondary stakeholders, *Academy of Management Journal*, forthcoming; K. Favaro, 2013, We're from corporate and we are here to help: Understanding the real value of corporate strategy and the head office, *Strategy+Business Online*, www.strategy-business.com, April 8; D. Collis, D. Young, & M. Goold, 2007, The size, structure, and performance of corporate headquarters, *Strategic Management Journal*, 28: 283–405.

10. M. Kleinbaum & T. E. Stuart, 2014, Inside the black box of the corporate staff: Social networks and the implementation of corporate strategy, *Strategic Management Journal*, 35: 24–47; G. Kenny, 2012, Diversification: Best practices of the leading companies, *Journal of*

Business Strategy, 33(1): 12–20; D. Miller, 2006, Technological diversity, related diversification performance, *Strategic Management Journal*, 27: 601–619.

11. D. D. Bergh, 2001, Diversification strategy research at a crossroads: Established, emerging and anticipated paths. In M. A. Hitt, R. E. Freeman, & J. S. Harrison (eds.), *Handbook of Strategic Management*, Oxford, U.K.: Blackwell Publishers, 363–383.

12. S. F. Matusik & M. A. Fitza, 2012, Diversification in the venture capital industry: Leveraging knowledge under uncertainty, *Strategic Management Journal*, 33: 407–426.

13. J. R. Lecuona & M. Reitzig, 2014, Knowledge worth having in 'excess': The value of tacit and firm-specific human resource slack, *Strategic Management Journal*, 35: 954–973; G. Ray, X. Ling, & J. B. Barney, 2013, Impact of information technology capital on firm scope and performance: The role of asset characteristics, *Academy of Management Journal*, 56: 1125–1147.

14. D. H. Zhu & G. Chen, 2015, CEO narcissism and the impact of prior board experience on corporate strategy, *Administrative Science Quarterly*, 60: 31–65; J. J. Marcel, 2009, Why top management team characteristics matter when employing a chief operating officer: A strategic contingency perspective, *Strategic Management Journal*, 30: 647–658.

15. R. P. Rumelt, 1974, *Strategy, Structure, and Economic Performance*, Boston: Harvard Business School; L. Wrigley, 1970, *Divisional Autonomy and Diversification* (Ph.D. dissertation), Harvard Business School.

16. 2015, Tabasco Products, www.tabasco.com, March 24.

17. 2015, United Parcel Service 2014 Annual Report, www.ups.com, March 24.

18. R. Rumelt, 2011, *Good Strategy/Bad Strategy: The Difference and Why It Matters*, New York: Crown Business Publishing.

19. L. R. Gomez-Mejia, J. T. Campbell, G. Martin, R. E. Hoskisson, M. Makri, & D. G. Sirmon, 2014, Socioemotional wealth as a mixed gamble: Revisiting family firm R&D investments with the behavioral agency model, *Entrepreneurship: Theory & Practice*, 38: 1351–1374; L. R. Gomez-Mejia, M. Makri, & M. L. Kintana, 2010, Diversification decisions in family controlled firms, *Journal of Management Studies*, 47: 223–252.

20. 2015, About SANY, www.sanygroup.com, accessed on March 27.

21. A. Barroso & M. S. Giarratana, 2013, Product proliferation strategies and firm performance: The moderating role of product space complexity, *Strategic Management Journal*, 34: 1435–1452.

22. 2015, Publicis Groupe, Wikipedia, http://en.wikipedia.org/wiki/Publicis, March 24.

23. J.-H. Lee & A. S. Gaur, 2013, Managing multi-business firms: A comparison between Korean chaebols and diversified U.S. firms, *Journal of World Business*, 48: 443–454; J. L. Stimpert, I. M. Duhaime, & J. Chesney, 2010, Learning to manage a large diversified firm, *Journal of Leadership and Organizational Studies*, 17: 411–425.

24. G. Smith, 2015, Hutchison Whampoa close to buying UK's 02 for $15 billion, *Fortune*, www.fortune.com, February 3; 2015, Hutchison Whampoa Limited 2014 Annual Report, www.hutchison-whampoa.com, accessed March 25, 2015.

25. R. E. Hoskisson, W, Shi, X. Yi, & J. Jing, 2013, The evolution and strategic positioning of private equity firms, *Academy of Management Perspectives*, 27: 22–38.

26. T. M. Alessandri & A. Seth, 2014, The effects of managerial ownership on international and business diversification: Balancing incentives and risks, *Strategic Management Journal*, 35: 2064–2075; C.-N. Chen & W. Chu, 2012, Diversification, resource concentration and business group performance: Evidence from Taiwan, *Asia Pacific Journal of Management*, 29: 1045–1061.

27. S. Pathak, R. E. Hoskisson, & R. A. Johnson, 2014, Settling up in CEO compensation: The impact of divestiture intensity and contextual factors in refocusing firms, *Strategic Management Journal*, 35: 1124–1143; D. H. Ming Chng, M. S. Rodgers, E. Shih, & X.-B. Song, 2012, When does incentive compensation motivate managerial behavior? An experimental investigation of the fit between incentive compensation, executive core self-evaluation and firm performance, *Strategic Management Journal*, 33: 1343–1362; J. E. Core & W. R. Guay, 2010, Is CEO pay too high and are incentives too low? A wealth-based contracting framework, *Academy of Management Perspectives*, 24: 5–19.

28. C. Chadwick, J. F. Super, & K. Kwon, 2015, Resource orchestration in practice: CEO emphasis on SHRM, commitment-based HR systems, and firm performance, *Strategic Management Journal*, 36: 360–376; D. G. Sirmon, M. A. Hitt, R. D. Ireland, & B. A. Gilbert, 2011, Resource orchestration to create competitive advantage: Breadth, depth and life cycle effects, *Journal of Management*, 37: 1390–1412.

29. T. Zahavi & D. Lavie, 2013, Intra-industry diversification and firm performance, *Strategic Management Journal*, 34: 978–998; H. Tanriverdi & C.-H. Lee, 2008, Within-industry diversification and firm performance in the presence of network externalities: Evidence from the software industry, *Academy of Management Journal*, 51: 381–397.

30. F. Bauer & K. Matzler, 2014, Antecedents of M&A success: The role of strategic complementarity, cultural fit, and degree and speed of integration, *Strategic Management Journal*, 35: 269–291; M. E. Graebner, K. M. Eisenhardt, & P. T. Roundy, 2010, Success and failure of technology acquisitions: Lessons for buyers and sellers, *Academy of Management Perspectives*, 24: 73–92.

31. G. M. Kistruck, I. Qureshi, & P. W. Beamish, 2013, Geographic and product diversification in charitable organizations, *Journal of Management*, 39: 496–530.

32. A. Arora, S. Belenzon, & L. A. Rios, 2014, Make, buy, organize: The interplay between research, external knowledge, and firm structure, *Strategic Management Journal*, 35: 317–337; F. Neffke & M. Henning, 2013, Skill relatedness and firm diversification, *Strategic Management Journal*, 34: 297–316.

33. Y. Chen, Y. Jiang, C. Wang, & W. C. Hsu, 2014, How do resources and diversification strategy explain the performance consequences of internationalization?, *Management Decision*, 52, 897–915; M. Makri, M. A. Hitt, & P. J. Lane, 2010, Complementary technologies, knowledge relatedness and invention outcomes in high technology mergers and acquisitions, *Strategic Management Journal*, 31: 602–628.

34. A. V. Sakhartov & T. B. Folta, 2014, Resource relatedness, redeployability, and firm value, *Strategic Management Journal*, 35: 1781–1797; D. Miller, 2006, Technological diversity, related diversification, and firm performance, *Strategic Management Journal*, 27: 601–619.

35. M. V. S. Kumar, 2013, The costs of related diversification: The impact of core business on the productivity of related segments, *Organization Science*, 24: 1827–1846.

36. M. A. Hitt, D. King, H. Krishnan, M. Makri, M. Schijven, K. Shimizu, & H. Zhu, 2012, Creating value through mergers and acquisitions: Challenges and opportunities. In D. Faulkner, S. Teerikangas, & R. Joseph (eds.), *Oxford Handbook of Mergers and Acquisitions*, Oxford, U.K.: Oxford University Press, 2012, 71–113; P. Puranam & K. Srikanth, 2007, What they know vs. what they do: How acquirers leverage technology acquisitions, *Strategic Management Journal*, 28: 805–825.

37. E. R. Feldman, 2014, Legacy divestitures: Motives and implications, *Organization Science*, 25: 815–832; L. B. Lien, 2013, Can the survivor principle survive diversification? *Organization Science*, in press; D. D. Bergh, 1995, Size and relatedness of units sold: An agency theory and resource-based perspective, *Strategic Management Journal*, 16: 221–239.

38. M. Lubatkin & S. Chatterjee, 1994, Extending modern portfolio theory into the domain of corporate diversification: Does it apply? *Academy of Management Journal*, 37: 109–136.

39. M. Menz, S. Kunisch, & D. J. Collis, 2015, The corporate headquarters in the contemporary corporation: Advancing a multimarket firm perspective, *Academy of Management Annals*, forthcoming; T. Kono, 1999, A strong head office makes a strong company, *Long Range Planning*, 32: 225–236.

40. A. Caimo & A. Lomi, 2015, Knowledge sharing in organizations: A Bayesian analysis of the role of reciprocity and formal structure. *Journal of Management*, 41: 665–691; Puranam & Srikanth, What they know vs. what they do; F. T. Rothaermel, M. A. Hitt, & L. A. Jobe, 2006, Balancing vertical integration and strategic outsourcing: Effects on product portfolio, product success, and firm performance, *Strategic Management Journal*, 27: 1033–1056.

41. M. Cui & S. L. Pan, 2015, Developing focal capabilities for e-commerce adoption: A resource orchestration perspective, *Information & Management*, 52: 200–209.

42. C. Huston, 2013, The value of a good name, *Wall Street* Journal, July 18, B5; J. Thottam, 2008, Branson's flight plan, *Time*, April 28, 40.

43. 2015, Operations overview, Honda Motor Company, www.honda.com, Accessed March 29.

44. N. D. Nguyen & A, Aoyama, A. 2014, Achieving efficient technology transfer through a specific corporate culture facilitated by management practices, *Journal of High Technology Management Research*, 25: 108–122; L. C. Thang, C. Rowley, T. Quang, & M. Warner, 2007, To what extent can management practices be transferred between countries?: The case of human resource management in Vietnam, *Journal of World Business*, 42: 113–127; G. Stalk Jr., 2005, Rotate the core, *Harvard Business Review*, 83(3): 18–19.

45. U. Andersson, P. J. Buckley, & H. Dellestrand, 2015, In the right place at the right time!: The influence of knowledge governance tools on knowledge transfer and utilization in MNEs, *Global Strategy Journal*, 5: 27–47; J. A. Martin & K. M. Eisenhardt, 2010, Rewiring: Cross-business unit collaborations in multibusiness organizations, *Academy of Management Journal*, 53: 265–301.

46. T. Hutzschenreuter & J. Horstkotte, 2013, Performance effects of top management team demographic faultlines in the process of product diversification, *Strategic Management Journal*, 34: 704–726.

47. E. Linares-Navarro, T. Pedersen, & J. Pla-Barber, 2014, Fine slicing of the value chain and offshoring of essential activities: Empirical evidence from European multinationals, *Journal of Business Economics & Management*, 15: 111–134; S. Gupta, A. Woodside, C. Dubelaar, & D. Bradmore, 2009, Diffusing knowledge-based core competencies for leveraging innovation strategies: Modeling

outsourcing to knowledge process organizations (KPOs) in pharmaceutical networks, *Industrial Marketing Management*, 38: 219–227.

48. A. Pehrsson, 2010, Business-relatedness and the strategy of moderations: Impacts on foreign subsidiary performance, *Journal of Strategy and Management*, 3: 110–133; S. Chatterjee & J. Singh, 1999, Are trade-offs inherent in diversification moves? A simultaneous model for type of diversification and mode of expansion decisions, *Management Science*, 45: 25–41.

49. D. Cimilluca, D. Mattioli, & A. Gasparro, 2015, Brazil's 3G in serious talks for Kraft, *Wall Street Journal*, www.wsj.com, March 25.

50. A. Ewing, 2014, Ericsson looks for a home in the cloud, *Bloomberg Businessweek*, November 17, 36–37.

51. H. Kai-Yu & F. Vermeulen, 2014, The structure of competition: How competition between one's rivals influences imitative market entry, *Organization Science*, 25: 299–319; L. Fuentelsaz & J. Gomez, 2006, Multipoint competition, strategic similarity and entry into geographic markets, *Strategic Management Journal*, 27: 477–499; J. Gimeno & C. Y. Woo, 1999, Multimarket contact, economies of scope, and firm performance, *Academy of Management Journal*, 42: 239–259.

52. M. J. De La Merced, 2015, Smucker to buy Big Heart Pet Brands for $5.8 billion, *New York Times*, www.nyt.com, February 3.

53. F. Brahm & J. Tarziján, 2014, Transactional hazards, institutional change, and capabilities: Integrating the theories of the firm, *Strategic Management Journal*, 35: 224–245; T. A. Shervani, G. Frazier, & G. Challagalla, 2007, The moderating influence of firm market power on the transaction cost economics model: An empirical test in a forward channel integration context, *Strategic Management Journal*, 28: 635–652.

54. N. Lahiri & S. Narayanan, 2013, Vertical integration, innovation and alliance portfolio size: Implications for firm performance, *Strategic Management Journal*, 34: 1042–1064; D. J. Teece, 2012, *Strategy, Innovation and the Theory of the Firm*, Northampton, MA: Edward Elgar Publishing Ltd.

55. R. Kapoor & J. M. Lee, 2013, Coordinating and competing in ecosystems: How organizational forms shape new technology investments, *Strategic Management Journal*, 34: 274–296; R. Carter & G. M. Hodgson, 2006, The impact of empirical tests of transaction cost economics on the debate on the nature of the firm, *Strategic Management Journal*, 27: 461–476; O. E. Williamson, 1996, Economics and organization: A primer, *California Management Review*, 38(2): 131–146.

56. R. Kapoor, 2013, Persistence of integration in the face of specialization: How firms navigated the winds of disintegration

and shaped the architecture of the semiconductor industry, *Organization Science*, 24: 1195–1213; S. Novak & S. Stern, 2008, How does outsourcing affect performance dynamics? Evidence from the automobile industry, *Management Science*, 54: 1963–1979.

57. C. Weigelt & D. J. Miller, 2013, Implications of internal organization structure for firm boundaries *Strategic Management Journal*, 34: 1411–1434; E. Rawley, 2010, Diversification, coordination costs and organizational rigidity: Evidence from microdata, *Strategic Management Journal*, 31: 873–891.

58. M. Bucheli & M. Kim, 2015, Attacked from both sides: A dynamic model of multinational corporations' strategies for protection of their property rights, *Global Strategy Journal*, 5: 1–26; C. Wolter & F. M. Veloso, 2008, The effects of innovation on vertical structure: Perspectives on transaction costs and competences, *Academy of Management Review*, 33: 586–605.

59. W. L. Tate, L. M. Ellram, T. Schoenherr, & K. L. Petersen, 2014, Global competitive conditions driving the manufacturing location decision, *Business Horizons*, 57: 381–390; T. Hutzschenreuter & F. Grone, 2009, Changing vertical integration strategies under pressure from foreign competition: The case of U.S. and German multinationals, *Journal of Management Studies*, 46: 269–307.

60. 2015, Flextronics International Ltd., www.flextronics.com, March 28.

61. S. Cabral, B. Quelin, & W. Maia, 2014, Outsourcing failure and reintegration: The influence of contractual and external factors, *Long Range Planning*, 47: 365–378.

62. J. Sears & G. Hoetker, 2014, Technological overlap, technological capabilities, and resource recombination in technological acquisitions, *Strategic Management Journal*, 35: 48–67; K. M. Eisenhardt & D. C. Galunic, 2000, Coevolving: At last, a way to make synergies work, *Harvard Business Review*, 78(1): 91–111.

63. O. Schilke, 2014, On the contingent value of dynamic capabilities for competitive advantage: The nonlinear moderating effect of environmental dynamism, *Strategic Management Journal*, 35: 179–203; P. David, J. P. O'Brien, T. Yoshikawa, & A. Delios, 2010, Do shareholders or stakeholders appropriate the rents from corporate diversification? The influence of ownership structure, *Academy of Management Journal*, 53: 636–654; J. A. Nickerson & T. R. Zenger, 2008, Envy, comparison costs, and the economic theory of the firm, *Strategic Management Journal*, 13: 1429–1449.

64. M. Gottfried, 2015, Walt Disney has built a better mousetrap, *Wall Street Journal*, Feb 5, C8.

65. T. Zenger, 2013, Strategy: The uniqueness challenge, *Harvard Business Review*, 91(11): 52–58.

66. F. Anjos & C. Fracassi, 2015, Shopping for Information? Diversification and the Network of Industries, *Management Science*, 61: 161–183; C. Rudolph & B. Schwetzler, 2013, Conglomerates on the rise again? A cross-regional study on the impact of the 2008–2009 financial crisis on the diversification discount, *Journal of Corporate Finance*, 22: 153–165; D. W. Ng, 2007, A modern resource-based approach to unrelated diversification. *Journal of Management Studies*, 44: 1481–1502.

67. Porter, *Competitive Advantage*.

68. G. Matvos & A. Seru, 2014, Resource allocation within firms and financial market dislocation: Evidence from diversified conglomerates, *Review of Financial Studies*, 27: 1143–1189; D. Collis, D. Young, & M. Goold, 2007, The size, structure, and performance of corporate headquarters, *Strategic Management Journal*, 28: 283–405; O. E. Williamson, 1975, *Markets and Hierarchies: Analysis and Antitrust Implications*, NY: Macmillan Free Press.

69. A. Ataullah, I. Davidson, H. Le, & G. Wood, 2014, Corporate diversification, information asymmetry and insider trading, *British Journal of Management*, 25: 228–251.

70. B. N. Cline, J. L. Garner, & S. A. Yore, 2014, Exploitation of the internal capital market and the avoidance of outside monitoring, *Journal of Corporate Finance*, 25: 234–250; R. Aggarwal & N. A. Kyaw, 2009, International variations in transparency and capital structure: Evidence from European firms. *Journal of International Financial Management & Accounting*, 20: 1–34.

71. D. Buchuk, B. Larrain, F. Muñoz, & I. F. Urzúa, 2014, The internal capital markets of business groups: Evidence from intra-group loans, *Journal of Financial Economics*, 112: 190–212.

72. M. Sengul & J. Gimeno, 2013, Constrained delegation: Limiting subsidiaries' decision rights and resources in firms that compete across multiple industries, *Administrative Science Quarterly*, 58: 420–471; E. Dooms & A. A. Van Oijen, 2008, The balance between tailoring and standardizing control, *European Management Review*, 5: 245–252; M. E. Raynor & J. L. Bower, 2001, Lead from the center: How to manage divisions dynamically, *Harvard Business Review*, 79(5): 92–100.

73. G. Smith, 2015, Siemens' long-feared slimdown isn't as drastic as feared, *Fortune*, www.fortune.com; B. Quint. 2009, Companies deal with tough times through diversification, *Information Today*, 26: 7–8.

74. H. Zhu & C. Chung, 2014, Portfolios of political ties and business group strategy in emerging economies: Evidence from Taiwan, *Administrative Science Quarterly*, 59: 599–638; S. L. Sun, X. Zhoa, & H. Yang, 2010, Executive compensation in Asia: A critical review, *Asia Pacific Journal of Management*, 27: 775–802; A. Delios, D. Xu, & P. W. Beamish, 2008, Within-country product diversification and foreign subsidiary performance, *Journal of International Business Studies*, 39: 706–724.

75. S. F. Karabag & C. Berggren, 2014, Antecedents of firm performance in emerging economies: Business groups, strategy, industry structure, and state support, *Journal of Business Research*, 67: 2212–2223; Lee, Park, Shin, Disappearing internal capital markets: Evidence from diversified business groups in Korea; A. Chakrabarti, K. Singh, & I. Mahmood, 2006, Diversification and performance: Evidence from East Asian firms, *Strategic Management Journal*, 28: 101–120.

76. S. Schönhaar, U. Pidun, & M. Nippa, M. 2014, Transforming the business portfolio: How multinationals reinvent themselves, *Journal of Business Strategy*, 35(3): 4–17; D. D. Bergh, R. A. Johnson, & R. L. Dewitt, 2008, Restructuring through spin-off or sell-off: Transforming information asymmetries into financial gain, *Strategic Management Journal*, 29: 133–148; C. Decker & M. Mellewigt, 2007, Thirty years after Michael E. Porter: What do we know about business exit? *Academy of Management Perspectives*, 2: 41–55; S. J. Chang & H. Singh, 1999, The impact of entry and resource fit on modes of exit by multibusiness firms, *Strategic Management Journal*, 20: 1019–135.

77. Hoskisson, Wei, Yi, Jing, The evolution and strategic positioning of private equity firms.

78. 2015, About us, Danaher, www.danaher.com, March 30; S. Ward, 2014, Danaher's best recent deal: Its shares, *Barron's*, June 9, 21.

79. D. H. Frank & T. Obloj, 2014, Firm-specific human capital, organizational incentives, and agency costs: Evidence from retail banking, *Strategic Management Journal*, 35: 1279–1301; R. Coff, 2003, Bidding wars over R&D-intensive firms: Knowledge, opportunism, and the market for corporate control, *Academy of Management Journal*, 46: 74–85.

80. I. Ioannou, 2014, When do spinouts enhance parent firm performance? Evidence from the U.S. automobile industry, 1890–1986, *Organization Science*, 25: 529–551; J. Xia & S. Li, 2013, The divestiture of acquired subunits: A resource-dependence approach, *Strategic Management Journal*, 34: 131–148; C. Moschieri & J. Mair, 2012, Managing divestitures through time—Expanding current knowledge, *Academy of Management Perspectives*, 26: 35–50.

81. T. W. Tong, J. J. Reuer, B. B. Tyler, & S. Zhang, 2015, Host country executives' assessments of international joint ventures and divestitures: An experimental approach, *Strategic Management Journal*, 36: 254–275; H. Berry, 2013, When do firms divest foreign operations? *Organization Science*, 24: 246–261; D. Ma, 2012, A relational view

of organizational restructuring: The case of transitional China, *Management and Organization Review*, 8: 51–75.

82. P. Pautler, 2015, A brief history of the FTC's Bureau of Economics: Reports, mergers, and information regulation. *Review of Industrial Organization*, 46: 59–94; M. Lubatkin, H. Merchant, & M. Srinivasan, 1997, Merger strategies and shareholder value during times of relaxed antitrust enforcement: The case of large mergers during the 1980s, *Journal of Management*, 23: 61–81.

83. D. P. Champlin & J. T. Knoedler, 1999, Restructuring by design? Government's complicity in corporate restructuring, *Journal of Economic Issues*, 33: 41–57.

84. R. M. Scherer & D. Ross, 1990, *Industrial Market Structure and Economic Performance*, Boston: Houghton Mifflin.

85. A. Shleifer & R. W. Vishny, 1994, Takeovers in the 1960s and 1980s: Evidence and implications. In R. P. Rumelt, D. E. Schendel, & D. J. Teece (eds.), *Fundamental Issues in Strategy*, Boston: Harvard Business School Press, 403–422.

86. S. Chatterjee, J. S. Harrison, & D. D. Bergh, 2003, Failed takeover attempts, corporate governance and refocusing, *Strategic Management Journal*, 24: 87–96; Lubatkin, Merchant, & Srinivasan, Merger strategies and shareholder value; D. J. Ravenscraft, & R. M. Scherer, 1987, *Mergers, Sell-Offs and Economic Efficiency*, Washington, DC: Brookings Institution, 22.

87. D. A. Zalewski, 2001, Corporate takeovers, fairness, and public policy, *Journal of Economic Issues*, 35: 431–437; P. L. Zweig, J. P. Kline, S. A. Forest, & K. Gudridge, 1995, The case against mergers, *BusinessWeek*, October 30, 122–130.

88. E. J. Lopez, 2001, New anti-merger theories: A critique, *Cato Journal*, 20: 359–378; 1998, The trustbusters' new tools, *The Economist*, May 2, 62–64.

89. D. Bush & B. D. Gelb, 2012 Anti-trust enforcement: An inflection point? *Journal of Business Strategy*, 33(6): 15–21.

90. M. C. Jensen, 1986, Agency costs of free cash flow, corporate finance, and takeovers, *American Economic Review*, 76: 323–329.

91. M. A. Hitt, J. S. Harrison, & R. D. Ireland, 2001, *Mergers and Acquisitions: A Guide to Creating Value for Stakeholders*, NY: Oxford University Press.

92. M. T. Brouwer, 2008, Horizontal mergers and efficiencies; theory and antitrust practice, *European Journal of Law and Economics*, 26: 11–26.

93. T. Afza, C. Slahudin, & M. S. Nazir, 2008, Diversification and corporate performance: An evaluation of Pakistani firms, *South Asian Journal of Management*, 15: 7–18; J. M. Shaver, 2006, A paradox of synergy: Contagion and capacity effects in mergers and acquisitions, *Academy of Management Journal*, 31: 962–976.

94. C. Sundaramurthy, K. Pukthuanthong, & Y. Kor, 2014, Positive and negative synergies between the CEO's and the corporate board's human and social capital: A study of biotechnology firms, *Strategic Management Journal*, 35: 845–868; Bauer & Matzler, Antecedents of M&A success: The role of strategic complementarity, cultural fit, and degree and speed of integration;

95. L. E. Palich, L. B. Cardinal, & C. C. Miller, 2000, Curvilinearity in the diversification-performance linkage: An examination of over three decades of research, *Strategic Management Journal*, 21: 155–174.

96. J. P. O'Brien, P. David, T. Yoshikawa, & A. Delios, 2014, How capital structure influences diversification performance: A transaction cost perspective, *Strategic Management Journal*, 35: 1013–1031; Sirmon, Hitt, Ireland, & Gilbert, Resource orchestration to create competitive advantage; A. E. Bernardo & B. Chowdhry, 2002, Resources, real options, and corporate strategy, *Journal of Financial Economics*, 63: 211–234.

97. T. B. Mackey & J. B. Barney, 2013, Incorporating opportunity costs in strategic management research: The value of diversification and payout as opportunities forgone when reinvesting in the firm, *Strategic Organization*, 11: 347–363; W. H. Tsai, Y. C. Kuo, J.-H. Hung, 2009, Corporate diversification and CEO turnover in family businesses: Self-entrenchment or risk reduction? *Small Business Economics*, 32: 57–76; N. W. C. Harper & S. P. Viguerie, 2002, Are you too focused? *McKinsey Quarterly*, Mid-Summer, 29–38.

98. J. W. Miller, 2015, Alcoa looks to shed more capacity, *Wall Street Journal*, March 10, B3

99. J. W. Miller, 2015, Alcoa makes deal to broaden reach in aircraft industry, *Wall Street Journal*, March 10, B3.

100. Sakhartov & Folta, Resource relatedness, redeployability, and firm value; T. B. Folta & J. P. O'Brien, 2008, Determinants of firm-specific thresholds in acquisition decisions, *Managerial and Decision Economics*, 29: 209–225.

101. N. M. Kay & A. Diamantopoulos, 1987, Uncertainty and synergy: Towards a formal model of corporate strategy, *Managerial and Decision Economics*, 8: 121–130.

102. R. W. Coff, 1999, How buyers cope with uncertainty when acquiring firms in knowledge-intensive industries: Caveat emptor, *Organization Science*, 10: 144–161.

103. P. B. Carroll & C. Muim 2008, 7 ways to fail big, *Harvard Business Review*, 86(9): 82–91.

104. Y. R. Choi, S. A. Zahra, T. Yoshikawa, & B. H. Han, 2015, Family ownership and R&D investment: The role of growth opportunities and business group membership, *Journal of Business Research*, 68: 1053–1061; S. K. Kim, J. D. Arthurs, A. Sahaym, & J. B. Cullen, 2013, Search behavior of the diversified firm: The impact of fit on innovation,

Strategic Management Journal, 34: 999–1009; J. Kang, 2013, The relationship between corporate diversification and corporate social performance, *Strategic Management Journal*, 34: 94–109.

105. Sears & Hoetker, Technological overlap, technological capabilities, and resource recombination in technological acquisitions; D. G. Sirmon, S. Gove, & M. A. Hitt, 2008, Resource management in dyadic competitive rivalry: The effects of resource bundling and deployment, *Academy of Management Journal*, 51: 919–935; S. J. Chatterjee & B. Wernerfelt, 1991, The link between resources and type of diversification: Theory and evidence, *Strategic Management Journal*, 12: 33–48.

106. G. Ertug & F. Castellucci, 2015, Who shall get more? How intangible assets and aspiration levels affect the valuation of resource providers, *Strategic Organization*, 13: 6–31; O'Brien, David, Yoshikawa, & Delios, How capital structure influences diversification performance; E. N. K. Lim, S. S. Das, & A. Das, 2009, Diversification strategy, capital structure, and the Asian financial crisis (1997–1998): Evidence from Singapore firms, *Strategic Management Journal*, 30: 577–594; W. Keuslein, 2003, The Ebitda folly, *Forbes*, March 17, 165–167.

107. C. Zillman, 2014, Michael Dell: Long live the PC, *Fortune*, www.fortune.com, May 23;

108. L. Capron & J. Hull 1999, Redeployment of brands, sales forces, and general marketing management expertise following horizontal acquisitions: A resource-based view, *Journal of Marketing*, 63: 41–54.

109. C. Mims, 2015, In battery revolution, a clean leap forward, *Wall Street Journal*, March 16, B4.

110. M. V. S. Kumar, 2009, The relationship between product and international diversification: The effects of short-run constraints and endogeneity. *Strategic Management Journal*, 30: 99–116; C. B. Malone & L. C. Rose, 2006. Intangible assets and firm diversification, *International Journal of Managerial Finance*, 2: 136–153.

111. J. Chekler, 2015, Alvarez & Marsal to launch investment arm, *Wall Street Journal*, www.wsj.com, March 25.

112. M. Rogan & O. Sorenson, 2014, Picking a (poor) partner: A relational perspective on acquisitions, *Administrative Science Quarterly*, 59: 301–329; C. Moschieri, 2011, The implementation and structuring of divestitures: The unit's perspective, *Strategic Management Journal*, 32: 368–401; K. Shimizu & M. A. Hitt, 2005, What constrains or facilitates divestitures of formerly acquired firms? The effects of organizational inertia, *Journal of Management*, 31: 50–72.

113. J. Bunge & L. Hoffman, 2014, Tables turn for Hillshire CEO as an acquirer becomes prey, *Wall Street Journal*, June 2, B1; D. Cimilluca & R. Van Daalen, 2013,. A year after its creation, Sara Lee coffee spinoff fetches

$9.8 billion. *Wall Street Journal*, April 13, B3; D. Cimilluca & J. Jargon, 2009, Corporate news: Sara Lee weighs sale of European business, *Wall Street Journal*, March 13, B3.

114. M. van Essen, J. Otten, & E. J. Carberry, 2015, Assessing managerial power theory: A meta-analytic approach to understanding the determinants of CEO compensation, *Journal of Management*, 41: 164–202; A. J. Nyberg, I. S. Fulmer, B. Gerhart, & M. A. Carpenter, 2010, Agency theory revisited: CEO return, and shareholder interest alignment, *Academy of Management Journal*, 53: 1029–1049.

115. X. Castañer & N. Kavadis, 2013, Does good governance prevent bad strategy? A study of corporate governance, financial diversification, and value creation by French corporations, 2000–2006, *Strategic Management Journal*, 34: 863–876; D. Souder, Z. Simsek, & S. G. Johnson, 2012, The differing effects of agent and founder CEOs on the firm's market expansion, *Strategic Management Journal*, 33: 23–41; R. E. Hoskisson, M. W. Castleton, & M. C. Withers, 2009, Complementarity in monitoring and bonding: More intense monitoring leads to higher executive compensation, *Academy of Management Perspectives*, 23: 57–74.

116. D. E. Black, S. S. Dikolli, & S. D. Dyreng, 2014, CEO pay-for-complexity and the risk of managerial diversion from multinational diversification, *Contemporary Accounting Research*, 31: 103–135; Pathak, Hoskisson, & Johnson, 2014.

117. E. M. Fich, L. T. Starks, & A. S. Yore, 2014, CEO deal-making activities and compensation, *Journal of Financial Economics*, 114: 471–492; M. van Essen, P. P. Heugens, J. Otto, & J. van Oosterhout, 2012, An institution-based view of executive compensation: A multilevel meta-analytic test, *Journal of International Business Studies*, 43: 396–423; Y. Deutsch, T. Keil, & T. Laamanen, 2011, A dual agency view of board compensation: The joint effects of outside director and CEO options on firm risk, *Strategic Management Journal*, 32: 212–227.

118. R. Krause, K. A. Whitler, & M. Semadeni, 2014, Power to the principals! An experimental look at shareholder say-on-pay voting, *Academy of Management Journal*, 57: 94–115.

119. Zhu & Chen, CEO narcissism and the impact of prior board experience on corporate strategy; A. J. Wowak & D. C. Hambrick, 2010, A model of person-pay interaction: How executives vary in their responses to compensation arrangements, *Strategic Management Journal*, 31: 803–821; J. Bogle, 2008, Reflections on CEO compensation, *Academy of Management Perspectives*, 22: 21–25.

120. E. Y. Rhee & P. C. Fiss, 2014, Framing controversial actions: Regulatory focus, source credibility, and stock market reaction to poison pill adoption, *Academy of Management Journal*, 57: 1734–1758; M. Kahan & E. B. Rock, 2002, How I learned to stop worrying and love the pill: Adaptive responses to takeover law, *University of Chicago Law Review*, 69: 871–915.

121. B. W. Benson, W. N. Davidson, T. R. Davidson, & H. Wang, 2015, Do busy directors and CEOs shirk their responsibilities? Evidence from mergers and acquisitions, *Quarterly Review of Economics & Finance*, 55: 1–19; R. C. Anderson, T. W. Bates, J. M. Bizjak, & M. L. Lemmon, 2000, Corporate governance and firm diversification, *Financial Management*, 29: 5–22; J. D. Westphal, 1998, Board games: How CEOs adapt to increases in structural board independence from management, *Administrative Science Quarterly*, 43: 511–537.

122. C. E. Devers, G. Mcnamara, J. Haleblian, & M. E. Yoder, 2013, Do they walk the talk? Gauging acquiring CEO and director confidence in the value creation potential of announced acquisitions, *Academy of Management Journal*, 56: 1679–1702; S. M. Campbell, A. J. Ward, J. A. Sonnenfeld, & B. R. Agle, 2008, Relational ties that bind: Leader-follower relationship dimensions and charismatic attribution, *Leadership Quarterly*, 19: 556–568; M. Wiersema, 2002, Holes at the top: Why CEO firings backfire, *Harvard Business Review*, 80(12): 70–77.

123. R. E. Hoskisson, J. D. Arthurs, R. E. White, & C. M. Wyatt, 2013. Multiple agency theory: An emerging perspective on corporate governance. In M. Wright, D. S. Siegel, K. Keasey, & I. Filatotchev (eds.), *The Oxford Handbook of Corporate Governance*, Oxford: Oxford University Press; D. Allcock & I. Filatotchev, 2010, Executive incentive schemes in initial public offerings: The effects of multiple-agency conflicts and corporate governance, *Journal of Management*, 36: 663–686; N. Wasserman, 2006, Stewards, agents, and the founder discount: Executive compensation in new ventures, *Academy of Management Journal*, 49: 960–976.

124. E. F. Fama, 1980, Agency problems and the theory of the firm, *Journal of Political Economy*, 88: 288–307.

125. H. Kim, R. E. Hoskisson, & S. Lee, 2015, Why strategic factor markets matter: 'New' multinationals' geographic diversification and firm profitability, *Strategic Management Journal*, 36: 518–536; M. Y. Brannen & M. F. Peterson, 2009, Merging without alienating: Interventions promoting cross-cultural organizational integration and their limitations, *Journal of International Business Studies*, 40: 468–489; M. L. A. Hayward, 2002, When do firms learn from their acquisition experience? Evidence from 1990–1995, *Strategic Management Journal*, 23: 21–39.

126. R. E. Hoskisson, R. A. Johnson, L. Tihanyi, & R. E. White, 2005, Diversified business groups and corporate refocusing in emerging economies, *Journal of Management*, 31: 941–965.

127. R. Chittoor, P. Kale, & P. Puranam, 2015. Business groups in developing capital markets: Towards a complementarity perspective, *Strategic Management Journal*, forthcoming; C. N. Chung & X. Luo, 2008, Institutional logics or agency costs: The influence of corporate governance models on business group restructuring in emerging economies, *Organization Science*, 19: 766–784; W. P. Wan & R. E. Hoskisson, 2003, Home country environments, corporate diversification strategies, and firm performance, *Academy of Management Journal*, 46: 27–45.

7

Merger and Acquisition Strategies

Studying this chapter should provide you with the strategic management knowledge needed to:

7-1 Explain the popularity of merger and acquisition strategies in firms competing in the global economy.

7-2 Discuss reasons why firms use an acquisition strategy to achieve strategic competitiveness.

7-3 Describe seven problems that work against achieving success when using an acquisition strategy.

7-4 Name and describe the attributes of effective acquisitions.

7-5 Define the restructuring strategy and distinguish among its common forms.

7-6 Explain the short- and long-term outcomes of the different types of restructuring strategies.

MERGERS AND ACQUISITIONS: PROMINENT STRATEGIES FOR FIRMS SEEKING TO ENHANCE THEIR PERFORMANCE

"Companies are turning to the capital markets at a record pace to fund acquisitions" read the headlines in mid-2015. At that point in time, U.S. firms had already raised roughly $206.3 billion to support their intended merger and acquisition activity. On a world-wide scale, announced and completed mergers and acquisitions (M&A) by mid-2015 totaled $1.47 trillion. This total was a 30 percent increase from the same time in 2014 and was the highest amount allocated to implement merger and acquisition strategies since 2007. If this pace continued through the end of 2015, the total global value of M&A transactions would exceed $3.7 trillion. At the time, many executives anticipated that this robust amount of M&A activity would likely continue and perhaps become even stronger in the next few years. But why? What causes firms to use strategies that call for them to either merge with another or acquire another firm? (As we explain later, a merger finds firms combining themselves as coequals, while acquisitions find the target firm being purchased by the acquiring firm.)

BhFoton/Shutterstock.com

As we discuss next, the influences on firms' decisions to use mergers and acquisitions' strategies are varied and interesting. The discussion of these influences in the Opening Case reinforces the discussion in the chapter about specific reasons why firms choose to implement these strategies.

The need to create value for stakeholders is a primary influence on firms' decisions to engage in M&A activity. Firms create value in multiple ways, including through the successful implementation of their business-level, diversification, international and cooperative strategies. Sometimes though, firms can create additional value by merging with another company or acquiring a firm. This is the case for life sciences companies today where weak R&D pipelines are yielding too few products, increasing the difficulty of creating sufficient amounts of value for stakeholders as a result. An analyst of this industry recently suggested that "this pressure to create value is driving M&A, divestitures, and restructurings at unprecedented levels throughout the industry." (We discuss restructuring strategies, including those involving divestitures, later in the chapter.) For firms in this industry, specific influences resulting in decisions to engage in M&A activity include patent expirations, pricing pressures, and growth opportunities in foreign and emerging markets.

Increasing confidence in a firm's domestic economy, and perhaps in global economies as well, is another influence on M&A activity. Observers of business conditions in the world are now concluding that the after effects of the 2007/2008 global crisis on companies have largely faded, resulting in boards of directors becoming more confident that their company should pursue all feasible strategies with the potential to increase firm value. This is particularly the case when growth in a firm's domestic market is stagnant or declining. This appears to be the situation facing a number of Japanese firms today in that although a number of them have significant amounts of cash on hand, their domestic markets are shrinking in size. Accordingly, these firms are examining what they believe are attractive merger and acquisition opportunities outside of Japan. These firms do indeed seem eager to engage in M&A activity as indicated by the fact that they paid an average premium of 46 percent for the acquisitions they completed during 2015's first quarter.

But companies interested in implementing M&A strategies sometimes face hurdles in their attempts to do so. Firms seeking to merge with or acquire Chinese firms often face complicated trade barriers and other rules, procedures, and laws that are in place to protect domestic firms. Honeywell International, Inc., for example, is frustrated with the pace of the acquisitions it has been able to finalize recently in China. The firm seeks to complete $10 billion in M&A activity in China by the end of 2018, although it is not confident that this goal will be reached. The U.K. government is looking more carefully at companies' attempts to acquire British firms. Mainly, government officials believe that at least some and potentially many of these transactions are against the public's interest and may pose a risk to the continuing employment of local/native workers. Thus, while certain factors influence a firm's decision to use M&A strategies, the reality is that some conditions may prevent them from being able to do so, at least in certain situations.

Sources: 2015, M&A trends report 2015, Deloitte, www2.deloitte.com, April 21; 2015, For life sciences CFOs: Using M&A to drive shareholder value, Deloitte, www2.deloitte.com, April 21; D. Cimilluca, D. Mattioli, & S. Raice, 2015, Rising optimism fuels deal rebound, *Wall Street Journal Online*, www.wsj.com, April 8; A. Fukase, 2015, Japanese M&A overseas takes off, *Wall Street Journal Online*, www.wsj.com, April 28; W. Ma, 2015, China's lower growth goal doesn't spook foreign companies, *Wall Street Journal Online*, www.wsj.com, March 5; L Wei & B. Spegele, 2015, China considering mergers among its big state oil companies, *Wall Street Journal Online*, www.wsj.com, February 17.

We examined corporate-level strategy in Chapter 6, focusing on types and levels of product diversification strategies firms use to create value for stakeholders and competitive advantages for the firms. As noted in that chapter, diversification allows a firm to create value by productively using excess resources to exploit new opportunities.[1] In this chapter, we explore merger and acquisition strategies. Firms throughout the world use these strategies, often in concert with diversification strategies, to become more diversified. In other words, firms often become more diversified by completing mergers and/or acquisitions. As we discuss in this chapter, although a popular strategy for small corporations[2] as well as large ones, using these strategies does not always lead to the success firms seek.[3] And as described in the Opening Case, certain conditions may preclude a firm from engaging in merger and acquisition activity, even though various factors are influencing it to try to do so.

A key objective of this chapter is to explain how firms can successfully use merger and acquisition strategies to create stakeholder value and competitive advantages.[4] To reach this objective, we first explain the continuing popularity of merger and acquisition strategies. As part of this explanation, we describe the differences between mergers, acquisitions, and takeovers. We next discuss specific reasons why firms choose to use merger and acquisition strategies and some of the problems organizations may encounter when doing so. We then describe the characteristics associated with effective acquisitions (we focus on acquisition strategies in the chapter) before closing the chapter with a discussion of different types of restructuring strategies. Restructuring strategies are commonly used to correct or deal with the results of ineffective mergers and acquisitions.

7-1 The Popularity of Merger and Acquisition Strategies

Merger and acquisition (M&A) strategies have been popular among U.S. firms for many years. Some believe that these strategies played a central role in the restructuring of U.S. businesses during the 1980s and 1990s and that they continue generating these types of benefits in the twenty-first century.[5] As discussed in other parts of this chapter, mergers and acquisitions are also occurring with greater frequency in many regions of the world.[6]

In the final analysis, firms use these strategies for the purpose of trying to create more value for all stakeholders.

Although popular as a way of creating value and earning above-average returns, it is challenging to effectively implement merger and acquisition strategies. This is particularly true for the acquiring firms in that some research results indicate that shareholders of the acquired firms often earn above-average returns from acquisitions, while shareholders of the acquiring firms typically earn returns that are close to zero.[7] Moreover, in approximately two-thirds of all acquisitions, the acquiring firm's stock price falls immediately after the intended transaction is announced. This negative response reflects investors' skepticism about the likelihood that the acquirer will be able to achieve the synergies required to justify the premium to purchase the target firm.[8]

Discussed more fully later in the chapter, paying excessive premiums to acquire firms can negatively influence the results a firm achieves through an acquisition strategy. Determining the worth of a target firm is difficult; this difficulty increases the likelihood a firm will pay a premium to acquire a target. Premiums are paid when those leading an acquiring firm conclude that the target firm would be worth more under its ownership than it would be as part of any other ownership arrangement or if it were to remain as an independent company. Recently, for example, Alexion Pharmaceuticals, Inc. paid a 124 percent premium to buy Synageva BioPharma Corp. Although Synageva did not have a product on the market at the time of the transaction, it was in late-stage development of a promising treatment for a rare genetic disease. Alexion placed high value on both this product and Synageva's overall innovation capabilities, factors that influenced the decision to pay a premium. The following comment from Alexion's CEO shows why the firm paid a premium to acquire a particular company:

> A **merger** is a strategy through which two firms agree to integrate their operations on a relatively coequal basis.

"We think the valuation is appropriate because we think Synageva is so much more valuable in our hand than anyone else's hands."[9]

This may in fact be the case. Overall though, paying a premium that exceeds the value of a target once integrated with the acquiring firm can result in negative outcomes.[10]

7-1a Mergers, Acquisitions, and Takeovers: What Are the Differences?

A **merger** is a strategy through which two firms agree to integrate their operations on a relatively coequal basis. A proposed merger of equals between two Canadian mining firms—Alamos Gold Inc. and AuRico Gold Inc.—was announced in mid-2015. This merger between two smaller miners was being considered so the combined firms could generate synergies through cost savings and a joint focus on low-risk mining operations. Openly stating that the merger was viewed by both firms as a merger of equals, Alamos' CEO stated that "the combination of diversified production from three mines and a pipeline of low-cost growth projects in safe

Hand-out/AURICO GOLD INC./Newscom

Pictured here are individual employees from two companies—Alamos Gold Inc. and AuRico Gold Inc.—who will now work together in the same company as a result of a merger.

jurisdictions equate to a leading gold intermediate and a significant re-rate opportunity for our collective shareholders."[11]

Even though the transaction that was proposed to take place between Alamos and AuRico was to be a merger of equals, evidence suggests that finalizing a proposal for firms to merge on an equal or a relatively equal basis is difficult. In an analyst's words:

"A merger of equals: It's how executives love to present big corporate tie-ups. The reality is that it isn't easy working out how to share control of multibillion-dollar businesses among strong-willed executives and reassure shareholders, wary of how management infighting can destroy value in meagdeals."[12]

On a practical basis, deciding who will lead the merged firm, how to fuse what are often disparate corporate cultures, and how to reach an agreement about the value of each company prior to the merger are issues that commonly affect firms' efforts to merge on a coequal basis.

To more fully consider issues such as these and others that surface when firms propose to merge as equals, we discuss the merger between Swiss-based Holcim Ltd. and French-based Lafarge SA in the Strategic Focus. Prior to deciding to merge, Holcim and Lafarge were long-time competitors. As we discuss, the route to finalizing this merger was not without challenges.

An **acquisition** is a strategy through which one firm buys a controlling, or 100 percent, interest in another firm with the intent of making the acquired firm a subsidiary business within its portfolio. After the acquisition is completed, the management of the acquired firm reports to the management of the acquiring firm.

Although most mergers that are completed are friendly in nature, acquisitions can be friendly or unfriendly. A **takeover** is a special type of acquisition where the target firm does not solicit the acquiring firm's bid; thus, takeovers are unfriendly acquisitions. As explained in Chapter 10, firms have developed defenses (mostly corporate governance devices) that can be used to prevent an unrequested and undesired takeover bid from being successful.[13]

Commonly, firms think of unsolicited bids as "hostile" takeovers. When such a bid is received, the takeover target may try to determine the highest amount the acquiring firm is willing to pay, even while simultaneously using defense mechanisms to prevent a takeover attempt from succeeding. Multiple exchanges may take place between a potential acquirer and its target before a resolution to the unsolicited bid is reached; and these exchanges can become quite complicated. The exchanges among Teva Pharmaceutical, Mylan N.V., and Perrigo Company that were initiated in the spring of 2015 demonstrate this complexity. Mylan made a hostile bid for Perrigo before receiving a hostile bid itself from Teva. The following comment captures the complexity of this situation:

"But Teva says it doesn't want Mylan if Mylan buys Perrigo, Perrigo rebuffed Mylan's offer, and earlier, Mylan said it wasn't thrilled with Teva's takeover interest."[14]

As the three firms worked to sort out the matter, some felt that the price firms would ultimately be willing to pay to complete an intended transaction would decide the fate of the hostile takeover bids involving the three firms.

On a comparative basis, acquisitions are more common than mergers and takeovers. Accordingly, we focus the remainder of this chapter's discussion on acquisitions.

7-2 Reasons for Acquisitions

In this section, we discuss reasons why firms decide to acquire another company. As this discussion shows, there are many unique reasons that firms choose to use an acquisition strategy.

An **acquisition** is a strategy through which one firm buys a controlling, or 100 percent, interest in another firm with the intent of making the acquired firm a subsidiary business within its portfolio.

A **takeover** is a special type of acquisition where the target firm does not solicit the acquiring firm's bid; thus, takeovers are unfriendly acquisitions.

Strategic **Focus**

A Merger of Equals: Making It Happen Isn't Easy!

Founded in France in 1833, Lafarge became a successful global industrial company specializing in three product areas—cement, construction aggregates, and concrete. The other party in a "merger of equals," that required well over a year to design and bring to the conclusion the firms intended, is Holcim, a materials and aggregates company that was founded in Switzerland in 1912. Holcim's global ambitions were obvious early when the firm expanded into France and throughout Europe and the Middle East during the 1920s. This expansion resulted in long-term and active competitions between Lafarge and Holcim.

In April of 2014, Lafarge and Holcim announced that they had settled on terms that would result in a merger of equals and that, accordingly, they were prepared to seek regulatory approval of the proposed transaction. Obtaining such approvals was anticipated to be challenging given that the diversity of the independent firms' global operations meant that 15 or so different jurisdictions could potentially object to a merger between the firms.

What influenced Lafarge and Holcim to want to merge as coequals given the difficulties of doing so? The prevailing thought is that mergers of equals are always more fragile to bring about in light of the need to effectively meld what are commonly two different cultures and specify the leadership structure that will be used to operate the newly-created firm. These issues are in addition to a core one of identifying the financial aspects of the transactions that will appeal to each firm's shareholders.

In spite of challenges such as these, Lafarge and Holcim thought that merging as equals would create a firm with enhanced and significant competitive abilities. Leaders of the two firms concluded that together LafargeHolcim, the agreed upon name for the combined firm, would have the most balanced and diversified portfolio in the building materials industry. The firms anticipated that integrating their operations would generate approximately $1.5 billion in annual cost savings. In an overall sense, company leaders thought that the anticipated positive benefits of merging would come about primarily as a result of being able to meld Holcim's marketing strengths with Lafarge's innovation capabilities.

Perhaps not unexpectedly, the transaction proposed between Lafarge and Holcim almost fell apart. This happened in March of 2015 when Holcim's board, "after first agreeing to a $44 billion merger with Lafarge, rejected the deal's terms as undervaluing Holcim. Corporate leadership also was a concern." This objection surfaced after the firms had received regulatory approvals from key jurisdictions, including the European Union, India, and the United States, regarding the number of divestitures of units they would make to prevent them from having highly concentrated positions in different global markets. At the core of the dispute was the conviction among Holcim's

board members that the financial terms should be more attractive for their shareholders and that Lafarge's CEO should not be appointed as CEO of the newly-created firm. One reason for these convictions was that in the nearly one year since terms of the initial merger were agreed upon, Holcim's "operating performance and share price had outperformed those of Lafarge." After restructuring the financing of the transaction and agreeing that a different CEO would be appointed for the new firm, 94 percent of Holcim's shareholders approved the transaction's terms.

After dealing with challenges, LafargeHolcim became a firm that was a merger of equals in July 2015. Speaking to the future, one board member said that "this isn't just another merger. It is an opportunity to create a new Number One in our industry." Assuming that this merger of equals achieves the potential some anticipate, all of the work required to bring it about will be validated. Going forward though, implementation challenges may come into play, at least in the short term, given the potential

FRANCK FIFE/AFP/Getty Images

Shown here left to right shaking hands during an announcement of their firms' intention to merge are Rolf Soiron, the chair of Holcim's board of directors and Bruno Lafont, CEO of Lafarge SA. Later, Eric Olsen was selected as the CEO of the newly formed firm, called LafargeHolcim.

incompatibility of Holcim's decentralized management approach with the more centralized approach that characterized Lafarge when it competed as an independent firm. Those leading the integration processes associated with the details of combining the two firms will need to pay close attention to this issue.

Sources: 2015, Holcim and Lafarge obtain merger clearances in the United States and Canada paving the way to closing their merger, *Holcim Home Page*, www.holcim. com, May 4; 2015, Lafarge to cut 380 jobs ahead of merger with Holcim, *Global Cement*, www.globalcement.com, May 19; M. Curtin, 2015, Holcim-Lafarge shows 'merger of equals' doesn't equal smooth sailing, *Wall Street Journal Online*, www.wsj. com, March 16; M. Curtin, 2015, A 'merger of equals' is more fragile, *Wall Street Journal Online*, www.wsj.com, March 16; J. Franklin, 2015, Holcim and Lafarge name post-merger board candidates, *Reuters*, www.reuters.com, April 14; J. Revill, 2015, Holcim moves step closer to Lafarge merger, *Wall Street Journal Online*, www.wsj.com, May 8.

7-2a   Increased Market Power

Achieving greater market power is a primary reason for acquisitions.[15] Defined in Chapter 6, *market power* exists when a firm is able to sell its goods or services above competitive levels or when the costs of its primary or support activities are lower than those of its competitors. Market power usually is derived from the size of the firm, the quality of the resources it uses to compete, and its share of the market(s) in which it competes.[16] Therefore, most acquisitions that are designed to achieve greater market power entail buying a competitor, a supplier, a distributor, or a business in a highly related industry so a core competence can be used to gain competitive advantage in the acquiring firm's primary market.

Next, we discuss how firms use horizontal, vertical, and related types of acquisitions to increase their market power. Active acquirers simultaneously pursue two or all three types of acquisitions in order to do this. Evidence suggests, for example, that Amazon "for years has been expanding the scale and scope of its operation, both horizontally and vertically."[17] These three types of acquisitions, and proposed mergers as well, are subject to regulatory review by various governmental entities. Sometimes these reviews bring about the dissolution of proposed transactions. In 2015 for example, Comcast abandoned its effort to acquire Time Warner for $45.2 billion in light of opposition to the transaction, primarily from the U.S. Department of Justice.[18]

Horizontal Acquisitions

The acquisition of a company competing in the same industry as the acquiring firm is a *horizontal acquisition*. Horizontal acquisitions increase a firm's market power by exploiting cost-based and revenue-based synergies.[19] Horizontal acquisitions occur frequently in the pharmaceutical industry. An indication of this is the fact that, in the first few months of 2015, intended or completed horizontal acquisitions reached a combined value of roughly $180 billion. With respect to a specific firm, Mylan N.V. became the second largest generic drug seller in the United States by acquiring a number of firms in its industry over the past few years.[20] Research suggests that horizontal acquisitions result in higher performance when the firms have similar characteristics,[21] such as strategy, managerial styles, and resource allocation patterns. Similarities in these characteristics, as well as previous alliance management experience, support efforts to integrate the acquiring and the acquired firm. Horizontal acquisitions are often most effective when the acquiring firm effectively integrates the acquired firm's assets with its own, but only after evaluating and divesting excess capacity and assets that do not complement the newly combined firm's core competencies.[22]

Vertical Acquisitions

A *vertical acquisition* refers to a firm acquiring a supplier or distributor of one or more of its products. Through a vertical acquisition, the newly formed firm controls additional parts of the value chain (see Chapter 3),[23] which is how vertical acquisitions lead to increased market power.

Through vertical integration, a firm has an opportunity to appropriate value being generated in a part of the value chain in which it does not currently compete and to better control its own destiny in terms of costs and access. These factors influenced Delta Air Lines' decision in 2012 to purchase a refinery.[24] Owning access to a source of what could become jet fuel reduces the likelihood that a raw material critical to the firm's operations would become unavailable to it or that Delta would be subjected to market forces in terms of having access to the raw material. Identical logic explains Italian confectionary giant Ferrero's purchase of Oltan Gida, Turkey's largest hazelnut company, because having ready access to a steady flow of a key ingredient at an attractive price has the potential to positively affect the firm's efforts to earn above-returns.[25]

Related Acquisitions

Acquiring a firm in a highly related industry is called a *related acquisition*. Through a related acquisition, firms seek to create value through the synergy that can be generated by integrating some of their resources and capabilities.

Cisco Systems designs, manufacturers, and sells networking equipment. Over time though, the firm has engaged in related acquisitions, primarily as a foundation for being able to compete aggressively in other product markets. For example, as software becomes a more integral aspect of all networking products, the firm is making plans to acquire small- and medium-sized software companies. Such purchases appear to support the belief that Cisco is committed to competing successfully in the SDN (software-defined networking) space. Over the past few years, Cisco acquired Insieme Metworks, Tail-F, and Cariden to elaborate its SDN plans. Acquiring companies in related industries is a common practice for Cisco, and it is a practice that, in some analysts' eyes, has "opened up market opportunities on many occasions throughout the firm's history."[26]

7-2b Overcoming Entry Barriers

Barriers to entry (introduced in Chapter 2) are factors associated with a market, or the firms currently operating in it, that increase the expense and difficulty new firms encounter when trying to enter that particular market. For example, well-established competitors may have economies of scale in manufacturing or servicing their products. In addition, enduring relationships with customers often create loyalties that are difficult for new entrants to overcome. When facing differentiated products, new entrants typically must spend considerable resources to advertise their products and may find it necessary to sell below competitors' prices to entice new customers.

Facing the entry barriers that economies of scale and differentiated products create, a new entrant may find that acquiring an established company is more effective than entering the market as a competitor offering a product that is unfamiliar to current buyers. In fact, the higher the barriers to market entry, the greater the probability that a firm will acquire an existing firm to overcome them. For example, Scripps Networks Interactive, Inc., the niched lifestyle-cable-channel with a portfolio including the Food Network, HGTV, and Travel Channel, wants to expand internationally, given the growth potential of markets outside the United States. Rather than establish its own operations in multiple international markets, Scripps is acquiring existing firms to overcome entry barriers that exist for various reasons, such as product loyalty. Recently, Scripps took a controlling stake in Polish TV operator TVN with the possibility of purchasing the remaining part of the firm in the future.[27] In light of TVN's "incredible portfolio of channels and services," Scripps' executives saw this transaction as "an important milestone in the ongoing strategic development of the firm's international business."[28]

As this discussion suggests, a key advantage of using an acquisition strategy to overcome entry barriers is that the acquiring firm gains immediate access to a market that is attractive to it. This can be especially important for firms seeking to enter international markets, as is the case for Scripps Networks Interactive. We further discuss cross-border acquisitions next.

Cross-Border Acquisitions

Acquisitions made between companies with headquarters in different countries are called *cross-border acquisitions.*[29] Historically, North American and European companies were the most active acquirers of companies outside their domestic markets. However, today's global competitive landscape is one in which firms from economies throughout the world are engaging in cross-border acquisitions, and for a host of reasons. In the Strategic Focus, we discuss different cross-border acquisitions that are being pursued or have been completed recently and are products of different strategic rationales.

Different Strategic Rationales Driving Cross-Border Acquisitions

As is true for acquisitions between firms headquartered in the same nation, a clear strategic rationale should be the foundation for all cross-border acquisitions. The decision to acquire a company should be carefully identified, examined, and agreed upon by key decision makers throughout the firm prior to finalizing an acquisition decision. The most successful acquisitions, including cross-border ones, are products of a rational decision process that is grounded in careful analysis of a proposed transaction with its strategic rationale as a guiding force.

The strategic rationale sometimes finds firms deciding to acquire ownership percentages of target firms to see if a full acquisition is warranted at a later date. This seems to be the situation with Alibaba Group Holding Limited, the Chinese-based company that is the world's largest e-commerce platform as measured by volume of transactions. Today though, China remains the firm's primary focus. Saying that the firm "must absolutely globalize and it must be a successful effort," Alibaba's CEO has committed the firm to thinking globally and taking actions accordingly. With the strategic rationale of "becoming more global" as a driver, the firm is acquiring parts of firms outside its home market, including its 9 percent purchase of U.S. online retailer Zulily, Inc. and its investments in mobile messaging app-maker Tango, also a U.S. firm. The following statement describes the rationale or logic driving Alibaba's acquisitions:

"We have made, and intend to continue to make, strategic investments and acquisitions to expand our user base, enhance our cloud computing business, add complementary products and technologies and further strengthen our ecosystem."

While some of Alibaba's strategic acquisitions will take place in China, a host of others will be cross-border transactions.

In other cases, altering a firm's competitive scope provides a strategic rationale for cross-border acquisitions. For example, based in Oxford, England, Circassia Pharmaceuticals PLC recently acquired Swedish-listed Aerocrine AB. Historically, Circassia competed with a laser-like focus on a single technology platform used to produce allergy vaccines. Aerocrine is an asthma-diagnostic company. Thus, the acquisition finds Circassia moving into the asthma market. According to Circassia's CEO, this transactions moves the firm closer to its goal of becoming "a self-sustaining specialty biopharmaceutical company focused on allergy and asthma."

Based in Spain, Banco Popular Español S.A. is pursuing acquisitions outside its home market. The bank's CEO noted that the rationale for this action is to prevent the firm from being too dependent on a single economy when that economy suffers from an economic downturn. In his words:

"In future crises, we would like the bank to be more diversified so we don't have the same level of dependence on a single economy that we have now. This will be a limited diversification, mainly in Latin America and done in a very gradual way over time without rushing."

Thus, it seems that the bank is committed to carefully examine each target before concluding that it should be acquired.

Zulily.PNG

Alibaba has taken an ownership position in U.S.-based Zulily (an e-commerce company) for the purpose of becoming a more global firm.

In mid-2015, Altice SA, a Luxembourg-based cable-and-telecom company controlled by French cable investor Patrick Drahi, was in advanced talks to buy U.S. firm Suddenlink in a transaction valued at between $8 and $10 billion. Already possessing communications companies from France to the Caribbean, many of which were acquired, adding Suddenlink to the fold would result in Altice being one of the world's largest cable and broadband market companies. An analyst captures Drahi's rationale for the string of cross-border acquisitions Altice has completed and intends to complete in the future in the following manner:

"Mr. Drahi has been betting that the future of the telecom industry lies in combining cable and broadband operators with mobile companies to offer clients higher-priced bundles combining television, broadband, fixed telephony, and mobile services."

The high degree of fragmentation in the global telecommunications market seems to yield opportunities for aggressive investors, such as Drahi, to gain value by consolidated firms on a global basis, using cross-border acquisitions in part to do so.

Thus, multiple reasons drive the decision to complete cross-border acquisitions. As we've noted, we can expect the most successful of these transactions, including the ones described here, to be based on a strong strategic rationale.

Sources: R. Bender, S. Ramachandran, & S. Raice, 2015, Altice in advanced talks to buy cable company Suddenlink, *Wall Street Journal Online*, www.wsj.com, May 19; J. Neumann, 2015, Spain's Banco Popular seeking acquisitions abroad, *Wall Street Journal Online*, www.wsj.com, May 18; D. Roland, 2015, U.K. biotech Circassia moves into asthma with two acquisitions, *Wall Street Journal Online*, www.wsj.com, May 15; C. Tejada, 2015, Alibaba to focus on expansion abroad, CEO says, *Wall Street Journal Online*, www.wsj.com, May 14; M. J. de la Merced, 2014, Alibaba's acquisition strategy focused: Focused largely on China and mobile, *New York Times*, www.nytimes.com, May 7.

Firms should recognize that cross-border acquisitions such as the ones discussed in the Strategic Focus are not risk free, even when a strong strategic rationale undergirds the completed transactions. China, for example, is a country with political and legal obstacles that increase acquisition risk.[30] Being able to conduct an effective due-diligence process when acquiring a company in China can be difficult where the target firm's financial data and corporate governance practices may lack complete transparency.[31] For instance, believing that the firm was going to be "its Chinese business card," Caterpillar, an earthmoving equipment company, acquired Chinese manufacturing company Siwei. After completing the purchase however, Caterpillar said it discovered "deliberate, multi-year, coordinated accounting misconduct at Siwei." Following complicated efforts to sort through everything, Caterpillar had to write down 86 percent of its $677 million purchase of Siwei.[32] Thus, firms must carefully study the risks as well as the potential benefits when contemplating cross-border acquisitions.

7-2c Cost of New Product Development and Increased Speed to Market

Developing new products internally and successfully introducing them into the marketplace often requires significant investment of a firm's resources, including time, making it difficult to quickly earn a profitable return.[33] Because an estimated 88 percent of innovations fail to achieve adequate returns, concerns exist in firms about their ability to achieve adequate returns from the capital they invest to develop and commercialize new products. Potentially contributing to these less-than-desirable rates of return is the successful imitation of approximately 60 percent of innovations within four years after the patents are obtained. These types of outcomes may lead managers to perceive internal product development as a high-risk activity.[34]

An acquisition strategy is another course of action a firm can take to gain access to new products and to current products that are new to it. Compared with internal product development processes, acquisitions provide more predictable returns as well as faster market entry. Returns are more predictable because the performance of the acquired firm's products can be assessed prior to completing the acquisition.[35]

WelchAllyn is a leading global manufacturer of medical diagnostic equipment. With a desire to provide diagnostic tools to doctors and nurses through which they can provide better healthcare to patients, WelchAllyn is completing a number of acquisitions to adapt to the rapidly changing health care environment. Rather than relying on internal innovation to produce all the new products it wants to sell, this firm has chosen to acquire solid companies through which it can quickly gain access to products that are related to its own and that target the same customers. Recently, for example, WelchAllyn acquired Scale-Tronix, a small firm that manufacturers "medical scales and patient weighing systems for hospitals, clinics, and extended-care facilities."[36] Scale-Tronix's specialization in a complete line of scales for use in the health care field allows WelchAllyn to immediately expand the scope of its product offerings to its customers.

7-2d　Lower Risk Compared to Developing New Products

The outcomes of an acquisition can be estimated more easily and accurately than the outcomes of an internal product development process; as such, managers may view acquisitions as less risky.[37] However, firms should be cautious when using acquisitions to reduce risk relative to the risk incurred when developing new products internally. Indeed, even though research suggests acquisition strategies are a common means of avoiding risky internal ventures (and therefore risky R&D investments), acquisitions may also become a substitute for internal innovation.

Over time, being dependent on others for innovation leaves a firm vulnerable and less capable of mastering its own destiny when it comes to using innovation as a driver of wealth creation. Thus, a clear strategic rationale, such as the ones influencing the cross-border acquisitions described in a Strategic Focus in this chapter, should drive each acquisition a firm chooses to complete. If a firm is being acquired to gain access to a specific innovation or to a target's innovation-related capabilities, the acquiring firm should be able to specify how the innovation is or the innovation-based skills are to be integrated with its operations for strategic purposes.

7-2e　Increased Diversification

Acquisitions are also used to diversify firms. Based on experience and the insights resulting from it, firms typically find it easier to develop and introduce new products in markets they are currently serving. In contrast, it is difficult for companies to develop products that differ from their current lines for markets in which they lack experience. Thus, it is relatively uncommon for a firm to develop new products internally to diversify its product lines.[38]

Acquisition strategies can be used to support the use of both related and unrelated diversification strategies. As we mentioned in Chapter 6, Campbell Soup uses a related constrained strategy. This global food company generates annual revenue in excess of $8 billion. In addition to the iconic soups, the firm's brands include Pepperidge Farm cookies, Arnott's Kjeldsens and Royal Dansk biscuits, and Pace Mexican sauce, among many others. Campbell recently restructured around product categories rather than geographies and brand groups. Americas Simple Meals and Beverages, Global Biscuits and Snacks, and Packaged Fresh are the three new business units. The firm's new structure is thought to be one that "will align the organization of the company's businesses with its core growth strategies."[39] One outcome from this reorganization is that Campbell feels it is better positioned to acquire "brands that are more popular and present greater growth opportunities."[40] Of course, given the firm's related constrained diversification strategy, brands that are acquired will share some similarities with those in one of the firm's newly-developed product categories.

Pictured here are some of the products from Campbell Soup Co.'s new business unit called Packaged Fresh.

Campbell Soup Company

In contrast to Campbell Soup, Samsung Group, a huge conglomerate, uses an unrelated diversification strategy to further diversify its operations. Headquartered in Suwon, South Korean, Samsung's portfolio recently included almost 70 companies competing in unrelated areas such as electronics, construction, life insurance, and fashion. It is South Korea's largest chaebol, or business conglomerate. Samsung Electronics, one of the firm's three core units, features three businesses that are well known to consumers throughout the world—mobile devices such as smartphones, consumer electronics (televisions and home appliances), and electronics components such as semiconductors and display panels. With roughly $56 billion in cash in mid-2015, Samsung intended to use some of this cash to complete what one observer called a "string of seemingly unrelated M&A deals." A printing-solutions company, a mobile payments start-up firm, and a battery-making affiliate are three recent acquisitions that appear to have the potential to increase the firm's level of diversification as it enters new competitive arenas.[41]

Firms using acquisition strategies should be aware that, in general, the more related the acquired firm is to the acquiring firm, the greater is the probability that the acquisition will be successful.[42] Thus, horizontal acquisitions and related acquisitions tend to contribute more to the firm's strategic competitiveness than do acquisitions of companies operating in product markets that differ from those in which the acquiring firm competes. Nonetheless, the unrelated diversification strategy, such as the one Samsung is implementing, can also lead to success when used in ways that enhance firm value.

7-2f Reshaping the Firm's Competitive Scope

As discussed in Chapter 2, the intensity of competitive rivalry is an industry characteristic that affects a firm's profitability.[43] To reduce the negative effect of an intense rivalry on financial performance, firms may use acquisitions to lessen their product and/or market dependencies. Reducing a company's dependence on specific products or markets shapes the firm's competitive scope. For example, Campbell Soup's intention to increase its position in organic foods in its new Packaged Fresh unit reduces its dependence on traditional and nongrowth areas such as soups. If Campbell continues to emphasize its Packaged Fresh units, perhaps through internal growth as well as acquisitions, the firm's competitive scope will change.

7-2g Learning and Developing New Capabilities

Firms sometimes complete acquisitions to gain access to capabilities they lack. Research shows that firms can broaden their knowledge base and reduce inertia through acquisitions[44] and that they increase the potential of their capabilities when they acquire diverse talent through cross-border acquisitions.[45] Of course, firms are better able to learn these acquired capabilities if they share some similar properties with the firm's current capabilities. Thus, firms should seek to acquire companies with different but related and complementary capabilities as a path to building their own knowledge base.

CenturyLink is a U.S.-based, multinational, communications corporation. The firm provides communications and data services to businesses, governmental agencies, and residential homes. With a focus on developing its capabilities to serve customers' needs for large-scale big data analytics, CenturyLink recently acquired Orchestrate, a firm that "offers a fully managed database service for rapid application development." The acquisition strengthened CenturyLink's cloud platform capabilities, primarily by integrating Orchestrate's experienced data services team with CenturyLink's own product development and technology organization.[46] By integrating their capabilities, the firms hope that they are enhancing their learning capabilities as a path to better serving customers dealing with big data analytics.

7-3 Problems in Achieving Acquisition Success

Effective and appropriate use of the acquisition strategies discussed in this chapter can facilitate firms' efforts to earn above-average returns. However, even when pursued for value-creating reasons, acquisition strategies are not problem-free. Reasons for the use of acquisition strategies and potential problems with such strategies are shown in Figure 7.1.

Figure 7.1 Reasons for Acquisitions and Problems in Achieving Success

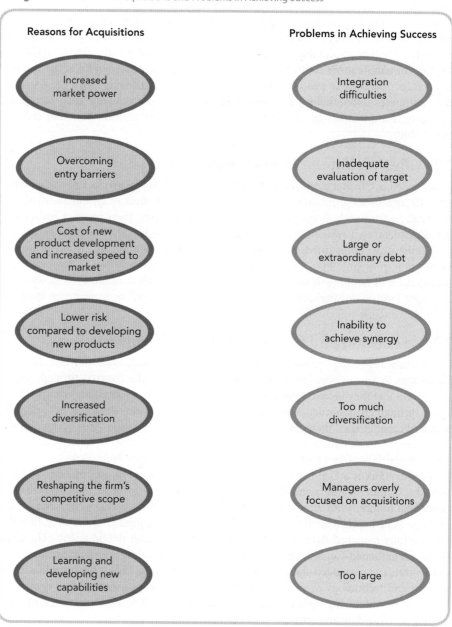

Table 7.1 Attributes of Successful Acquisitions

Attributes	Results
1. Acquired firm has assets or resources that are complementary to the acquiring firm's core business	1. High probability of synergy and competitive advantage by maintaining strengths
2. Acquisition is friendly	2. Faster and more effective integration and possibly lower premiums
3. Acquiring firm conducts effective due diligence to select target firms and evaluate the target firm's health (financial, cultural, and human resources)	3. Firms with strongest complementarities are acquired and overpayment is avoided
4. Acquiring firm has financial slack (cash or a favorable debt position)	4. Financing (debt or equity) is easier and less costly to obtain
5. Merged firm maintains low to moderate debt position	5. Lower financing cost, lower risk (e.g., of bankruptcy), and avoidance of trade-offs that are associated with high debt
6. Acquiring firm has a sustained and consistent emphasis on R&D and innovation	6. Maintain long-term competitive advantage in markets
7. Acquiring firm manages change well and is flexible and adaptable	7. Faster and more effective integration facilitates achievement of synergy

Research suggests that perhaps 20 percent of mergers and acquisitions are successful, approximately 60 percent produce disappointing results, and the remaining 20 percent are clear failures; and evidence suggests that technology acquisitions have even higher failure rates.[47] In general, though, companies appear to be increasing their ability to achieve success with acquisition strategies. Later, we discuss a number of attributes that are associated with successful acquisitions (the attributes appear in Table 7.1). In spite of this increasing success, firms using acquisition strategies should be aware of problems that tend to affect acquisition success when problems do surface. We show these problems in Figure 7.1 and discuss them next.

7-3a Integration Difficulties

The importance of a successful integration should not be underestimated.[48] Indeed, some believe that the integration process is the strongest determinant of whether either a merger or an acquisition will be successful. This belief highlights the fact that post-acquisition integration is often a complex set of organizational processes that is difficult and challenging. The processes tend to generate uncertainty and often resistance because of cultural clashes and organizational politics.[49] How people are treated during the integration process relative to perceptions of fairness is an important issue to consider when trying to integrate the acquiring and acquired firms. Among the challenges associated with integration processes are the need to:

- meld two or more unique corporate cultures
- link different financial and control systems
- build effective working relationships (particularly when management styles differ)
- determine the leadership structure and those who will fill it for the integrated firm.[50]

These types of challenges, and others as well, may affect Nokia's proposed acquisition of Alcatel-Lucent.

In mid-2015, Finnish telecommunications company Nokia was in advanced talks to acquire its French Rival Alcatel-Lucent. If completed, the transaction would create the second largest mobile equipment manufacturer in the world. Benefits sought through this acquisition included those of giving Nokia a stronger position in the United States, creating synergy through cost reductions achieved by eliminating duplicative processes and operations, and increasing the newly-formed firm's pricing power, partly as a result of its size. The reaction to the proposed transaction was generally positive, with one analyst suggesting that being left to fend for themselves as independent firms and "as subscale players in a fiercely competitive market (was), arguably, a worse alternative" compared to completing the acquisition.[51]

In spite of the overall positive reaction to the proposed transaction, concerns were simultaneously raised about how effectively Nokia and Alcatel-Lucent would be able to complete the integration process. Highlighting this matter, one analyst said that the implementation of the acquisition would be much "messier" than would structuring the deal's finances. Among the issues associated with integration were those related to the fact that telecommunications' firms are "notoriously difficult to integrate" and the need to carefully involve customers with the combined firm's efforts to integrate the two firms' different operating platforms. Given that both firms had been independently trying to restructure prior to the announced acquisition, others wondered if the anticipated cost savings were overly optimistic.[52] Thus, those involved with integrating Nokia and Alcatel-Lucent seem to be facing integration-related challenges.

7-3b   Inadequate Evaluation of Target

Due diligence is a process through which a potential acquirer evaluates a target firm for acquisition. In an effective due-diligence process, hundreds of items are examined in areas as diverse as the financing for the intended transaction, differences in cultures between the acquiring and target firm, tax consequences of the transaction, and actions that would be necessary to successfully meld the two workforces. Due diligence is commonly performed by investment bankers such as Deutsche Bank, Goldman Sachs, and Morgan Stanley, as well as accountants, lawyers, and management consultants specializing in that activity, although firms actively pursuing acquisitions may form their own internal due-diligence team. Even in instances when a company does its own due diligence, companies almost always work with intermediaries such as large investment banks to facilitate their due-diligence efforts. Interestingly, research suggests that acquisition performance increases with the number of due-diligence–related transactions facilitated by an investment bank, but decreases when the relationship with a particular investment bank becomes exclusive.[53] Thus, using investment banks as part of the due-diligence process a firm completes to examine a proposed merger or acquisition is a complex matter requiring careful managerial attention.

As noted earlier in the chapter, the due diligence Caterpillar performed prior to acquiring Chinese firm Siwei was inadequate and ineffective. Although due diligence often focuses on evaluating the accuracy of the financial position and accounting standards used (a financial audit), due diligence also needs to examine the quality of the strategic fit and the ability of the acquiring firm to effectively integrate the target to realize the potential gains from the deal.[54] A comprehensive due-diligence process reduces the likelihood an acquiring firm will have the experience Caterpillar did as a result of acquiring Siwei.

Early evidence suggests that French IT services company Cap Gemini S.A. completed an effective due-diligence process prior to deciding to spend $4.04 billion to acquire U.S.-based iGate Corporation. At the time, this was the 10th largest acquisition of a U.S.-based technology firm by a European company. Noting that the deal made sense for both parties largely because of complementarities in their businesses and the positive nature of the transaction from a financial perspective, analysts felt that there was a strong fit between the firms and that the acquisition had a strong strategic rationale for Cap Gemini.

In this respect, one observer said that "the added huge bonus for Cap Gemini is that it gives them, in one move, a great presence and foothold in the U.S. market, which has always been a challenge for them as a Europe-centric provider. This boosts their presence and revenue in the largest market for global sourcing and gives them a credible offering for the U.S. market."[55] Even with these positives, the firms will have to work diligently to avoid problems during the integration process.

Commonly, firms are willing to pay a premium to acquire a company they believe will increase their ability to earn above-average returns. Determining the precise premium that is appropriate to pay is challenging. While the acquirer can estimate the value of anticipated synergies, it is just that—an estimate. Only after working to integrate the firms and then engaging in competitive actions in the marketplace will the absolute value of synergies be known.

When firms overestimate the value of synergies or the value of future growth potential associated with an acquisition, the premium they pay may prove to be too large. Excessive premiums can have dilutive effects on the newly formed firm's short- and long-term earning potential. In November 2011, for example, Gilead Sciences paid an 89 percent premium to acquire Pharmasset.[56] At first glance, this premium seems excessive. However, since the acquisition was completed, Gilead's stock price has soared. Moreover, the firm's hepatitis C drug franchise, to which Gilead obtain access by acquiring Pharmasset, reached sales of $12.4 billion in 2014 and was seen as a huge success. In this instance then, it seems that the premium Gilead paid to acquire Pharmasset was not excessive. The managerial challenge is to effectively examine each acquisition target for the purpose of determining the amount of premium that is appropriate for the acquiring firm to pay.

7-3c Large or Extraordinary Debt

To finance a number of acquisitions completed during the 1980s and 1990s, some companies significantly increased their debt levels. Although firms today are more prudent about the amount of debt they'll accept to complete an acquisition, those evaluating the possibility of an acquisition for their company need to be aware of the problem that taking on too much debt can create. In this sense, firms using an acquisition strategy want to verify that their purchases do not create a debt load that overpowers their ability to remain solvent and vibrant as a competitor.

A financial innovation called junk bonds supported firms' earlier efforts to take on large amounts of debt when completing acquisitions. *Junk bonds*, which are used less frequently today and are now more commonly called high-yield bonds, are a financing option through which risky acquisitions are financed with money (debt) that provides a large potential return to lenders (bondholders). Because junk bonds are unsecured obligations that are not tied to specific assets for collateral, interest rates for these high-risk debt instruments sometimes reached between 18 and 20 percent during the 1980s.[57] Additionally, interest rates for these types of bonds tend to be quite volatile, a condition that potentially exposes companies to greater financial risk.[58] Some prominent financial economists viewed debt as a means to discipline managers, causing the managers to act in the shareholders' best interests.[59] Managers adopting this perspective are less concerned about the amount of debt their firm assumes when acquiring other companies. However, the perspective that debt disciplines managers is not as widely supported today as was the case in the past.[60]

Bidding wars, through which an acquiring firm overcommits to the decision to acquire a target, can result in large or extraordinary debt. While finance theory suggests that managers will make rational decisions when seeking to complete an acquisition, other research suggests that rationality may not always drive the acquisition decision. Hubris, escalation of commitment to complete a particular transaction, and self-interest sometimes influence executives to pay a large premium which, in turn, may result in taking on too much debt to acquire a target. Executives need to be aware of these possibilities and challenge themselves to engage in rational decision making only when dealing with an acquisition strategy.

7-3d Inability to Achieve Synergy

Derived from *synergos*, a Greek word that means "working together," *synergy* exists when the value created by units working together exceeds the value that those units could create working independently (see Chapter 6). That is, synergy exists when assets are worth more when used in conjunction with each other than when they are used separately. For shareholders, synergy generates gains in their wealth that they could not duplicate or exceed through their own portfolio diversification decisions.[61] Synergy is created by the efficiencies derived from economies of scale and economies of scope and by sharing resources (e.g., human capital and knowledge) across the businesses in the newly created firm's portfolio.[62]

A firm develops a competitive advantage through an acquisition strategy only when a transaction generates private synergy. *Private synergy* is created when combining and integrating the acquiring and acquired firms' assets yield capabilities and core competencies that could not be developed by combining and integrating either firm's assets with another company. Private synergy is possible when firms' assets are complementary in unique ways; that is, the unique type of asset complementarity is not always possible simply by combining two companies' sets of assets with each other.[63] Although difficult to create, the attractiveness of private synergy is that because of its uniqueness, it is difficult for competitors to understand and imitate, meaning that a competitive advantage results for the firms able to create it.

It is possible that Southwest Airlines' acquisition of AirTran has created private synergy. Among other outcomes, this acquisition added 21 cities to Southwest's network; 7 of these are international locations. Previous to the acquisition, Southwest serviced only U.S. cities. In commenting about the results of this transaction, an observer said that "Southwest has done a commendable job integrating AirTran. Southwest smoothly absorbed AirTran's Atlanta operations, making them similar to the rest of its focus cities, rather than remaining a hub."[64] Very importantly, as a firm using the cost leadership strategy, Southwest's integrated cost structure still allows it to have lower costs than its rivals, including JetBlue. The lowest cost position is the firm's competitive advantage. Early financial results are also impressive in that, following the acquisition, Southwest's profit grew from $178 million in 2011 to $421 million in 2012, $754 million in 2013, and $946 million in 2014. Thus, the evidence suggests that the acquiring firm, Southwest, and the acquired firm, AirTran, were able to create private synergy by combing the two firms.

A firm's ability to account for costs that are necessary to create anticipated revenue and cost-based synergies affects its efforts to create private synergy. Firms experience several expenses when seeking to create private synergy through acquisitions. Called transaction costs, these expenses are incurred when firms use acquisition strategies to create synergy.[65] Transaction costs may be direct or indirect. Direct costs include legal fees and charges from investment bankers who complete due diligence for the acquiring firm. Indirect costs include managerial time to evaluate target firms and then to complete negotiations, as well as the loss of key managers and employees following an acquisition.[66] After acquiring Canadian-based Wheels Group Inc., Radiant Logistics' earnings were affected by short-term, nonrecurring transaction costs associated with the acquisition. As a mid-size freight forwarder based in the United States, Radiant acquired Wheels in order to extend its "geographic reach and customer bases by consolidating operators in a fragmented market."[67] Company officials expected the newly formed firm to quickly return to profitability following payment of the nonrecurring acquisition costs. Firms tend to underestimate the sum of indirect costs when specifying the value of the synergy that may be created by integrating the acquired firm's assets with the acquiring firm's assets.

7-3e Too Much Diversification

As explained in Chapter 6, diversification strategies, when used effectively, can help a firm earn above-average returns. In general, firms using related diversification strategies outperform those employing unrelated diversification strategies. However, conglomerates formed by using an unrelated diversification strategy also can be successful.

At some point, however, firms can become overdiversified. The level at which this happens varies across companies because each firm has different capabilities to manage diversification. Recall from Chapter 6 that related diversification requires more information processing than does unrelated diversification. Because of this need to process additional amounts of information, related diversified firms become overdiversified with a smaller number of business units than do firms using an unrelated diversification strategy.[68] Regardless of the type of diversification strategy implemented, however, the firm that becomes overdiversified will experience a decline in its performance and likely a decision to divest some of its units.[69] Commonly, such divestments, which tend to reshape a firm's competitive scope, are part of a firm's restructuring strategy. (Restructuring is discussed in greater detail later in the chapter.)

Even when a firm is not overdiversified, a high level of diversification can have a negative effect on its long-term performance. For example, the scope created by additional amounts of diversification often causes managers to rely on financial rather than strategic controls to evaluate business units' performance (financial and strategic controls are discussed in Chapters 11 and 12). Top-level executives often rely on financial controls to assess the performance of business units when they do not have a rich understanding of business units' objectives and strategies. Using financial controls, such as return on investment (ROI), causes individual business-unit managers to focus on short-term outcomes at the expense of long-term investments. Reducing long-term investments to generate short-term profits can negatively affect a firm's overall performance ability.[70]

Another problem resulting from overdiversification is the tendency for acquisitions to become substitutes for innovation. Typically, managers have no interest in acquisitions substituting for internal R&D efforts; however, a reinforcing cycle evolves. Costs associated with acquisitions may result in fewer allocations to activities, such as R&D, that are linked to innovation. Without adequate support, a firm's innovation skills begin to atrophy. Without internal innovation skills, a key option available to a firm to gain access to innovation is to complete additional acquisitions. Evidence suggests that a firm using acquisitions as a substitute for internal innovations eventually encounters performance problems.[71]

7-3f Managers Overly Focused on Acquisitions

Typically, a considerable amount of managerial time and energy is required for acquisition strategies to be used successfully. Activities with which managers become involved include:

- searching for viable acquisition candidates
- completing effective due-diligence processes
- preparing for negotiations
- managing the integration process after completing the acquisition

Top-level managers do not personally gather all of the information and data required to make acquisitions. However, these executives do make critical decisions regarding the firms to be targeted, the nature of the negotiations, and so forth. Company experiences show that participating in and overseeing the activities required for making acquisitions can divert managerial attention from other matters that are necessary for long-term competitive success, such as identifying and taking advantage of other opportunities and interacting with important external stakeholders.[72]

Both theory and research suggest that managers can become overly involved in the process of making acquisitions.[73] One observer suggested, "some executives can become preoccupied with making deals—and the thrill of selecting, chasing, and seizing a target."[74] The over-involvement can be surmounted by learning from mistakes and by not having too much agreement in the boardroom. Dissent is helpful to make sure that all sides of a question are considered. For example, research suggests that there may be group bias in the decision making of boards of directors regarding acquisitions. The research suggests that possible group polarization leads to either higher premiums paid or lower premiums paid after group discussions about potential premiums for target firms.[75] When failure does occur, leaders may be tempted to blame the failure on others and on unforeseen circumstances rather than on their excessive involvement in the acquisition process. Finding the appropriate degree of involvement with the firm's acquisition strategy is a challenging, yet important, task for top-level managers.

7-3g Too Large

Most acquisitions result in a larger firm, which should create or enhance economies of scale. In turn, scale economies can lead to more efficient operations—for example, two sales organizations can be integrated using fewer sales representatives because the combined sales force can sell the products of both firms (particularly if the products of the acquiring and target firms are highly related).[76] However, size can also increase the complexity of the managerial challenge and create diseconomies of scope; that is, not enough economic benefit to outweigh the costs of managing the more complex organization created through acquisitions.

Thus, while many firms seek increases in size because of the potential economies of scale and enhanced market power size creates, at some level, the additional costs required to manage the larger firm will exceed the benefits of the economies of scale and additional market power. The complexities generated by the larger size often lead managers to implement more bureaucratic controls to manage the combined firm's operations. *Bureaucratic controls* are formalized supervisory and behavioral rules and policies designed to ensure consistency of decisions and actions across a firm's units. However, across time, formalized controls often lead to relatively rigid and standardized managerial behavior.[77] Certainly, in the long run, the diminished flexibility that accompanies rigid and standardized managerial behavior may produce less innovation. Because of innovation's importance to competitive success, the bureaucratic controls resulting from a large organization that might be built at least in part by using an acquisition strategy can negatively affect a firm's performance. Thus, managers may decide their firm should complete acquisitions in the pursuit of increased size as a path to profitable growth. At the same time, managers should avoid allowing their firm to get to a point where acquisitions are creating a degree of size that increases its inefficiency and ineffectiveness.

7-4 Effective Acquisitions

As we've noted, acquisition strategies do not always lead to above-average returns for the acquiring firm's shareholders.[78] Nonetheless, some companies are able to create value when using an acquisition strategy.[79] Research evidence suggests that the probability of being able to create value through acquisitions increases when the nature of the acquisition and the processes used to complete it are consistent with the "attributes of successful acquisitions" shown in Table 7.1.[80] For example, when the target firm's assets are complementary to the acquired firm's assets, an acquisition is more successful. With complementary assets, the integration of two firms' operations has a higher probability of creating synergy. In fact, integrating two firms with complementary assets frequently produces unique capabilities and core competencies. With complementary assets, the acquiring firm can maintain its focus on core businesses and leverage the complementary assets and capabilities from the acquired firm. In effective acquisitions, targets are often selected and "groomed" by establishing a working relationship prior to the acquisition.[81] As discussed in Chapter 9, firms sometimes form strategic alliances to test the feasibility of a future merger or acquisition between them, an experience that can also contribute to acquisition success.

Research evidence also shows that friendly acquisitions facilitate integration of the acquiring and acquired firms. Of course, a target firm's positive reaction to a bid from the acquiring firm increases the likelihood that a friendly transaction will take place. For example, AdvancedCath responded positively to being acquired by TE Connectivity, a world leader in designing and managing highly-engineered connectors, sensors, and electronic components that are sold to manufacturers who integrate them into their products. AdvancedCath is a leading source of catheter systems, products that complement those included in TE's Medical business unit. Commenting about the value the acquisition creates for his firm, AdvancedCath's CEO said that "with TE's global footprint, we can provide better support to our global customers as they progress through development, clinical trials, and volume manufacturing."[82] After completing a friendly acquisition, firms collaborate to create synergy while integration their operations.[83] This is in contrast to hostile takeovers, situations in which common disagreements, such as those concerned with the combined firm's leadership structure and operational methods that will be used in the newly created firm, strongly increase the difficulty associated with attempts to create synergy through the integration process.

Additionally, effective due-diligence processes involving the deliberate and careful selection of target firms and an evaluation of the relative health of those firms (financial health, cultural fit, and the value of human resources) contribute to successful acquisitions.[84] Financial slack in the form of debt equity or cash, in both the acquiring and acquired firms, also frequently contributes to acquisition success. Even though financial slack provides access to financing for the acquisition, it is still important to maintain a low or moderate level of debt after the acquisition to keep debt costs low. When substantial debt is used to finance acquisitions, companies with successful acquisitions reduce the debt quickly, partly by selling off assets from the acquired firm, especially noncomplementary or poorly performing assets. For these firms, debt costs do not preclude long-term investments in areas such as R&D, and managerial discretion in the use of cash flow is relatively flexible.

Another attribute of successful acquisition strategies is an emphasis on innovation, as demonstrated by continuing investments in R&D activities.[85] Innovation is critical to the anticipated success of Nokia's proposed acquisition of Alcatel-Lucent. According to Nokia officials, "the combined company will have unparalleled innovation capabilities, with Alcatel-Lucent's Bell Labs and Nokia's FutureWorks as well as Nokia Technologies." The initial combination of the two firms would create a R&D staff in excess of 40,000 with an allocation of EUR 4.7 billion in R&D in the first year.[86] Thus, this acquisition appears to satisfy the criterion of emphasizing innovation in a newly created firm.

Flexibility and adaptability are the final two attributes of successful acquisitions. When executives of both the acquiring and the target firms have experience in managing change and learning from acquisitions, they are more skilled at adapting their capabilities to new environments.[87] As a result, they are more adept at integrating the two organizations, which is particularly important when firms have different organizational cultures.

As we have explained, firms using an acquisition strategy seek to create wealth and earn above-average returns. Sometimes, though, the results of an acquisition strategy fall short of expectations. When this happens, firms consider using restructuring strategies.

7-5 Restructuring

Restructuring is a strategy through which a firm changes its set of businesses or its financial structure.[88] Restructuring is a global phenomenon.[89] Historically, divesting businesses from company portfolios and downsizing have accounted for a large percentage of firms' restructuring strategies. Commonly, firms focus on fewer products and markets following restructuring.

Although restructuring strategies are generally used to deal with acquisitions that are not reaching expectations, firms sometimes use restructuring strategies because of changes they have detected in their external environment. For example, opportunities sometimes surface in a firm's external environment that a diversified firm can pursue because of the capabilities it has formed by integrating firms' operations. In such cases, restructuring may be appropriate to position the firm to create more value for stakeholders, given environmental changes and the opportunities associated with them.[90]

As discussed next, firms use three types of restructuring strategies: downsizing, downscoping, and leveraged buyouts.

7-5a Downsizing

Downsizing is a reduction in the number of a firm's employees and, sometimes, in the number of its operating units; but, the composition of businesses in the company's portfolio may not change through downsizing. Thus, downsizing is an intentional managerial strategy that is used for the purpose of improving firm performance. In contrast, organizational decline, which too often results in a reduction of a firm's resources including the number of its employees and potentially in the number of its units, is an unintentional outcome of what turned out to be a firm's ineffective competitive actions.[91] When downsizing, firms make intentional decisions about resources to retain and resources to eliminate. Organizational decline however, finds firms losing access to an array of resources, many of which are critical to current and future performance. Thus, downsizing is a legitimate strategy and is not necessarily a sign of organizational decline.[92]

Downsizing can be an appropriate strategy to use after completing an acquisition, particularly when there are significant operational and/or strategic relationships between the acquiring and the acquired firm. In these instances, the newly formed firm may have excess capacity in functional areas such as sales, manufacturing, distribution, human resource management, and so forth. In turn, excess capacity may prevent the combined firm from realizing anticipated synergies and the reduced costs associated with them.[93] Managers should remember that, as a strategy, downsizing will be far more effective when they consistently use human resource practices that ensure procedural justice and fairness in downsizing decisions.[94]

7-5b Downscoping

Downscoping refers to divestiture, spin-off, or some other means of eliminating businesses that are unrelated to a firm's core businesses. Downscoping has a more positive effect on firm performance than does downsizing[95] because firms commonly find that

Restructuring is a strategy through which a firm changes its set of businesses or its financial structure.

downscoping causes them to refocus on their core business.[96] Managerial effectiveness increases because the firm has become less diversified, allowing the top management team to better understand and manage the remaining businesses.[97]

Firms often use the downscoping and downsizing strategies simultaneously. When doing this, firms need to avoid layoffs of key employees, as such layoffs might lead to a loss of one or more core competencies. Instead, a firm that chooses to simultaneously engage in downscoping and downsizing should intentionally become smaller as a result of decisions made to reduce the diversity of businesses in its portfolio, allowing it to focus on its core areas as a result.[98]

In general, U.S. firms use downscoping as a restructuring strategy more frequently than do European companies—in fact, the trend not too long ago in Europe, Latin America, and Asia was to build conglomerates. In Latin America, these conglomerates are called *grupos*. More recently though, many Asian and Latin American conglomerates have chosen to downscope their operations as a path to refocusing on their core businesses. This recent downscoping trend has occurred simultaneously with increasing globalization and with more open markets that have greatly enhanced competition.[99]

7-5c Leveraged Buyouts

A *leveraged buyout* (LBO) is a restructuring strategy whereby a party (typically a private equity firm) buys all of a firm's assets in order to take the firm private.[100] Once a private equity firm completes this type of transaction, the target firm's company stock is no longer traded publicly.

Traditionally, leveraged buyouts were used as a restructuring strategy to correct for managerial mistakes or because the firm's managers were making decisions that primarily served their own interests rather than those of shareholders.[101] However, some firms complete leveraged buyouts for the purpose of building firm resources and expanding their operations rather than simply to restructure a distressed firm's assets.

Significant amounts of debt are commonly incurred to finance a buyout; hence, the term *leveraged* buyout. To support debt payments and to downscope the company to concentrate on the firm's core businesses, the new owners may quickly sell a number of assets. Indeed, it is not uncommon for those buying a firm through an LBO to restructure the firm to the point that it can be sold at a profit within a five- to eight-year period.

Management buyouts (MBOs), employee buyouts (EBOs), and whole-firm buyouts, in which one company or partnership purchases an entire company instead of a part of it, are the three types of LBOs. In part because of managerial incentives, MBOs, more so than EBOs and whole-firm buyouts, have been found to lead to downscoping, increased strategic focus, and improved performance.[102] Research shows that management buyouts can lead to greater entrepreneurial activity and growth.[103] As such, buyouts can represent a form of firm rebirth to facilitate entrepreneurial efforts and stimulate strategic growth and productivity.[104]

7-5d Restructuring Outcomes

The short- and long-term outcomes that result from use of the three restructuring strategies are shown in Figure 7.2. As indicated, downsizing typically does not lead to higher firm performance.[105] In fact, some research results show that downsizing contributes to lower returns for both U.S. and Japanese firms. The stock markets in the firms' respective nations evaluate downsizing negatively, believing that it has long-term negative effects on the firms' efforts to achieve strategic competitiveness. Investors also seem to conclude that downsizing occurs as a consequence of other problems in a company.[106] This assumption may be caused by a firm's diminished corporate reputation when a major downsizing is announced.[107]

Figure 7.2 Restructuring and Outcomes

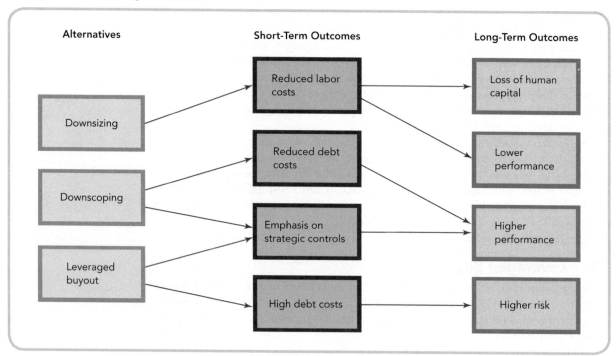

The loss of human capital is another potential problem of downsizing (see Figure 7.2). Losing employees with many years of experience with the firm represents a major loss of knowledge. As noted in Chapter 3, knowledge is vital to competitive success in the global economy. Research also suggests that a loss of valuable human capital can also spill over into dissatisfaction of customers.[108] Thus, in general, downsizing may be of more tactical (or short-term) value than strategic (or long-term) value, meaning that firms should exercise caution when restructuring through downsizing.

Compared to downsizing and leveraged buyouts, downscoping generally leads to more positive outcomes in both the short and long term. Downscoping's desirable long-term outcome of higher performance is a product of reduced debt costs and the emphasis on strategic controls derived from concentrating on the firm's core businesses. In so doing, the refocused firm should be able to increase its ability to compete.[109]

Whole-firm LBOs have been hailed as a significant innovation in the financial restructuring of firms. However, this type of restructuring can be complicated, especially when cross-border transactions are involved[110]; moreover, they can involve negative trade-offs.[111] First, the resulting large debt increases the firm's financial risk, as is evidenced by the number of companies that filed for bankruptcy in the 1990s after executing a whole-firm LBO. Sometimes, the intent of the owners to increase the efficiency of the acquired firm and then sell it within five to eight years creates a short-term and risk-averse managerial focus.[112] As a result, these firms may fail to invest adequately in R&D or take other major actions designed to maintain or improve the company's ability to compete successfully against rivals.[113] Because buyouts more often result in significant debt, most LBOs have been completed in mature industries where stable cash flows are the norm. Stable cash flows support the purchaser's efforts to service the debt obligations assumed as a result of taking a firm private.

SUMMARY

- Mergers and acquisitions as a strategy are popular for companies based in countries throughout the world. Through this strategy, firms seek to create value and outperform rivals. Globalization and deregulation of multiple industries in many of the world's economies are two of the reasons for this popularity among both large and small firms.

- Firms use acquisition strategies to

  - increase market power

  - overcome entry barriers to new markets or regions

  - avoid the costs of developing new products and increase the speed of new market entries

  - reduce the risk of entering a new business

  - become more diversified

  - reshape their competitive scope by developing a different portfolio of businesses

  - enhance their learning as the foundation for developing new capabilities

- Among the problems associated with using an acquisition strategy are

  - the difficulty of effectively integrating the firms involved

  - incorrectly evaluating the target firm's value

  - creating debt loads that preclude adequate long-term investments (e.g., R&D)

  - overestimating the potential for synergy

  - creating a firm that is too diversified

  - creating an internal environment in which managers devote increasing amounts of their time and energy to analyzing and completing the acquisition

  - developing a combined firm that is too large, necessitating extensive use of bureaucratic, rather than strategic, controls

- Effective acquisitions have the following characteristics:

  - the acquiring and target firms have complementary resources that are the foundation for developing new capabilities

  - the acquisition is friendly, thereby facilitating integration of the firms' resources

  - the target firm is selected and purchased on the basis of completing a thorough due-diligence process

  - the acquiring and target firms have considerable slack in the form of cash or debt capacity

  - the newly formed firm maintains a low or moderate level of debt by selling off portions of the acquired firm or some of the acquiring firm's poorly performing units

  - the acquiring and acquired firms have experience in terms of adapting to change

  - R&D and innovation are emphasized in the new firm

- Restructuring is used to improve a firm's performance by correcting for problems created by ineffective management. Restructuring by downsizing involves reducing the number of employees and hierarchical levels in the firm. Although it can lead to short-term cost reductions, the reductions may be realized at the expense of long-term success because of the loss of valuable human resources (and knowledge) and overall corporate reputation.

- The goal of restructuring through downscoping is to reduce the firm's level of diversification. Often, the firm divests unrelated businesses to achieve this goal. Eliminating unrelated businesses makes it easier for the firm and its top-level managers to refocus on the core businesses.

- Through a leveraged buyout (an LBO), a firm is purchased so that it can become a private entity. LBOs usually are financed largely through debt, although limited partners (institutional investors) are becoming more prominent. General partners have a variety of strategies, and some emphasize equity versus debt when limited partners have a longer time horizon. Management buyouts (MBOs), employee buyouts (EBOs), and whole-firm LBOs are the three types of LBOs. Because they provide clear managerial incentives, MBOs have been the most successful of the three. Often, the intent of a buyout is to improve efficiency and performance to the point where the firm can be sold successfully within five to eight years.

- Commonly, restructuring's primary goal is gaining or reestablishing effective strategic control of the firm. Of the three restructuring strategies, downscoping is aligned most closely with establishing and using strategic controls and usually improves performance more on a comparative basis.

KEY TERMS

acquisition 208
merger 207

restructuring 224
takeover 208

REVIEW QUESTIONS

1. Why are merger and acquisition strategies popular in many firms competing in the global economy?

2. What reasons account for firms' decisions to use acquisition strategies as a means to achieving strategic competitiveness?

3. What are the seven primary problems that affect a firm's efforts to successfully use an acquisition strategy?

4. What are the attributes associated with a successful acquisition strategy?

5. What is the restructuring strategy, and what are its common forms?

6. What are the short- and long-term outcomes associated with the different restructuring strategies?

Mini-Case

Strategic Acquisitions and Accelerated Integration of Those Acquisitions are a Vital Capability of Cisco Systems

Cisco Systems is in the business of building the infrastructure that allows the Internet to work. As the Internet evolved, however, Cisco's business was required to change with this evolution. As part of its advancement, Cisco Systems has used an acquisition strategy to build network products and extend its reach into new areas, both related and unrelated. In the beginning, digital connectivity was important through e-mail and Web browsing and searches. This evolved into a network economy facilitating e-commerce, digital supply chains, and digital collaboration. Subsequently, the digital interaction phase moved Cisco into developing infrastructure for social media, mobile and cloud computing, and digital video. The next stage seems to be "the Internet of everything" connecting people, processes, and data. This will require the basic core in routing, switching, and services, as well as large data centers to facilitate visualization through cloud computing. Video and collaboration as well as basic architecture of the business will be transforming to become the base strategic business blocks. Furthermore, the need to have strong digital security will be paramount.

Cisco has entered many aspects of the business in which it competes through acquisitions. For instance, in 2012, Cisco acquired TV software developer NDS for $5 billion. NDS Group develops software for television networks. In particular, its solutions allow pay-TV providers to deliver digital content to TVs, DVRs, PCs, and other multimedia devices. It provides solutions that protect digital content so that only paid subscribers can access it. Because of Cisco's customer-driven focus, it has sought to help its customers capture these market transitions and meet their particular needs. Of course, Cisco also builds the routers that allow video data and e-mail communications to come together through their blade servers (individual and modular servers that cut down on cabling). These routers and servers support cloud computing for the mobile devices that deliver the video that NDS software enables on desktop and mobile devices.

Also in 2012, Cisco purchased Meraki for $1.2 billion. Meraki provides solutions that optimize services in the cloud. For instance, it offers mid-sized customers Wi-Fi, switching, security, and mobile device management centrally from a set of cloud servers. For instance, if you are a guest at a university or other company campus it supports, you can bring your own personal device into the network, which allows guest networking and facilitates application controls. It manages the firewall and other advanced networking services to protect security as well.

John Chambers, Cisco CEO, has helped the firm move through the many transitions noted earlier. In the IT sector, 90 percent of acquisitions fail. However, as Chambers notes, "although Cisco does better than anyone else, we know that a third of our acquisitions won't work." Chambers worked for companies that did not successfully make transitions. Wang Laboratories missed a transition, and after experiencing this as an executive, Chambers learned to have a "healthy paranoia." He adds, "more than anything, I've tried to make Cisco a company that can see big transitions and move." One way they do this is to "listen to the customers very closely" to understand the necessary changes.

As Cisco makes the transition into the all-everything network, not only must it manage the cloud, but it also must provide service to the mobile devices that work in cellular networks. Accordingly, Cisco also acquired Intucell, a self-optimizing network software developer, for $475 million. It likewise acquired Truviso, Inc., a provider of network data analysis and reporting software, for an undisclosed price (Truviso was partly owned by venture capital firms and was headquartered in Israel). Most recently, Cisco acquired Ubiquisys, which cuts cellular carriers' costs "by shifting traffic from congested towers to more targeted locations inside an office, home or public space, which also boosts the service's reliability." This shifting-traffic approach is especially efficient when seeking to improve "coverage in crowded areas such as stadiums, convention centers and subway stations." These acquisitions help cellular network customers manage their products in the network more efficiently in the delivery of data, e-mail, and video services. As you can see, for this series of acquisitions, Cisco has used acquisitions strategically to move into new areas as its environment changes, to learn about new technologies, and to gain knowledge on new technologies as it experiences these transitions.

In the process of this rapid change, Cisco has developed a distinct ability to integrate acquisitions. When Cisco contemplates an acquisition, along with financial due diligence to make sure that it is paying the right price, it develops a detailed plan for possible post-merger integration. It begins communicating early with stakeholders about integration plans and conducts rigorous post-mortems to identify ways "to make subsequent integrations more efficient and effective." Once a deal is completed, this allows the company to hit the ground running when the deal becomes public. Cisco is ready "from Day 1 to explain how the two companies are going to come together and provide unique value and how the integration effort itself will be structured to realize value." The firm does not "want the [acquired] organization to go in limbo," which can happen if the integration process is not well thought out. Also, during the integration process, it is important to know how far the integration should go. Sometimes integration is too deep, and value that was being sought in the acquisition is destroyed. Sometimes it may even pay to keep the business separate from Cisco's other operations to allow the business to function without integration until the necessary learning is complete. "Cisco learned the hard way that complex deals require you to know at a high level of detail how you're going to drive value."

Sources: L. Capron, 2013, Cisco's corporate development portfolio: A blend of building, borrowing, and buying, *Strategy & Leadership*, 41(2): 27–30; D. FitzGerald & S. Chaudhuri, 2013, Corporate news: Cisco doubles down on small-cell transmitters with Ubiquisys, *Wall Street Journal*, April 4, B7; T. Geron, 2012, Meraki-Cisco deal a boost for Sequoia, Google-connected VCs, *Forbes*, November 19, 18; R. Karlgaard, 2012, Cisco's Chambers: Driving change, *Forbes*, February 22, 68; A. Moscaritolo, 2012, Cisco to acquire TV software developer NDS for $5 billion, *PC Magazine*, March 1; B. Worthern, D. Cimilluca, & A. Das, 2012, Cisco hedges bet on video delivery, *Wall Street Journal*, March 16, B1; R. Myers, 2011, Integration acceleration, *CFO*, 27: 52–57.

Case Discussion Questions

1. Of the "Reasons for Acquisitions" section in the chapter, which reasons are the primary drivers of Cisco's acquisition strategy?

2. Of the acquisitions Cisco has completed, which ones are horizontal acquisitions and which ones are vertical acquisitions? Which of these acquisitions do you believe have the strongest likelihood of being successful and why?

3. Explain John Chambers' views about acquisitions. How have his views affected the nature of Cisco's acquisition strategy?

4. Describe the core plan Cisco has in place to guide the integration of an acquired firm into its operations. What are the strengths of this plan, and what are its potential weaknesses?

NOTES

1. M. Menz, S. Kunisch, & D. J. Collis, 2015, The corporate headquarters in the contemporary corporation: Advancing a multimarket firm perspective, *Academy of Management Annals*, 9: 633–714; M. Gruber, I. C. MacMillan, & J. D. Thompson, 2012, From minds to markets: How human capital endowments shape market opportunity identification of technology start-ups, *Journal of Management*, 38: 1421–1449; D. J. Teece, 2010, Alfred Chandler and "capabilities" theories of strategy and management, *Industrial and Corporate Change*, 19: 297–316.

2. R. Ragozzino & D. P. Blevins, 2015, Venture-backed firms: How does venture capital involvement affect their likelihood of going public or being acquired? *Entrepreneurship Theory and Practice*, in press; H. R. Greve, 2011, Positional rigidity: Low performance and resource acquisition in large and small firms, *Strategic Management Journal*, 32: 103–114; R. Ragozzino & J. J. Reuer, 2010, The opportunities and challenges of entrepreneurial acquisitions, *European Management Review*, 70: 80–90.

3. P.-X. Meschi & E. Metais, 2015, Too big to learn: The effects of major acquisition failures on subsequent acquisition divestment, *British Journal of Management*, in press; K. Muehlfeld, P. Rao Sahib, & A. Van Witteloostuijn, 2012, A contextual theory of organizational learning from failures and successes: A study of acquisition completion in the global newspaper industry, 1981–2008, *Strategic Management Journal*, 33: 938–964; M. A. Hitt, D. King, H. Krishnan, M. Makri, M. Schijven, K. Shimizu, & H. Zhu, 2009, Mergers and acquisitions: Overcoming pitfalls, building synergy and creating value, *Business Horizons*, 52: 523–529.

4. D. A. Basuil & D. K. Datta, 2015, Effects of industry- and region-specific acquisition experience on value creation in cross-border acquisitions: The moderating role of cultural similarity, *Journal of Management Studies*, in press; A. S. Gaur, S. Malhotra, & P. Zhu, 2013, Acquisition announcements and stock market valuations of acquiring firms' rivals: A test of the growth probability hypothesis in China, *Strategic Management Journal*, 34: 215–232; G. M. McNamara, J. Haleblian, & B. J. Dykes, 2008, The performance implications of participating in an acquisition wave: Early mover advantages, bandwagon effects, and the moderating influence of industry characteristics and acquirer tactics, *Academy of Management Journal*, 51: 113–130.

5. C. Moschieri & J. M. Campa, 2014, New trends in mergers and acquisitions: Idiosyncrasies of the European market,

Journal of Business Research, 67: 1478–1485; J. J. Reuer, T. W. Tong, & C. Wu, 2012, A signaling theory of acquisition premiums: Evidence from IPO targets, *Academy of Management Journal*, 55: 667–683.

6. J. B. Edwards, 2015, M&A deal-makers are dealing in 2014: A commentary, *Journal of Corporate Accounting & Finance*, 26: 19–24.

7. J. S. Ang & A. K. Ismail, 2015, What premiums do target shareholders expect? Explaining negative returns upon offer announcement, *Journal of Corporate Finance*, 30: 245–256; M. Cornett, B. Tanyeri, & H. Tehranian, 2011, The effect of merger anticipation on bidder and target firm announcement period returns, *Journal of Corporate Finance*, 17: 595–611.

8. A. Kaul & X. (Brian) Wu, 2015, A capabilities-based perspective on target selection in acquisitions, *Strategic Management Journal*, in press; J. Cicon, J. Clarke, S. P. Ferris, & N. Jayaraman, 2014, Managerial expectations of synergy and the performance of acquiring firms: The contribution of soft data, *Journal of Behavioral Finance*, 15: 161–175; J. Sears & G. Hoetker, 2014, Technological overlap, technological capabilities, and resource recombination in technological acquisitions, *Strategic Management Journal*, 35: 48–67.

9. P. Loftus, J. D. Rockoff, & M. Farrell, 2015, Alexion-Synageva deal shows lure of rare-disease drugs, *Wall Street Journal Online*, www.wsj.com, May 6.

10. J.-Y. (Jay) Kim, S. Finkelstein, & J. Haleblian, 2015, All aspirations are not created equal: The differential effects of historical and social aspirations on acquisition behavior, *Academy of Management Journal*, in press; V. Ambrosini, C. Bowman, & R. Schoenberg, 2011, Should acquiring firms pursue more than one value creation strategy? An empirical test of acquisition performance, *British Journal of Management*, 22: 173–185; K. J. Martijn Cremers, V. B. Nair, & K. John, 2009, Takeovers and the cross-section of returns, *Review of Financial Studies*, 22: 1409–1445.

11. J. McKinnon, 2015, Canada's Alamos Gold and AuRico Gold to merge, *Wall Street Journal Online*, www.wsj.com, April 13.

12. M. Curtin, 2015, A 'merger of equals' is more fragile, *Wall Street Journal Online*, www.wsj.com, March 16.

13. N. Aktas, E. Croci, & S. A. Simsir, 2015, Corporate governance and takeover outcomes, *Corporate Governance: An International Review*, in press; M. Humphery-Jenner, 2014, Takeover defenses as drivers of innovation and value-creation, *Strategic Management Journal*, 35: 668–690.

14. R. Barusch, 2015, Dealpolitik: Three ways to look at the three-way pharma scrum,

Wall Street Journal Online, www.wsj.com, April 23.

15. K. Huschelrath & K. Muller, 2015, Market power, efficiencies, and entry evidence from an airline merger, *Managerial and Decision Economics*, 36: 239–255; J. Garcia-Quevedo, G. Pellegrino, & M. Vivarelli, 2014, R&D drivers and age: Are young firms different? *Research Policy*, 43: 1544–1556.

16. V. Bilotkach & P. A. Lakew, 2014, On sources of market power in the airline industry: Panel data evidence from the US airports, *Transportation Research Part A: Policy and Practice*, 59: 288–305; M. A. Hitt, D. King, H. Krishnan, M. Makri, M. Schijven, K. Shimizu, & H. Zhu, 2012, Creating value through mergers and acquisitions: Challenges and opportunities, in D. Faulkner, S. Teerikangas, & R. Joseph (eds.), *Oxford Handbook of Mergers and Acquisitions*, Oxford, U.K.: Oxford University Press, 71–113; J. Haleblian, C. E. Devers, G. McNamara, M. A. Carpenter, & R. B. Davison, 2009, Taking stock of what we know about mergers and acquisitions: A review and research agenda, *Journal of Management*, 35: 469–502.

17. P. Mourdoukoutas, 2014, Amazon's big problem, *Forbes*, www.forbes.com, May 7.

18. H. Furchtgott-Roth, 2015, Comcast and Time Warner Cable: Autopsy of a failed merger, *Forbes*, www.forbes.com, April 24.

19. D. Burghardt & M. Helm, 2015, Firm growth in the course of mergers and acquisitions, *Small Business Economicx*, 44: 889–904; D. K. Oler, J. S. Harrison, & M. R. Allen, 2008, The danger of misinterpreting short-window event study findings in strategic management research: An empirical illustration using horizontal acquisitions, *Strategic Organization*, 6: 151–184.

20. J. D. Rockoff & J. Walker, 2015, Meet pharma's newest movers and shakers, *Wall Street Journal Online*, www.wsj.com, April 22.

21. W. Moatti, C. R. Ren, J. Anand, & P. Dussauge, 2015, Disentangling the performance effects of efficiency and bargaining power in horizontal growth strategies: An empirical investigation in the global retail industry, *Strategic Management Journal*, 36: 745–757; C. E. Fee & S. Thomas, 2004, Sources of gains in horizontal mergers: Evidence from customer, supplier, and rival firms, *Journal of Financial Economics*, 74: 423–460.

22. T. H. Reus, B. T. Lamont, & K. M. Ellis, 2015, A darker side of knowledge transfer following international acquisitions, *Strategic Management Journal*, in press; G. E. Halkos & N. G. Tzeremes, 2013, Estimating the degree of operational efficiency gains from a potential bank merger and acquisition: A DEA bootstrapped approach, *Journal of*

Banking & Finance, 37: 1658–1668; L. Capron, W. Mitchell, & A. Swaminathan, 2001, Asset divestiture following horizontal acquisitions: A dynamic view, *Strategic Management Journal*, 22: 817–844.

23. C.-H. Chou, 2014, Strategic delegation and vertical integration, *Managerial and Decision Economics*, 35: 580–586; J. Shenoy, 2012, An examination of the efficiency, foreclosure, and collusion rationales for vertical takeovers, *Management Science*, 58: 1482–1501.

24. K. Favaro, 2015, Vertical integration 2.0: An old strategy makes a comeback, *Strategy & Business*, www.strategy-business.com, May 6.

25. N. Wilson, 2014, Nutella maker Ferrero buys Turkey's biggest Hazelnut company, *International Business Times*, www.ibtimes.co/uk, July 7.

26. P. Burrows, 2015, Cisco CEO says company remains in hunt for software makers, *Bloomberg*, www.bloomberg.com, February 19; C. Talbot, 2015, Cisco targets software companies for acquisition, *FierceEnterpriseCommunications*, www.fierceenterprisecommunications.com, February 23.

27. L. Beilfuss, 2015, Scripps Networks profit falls on acquisitions, restructuring costs, *Wall Street Journal Online*, www.wsj.com, May 7.

28. 2015, Scripps Networks Interactive to acquire controlling interest in Polish TV operator TVN, Scripps Networks Interactive Home Page, www.scrippsnetworksinteractive.com, March 16.

29. B. B. Fancis, I. Hasan, X. Sun, & M. Waisman, 2014, Can firms learn by observing? Evidence from cross-border M&As, *Journal of Corporate Finance*, 25: 202–215; I. Erel, R. C. Liao, & M. S. Weisbach, 2012, Determinants of cross-border mergers and acquisitions, *Journal of Finance*, 67: 1045–1082; K. Boeh, 2011, Contracting costs and information asymmetry reduction in cross-border M&A, *Journal of Management Studies*, 48: 568–590; R. Chakrabarti, N. Jayaraman, & S. Mukherjee, 2009, Mars-Venus marriages: Culture and cross-border M&A, *Journal of International Business Studies*, 40: 216–237.

30. Y. Chen, W. Li, & K. J. Lin, 2015, Cumulative voting: Investor protection or antitakeover? Evidence from family firms in China, *Corporate Governance: An International Review*, 23: 234–238; J. Lahart, 2012, Emerging risk for multinationals, *Wall Street Journal*, November 15, C12; Y. W. Chin, 2011, M&A under China's Anti-Monopoly Law, *Business Law Today*, 19: 1–5.

31. 2015, China 2015 regulatory transparency scorecard, *The US-China Business Council*, www.uschina.org, March; L. Burkitt, 2015, Nine out of 10 Chinese charities fail transparency text, report finds, *Wall Street Journal Online*, www.wsj.com, April 1.

32. 2014, Special report—How Caterpillar got bulldozed in China, *Reuters Industries*, www.reteurs.com, January 22; S. Montlake, 2013, Cat scammed, *Forbes*, March 4, 36–38.

33. H. Liu, X.-H. Ding, H. Guo, & J.-H. Luo, 2014, How does slack affect product innovation in high-tech Chinese firms: The contingent value of entrepreneurial orientation, *Asia Pacific Journal of Management*, 31: 47–68; L. Capron & W. Mitchell, 2012, *Build, Borrow or Buy: Solving the Growth Dilemma*, Cambridge: Harvard Business Review Press; G. K. Lee & M. B. Lieberman, 2010, Acquisition vs. internal development as modes of market entry, *Strategic Management Journal*, 31: 140–158.

34. H. Berends, M. Jelinek, I. Reymen, & R. Stultiens, 2014, Product innovation processes in small firms: Combining entrepreneurial effectuation and managerial causation, *Journal of Product Innovation Management*, 31: 616–635; H. Evanschitzky, M. Eisend, R. J. Calantone, & Y. Jiang, 2012, Success factors of product innovation: An updated meta-analysis, *Journal of Product Innovation Management*, 29: 21–37; H. K. Ellonen, P. Wilstrom, & A. Jantunen, 2009, Linking dynamic-capability portfolios and innovation outcomes, *Technovation*, 29: 753–762.

35. U. Stettner & D. Lavie, 2014, Ambidexterity under scrutiny: Exploration and exploitation via internal organization, alliances, and acquisitions, *Strategic Management Journal*, 35: 1903–1929; M. Makri, M. A. Hitt, & P. J. Lane, 2010, Complementary technologies, knowledge relatedness, and invention outcomes in high technology M&As, *Strategic Management Journal*, 31: 602–628; M. A. Hitt, R. E. Hoskisson, R. A. Johnson, & D. D. Moesel, 1996, The market for corporate control and firm innovation, *Academy of Management Journal*, 39: 1084–1119.

36. 2015, Welch Allyn continues acquisitions, buys scale maker, *Wall Street Journal Online*, www.wsj.com, May 6.

37. C. Grimpe & K. Hussinger, 2014, Resource complementarity and value capture in firm acquisitions: The role of intellectual property rights, *Strategic Management Journal*, 35: 1762–1780; W. P. Wan & D. W. Yiu, 2009, From crisis to opportunity: Environmental jolt, corporate acquisitions, and firm performance, *Strategic Management Journal*, 30: 791–801; G. Ahuja & R. Katila, 2001, Technological acquisitions and the innovation performance of acquiring firms: A longitudinal study, *Strategic Management Journal*, 22: 197–220.

38. O. Koryak, K. F. Mole, A. Lockett, J. C. Hayton, D. Ucbasaran, & G. P. Hodgkinson, 2015, Entrepreneurial leadership, capabilities and firm growth, *International Small Business Journal*, 33: 89–105; N. Zhou & A. Delios, 2012, Diversification and diffusion: A social

networks and institutional perspective, *Asia Pacific Journal of Management*, 29: 773–798; M. A. Hitt, R. E. Hoskisson, R. D. Ireland, & J. S. Harrison, 1991, Effects of acquisitions on R&D inputs and outputs, *Academy of Management Journal*, 34: 693–706.

39. 2015, Campbell announces plans for a reorganization of its business operations and appoints the presidents of its three new business divisions, Campbell Soup Home Page, www.campbellsoupcompany.com, January 29.

40. J. Kell, 2015, Campbell Soup is still searching for its recipe for success, *Fortune*, www.fortune, February 25.

41. M.-J. Lee, 2015, Samsung's latest acquisition: Utah-based Yesco Electronics, *Wall Street Journal Online*, www.wsj.com, March 5.

42. A. Chakrabarti & W. Mitchell, 2015, The role of geographic distance in completing related acquisitions: Evidence from U.S. chemical manufacturers, *Strategic Management Journal*, in press; F. Bauer & K. Matzler, 2014, Antecedents of M&A success: The role of strategic complementarity, cultural fit, and degree and speed of integration, *Strategic Management Journal*, 35: 269–291; T. Laamanen & T. Keil, 2008, Performance of serial acquirers: Toward an acquisition program perspective, *Strategic Management Journal*, 29: 663–672.

43. T. J. Hannigan, R. D. Hamilton, III, & R. Mudambi, 2015, Competition and competitiveness in the US airline industry, *Competitiveness Review*, 25: 134–155; D. G. Sirmon, S. Gove, & M. A. Hitt, 2008, Resource management in dyadic competitive rivalry: The effects of resource bundling and deployment, *Academy of Management Journal*, 51: 919–933.

44. S. Banerjee, J. C. Prabhu, & R. K. Chandy, 2015, Indirect learning: How emerging-market firms grow in developed markets, *Journal of Marketing*, 79: 10–28; A. Kaul, 2012, Technology and corporate scope: Firm and rival innovation as antecedents of corporate transactions, *Strategic Management Journal*, 33: 347–367; M. Zollo & J. J. Reuer, 2010, Experience spillovers across corporate development activities, *Organization Science*, 21: 1195–1212.

45. A. Hajro, 2015, Cultural influences and the mediating role of socio-cultural integration processes on the performance of cross-border mergers and acquisitions, *International Journal of Human Resource Management*, 26: 192–215; A. Ataullahm, H. Le, & A. S. Sahota, 2014, Employee productivity, employment growth, and the cross-border acquisitions by emerging market firms, *Human Resource Management*, 53: 987–1004; T. Gantumur & A. Stephan, 2012, Mergers & acquisitions and innovation performance in the telecommunications equipment industry, *Industrial & Corporate Change*, 21: 277–314.

46. 2015, CenturyLink acquires Orchestrate to enhance cloud platform with new database capabilities, CenturyLink Home Page, www.centurylink.com, April 20.

47. M. G. Colombo & L. Rabbiosi, 2014, Technological similarity, post-acquisition R&D reorganization, and innovation performance in horizontal acquisitions, *Research Policy*, 2014, 43: 1039–1054; M. E. Graebner, K. M. Eisenhardt, & P. T. Roundy, 2010, Success and failure in technology acquisitions: Lessons for buyers and sellers, *Academy of Management Perspectives*, 24, 73–92; J. A. Schmidt, 2002, Business perspective on mergers and acquisitions, in J. A. Schmidt (ed.), *Making Mergers Work*, Alexandria, VA: Society for Human Resource Management, 23–46.

48. A. Trichterborn, D. Z. Knyphausen-Aufseb, & L. Schweizer, 2015, How to improve acquisition performance: The role of a dedicated M&A function, M&A learning process, and M&A capability, *Strategic Management Journal*, in press; A. Zaheer, X. Castañer, & D. Souder, 2013, Synergy sources, target autonomy, and integration in acquisitions, *Journal of Management*, 39: 604–632; K. M. Ellis, T. H. Reus, & B. T. Lamont, 2009, The effects of procedural and informational justice in the integration of related acquisitions, *Strategic Management Journal*, 30: 137–161.

49. R. Shen, Y. Tang, & G. Chen, 2014, When the role fits: How firm status differentials affect corporate takeovers, *Strategic Management Journal*, 35: 2012–2030; T. H. Reus, 2012, Culture's consequences for emotional attending during cross-border acquisition implementation, *Journal of World Business*, 47: 342–351.

50. H. Zhu, J. Xia, & S. Makino, 2015, How do high-technology firms create value in international M&A? Integration, autonomy and cross-border contingencies, *Journal of World Business*, in press; J. Q. Barden, 2012, The influences of being acquired on subsidiary innovation adoption, *Strategic Management Journal*, 33: 1269–1285; H. G. Barkema & M. Schijven, 2008, Toward unlocking the full potential of acquisitions: The role of organizational restructuring, *Academy of Management Journal*, 51: 696–722.

51. T. Hua, 2015, Nokia can't cut its way to success with Alcatel, *Wall Street Journal Online*, wsj.com, April 14.

52. T. Hua, 2015, Nokia's ambitions could crack under integration pressure, *Wall Street Journal Online*, www.wsj.com, April 15.

53. S. F. Rockart & N. Dutt, 2015, The rate and potential of capability development trajectories, *Strategic Management Journal*, 36: 53–75; A. Sleptsov, J. Anand, & G. Vasudeva, 2013, Relationship configurations with information intermediaries: The effect of firm-investment bank ties on expected acquisition performance, *Strategic Management Journal*, 34: 957–977.

54. J. B. Edwards, 2014, The urge to merge, *Journal of Corporate Accounting & Finance*, 25: 51–55; R. Duchin & B. Schmidt, 2013, Riding the merger wave: Uncertainty, reduced monitoring, and bad acquisitions, *Journal of Financial Economics*, 107: 69–88; J. DiPietro, 2010, Responsible acquisitions yield growth, *Financial Executive*, 26: 16–19.

55. 2015, Capgemini to acquire iGate for $4 billion, *livemint*, www.livemint.com, April 28.

56. J. Wieczner, 2015, Fat pharma: Pfizer-Hospira and the top 10 overpriced drug deals ever, *Fortune*, www.fortune.com, February 6.

57. B. Becker & V. Ivashiina, 2015, Reaching for yield in the bond market, *Journal of Finance*, in press; G. Yago, 1991, *Junk Bonds: How High Yield Securities Restructured Corporate America*, NY: Oxford University Press, 146–148.

58. D. H. Kim & D. Stock, 2014, The effect of interest rate volatility and equity volatility on corporate bond yield spreads: A comparison of noncallables and callables, *Journal of Corporate Finance*, 26: 20–35.

59. M. C. Jensen, 1986, Agency costs of free cash flow, corporate finance, and takeovers, *American Economic Review*, 76: 323–329.

60. I. M. Pandey & V. Ongpipattanakul, 2015, Agency behavior and corporate restructuring choices during performance decline in an emerging economy, *International Journal of Managerial Finance*, 11: 244–267; S. Guo, E. S. Hotchkiss, & W. Song, 2011, Do buyouts (still) create value? *Journal of Finance*, 66: 479–517.

61. K. Craninckx & N. Huyghebaert, 2015, Large shareholders and value creation through corporate acquisitions in Europe: The identity of the controlling shareholder matters, *European Management Journal*, 33: 116–131; M. Rahman & M. Lambkin, 2015, Creating or destroying value through mergers and acquisitions: A marketing perspective, *Industrial Marketing Management*, 46: 24–35; S. W. Bauguess, S. B. Moeller, F. P. Schlingemann, & C. J. Zutter, 2009, Ownership structure and target returns, *Journal of Corporate Finance*, 15: 48–65; H. Donker & S. Zahir, 2008, Takeovers, corporate control, and return to target shareholders, *International Journal of Corporate Governance*, 1: 106–134.

62. J. Jaffe, J. Jindra, D. Pedersen, & T. Voetmann, 2015, Returns to acquirers of public and subsidiary targets, *Journal of Corporate Finance*, 31: 246–270; C. Tantalo & R. L. Priem, 2015, Value creation through stakeholder synergy, *Strategic Management Journal*, in press; Y. M. Zhou, 2011, Synergy, coordination costs, and diversification choices, *Strategic Management Journal*, 32: 624–639.

63. G. Speckbacher, K. Neumann, & W. H. Hoffmann, 2015, Resource relatedness and the mode of entry into new businesses: Internal resource accumulation vs. access

by collaborative arrangement, *Strategic Management Journal*, in press; J. B. Barney, 1988, Returns to bidding firms in mergers and acquisitions: Reconsidering the relatedness hypothesis, *Strategic Management Journal*, 9 (Special Issue): 71–78.

64. Trefis team, 2014, What has AirTran done for Southwest Airlines? *Forbes*, www.forbes.com, December 11.

65. A. Chakrabarti, 2015, Organizational adaptation in an economic shock: The role of growth reconfiguration, *Strategic Management Journal*, in press; O. E. Williamson, 1999, Strategy research: Governance and competence perspectives, *Strategic Management Journal*, 20: 1087–1108.

66. R. Stunda, 2014, The market impact of mergers and acquisitions on firms in the U.S., *Journal of Accounting and Taxation*, 6: 30–37; S. Snow, 2013, How to avoid a post-acquisition idea slump, *Fast Company*, February, 50; M. Cleary, K. Hartnett, & K. Dubuque, 2011, Road map to efficient merger integration, *American Banker*, March 22, 9; S. Chatterjee, 2007, Why is synergy so difficult in mergers of related businesses? *Strategy & Leadership*, 35: 46–52.

67. P. Page, 2015, Canada acquisition weighs on Radiant's earnings in recent quarter, *Wall Street Journal Online*, www.wsj.com, May 18.

68. P.-X. Meschi & E. Metais, 2015, Too big to learn: The effects of major acquisition failures on subsequent acquisition divestment, *British Journal of Management*, in press; W. P. Wan, R. E. Hoskisson, J. C. Short, & D. W. Yiu, 2011, Resource-based theory and corporate diversification: Accomplishments and opportunities, *Journal of Management*, 37: 1335–1368; E. Rawley, 2010, Diversification, coordination costs and organizational rigidity: Evidence from microdata, *Strategic Management Journal*, 31: 873–891.

69. S. Schonhaar, U. Pidun, & M. Nippa, 2014, Transforming the business portfolio: How multinational reinvent themselves, *Journal of Business Strategy*, 35: 4–17; S. Pathak, R. E. Hoskisson, & R. A. Johnson, 2014, Settling up in CEO compensation: The impact of divestiture intensity and contextual factors in refocusing firms, *Strategic Management Journal*, 35: 1124–1143; M. L. A. Hayward & K. Shimizu, 2006, De-commitment to losing strategic action: Evidence from the divestiture of poorly performing acquisitions, *Strategic Management Journal*, 27: 541–557.

70. J. B. Edwards, 2015, M&A deal-makers are dealing in 2014: A commentary, *Journal of Corporate Accounting & Finance*, 26: 19–24; J. Hagedoorn & N. Wang, 2012, Is there complementarity or substitutability between internal and external R&D strategies? *Research Policy*, 41: 1072–1083; P. David, J. P. O'Brien, T. Yoshikawa, & A. Delios, 2010, Do shareholders or

stakeholders appropriate the rents from corporate diversification? The influence of ownership structure, *Academy of Management Journal*, 53: 636–654; R. E. Hoskisson & R. A. Johnson, 1992, Corporate restructuring and strategic change: The effect on diversification strategy and R&D intensity, *Strategic Management Journal*, 13: 625–634.

71. F. Szucs, 2014, M&A and R&D: Asymmetric effects on acquirers and targets? *Research Policy*, 43: 1264–1273; R. D. Banker, S. Wattal, & J. M. Plehn-Dujowich, 2011, R&D versus acquisitions: Role of diversification in the choice of innovation strategy by information technology firms, *Journal of Management Information Systems*, 28: 109–144; J. L. Stimpert, I. M. Duhaime, & J. Chesney, 2010, Learning to manage a large diversified firm, *Journal of Leadership and Organizational Studies*, 17: 411–425; T. Keil, M. V. J. Maula, H. Schildt, & S. A. Zahra, 2008, The effect of governance modes and relatedness of external business development activities on innovative performance, *Strategic Management Journal*, 29: 895–907.

72. B. E. Perrott, 2015, Building the sustainable organization: An integrated approach, *Journal of Business Strategy*, 36: 41–51; A. Kacperczyk, 2009, With greater power comes greater responsibility? Takeover protection and corporate attention to stakeholders, *Strategic Management Journal*, 30: 261–285; M. L. Barnett, 2008, An attention-based view of real options reasoning, *Academy of Management Review*, 33: 606–628.

73. M. V. S. Kumar, J. Dixit, & B. Francis, 2015, The impact of prior stock market reactions on risk taking in acquisitions, *Strategic Management Journal*, in press; J. A. Martin & K. J. Davis, 2010, Learning or hubris? Why CEOs create less value in successive acquisitions, *Academy of Management Perspectives*, 24: 79–81; M. L. A. Hayward & D. C. Hambrick, 1997, Explaining the premiums paid for large acquisitions: Evidence of CEO hubris, *Administrative Science Quarterly*, 42: 103–127; R. Roll, 1986, The hubris hypothesis of corporate takeovers, *Journal of Business*, 59: 197–216.

74. F. Vermeulen, 2007, Business insight (a special report): Bad deals: Eight warning signs that an acquisition may not pay off, *Wall Street Journal*, April 28, R10.

75. D. H. Zhu, 2013, Group polarization on corporate boards: Theory and evidence on board decisions about acquisition premiums, *Strategic Management Journal*, 34: 800–822.

76. G. Kling, A. Ghobadian, M. A. Hitt, U. Weitzel, & N. O'Regan, 2014, The effects of cross-border and cross-industry mergers and acquisitions on home-region and global multinational enterprises, *British Journal of Management*, 25: S116–S132; V. Swaminathan, F. Murshed, & J. Hulland,

2008, Value creation following merger and acquisition announcements: The role of strategic emphasis alignment, *Journal of Marketing Research*, 45: 33–47.

77. O.-P. Kauppila, 2014, So, what am I supposed to do? A multilevel examination of role clarity, *Journal of Management Studies*, 51: 737–763; M. Wagner, 2011, To explore or to exploit? An empirical investigation of acquisitions by large incumbents, *Research Policy*, 40: 1217–1225; H. Greve, 2011, Positional rigidity: Low performance and resource acquisition in large and small firms, *Strategic Management Journal*, 32: 103–114.

78. D. N. Angwin, S. Paroutis, & R. Connell, 2015, Why good things don't happen: The micro-foundations of routines in the M&A process, *Journal of Business Research*, 68: 1367–1381; E. Gomes, D. N. Angwin, Y. Weber, & S. Tarba, 2013, Critical success factors through the mergers and acquisitions process: Revealing pre- and post-M&A connections for improved performance, *Thunderbird International Business Review*, 55: 13–35; M. Cording, P. Christmann, & C. Weigelt, 2010, Measuring theoretically complex constructs: The case of acquisition performance, *Strategic Organization*, 8: 11–41.

79. D. Gamache, G. McNamara, M. Mannor, & R. Johnson, 2015, Motivated to acquire? The impact of CEO regulatory focus on firm acquisitions, *Academy of Management Journal*, inn press; A. Riviezzo, 2013, Acquisitions in knowledge-intensive industries: Exploring the distinctive characteristics of the effective acquirer, *Management Research Review*, 36: 183–212; S. Chatterjee, 2009, The keys to successful acquisition programmes, *Long Range Planning*, 42: 137–163.

80. O. Ahlers, A. Hack, & F. W. Kellermanns, 2014, Stepping into the buyers' shoes: Looking at the value of family firms through the eyes of private equity investors, *Journal of Family Business Strategy*, 6: 384–396; M. A. Hitt, R. D. Ireland, J. S. Harrison, & A. Best, 1998, Attributes of successful and unsuccessful acquisitions of U.S. firms, *British Journal of Management*, 9: 91–114.

81. S. R. Jory & T. N. Nog, 2014, Cross-border acquisitions of state-owned enterprises, *Journal of International Business Studies*, 45: 1096–1114; K. Uhlenbruck, M. A. Hitt, & M. Semadeni, 2006, Market value effects of acquisitions involving Internet firms: A resource-based analysis, *Strategic Management Journal*, 27: 899–913.

82. 2015, TE Connectivity to acquire AdvancedCath, *Pr NewsWire*, www.prnewswire.com, March 4.

83. M. Humphery-Jenner, 2014, Takeover defenses, innovation, and value creation: Evidence from acquisition decisions, *Strategic Management Journal*, 35: 668–690; A. Rouzies & H. L. Colman, 2012,

Identification processes in post-acquisition integration: The role of social interactions, *Corporate Reputation Review*, 15: 143–157; D. K. Ellis, T. Reus, & B. Lamont, 2009, The effects of procedural and informational justice in the integration of related acquisitions, *Strategic Management Journal*, 30: 137–161.

84. S. Graffin, J. Haleblian, & J. T. Kiley, 2015, Ready, AIM, acquire: Impression offsetting and acquisitions, *Academy of Management Journal*, in press; R. Agarwal, J. Anand, J. Bercovitz, & R. Croson, 2012, Spillovers across organizational architectures: The role of prior resource allocation and communication in post-acquisition coordination outcomes, *Strategic Management Journal*, 33: 710–733; M. E. Graebner, 2009, Caveat venditor: Trust asymmetries in acquisitions of entrepreneurial firms, *Academy of Management Journal*, 52: 435–472.

85. F. Szucs, 2014, M&A and R&D: Asymmetric effects on acquirers and targets? *Research Policy*, 43: 1264–1273; Y. Suh, J. You, & P. Kim, 2013, The effect of innovation capabilities and experience on cross-border acquisition performance, *Global Journal of Business Research*, 7: 59–74; J. Jwu-Rong, H. Chen-Jui, & L. Hsieh-Lung, 2010, A matching approach to M&A, R&D, and patents: Evidence from Taiwan's listed companies, *International Journal of Electronic Business Management*, 8: 273–280.

86. 2015, Nokia and Alcaltel-Lucent to combine to create an innovation leader in next generation technology and services for an IP connected world, Nokia Home Page, www.nokia.com, April 15.

87. D. N. Angwin & M. Meadows, 2015, New integration strategies for post-acquisition management, *Long Range Planning*, in press; K. H. Heimeriks, M. Schijven, & S. Gates, 2013, Manifestations of higher-order routines: The underlying mechanisms of deliberate learning in the context of postacquisition integration, *Academy of Management Journal*, 55: 703–726; M. L. McDonald, J. D. Westphal, & M. E. Graebner, 2008, What do they know? The effects of outside director acquisition experience on firm acquisition performance, *Strategic Management Journal*, 29: 1155–1177.

88. M. McCann & R. Ackrill, 2015, Managerial and disciplinary responses to abandoned acquisitions in bidding firms: A new perspective, *Corporate Governance: An International Review*, in press; C. Moschieri & J. Mair, 2012, Managing divestitures through time—Expanding current knowledge, *Academy of Management Perspectives*, 26: 35–50; D. Lee & R. Madhaven, 2010, Divestiture and firm performance: A meta-analysis, *Journal of Management*, 36: 1345–1371.

89. N. Kavadis & X. Castaner, 2015, Who drives corporate restructuring? Co-existing

owners in French firms, *Corporate Governance: An International Review*, in press; Y. G. Suh & E. Howard, 2009, Restructuring retailing in Korea: The case of Samsung-Tesco, *Asia Pacific Business Review*, 15: 29–40; Z. Wu & A. Delios, 2009, The emergence of portfolio restructuring in Japan, *Management International Review*, 49: 313–335.

90. E. R. Feldman, 2015, Corporate spinoffs and analysts' coverage decisions: The implications for diversified firms, *Strategic Management Journal*, in press; A. Fortune & W. Mitchell, 2012, Unpacking firm exit at the firm and industry levels: The adaptation and selection of firm capabilities, *Strategic Management Journal*, 33: 794–819; J. L. Morrow, Jr., D. G. Sirmon, M. A. Hitt, & T. R. Holcomb, 2007, Creating value in the face of declining performance: Firm strategies and organizational recovery, *Strategic Management Journal*, 28: 271–283.

91. W. McKinley, S. Latham, & M. Braun, 2014, Organizational decline and innovation: Turnarounds and downward spirals, *Academy of Management Review*, 39: 88–110.

92. C. Tangpong, M. Agebe, & Z. Li, 2015, A temporal approach to retrenchment and successful turnaround in declining firms, *Journal of Management Studies*, in press; H. A. Krishnan, M. A. Hitt, & D. Park, 2007, Acquisition premiums, subsequent workforce reductions and post-acquisition performance, *Journal of Management*, 44: 709–732.

93. I. Paeleman & T. Vanacker, 2015, Less is more, or not? On the interplay between bundles of slack resources, firm performance and firm survival, *Journal of Management Studies*, in press; D. K. Lim, N. Celly, E. A. Morse, & W. Rowe, 2013, Rethinking the effectiveness of asset and cost retrenchment: The contingency effects of a firm's rent creation mechanism, *Strategic Management Journal*, 34: 42–61.

94. L. S. Alberet, D. G. Allen, J. E. Biggane, & Q. (Kathy) Ma, 2015, Attachment and responses to employment dissolution, *Human Resource Management*, 25: 94–106; R. Iverson & C. Zatzick, 2011, The effects of downsizing on labor productivity: The value of showing consideration for employees' morale and welfare in high-performance work systems, *Human Resource Management*, 50: 29–43; C. O. Trevor & A. J. Nyberg, 2008, Keeping your headcount when all about you are losing theirs: Downsizing, voluntary turnover rates, and the moderating role of HR practices, *Academy of Management Journal*, 51: 259–276.

95. T. J. Chemmanur, K. Krishnan, & D. K. Nandy, 2014, The effects of corporate spin-offs on productivity, *Journal of Corporate Finance*, 27: 72–98; R. E. Hoskisson & M. A. Hitt, 1994, *Downscoping: How to Tame the Diversified Firm*, NY: Oxford University Press.

96. E. R. Feldman, R. (Raffi) Amit, & B. Villalonga, 2015, Corporate divestitures and family control, *Strategic Management Journal*, in press; A. T. Nicolai, A. Schulz, & T. W. Thomas, 2010, What Wall Street wants—Exploring the role of security analysts in the evolution and spread of management concepts, *Journal of Management Studies*, 47: 162–189; L. Dranikoff, T. Koller, & A. Schneider, 2002, Divestiture: Strategy's missing link, *Harvard Business Review*, 80(5): 74–83.

97. A. Nadolska & H. G. Barkema, 2014, Good learners: How top management teams affect the success and frequency of acquisitions, *Strategic Management Journal*, 35: 1483–1507; R. E. Hoskisson & M. A. Hitt, 1990, Antecedents and performance outcomes of diversification: A review and critique of theoretical perspectives, *Journal of Management*, 16: 461–509.

98. E. Vidal & W. Mitchell, 2015, Adding by subtracting: The relationship between performance feedback and resource reconfiguration through divestitures, *Organization Science*, in press; S. Schonhaar, U. Pidun, & M. Nippa, 2014, Transforming the business portfolio: How multinationals reinvent themselves, *Journal of Business Strategy*, 35: 4–17.

99. W. G. Xavier, R. Bandeira-de-Mello, & R. Marcon, 2014, Institutional environment and business groups' resilience in Brazil, *Journal of Business Research*, 67: 900–907; H. Berry, 2013, When do firms divest foreign operations? *Organization Science*, 24: 246–261; C. Chi-Nien & L. Xiaowei, 2008, Institutional logics or agency costs: The influence of corporate governance models on business group restructuring in emerging economies, *Organization Science*, 19: 766–784; R. E. Hoskisson, R. A. Johnson, L. Tihanyi, & R. E. White, 2005, Diversified business groups and corporate refocusing in emerging economies, *Journal of Management*, 31: 941–965.

100. H. D. Park & P. C. Patel, 2015, How does ambiguity influence IPO underpricing? The role of the signaling environment, *Journal of Management Studies*, in press.

101. A. N. Link, C. J. Ruhm, & D. S. Siegel, 2014, Private equity and the innovation strategies of entrepreneurial firms: Empirical evidence form the small business innovation research program, *Managerial and Decision Economics*, 35: 103–113; S. N. Kaplan & P. Stromberg, 2009, Leveraged buyouts and private equity, *Journal of Economic Perspectives*, 23: 121–146.

102. S. Pathak, R. E. Hoskisson, & R. A. Johnson, 2014, Settling up in CEO compensation: The impact of divestiture intensity and contextual factors in refocusing firms, *Strategic Management Journal*, 35: 1124–1143; N. Wilson, M. Wright, D. S. Siegel, & L. Scholes, 2012, Private equity portfolio company performance during the global recession, *Journal of Corporate Finance*, 18:

193–205; R. Harris, D. S. Siegel, & M. Wright, 2005, Assessing the impact of management buyouts on economic efficiency: Plant-level evidence from the United Kingdom, *Review of Economics and Statistics*, 87: 148–153.

103. E. Autio, M. Kenney, P. Mustar, D. Siegel, & M. Wright, 2014, Entrepreneurial innovation: The importance of context, *Research Policy*, 43: 1097–1108; H. Bruining, E. Verwaal, & M. Wright, 2013, Private equity and entrepreneurial management in management buy-outs, *Small Business Economics*, 40: 591–605; M. Meuleman, K. Amess, M. Wright, & L. Scholes, 2009, Agency, strategic entrepreneurship, and the performance of private equity-backed buyouts, *Entrepreneurship Theory and Practice*, 33: 213–239.

104. F. Castellaneta & O. Gottschalg, 2015, Does ownership matter in private equity? The sources of variance in buyouts' performance, *Strategic Management Journal*, in press; W. Kiechel III, 2007, Private equity's long view, *Harvard Business Review*, 85(4): 18–20; M. Wright, R. E. Hoskisson, & L. W. Busenitz, 2001, Firm rebirth: Buyouts as facilitators of strategic growth and entrepreneurship, *Academy of Management Executive*, 15: 111–125.

105. Y.-Y. Ji, J. P. Guthrie, & J. G. Messersmith, 2014, The tortoise and the hare: The impact of employment instability on firm performance, *Human Resource Management Journal*, 24: 355–373; E. G. Love & M. Kraatz, 2009, Character, conformity, or the bottom line? How and why downsizing affected corporate reputation, *Academy of Management Journal*, 52: 314–335; J. P. Guthrie & D. K. Datta, 2008, Dumb and dumber: The impact of downsizing on firm performance as moderated by industry conditions, *Organization Science*, 19: 108–123.

106. M. Brauer & T. Laamanen, 2014, Workforce downsizing and firm performance: An organizational routine perspective, *Journal of Management Studies*, 51: 1311–1333; H. A. Krishnan & D. Park, 2002, The impact of work force reduction on subsequent performance in major mergers and acquisitions: An exploratory study, *Journal of Business Research*, 55: 285–292; P. M. Lee, 1997, A comparative analysis of layoff announcements and stock price reactions in the United States and Japan, *Strategic Management Journal*, 18: 879–894.

107. S. Mariconda & F. Lurati, 2015, Ambivalence and reputation stability: An experimental investigation on the effects of new information, *Corporate Reputation Review*, 18: 87–98; D. J. Flanagan & K. C. O'Shaughnessy, 2005, The effect of layoffs on firm reputation, *Journal of Management*, 31: 445–463.

108. J. Habel & M. Klarmann, 2015, Customer reactions to downsizing: When and how is satisfaction affected? *Journal of the*

Academy of Marketing Science, in press;
P. Williams, K. M. Sajid, & N. Earl, 2011,
Customer dissatisfaction and defection:
The hidden costs of downsizing, *Industrial
Marketing Management*, 40: 405–413.

109. F. Bertoni & A. P. Groh, 2014, Cross-border
investments and venture capital exits
in Europe, *Corporate Governance: An
International Review*, 22: 84–99;
C. Moschieri & J. Mair, 2011, Adapting for
innovation: Including divestitures in the
debate, *Long Range Planning*, 44: 4–25;
K. Shimizu & M. A. Hitt, 2005, What constrains
or facilitates divestitures of formerly
acquired firms? The effects of organizational
inertia, *Journal of Management*, 31: 50–72.

110. J X. Cao, D. Cumming, M. Qian, & X. Wang,
2015, Cross-border LBOs, *Journal of Banking
and Finance*, 50: 69–80.

111. K. Cao, J. Coy, & T. Nguyen, 2015, The
likelihood of management involvement, offer
premiums, and target shareholder wealth
effects: Evidence from the 2002–2007 LBO
wave, *Research in International Business and
Finance*, in press; P. G. Klein, J. L. Chapman, &
M. P. Mondelli, 2013, Private equity and
entrepreneurial governance: Time for a
balanced view, *Academy of Management
Perspectives*, 27: 39–51; D. T. Brown, C. E. Fee, &
S. E. Thomas, 2009, Financial leverage and
bargaining power with suppliers: Evidence
from leveraged buyouts, *Journal of Corporate
Finance*, 15: 196–211.

112. H.-C. Huang, Y.-C. Su, & Y.-H. Chang,
2014, Dynamic return-order imbalance
relationship response to leveraged buyout
announcements, *Global Journal of Business
Research*, 8: 55–63; S. B. Rodrigues &

J. Child, 2010, Private equity, the
minimalist organization and the quality of
employment relations, *Human Relations*,
63: 1321–1342; G. Wood & M. Wright, 2009,
Private equity: A review and synthesis,
*International Journal of Management
Reviews*, 11: 361–380.

113. L. Bouvier & T. M. Misar, 2015, Design and
impacts of securitized leveraged buyouts,
Cogent Economics & Finance, 3: http://
dx.doi.org/10.1080/23322039.2015.1009307;
M. Goergen, N. O'Sullivan, & G. Wood, 2011,
Private equity takeovers and employment
in the UK: Some empirical evidence,
*Corporate Governance: An International
Review*, 19: 259–275; W. F. Long &
D. J. Ravenscraft, 1993, LBOs, debt, and
R&D intensity, *Strategic Management
Journal*, 14 (Special Issue): 119–135.

8

International Strategy

Studying this chapter should provide you with the strategic management knowledge needed to:

8-1   Explain incentives that can influence firms to use an international strategy.

8-2   Identify three basic benefits firms achieve by successfully implementing an international strategy.

8-3   Explore the determinants of national advantage as the basis for international business-level strategies.

8-4   Describe the three international corporate-level strategies.

8-5   Discuss environmental trends affecting the choice of international strategies, particularly international corporate-level strategies.

8-6   Explain the five modes firms use to enter international markets.

8-7   Discuss the two major risks of using international strategies.

8-8   Discuss the strategic competitiveness outcomes associated with international strategies, particularly with an international diversification strategy.

8-9   Explain two important issues firms should have knowledge about when using international strategies.

NETFLIX IGNITES GROWTH THROUGH INTERNATIONAL EXPANSION, BUT SUCH GROWTH ALSO FIRES UP THE COMPETITION

Netflix has been pursuing a typical international strategy by developing strong capabilities in technological innovation domestically and then using that base technology to expand abroad. Its technology is focused on understanding customer viewing patterns and providing content that matches that pattern as well as having a broad selection of content produced by network television and movie studios in addition to its own original content, which has become a strong force in the market (see examples in Chapter 1 and Chapter 4).

However, Netflix has reached a near saturation point in the domestic U.S. market. As an obvious extension, it has begun to extend its services abroad in countries that are close culturally and geographically to its U.S. customer base, such as Canada, Nordic, and Latin American countries. Although it is trying to foster more growth by partnering with firms such as Marriott for access to its hotel entertainment systems, Netflix's primary growth is coming from its international expansion efforts which allow it to share its cost across a broader range of countries and a larger subscriber base. In the fourth quarter of 2014, Netflix added 1.9 million U.S. streaming subscribers, but this was down from 2.4 million in the period a year earlier. However, overall in 2014 it added 4.3 million streaming customers, exceeding its 4 million forecast, primarily driven because foreign markets grew faster than expected. Netflix already has some services in approximately 50 countries. In the first quarter of 2015, it expanded into Australia and New Zealand. It is also exploring the opportunity of obtaining a government license to offer its streaming services in China.

Getty Images

Netflix's international growth strategy has some confounding complexities. First, Netflix must seek global licenses with its contract video and movie content providers. However, the content providers want to distribute their content in international markets as well, and thus Netflix will have to pay more for the content to get a global license, in addition to the costs of initial start-up and licensing in new foreign countries. This drives up the costs of pursuing its global strategy, at least in the short term.

Second, as it pursues its global streaming strategy, there are both increased domestic competition for subscriber growth as well as new entrants into foreign markets as they see the opportunity that Netflix is trying to realize. For example, Alibaba, whose home country is China, recently indicated that it would start up its own video streaming service and even contracted to produce original content, copying Netflix's strategy (see the opening case in Chapter 1). Interestingly, there is some speculation that Alibaba, given its huge size and recent cash from an initial public offering (IPO), would seek to purchase Netflix as a way of fostering its entry push into the U.S. In addition, Netflix has many other domestic streaming competitors, including Amazon and Hulu.

For example, in the United States, Hulu has been increasing its subscriber base substantially by partnering with television networks to get their best content. Netflix had been cherry-picking this content with lower contractual pricing, but it is having to pay more, and as such, Netflix is not choosing as much prime content. Meanwhile, Hulu has a better relationship with the television networks because it was originally founded and partly owned by the networks. As such, Hulu is willing to pay a higher price for the premium television network video content. This strategy has helped increase its subscriber base from 6 million in 2014 to potentially 9 million in 2015. Furthermore, the television network producers see Netflix as a competitor because it is now producing its own video television content for its subscriber base. A positive for Netflix, though, is that it can use its propriety video content globally without the contractual complexities noted earlier.

In summary, although the international expansion strategy has facilitated growth and profits for Netflix through sharing costs and expenses across a large subscriber base, it has also increased the complexity of its management structure. Additionally, the difficulty in global contracting for top-level domestic U.S. content has increased both international and domestic competition as it has pursued its international strategy.

Sources: M. Armenta & S. Ramachandran, 2015, Business news: Netflix builds steam abroad—International operations spilled red ink but growth in number of subscribers propels the stock higher, *Wall Street Journal*, April 16, B3; B. Darrow, 2015, Alibaba to opening streaming video service in China, *Fortune*, www.fortune.com, June 15; K. Hagey & S. Ramachandran, 2015, Hulu courts TV networks in bid to catch up with Netflix, *Wall Street Journal*, A1, A2; J. Lansing, 2015, TV everywhere: The thundering head, *Broadcasting & Cable*, May 11, 19; S. Ramachandran, 2015, Netflix steps up foreign expansion, subscriber additions top streaming service's forecast, helped by growth in markets abroad, *Wall Street Journal*, www.wsj.com, January 21; A. Tracy, 2015, Marriott and Netflix have partnered up, *Forbes*, June 10, 22; F. Video, 2015, Netflix eyes China for continued global expansion, *Fortune*, www.fortune.com, June 11; S. Saghoee, 2014, Who could buy Netflix?, *Fortune*, www.fortune.com, November 18.

Our description of Netflix's competitive actions in this chapter's Opening Case (e.g., international expansion strategy) highlights the importance of international markets for this firm. Netflix is using its growth in international markets to overcome weakening subscriber growth in its U.S. market. Being able to effectively compete in countries and regions outside a firm's domestic market is increasingly important to firms of all types, as exemplified by Netflix. One reason for this is that the effects of globalization continue to reduce the number of industrial and consumer markets in which only domestic firms can compete successfully. In place of what historically were relatively stable and predictable domestic markets, firms across the globe find they are now competing in globally oriented industries—industries in which firms must compete in all world markets where a consumer or commercial good or service is sold in order to be competitive.[1] Unlike domestic markets, global markets are relatively unstable and much less predictable.

The purpose of this chapter is to discuss how international strategies can be a source of strategic competitiveness for firms competing in global markets. To do this, we examine a number of topics (see Figure 8.1). After describing incentives that influence firms to identify international opportunities, we discuss three basic benefits that can accrue to firms that successfully use international strategies. We then turn our attention to the international strategies available to firms. Specifically, we examine both international business-level strategies and international corporate-level strategies. The five modes of entry firms can use to enter international markets for implementing their international strategies are then examined. Firms encounter economic and political risks when using international strategies. Some refer to these as economic and political institutions.[2] These risks must be effectively managed if the firm is to achieve the desired outcomes of higher performance and enhanced innovation. After discussing the outcomes firms seek when using international strategies, the chapter closes with mention of two cautions about international strategy that should be kept in mind.

Figure 8.1 Opportunities and Outcomes of International Strategy

Identify International Opportunities	Explore Resources and Capabilities	Use Core Competencies	Strategic Competitiveness Outcomes
Basic Benefits	International Strategies	Modes of Entry	

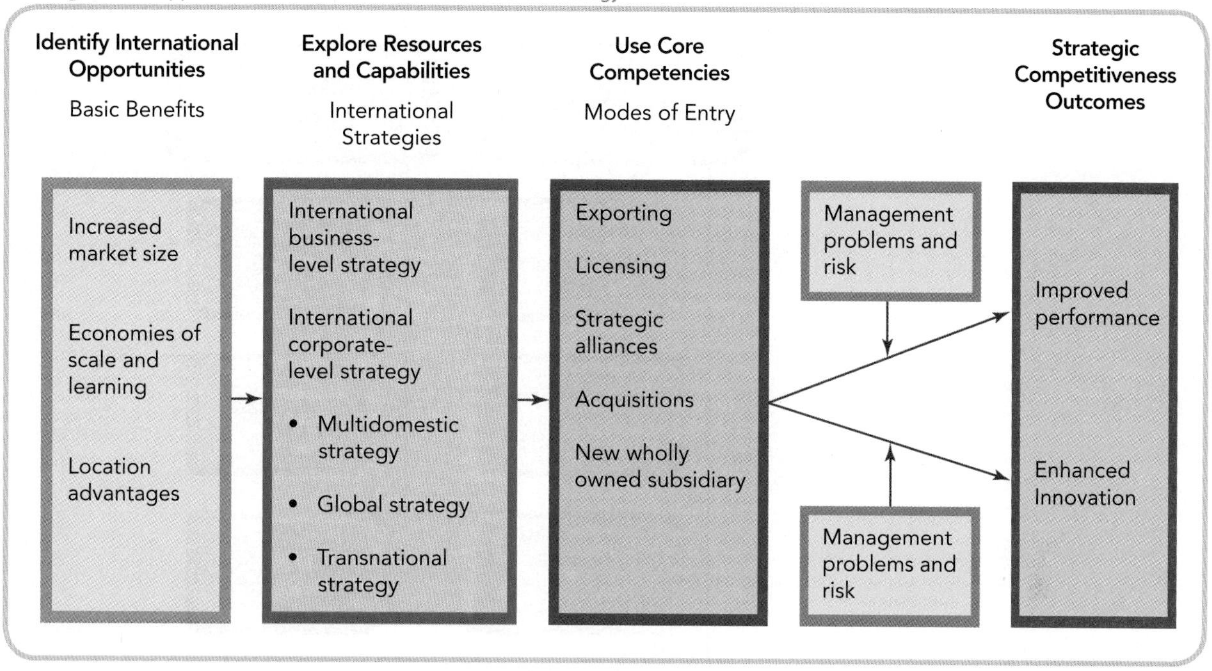

8-1 Identifying International Opportunities

An **international strategy** is a strategy through which the firm sells its goods or services outside its domestic market.[3] In some instances, firms using an international strategy become quite diversified geographically as they compete in numerous countries or regions outside their domestic market. This is the case for Netflix in that it competes in about 50 countries. In other cases, firms engage in less international diversification because they compete in a smaller number of markets outside their "home" market.

There are incentives for firms to use an international strategy and to diversify their operations geographically, and they can gain three basic benefits when they successfully do so.[4] We show international strategy's incentives and benefits in Figure 8.2.

8-1a Incentives to Use International Strategy

Raymond Vernon expressed the classic rationale for an international strategy.[5] He suggested that typically a firm discovers an innovation in its home-country market, especially in advanced economies such as those in Germany, France, Japan, Sweden, Canada, and the United States. Often demand for the product then develops in other countries, causing a firm to export products from its domestic operations to fulfil demand. Continuing increases in demand can subsequently justify a firm's decision to establish operations outside of its domestic base, as illustrated in the Opening Case on Netflix. As Vernon noted, engaging in an international strategy has the potential to help a firm extend the life cycle of its product(s).

Gaining access to needed and potentially scarce resources is another reason firms use an international strategy. Key supplies of raw material—especially minerals and energy—are critical to firms' efforts in some industries to manufacture their products. Energy and mining companies have access to the raw materials, through their worldwide operations, which they in turn sell to manufacturers requiring those resources. Rio Tinto Group is

An **international strategy** is a strategy through which the firm sells its goods or services outside its domestic market.

Figure 8.2 Incentives and Basic Benefits of International Strategy

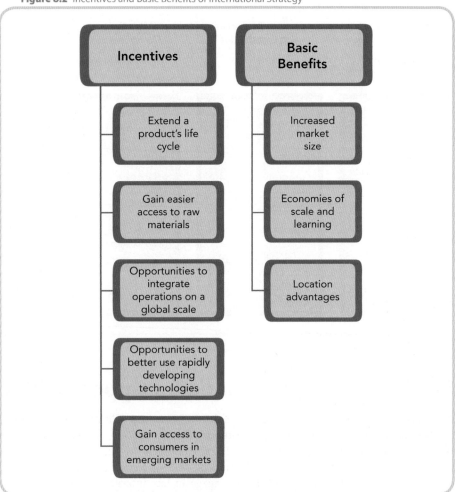

a leading international mining corporation. Operating as a global organization, the firm has 71,000 employees across six continents to include Australia, North America, South America, Europe, Asia, and Africa. Rio Tinto uses its capabilities of technology and innovation (see first incentive noted above), exploration, marketing, and operational processes to identify, extract, and market mineral resources throughout the world.[6] In other industries where labor costs account for a significant portion of a company's expenses, firms may choose to establish facilities in other countries to gain access to less expensive labor. Clothing and electronics manufacturers are examples of firms pursuing an international strategy for this reason.

Increased pressure to integrate operations on a global scale is another factor influencing firms to pursue an international strategy. As nations industrialize, the demand for some products and commodities appears to become more similar. This borderless demand for globally branded products may be due to growing similarities in lifestyle in developed nations. Increases in global communications also facilitate the ability of people in different countries to visualize and model lifestyles in other cultures. In an increasing number of industries, technology drives globalization because the economies of scale necessary to reduce costs to the lowest level often require an investment greater than that needed to meet domestic market demand. Moreover, in emerging markets, the increasingly rapid adoption of technologies such as the Internet and mobile applications permits greater integration of trade, capital, culture, and labor. For instance, Vietnam is experiencing a "mobile revolution." In 2015, over 40 percent of the population has smartphones and access to the Internet, compared to 12 percent ten years ago. This is driving $4 billion in e-commerce business in 2015 versus $700 million in 2012.[7] In this sense, technologies are the foundation for efforts to bind together disparate markets and operations across the world. International strategy also makes it possible for firms to use technologies to organize their operations into a seamless whole.[8]

The potential of large demand for goods and services from people in emerging markets such as China and India is another strong incentive for firms to use an international strategy.[9] This is the case for French-based Carrefour S.A. This firm is the world's second-largest retailer (behind only Walmart) and the largest retailer in Europe. Carrefour operates five main grocery store formats—hypermarkets, supermarkets, cash & carry, hypercash stores, and convenience stores. The firm also sells products online.[10] In some areas of the world, Carrefour performed poorly and in 2014. For example, it withdrew from India as did another large U.K. retailer, Tesco. One observer concluded that "both Carrefour and Tesco have been withdrawing from non-core international markets where they cannot see long-term returns. Both had neglected their core domestic operations and saw sales at home suffer."[11] Both companies have been attempting to fine tune their business models in both domestic and international locations.

Even though India differs from Western countries in many respects, such as culture, politics, and the precepts of its economic system, it offers a huge potential market, and the government is becoming more supportive of foreign direct investment.[12] Differences among Chinese, Indian, and Western-style economies and cultures make the successful use of an international strategy challenging. As such, firms seeking to meet customer demands in emerging markets must learn how to manage an array of political and economic risks, which we discuss later in the chapter.[13]

We've now discussed incentives that influence firms to use international strategies. Firms derive three basic benefits by successfully using international strategies:

1. increased market size
2. increased economies of scale and learning
3. development of a competitive advantage through location (e.g., access to low-cost labor, critical resources, or customers).

These benefits will be examined here in terms of both their costs (e.g., higher coordination expenses and limited access to knowledge about host country political influences)[14] and their challenges.

8-1b   Three Basic Benefits of International Strategy

As noted, effectively using one or more international strategies can result in three basic benefits for the firm. These benefits facilitate the firm's effort to achieve strategic competitiveness (see Figure 8.1) when using an international strategy.

Increased Market Size

Firms can expand the size of their potential market—sometimes dramatically—by using an international strategy to establish stronger positions in markets outside their domestic market. As noted, access to additional consumers is a key reason Carrefour sees international markets such as China as a major source of growth.

China's WH Group (formerly known as Shuanghui International) acquired the U.S. based, Smithfield Foods, Inc., a large pork producer in the U.S. Pork consumption accounts for more than 60 percent of the total meat consumption in China creating an opportunity for foreign pork producers to export more pork to China and overcome potential trade barriers in doing so. The acquisition also helps WH Group to upgrade its global image, while providing the resources that Smithfield needed. It allows both firms to expand their market size as well.[15]

Firms such as Netflix, Carrefour, and WH Group understand that effectively managing different consumer tastes and practices linked to cultural values or traditions in different markets is challenging. Nonetheless, they accept this challenge because of the potential to enhance the firms' size and performance. Other firms accept the challenge of successfully implementing an international strategy largely because of limited growth opportunities in their domestic market. This appears to be at least partly the case for major competitors Coca-Cola and PepsiCo, firms that have not been able to generate significant growth in their U.S. domestic and North American markets for some time. Indeed, most of these firms' growth is occurring in international markets. An international market's overall size also has the potential to affect the degree of benefit a firm can accrue as a result of using an international strategy. In general, larger international markets offer higher potential returns and pose less risk for the firm choosing to invest in those markets. Also related is the strength of the science base of the international markets in which a firm may compete. This is important because scientific knowledge and human capital are needed to facilitate efforts to more effectively sell and/or produce products that create value for customers.[16]

Economies of Scale and Learning

By expanding the number of markets in which they compete, firms may be able to enjoy economies of scale, particularly in manufacturing operations. More broadly, firms able to make continual process improvements enhance their ability to reduce costs while, hopefully, increasing the value their products create for customers. For example, rivals Airbus SAS and Boeing have multiple manufacturing facilities and outsource some activities to firms located throughout the world, partly for the purpose of developing economies of scale as a source of being able to create value for customers.

Economies of scale are critical in a number of settings in addition to the airline manufacturing industry. Automobile manufacturers certainly seek economies of scale as a benefit of their international strategies. Ford Motor Company employs 224,000 people worldwide and operates in six global regions: North America, Central and South America, Europe, Middle East, Africa, and Asia Pacific. Ford is planning on increasing sales in each region, especially in Asia.[17] Overall, Ford seeks to increase the annual number of products it sells outside of North America, for example, it increased its market share in Europe in 2014. Demonstrating the use of this international strategy is the fact that Ford is now run as a single global business developing cars and trucks that can be built and sold throughout the world.[18] Firms may also be able to exploit core competencies in international markets through resource and knowledge sharing between units and network partners across country borders.[19] By sharing resources and knowledge in this manner, firms can learn how to create synergy, which in turn can help each firm learn how to produce higher quality products at a lower cost.

Operating in multiple international markets also provides firms with new learning opportunities,[20] perhaps even in terms of research and development (R&D) activities. Increasing the firm's R&D ability can contribute to its efforts to enhance innovation, which is critical to both short- and long-term success. However, research results suggest that to take advantage of international R&D investments, firms need to already have a strong R&D system in place to absorb knowledge resulting from effective R&D activities.[21]

Location Advantages

Locating facilities outside their domestic market can sometimes help firms reduce costs. This benefit of an international strategy accrues to the firm when its facilities in international locations provide easier access to lower cost labor, energy, and other natural resources. Other location advantages include access to critical supplies and to customers. Once positioned in an attractive location, firms must manage their facilities effectively to gain the full benefit of a location advantage.[22]

A firm's costs, particularly those dealing with manufacturing and distribution, as well as the nature of international customers' needs affect the degree of benefit it can capture through a location advantage.[23] Cultural influences may also affect location advantages and disadvantages. International business transactions are easier for a firm to complete when there is a strong cultural match with which the firm is involved while implementing its international strategy.[24] Finally, physical distances influence a firms' location choices as well as how it manages facilities in the chosen locations.[25]

8-2 International Strategies

Firms choose to use one or both basic types of international strategy: business-level international strategy and corporate-level international strategy. At the business-level, firms select from among the generic strategies of cost leadership, differentiation, focused cost leadership, focused differentiation, and integrated cost leadership/ differentiation. At the corporate level, multidomestic, global, and transnational international strategies (the transnational is a combination of the multidomestic and global strategies) are considered. To contribute to the firm's efforts to achieve strategic competitiveness in the form of improved performance and enhanced innovation (see Figure 8.1), each international strategy the firm uses must be based on one or more core competencies.[26]

8-2a International Business-Level Strategy

Firms considering the use of any international strategy first develop domestic-market strategies (at the business level and at the corporate level if the firm has diversified at the product level). This is important because the firm may be able to use some of the capabilities and core competencies it has developed in its domestic market as the foundation for competitive success in international markets, as illustrated in the Opening Case on Netflix. However, research results indicate that the value created by relying on capabilities and core competencies developed in domestic markets as a source of success in international markets diminishes as a firm's geographic diversity increases.[27]

As we know from our discussion of competitive dynamics in Chapter 5, firms do not select and then use strategies in isolation of market realities. In the case of international strategies, conditions in a firm's domestic market affect the degree to which the firm can build on capabilities and core competencies it established to create capabilities and core competencies in international markets. The reason is grounded in Michael Porter's analysis of why some nations are more competitive than other nations and why and how some industries within nations are more competitive relative to those industries in other nations. Porter's core argument is that conditions or factors in a firm's home base—that is, in its domestic market—either hinder or support the firm's efforts to use an international business-level strategy for the purpose of establishing a competitive advantage in international markets. Porter identifies four factors as determinants of a national advantage that some countries possess (see Figure 8.3).[28] Interactions among these four factors influence a firm's choice of international business-level strategy.

Figure 8.3 Determinants of National Advantage

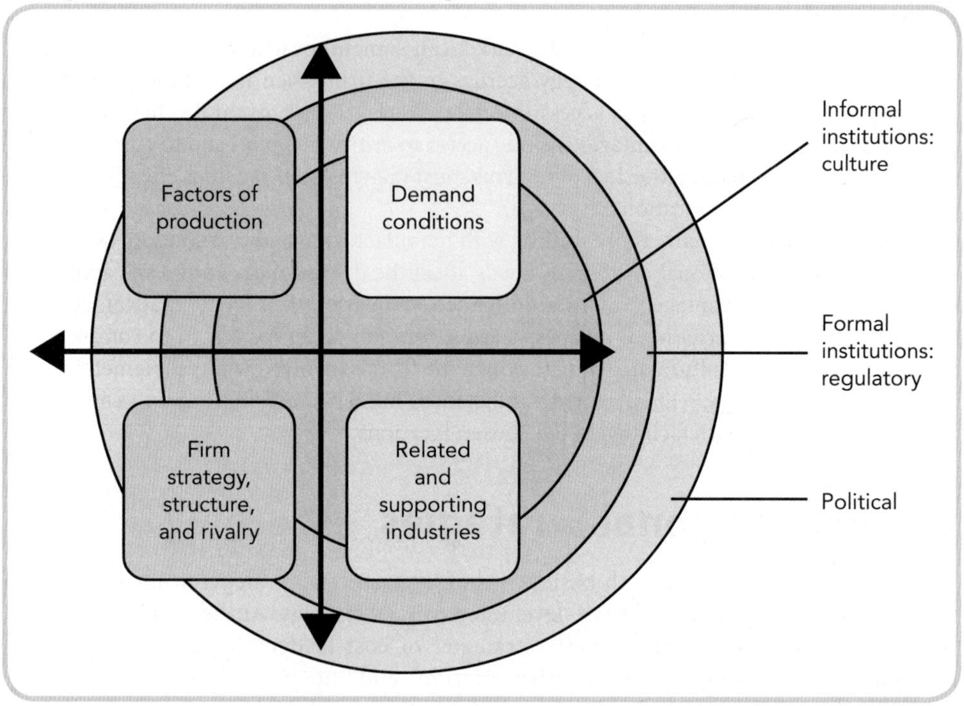

The first determinant of national advantage is factors of production. This determinant refers to the inputs necessary for a firm to compete in any industry. Labor, land, natural resources, capital, and infrastructure (transportation, delivery, and communication systems) represent such inputs. There are basic factors (natural and labor resources) and advanced factors (digital communication systems and a highly educated workforce). Other factors of production are generalized (highway systems and the supply of debt capital) and specialized (skilled personnel in a specific industry, such as the workers in a port that specialize in handling bulk chemicals). If a country possesses advanced and specialized production factors, it is likely to serve an industry well by spawning strong home-country competitors that also can be successful global competitors.

Ironically, countries often develop advanced and specialized factors because they lack critical basic resources. For example, South Korea lacks abundant natural resources but has a workforce with a strong work ethic, a large number of engineers, and systems of large firms to create an expertise in manufacturing. Similarly, Germany developed a strong chemical industry, partly because Hoechst and BASF spent years creating a synthetic indigo dye to reduce their dependence on imports, unlike the United Kingdom, whose colonies provided large supplies of natural indigo.[29]

The second factor or determinant of national advantage, demand conditions, is characterized by the nature and size of customers' needs in the home market for the products firms competing in an industry produce. Meeting the demand generated by a large number of customers creates conditions through which a firm can develop scale-efficient facilities and enhance the capabilities, and perhaps core competencies, required to use those facilities. Once enhancements are in place, the probability that the capabilities and core competencies will benefit the firm as it diversifies geographically increases.

This is the case for Chiquita Brands International, which spent years building its businesses and developing economies of scale and scale efficient facilities, however, it diversified into too many different product lines. In recent years it has refocused the firm on its bananas and packaged salad product lines. Now, Chiquita produces almost one-third of the bananas it sells on its own farms in Latin America. It is the market leader in bananas in Europe and is number two in the market in North America. Chiquita is using its capabilities and core competencies in growing and distributing its brand bananas in its international markets. However, in 2015 it was purchased by Brazil's Cutrale Group which added Chiquita brand bananas and fresh packaged salads to its fruit business in oranges, apples, and peaches.[30]

The third factor in Porter's model of the determinants of national advantage is related and supporting industries. Italy has become the leader in the shoe industry because of related and supporting industries. For example, a well-established leather-processing industry provides the leather needed to construct shoes and related products. Also, many people travel to Italy to purchase leather goods, providing support in distribution. Supporting industries in leather-working machinery and design services also contribute to the success of the shoe industry. In fact, the design services industry supports its own related industries, such as ski boots, fashion apparel, and furniture. In Japan, cameras and copiers are related industries. Similarly, Germany is known for the quality of its machine tools and Belgium is known for skilled manufacturing (supporting and related industries are important in these two settings also).

Firm strategy, structure, and rivalry make up the final determinant of national advantage and also foster the growth of certain industries. The types of strategy, structure, and rivalry among firms vary greatly from nation to nation. The excellent technical training system in Germany fosters a strong emphasis on continuous product and process improvements. In Italy, the national pride of the country's designers spawns strong industries not only in shoes but also sports cars, fashion apparel, and furniture. In the United States, competition among computer manufacturers and software producers contributes to further development of these industries.

The four determinants of national advantage (see Figure 8.3) emphasize the structural characteristics of a specific economy that contribute to some degree to national advantage and influence the firm's selection of an international business-level strategy. Policies of individual governments also affect the nature of the determinants as well as how firms compete within the boundaries governing bodies establish and enforce within a particular economy.[31] While studying their external environment (see Chapter 2), firms considering the possibility of using an international strategy need to gather information and data that will allow them to understand the effects of governmental policies and their enforcement on the nation's ability to establish advantages relative to other nations. Likewise, firms need to understand the relative degree of increased competitiveness the entering firm might receive by examining the country resources necessary to help the firm compete on a global basis in a focal industry.

Leading companies should recognize that a firm based in a country with a national competitive advantage is not guaranteed success as it implements its chosen international business-level strategy. The actual strategic choices managers make may be the most compelling reasons for success or failure as firms diversify geographically. Accordingly, the factors illustrated in Figure 8.3 are likely to produce the foundation for a firm's competitive advantages only when it develops and implements an appropriate international business-level strategy that takes advantage of distinct country factors. Thus, these distinct country factors should be thoroughly considered when making a decision about which international business-level strategy to use. The firm will then make continuous adjustments to its international business-level strategy in light of the nature of competition it encounters in different international markets and in light of customers' needs. Lexus, for example, does not have the share of the luxury car market in China that it desires. Accordingly, Toyota (Lexus' manufacturer) is adjusting how it implements its international differentiation business-level strategy in China to better serve customers. However, it is still far behind other luxury brands such as BMW, Audi, and Cadillac which are growing faster than Lexus. Several analysts noted that it was not getting the traction desired in part because Toyota decided not to put a production facility in China, thus having to pay a 25 percent tariff for each vehicle sold.[32]

8-2b   International Corporate-Level Strategy

A firm's international business-level strategy is also based, at least partially, on its international corporate-level strategy. Some international corporate-level strategies give individual country units the authority to develop their own business-level strategies, while others dictate the business-level strategies in order to standardize the firm's products and sharing of resources across countries.[33]

International corporate-level strategy focuses on the scope of a firm's operations through geographic diversification.[34] International corporate-level strategy is required when the firm operates in multiple industries that are located in multiple countries or regions (e.g., Southeast Asia or the European Union) and in which it sells multiple products. The headquarters unit guides the strategy, although as noted, business- or country-level managers can have substantial strategic input depending on the type of international corporate-level strategy the firm uses. The three international corporate-level strategies are shown in Figure 8.4; the international corporate-level strategies vary in terms of two dimensions—the need for global integration and the need for local responsiveness.

Multidomestic Strategy

A **multidomestic strategy** is an international strategy in which strategic and operating decisions are decentralized to the strategic business units in individual countries or

A **multidomestic strategy** is an international strategy in which strategic and operating decisions are decentralized to the strategic business units in individual countries or regions for the purpose of allowing each unit the opportunity to tailor products to the local market.

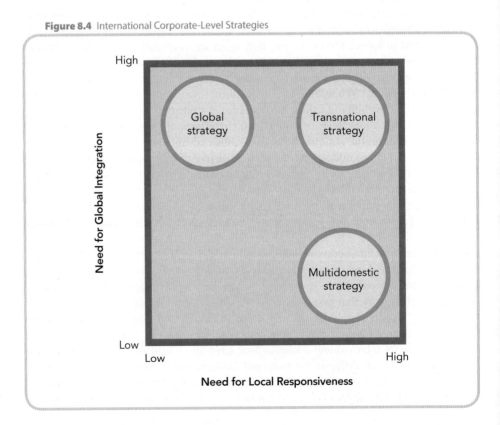

Figure 8.4 International Corporate-Level Strategies

regions for the purpose of allowing each unit the opportunity to tailor products to the local market.[35] With this strategy, the firm's need for local responsiveness is high while its need for global integration is low. Influencing these needs is the firm's belief that consumer needs and desires, industry conditions (e.g., the number and type of competitors), political and legal structures, and social norms vary by country. Thus, a multidomestic strategy focuses on competition within each country because market needs are thought to be segmented by country boundaries. To meet the specific needs and preferences of local customers, country or regional managers have the autonomy to customize the firm's products. Therefore, these strategies should maximize a firm's competitive response to the idiosyncratic requirements of each market.[36] The multidomestic strategy is most appropriate for use when the differences between the markets a firm serves and the customers in them are significant.

The use of multidomestic strategies usually expands the firm's local market share because the firm can pay attention to the local clientele's needs. However, using a multidomestic strategy results in less knowledge sharing for the corporation as a whole because of the differences across markets, decentralization, and the different international business-level strategies employed by local units.[37] Moreover, multidomestic strategies do not allow the development of economies of scale and thus can be more costly.

Unilever is a large European consumer products company selling products in over 180 countries. The firm has more than 400 global brands that are grouped into three business units—foods, home care, and personal care. Historically, Unilever has used a highly decentralized approach for the purpose of managing its global brands. This approach allows regional managers considerable autonomy to adapt the characteristics of specific products to satisfy the unique needs of customers in different markets. More recently however, Unilever has sought to increase the coordination between its independent subsidiaries in order to establish an even stronger global brand presence. One way coordination is achieved is by having the presidents of each of the five global regions serve as members of the top management team.[38] As such, Unilever may be transitioning from a multidomestic strategy to a transnational strategy.

Global Strategy

A **global strategy** is an international strategy in which a firm's home office determines the strategies that business units are to use in each country or region.[39] This strategy indicates that the firm has a high need for global integration and a low need for local responsiveness. These needs indicate that, compared to a multidomestic strategy, a global strategy seeks greater levels of standardization of products across country markets. The firm using a global strategy seeks to develop economies of scale as it produces the same, or virtually the same, products for distribution to customers throughout the world who are assumed to have similar needs. The global strategy offers greater opportunities to take innovations developed at the corporate-level, or in one market, and apply them in other markets.[40] Improvements in global accounting and financial reporting standards facilitate use of this strategy.[41] A global strategy is most effective when the differences between markets and the customers the firm is serving are insignificant.

Efficient operations are required to successfully implement a global strategy. Increasing the efficiency of a firm's international operations mandates resource sharing and greater coordination and cooperation across market boundaries. Centralized decision making as designed by headquarters details how resources are to be shared and coordinated across markets. Research results suggest that the outcomes a firm achieves by using a global strategy become more desirable when the strategy is used in areas in which regional integration among countries is occurring.[42]

A **global strategy** is an international strategy in which a firm's home office determines the strategies that business units are to use in each country or region.

As illustrated in the following Strategic Focus, IKEA has implemented the global strategy. IKEA has centralized a number of its activities, including design and packaging. Accordingly, it integrates and centralizes some support functions from the firm's value chain (see Chapter 3). This integration and centralization brings about the types of benefits sought by firms when using a global strategy. Significant cost savings increases the productivity of the involved support functions, which foster economies of scale benefiting IKEA.

Strategic **Focus**

Furniture Giant IKEA's Global Strategy

Founded in Sweden, IKEA has pursued a global strategy in developing its well-designed, inexpensive retail furniture strategy. As with most companies pursuing a global strategy, it emphasizes global efficiencies.

One particular approach that IKEA has used is to reduce shipping weight by efficient packaging. Efficient packaging and the associated benefit of lower transportation costs "is at the heart of IKEA's ability to stay affordable." For example, in 2011 the company cut the price of its Bjursta label dining table to €199 from €279 by making the table legs hollow thus reducing weight and raw material costs. "Instead of changing products once they have hit shelves, IKEA is increasingly designing things with packaging and manufacturing in mind from the start." A tradeoff they have experienced is that packaging can become too efficient at the expense of consumer frustration at the complexity of assembly once the product is in the home. So, simple assembly is also an important criteria.

In 2015, IKEA plans to open 13 new stores adding to its current total of 315. It is seeking to buy land in India to open its first locations. Furthermore, the firm is ramping up its focus on online shopping, currently available only in 13 of 27 country locations. It saw 1.5 billion online visits in 2014, up from 200 million in the prior year, which also exceeds its visits to physical stores. Ikea is expanding this strategy by increasing its "click-and-collect merchandising approach where people order online and pick-up the merchandise at a physical location."

IKEA is also focusing on developing city-center stores with a smaller range of products compared to its majority of suburban store locations. However, the suburban stores will likely be maintained as its central focus. Even when in a suburban location, IKEA seeks to be within walking distance of transportation hubs such as subway stations.

Although, IKEA is focused on efficiency, it also takes a long time to study each new country market entry. It focuses on where a growing middle-class is developing. It has entered China,

is planning on a strong entry into India, and is considering Brazil as well. All of these economies have a growing middle-class. Even in these countries, IKEA is focusing on "flat packing, transporting, and reassembling its quirky Swedish-styling all across the planet."

One of IKEA's latest strategies to improve its image is to develop a sounder approach to sustainability. Accordingly, its store roofs are outfitted with solar panels, and it will operate 314 wind turbines in 9 countries, putting the company on tract to be energy independent by 2020. IKEA recycles left over wood scraps from their furniture as well as the soft plastic film used in packaging to make the Skrutt desk pads it sells. It's also starting to phase out non-LED light bulbs in its stores and has begun selling solar panels. With this strategy, IKEA expects to be seen as a company that takes its social and environmental responsibility seriously as it expands internationally. But in the process, it also expects to lower its costs.

Face to Face/UPPA/Photoshot

The founding CEO of IKEA, Ingvar Kamprad, in front of one of IKEA's store fronts.

Sources: S. Chaudhury, 2015, IKEA's favorite design idea: Shrink the box, *Wall Street Journal*, June 18, B10; B. Kowitt, 2015, How IKEA took over the world, *Fortune*, www.fortune.com, March 13; M. Locker, 2015, IKEA is getting into the wedding business, *Time*, www.time.com, April 20; A. Molin, 2015, IKEA builds momentum in Europe, *Wall Street Journal*, www.wsj.com, January 29; J. Sanburn, F. Trianni, & D. Tsai, 2015, Find out why you overshop in IKEA, *Time*, www.time.com, March 17; C. Zillman, 2015, Here's how IKEA is fighting climate change, *Fortune*, www.fortune.com, June 11.

Because of increasing global competition and the need to simultaneously be cost efficient and produce differentiated products, the number of firms using a transnational international corporate-level strategy is increasing.

Transnational Strategy

A **transnational strategy** is an international strategy through which the firm seeks to achieve both global efficiency and local responsiveness. Realizing the twin goals of global integration and local responsiveness is difficult because global integration requires close global coordination while local responsiveness requires local flexibility. "Flexible coordination"—building a shared vision and individual commitment through an integrated network—is required to implement the transnational strategy. Such integrated networks allow a firm to manage its connections with customers, suppliers, partners, and other parties more efficiently rather than using arm's-length transactions.[43] The transnational strategy is difficult to use because of its conflicting goals (see Chapter 11 for more on the implementation of this and other corporate-level international strategies). On the positive side, effectively implementing a transnational strategy can produce higher performance than implementing either the multidomestic or global strategies if the circumstances are right.[44]

Transnational strategies are becoming increasingly necessary to successfully compete in international markets. Reasons for this include the fact that continuing increases in the number of viable global competitors challenge firms to reduce their costs. Simultaneously, the increasing sophistication of markets with greater information flows, made possible largely by the diffusion of the Internet and the desire for specialized products to meet consumers' unique needs, pressures firms to differentiate their products in local markets. Differences in culture and institutional environments also require firms to adapt their products and approaches to local environments. However, some argue that transnational strategies are not required to successfully compete in international markets. Those holding this view suggest that most multinational firms try to compete at the regional level (e.g., the European Union) rather than at the country level. To the degree this is the case, the need for the firm to simultaneously offer relatively unique products that are adapted to local markets and to produce those products at lower costs permitted by developing scale economies is reduced.[45]

The complexities of competing in global markets increase the need for the use of a transnational strategy. Mondelēz International was created as a spinoff company from Kraft, which separated its domestic grocery products in order to focus on its high-growth snack foods business, in which it has 80 percent of sales come from foreign markets. Mondelēz had $34 billion in revenue in 2014 and has power brands (brands that are globally known and respected) and local brands.[46] So, because it globally integrates its operations to standardize and maintain its power brands while simultaneously developing and marketing local brands that are specialized to meet the needs of local customers, Mondelēz pursues the transnational strategy. It is the global market leader in biscuits, chocolate, candy, and powdered beverages, and it holds the number two position in the global markets for chewing gum and coffee. About 45 percent of its sales come from fast-growing, emerging markets and with the variety of brands offered, it must adjust its strategy accordingly. For instance, besides having recently signed a global agreement

> A **transnational strategy** is an international strategy through which the firm seeks to achieve both global efficiency and local responsiveness.

Pictured above are many of the international brands that Mondelez manages globally while implementing the transnational strategy.

with Google for online and social media advertising, Mondelēz has to decide "if a brand is a local, regional, or global priority and adjust spend accordingly."[47]

Next we discuss trends in the global environment that are affecting the choices firms make when deciding which international corporate-level strategies to use and in which international markets to compete.

8-3   Environmental Trends

Although the transnational strategy is difficult to implement, an emphasis on global efficiency is increasing as more industries, and the companies competing within them, encounter intensified global competition. Magnifying the scope of this issue is the fact that, simultaneously, firms are experiencing demands for local adaptations of their products. These demands can be from customers (for products to satisfy their tastes and preferences) and from governing bodies (for products to satisfy a country's regulations). In addition, most multinational firms desire coordination and sharing of resources across country markets to hold down costs, as demonstrated in the Opening Case on Netflix.[48]

Because of these conditions, some large multinational firms with diverse products use a multidomestic strategy with certain product lines and a global strategy with others when diversifying geographically. Many multinational firms may require this type of flexibility if they are to be strategically competitive, in part due to trends that change over time.

Liability of foreignness and regionalization are two important trends influencing a firm's choice and use of international strategies, particularly international corporate-level strategies. We discuss these trends next.

8-3a   Liability of Foreignness

The dramatic success of Japanese firms such as Toyota and Sony in the United States and other international markets in the 1980s was a powerful jolt to U.S. managers. This success awakened U.S. managers to the importance of international competition and the fact that many markets were rapidly becoming globalized. In the twenty-first century, Brazil, Russia, India, and China (BRIC) represent major international market opportunities for firms from many countries, including the United States, Japan, Korea, and members of the European Union. In addition, emerging economies such as Indonesia, Malaysia, Mexico, Colombia, Kenya, and Poland have shown rapid growth, internet penetration, and improving rule of law.[49] However, even if foreign markets seem attractive, as appears to be the case with the BRIC countries and other growing economies, there are legitimate concerns for firms considering entering these markets. This is the *liability of foreignness*,[50] a set of costs associated with various issues firms face when entering foreign markets, including unfamiliar operating environments; economic, administrative, and cultural differences; and the challenges of coordination over distances.[51] Four types of distances commonly associated with liability of foreignness are cultural, administrative, geographic, and economic.[52]

Walt Disney Company's experience while opening theme parks in foreign countries demonstrates the liability of foreignness. For example, Disney suffered "lawsuits in France, at Disneyland Paris, because of the lack of fit between its transferred personnel policies and the French employees charged to enact them."[53] Disney executives learned from this experience and from building the firm's theme park in Hong Kong, and the company "went out of its way to tailor the park to local tastes."[54] Thus, as with Walt Disney Company, firms thinking about using an international strategy to enter foreign markets must be aware of the four types of distances they'll encounter when doing so and determine actions to take to reduce the potentially negative effects associated with those distances.

8-3b Regionalization

Regionalization is a second global environmental trend influencing a firm's choice and use of international strategies. This trend is becoming prominent largely because *where* a firm chooses to compete can affect its strategic competitiveness.[55] As a result, the firm considering using international strategies must decide if it should enter individual country markets or if it would be better served by competing in one or more regional markets.

Currently, the global strategy is used less frequently. It remains difficult to successfully implement even when the firm uses Internet-based strategies, although country borders matter less when e-commerce matters more.[56] In addition, the amount of competition vying for a limited amount of resources and customers can limit a firm's focus to a specific region rather than on country-specific markets that are located in multiple parts of the world. A regional focus allows a firm to marshal its resources to compete effectively rather than spreading their limited resources across multiple country-specific international markets.[57]

However, a firm that competes in industries where the international markets differ greatly (in which it must employ a multidomestic strategy) may wish to narrow its focus to a particular region of the world. In so doing, it can better understand the cultures, legal and social norms, and other factors that are important for effective competition in those markets. For example, a firm may focus on Asian markets only, rather than competing simultaneously in the Middle East, Europe, and Asia or the firm may choose a region of the world where the markets are more similar and coordination and sharing of resources would be possible. In this way, the firm may be able to better understand the markets in which it competes, as well as achieve some economies, even though it may have to employ a multidomestic strategy. Research suggests that most large retailers are better at focusing on a particular region rather than being truly global.[58] Firms commonly focus much of their international market entries on countries adjacent to their home country, which might be referred to as their home region.[59]

Countries that develop trade agreements to increase the economic power of their regions may promote regional strategies. The European Union and South America's Organization of American States (OAS) are country associations that developed trade agreements to promote the flow of trade across country boundaries within their respective regions.[60] Many European firms acquire and integrate their businesses in Europe to better coordinate pan-European brands as the European Union tries to create unity across the European markets. This process is likely to continue as new countries are added to the agreement, some international firms may prefer to focus on regions rather than multiple country markets when entering international markets.

The North American Free Trade Agreement (NAFTA), signed by the United States, Canada, and Mexico in 1993, facilitates free trade across country borders in North America. NAFTA loosens restrictions on international strategies within this region and provides greater opportunity for regional international strategies.[61]

Most firms enter regional markets sequentially, beginning in markets with which they are more familiar. They also introduce their largest and strongest lines of business into these markets first, followed by other product lines once the initial efforts are deemed successful. The additional product lines typically are introduced in the original investment location.[62] However, research also suggests that the size of the market and industry characteristics can influence this decision.[63]

Regionalization is important to most multinational firms, even those competing in many regions across the globe. For example, most large multinational firms have organizational structures that group operations within the same region (across countries) for managing and coordination purposes. Managing businesses by regions helps multinational enterprises (MNEs) deal with the complexities and challenges of operating in multiple international markets. As the Opening Case on Netflix suggests, managing across regions creates more costs, notwithstanding the benefits.

After selecting its business- and corporate-level international strategies, the firm determines how it will enter the international markets in which it has chosen to compete. We turn to this topic next.

8-4 Choice of International Entry Mode

Five modes of entry into international markets are available to firms. We show these entry modes and their characteristics in Figure 8.5. Each means of market entry has its advantages and disadvantages, suggesting that the choice of entry mode can affect the degree of success the firm achieves by implementing an international strategy.[64] Many firms competing in multiple markets may use one or more or all five entry modes.[65]

Figure 8.5 Modes of Entry and their Characteristics

Type of Entry	Characteristics
Exporting	High cost, low control
Licensing	Low cost, low risk, little control, low returns
Strategic alliances	Shared costs, shared resources, shared risks, problems of integration (e.g., two corporate cultures)
Acquisitions	Quick access to new markets, high costs, complex negotiations, problems of merging with domestic operations
New wholly owned subsidiary	Complex, often costly, time consuming, high risk, maximum control, potential above-average returns

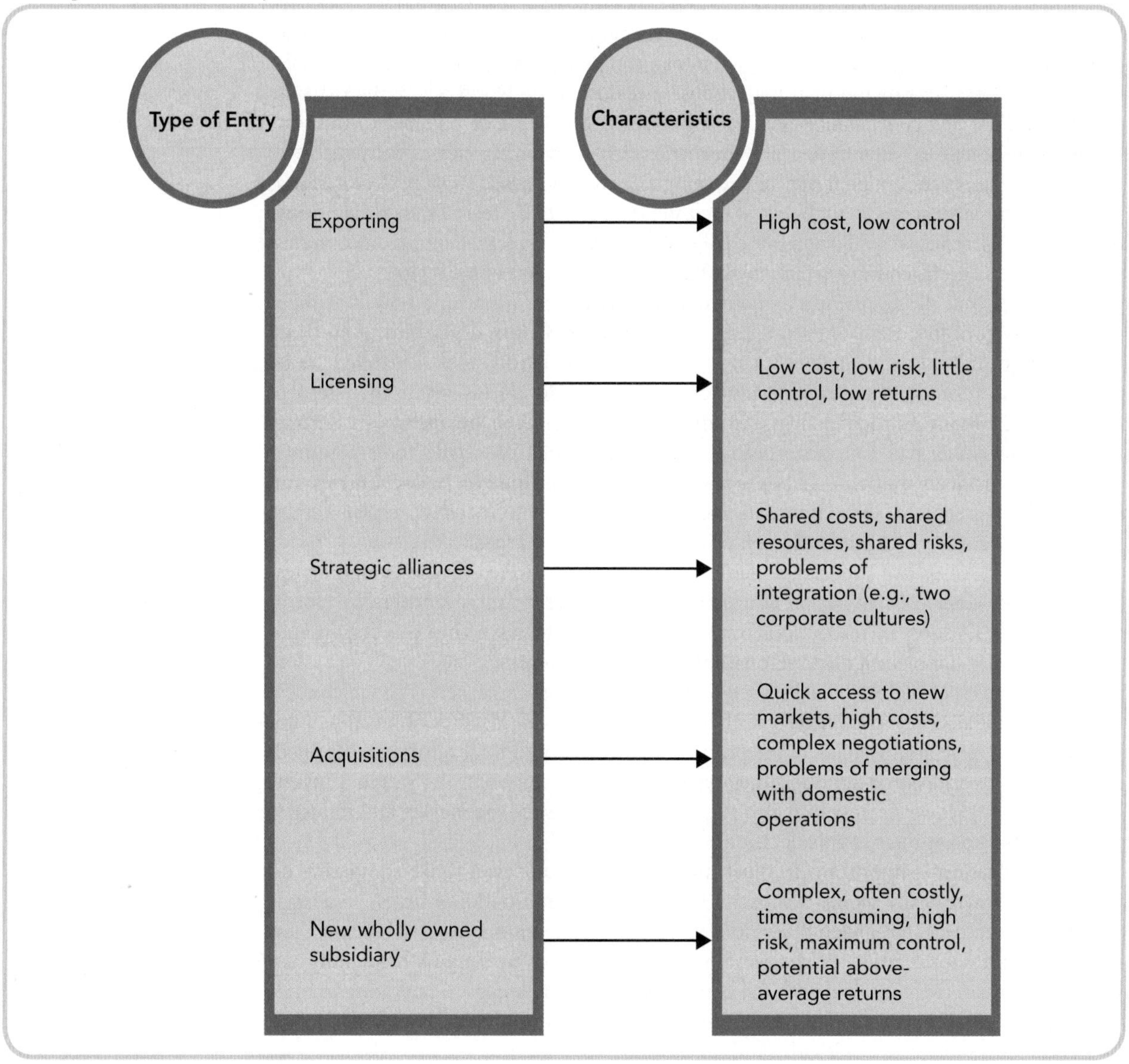

8-4a Exporting

For many firms, exporting is the initial mode of entry used.[66] *Exporting* is an entry mode through which the firm sends products it produces in its domestic market to international markets. Exporting is a popular entry mode choice for small businesses to initiate an international strategy.[67]

The number of small U.S. firms using an international strategy is increasing, with some predicting that up to 50 percent of small U.S. firms will be involved in international trade by 2018, most of them through export.[68] By exporting, firms avoid the expense of establishing operations in host countries (e.g., in countries outside their home country) in which they have chosen to compete. However, firms must establish some means of marketing and distributing their products when exporting. Usually, contracts are formed with host-country firms to handle these activities. Potentially high transportation costs to export products to international markets and the expense of tariffs placed on the firm's products as a result of host countries' policies are examples of exporting costs. The loss of some control when the firm contracts with local companies in host countries for marketing and distribution purposes can be expensive, making it harder for the exporting firm to earn profits.[69] Evidence suggests that, in general, using an international cost leadership strategy when exporting to developed countries has the most positive effect on firm performance, while using an international differentiation strategy with larger scale when exporting to emerging economies leads to the greatest amount of success. In either case, younger firms with a strong management team and market orientation capabilities are more successful.[70]

Firms export mostly to countries that are closest to their facilities because usually transportation costs are lower and there is greater similarity between geographic neighbors. For example, the United States' NAFTA partners, Mexico and Canada, account for more than half of the goods exported from the state of Texas. The Internet has also made exporting easier. Firms of any size can use the Internet to access critical information about foreign markets, examine a target market, research the competition, and find lists of potential customers.[71] Governments also use the Internet to support the efforts of those applying for export and import licenses, facilitating international trade among countries while doing so.

8-4b Licensing

Licensing is an entry mode in which an agreement is formed that allows a foreign company to purchase the right to manufacture and sell a firm's products within a host country's market or a set of host countries' markets.[72] The licensor is normally paid a royalty on each unit produced and sold. The licensee takes the risks and makes the monetary investments in facilities for manufacturing, marketing, and distributing products. As a result, licensing is possibly the least costly form of international diversification. As with exporting, licensing is an attractive entry mode option for smaller firms, and potentially for newer firms as well.[73]

China, a country accounting for almost one-third of all cigarettes smoked worldwide, is obviously a huge market for this product. U.S. cigarette firms want to have a strong presence in China but have had trouble entering this market, largely because of successful lobbying by state-owned tobacco firms against such entry. Because of these conditions, cigarette manufacturer Philip Morris International (PMI) had an incentive to form a deal with these state-owned firms. Accordingly, PMI and the China National Tobacco Corporation (CNTC) completed a licensing agreement at the end of 2005. This agreement provides CNTC access to the most famous brand in the world, Marlboro.[74] Because it is a licensing agreement rather than a foreign direct investment by PMI, China maintains control of distribution. The Marlboro brand was launched at two Chinese manufacturing plants in 2008. The Chinese state-owned tobacco monopoly, as part of the agreement, also receives PMI's help through a joint venture in distributing its own brands in select foreign markets. The Chinese cigarettes have also been distributed in other countries such as the Czech Republic and Poland.[75]

Another potential benefit of licensing as an entry mode is the possibility of earning greater returns from product innovations by selling the firm's innovations in international markets as well as in the domestic market.[76] Firms can obtain a larger market for their innovative new products, which helps them to pay off the R&D costs to develop them and to earn a faster return on the innovations than if they only sell them in domestic markets. This is done with little risk and without additional investment costs.

Licensing also has disadvantages. For example, after a firm licenses its product or brand to another party, it has little control over selling and distribution. Developing licensing agreements that protect the interests of both parties, while supporting the relationship embedded within an agreement, helps prevent this potential disadvantage.[77] In addition, licensing provides the least potential returns because returns must be shared between the licensor and the licensee. Another disadvantage is that the international firm may learn the technology of the party with whom it formed an agreement and then produce and sell a similar competitive product after the licensing agreement expires. In a classic example, Komatsu first licensed much of its technology from International Harvester, Bucyrus-Erie, and Cummins Engine to compete against Caterpillar in the earthmoving equipment business. Komatsu then dropped these licenses and developed its own products using the technology it gained from the U.S. companies.[78] Because of potential disadvantages, the parties to a licensing arrangement should finalize an agreement only after they are convinced that both parties' best interests are protected.

8-4c   Strategic Alliances

Increasingly popular as an entry mode among firms using international strategies,[79] a *strategic alliance* finds a firm collaborating with another company in a different setting in order to enter one or more international markets.[80] Firms share the risks and the resources required to enter international markets when using strategic alliances.[81] Moreover, because partners bring their unique resources together for the purpose of working collaboratively, strategic alliances can facilitate developing new capabilities and possibly core competencies that may contribute to the firm's strategic competitiveness.[82] Indeed, developing and learning how to use new capabilities and/or competencies (particularly those related to technology) is often a key purpose for which firms use strategic alliances as an entry mode.[83] Firms should be aware that establishing trust between partners is critical for developing and managing technology-based capabilities while using strategic alliances.[84]

French-based Limagrain is the fourth largest seed company in the world through its subsidiary Vilmorin & Cie. An international agricultural cooperative group specializing in field seeds, vegetable seeds, and cereal products, part of Limagrain's strategy calls for it to continue to enter and compete in additional international markets. Limagrain is using strategic alliances as an entry mode. In 2011, the firm formed a strategic alliance with the Brazilian seed company Sementes Guerra in Brazil. The joint venture is named Limagrain Guerra do Brasil. Corn is the focus of the joint venture between these companies. Guerra is a family-owned company engaged in seed research; the production of corn, wheat, and soybeans; and the distribution of those products to farmers in Brazil and neighboring countries. Limagrain also had an earlier, successful joint venture with KWS in the United States. This venture, called AgReliant Genetics, focused primarily on corn and soybeans.[85]

Not all alliances formed for the purpose of entering international markets are successful.[86] Incompatible partners and conflict between the partners are primary reasons for failure when firms use strategic alliances as an entry mode. Another issue is that international strategic alliances are especially difficult to manage. Trust is an important aspect of alliances and must be carefully managed. The degree of trust between partners strongly influences alliance success. The probability of alliance success increases as the amount of trust between partners expands. Efforts to build trust are affected by at least four fundamental issues: the initial condition of the relationship, the negotiation process to arrive at an agreement, partner interactions, and external events.[87] Trust is also influenced by the country cultures involved and the relationships between the countries' governments (e.g., degree of political differences) where the firms in the alliance are home based.[88] Firms should be aware of these issues when trying to appropriately manage trust.

Research has shown that equity-based alliances, over which a firm has more control, are more likely to produce positive returns.[89] (We discuss equity-based and other types of strategic alliances in Chapter 9.) However, if trust is required to develop new capabilities through an alliance, equity positions can serve as a barrier to the necessary relationship building. Trust can be an especially important issue when firms have multiple partners supplying raw materials and/or services in their value chain (often referred to as outsourcing).[90] If conflict in a strategic alliance formed as an entry mode is not manageable, using acquisitions to enter international markets may be a better option.[91]

8-4d Acquisitions

When a firm acquires another company to enter an international market, it has completed a cross-border acquisition. Specifically, a *cross-border acquisition* is an entry mode through which a firm from one country acquires a stake in or purchases all of a firm located in another country.[92]

As free trade expands in global markets, firms throughout the world are completing a larger number of cross-border acquisitions. The ability of cross-border acquisitions to provide rapid access to new markets is a key reason for their growth. In fact, of the five entry modes, acquisitions often are the quickest means for firms to enter international markets.[93]

For example, two European supermarket chains have been seeking a merger which will have significant effects in the U.S. market. The proposed $29 billion merger between Ahold, the Dutch owner of the Stop and Shop and Giant chains in the United States, with Delhaize, the Belgian operator of American chains Food Lion and Hannaford, would give the merged Ahold-Delhaize combination a 4.6 percent share of the U.S. grocery market, making it the fourth-largest player by revenue. This would give the combined European-based firms a major footprint on the East Coast and over 2,000 stores in the United States. Ahold also owns Peapod, a large online grocer in the United States thus strengthening its stake in United States markets. Ahold owns the leading grocery chain in the Netherlands, Heijn, and has stores in Belgium and the Czech Republic. Delhaize owns its namesake store in Belgium, Alpha Beta chains in Greece, and other stores in Eastern Europe.[94]

LAURIE DIEFFEMBACQ/Getty Images

The CEOs of Ahold, Dick Boer (left), and Belgian rival Delhaize, Frans Mullerand Delhaize, shake hands prior to announcing the merger of these giant food distribution chains in a significant cross-border merger.

Interestingly, firms use cross-border acquisitions less frequently to enter markets where corruption affects business transactions and, hence, the use of international strategies. A firm's preference is to use joint ventures to enter markets in which corruption is an issue, rather than using acquisitions. (Discussed fully in Chapter 9, a joint venture is a type of strategic alliance in which two or more firms create a legally independent company and share their resources and capabilities to operate it.) However, these ventures fail more often, although this is less frequently the case for firms experienced with entering "corrupt" markets. When acquisitions are made in such countries, acquirers commonly pay smaller premiums to purchase firms.[95]

Although increasingly popular, acquisitions as an entry mode are not without costs, nor are they easy to successfully complete and operate. Cross-border acquisitions have some of the disadvantages of domestic acquisitions (see Chapter 7). In addition, they often require debt financing to complete, which carries an extra cost. Another issue for firms to consider is that negotiations for cross-border acquisitions can be exceedingly complex and are generally more complicated than are the negotiations associated with domestic acquisitions. Dealing with the legal and regulatory requirements in the target firm's country and obtaining appropriate information to negotiate an agreement are also frequent problems. Finally, the merging of the new firm into the acquiring firm is often more complex than is the case with domestic acquisitions. The firm completing the cross-border acquisition must deal not only with different corporate cultures, but also with potentially different social cultures and practices.[96] These differences make integrating the two firms after the acquisition more challenging because it is difficult to capture the potential synergy when integration is slowed or stymied because of cultural differences.[97] Therefore, while cross-border acquisitions are popular as an entry mode primarily because they provide rapid access to new markets, firms considering this option should be fully aware of the costs and risks associated with using it.

8-4e New Wholly Owned Subsidiary

A **greenfield venture** is an entry mode through which a firm invests directly in another country or market by establishing a new wholly owned subsidiary. The process of creating a greenfield venture is often complex and potentially costly, but this entry mode affords maximum control to the firm and has the greatest amount of potential to contribute to the firm's strategic competitiveness as it implements international strategies. This potential is especially true for firms with strong intangible capabilities that might be leveraged through a greenfield venture.[98] Moreover, having additional control over its operations in a foreign market is especially advantageous when the firm has proprietary technology.

Research also suggests that "wholly owned subsidiaries and expatriate staff are preferred" in service industries where "close contacts with end customers" and "high levels of professional skills, specialized know-how, and customization" are required.[99] Other research suggests that, as investments, greenfield ventures are used more prominently when the firm's business relies significantly on the quality of its capital-intensive manufacturing facilities. In contrast, cross-border acquisitions are more likely to be used as an entry mode when a firm's operations are human-capital intensive—for example, if a strong local union and high cultural distance (between the countries involved) would cause difficulty in transferring knowledge to a host nation through a greenfield venture.[100]

The risks associated with greenfield ventures are significant in that the costs of establishing a new business operation in a new country or market can be substantial. To support the operations of a newly established operation in a foreign country, the firm may have to acquire knowledge and expertise about the new market by hiring either host-country nationals, possibly from competitors, or through consultants, which can be costly.

A **greenfield venture** is an entry mode through which a firm invests directly in another country or market by establishing a new wholly owned subsidiary.

This new knowledge and expertise often is necessary to facilitate the building of new facilities, establishing distribution networks, and learning how to implement marketing strategies that can lead to competitive success in the new market.[101] Importantly, while taking these actions, the firm seeks to maintain control over the technology, marketing, and distribution of its products. Research also suggests that when the country risk is high, firms prefer to enter with joint ventures instead of greenfield investments. However, if firms have previous experience in a country, they prefer to use a wholly owned greenfield venture rather than a joint venture.[102]

China has been an attractive market for foreign retailers (e.g., Walmart) because of its large population, the growing economic capabilities of Chinese citizens, and the opening of the Chinese market to foreign firms. For example, by 2005 more than 300 foreign retailers had entered China, many of them using greenfield ventures. Of course, China is a unique environment, partly because of its culture, but more so because of the government control and intervention. Good relationships with local and national government officials are quite important to foreign firms' success in China. Because of these complexities and the challenges they present, foreign retailers' success in this market has been mixed despite the substantial opportunities that exist there. Expansion, however, is going to be more difficult, given how popular the online retailer Alibaba and its affiliates and competitors have become. Thus great care should be exercised when selecting the best mode for entering particular markets, as we discuss next.[103]

8-4f Dynamics of Mode of Entry

Several factors affect the firm's choice about how to enter international markets. Market entry is often achieved initially through exporting, which requires no foreign manufacturing expertise and investment only in distribution. Licensing can facilitate the product improvements necessary to enter foreign markets, as in the Komatsu example. Strategic alliances are a popular entry mode because they allow a firm to connect with an experienced partner already in the market. Partly because of this, geographically diversifying firms often use alliances in uncertain situations, such as an emerging economy where there is significant risk (e.g., Venezuela). However, if intellectual property rights in the emerging economy are not well protected, the number of firms in the industry is growing fast, and the need for global integration is high, other entry modes such as a joint venture (see Chapter 9) or a wholly owned subsidiary are preferred.[104] In the final analysis though, all three modes—export, licensing, and strategic alliance—can be effective means of initially entering new markets and for developing a presence in those markets.

Acquisitions, greenfield ventures, and sometimes joint ventures are used when firms want to establish a strong presence in an international market. Aerospace firms Airbus and Boeing have used joint ventures, especially in large markets, to facilitate entry, while military equipment firms such as Thales SA have used acquisitions to build a global presence. Japanese auto manufacturer Toyota has established a presence in the United States through both greenfield ventures and joint ventures. Because of Toyota's highly efficient manufacturing processes, the firm wants to maintain control over manufacturing when possible. As such, it is opening a new regional center to bring together supplier coordination and regional North American research in Michigan as well as opening a new North American headquarters facility in Texas.[105] Both acquisitions and greenfield ventures are likely to come at later stages in the development of a firm's international strategies.

Thus, to enter a global market, a firm selects the entry mode that is best suited to its situation. In some instances, the various options will be followed sequentially, beginning with exporting and eventually leading to greenfield ventures. In other cases, the firm may use several, but not all, of the different entry modes, each in different markets. The decision regarding which entry mode to use is primarily a result of the industry's competitive conditions; the country's situation and government policies; and the firm's unique set of resources, capabilities, and core competencies.

FEMSA, the large multibusiness Mexican firm, has been expanding its operations into multiple countries in recent years. Most of its expansion has been into other Latin American countries (where it better understands the culture and markets). A recent acquisition in Brazil has capped a series of acquisitions to become a powerhouse in bottling and distribution. In fact, FEMSA is Coca-Cola's largest bottler worldwide, including some operations in Asia. Its most common mode of entry has been acquisitions. It has considerable experience with acquisitions given that a large amount of its domestic growth has also come from acquisitions.[106]

8-5 Risks in an International Environment

International strategies are risky, particularly those that would cause a firm to become substantially more diversified in terms of geographic markets served. Firms entering markets in new countries encounter a number of complex institutional risks.[107] Political and economic risks cannot be ignored by firms using international strategies (see specific examples of political and economic risks in Figure 8.6).

8-5a Political Risks

Political risks "denote the probability of disruption of the operations of multinational enterprises by political forces or events whether they occur in host countries, home country, or result from changes in the international environment."[108] Possible disruptions to a firm's operations when seeking to implement its international strategy create numerous problems, including uncertainty created by government regulation; the existence of many, possibly conflicting, legal authorities or corruption; and the potential nationalization of private assets.[109] Firms investing in other countries, when implementing their

Figure 8.6 Risks in the International Environment

international strategy, may have concerns about the stability of the national government and the effects of unrest and government instability on their investments or assets.[110] A recent study also suggests that political risk in one country often spreads to others, as in the Arab Spring revolutions among many mid-eastern countries.[111] To deal with these concerns, firms should conduct a political risk analysis of the countries or regions they may enter using one of the five entry modes. Through political risk analysis, the firm examines potential sources and factors of noncommercial disruptions of their foreign investments and the operations flowing from them.[112] However, occasionally firms might use political (institutional) weaknesses as an opportunity to transfer activities or practices that stakeholders see as undesirable for their operations in the home country to a new market so they can continue earning returns on these questionable practices.[113]

FIFA, the international soccer federation which sponsors world cup soccer matches along with its regional and country affiliates, have come under heavy scrutiny for possible corrupt practices, as illustrated in the Strategic Focus. Much of the alleged corruption that has taken place has been indirectly supported by the nature of the governments and institutions in which soccer is popular, especially in less developed countries. Bribes were alleged to have been paid for Africa to receive the World Cup and the recent decisions by FIFA to host the games in Russian and Qatar in 2018 and 2022 have come under question.[114] Many of the countries, for example Brazil and Paraguay, are seeking to overhaul their country soccer regulating bodies because of the scandal.[115]

Russia has experienced a relatively high level of institutional instability in the years following its revolutionary transition to a more democratic government. In an effort to regain more central control and reduce the decentralized chaos, Russian leaders took actions such as prosecuting powerful private firm executives, seeking to gain state control of firm assets, and not approving some foreign acquisitions of Russian businesses. The initial institutional instability, followed by the actions of the central government, caused some firms to delay or avoid significant foreign direct investment in Russia. The riskiness of the situation has worsened as Russia has taken the Crimea from Ukraine and used proxy rebels to fight in Eastern Ukraine. "The resulting U.S. and European Union sanctions, in conjunction with falling oil prices, sent the Russian economy into a tailspin. The ruble lost half its value, and, despite a muted recovery in oil and a boost to industry from the devaluation, Russia's economy is set to shrink by 2.7 percent this year [2015], according to a World Bank report."[116]

8-5b Economic Risks

Economic risks include fundamental weaknesses in a country or region's economy with the potential to cause adverse effects on firms' efforts to successfully implement their international strategies. As illustrated in the example of Russian institutional instability and property rights, political risks and economic risks are interdependent. If firms cannot protect their intellectual property, they are highly unlikely to use a means of entering a foreign market that involves significant and direct investments. Therefore, countries need to create, sustain, and enforce strong intellectual property rights in order to attract foreign direct investment.[117]

In emerging economies, one of the significant economic risks is the availability of important infrastructure to allow large industry players, such as miners, to have sufficient electrical power in national grids to meet their power usage requirements. Often, inefficient, state-owned electric power producers are forced to run intermittent blackouts, which is devastating for continuous process manufacturing and refining such as found in the mining industry. South Africa used to have a reliable electrical power grid. However the state-owned electrical utility, Eskom Holdings Ltd., has neglected to build new power plants and sufficiently maintain current operating generating plants.

The Global Soccer Industry and the Effect of the FIFA Scandal

The Fédération Internationale de Football Association (FIFA) was founded in Paris in 1904 and was initially comprised of only European nations. By World War II, FIFA had added a few South American members. Newly independent states in Africa, Asia, and the Caribbean joined later. However it continued to be governed "as though it was an exclusive European club"—until 1974 when João Havelange, a Brazilian, won election as FIFA's president. Havelange was able to transform the organization and expand the World Cup competition to teams from nations outside Europe and South America and made the tournament a major money making enterprise. With the amount of exposure and money involved, companies desire sponsorship rights because of the advertising potential. Adidas AG and Coca-Cola were original sponsors. Havelange also oversaw significant increases in revenue from television rights. In the process, Havelange was alleged to have participated in much corruption and eventually was suspected of amassing $50 million in bribes.

Havelange facilitated the election of Sepp Blatter who became FIFA president in 1998 and continued to follow Havelange's approach to politics. After FIFA became a worldwide organization, especially in developing countries in Latin America, Africa, and the Caribbean, more allegations of corruption surfaced. One analyst suggested that "FIFA could not have developed soccer in poorer countries without corrupt practices." Of course, there has also been corruption in more developed countries in the United Kingdom and other places, including the United States, although normally not through blatant bribery as has been discovered over time by FIFA officials. On May 27, 2015, the United States Department of Justice and the FBI announced a long list of indictments and simultaneous arrests of FIFA officials were made at the Zurich FIFA meetings in Switzerland. Several days after the indictment, though he was not officially indicted, Blatter stepped down from his long presidency.

In order to understand the amount of exposure and money involved, an estimated one billion people watched at least some of the 2010 World Cup Final. In the same year the National Football League's Super Bowl accumulated only 114.4 million worldwide viewers. Given the massive exposure, it is no wonder that sponsors as well as television and media outlets want to be involved. However, sponsors do not want to be associated with a large scandal. Coca-Cola, Adidas, Nike, McDonald's, and Hyundai Motor were all said to be "deeply concerned" about the FBI allegations and the indictments brought recently by the United States Department of Justice against a growing list of regional and country level

FIFA-affiliated executives who were identified as having participated in the alleged corruption.

Many of the sponsors are cautious about supporting an organization that has been as tainted politically as has FIFA. Apparently, the way the corruption has been pursued is through intermediaries who are paid exorbitant amounts for contracts that they helped to establish; then these intermediaries funnel the bribes to the leaders of the regional and country FIFA related associations. For example, in order for Nike to get a contract in the soccer-crazed country of Brazil, it paid a sports marketing agency, Traffic Brazil, $30 million between 1996 and 1999 which Traffic Brazil used, in part, for bribes and kick-backs. This allowed Nike to sign a 10-year, $160 million agreement to become a co-sponsor of the CBF, the Brazilian soccer confederation. Nike's strategic intent for the deal was to better compete with its chief overseas rival, Adidas. In 2014, the World Cup was held in Brazil, and Nike had $2.3 billion in sales of soccer products, an annual increase of 21 percent, compared with $2.29 billion in sales for Adidas, which was up 20 percent over its previous year. These figures illustrate how strong the incentives are for sponsors as well as for media outlets to participate; the advertising potential and selling opportunities are enormous for those involved.

VALERIANO DI DOMENICO/Getty Images

Former FIFA President, Sepp Blatter, speaking during a press conference at the headquarters of the world's football governing body in Zurich shortly before stepping down from his FIFA leadership position.

However, because of the weak institutional infrastructure in many countries around the world where the game of soccer is played, there is opportunity for corruption. Apparently, many involved in the FIFA infrastructure globally, regionally, and within specific countries have taken advantage of this opportunity. For example, Paraguay has been the headquarters for the Latin American regional confederation known as CONMEBOL. CONMEBOL has been centered in Paraguay since 1998 when Nicolás Leoz, a Paraguayan business man and president of the Latin American Confederation, negotiated to have the confederation headquartered there by having the Paraguay parliament secure prosecutorial immunity for the organization. In essence, this gave the federation license to act in ways that would protect it against local law enforcement officials, just as a local embassy would have exemption from prosecution in a particular foreign country. As such, this allowed the local confederation to pursue deals under the table. Leoz was charged in the FIFA indictments by the U.S. Department of Justice, along with 13 other FIFA officials, of bribery and money laundering schemes related to funds he received from sports marketing firms during his tenure at CONMEBOL. Interestingly, following the indictment, Paraguay's congress moved quickly to repeal the prosecutorial immunity for the CONMEBOL federation.

Likewise, many other legal and investigative organizations in Switzerland, Latin America, and around the world, including INTERPOL, an international investigation organization, have begun to initiate their own enquiries. Many fans in the soccer world have been excited about these indictments because many have felt that the corruption was hurting the game. People were profiting in illegal ways that created corruption throughout many organizations associated with the game of soccer. This Strategic Focus outlines a main danger of working in countries where many participate in corrupt practices which are indirectly sponsored by the government. This is not to say officials in more developed governments are not also corrupt, but the rule of law is not as strong in many developing countries.

Sources: 2015, A timeline of the FIFA scandal, *LA Times*, www.latimes.com, June 2; P. Blake, 2015, FIFA scandal: Why the US is policing a global game, *BBC News*, www.bbc.com, May 28; M. Futterman, A. Viswanatha, & C. M. Matthews, 2015, Soccer's geyser of cash, *Wall Street Journal*, May 28, A1, A10; S. Germano, 2015, Nike is cooperating with investigators, *Wall Street Journal*, May 28, A11; P. Keirnan, R. Jelmayer, & L. Magalhaes, 2015, Soccer boss learned ropes from his Brazilian mentor, *Wall Street Journal*, May 30–31, A4; K. Malic, 2015, The corruption rhetoric of the FIFA scandal, *New York Times*, www.nytimes.com, June 16; S. S. Munoz, 2015, FIFA pro shows soccer state within a state, *Wall Street Journal*, June 20–21, A7; S. Varinca, T. Micklel, & J. Robinson, 2015, Scandal pressures soccer's sponsors, *Wall Street Journal*, May 29, A1, A8; A. Viswanatha, S. Germano, & P. Kowsmann, 2015, U.S. probes Nike Brazil money, *Wall Street Journal*, June 13–14, B1, B4; M. Yglesias & J. Stromberg, 2015, FIFA's huge corruption and bribery scandal, explained, *VOX*, www.vox.com, June 3; C. Zillman, 2015, Here's how major FIFA sponsors are reacting to the scandal, *Fortune*, www.fortune.com, May 28.

As such, power outages have been intermittent and lasting up to 12 hours. This has caused a significant decrease in productivity for the dominant industry, mining, which produces 60 percent of South Africa's exports. The mining industry uses 15 percent of the country's electricity, and, as such, Eskom negotiates with each large commercial customer to reduce its power input at peak times. ArcelorMittal S.A., a large steel firm, has been losing $130,000 an hour because it has had to dial back its power usage "almost daily." DRDGOLD's gold production dropped 3 percent in the last 3 months of 2014 because of power outages. As this example suggests, infrastructure can be a significant economic risk in emerging or partially developed economies such as South Africa.[118]

Another economic risk is the perceived security risk of a foreign firm acquiring firms that have key natural resources or firms that may be considered strategic in regard to intellectual property. For instance, many Chinese firms have been buying natural resource firms in Australia and Latin America. as well as manufacturing assets in the United States.

Bloomberg/Getty Images

Darkness surrounding residential homes due to blackout by Eskom Holdings SOC Ltd. in the Troyeville suburb of Johannesburg, South Africa, in 2014.

This has made the governments of the key resource firms nervous about such strategic assets falling under the control of state-owned Chinese firms.[119] Terrorism has also been of concern. Indonesia has difficulty competing for investment against China and India, countries that are viewed as having fewer security risks.

As noted earlier, the differences and fluctuations in the value of currencies is among the foremost economic risks of using an international strategy.[120] This is especially true as the level of the firm's geographic diversification increases to the point where the firm is trading in a large number of currencies. The value of the dollar relative to other currencies can affect the value of the international assets and earnings of U.S. firms. For example, an increase in the value of the U.S. dollar can reduce the value of U.S. multinational firms' international assets and earnings in other countries. Furthermore, the value of different currencies can, at times, dramatically affect a firm's competitiveness in global markets because of its effect on the prices of goods manufactured in different countries. An increase in the value of the dollar can harm U.S. firms' exports to international markets because of the price differential of the products. For example, Johnson & Johnson recently reported that the firm's international results were impacted negatively by the increased value of the dollar, while Unilever's results were positive due to the decreased value of the euro relative to the dollar.[121] Thus, government oversight and control of economic and financial capital, as well as corporate governance rules in a country, affect not only local economic activity, but also foreign investments in the country.[122]

8-6 Strategic Competitiveness Outcomes

As previously discussed, international strategies can result in three basic benefits (increased market size; economies of scale and learning; and location advantages) for firms. These basic benefits are gained when the firm successfully manages political, economic, and other institutional risks while implementing its international strategies. In turn, these benefits are critical to the firm's efforts to achieve strategic competitiveness (as measured by improved performance and enhanced innovation—see Figure 8.1).

Overall, the degree to which firms achieve strategic competitiveness through international strategies is expanded or increased when they successfully implement an international diversification strategy. As an extension or elaboration of international strategy, an **international diversification strategy** is a strategy through which a firm expands the sales of its goods or services across the borders of global regions and countries into a potentially large number of geographic locations or markets. Instead of entering one or just a few markets, the international diversification strategy finds firms using international business-level and international corporate-level strategies for the purpose of entering multiple regions and markets in order to sell their products.

8-6a International Diversification and Returns

Evidence suggests numerous reasons for firms to use an international diversification strategy,[123] meaning that international diversification should be related positively to a firm's performance as measured by the returns it earns on its investments. Research has shown that as international diversification increases, a firm's returns decrease initially but then increase quickly as it learns how to manage the increased geographic diversification it has created.[124] In fact, the stock market is particularly sensitive to investments in international markets. Firms that are broadly diversified into multiple international markets usually achieve the most positive stock returns, especially when they diversify geographically into core business areas.[125]

An **international diversification strategy** is a strategy through which a firm expands the sales of its goods or services across the borders of global regions and countries into a potentially large number of geographic locations or markets.

Many factors contribute to the positive effects of international diversification, such as private versus government ownership, potential economies of scale and experience, location advantages, increased market size, and the opportunity to stabilize returns. The stabilization of returns through international diversification helps reduce a firm's overall risk.[126] Large, well-established firms and entrepreneurial ventures can both achieve these positive outcomes by successfully implementing an international diversification strategy. As described in an earlier example, FEMSA was using an acquisition strategy to increase its international diversification. FEMSA's financial results suggest that it has achieved positive returns from this strategy.

8-6b   Enhanced Innovation

In Chapter 1, we indicated that developing new technology is at the heart of strategic competitiveness. As noted in our discussion of the determinants of national advantage (see Figure 8.3), a nation's competitiveness depends, in part, on the capacity of its industries to innovate. Eventually and inevitably, competitors outperform firms that fail to innovate. Therefore, the only way for individual nations and individual firms to sustain a competitive advantage is to upgrade it continually through innovation.[127]

An international diversification strategy creates the potential for firms to achieve greater returns on their innovations (through larger or more numerous markets) while reducing the often substantial risks of R&D investments. Additionally, international diversification may be necessary to generate the resources required to sustain a large-scale R&D operation. An environment of rapid technological obsolescence makes it difficult to invest in new technology and the capital-intensive operations necessary to compete in such an environment. Firms operating solely in domestic markets may find such investments difficult because of the length of time required to recoup the original investment. However, diversifying into a number of international markets improves a firm's ability to appropriate additional returns from innovation before domestic competitors can overcome the initial competitive advantage created by the innovation.[128] In addition, firms moving into international markets are exposed to new products and processes. If they learn about those products and processes and integrate this knowledge into their operations, further innovation can be developed. To incorporate the learning into their own R&D processes, firms must manage those processes effectively in order to absorb and use the new knowledge to create further innovations.[129] For a number of reasons then, international strategies and certainly an international diversification strategy provide incentives for firms to innovate.[130]

The relationship among international geographic diversification, innovation, and returns is complex. Some level of performance is necessary to provide the resources the firm needs to diversify geographically; in turn, geographic diversification provides incentives and resources to invest in R&D. Effective R&D should enhance the firm's returns, which then provide more resources for continued geographic diversification and investment in R&D.[131] Of course, the returns generated from these relationships increase through effective managerial practices. Evidence suggests that more culturally diverse top management teams often have a greater knowledge of international markets and their idiosyncrasies, but their orientation to expand internationally can be affected by the nature of their incentives.[132] Moreover, managing the business units of a geographically diverse multinational firm requires skill, not only in managing a decentralized set of businesses, but also coordinating diverse points of view emerging from businesses located in different countries and regions. Firms able to do this increase the likelihood of outperforming their rivals.[133]

8-7 The Challenge of International Strategies

Effectively using international strategies creates basic benefits and contributes to the firm's strategic competitiveness. However, for several reasons, attaining these positive outcomes is difficult.

8-7a Complexity of Managing International Strategies

Pursuing international strategies, particularly an international diversification strategy, typically leads to growth in a firm's size and the complexity of its operations. In turn, larger size and greater operational complexity make a firm more difficult to manage. At some point, size and complexity either cause the firm to become virtually unmanageable or increase the cost of its management beyond the value created using international strategies. Different cultures and institutional practices (e.g., those associated with governmental agencies) that are part of the countries in which a firm competes when using an international strategy also can create difficulties.[134]

Firms have to build on their capabilities and other advantages to overcome the challenges encountered in international markets. For example, some firms from emerging economies that hold monopolies in their home markets can invest the resources gained there to enhance their competitiveness in international markets (because they don't have to be concerned about competitors in home markets).[135] The key is for firms to overcome the various liabilities of foreignness regardless of their source.

8-7b Limits to International Expansion

Learning how to effectively manage an international strategy improves the likelihood of achieving positive outcomes such as enhanced performance. However, at some point, the degree of geographic and possibly product diversification the firm's international strategies bring about causes the returns from using the strategies to level off and eventually become negative.[136]

There are several reasons for the limits to the positive effects of the diversification associated with international strategies. First, greater geographic dispersion across country borders increases the costs of coordination between units and the distribution of products. This is especially true when firms have multiple locations in countries that have diverse subnational institutions. Second, trade barriers, logistical costs, cultural diversity, and other differences by country (e.g., access to raw materials and different employee skill levels) greatly complicate the implementation of an international strategy.[137]

Institutional and cultural factors can be strong barriers to the transfer of a firm's core competencies from one market to another.[138] Marketing programs often have to be redesigned and new distribution networks established when firms expand into new markets. In addition, firms may encounter different labor costs and capital expenses. In general, it becomes increasingly difficult to effectively implement, manage, and control a firm's international operations with increases in geographic diversity.[139]

The amount of diversification in a firm's international operations that can be managed varies from company to company and is affected by managers' abilities to deal with ambiguity and complexity. The problems of central coordination and integration are mitigated if the firm's international operations compete in friendly countries that are geographically close and have cultures similar to its own country's culture. In that case, the firm is likely to encounter fewer trade barriers, the laws and customs are better understood, and the product is easier to adapt to local markets.[140] For example, U.S. firms may find it less difficult to expand their operations into Mexico, Canada, and Western European countries than into Asian countries.

The relationships between the firm using an international strategy and the governments in the countries in which the firm is competing can also be constraining.[141] The reason for this is that the differences in host countries' governmental policies and practices can be substantial, creating a need for the focal firm to learn how to manage what can be a large set of different enforcement policies and practices. At some point, the differences create too many problems for the firm to be successful. Using strategic alliances is another way firms can deal with this limiting factor. Partnering with companies in different countries allows the foreign-entering firm to rely on its partner to help deal with local laws, rules, regulations, and customs. But these partnerships are not risk free and managing them tends to be difficult.[142]

SUMMARY

- The use of international strategies is increasing. Multiple factors and conditions are influencing the increasing use of these strategies, including opportunities to

  - extend a product's life cycle

  - gain access to critical raw materials, sometimes including relatively inexpensive labor

  - integrate a firm's operations on a global scale to better serve customers in different countries

  - better serve customers whose needs appear to be more alike today as a result of global communications media and the Internet's capabilities to inform

  - meet increasing demand for goods and services that is surfacing in emerging markets

- When used effectively, international strategies yield three basic benefits: increased market size, economies of scale and learning, and location advantages. Firms use international business-level and international corporate-level strategies to geographically diversify their operations.

- International business-level strategies are usually grounded in one or more home-country advantages. Research suggests that there are four determinants of national advantage: factors of production; demand conditions; related and supporting industries; and patterns of firm strategy, structure, and rivalry.

- There are three types of international corporate-level strategies. A multidomestic strategy focuses on competition within each country in which the firm competes. Firms using a multidomestic strategy decentralize strategic and operating decisions to the business units operating in each country, so that each unit can tailor its products to local conditions. A global strategy assumes more standardization of products across country boundaries; therefore, a competitive strategy is centralized and controlled by the home office. Commonly, large multinational firms, particularly those with multiple diverse products being sold in many different markets, use a

multidomestic strategy with some product lines and a global strategy with others.

- A transnational strategy seeks to integrate characteristics of both multidomestic and global strategies for the purpose of being able to simultaneously emphasize local responsiveness and global integration.

- Two global environmental trends—liability of foreignness and regionalization—are influencing firms' choices of international strategies as well as their implementation. Liability of foreignness challenges firms to recognize that distance between their domestic market and international markets affects how they compete. Some firms choose to concentrate their international strategies on regions (e.g., the EU and NAFTA) rather than on individual country markets.

- Firms can use one or more of five entry modes to enter international markets. Exporting, licensing, strategic alliances, acquisitions, and new wholly owned subsidiaries, often referred to as greenfield ventures, are the five entry modes. Most firms begin with exporting or licensing because of their lower costs and risks. Later they often use strategic alliances and acquisitions as well. The most expensive and risky means of entering a new international market is establishing a new wholly owned subsidiary (greenfield venture). On the other hand, such subsidiaries provide the advantages of maximum control by the firm and, if successful, the greatest returns. Large, geographically diversified firms often use most or all five entry modes across different markets when implementing international strategies.

- Firms encounter a number of risks when implementing international strategies. The two major categories of risks firms need to understand and address when diversifying geographically through international strategies are political risks (risks concerned with the probability that a firm's operations will be disrupted by political forces or events, whether they occur in the firm's domestic market or in the markets the firm has entered to implement its international strategies) and economic risks (risks resulting from fundamental weaknesses in a country's or a region's economy with the potential to adversely affect a firm's ability to implement its international strategies).

■ Successful use of international strategies (especially an international diversification strategy) contributes to a firm's strategic competitiveness in the form of improved performance and enhanced innovation. International diversification facilitates innovation in a firm because it provides a larger market to gain greater and faster returns from investments in innovation. In addition, international diversification can generate the resources necessary to sustain a large-scale R&D program.

■ In general, international diversification helps to achieve above-average returns, but this assumes that the

diversification is effectively implemented and that the firm's international operations are well managed. International diversification provides greater economies of scope and learning which, along with greater innovation, help produce above-average returns.

■ A firm using international strategies to pursue strategic competitiveness often experiences complex challenges that must be overcome. Some limits also constrain the ability to manage international expansion effectively. International diversification increases coordination and distribution costs, and management problems are exacerbated by trade barriers, logistical costs, and cultural diversity, among other factors.

KEY TERMS

global strategy 247
greenfield venture 256
international strategy 239

international diversification strategy 262
multidomestic strategy 246
transnational strategy 248

REVIEW QUESTIONS

1. What incentives influence firms to use international strategies?

2. What are the three basic benefits firms can achieve by successfully using an international strategy?

3. What four factors are determinants of national advantage and serve as a basis for international business-level strategies?

4. What are the three international corporate-level strategies? What are the advantages and disadvantages associated with these individual strategies?

5. What are some global environmental trends affecting the choice of international strategies, particularly international corporate-level strategies?

6. What five entry modes do firms consider as paths to use to enter international markets? What is the typical sequence in which firms use these entry modes?

7. What are political risks and what are economic risks? How should firms approach dealing with these risks?

8. What are the strategic competitiveness outcomes firms can reach through international strategies, and particularly through an international diversification strategy?

9. What are two important issues that can potentially affect a firm's ability to successfully use international strategies?

Mini-Case

An International Strategy Powers ABB's Future

ABB, headquartered in Zurich, Switzerland, is a major competitor in the power and automation technologies industries across the major markets globally. It has 140,000 employees operating in almost 100 countries. In fact, it has five major businesses—power products, power systems, discrete automation, low voltage products, and process

automation. It operates in eight major regions: (1) Northern Europe, (2) Central Europe, (3) the Mediterranean, (4) North America, (5) South America, (6) India, the Middle East, and Africa, (7) North Asia, and (8) South Asia. Over time, ABB has been a successful company using its geographic diversification across the globe to its advantage.

It also exemplifies the difficulty of managing an international strategy and operations. For example, its power systems business has experienced performance problems in recent years due to poor performance in some countries due primarily to the economy downturn. Notwithstanding the difficulty of managing in emerging economies, much of its growth is focused on improving country infrastructure such as power systems and grids. In 2014, the firm announced that the Asia, Middle East, and Africa (AMEA) region currently contributes about 37 percent of ABB's total revenue, or about $15.3 billion, and "emerging markets were planned to contribute to two-thirds of the forecast growth between 2015 and 2020."

In recent years, most of ABB's entries to new markets and expansions in existing markets have come from acquisitions of existing businesses in those markets. Recently, it acquired Siemens' solar energy business, Power-One, and U.S.-based Los Gatos Research, a manufacturer of gas analyzers used in environmental monitoring and research. The purchase of Power-One represents a major risk as the solar power industry is in a downturn. Yet some analysts predict a brighter future for the industry over the long term. ABB also uses other modes of entry and expansion, exemplified by the 2013 joint venture with China's Jiangsu Jinke Smart Electric Company to design, manufacture, and provide follow-up service on high voltage instrument transformers. It also recently procured major contracts for business in Brazil and South Africa.

Partly due to the global economic recession that began in 2008, recent weak economic performance, and some poor expansion decisions, ABB's performance has been weaker than expected. As a result, the CEO and chief technology officer announced their resignations in 2013. Despite these changes, ABB is a highly respected global brand, and, after its recent changes (e.g., closing some country operations), its revenues and earnings have started to rise. These positive changes have been largely attributed to the success of its North American businesses. Its acquisitions of Baldor (maker of industrial motors) in 2010 and Thomas & Betts in 2012 greatly enhanced its North American operations and revenues. It has also had success in manufacturing equipment and robots with its robotics business headquartered in the United States. It is even moving to help small companies, such as ones in the beer industry, to automate their production processes. Therefore, even in turbulent times, ABB's future looks bright.

Sources: 2015, About ABB, www.abb.com, accessed on June 18; J. R. Hagerty, 2015, Meet the new robots, *Wall Street Journal*, June 3, R1–R2; 2104, Emerging markets key to ABB's growth strategy, *MEED: Middle East Economic Digest*, September 12, 14; J. Revill, 2014, Robots keep the beer flowing. *Wall Street* Journal, December 27, B4; 2013, ABB procures contract in Brazil, *Zacks Equity Research*, www.zacks.com, May 14; 2013, ABB's South African project, *Zacks Equity Research*, www.zacks.com, May 13; P. Winters, 2013, ABB loses Banerjee after Hogan's decision to step down, *Bloomberg Businessweek*, www.businessweek.com, May 13; J. Revill & A. Morse, 2013, ABB CEO to resign, *Wall Street Journal*, www.wsj.com, May 10; 2013, ABB strengthens footprints in China, *Zacks Equity Research*, www.zacks.com, May 10; J. Revill, 2013, ABB buys US gas analyzer company Los Gatos Research, *Wall Street Journal*, www.wsj.com, May 3; 2013, ABB/Power-One: Shining example, *Financial Times*, www.ft.com, April 22; W. Pentland, 2013, ABB gambles big on solar power, *Forbes*, www.forbes.com, April 22; M. Scott, 2013, ABB to buy Power-One for $1 billion, *New York Times Dealbook*, http://dealbook.nytimes.com, April 22; J. Shotter, 2013, ABB boosted by US ventures, *Financial Times*, www.ft.com, February 14; J. Shotter, 2012, ABB overhauls power systems division, *Financial Times*, www.ft.com, December 14.

Case Discussion Questions

1. What are the dominant reason's for ABB to enter into international markets?

2. Which corporate international strategy would you classify ABB as using? Explain your answer.

3. Why has ABB used acquisitions and joint ventures as dominant entry modes in international markets?

4. What are the main political and economic risks that ABB must deal with given that it has a strong focus on entering emerging economies?

5. What are the significant organizational complexities that ABB encounters as it tries to manage its international strategy?

NOTES

1. C. G. Asmussen & N. J. Foss, 2014, Competitive advantage and the existence of the multinational corporation: Earlier research and the role of frictions, *Global Strategy Journal*, 4: 49–54; C. N. Pitellis & D. J. Teece, 2012, Cross-border market co-creation, dynamic capabilities and the entrepreneurial theory of the multinational enterprise. In D. J. Teece (ed.), *Strategy, Innovation and the Theory of the Firm*, Cheltenham, U.K.: Edward Elgar, 341–364; M. J. Nieto & A. Rodriguez, 2011, Offshoring of R&D: Looking abroad to improve innovation performance, *Journal of International Business Studies*, 42: 345–361.

2. S. K. Majumdar & A. Bhattacharjee, 2014, Firms, markets, and the state: Institutional change and manufacturing sector profitability variances in India, *Organization Science*, 25: 509–528; R. M. Holmes, T. Miller, M. A. Hitt, & M. P. Salmador, 2013, The interrelationship among informal institutions, formal institutions and inward foreign direct investment, *Journal of Management*, 39: 531–566.

3. A. Gaur & A. Delios, 2015, International diversification of emerging market firms: The role of ownership structure and group affiliation, *Management International Review*, 55: 235–253; J.-L. Arregle, L. Naldi, M. Nordqvist, & M. A. Hitt, 2012, Internationalization of family-controlled firms: A study of the effects of external involvement in governance, *Entrepreneurship Theory and Practice*, 36: 1115–1143; M. A. Hitt, L. Tihanyi, T. Miller, & B. Connelly, 2006, International diversification: Antecedents, outcomes and moderators, *Journal of Management*, 32: 831–867.

4. H. Kim, R. E. Hoskisson, & S. Lee, 2015, Why strategic factor markets matter: 'New' multinationals' geographic diversification and firm profitability, *Strategic Management Journal*, 36: 518–536; M. F. Wiersema & H. P. Bowen, 2011, The relationship between international diversification and firm performance: Why it remains a puzzle, *Global Strategy Journal*, 1: 152–170.

5. R. Vernon, 1996, International investment and international trade in the product cycle, *Quarterly Journal of Economics*, 80: 190–207.

6. 2015, Our strategy, Rio Tinto homepage, www.riotinto.com, accessed on June 16.

7. J. Hookway, Vietnam's mobile revolution, *Wall Street Journal*, June 15, B4.

8. M. J. Mol & C. Brewster, 2014, The outsourcing strategy of local and multinational firms: A supply base perspective, *Global Strategy Journal*, 4: 20–34; J. Li, Y. Li, & D. Shapiro, 2012, Knowledge seeking and outward FDI of emerging market firms: The moderating effect of inward FDI, *Global Strategy Journal*, 2: 277–295.

9. J. P. Murmann, S. Z. Ozdemir, & D. Sardana, 2015, The role of home country demand in the internationalization of new ventures, *Research Policy*, 44: 1207–1225; K. E. Meyer, R. Mudambi, & R. Nanula, 2011, Multinational enterprises and local contexts: The opportunities and challenges of multiple embeddedness, *Journal of Management Studies*, 48: 235–252.

10. 2015, Our stores, Carrefour Group homepage, www.carrefour.com, June 18.

11. D. Gray, 2014, What Tesco can learn from Carrefour, *Stores Magazine*, September, 66.

12. V. Mallet, 2014, Narendra Modi prepares to raise India's FDI limits, *Financial Times*, www.ft.com, May 30; T. R. Annamalai & A. Deshmukh, 2011, Venture capital and private equity in India: An analysis of investments and exits, *Journal of Indian Business Research*, 3: 6–21.

13. S. L. Fourné, J. P. Jansen, & T. M. Mom, 2014, Strategic agility in MNEs: Managing tensions to capture opportunities across emerging and established markets, *California Management Review*, 56(3): 13–38; R. Ramamurti, 2012, What is really different about emerging market multinationals? *Global Strategy Journal*, 2: 41–47.

14. P. Regnér & J. Edman, 2014, MNE institutional advantage: How subunits shape, transpose and evade host country institutions, *Journal of International Business Studies*, 45: 275–302; M. Carney, E. R. Gedajlovic, P. M. A. R. Heugens, M. van Essen, & J. van Oosterhout, 2011, Business group affiliation, performance, context, and strategy: A meta-analysis, *Academy of Management Journal*, 54: 437–460; B. Elango, 2009, Minimizing effects of "liability of foreignness": Response strategies of foreign firm in the United States, *Journal of World Business*, 44: 51–62.

15. 2013, Midrange growth strategy starting from fiscal year 2013, News Release, www.takeda.com, May 9; K. Inagaki & J. Osawa, 2011, Takeda, Toshiba make $16 billion M&A push, *Wall Street Journal*, www.wsj.com, May 20; K. Iagaki, 2011, Takeda buys Nycomed for $14 billion, *Wall Street Journal*, www.wsj.com, May 20.

16. K. Kalasin, P. Dussauge, & M. Rivera-Santos, 2014, the expansion of emerging economy firms into advanced markets: The influence of intentional path-breaking change, *Global Strategy Journal*, 4: 75–103; A. Verbeke & W. Yuan, 2013, The drivers of multinational enterprise subsidiary entrepreneurship in China: A resource-based view perspective, *Journal of Management Studies*, 50: 236–258; S. B. Choi, S. H. Lee, & C. Williams, 2011, Ownership and firm innovation in transition economy: Evidence from China, *Research Policy*, 40: 441–452.

17. 2015, Corporate, Ford Motor Company, www.ford.com, accessed June 19; N. E. Boudette, 2011, Ford forecasts sharp gains from Asian sales, *Wall Street Journal*, www.wsj.com, June 8.

18. D. McCann, 2014, One Ford, One Finance. *CFO*, July, 16–17.

19. R. Erkelens, B. Hooff, M. Huysman, & P. Vlaar, 2015, Learning from locally embedded knowledge: Facilitating organizational learning in geographically dispersed settings, *Global Strategy Journal*, 5: 177–197; A. H. Kirka, G. T. Hult, S. Deligonul, M. Z. Perry, & S. T. Cavusgil, 2012, A multilevel examination of the drivers of firm multinationality: A meta-analysis, *Journal of Management*, 38: 502–530; L. Nachum & S. Song, 2011, The MNE as a portfolio: Interdependencies in MNE growth trajectory, *Journal of International Business Studies*, 42: 381–405.

20. M. Kim, 2015, Geographic scope, isolating mechanisms, and value appropriation, *Strategic Management Journal*, in press; G. Qian, T. A. Khoury, M. W. Peng, & Z. Qian, 2010, The performance implications of intra- and inter-regional geographic diversification, *Strategic Management Journal*, 31: 1018–1030; H. Zou & P. N. Ghauri, 2009, Learning through international acquisitions: The process of knowledge acquisition in China, *Management International Review*, 48: 207–226.

21. R. Sambharya & J. Lee, 2014, Renewing dynamic capabilities globally: An empirical study of the world's largest MNCs, *Management International Review*, 54: 137–169; Y. Zhang, H. Li, Y. Li, & L.-A. Zhou, 2010, FDI spillovers in an emerging market: The role of foreign firms' country origin diversity and domestic firms' absorptive capacity, *Strategic Management Journal*, 31: 969–989; J. Song & J. Shin, 2008, The paradox of technological capabilities: A study of knowledge sourcing from host countries of overseas R&D operations, *Journal of International Business Studies*, 39: 291–303.

22. N. Hashai & P. J. Buckley, 2014, Is competitive advantage a necessary condition for the emergence of the multinational enterprise? *Global Strategy Journal*, 4: 35–48; F. J. Froese, 2013, Work values of the next generation of business leaders in Shanghai, Tokyo and Seoul, *Asia Pacific Journal of Management*, 30: 297–315.

23. F. Lo & F. Lin, 2015, Advantage transfer on location choice and subsidiary performance, *Journal of Business Research*, 68: 1527–1531; A. Gambardella & M. S. Giarratana, 2010, Localized knowledge

spillovers and skill-based performance, *Strategic Entrepreneurship Journal*, 4: 323–339; A. M. Rugman & A. Verbeke, 2009, A new perspective on the regional and global strategies of multinational services firms, *Management International Review*, 48: 397–411.

24. C. Peeters, C. Dehon, & P. Garcia-Prieto, 2015, The attention stimulus of cultural differences in global services sourcing, *Journal of International Business Studies*, 46: 241–251; O. Shenkar, 2012, Cultural distance revisited: Towards a more rigorous conceptualization and measurement of cultural differences, *Journal of International Business Studies*, 43: 1–11; R. Chakrabarti, Gupta-Mukherjee, & N. Jayaraman, 2009, Mars-Venus marriages: Culture and cross-border M&A, *Journal of International Business Studies*, 40: 216–236.

25. S. L. Sun, M. W. Peng, R. P. Lee, & W. Tan, 2015, Institutional open access at home and outward internationalization, *Journal of World Business*, 50: 234–246; B. T. McCann & G. Vroom, 2010, Pricing response to entry and agglomeration effects, *Strategic Management Journal*, 31: 284–305.

26. Sambharya & Lee, Renewing dynamic capabilities globally: An empirical study of the world's largest MNCs; Y. Y. Chang, Y. Gong, & M. Peng, 2012, Expatriate knowledge transfer, subsidiary absorptive capacity and subsidiary performance, *Academy of Management Journal*, 55: 927–948; P. Kappen, 2011, Competence-creating overlaps and subsidiary technological evolution in the multinational corporation, *Research Policy*, 40: 673–686.

27. H. Liang, B. Ren, & S. L. Sun, 2015, An anatomy of state control in the globalization of state-owned enterprises, *Journal of International Business Studies*, 46: 223–240; Y. Fang, M. Wade, A. Delios, & P. W. Beamish, 2013, An exploration of multinational enterprise knowledge resources and foreign subsidiary performance, *Journal of World Business*, 48: 30–38; A. Arino, 2011, Building the global enterprise: Strategic assembly, *Global Strategy Journal*, 1: 47–49.

28. M. E. Porter, 1990, *The Competitive Advantage of Nations*, NY: The Free Press.

29. Ibid., 84.

30. D. Dulaney, 2014, Chiquita agrees to $742 million buyout, *Wall Street Journal*, www.wsj.com, October 28; D. Englander, 2013, Chiquita Brands—Stocks with appeal, *Wall Street Journal*, www.wsj.com, April 28.

31. M. Bucheli & M. Kim, 2015, Attacked from both sides: A dynamic model of multinational corporations' strategies for protection of their property rights, *Global Strategy Journal*, 5: 1–26; C. Wang, J. Hong, M. Kafouros, & M. Wright, 2012, Exploring the role of government involvement in outward FDI from emerging economies, *Journal of International Business Studies*, 43: 655–676; J. Nishimura & H. Okamuro,

2011, Subsidy and networking: The effects of direct and indirect support programs of the cluster policy, *Research Policy*, 40: 714–727.

32. C. Trundell & Y Hagiwara, 2015, Lexus flag China ambitions with new ES's Shanghai debut, *Bloomberg Business*, www.bloombergbusiness.com, April 9.

33. S. Song, M. Makhija, & S. Lee, 2014, Within-country growth options versus across-country switching options in foreign direct investment, *Global Strategy Journal*, 4: 127–142.

34. Kim, Hoskisson, & Lee, Why strategic factor markets matter: 'New multinationals' geographic diversification and firm profitability; M. Musteen, D. K. Datta, & J. Francis, 2014, Early internationalization by firms in transition economies into developed markets: The role of international networks, *Global Strategy Journal*, 4: 221–237.

35. R. Qu & Z. Zhang, 2015, Market orientation and business performance in MNC foreign subsidiaries—moderating effects of integration and responsiveness, *Journal of Business Research*, 68: 919–924.

36. W. Aghina, A. De Smet, & S Heywood, 2014, The past and future of global organizations, *McKinsey Quarterly*, March, 97–106; S. Zaheer & L. Nachum, 2011, Sense of place: From location resources to MNE locational capital, *Global Strategy Journal*, 1: 96–108; N. Guimaraes-Costs & M. P. E. Cunha, 2009, Foreign locals: A liminal perspective of international managers, *Organizational Dynamics*, 38: 158–166.

37. S. C. Schleimer & T. Pedersen, T. 2014, The effects of MNC parent effort and social structure on subsidiary absorptive capacity, *Journal of International Business Studies*, 45: 303–320; J.-S. Chen & A. S. Lovvorn, 2011, The speed of knowledge transfer within multinational enterprises: The role of social capital, *International Journal of Commerce and Management*, 21: 46–62; H. Kasper, M. Lehrer, J. Muhlbacher, & B. Muller, 2009, Integration-responsiveness and knowledge-management perspectives on the MNC: A typology and field study of cross-site knowledge-sharing practices, *Journal of Leadership & Organizational Studies*, 15: 287–303.

38. 2015, Introduction to Unilever global, Unilever homepage, www.unilever.com, accessed on June 19; J. Neff, 2008, Unilever's CMO finally gets down to business, *Advertising Age*, July 11.

39. K. E. Meyer & S. Estrin, 2014, Local context and global strategy: Extending the integration responsiveness framework to subsidiary strategy, *Global Strategy Journal*, 4: 1–19; M. P. Koza, S. Tallman, & A. Ataay, 2011, The strategic assembly of global firms: A microstructural analysis of local learning and global adaptation, *Global Strategy Journal*, 1: 27–46; P. J. Buckley, 2009, The impact of the global factory on economic

development, *Journal of World Business*, 44: 131–143.

40. H. Berry, 2014, Global integration and innovation: Multicountry knowledge generation within MNCs, *Strategic Management Journal*, 35: 869–890; A. Zaheer & E. Hernandez, 2011, The geographic scope of the MNC and its alliance portfolio: Resolving the paradox of distance, *Global Strategy Journal*, 1: 109–126.

41. C. Wang, 2014, Accounting standards harmonization and financial statement comparability: Evidence from transnational information transfer, *Journal of Accounting Research*, 52: 955–992; L. Hail, C. Leuz, & P. Wysocki, 2010, Global accounting convergence and the potential adoption of IFRS by the U.S. (part II): Political factors and future scenarios for U.S. accounting standards, *Accounting Horizons*, 24: 567–581; R. G. Barker, 2003, Trend: Global accounting is coming, *Harvard Business Review*, 81(4): 24–25.

42. J. U. Kim & R. V. Aguilera, 2015, The world is spiky: An internationalization framework for a semi-globalized world, *Global Strategy Journal*, 5: 113–132; J.-L. Arregle, T. Miller, M. A. Hitt, & P. W. Beamish, 2013, Do regions matter? An integrated institutional and semiglobalization perspective on the internationalization of MNEs, *Strategic Management Journal*, 34: 910–934; L. H. Shi, C. White, S. Zou, & S. T. Cavusgil, 2010, Global account management strategies: Drivers and outcomes, *Journal of International Business Studies*, 41: 620–638.

43. S. Morris, R. Hammond, & S. Snell, 2014, A microfoundations approach to transnational capabilities: The role of knowledge search in an ever-changing world, *Journal of International Business Studies*, 45: 405–427; R. Greenwood, S. Fairclough, T. Morris, & M. Boussebaa, 2010, The organizational design of transnational professional service firms, *Organizational Dynamics*, 39: 173–183.

44. K. J. Breunig, R. Kvålshaugen, & K. M. Hydle, 2014, Knowing your boundaries: Integration opportunities in international professional service firms, *Journal of World Business*, 49: 502–511; C. Stehr, 2010, Globalisation strategy for small and medium-sized enterprises, *International Journal of Entrepreneurship and Innovation Management*, 12: 375–391; A. M. Rugman & A. Verbeke, 2008, A regional solution to the strategy and structure of multinationals, *European Management Journal*, 26: 305–313.

45. X. Zhang, W. Zhong, & S. Makino, 2015, Customer involvement and service firm internationalization performance: An integrative framework, *Journal of International Business Studies*, 46: 355–380; 2010, Regional resilience: Theoretical and empirical perspectives, *Cambridge Journal of Regions, Economy and Society*, 3–10; Rugman & Verbeke, A regional

solution to the strategy and structure of multinationals.

46. 2015, Unleashing a global snacking powerhouse, Mondelez International, www.mondelezinternational.com, accessed on June 22.

47. A. Millington, 2015, Mondelez splashes £10m to grow savoury snacks business as it looks to balance its portfolio, *Marketing Week*, www.marketingweek.com, April 10.

48. M. W. Peng & Y. Jiang, 2010, Institutions behind family ownership and control in large firms, *Journal of Management Studies*, 47: 253–273; A. M. Rugman & A. Verbeke, 2003, Extending the theory of the multinational enterprise: Internationalization and strategic management perspectives, *Journal of International Business Studies*, 34: 125–137.

49. I. Bremmer, E. Fry, & D. Shanker, 2015 The new world of business, *Fortune*, February 1, 86–92; D. Klonowski, 2011, Private equity in emerging markets: Stacking up the BRICs, *Journal of Private Equity*, 14: 24–37.

50. F. Jiang, L. Liu, & B. W. Stening, 2014, Do Foreign Firms in China Incur a Liability of Foreignness? The Local Chinese Firms' Perspective, *Thunderbird International Business Review*, 56: 501–518; J. Mata & E. Freitas, 2012, Foreignness and exit over the life cycle of firms, *Journal of International Business Studies*, 43: 615–630. R. G. Bell, I. Filatotchev, & A. A. Rasheed, 2012, The liability of foreignness, in capital markets: Sources and remedies, *Journal of International Business Studies*, 43: 107–122.

51. J. Aguilera-Caracuel, E. M. Fedriani, & B. L. Delgado-Márquez, 2014, Institutional distance among country influences and environmental performance standardization in multinational enterprises, *Journal of Business Research*, 67: 2385–2392; R. Salomon & Z. Wu, 2012, Institutional distance and local isomorphism strategy, *Journal of International Business Studies*, 43: 347–367.

52. T. Hutzschenreuter, I. Kleindienst, & S. Lange, 2014, Added psychic distance stimuli and MNE performance: Performance effects of added cultural, governance, geographic, and economic distance in MNEs' international expansion, *Journal of International Management*, 20: 38–54; J. T. Campbell, L. Eden, & S. R. Miller, 2012, Multinationals and corporate social responsibility in host countries: Does distance matter? *Journal of International Business Studies*, 43: 84–106; P. Ghemawat, 2001, Distance still matters, *Harvard Business Review*, 79(8): 137–145.

53. N. Y. Brannen, 2004, When Mickey loses face: Recontextualization, semantic fit and semiotics of foreignness, *Academy of Management Review*, 29: 593–616.

54. M. Schuman, 2006, Disney's Hong Kong headache, *Time*, www.time.com, May 8.

55. G. Suder, P. W. Liesch, S. Inomata, I. Mihailova, & B. Meng, 2015, The evolving geography of production hubs and regional value chains across East Asia: Trade in value-added, *Journal of World Business*, 50: 404–416; Arregle, Miller, Hitt, & Beamish, Do regions matter?; J. Cantwell & Y. Zhang, 2011, Innovation and location in the multinational firm, *International Journal of Technology Management*, 54: 116–132.

56. L. Stevens, 2015, Borders matter less and less in e-commerce, *Wall Street Journal*, June 24, B8; K. Ito & E. L. Rose, 2010, The implicit return on domestic and international sales: An empirical analysis of U.S. and Japanese firms, *Journal of International Business Studies*, 41: 1074–1089; A. M. Rugman & A. Verbeke, 2007, Liabilities of foreignness and the use of firm-level versus country level data: A response to Dunning et al. (2007), *Journal of International Business Studies*, 38: 200–205.

57. A. Ghobadian, A. M. Rugman, & R. L. Tung, 2014, Strategies for firm globalization and regionalization, *British Journal of Management*, 25: S1–S5; Arregle, Miller, Hitt, & Beamish, Do regions matter?; E. R. Banalieva, M. D. Santoro, & R. J. Jiang, 2012, Home region focus and technical efficiency of multinational enterprises: The moderating role of regional integration, *Management International Review*, 52: 493–518.

58. B. V. Dimitrova, B. Rosenbloom, & T. L. Andras, 2014, Does the degree of retailer international involvement affect retailer performance? *International Review of Retail, Distribution & Consumer Research*, 24: 243–277; A. M. Rugman & S. Girod, 2003, Retail multinationals and globalization: The evidence is regional, *European Management Journal*, 21: 24–37.

59. D. E. Westney, 2006, Review of the regional multinationals: MNEs and global strategic management (book review), *Journal of International Business Studies*, 37: 445–449.

60. S. Arita & K. Tanaka, 2014, Heterogeneous multinational firms and productivity gains from falling FDI barriers, *Review of World Economics*, 150: 83–113; R. D. Ludema, 2002, Increasing returns, multinationals and geography of preferential trade agreements, *Journal of International Economics*, 56: 329–358.

61. L Caliendo & F. Parro, 2015, Estimates of the trade and welfare effects of NAFTA, *Review of Economic Studies*, 82: 1–44; M. Aspinwall, 2009, NAFTA-ization: Regionalization and domestic political adjustment in the North American economic area, *Journal of Common Market Studies*, 47: 1–24.

62. N. Åkerman, 2015, Knowledge-acquisition strategies and the effects on market knowledge—profiling the internationalizing firm, *European Management Journal*, 33: 79–88; D. Zu & O. Shenar, 2002, Institutional distance and the multinational enterprise, *Academy of Management Review*, 27: 608–618.

63. P. J. Buckley & N. Hashai, 2014, The role of technological catch up and domestic market growth in the genesis of emerging country based multinationals, *Research Policy*, 43: 423–437; A. Ojala, 2008, Entry in a psychically distant market: Finnish small and medium-sized software firms in Japan, *European Management Journal*, 26: 135–144.

64. V. Hernández & M. J. Nieto, 2015, The effect of the magnitude and direction of institutional distance on the choice of international entry modes, *Journal of World Business*, 50: 122–132; K. D. Brouthers, 2013, Institutional, cultural and transaction cost influences on entry mode choice and performance, *Journal of International Business Studies*, 44: 1–13.

65. J.-F. Hennart & A. H. L. Slangen, A. 2015, Yes, we really do need more entry mode studies! A commentary on Shaver, *Journal of International Business Studies*, 46: 114–122; B. Maekelburger, C. Schwens, & R. Kabst, 2012, Asset specificity and foreign market entry mode choice of small and medium-sized enterprises: The moderating influence of knowledge safeguards and institutional safeguards, *Journal of International Business Studies*, 43: 458–476.

66. S. Gerschewski, E. L. Rose, & V. J. Lindsay, 2015, Understanding the drivers of international performance for born global firms: An integrated perspective, *Journal of World Business*, 50: 558–575; C. A. Cinquetti, 2009, Multinationals and exports in a large and protected developing country, *Review of International Economics*, 16: 904–918.

67. S. T. Cavusgil & G. Knight, 2015, The born global firm: An entrepreneurial and capabilities perspective on early and rapid internationalization, *Journal of International Business Studies*, 46: 3–16; P. Ganotakis & J. H. Love, 2012, Export propensity, export intensity and firm performance: The role of the entrepreneurial founding team, *Journal of International Business Studies*, 43: 693–718.

68. I. Zander, P. McDougall-Covin, & E. L. Rose, 2015, Born globals and international business: Evolution of a field of research, *Journal of International Business Studies*, 46: 27–35; M. Bandyk, 2008, Now even small firms can go global, *U.S. News & World Report*, March 10, 52.

69. S. Sui & M. Baum, 2014, Internationalization strategy, firm resources and the survival of SMEs in the export market, *Journal of International Business Studies*, 45: 821–841; B. Cassiman & E. Golovko, 2010, Innovation and internationalization through exports, *Journal of International Business Studies*, 42: 56–75.

70. E. Golovko & G. Valentini, 2014, Selective learning-by-exporting: Firm size and product versus process innovation, *Global Strategy Journal*, 4: 161–180; X. He, K. D. Brouthers, & I. Filatotchev, 2013, Resource-based and institutional perspectives on export channel selection and export performance, *Journal of

Management, 39: 27–47; M. Hughes, S. L. Martin, R. E. Morgan, & M. J. Robson, 2010, Realizing product-market advantage in high-technology international new ventures: The mediating role of ambidextrous innovation, *Journal of International Marketing*, 18: 1–21.

71. A. Troianovski, 2014, German seeds web shopping in the developing world, *Wall Street Journal*, January 14, A1, A12; P. Ganotakis & J. H. Love, 2011, R&D, product innovation, and exporting: Evidence from UK new technology-based firms, *Oxford Economic Papers*, 63: 279–306; M. Gabrielsson & P. Gabrielsson, 2011, Internet-based sales channel strategies of born global firms, *International Business Review*, 20: 88–99.

72. B. Bozeman, H. Rimes, & J. Youtie, J. 2015, The evolving state-of-the-art in technology transfer research: Revisiting the contingent effectiveness model, *Research Policy*, 44: 34–49; P. S. Aulakh, M. Jiang, & Y. Pan, 2010, International technology licensing: Monopoly rents transaction costs and exclusive rights, *Journal of International Business Studies*, 41: 587–605; R. Bird & D. R. Cahoy, 2008, The impact of compulsory licensing on foreign direct investment: A collective bargaining approach, *American Business Law Journal*, 45: 283–330.

73. M. Bianchi, M. Frattini, J. Lejarraga, & A. Di Minin, 2014, Technology exploitation paths: combining technological and complementary resources in new product development and licensing, *Journal of Product Innovation Management*, 31: 146–169; M. S. Giarratana, & S. Torrisi, 2010, Foreign entry and survival in a knowledge-intensive market: Emerging economy countries' international linkages, technology competences, and firm experience, *Strategic Entrepreneurship Journal*, 4: 85–104; U. Lichtenthaler, 2008, Externally commercializing technology assets: An examination of different process stages, *Journal of Business Venturing*, 23: 445–464.

74. N. Byrnes & F. Balfour, 2009, Philip Morris unbound, *BusinessWeek*, May 4, 38–42.

75. 2015, PMI around the world, Philip Morris International homepage, www.pmi.com, accessed on June 23.

76. J. Li-Ying & Y. Wang, 2015, Find them home or abroad? The relative contribution of international technology in-licensing to "indigenous innovation" in China, *Long Range Planning*, 48: 123–134; E. Dechenaux, J. Thursby, & M. Thursby, 2011, Inventor moral hazard in university licensing: The role of contracts, *Research Policy*, 40: 94–104; S. Hagaoka, 2009, Does strong patent protection facilitate international technology transfer? Some evidence from licensing contrasts of Japanese firms, *Journal of Technology Transfer*, 34: 128–144.

77. A. Agarwal, I. Cockburn, & I. Zhang, L. Deals not done: Sources of failure in the market for ideas, *Strategic Management Journal*, 36: 976–986; U. Lichtenthaler, 2011, The evolution of technology licensing management: Identifying five strategic approaches, *R&D Management*, 41: 173–189; M. Fiedler & I. M. Welpe, 2010, Antecedents of cooperative commercialisation strategies of nanotechnology firms, *Research Policy*, 39: 400–410.

78. C. A. Barlett & S. Rangan, 1992, Komatsu Limited. In C. A. Bartlett & S. Ghoshal (eds.), *Transnational Management: Text, Cases and Readings in Cross-Border Management*, Homewood, IL: Irwin, 311–326.

79. F. J. Contractor & J. J. Reuer, 2014, Structuring and governing alliances: New directions for research, *Global Strategy Journal*, 4: 241–256; S. Veilleux, N. Haskell, & F. Pons, 2012, Going global: How smaller enterprises benefit from strategic alliances, *Journal of Business Strategy*, 33(5): 22–31; C. Schwens, J. J. Eiche, & R. Kabst, 2011, The moderating impact of informal institutional distance and formal institutional risk on SME entry mode choice, *Journal of Management Studies*, 48: 330–351.

80. J. J. Reuer & R. Ragozzino, 2014, Signals and international alliance formation: The roles of affiliations and international activities, *Journal of International Business Studies*, 45: 321–337; T. Barnes, S. Raynor, & J. Bacchus, 2012, A new typology of forms of international collaboration, *Journal of Business and Strategy*, 5: 81–102; S. Prashantham & S. Young, 2011, Post-entry speed of international new ventures, *Entrepreneurship Theory and Practice*, 35: 275–292.

81. F. J. Contractor & J. A. Woodley, 2015, How the alliance pie is split: Value appropriation by each partner in cross-border technology transfer alliances, *Journal of World Business*, 50: 535–547; Z. Bhanji & J. E. Oxley, 2013, Overcoming the dual liability of foreignness and privateness in international corporate citizenship partnerships, *Journal of International Business Studies*, 44: 290–311; J. S. Harrison, M. A. Hitt, R. E. Hoskisson, & R. D. Ireland, 2001, Resource complementarity in business combinations: Extending the logic to organization alliances, *Journal of Management*, 27: 679–690.

82. W. Shi, S. L. Sun, B. C. Pinkham, & M. W. Peng, 2014, Domestic alliance network to attract foreign partners: Evidence from international joint ventures in China, *Journal of International Business Studies*, 45: 338–362; R. A. D'Aveni, G. B. Dagnino, & K. G. Smith, 2010, The age of temporary advantage, *Strategic Management Journal*, 31: 1371–1385; M. A. Hitt, D. Ahlstrom, M. T. Dacin, E. Levitas, & L. Svobodina, 2004, The institutional effects on strategic alliance

partner selection in transition economies: China versus Russia, *Organization Science*, 15: 173–185.

83. Z. Khan, R. R. Sinkovics, & Y. K. Lew, 2015, International joint ventures as boundary spanners: Technological knowledge transfer in an emerging economy, *Global Strategy Journal*, 5: 48–68; G. Vasudeva, J. W. Spencer, & H. J. Teegen, 2013, Bringing the institutional context back in: A cross-national comparison of alliance partner selection and knowledge acquisition, *Organization Science*, 24: 319–338; R. A. Corredoira & L. Rosenkopf, 2010, Should auld acquaintance be forgot? The reverse transfer of knowledge through mobility ties, *Strategic Management Journal*, 31: 159–181.

84. X. Jiang, F. Jiang, X. Cai, & H. Liu, 2015, How does trust affect alliance performance? The mediating role of resource sharing, *Industrial Marketing Management*, 45: 128–138; J-P. Roy, 2012, IJV partner trustworthy behavior: The role of host country governance and partner selection criteria, *Journal of Management Studies*, 49: 332–355; M. J. Robson, C. S. Katsikeas, & D. C. Bello, 2008, Drivers and performance outcomes of trust in international strategic alliances: The role of organizational complexity, *Organization Science*, 19: 647–668.

85. 2015, A culture of partnership in favor of collective intelligence, Limagrain, www.limagrain.com, accessed on June 23; 2011, Limagrain signs strategic alliance to enter Brazilian corn market, *Great Lakes Hybrids*, www.greatlakeshybrids.com, February 14.

86. M. del Mar Benavides-Espinosa & D. Ribeiro-Soriano, 2014, Cooperative learning in creating and managing joint ventures, *Journal of Business Research*, 67: 648–655; S. Kotha & K. Srikanth, 2013, Managing a global partnership model: Lessons from the Boeing 787 'dreamliner' program, *Global Strategy Journal*, 3: 41–66; C. Schwens, J. Eiche, & R. Kabst, 2011, The moderating impact of informal institutional distance and formal institutional risk on SME entry mode choice, *Journal of Management Studies*, 48: 330–351.

87. R. Kumar, 2014, Managing ambiguity in strategic alliances, *California Management Review*, 56(4): 82–102; Y. Luo, O. Shenkar, & H. Gurnani, 2008, Control-cooperation interfaces in global strategic alliances: A situational typology and strategic responses, *Journal of International Business Studies*, 39: 428–453.

88. I. Arikan & O. Shenkar, 2013, National animosity and cross-border alliances, *Academy of Management Journal*, 56:516–1544; T. K. Das, 2010, Interpartner sensemaking in strategic alliances: Managing cultural differences and internal tensions, *Management Decision*, 48: 17–36.

89. A. Iriyama & R. Madhavan, 2014, Post-formation inter-partner equity transfers in international joint ventures: the role

of experience, *Global Strategy Journal*, 4: 331–348; B. B. Nielsen, 2010, Strategic fit, contractual, and procedural governance in alliances, *Journal of Business Research*, 63: 682–689; D. Li, L. Eden, M. A. Hitt, & R. D. Ireland, 2008, Friends, acquaintances and stranger? Partner selection in R&D alliances, *Academy of Management Journal*, 51: 315–334.

90. A. M. Joshi & N. Lahiri, 2015, Language friction and partner selection in cross-border R&D alliance formation, *Journal of International Business Studies*, 46: 123–152; P. D. O. Jensen & B. Petersen, 2013, Global sourcing of services: Risk, process and collaborative architecture, *Global Strategy Journal*, 3: 67–87.

91. T. W. Tong, J. J. Reuer, B. B. Tyler, & S. Zhang, 2015, Host country executives' assessments of international joint ventures and divestitures: An experimental approach, *Strategic Management Journal*, 36: 254–275; S.-F. S. Chen, 2010, A general TCE model of international business institutions; market failure and reciprocity, *Journal of International Business Studies*, 41: 935–959; J. Wiklund & D. A. Shepherd, 2009, The effectiveness of alliances and acquisitions: The role of resource combination activities, *Entrepreneurship Theory and Practice*, 33:193–212.

92. G. Kling, A. Ghobadian, M. A. Hitt, U. Weitzel, & N. O'Regan, 2014, The effects of cross-border and cross-industry mergers and acquisitions on home-region and global multinational enterprises, *British Journal of Management*, 25: S116–S132.

93. A. Arslan & Y. Wang, Y. 2015, Acquisition entry strategy of Nordic multinational enterprises in China: An analysis of key determinants, *Journal of Global Marketing*, 28: 32–51; A. Guar, S. Malhotra, & P. Zhu, 2013, Acquisition announcements and stock market valuations of acquiring firms' rivals: A test of the growth probability hypothesis in China, *Strategic Management Journal*, 34: 215–232; M. A. Hitt & V. Pisano, 2003, The cross-border merger and acquisition strategy, *Management Research*, 1: 133–144.

94. I. Walker & A. Gasparro, 2015, Merge unites major supermarket players, *Wall Street Journal*, June 25, B1

95. P. C. Narayan & M. Thenmozhi, 2014, Do cross-border acquisitions involving emerging market firms create value: Impact of deal characteristics, *Management Decision*, 52: 1–23; S. Malhotra, P.-C. Zhu, & W. Locander, 2010, Impact of host-country corruption on U.S. and Chinese cross-border acquisitions, *Thunderbird International Business Review*, 52: 491–507; P. X. Meschi, 2009, Government corruption and foreign stakes in international joint ventures in emerging economies, *Asia Pacific Journal of Management*, 26: 241–261.

96. F. J. Contractor, S. Lahiri, B. Elango, & S. K. Kundu, Institutional, cultural and industry related determinants of ownership choices in emerging market FDI acquisitions, *International Business Review*, 23: 931–941; J. Li & C. Qian, 2013, Principal-principal conflicts under weak institutions: A study of corporate takeovers in China, *Strategic Management Journal*, 34: 498–508; A. Madhok & M. Keyhani, 2012, Acquisitions as entrepreneurship: Asymmetries, opportunities, and the internationalization of multinationals from emerging economies, *Global Strategy Journal*, 2: 26–40.

97. S. Lee, J. Kim, & B. I. Park, 2015, Culture clashes in cross-border mergers and acquisitions: A case study of Sweden's Volvo and South Korea's Samsung, *International Business Review*, 24: 580–593; E. Vaara, R. Sarala, G. K. Stahl, & I. Bjorkman, 2012, *Journal of Management Studies*, 49: 1–27; D. R. Denison, B. Adkins, & A. Guidroz, 2011, Managing cultural integration in cross-border mergers and acquisitions. In W. H. Mobley, M. Li, & Y. Wang (eds.), *Advances in Global Leadership*, vol. 6, Bingley, U.K.: Emerald Publishing Group, 95–115.

98. U. Stettner & D. Lavie, 2014, Ambidexterity under scrutiny: Exploration and exploitation via internal organization, alliances, and acquisitions, *Strategic Management Journal*, 35: 1903–1929; S.-J. Chang, J. Chung, & J. J. Moon, 2013, When do wholly owned subsidiaries perform better than joint ventures? *Strategic Management Journal*, 34: 317–337; Y. Fang, G.-L. F. Jiang, S. Makino, & P. W. Beamish, 2010, Multinational firm knowledge, use of expatriates, and foreign subsidiary performance, *Journal of Management Studies*, 47: 27–54.

99. S. Lahiri, B. Elango, & S. K. Kundu, 2014, Cross-border acquisition in services: Comparing ownership choice of developed and emerging economy MNEs in India, *Journal of World Business*, 49: 409–420; C. Bouquet, L. Hebert, & A. Delios, 2004, Foreign expansion in service industries: Separability and human capital intensity, *Journal of Business Research*, 57: 35–46.

100. O. Bertrand & L. Capron, L. 2015, Productivity enhancement at home via cross-border acquisitions: The roles of learning and contemporary domestic investments, *Strategic Management Journal*, 36: 640–658; C. Schwens, J. Eiche, & R. Kabst, 2011, The moderating impact of informal institutional distance and formal institutional risk on SME entry mode choice, *Journal of Management Studies*, 48: 330–351; K. F. Meyer, S. Estrin, S. K. Bhaumik, & M. W. Peng, 2009, Institutions, resources, and entry strategies in emerging economies, *Strategic Management Journal*, 30: 61–80.

101. G. O. White, T. A. Hemphill, J. R. Joplin, & L. A. Marsh, 2014, Wholly owned foreign subsidiary relation-based strategies in volatile environments, *International Business Review*, 23: 303–312; Chang, Chung & Moon, When do wholly owned subsidiaries perform better than joint ventures?; K. D. Brouthers & D. Dikova, 2010, Acquisitions and real options: The greenfield alternative, *Journal of Management Studies*, 47: 1048–1071.

102. 2015. Walmart's China expansion won't be easy, *Fortune*, www.fortune.com, May 6; Y. Parke & B. Sternquist, 2008, The global retailer's strategic proposition and choice of entry mode, *International Journal of Retail & Distribution Management*; 36: 281–299.

103. X. He, J. Zhang, & J. Wang, 2015, Market seeking orientation and performance in China: The impact of institutional environment, subsidiary ownership structure and experience. *Management International Review*, 55: 389–419; L. Q. Siebers, 2012, Foreign retailers in China: The first ten years, *Journal of Business Strategy*, 33(1): 27–38.

104. White, Hemphill, Joplin, & Marsh, Wholly owned foreign subsidiary relation-based strategies in volatile environments; A. M. Rugman, 2010, Reconciling internalization theory and the eclectic paradigm, *Multinational Business Review*, 18: 1–12; J. Che & G. Facchini, 2009, Cultural differences, insecure property rights and the mode of entry decision, *Economic Theory*, 38: 465–484.

105. J. Muller, 2015, Toyota is laying down deeper roots in Michigan. *Forbes*, June 11, 24.

106. 2014, Corporate with the best regional strategy, *LatinFinance*, July–August, 31.

107. A. Cuervo-Cazurra, A. Inkpen, A. Musacchio, & K. Ramaswamy, 2014, Governments as owners: State-owned multinational companies, *Journal of International Business Studies*, 45: 919–942; B. Batjargal, M. Hitt, A. S. Tsui, J.-L. Arregle, J. Webb, & T. Miller, 2013, Institutional polycentrism, entrepreneurs' social networks and new venture growth, *Academy of Management Journal*, 56: 1024–1049.

108. C. Giersch, 2011, Political risk and political due diligence, *Global Risk Affairs*, www.globalriskaffairs.com, March 4.

109. G. G. Goswami & S. Haider, 2014, Does political risk deter FDI inflow? An analytical approach using panel data and factor analysis, *Journal of Economic Studies*, 41: 233–252; J. Li & Y. Tang, 2010, CEO hubris and firm risk taking in China: The moderating role of managerial discretion, *Academy of Management Journal*, 53: 45–68; I. Alon & T. T. Herbert, 2009, A stranger in a strange land: Micro political risk and the multinational firm, *Business Horizons*, 52: 127–137; P. Rodriguez, K. Uhlenbruck, & L. Eden, 2003, Government corruption and the entry strategies of multinationals, *Academy of Management Review*, 30: 383–396.

110. A. Jiménez, I. Luis-Rico, & D. Benito-Osorio, 2014, The influence of political risk on the scope of internationalization of regulated companies: Insights from a Spanish sample, *Journal of World Business*, 49: 301–311; D. Quer, E. Claver, & L. Rienda, 2012, Political risk, cultural distance, and outward foreign direct investment: Empirical evidence from large Chinese firms, *Asia Pacific Journal of Management*, 29: 1089–1104; O. Branzei & S. Abdelnour, 2010, Another day, another dollar: Enterprise resilience under terrorism in developing countries, *Journal of International Business Studies*, 41: 804–825.

111. G. Bekaert, C. R. Harvey, C. T. Lundblad, & S. Siegel, 2014, Political risk spreads, *Journal of International Business Studies*, 45: 471–493.

112. C. L. Brown, S. T. Cavusgil, & A. W. Lord, 2015, Country-risk measurement and analysis: A new conceptualization and managerial tool, *International Business Review*, 24: 246–265; Giersch, Political risk and political due diligence.

113. D. L. Keig, L. E. Brouthers, & V. B. Marshall, 2015, Formal and informal corruption environments and multinational enterprise social irresponsibility, *Journal of Management Studies*, 52: 89–116; J. Surroca, J. A. Tribo, & S. A. Zahra, 2013, Stakeholder pressure on MNEs and the transfer of socially irresponsible practices to subsidiaries, *Academy of Management Journal*, 56: 549–572.

114. A. Flynn, 2015, Questions re-emerge on World Cup venues, *Wall Street Journal*, May 28, A10.

115. R. Johnson, R. Jelmaye, & L. Magalhaes, Scandal spurs overhaul of Brazil's soccer body, *Wall Street Journal*, June 12, A9.

116. O. Matthews, 2015, Russia retreats. *Newsweek Global*, June 19, 12–16.

117. C. Grimpe & K. Hussinger, 2014, Resource complementarity and value capture in firm acquisitions: The role of intellectual property rights, *Strategic Management Journal*, 35: 1762–1780.

118. A. Wexler, 2015, Power outages mar South Africa's economic expansion, *Wall Street Journal*, www.wsj.com, May 8.

119. P. Kiernan & P. Trevisani, 2015, China seeks to keep its ties tight with South America, *Wall Street Journal*, May 20, A14; G. Fornes & A. Butt-Philip, 2011, Chinese MNEs and Latin America: A review, *International Journal of Emerging Markets*, 6: 98–117; S. Globerman & D. Shapiro, 2009, Economic and strategic considerations surrounding Chinese FDI in the United States, *Asia Pacific Journal of Management*, 26: 163–183.

120. E. Beckmann & H. Stix, 2015, Foreign currency borrowing and knowledge about exchange rate risk, *Journal of Economic Behavior & Organization*, 11: 21–16; C. R. Goddard, 2011, Risky business: Financial-sector liberalization and China, *Thunderbird International Business Review*, 53: 469–482; I. G. Kawaller, 2009, Hedging

currency exposures by multinationals: Things to consider, *Journal of Applied Finance*, 18: 92–98.

121. P. Loftus & T. Stynes, 2015, J&J'S weak results tied to U.S. Dollar, device revenues, *Wall Street Journal*, April 15, B6; P. Evans, 2015, Unilever gets boost from Euro's weakness, *Wall Street Journal*, April 17, B6.

122. R. G. Bell, I. Filatotchev, & R. Aguilera, 2014, Corporate governance and investors' perceptions of foreign IPO value: An institutional perspective, *Academy of Management Journal*, 57: 301–320.

123. M. Alessandri & A. Seth, 2014, The effects of managerial ownership on international and business diversification: Balancing incentives and risks, *Strategic Management Journal*, 35: 2064–2075; F. J. Contractor, 2012, Why do multinational firms exist? A theory note about the effect of multinational expansion on performance and recent methodological critiques, *Global Strategy Journal*, 2: 318–331; P. David, J. P. O'Brien, T. Yoshikawa, & A. Delios, 2010, Do shareholders or stakeholders appropriate the rents from corporate diversification? The influence of ownership structure, *Academy of Management Journal*, 53: 636–654.

124. L. Zhou & A. Wu, A. 2014, Earliness of internationalization and performance outcomes: Exploring the moderating effects of venture age and international commitment, *Journal of World Business*, 49: 132–142; L. Li, 2007, Multinationality and performance: A synthetic review and research agenda, *International Journal of Management Reviews*, 9: 117–139; J. A.Doukas & O. B. Kan, 2006, Does global diversification destroy firm value? *Journal of International Business Studies*, 37: 352–371

125. H. Tan & J. A. Mathews, 2015, Accelerated internationalization and resource leverage strategizing: The case of Chinese wind turbine manufacturers, *Journal of World Business*, 50: 417–427; J. H. Fisch, 2012, Information costs and internationalization performance, *Global Strategy Journal*, 2: 296–312; S. E. Christophe & H. Lee, 2005, What matters about internationalization: A market-based assessment, *Journal of Business Research*, 58: 636–643.

126. S. Kraus, T. C. Ambos, F. Eggers, & B. Cesinger, 2015, Distance and perceptions of risk in internationalization decisions, *Journal of Business Research*, 68: 1501–1505; H. Berry, 2013, When do firms divest foreign operations? *Organization Science*, 24: 246–261; T. J. Andersen, 2011, The risk implications of multinational enterprise, *International Journal of Organizational Analysis*, 19: 49–70.

127. Berry, Global integration and innovation: Multi-country knowledge generation within MNCs; A. Y. Lewin, S. Massini, & C. Peeters, 2011, Microfoundations of internal and external absorptive capacity routines, *Organization Science*, 22: 81–98.

128. P. C. Patel, S. A. Fernhaber, P. P. McDougal-Covin, & R. P. van der Have, 2014, Beating competitors to international markets: The value of geographically balanced networks for innovation, *Strategic Management Journal*, 35: 691–711.

129. S. Awate, M. M. Larsen, & R. Mudambi, 2015, Accessing vs sourcing knowledge: A comparative study of R&D internationalization between emerging and advanced economy firms, *Journal of International Business Studies*, 46: 63–86; O. Bertrand & M. J. Mol, 2013, The antecedents and innovation effects of domestic and offshore R&D outsourcing: The contingent impact of cognitive distance and absorptive capacity, *Strategic Management Journal*, 34: 751–760; B. S. Reiche, 2012, Knowledge benefits of social capital upon repatriation: A longitudinal study of international assignees, *Journal of Management Studies*, 49: 1052–1072.

130. J. Alcacer & J. Oxley, 2014, Learning by supplying, *Strategic Management Journal*, 35: 204–223; G. R. G. Benito, R. Lunnan & S. Tomassen, 2011, Distant encounters of the third kind: Multinational companies locating divisional headquarters abroad, *Journal of Management Studies*, 48: 373–394; M. A. Hitt, L. Tihanyi, T. Miller, & B. Connelly, 2006, International diversification: Antecedents, outcomes, and moderators, *Journal of Management*, 32: 831–867.

131. R. Belderbos, B. Lokshin, & B. Sadowski, 2015, The returns to foreign R&D, *Journal of International Business Studies*, 46, 491–504; I. Guler & A. Nerkar, 2012, The impact of global and local cohesion on innovation in the pharmaceutical industry, *Strategic Management Journal*, 33: 535–549.

132. M. Alessandri & A. Seth, 2014, The effects of managerial ownership on international and business diversification: Balancing incentives and risks, *Strategic Management Journal*, 35: 2064–2075; X. Fu, 2012, Foreign direct investment and managerial knowledge spillovers through diffusion of management practices, *Journal of Management Studies*, 49: 970–999; D. Holtbrugge & A. T. Mohr, 2011, Subsidiary interdependencies and international human resource management practices in German MNCs, *Management International Review*, 51: 93–115.

133. B. B. Nielsen & S. Nielsen, 2013, Top management team nationality diversity and firm performance: A multilevel study. *Strategic Management Journal*, 34, 373–382; M. Halme, S. Lindeman, & P. Linna, 2012, Innovation for inclusive business: Intrapreneurial bricolage in multinational corporations, *Journal of Management Studies*, 49: 743–784; I. Filatotchev & M. Wright, 2010, Agency perspectives on corporate governance of multinational enterprises, *Journal of Management Studies*, 47: 471–486.

134. C. Hsu, Y. Lien, & H. Chen, H. 2015, R&D internationalization and innovation performance, *International Business Review*, 24: 187–195; J. I. Siegel & S. H. Schwartz, 2013, Egalitarianism, cultural distance and foreign direct investment: A new approach, *Organization Science*, 24: 1174–1194; G. A. Shinkle & A. P. Kriauciunas, 2012, The impact of current and founding institutions on strength of competitive aspirations in transition economies, *Strategic Management Journal*, 33: 448–458.

135. R. Chittoor, P. S. Aulakh, & S. Ray, 2015, Accumulative and assimilative learning, institutional infrastructure, and innovation orientation of developing economy firms, *Global Strategy Journal*, 5: 133–153; P. C. Nell & B. Ambos, 2013, Parenting advantage in the MNC: An embeddedness perspective on the value added by headquarters, *Strategic Management Journal*, 34: 1086–1103; J.-F. Hennart, 2012, Emerging market multinationals and the theory of the multinational enterprise, *Global Strategy Journal*, 2: 168–187.

136. S. Schmid & T. Dauth, 2014, Does internationalization make a difference? Stock market reaction to announcements of international top executive appointments, *Journal of World Business*, 49: 63–77; Wiersema & Bowen, The relationship between international diversification and firm performance; C.-F. Wang, L.-Y. Chen, & S.-C. Change, 2011, International diversification and the market

value of new product introduction, *Journal of International Management*, 17: 333–347.

137. J. U. Kim & R. V. Aguilera, 2015, The world is spiky: An internationalization framework for a semi-globalized world, *Global Strategy Journal*, 5: 113–132; R. Belderbos, T. W. Tong, & S. Wu, 2013, Multinationality and downside risk: The roles of option portfolio and organization, *Strategic Management Journal*, in press; W. Shi, S. L. Sun, & M. W. Peng, 2012, Sub-national institutional contingencies, network positions and IJV partner selection, *Journal of Management Studies*, 49: 1221–1245.

138. P. Regnér & J. Edman, J. 2014, MNE institutional advantage: How subunits shape, transpose and evade host country institutions, *Journal of International Business Studies*, 45: 275–302; B. Baik, J.-K. Kang, J.-M. Kim, & J. Lee, 2013, The liability of foreignness in international equity investments: Evidence from the U.S. stock market, *Journal of International Business Studies*, 44: 391–411.

139. S. Song, 2014, Entry mode irreversibility, host market uncertainty, and foreign subsidiary exits, *Asia Pacific Journal of Management*, 31: 455–471; S.-H. Lee & S. Song, 2012, Host country uncertainty, intra-MNC production shifts, and subsidiary performance, *Strategic Management Journal*, 33: 1331–1340.

140. D. W. Williams & D. A. Grégoire, 2015, Seeking commonalities or avoiding differences? Re-conceptualizing distance and its effects on internationalization

decisions, *Journal of International Business Studies*, 46: 253–284; L. Berchicci, A. King, & C. L. Tucci, 2011, Does the apple always fall close to the tree? The geographical proximity choice of spin-outs, *Strategic Entrepreneurship Journal*, 5: 120–136; A. Ojala, 2008, Entry in a psychically distant market: Finnish small and medium-sized software firms in Japan, *European Management Journal*, 26: 135–144.

141. W. Shi, R. E. Hoskisson, & Y. Zhang, 2015. A geopolitical perspective into the opposition to globalizing state-owned enterprises in target states. *Global Strategy Journal*, in press; M. L. L. Lam, 2009, Beyond credibility of doing business in China: Strategies for improving corporate citizenship of foreign multinational enterprises in China, *Journal of Business Ethics*, 87: 137–146.

142. M. H. Ho & F. Wang, 2015, Unpacking knowledge transfer and learning paradoxes in international strategic alliances: Contextual differences matter, *International Business Review*, 24: 287–297; E. Fang & S. Zou, 2010, The effects of absorptive capacity and joint learning on the instability of international joint ventures in emerging economies, *Journal of International Business Studies*, 41: 906–924; D. Lavie & S. Miller, 2009, Alliance portfolio internationalization and firm performance, *Organization Science*, 19: 623–646.

9

Cooperative Strategy

Studying this chapter should provide you with the strategic management knowledge needed to:

9-1   Define cooperative strategies and explain why firms use them.

9-2   Define and discuss the three major types of strategic alliances.

9-3   Name the business-level cooperative strategies and describe their use.

9-4   Discuss the use of corporate-level cooperative strategies.

9-5   Understand the importance of cross-border strategic alliances as an international cooperative strategy.

9-6   Explain cooperative strategies' risks.

9-7   Describe two approaches used to manage cooperative strategies.

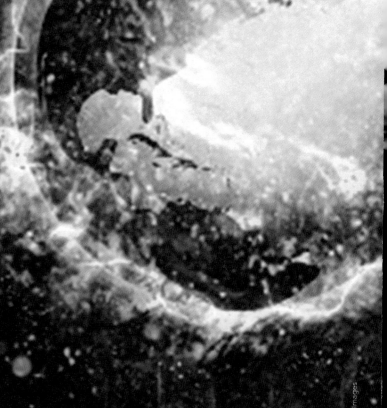

© RomanOkopny/Getty Images

GOOGLE, INTEL, AND TAG HEUER: COLLABORATING TO PRODUCE A SMARTWATCH

When using different types of cooperative strategies, firms commit to sharing some of their unique resources in order to reach an objective that is important to all participants. A key reason cooperative strategies are used is that individual firms sometimes identify opportunities they can't pursue because they lack the type and/or quantity of resources needed to do so.

Some partnerships are formed between similar firms who desire to develop scale economies to enhance their competitiveness. For years, automobile manufacturers have formed large numbers of partnerships for this reason. In other instances, firms competing in different industries uniquely combine their unique resources to pursue what they believe is a value-creating shared objective. This reason describes the rationale driving the partnership Google, Intel and TAG Heuer have formed to design and produce a smartwatch. A number of observers of the partnership among these three firms viewed it positively given their conclusion that TAG Heuer lacked the technology skills to build a competitive smartwatch while the Silicon Valley firms lacked the design skills to do so successfully.

FABRICE COFFRINI/AFP/Getty Images

In part, the decision Google, Intel and TAG Heuer made to collaborate is a strategic action taken in response to Apple's introduction of the iWatch. A common opinion among those leading Swiss watch manufacturing companies is that the worst decision that could be made would be for the companies to fail to respond to the iWatch. Google, Intel and TAG Heuer believe they are uniquely qualified to respond to the iWatch given the technology used to produce it and in light of Apple's decision to offer "upscale" luxury versions of the product, priced initially between $10,000 and $17,000. Recognizing the threat of smartwatches, other Swiss watchmakers, in addition to TAG Heuer, are taking action. "Swatch, Breitling, Montblanc, and Frederique Constant are among those that have entered the fray, with products ranging from a messaging device that clips to a watch strap to a gold-plated watch containing a fitness tracker." Supporting the decision among all of these firms to be involved with smartwatches is the size of the market for this product. In 2014, 4.6 million smartwatches were sold globally. Analysts thought the market for this product might jump to as many as 30 million units in 2015. In contrast, the number of Swiss watches sold in 2015 was expected to decline by 6.3 percent from the number sold a year earlier.

TAG Heuer CEO Jean-Claude Biver describes the nature of the alliance his firm has formed with Google and Intel as follows: "Swiss watchmaking and Silicon Valley is a marriage of technological innovation with watchmaking credibility. Our collaboration provides a rich host of synergies, forming a win-win partnership, and the potential for our three companies is enormous." In essence then, he believes that Google and Intel bring unique technological innovation to the partnership while his firm brings its reputation and skills as a successful manufacturer of luxury Swiss watches. Part of the reason TAG Heuer's watches are thought of as a luxury good is that the firm is a unit of French luxury giant LVMH Moet Hennessy Louis Vuitton SA. Influencing the formation of this alliance is Google's desire to demonstrate that its software can effectively power wearables, Intel's desire to show how its chips can be used in wearables, and TAG Heuer's desire to design and produce more technologically sophisticated watches that meet the needs of today's tech-savvy consumers. To expand their footprint in luxury goods, both Google and Intel have established additional alliances. Intel is collaborating with Luxottica Group SpA to produce smart eyewear and Google is partnering with the same firm to create new designs of Google Glass.

As is the case with all strategies, alliances such as the one among Google, Intel and TAG Heuer are not risk free. The degree to which the cultures of technology firms that are strongly oriented to producing innovation after innovation with the precision-oriented culture of a luxury Swiss watchmaker can be successfully integrated is an important concern. Another risk is that the significant amount of coordination that will be required to integrate the firms' operations that are based in different countries along with all of the companies that are involved with the international electronics supply chain may not be achieved efficiently. In spite of these potential risks, the opportunity to innovate in a rapidly expanding global market seems to be more than sufficient to support the decision among Google, Intel and TAG Heuer to collaboratively design and produce a novel smartwatch.

Sources: A. Chen, 2015, Google, Intel, TAG Heuer to collaborate on Swiss smartwatch, *Wall Street Journal Online*, //www.wsj.com, March 19; M. Clerizol, 2015, There's something in the way they move, *Wall Street Journal Online*, www.wsj.com, March 18; L. Dignan, 2015, Can TAG Heuer, Intel, Google collaborate and create a smart enough watch? *ZDNET Online*, www.zdnet.com, March 19; S. Kessler, 2015, Intel, Google, and TAG Heuer announce a Swiss smartwatch, *Fast Company Online*, www.fastcompany.com, March, 19; J. Newman, 2015, TAG Heuer, Google, and Intel get together to announce a conceptual smartwatch, *PCWorld Online*, www.pcworld.com, March 19; J. Revill, 2015, Swiss watchmakers rise to the smartwatch challenge, *Wall Street Journal Online*, www.wsj.com, March 19; K. Sintumuang, 2015, Will the Apple watch eclipse the classic Swiss watch? *Wall Street Journal Online*, www.wsj.com, April 17.

In describing the multiple arenas in which Google competes in Chapter 5's Opening Case, we mentioned the firm's plans to enter the smartwatch market. In this chapter's Opening Case, we describe in detail the actions Google is taking to do this. More specifically, we describe the cooperative strategy Google, Intel, and TAG Heuer have formed in order to apply technological innovations to compete in the world of luxury fashion. None of these firms could produce the particular type of smartwatch the collaborators plan to develop without the other two partners. This collaboration is one through which each company is using some of its unique resources (as well as the capabilities and core competencies that flow from them) in order to design, produce, and then launch a product into a specific market. It is the specific combination of each firm's unique resources through which a particular smartwatch is to be developed. Thus, as is the case for all companies implementing cooperative strategies, these three firms intend to use their resources in ways that will create the greatest amount of value for stakeholders.[1]

Forming a cooperative strategy like the one among Google, Intel, and TAG Heuer has the potential to help companies reach an objective that is important to all of them, such as firm growth. Specifically, a **cooperative strategy** is a means by which firms collaborate to achieve a shared objective.[2] Cooperating with others is a strategy firms use to create value for a customer that it likely could not create by itself. As noted above, this is the situation for Google, Intel, and TAG Heuer in that none of these firms could create the specific smartwatch the firms intended to develop without the combination of the three companies' resources. (Throughout this chapter, the term "resources" is used comprehensively and refers to a firm's capabilities as well as its resources.)

Firms also try to create competitive advantages when using a cooperative strategy.[3] A competitive advantage developed through a cooperative strategy often is called a *collaborative* or *relational* advantage,[4] indicating that the relationship that develops among collaborating partners is commonly the basis on which to build a competitive advantage. Importantly, successfully using cooperative strategies finds a firm outperforming its rivals in terms of strategic competitiveness and above-average returns,[5] often because they've been able to form a competitive advantage.

A **cooperative strategy** is a means by which firms collaborate to achieve a shared objective.

We examine several topics in this chapter. First, we define and offer examples of different strategic alliances as primary types of cooperative strategies. We focus on strategic alliances because firms use them more frequently than other types of cooperative relationships. In succession, we describe business-level, corporate-level, international, and network cooperative strategies. The chapter closes with a discussion of the risks of using cooperative strategies as well as how effectively managing the strategies can reduce these risks.

9-1 Strategic Alliances as a Primary Type of Cooperative Strategy

A **strategic alliance** is a cooperative strategy in which firms combine some of their resources to create a competitive advantage. Strategic alliances involve firms with some degree of exchange and sharing of resources to jointly develop, sell, and service goods or services.[6] In addition, firms use strategic alliances to leverage their existing resources while working with partners to develop additional resources as the foundation for new competitive advantages.[7] To be certain, the reality today is that strategic alliances are a vital strategy that firms use as a means to try to outperform rivals.[8]

An alliance involving Juniper and Aruba Networks is an example of a partnership that has been formed to combine individual firms' unique resources in order to create competitive advantages as a path to outperforming rivals. To enhance their ability to innovate as a way to solve complex enterprise problems, Juniper and Aruba formed an alliance through which they are collaborating at both the product development stage and the sales stage by leveraging their client relationships and reseller networks. Commenting about this alliance, one analyst indicated that Juniper will contribute "its expertise in wired infrastructure (enterprise switches and routers) (while) Aruba provides its wireless mobility solutions."[9]

Before describing three types of major strategic alliances and reasons for their use, we need to note that, for all cooperative strategies, success is more likely when partners behave cooperatively. Actively solving problems, being trustworthy, and consistently pursuing ways to combine partners' resources to create value are examples of cooperative behavior known to contribute to alliance success.[10]

9-1a Types of Major Strategic Alliances

Joint ventures, equity strategic alliances, and nonequity strategic alliances are the three major types of strategic alliances that firms use. The ownership arrangement is a key difference among these alliances.

A **joint venture** is a strategic alliance in which two or more firms create a legally independent company to share some of their resources to create a competitive advantage. Typically, partners in a joint venture own equal percentages and contribute equally to the venture's operations. Often formed to improve a firm's ability to compete in uncertain competitive environments, joint ventures can be effective in establishing long-term relationships and in transferring tacit knowledge between partners.

GM and China-based SAIC Motor Corp., China's largest automobile manufacturer by sales volume, recently formed a joint venture to develop new cars that cater specifically to Chinese tastes. Called Shanghai GM Co., each partner owns 50 percent of this cooperative strategy. The partners intend to invest a total of 100 billion yuan, or approximately $16.4 billion, between 2016 and 2020 for the purpose of developing at least "10 all-new or face-lift" models during each of the five years included within the investment time horizon. Part of the investment is to be allocated to bring green technologies to China. Using some green technologies to produce automobiles is a key way the joint venture's products are to be differentiated from those produced by competitors.[11] Demonstrating the complexities

A **strategic alliance** is a cooperative strategy in which firms combine some of their resources to create a competitive advantage.

A **joint venture** is a strategic alliance in which two or more firms create a legally independent company to share some of their resources to create a competitive advantage.

This is a photo of the Shanghai GM facility where the work of the firms' joint venture takes place.

Shanghai GM.PNG

associated with being a successful competitor in today's business environment is the fact that SAIC also has a joint venture with Volkswagen AG. Among other products, the SAIC-VW joint venture manufacturers the Tiguan sport-utility model, which is the number one foreign-brand SUV being sold in China.[12]

Because it can't be codified, tacit knowledge, which is increasingly critical to firms' efforts to develop competitive advantages, is learned through experiences such as those taking place when people from partner firms work together in a joint venture.[13] Overall, a joint venture may be the optimal type of cooperative arrangement when firms need to combine their resources to create a competitive advantage that is substantially different from any they possess individually and when the partners intend to compete in highly uncertain environments.

An **equity strategic alliance** is an alliance in which two or more firms own different percentages of a company that they have formed by combining some of their resources to create a competitive advantage. Many foreign direct investments in China by multinational corporations are completed through equity strategic alliances. For example, Boston Scientific has formed an alliance with Frankenman Medical Equipment Company, a firm with headquarters in Suzhou, China. Boston Scientific will become a shareholder of Frankenman and will also provide "services and expertise to Frankenman to support its continued growth, development pipeline, and manufacturing capabilities." This alliance will combine Boston Scientific's capabilities related to less invasive endoscopic technologies with Frankenman's local market expertise.[14] Likewise, many Chinese firms, particularly those that are state owned, use equity alliances to engage in outward foreign direct investment.[15]

Firms sometimes form equity alliances in order to refocus their strategy as a means of creating a competitive advantage. This appears to be the case with the alliance Johnson Controls recently developed with Yanfeng Automotive Trim Systems Co., Ltd. Called Yanfeng Automotive Interiors, the alliance will produce and sell cockpit systems, floor consoles, and instrument panels in India, Japan, China, Europe, and the United States. Johnson has a 30 percent stake in the partnership, while Yanfeng holds a 70 percent interest. This relationship finds Johnson spinning off its automotive-interiors business to the alliance. Analysts viewed the forming of this partnership as a move by Johnson to focus on its higher-margin, non-auto businesses such as "York heating and air-conditioning equipment for commercial buildings."[16]

A **nonequity strategic alliance** is an alliance in which two or more firms develop a contractual relationship to share some of their resources to create a competitive advantage.[17] In this type of alliance, firms do not establish a separate independent company and therefore do not take equity positions. For this reason, nonequity strategic alliances are less formal, demand fewer partner commitments than do joint ventures and equity strategic alliances, and generally do not foster an intimate relationship between partners; nonetheless, research evidence indicates that they can create value for the involved firms.[18] The relative informality and lower commitment levels characterizing nonequity strategic alliances make them unsuitable for complex projects where success requires partners to be able to effectively transfer tacit knowledge to each other.[19] Licensing agreements, distribution agreements, and supply contracts are examples of nonequity strategic alliances.

An **equity strategic alliance** is an alliance in which two or more firms own different percentages of the company they have formed by combining some of their resources to create a competitive advantage.

A **nonequity strategic alliance** is an alliance in which two or more firms develop a contractual relationship to share some of their resources to create a competitive advantage.

Commonly, outsourcing arrangements are organized in the form of a nonequity strategic alliance. (Discussed in Chapter 3, *outsourcing* is the purchase of a value-chain activity or a support-function activity from another firm.) Apple Inc. and most other companies involved with selling computers, tablets, and smartphones use nonequity strategic alliances to outsource most or all of the activities required to manufacture their products. Apple, for example, has traditionally outsourced most of its manufacturing to Foxconn Technology Group. Recently, Foxconn, with most of its production facilities located in China, was manufacturing 70 percent of all iPhone 6 phones.[20] Firms often choose to use nonequity strategic alliances to outsource manufacturing activities to Chinese companies because of the cost efficiencies those firms generate through scale economies.[21] This collaborative pattern between a product designer such as Apple and

Courtesy of ZDnet

This is a Foxconn employee who is working to produce iPhone 6s for Apple.

a manufacturer such as Foxconn is likely to continue. One reason for this is that Foxconn, for example, works within an ecosystem of firms that supply it with the component parts it requires to manufacture products for its customers. Effective ecosystems, such as the one in which Foxconn operates, create value that is difficult for competitors to imitate.[22]

9-1b Reasons Firms Develop Strategic Alliances

Cooperative strategies are an integral part of the competitive landscape and are quite important to many companies. The fact that alliances can account for up to 25 percent or more of a typical firm's sales revenue demonstrates their importance. In addition to partnerships among for-profit organizations, alliances are also formed between educational institutions and individual companies for the purpose of commercializing ideas flowing from basic research projects that are completed at universities.[23] Moreover, in addition to dyadic partnerships where two firms form a collaborative relationship for competitive purposes, competition now occurs between large alliances themselves in some industries. This pattern of competition exists in the global airline industry where individual airlines compete against each other but simultaneously join alliances (such as Star, OneWorld and SkyTeam) which in turn compete against each other.[24] The array of alliances with which firms are involved highlight the various options available to companies seeking to increase their competitiveness by cooperating with others.

Overall, there are many reasons firms choose to participate in strategic alliances. We mention two key reasons here and discuss additional ones below by explaining how strategic alliances may help firms improve their competitiveness while competing in either slow-, fast-, or standard-cycle markets.

Making it possible for firms to create value they couldn't generate by acting independently and entering markets more rapidly combine to form the first important reason firms form strategic alliances.[25] The partnership formed among online news publishers *The Guardian*, *CNN International*, *Financial Times*, and *The Economist* for the purpose of making it possible for advertisers to reach online audiences with scale demonstrates this reason. Called Pangea, those forming this alliance concluded that the collaboration would help the firms efficiently expand on a global basis. In commenting about this, one firm's executive said that "we've come together to ensure the quality that's represented by these publisher brands is now available at scale."[26]

A second major reason firms form strategic alliances is that most (if not all) companies lack the full set of resources needed to pursue all identified opportunities and reach their objectives in the process of doing so, a reality indicating that partnering with others will increase the probability of reaching firm-specific performance objectives. Given constrained resources, firms can collaborate for a number of purposes, including those of reaching new customers and broadening both the product offerings and the distribution of their products without adding significantly to their cost structures.

Through the partnership between Expedia and Latin American online travel leader Decolar.com, which operates the Portuguese Decolar.com and Spanish Despegar.com websites, both firms are deriving important benefits that neither could access acting independently. In this sense, the partnership "...offers Expedia better exposure to the Latin American travelers (while) Decolar benefits by expanding its portfolio of international hotel supply through Expedia."[27]

As we discussed in Chapter 5, when considering competitive rivalry and competitive dynamics, unique competitive conditions characterize slow-, fast-, and standard-cycle markets.[28] As shown in Figure 9.1, these unique market types create different reasons for firms to use strategic alliances.

In short, *slow-cycle markets* are markets where the firm's competitive advantages are shielded from imitation for relatively long periods of time and where imitation is costly. Railroads and, historically, telecommunications, utilities, and financial services are

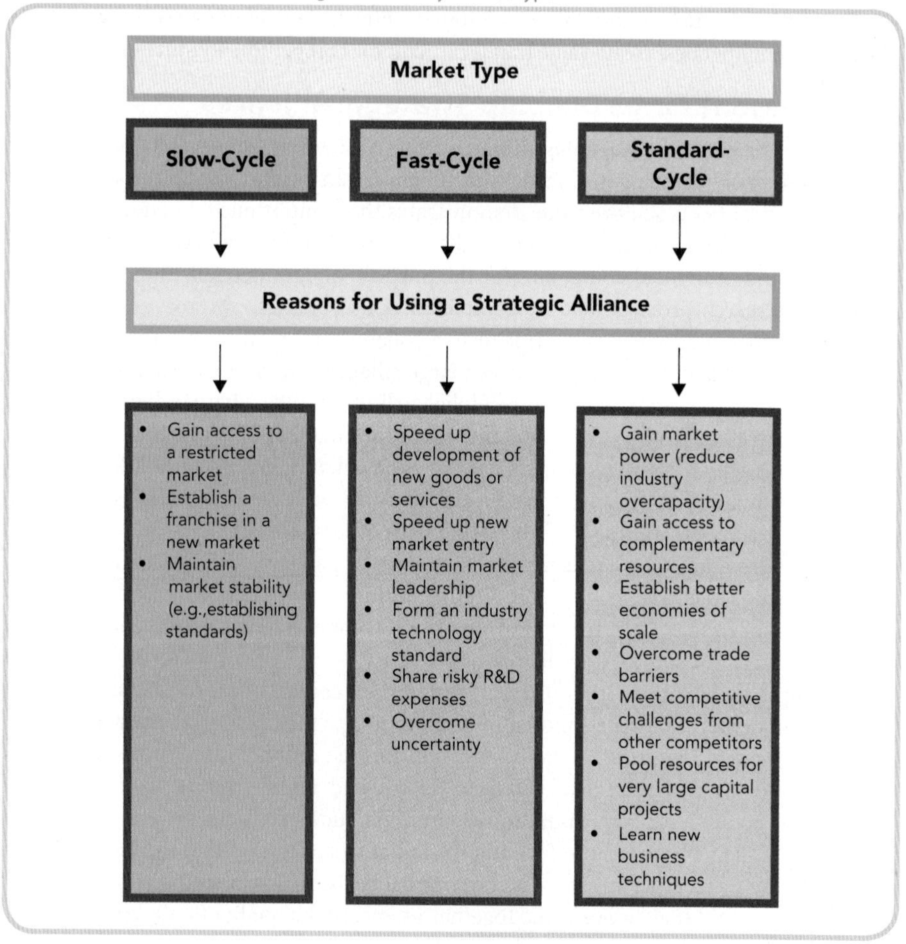

Figure 9.1 Reasons for Strategic Alliances by Market Type

industries characterized as slow-cycle markets. In *fast-cycle markets*, the firm's competitive advantages are not shielded from imitation, preventing their long-term sustainability. Competitive advantages are moderately shielded from imitation in *standard-cycle markets*, typically allowing them to be sustained for a longer period of time than in fast-cycle market situations, but for a shorter period of time than in slow-cycle markets.

Slow-Cycle Markets

Firms in slow-cycle markets often use strategic alliances to enter restricted markets or to establish a franchise in a new market. For example, Carnival Corporation, owner and operator of Carnival Cruise Line, recently formed two joint ventures with state-owned China Merchants Group, which is a conglomerate with businesses in financial investments and property development as well as transportation. One venture between the two firms focuses on shipbuilding while the second concentrates on developing new ports and travel destinations in and around China. The launching of China's first domestic cruise brand that will target Chinese customers is one outcome associated with the collaborations between the two companies. Carnival's interest with these joint ventures is to quickly scale up its operations in China where the cruise industry is beginning to grow rapidly. Similarly, China Merchants Group wants to partner with a major competitor in the cruise industry to better position itself for future growth.[29]

Slow-cycle markets are becoming rare in the twenty-first century competitive landscape for several reasons, including the privatization of industries and economies, the rapid expansion of the Internet's capabilities for quick dissemination of information, and the speed with which advancing technologies make quickly imitating even complex products possible.[30] Firms competing in slow-cycle markets should recognize the likelihood that in the future, they will encounter situations in which their competitive advantages become partially sustainable (in the instance of a standard-cycle market) or unsustainable (in the case of a fast-cycle market). Cooperative strategies can help firms transition from relatively sheltered markets, such as the travel cruise market in which Carnival Corporation competes, to more competitive ones.[31]

Fast-Cycle Markets

Fast-cycle markets are unstable, unpredictable, and complex; in a word, hypercompetitive.[32] Combined, these conditions virtually preclude establishing sustainable competitive advantages, forcing firms to constantly seek sources of new competitive advantages while creating value by using current ones. Alliances between firms with current excess resources and those with promising resources help companies competing in fast-cycle markets effectively transition from the present to the future and gain rapid entry into new markets. As such, a "collaboration mindset" is of paramount importance for firms competing in fast-cycle markets.[33]

Micron Technology, Inc. and Seagate Technology LLC are competitors in manufacturing storage solutions, a competitive arena in which establishing sustainable competitive advantages is all but impossible. Because of this, innovation is critical to their success as well as for

Shown here is a Carnival Cruise Line ship that may soon transport Chinese customers through the firm's joint venture with China Merchants Group.

think4photop/Shutterstock.com

others operating in this industry given the fast-cycle nature of the storage-solution market. Micron and Seagate recently formed a strategic alliance for the purpose of combining the firms' innovation and expertise. Resulting from this collaboration, the partners believe, will be an ability to provide customers with "industry-leading" storage solutions. In turn, Micron and Seagate believe that customers buying the products that will flow from the collaboration will themselves be able to innovate faster while producing their goods and services. As reflected by the following comment from a customer, those anticipating buying products from the firms' strategic alliance seem to believe that novel products will be available to them to purchase: "The strategic agreement between Micron and Seagate promises to deliver new and innovative flash-based storage solutions."[34]

Standard-Cycle Markets

In standard-cycle markets, alliances are more likely to be made by partners that have complementary resources. The alliances formed by airline companies are an example of standard-cycle market alliances.

When initially established, airline alliances were intended to allow firms to share their complementary resources to make it easier for passengers to fly between secondary cities in the United States and Europe. Today, airline alliances are mostly global in nature and are formed primarily so members can gain marketing clout, have opportunities to reduce costs, and have access to additional international routes.[35] Of these reasons, international expansion by having access to more international routes is the most important because these routes are the path to increased revenues and potential profits. To support efforts to control costs, alliance members jointly purchase some items and share facilities such as passenger gates, customer service centers, and airport passenger lounges when possible. For passengers, airline alliances create benefits such as less complicated ticket buying processes, easier connections for international flights, and the earning of frequent flyer miles.

There are three major airline alliances operating today. Star Alliance is the largest with 27 members. With 16 members, Oneworld Alliance is the smallest, while the 20-member SkyTeam Alliance is in between the other two alliances in terms of total number of members. All three alliances continue to add members to expand their geographic coverage and to respond to market trends, such as the increasing amount of travel from regions throughout the world to Asia. In general, most airline alliances, such as the three we mention here, are formed to help firms gain economies of scale and meet competitive challenges (see Figure 9.1). Code sharing agreements and the ability to reduce costs associated with operations, maintenance, and purchases are examples of how airline alliances help members gain economies of scale as a path to increasing their competitiveness.[36]

9-2   Business-Level Cooperative Strategy

A **business-level cooperative strategy** is a strategy through which firms combine some of their resources to create a competitive advantage by competing in one or more product markets. As discussed in Chapter 4, business-level strategy details what the firm intends to do to gain a competitive advantage in specific product markets. Thus, the firm forms a business-level cooperative strategy when it believes that combining some of its resources with those of one or more partners will create competitive advantages that it can't create by itself and will lead to success in a specific product market. We present the four business-level cooperative strategies in Figure 9.2.

9-2a   Complementary Strategic Alliances

Complementary strategic alliances are business-level alliances in which firms share some of their resources in complementary ways to create a competitive advantage.[37] Vertical and horizontal are the two dominant types of complementary strategic alliances (see Figure 9.2).

A **business-level cooperative strategy** is a strategy through which firms combine some of their resources to create a competitive advantage by competing in one or more product markets.

Complementary strategic alliances are business-level alliances in which firms share some of their resources in complementary ways to create a competitive advantage.

Figure 9.2 Business-Level Cooperative Strategies

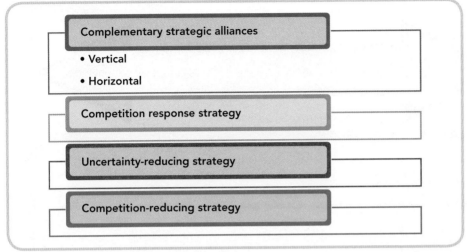

Vertical Complementary Strategic Alliance

In a *vertical complementary strategic alliance*, firms share some of their resources from different stages of the value chain for the purpose of creating a competitive advantage (see Figure 9.3).[38] Oftentimes, vertical complementary alliances are formed to adapt to environmental changes;[39] sometimes the changes represent an opportunity for partnering firms to innovate while adapting.[40]

Companies recognize that today's consumers are more connected than ever as they use various devices such as smartphone applications, GPS systems, and the wireless Internet. GE Lighting and Qualcomm Atheros, Inc. (a subsidiary of Qualcomm Incorporated) formed a vertical complementary alliance to bring another functionality to "tech savvy" shoppers. By combining Qualcomm's wireless technologies, which yield positioning information, with GE's LED bulbs that are used to light retail stores, these two firms are making it possible for retailers to "talk" to customers while they shop. The real-time connection this configuration creates allows "retailers to combine contextual information with location to create revolutionary new tools such as indoor navigation, infinite aisle, suggested items, product information, and special offers or coupons to those who opt in and download the retailer's app."[41]

Horizontal Complementary Strategic Alliance

A *horizontal complementary strategic alliance* is an alliance in which firms share some of their resources from the same stage (or stages) of the value chain for the purpose of creating a competitive advantage. Automobile manufacturers make frequent use of this type of alliance, as do pharmaceutical companies. In this regard, Sorrento Therapeutics, Inc. is collaborating with NantWorks LLC to develop "next generation immunotherapies

Ringo Chiu/ZUMA Press, Inc./Alamy

Mr. Patrick Soon-Shiong, pictured here, is the CEO of Nantworks LLC. This firm is collaborating with Sorrento Therapeutics to develop innovative drugs for the purpose of combating serious diseases such as cancer.

Figure 9.3 Vertical and Horizontal Complementary Strategic Alliances

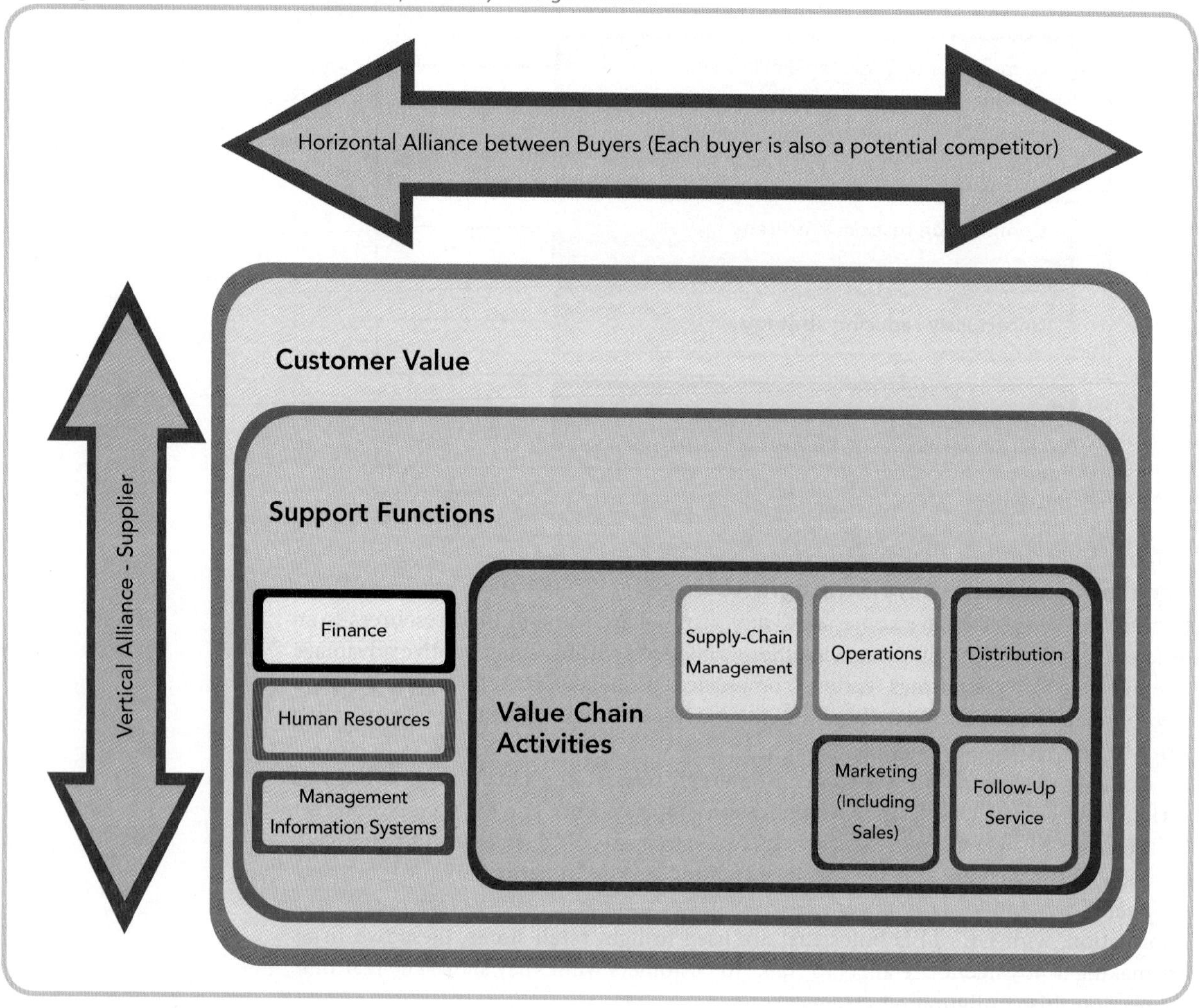

for cancer and autoimmune diseases."[42] More comprehensively, some of the world's largest pharmaceutical firms, including Pfizer, Bristol-Myers Squibb, GlaxoSmithKline and Eli Lilly, are sharing some of their proprietary assets through a collaboration organized by the U.S.-based National Institutes of Health. The primary purpose of this five-year partnership is to more quickly discover and produce drugs that cure challenging and, what historically have been, intractable diseases.[43]

Commonly, firms use complementary strategic alliances to focus on joint long-term product development and distribution opportunities.[44] For example, Boeing Company and Lockheed Martin Corporation recently formed a partnership "to defend their profitable Pentagon space rocket business with an all-new rocket equipped with reusable engines that could slash satellite-launch costs and provide a steppingstone to various commercial space ventures."[45] Thus, the essence of this collaboration is pursuing opportunities to find ways to monetize operations in space.

9-2b　Competition Response Strategy

As discussed in Chapter 5, competitors initiate competitive actions (strategic and tactical) to attack rivals and launch competitive responses (strategic and tactical) to their competitors' actions. Strategic alliances can be used at the business level to respond to competitors' attacks. The alliance among Google, Intel, and TAG Heuer that is discussed in the Opening Case is a strategic response to Apple's strategic action of introducing the iWatch. Because they can be difficult to reverse and expensive to operate, strategic alliances are primarily formed to take strategic rather than tactical actions and to respond to competitors' actions in a like manner.

In October of 2007, SABMiller and Molson Coors Brewing Company formed a partnership. At the time, these firms held the second and third largest shares of the U.S. brew market. When formed, MillerCoors LLC, the name of the partnership, commanded roughly 29 percent of the U.S. brew market. However, Anheuser-Busch held 49 percent of the market. Indeed, the MillerCoors collaboration was a response to the size and scale of Anheuser-Busch's operations. (Anheuser-Busch itself was acquired by InBev in 2008, an acquisition that created the world's largest brewer.) Indicating that the collaboration would result in significant cost reductions and an ability to generate economies of scale through the firms' combined operations, a company official said that "Miller and Coors will be a stronger, more competitive U.S. brewer than either company can be on its own." Analysts agreed with this assessment, with one person noting that the partnership would give the two companies "substantially more scale, which helps them with their retailers and their distributors and helps erode Anheuser Busch's No. 1 competitive advantage, which is their (market) share."[46] A successful collaboration in response to competitors for many years, MillerCoors today is struggling as it tries to compete against consumers' emerging preference for craft brews and cocktails instead of domestic lagers.[47] Thus, finding ways to effectively manage this alliance going forward is critical to its future.

9-2c Uncertainty-Reducing Strategy

Firms sometimes use business-level strategic alliances to hedge against risk and uncertainty, especially in fast-cycle markets.[48] These strategies are also used where uncertainty exists, such as in entering new product markets, especially those within emerging economies.

The relationship between hybrid vehicles and batteries that are needed to power them create a situation for which alliances are being formed to reduce uncertainty. More specifically, there is insufficient industry capacity among battery manufacturers to meet the demand for the type of batteries used in hybrids. This lack of a sufficient supply of electric batteries creates uncertainty for automobile manufacturers. To reduce this uncertainty, auto manufacturers are forming alliances. For example, Daimler AG formed a partnership with Tesla through which it buys Tesla batteries to use in its "smart" minicar as well as its Freightliner trucks. This collaboration continues even though Daimler recently sold its 4 percent ownership stake in Tesla.[49] Knowing that it has access to quality batteries through Tesla reduces Daimler's uncertainty with respect to a component part that is critical to building some of its products.

We further discuss Tesla in the Strategic Focus. As you will see, alliances are critical to this firm's current operations and will no doubt affect its ability to achieve success in the long term.

9-2d Competition-Reducing Strategy

Used to reduce competition, collusive strategies differ from strategic alliances in that collusive strategies are often an illegal cooperative strategy. Explicit collusion and tacit collusion are the two types of collusive strategies.

Explicit collusion exists when two or more firms negotiate directly to jointly agree about the amount to produce as well as the prices for what is produced.[50] Explicit collusion

Strategic **Focus**

Strategic Alliances as the Foundation for Tesla Motors' Operations

Founded in 2003, Tesla Motors, the manufacturer of electric vehicles, has formed many alliances as a means of competing during the early years of its life. For example, the company created a R&D partnership with Dana Holding Corporation initially for the purpose of jointly designing and producing a system capable of controlling the build-up of heat in its car batteries. Overall, Tesla has partnered with many companies working in the value chain that is used to produce its products. In this sense, alliances have been formed with suppliers, R&D experts, as well as original equipment manufacturers such as Daimler. One of the projects on which Daimler and Tesla are collaborating is the B-Class Electric Drive, an all-electric vehicle from Mercedes-Benz. Other partnerships that have been formed over the years include Tesla's nonequity strategic alliance with Sotira, a French company, and an equity alliance with Panasonic, a Japanese-based firm. The purpose of the partnership with Sotira is to manufacturer the carbon fiber bodies for its cars, while battery cells for the Tesla battery pack are produced through the collaboration with Panasonic.

Interestingly, its on-going work with batteries and recent hints from founder and CEO Elon Musk suggest that Tesla may, at is core, become a battery company rather than an automobile manufacturer. Appearing to support this possibility were comments indicating that Tesla intends to make and sell mega-batteries for homes and electric utility companies. The firm's decision to build and operate a 10-million-square-foot facility (dubbed the Gigafactory) to build batteries seems to reflect Tesla's capacity to build an array of batteries with different functionalities. With an initial investment of $5 billion, this factory was to be the largest lithium-ion-battery plant in the world. One goal of the Gigafactory is to "make batteries so cheap that electric cars can compete with conventional gasoline engines." Interestingly, the Gigafactory's size and scale allow Tesla to produce a quantity of batteries exceeding the firm's needs for its cars. In turn, analysts suggested that the company may seek additional partnerships as a way of continuing to develop innovative batteries and to sell some of the outputs from its plant.

In early 2015, Apple announced an internal project that was aimed at developing an Apple-branded electric vehicle. With a code-name "Titan," the initial work was oriented to designing a vehicle that resembles a minivan. Early assessments were that Apple intended to compete directly against Tesla if it decided to enter the electric vehicle market space. At the same time, the seriousness with which Apple is approaching this initial

design work is unknown, especially given the company's pattern of going so far as developing product prototypes before deciding to abandon a potential innovation. Additionally, the complexity of designing and producing an electric vehicle is such that several years would be required for Apple to introduce its product to the market, even if it chose to do so. Still, Apple's large investable assets and its innovative successes suggest that Tesla executives would be well served to carefully observe the firm's progress with respect to the Titan project.

Shown here is a Telsa Roadster and the electric battery pack that powers the car.

Other recent speculation regarding Tesla and Apple centered on the possibility of Apple acquiring Tesla, at a rumored cost of roughly $75 billion. In contrast, some analysts were suggesting that "some sort of joint venture or collaboration remains the smartest bet for both companies" (Apple and Tesla). As Tesla looks to its future, might the possibility of collaborating with another innovative firm, but one with significant financial resources, be a viable option? And from a broad perspective, might "a collaboration between the two tech giants, each with enormous clout and credibility, go a long way to converting the electric car from niche curiosity to mass consumer good?"

Sources: K. Finley, 2015, Tesla isn't an automaker. It's a battery company, *Wired*, www.wired.com, April 22; N. Gordon-Bloomfield, Move over Tesla: LG Chem now largest manufacturer of electric car battery packs thanks to Daimler deal, *Transport Evolved*, www.transportevolved.com, April 2; T. Lee, 2015, Apple, Tesla alliance still makes most sense for electric car, *San Francisco Chronicle Online*, www.sfchronicle.com, February 17; D. Wakabayashi & M. Ramsey, 2015, Apple gears up to challenge Tesla in electric cars, *Wall Street Journal Online*, www.wsj.com, February 13; C. Trudell & A. Ohnsman, 2014, Why the Tesla-Toyota partnership short-circuited, *Bloomberg News Online*, www.bloomberg.com, August. 7.

Doug Cheeseman/Getty Images

strategies are illegal in the United States and most developed economies (except in regulated industries). Accordingly, companies choosing to explicitly collude with other firms should recognize that competitors and regulatory bodies likely will challenge the acceptability of their competitive actions.

Tacit collusion exists when several firms in an industry indirectly coordinate their production and pricing decisions by observing each other's competitive actions and responses.[51] Tacit collusion tends to take place in industries dominated by a few large firms. "With tacit collusion, competitors don't agree to pricing, but since there are so few of them they all understand very well how their competition will behave, and are able to prevent dramatic prices slides by using this understanding."[52] Tacit collusion results in production output that is below fully competitive levels and above fully competitive prices. In addition to the effects on competition within a particular market, research suggests that tacit collusion between two firms can lead to less competition in other markets in which both firms operate.[53]

As suggested above, tacit collusion tends to be used as a competition-reducing, business-level strategy in industries with a high degree of concentration, such as the airline and breakfast cereal industries. Research in the airline industry suggests that tacit collusion reduces service quality and on-time performance.[54] Firms in these industries recognize their interdependence, which means that their competitive actions and responses significantly affect competitors' behavior toward them. Understanding this interdependence and carefully observing competitors can lead to tacit collusion.

Over time, four firms—Kellogg Company (producers of Kellogg's Corn Flakes, Fruit Loops, etc.), General Mills, Inc. (Cheerios, Lucky Charms, etc.), Ralcorp Holdings, now owned by ConAgra Foods (producing mostly private store brands), and Quaker Foods North America, a part of PepsiCo (Quaker Oatmeal, Cap'n Crunch, etc.)—have accounted for as much as 80 percent of sales volume in the ready-to-eat segment of the U.S. cereal market.[55] The global breakfast cereals market is expected to grow at roughly 4 percent annually for the next few years, reaching a total of $43.2 billion by 2019.[56] Some believe that the high degree of concentration in the global breakfast cereals industry results in prices to consumers that substantially exceed the costs companies incur to produce and sell their products. If prices are above the competitive level in this industry, it may be a possibility that the dominant firms use a tacit collusion cooperative strategy.

Mutual forbearance is a form of tacit collusion in which firms do not take competitive actions against rivals they meet in multiple markets. Rivals learn a great deal about each other when engaging in multimarket competition, including how to deter the effects of their rivals' competitive attacks and responses. Given what they know about each other as competitors, firms choose not to engage in what could be destructive competition in multiple product markets.[57]

In general, governments in free-market economies seek to determine how rivals can form cooperative strategies for the purpose of increasing their competitiveness without violating established regulations about competition.[58] However, this task is challenging when evaluating collusive strategies, particularly tacit ones. For example, the regulation of securities analysts through Regulation Fair Disclosure (Reg-FD) as established in the United States promoted more potential competition through competitive parity by eliminating privileged access to proprietary firm information as a critical source of competitive advantage. In doing so, research suggests that it led to more mutual forbearance among competing firms because they had more awareness of information possessed by their competitors, thus leading to more tacit collusion.[59] In the final analysis, individual companies must analyze the effect of a competition-reducing strategy on their performance and competitiveness and decide if pursuing such a strategy facilitates or inhibits their competitive success.

9-2e Assessing Business-Level Cooperative Strategies

Firms use business-level cooperative strategies to develop competitive advantages that can contribute to successful positions in individual product markets. Evidence suggests that complementary business-level strategic alliances, especially vertical ones, have the greatest probability of creating a competitive advantage and possibly even a sustainable one.[60] Horizontal complementary alliances are sometimes difficult to maintain because often they are formed between firms that compete against each other at the same time they are cooperating. Airline companies, for example, want to compete aggressively against others serving their markets and customers. However, the need to develop scale economies and to share resources (such as scheduling systems) dictates that alliances be formed so the companies can compete by using cooperative actions and responses while they simultaneously compete against one another through competitive actions and responses. The challenge in these instances is for each firm to find ways to create the greatest amount of value from their simultaneous competitive and cooperative actions.

Although strategic alliances designed to respond to competition and to reduce uncertainty can also create competitive advantages, these advantages often are more temporary than those developed through complementary (both vertical and horizontal) alliances. The primary reason for this is that complementary alliances have a stronger focus on creating value than do competition-reducing and uncertainty-reducing alliances, which are formed to respond to competitors' actions or reduce uncertainty rather than to attack competitors.

9-3 Corporate-Level Cooperative Strategy

A **corporate-level cooperative strategy** is a strategy through which a firm collaborates with one or more companies to expand its operations. Diversifying alliances, synergistic alliances, and franchising are the most commonly used corporate-level cooperative strategies (see Figure 9.4).

Firms use diversifying and synergistic alliances to improve their performance by diversifying their operations through a means other than or in addition to internal organic growth or a merger or acquisition.[61] When a firm seeks to diversify into markets in which the host nation's government prevents mergers and acquisitions, alliances become an especially appropriate option. Corporate-level strategic alliances are also attractive compared with mergers, and particularly acquisitions, because they require fewer resource commitments[62] and permit greater flexibility in terms of efforts to diversify partners'

A **corporate-level cooperative strategy** is a strategy through which a firm collaborates with one or more companies to expand its operations.

Figure 9.4 Corporate-Level Cooperative Strategies

Corporate-Level Cooperative Strategies		
Diversifying alliances	Synergistic alliances	Franchising

operations.[63] An alliance can be used as a way to determine whether the partners might benefit from a future merger or acquisition between them. This "testing" process often characterizes alliances formed to combine firms' unique technological resources and capabilities.[64]

9-3a   Diversifying Strategic Alliance

A **diversifying strategic alliance** is a strategy in which firms share some of their resources to engage in product and/or geographic diversification. Companies using this strategy typically seek to enter new markets (either domestic or outside of their home setting) with existing products or with newly developed products. Sikorsky Aircraft Corporation, a subsidiary of United Technologies Corporation, formed an alliance with Tata Advanced Systems partially to diversify where some of its products are produced. Through this partnership, Sikorsky's S-92 helicopter cabins are manufactured in India, as are more than 5,000 detailed aerospace components. This alliance allows Sikorsky to diversify the global supply chain that is critical to producing its products.[65]

9-3b   Synergistic Strategic Alliance

A **synergistic strategic alliance** is a strategy in which firms share some of their resources to create economies of scope. Similar to the business-level horizontal complementary strategic alliance, synergistic strategic alliances create synergy across multiple functions or multiple businesses between partner firms. The partnership between French-based Renault SA and Japan-based Nissan Motor Company that was formed in 1999 is a synergistic strategic alliance because, among other outcomes, the firms seek to create economies of scope by sharing their resources to develop manufacturing platforms that can be used to produce cars that will carry either the Renault or the Nissan brand. BMW relies on its collaboration with Chinese auto maker Brilliance (BBA is the name of this partnership) to produce engines in China as well as models including "BMW's 3-series and 5-series vehicles as well as the small X1 SUV."[66] This relationship is critical to BMW's efforts to maintain strong sales in China, a market in which roughly one-fifth of its total output is sold.

9-3c   Franchising

Franchising is a strategy in which a firm (the franchisor) uses a franchise as a contractual relationship to describe and control the sharing of its resources with its partners (the franchisees).[67] A *franchise* is a "form of business organization in which a firm that already has a successful product or service (the franchisor) licenses its trademark and method of doing business to other businesses (the franchisees) in exchange for an initial franchise fee and an ongoing royalty rate."[68] Often, the effectiveness of these strategic alliances is a product of how well the franchisor can replicate its success across multiple partners in a cost-effective way.[69] As with diversifying and synergistic strategic alliances, franchising is an alternative to pursuing growth through mergers and acquisitions. McDonald's, Choice Hotels International, Hilton International, Marriott International, Mrs. Fields Cookies, Subway, and Ace Hardware are well-known firms using the franchising corporate-level cooperative strategy.

Franchising is a particularly attractive strategy to use in fragmented industries, such as retailing, hotels and motels, and commercial printing. In fragmented industries, a large number of small and medium-sized firms compete as rivals; however, no firm or small set of firms has a dominant share, making it possible for a company to gain a large market share by consolidating independent companies through the contractual relationships that are a part of a franchise agreement.

A **diversifying strategic alliance** is a strategy in which firms share some of their resources to engage in product and/or geographic diversification.

A **synergistic strategic alliance** is a strategy in which firms share some of their resources to create economies of scope.

Franchising is a strategy in which a firm (the franchisor) uses a franchise as a contractual relationship to describe and control the sharing of its resources with its partners (the franchisees).

In the most successful franchising strategy, the partners (the franchisor and the franchisees) work closely together.[70] A primary responsibility of the franchisor is to develop programs to transfer to the franchisees the knowledge and skills that are needed to successfully compete at the local level.[71] In return, franchisees should provide feedback to the franchisor regarding how their units could become more effective and efficient.[72] Working cooperatively, the franchisor and its franchisees find ways to strengthen the core company's brand name, which is often the most important competitive advantage for franchisees operating in their local markets.[73]

9-3d Assessing Corporate-Level Cooperative Strategies

Costs are incurred to implement each type of cooperative strategy.[74] Compared with their business-level counterparts, corporate-level cooperative strategies commonly are broader in scope and more complex, making them relatively more challenging and costly to use.

In spite of these costs, firms can create competitive advantages and value for customers by effectively using corporate-level cooperative strategies.[75] Internalizing successful alliance experiences makes it more likely that the strategy will attain the desired advantages. In other words, those involved with forming and using corporate-level cooperative strategies can also use them to develop useful knowledge about how to succeed in the future. To gain maximum value from this knowledge, firms should organize it and verify that it is always properly distributed to those involved with forming and using alliances.

We explained in Chapter 6 that firms answer two questions when dealing with corporate-level strategy: in which businesses and product markets will the firm choose to compete and how will those businesses be managed? These questions are also answered as firms form corporate-level cooperative strategies. Thus, firms able to develop corporate-level cooperative strategies and manage them in ways that are valuable, rare, imperfectly imitable, and nonsubstitutable (see Chapter 3) develop a competitive advantage that is in addition to advantages gained through the activities completed to implement business-level cooperative strategies. (Later in the chapter, we further describe alliance management as another potential competitive advantage.)

9-4 International Cooperative Strategy

The new competitive landscape finds firms using cross-border transactions for several purposes. In Chapter 7, we discussed cross-border acquisitions—actions through which a company located in one country acquires a firm located in a different country. In Chapter 8, we described how firms use cross-border acquisitions as a way of entering international markets. Here in Chapter 9, we examine cross-border strategic alliances as a type of international cooperative strategy. Thus, as the discussions in Chapters 7, 8 and 9 show, firms engage in cross-border activities to achieve several related objectives.

A **cross-border strategic alliance** is a strategy in which firms with headquarters in different countries decide to combine some of their resources to create a competitive advantage. Taking place in virtually all industries, the number of cross-border alliances firms are completing continues to increase.[76] These alliances are sometimes formed instead of mergers and acquisitions, which can be riskier. Even though cross-border alliances can themselves be complex and hard to manage,[77] they have the potential to help firms use some of their resources to create value in locations outside their home market. The cross-border alliance between Renault and Nissan that we mentioned earlier is thought to be one of "the auto-industry's most successful cross-border alliances."[78] Through this collaboration, the partners cooperate in terms of development, procurement, and production processes partly in order to be able to create value in markets throughout the world that neither firm could create operating independently.

A **cross-border strategic alliance** is a strategy in which firms with headquarters in different countries decide to combine some of their resources to create a competitive advantage.

Limited domestic growth opportunities and foreign government economic policies are key reasons firms use cross-border alliances. As discussed in Chapter 8, local ownership is an important national policy objective in some nations. In India and China, for example, governmental policies reflect a strong preference to license local companies. Thus, in some countries, the full range of entry mode choices we described in Chapter 8 may not be available to firms seeking to geographically diversify. Indeed, investment by foreign firms in these instances may be allowed only through a partnership with a local firm, such as in a cross-border alliance. Important too is the fact that strategic alliances with local partners can help firms overcome certain liabilities of moving into a foreign country, including those related to a lack of knowledge of the local culture or institutional norms.[79] A cross-border strategic alliance can also help foreign partners from an operational perspective because the local partner has significantly more information about factors contributing to competitive success such as local markets, sources of capital, legal procedures, and politics.[80] Interestingly, research results suggest that firms with foreign operations have longer survival rates than domestic-only firms, although this is reduced if there are competition problems between foreign subsidiaries.[81]

In general, cross-border strategic alliances are more complex and risky than domestic strategic alliances. Complexity and, perhaps, risk may be factors associated with the alliance recently completed between Airbus Group NV and Korea Aerospace Industries Ltd. These firms are partnering to build at least 300 military and civilian helicopters in South Korea.[82] Complexity is suggested by the fact that the partners are committed to designing and producing "next-generation light civilian and military helicopters" that will satisfy South Korean customers. Risks include those of relying on unique, firm-specific cultures and practices as the foundation for designing next generation products in an acceptable time period and producing those products at acceptable costs. In spite of the risks, firms, such as Airbus and Korea Aerospace, choose to form and operate cross-border strategic alliances partly because companies competing internationally tend to outperform domestic-only competitors.

9-5 Network Cooperative Strategy

In addition to forming their own alliances with individual companies, an increasing number of firms are collaborating in multiple alliances called networks.[83] A **network cooperative strategy** is a strategy where several firms agree to form multiple partnerships to achieve shared objectives.

Through its Global Partner Network, Cisco has formed alliances with a host of companies including IBM, Emerson, Hitachi, CA Technologies Fujitsu, Intel, Nokia, and Wipro. Cisco uses alliances to drive its growth, differentiate itself from competitors, enter new businesses areas, and create competitive advantages. Recently, Cisco's annual revenues earned from its alliances exceeded $5 billion. Sometimes, several of the firms with which Cisco has formed individual alliances partner together to form a network to achieve shared objectives.[84]

Demonstrating the complexity of network cooperative strategies is the fact that Cisco also competes against a number of the firms with whom it has formed cooperative agreements, including network strategies. For example, Cisco is competing against IBM when selling and servicing its servers. At the same time, Cisco and IBM's alliance is very active as the two firms help organizations "find better ways to connect people, share critical data, and create analytic insights to improve"[85] their ability to earn above-average returns. Overall, the example of the simultaneous "cooperative and competitive" relationships between Cisco and IBM demonstrates how firms use network cooperative strategies

A **network cooperative strategy** is a strategy where several firms agree to form multiple partnerships to achieve shared objectives.

more extensively as a way of creating value for customers by offering many goods and services in many geographic (domestic and international) markets.

A network cooperative strategy is particularly effective when it is formed by geographically clustered firms,[86] as in California's Silicon Valley and Rome, Italy's aerospace cluster. Effective social relationships and interactions among partners while sharing their resources make it more likely that a network cooperative strategy will be successful,[87] as does having a productive *strategic center firm* (we discuss strategic center firms in detail in Chapter 11). Firms involved in networks gain information and knowledge from multiple sources. They can use these heterogeneous knowledge sets to produce more and better innovation. As a result, firms involved in networks of alliances tend to be more innovative.[88] However, there are disadvantages to participating in networks as a firm can be locked into its partnerships, precluding the development of alliances with others. In certain network configurations, such as Japanese *keiretsus*, firms in a network are expected to help other firms in that network whenever support is required. Such expectations can become a burden and negatively affect the focal firm's performance over time.[89]

9-5a   Alliance Network Types

An important advantage of a network cooperative strategy is that firms gain access to their partners' other partners. Having access to multiple collaborations increases the likelihood that additional competitive advantages will be formed as the set of shared resources expands.[90] In turn, being able to develop new resources further stimulates product innovations that are critical to strategic competitiveness in the global economy.

The set of strategic alliance partnerships that firms develop when using a network cooperative strategy is called an *alliance network*. Companies' alliance networks vary by industry characteristics. A *stable alliance network* is formed in mature industries where demand is relatively constant and predictable. Through a stable alliance network, firms try to extend their competitive advantages to other settings while continuing to profit from operations in their core, relatively mature industry. Thus, stable networks are built primarily to *exploit* the economies (scale and/or scope) that exist between the partners, such as in the airline and automobile industries.[91]

Dynamic alliance networks are used in industries characterized by frequent product innovations and short product life cycles.[92] The industries in which Apple and IBM compete are examples of this situation. Partly in response, these two firms recently formed a partnership through which they collaborate on business services. The purpose of the partnership is to "get more iPhones and iPads into corporate hands and more IBM services such as analytics, data storage, and supply-chain management onto mobile devices."[93] Of course, Apple and IBM each partner with a host of other firms to develop component parts that are critical to producing the products that are central to the success of their recently-formed partnership. Thus, a network of relationships

Shown in the middle here is representation of a strategic center firm with links to other firms in an alliance network.

Mathias Rosenthal/Shutterstock.com

among multiple companies is foundational to achieving the objectives Apple and IBM seek through their partnership.

In dynamic alliance networks, partners typically *explore* new ideas and possibilities with the potential to lead to product innovations, entries to new markets, and the development of new markets. These are outcomes sought by Apple and IBM through the collaboration described above. Research suggests that firms that help to broker relationships between companies remain important network participants as these networks change.[94] Often, large firms in industries such as software and pharmaceuticals create networks of relationships with smaller entrepreneurial startup firms in their search for innovation-based outcomes.[95] An important outcome for small firms successfully partnering with larger firms in an alliance network is the credibility they build by being associated with their larger collaborators.[96]

9-6 Competitive Risks with Cooperative Strategies

Stated simply, many cooperative strategies fail. In fact, evidence shows that two-thirds of cooperative strategies have serious problems in their first two years and that as many as 50 percent of them fail. This failure rate suggests that even when the partnership has potential complementarities and synergies, alliance success is elusive.[97] Although failure is undesirable, it can be a valuable learning experience, meaning that firms should carefully study a cooperative strategy's failure to gain insights with respect to how to form and manage future cooperative arrangements.[98] We show prominent cooperative strategy risks in Figure 9.5. We discuss a few cooperative strategies that have failed and possible reasons for those failures in the Strategic Focus.

One cooperative strategy risk is that a firm may act in a way that its partner thinks is opportunistic. BP plc and OAO Rosneft developed a joint venture to explore Russia's Arctic Ocean in search of oil. However, the investment by minority partners of this joint venture was driven down in value at one point by 50 percent over concern that the Russian government, Rosneft's dominant owner, would expropriate value from the deal.[99] In general, opportunistic behaviors surface either when formal contracts fail to prevent them or when an alliance is based on a false perception of

Figure 9.5 Managing Competitive Risks in Cooperative Strategies

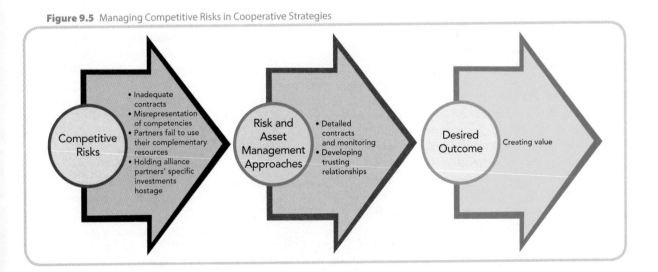

Strategic **Focus**

Failing to Obtain Desired Levels of Success with Cooperative Strategies

The complexity associated with most cooperative strategies increases the difficulty of successfully using them. One complexity is the fact that often, firms collaborating to complete certain projects are simultaneously competing with each other as well. As explained earlier, this reality describes the relationship between Cisco and IBM as well as those existing with airline companies that have joined one of the three major alliance networks (Star, Oneworld, and SkyTeam). Another complication is that firms sometimes form a partnership with a company that is itself a collaboration between other companies. Recently, for example, Ford Motor Company formed a joint venture with carbon manufacturer DowAksa, a firm that is itself a joint venture organized by Dow Chemical Company and Istanbul-based Aksa Akrilik Kimya Sanayii A.S. The purpose of the Ford/DowAksa collaboration is to find ways to develop cheaper grades of carbon fiber components that can be integrated into Ford's automobiles and trucks. Because it is much lighter than steel, carbon fiber helps auto manufacturers reduce the weight of their products which in turn facilitates their efforts to increase products' gas mileage. We see then that, for multiple reasons, the complexities of cooperative strategies increase the challenge of effectively implementing them and may contribute to alliance failure.

Redbox and Verizon terminated their relationship that was organized to become the streaming subscription components of Redbox's rental business after only two years. (Outerwall founded Redbox in partnership with McDonald's Ventures, LLC. McDonald's interest was to distribute DVDs through rental kiosks at its restaurants as a means of attracting customers and providing them with a unique service.) Competing against the likes of Netflix and Hulu Plus, Redbox's streaming service failed to attract a sufficient number of customers, perhaps in part because it was able to stream to customers only items that its competitors were also streaming. Unlike Netflix and Hulu Plus, Redbox was not developing its own original content as a means of creating unique value for customers. Because the service made available through the Redbox and Verizon collaboration was losing money and was not gaining a sufficient number of subscribers, the partners chose to terminate their relationship.

Carefully executing the operational details of a planned cooperative strategy is foundational to its performance and influences if it will succeed or fail. In mid-2015 for example, First Solar, Inc. and SunPower Corporation, the two largest U.S. solar-panel manufacturers were in the planning stages to form a joint venture that would own and operate some of the firms'

projects. The proposed partners believed that the collaboration would create value by combining "SunPower's polysilicon technology with First Solar's thin-film panels." However, SunPower recorded a loss in the first quarter of 2015, partly because of costs it was incurring to structure the proposed relationship with First Solar. This demonstrates the importance of identifying efficient as well as effective ways to structure a proposed collaboration between companies as a means of increasing the likelihood of operational success.

The handshake between partners suggests the cooperation that is needed between parties for business collaborations to succeed.

Earlier, we noted that MillerCoors, the joint venture formed between Molson Coors and SABMiller, is encountering difficulties. Some analysts believe that a reason for this is that, while the partnership had been very successful during its first six years in terms of substantially reducing costs by creating economies of scale, it had failed to increase the market shares held by two of its important products, Miller Lite and Coors Light. The situation with the MillerCoors partnership suggests that long-term cooperative strategy success results when partners find unique ways to create value for customers in addition to finding ways to reduce operating costs.

Sources: M. Armental, 2015, SunPower swings to loss on costs related to planned joint venture, *Wall Street Journal Online*, www.wsj.com, April 30; D. Harris, 2015, China joint ventures: How not to get burned, Above the Law, www.abovethelaw.com, February 9; Molson Coors, U.S. joint venture MillerCoors facing stiff challenges, *Wall Street Journal Online*, www.wsj.com, May 7; J. D. Stoll, 2015, Ford to develop carbon-fiber material for cars, *Wall Street Journal Online*, www.wsj.com, April 17; P. E. Farrell, 2014, The 7 deadly sins of joint ventures, *Entrepreneur*, www.entrepreneur.com, September 2; Q. Plummer, 2014, Redbox instant will be killed Oct. 7: A failed joint venture, Tech Times, www.techtimes.com, October 6.

partner trustworthiness. Typically, an opportunistic firm wants to acquire as much of its partner's tacit knowledge as it can.[100] Full awareness of what a partner wants in a cooperative strategy reduces the likelihood that a firm will suffer from another's opportunistic actions.[101]

Some cooperative strategies fail when it is discovered that a firm has misrepresented the resources it can bring to the partnership. This risk is more common when the partner's contribution is based on some of its intangible assets. Superior knowledge of local conditions is an example of an intangible asset that partners often fail to deliver. An effective way to deal with this risk may be to ask the partner to provide evidence that it does, in fact, possess the resources (even when they are largely intangible) it will share in the cooperative strategy.[102]

The cooperative relationships in the form of nonequity strategic alliances that are being created between some large pharmaceutical companies and outsourcing firms is potentially an example of the "misrepresentation of available resources" risk. As discussed in Chapter 3, pharmaceutical companies are outsourcing the monitoring of drug safety to firms claiming to have the requisite human capital skills needed to successfully complete various monitoring tasks. But is this the case? Not everyone is convinced. In fact, "critics of the (outsourcing) practice say drug monitoring is difficult, requiring deep experience and a knack for detective work in addition to knowledge of biochemistry and pharmacology, and that the shift toward outsourcing carries risks that deadly side effects will go unnoticed."[103] Thus, pharmaceutical companies may need to carefully monitor the quality of the human capital resource their partners provide for the purpose of completing what appears to be complicated monitoring work.

A firm's failure to make available to its partners the resources (such as the most sophisticated technologies) that it committed to the cooperative strategy is a third risk. This particular risk surfaces most commonly when firms form an international cooperative strategy, especially in emerging economies.[104] In these instances, different cultures and languages can cause misinterpretations of contractual terms or trust-based expectations.

A final risk is that one firm may make investments that are specific to the alliance while its partner does not. For example, the firm might commit resources to develop manufacturing equipment that can be used only to produce products associated with the alliance. If the partner isn't also making alliance-specific investments, the firm is at a relative disadvantage in terms of returns earned from the alliance compared with investments made to earn the returns.

9-7 Managing Cooperative Strategies

Although they are difficult to manage, cooperative strategies are an important means of growth and enhanced firm performance. Because the ability to effectively manage cooperative strategies is unevenly distributed across organizations in general, assigning managerial responsibility for a firm's cooperative strategies to a high-level executive or to a team improves the likelihood that the strategies will be well managed. In turn, being able to successfully manage cooperative strategies can itself be a competitive advantage.[105]

Those responsible for managing the firm's cooperative strategies should take the actions necessary to coordinate activities, categorize knowledge learned from previous experiences, and make certain that what the firm knows about how to effectively form and use cooperative strategies is in the hands of the right people at the right time. Firms must also learn how to manage both the tangible and intangible assets (such as knowledge) that are involved with a cooperative arrangement. Too often, partners concentrate on managing tangible assets at the expense of taking action to also manage a cooperative relationship's intangible assets.[106]

Cost minimization and opportunity maximization are the two primary approaches firms use to manage cooperative strategies[107] (see Figure 9.5). In the *cost-minimization* approach, the firm develops formal contracts with its partners. These contracts specify how the cooperative strategy is to be monitored and how partner behavior is to be controlled. The joint venture between GM China and SAIC Motor Corp. that we discussed earlier is being managed largely through formal contractual relationships. The goal of the cost-minimization approach is to minimize the cooperative strategy's cost and to prevent opportunistic behavior by a partner.

Maximizing a partnership's value-creating opportunities is the focus of the *opportunity-maximization* approach. In this case, partners are prepared to take advantage of unexpected opportunities to learn from each other and to explore additional marketplace possibilities. Less formal contracts, with fewer constraints on partners' behaviors, make it possible for partners to explore how their resources can be shared in multiple value-creating ways. This appears to be the approach being used to manage the Pangea partnership we discussed earlier that has been formed among online news publishers since for the beta-testing phrase, a central team with "commercial leadership and operational resources from all the member publishers" was organized.[108] Finding additional ways to collaborate was one of the objectives associated with the decision to organize this team.

Firms can successfully use both approaches to manage cooperative strategies. However, the costs to monitor the cooperative strategy are greater with cost minimization because writing detailed contracts and using extensive monitoring mechanisms is expensive, even though the approach is intended to reduce alliance costs. Although monitoring systems may prevent partners from acting in their own self-interests, they also often preclude positive responses to new opportunities that surface to productively use each alliance partner's unique resources. Thus, formal contracts and extensive monitoring systems tend to stifle partners' efforts to gain maximum value from their participation in a cooperative strategy and require significant resources to be put into place and used.[109]

The relative lack of detail and formality that is a part of the contract developed when using the opportunity-maximization approach means that firms need to trust that each party will act in the partnership's best interests. The psychological state of *trust* in the context of cooperative arrangements is the belief that a firm will not do anything to exploit its partner's vulnerabilities, even if it has an opportunity to do so. When partners trust each other, there is less need to write detailed formal contracts to specify each firm's alliance behaviors,[110] and the cooperative relationship tends to be more stable.[111] On a relative basis, trust tends to be more difficult to establish in international cooperative strategies than domestic ones. Differences in trade policies, cultures, laws, and politics that are part of cross-border alliances account for the increased difficulty.

Research showing that trust between partners increases the likelihood of success when using alliances highlights the benefits of the opportunity-maximization approach to managing cooperative strategies. Trust may also be the most efficient way to influence and control alliance partners' behaviors. Research indicates that trust can be a capability that is valuable, rare, imperfectly imitable, and often nonsubstitutable.[112] Thus, firms known to be trustworthy can have a competitive advantage in terms of how they develop and use cooperative strategies. Increasing the importance of trust in alliances is the fact that it is not possible to specify all operational details of a cooperative strategy in a formal contract. As such, being confident that its partner can be trusted reduces the firm's concern about its inability to contractually control all alliance details.

SUMMARY

- A cooperative strategy is one through which firms work together to achieve a shared objective. Strategic alliances, where firms combine some of their resources for the purpose of creating a competitive advantage, are the primary form of cooperative strategies. Joint ventures (where firms create and own equal shares of a new venture), equity strategic alliances (where firms own different shares of a newly created venture), and nonequity strategic alliances (where firms cooperate through a contractual relationship) are the three major types of strategic alliances. Outsourcing, discussed in Chapter 3, commonly occurs as firms form nonequity strategic alliances.

- Collusive strategies are the second type of cooperative strategies (with strategic alliances being the other). In many economies, explicit collusive strategies are illegal unless sanctioned by government policies. Increasing globalization has led to fewer government-sanctioned situations of explicit collusion. Tacit collusion, also called mutual forbearance, is a cooperative strategy through which firms tacitly cooperate to reduce industry output below the potential competitive output level, thereby raising prices above the competitive level.

- The reasons firms use strategic alliances vary by slow-cycle, fast-cycle, and standard-cycle market conditions. To enter restricted markets (slow cycle), to move quickly from one competitive advantage to another (fast cycle), and to gain market power (standard cycle) are among the reasons firms choose to use strategic alliances.

- Four business-level cooperative strategies are used to help the firm improve its performance in individual product markets:

  - Through vertical and horizontal complementary alliances, companies combine some of their resources to create value in different parts (vertical) or the same parts (horizontal) of the value chain

  - Competition response strategies are formed to respond to competitors' actions, especially strategic actions

  - Uncertainty-reducing strategies are used to hedge against the risks created by the conditions of uncertain competitive environments (such as new product markets)

  - Competition-reducing strategies are used to avoid excessive competition while the firm marshals its resources to improve its strategic competitiveness

  Complementary alliances have the highest probability of helping a firm form a competitive advantage; competition-reducing alliances have the lowest probability.

- Firms use corporate-level cooperative strategies to engage in product and/or geographic diversification. Through diversifying strategic alliances, firms agree to share some of their resources to enter new markets or produce new products. Synergistic alliances are ones where firms share some of their resources to develop economies of scope. Synergistic alliances are similar to business-level horizontal complementary alliances where firms try to develop operational synergy, except that synergistic alliances are used to develop synergy at the corporate level. Franchising is a corporate-level cooperative strategy where the franchisor uses a franchise as a contractual relationship to specify how resources will be shared with franchisees.

- As an international cooperative strategy, a cross-border strategic alliance is used for several reasons, including the performance superiority of firms competing in markets outside their domestic market and governmental restrictions on a firm's efforts to grow through mergers and acquisitions. Commonly, cross-border strategic alliances are riskier than their domestic counterparts, particularly when partners aren't fully aware of each other's reason for participating in the partnership.

- In a network cooperative strategy, several firms agree to form multiple partnerships to achieve shared objectives. A firm's opportunity to gain access "to its partner's other partnerships" is a primary benefit of a network cooperative strategy. Network cooperative strategies are used to form either a stable alliance network or a dynamic alliance network. In mature industries, stable networks are used to extend competitive advantages into new areas. In rapidly changing environments where frequent product innovations occur, dynamic networks are used primarily as a tool of innovation.

- Cooperative strategies aren't risk free. If a contract is not developed appropriately, or if a partner misrepresents its resources or fails to make them available, failure is likely. Furthermore, a firm may be held hostage through asset-specific investments made in conjunction with a partner, which may be exploited.

- Trust is an increasingly important aspect of successful cooperative strategies. Firms place high value on opportunities to partner with companies known for their trustworthiness. When trust exists, a cooperative strategy is managed to maximize the pursuit of opportunities between partners. Without trust, formal contracts and extensive monitoring systems are used to manage cooperative strategies. In this case, the interest is "cost minimization" rather than "opportunity maximization."

KEY TERMS

business-level cooperative strategy 284
complementary strategic alliances 284
cooperative strategy 278
corporate-level cooperative strategy 290
cross-border strategic alliance 292
diversifying strategic alliance 291
equity strategic alliance 280

franchising 291
joint venture 279
network cooperative strategy 293
nonequity strategic alliance 280
strategic alliance 279
synergistic strategic alliance 291

REVIEW QUESTIONS

1. What is the definition of cooperative strategy, and why is this strategy important to firms competing in the twenty-first century competitive landscape?

2. What is a strategic alliance? What are the three major types of strategic alliances that firms form for the purpose of developing a competitive advantage?

3. What are the four business-level cooperative strategies? What are the key differences among them?

4. What are the three corporate-level cooperative strategies? How do firms use each of these strategies for the purpose of creating a competitive advantage?

5. Why do firms use cross-border strategic alliances?

6. What risks are firms likely to experience as they use cooperative strategies?

7. What are the differences between the cost-minimization approach and the opportunity-maximization approach to managing cooperative strategies?

Mini-Case

Alliance Formation, Both Globally and Locally, in the Global Automobile Industry

The academic literature on alliances has some interesting recent findings, one of which is the rationale that because firms are often located in the same country, and often in the same region of the country, it is easier for them to collaborate on major projects. As such, they compete globally, but may cooperate locally. Historically, firms have learned to collaborate by establishing strategic alliances and forming cooperative strategies when there is intensive competition. This interesting paradox is due to several reasons. First, when there is intense rivalry, it is difficult to maintain market power. As such, using a cooperative strategy can reduce market power through better norms of competition; this pertains to the idea of "*mutual forbearance*". Another rationale that has emerged is based on the resource-based view of the firm (see Chapter 3).

To compete, firms often need resources that they don't have but may be found in other firms in or outside of the focal firm's home industry. As such, these "complementary resources" are another rationale for why large firms form joint ventures and strategic alliances within the same industry or in vertically related industries.

Because firms are co-located and have similar needs, it's easier for them to jointly work together, for example, to produce engines and transmissions as part of the powertrain. This is evident in the European alliance between Peugeot-Citroën and Opel-Vauxhall (owned by General Motors). It is also the reason for a recent U.S. alliance between Ford and General Motors in developing upgraded nine- and ten-speed transmissions. Furthermore, Ford and GM are looking to develop, together, eleven- and twelve-speed automatic transmissions to improve fuel efficiency and help the firms meet new federal guidelines regarding such efficiency.

In regard to resource complementarity, a very successful alliance was formed in 1999 by French-based Renault and Japan-based Nissan. Each of these firms lacked the necessary size to develop economies of scale and economies of scope that were critical to succeed in the 1990s and beyond in the global automobile industry. When the alliance was formed, each firm took an ownership stake in the other. The larger of the two companies, Renault, holds a 43.3 percent stake in Nissan, while Nissan has a 15 percent stake in Renault. It is interesting to note that Carlos Ghosn serves as the CEO of both companies. Over time, this corporate-level synergistic alliance has developed three values to guide the relationship between the two firms:

1. *trust* (work fairly, impartially, and professionally)
2. *respect* (honor commitments, liabilities, and responsibilities)
3. *transparency* (be open, frank, and clear)

Largely due to these established principles, the Renault-Nissan alliance is a recognized success. One could argue that the main reason for the success of this alliance is the complementary assets that the firms bring to the alliance; Nissan is strong in Asia, while Renault is strong in Europe. Together they have been able to establish other production locations, such as those in Latin America, which they may not have obtained independently.

Some firms enter alliances because they are "squeezed in the middle;" that is, they have moderate volumes, mostly for the mass market, but need to collaborate to establish viable economies of scale. For example, Fiat-Chrysler needs to boost its annual sales from $4.3 billion to something like $6 billion, and likewise needs to strengthen its presence in the booming Asian market to have enough global market power. As such, it is entering joint ventures with two undersized Japanese carmakers, Mazda and Suzuki. However, the past history of Mazda and Suzuki with alliances may be a reason for their not being overly enthusiastic about the prospects of the current alliances. Fiat broke up with GM, Chrysler with Daimler, and Mazda with Ford.

This is also the situation in Europe locally for Peugeot-Citroën of France, which is struggling for survival along with the GM European subsidiary, Opel-Vauxhall. More specifically, Peugeot-Citroën and Opel-Vauxhall have struck a tentative agreement to share platforms and engines to get the capital necessary for investment in future models. As such, in all these examples, the firms need additional market share, but also enough capital to make the investment necessary to realize more market power to compete.

In summary, there are a number of rationales why competitors not only compete but also cooperate in establishing strategic alliances and joint ventures in order to meet strategic needs for increased market power, take advantage of complementary assets, and cooperate with close neighbors, often in the same region of a country.

Sources: 2013, Markets and makers: Running harder, *Economist*, April 20, ss4–ss7; J. Boxell, 2013, Peugeot reaffirms push into BRICs, *Financial Times*, www.ft.com, February 7; D. Pearson & J. Bennett, 2013, Corporate news: GM, Peugeot pledge to deepen car alliance – Tough market in Europe has slowed progress, but automakers now see opportunities to cooperate outside the region, *Wall Street Journal Online*, www.wsj.com, January 10; J. B. White, 2013, Mazda uses alliances to boost sales, *Wall Street Journal Online*, www.wsj.com, January 27; T. Yu, M. Subramaniam, & A. A. Cannella, Jr., 2013, Competing globally, allying locally: Alliances between global rivals and host-country factors, *Journal of International Business Studies*, 44: 117-137; W. Kim, 2012, The voyage of the Renault-Nissan alliance: A successful venture, *Advances in Management*, 5(9): 25–29.

Case Discussion Questions

1. How can the resource-based view of the firm (see Chapters 1 and 3) help us understand why firms develop and use cooperative strategies such as strategic alliances and joint ventures?

2. What is the relationship between the core competencies a firm possesses, the core competencies the firm feels it needs, and decisions to form cooperative strategies?

3. What does it mean to say that the partners of an alliance have "complementary assets"? What complementary assets do Renault and Nissan share?

4. What are the risks associated with the corporate-level strategic alliance between Renault and Nissan? What have these firms done to mitigate these risks?

5. Is it possible that some of the firms mentioned in this Mini-Case (e.g., Renault, Nissan, Mazda, Peugot-Citroen, Opel-Vauxhall) might form a network cooperative strategy? If so, what conditions might influence a decision by these firms to form this particular type of strategy?

NOTES

1. B. B. Tyler & T. Caner, 2015, New product
    introductions below aspirations, slack and
    R&D alliances: A behavioral perspective,
    Strategic Management Journal, in press;
    O. Schilke, 2014, Second-order dynamic
    capabilities: How do they matter? *Academy
    of Management Perspectives*, 28: 368–380;
    U. Wassmer & P. Dussauge, 2012, Network
    resource stocks and flows: How do alliance
    portfolios affect the value of new alliance
    formations? *Strategic Management Journal*,
    33: 871–883.

2. A. L. Brito, E. P. Z. Brito, & L. H. Hashiba,
    2014, What type of cooperation with
    suppliers and customers leads to superior
    performance? *Journal of Business Research*,
    67: 952–959; R. A. Heidl, H. K. Steensma, &
    C. Phelps, 2014, Divisive faultlines and the
    unplanned dissolutions of multipartner
    alliances, *Organization Science*, 25: 1351–
    1371; D. Lavie, P. R. Haunschild, & P. Khanna,
    2012, Organizational differences, relational
    mechanisms, and alliance performance,
    Strategic Management Journal, 33:
    1453–1479.

3. Z. Khan, O. Shenkar, & Y. K. Lew, 2015,
    Knowledge transfer from international
    joint ventures to local suppliers in
    a developing economy, *Journal of
    International Business Studies*, in press.

4. S. J. D. Schillebeeckx, S. Chaturvedi,
    G. George, & Z. King, 2015, What do I want?
    The effects of individual aspiration and
    relational capability on collaboration
    preferences, *Strategic Management Journal*,
    in press; R. J. Arend, P. C. Patel, &
    H. D. Park, 2014, Explaining post-IPO venture
    performance through a knowledge-based
    view typology, *Strategic Management
    Journal*, 35: 376–397; J. H. Dyer & H. Singh,
    1998, The relational view: Cooperative
    strategy and sources of interorganizational
    competitive advantage, *Academy of
    Management Review*, 23: 660–679.

5. R. R. Kehoe & D. Tzabbar, 2015,
    Lighting the way or stealing the shine?
    An examination of the duality in star
    scientists' effects on firm innovative
    performance, *Strategic Management
    Journal*, 36: 709–727; R. Vandaie &
    A. Zaheer, 2014, Surviving bear hugs:
    Firm capability, large partner alliances, and
    growth, *Strategic Management Journal*,
    35: 566–577; J. Walter, F. W. Kellermanns, &
    C. Lechner, 2012, Decision making within
    and between organizations: Rationality,
    politics, and alliance performance, *Journal
    of Management*, 38: 1582–1610.

6. C. Lioukas & J. Reuer, 2015, Isolating trust
    outcomes from exchange relationships:
    Social exchange and learning benefits
    of prior ties in alliances, *Academy of
    Management Journal*, in press;
    J. Charterina & J. Landeta, 2013, Effects of

    knowledge-sharing routines and dyad-
    based investments on company innovation
    and performance: An empirical study
    of Spanish manufacturing companies,
    International Journal of Management,
    30: 197–216.

7. J. Wu & P. Olk, 2014, Technological
    advantage, alliances with customers, local
    knowledge and competitor identification,
    Journal of Business Research, 67: 2106–2114;
    J. L. Cummings & S. R. Holmberg, 2012,
    Best-fit alliance partners: The use of critical
    success factors in a comprehensive partner
    selection process, *Long Range Planning*,
    45: 136–159.

8. N. Rahman & H. J. Korn, 2014, Alliance
    longevity: Examining relational and
    operational antecedents, *Long Range
    Planning*, 47: 245–261; S. Xu, A. P. Fenik, &
    M. B. Shaner, 2014, Multilateral alliances
    and innovation output: The importance of
    equity and technological scope, *Journal of
    Business Research*, 67: 2403–2410.

9. Treflis team, 2014, Juniper collaborates with
    Aruba to expand converged networking
    solutions portfolio, *Forbes Online*, www.
    forbes.com, June 13.

10. Y. Liu & T. Ravichandran, 2015, Alliance
    experience, IT-enabled knowledge
    integration, and ex-ante value gains,
    Organization Science, 26: 511–530; J. Roy,
    2012, IJV partner trustworthy behaviour:
    The role of host country governance
    and partner selection criteria, *Journal of
    Management Studies*, 49: 332–355.

11. C. Murphy, 2015, GM China venture to
    spend $16 billion to develop new products,
    Wall Street Journal Online, www.wsj.com,
    April 19.

12. R. Yu, 2015, SAIC Motor's tie-ups with
    Volkswagen, GM rev up 2014 profit, *Wall
    Street Journal Online*, www.wsj.com, April 2.

13. J. H. Love, S. Roper, & P. Vahter, 2014,
    Learning from openness: The dynamics of
    breadth in external innovation linkages,
    Strategic Management Journal, 35:
    1703–1716; E. Chrysostome, R. Nigam, &
    C. Jarilowski, 2013, Revisiting strategic
    learning in international joint ventures:
    A knowledge creation perspective,
    International Journal of Management, 30(1):
    88–98; D. Tan & K. E. Meyer, 2011, Country-
    of-origin and industry FDI agglomeration
    of foreign investors in an emerging
    economy, *Journal of International Business
    Studies*, 42: 504–520.

14. 2015, Boston Scientific signs strategic
    alliance with Frankenman Medical
    Equipment Company, Boston
    Scientific Company Home Page, www.
    bostonscientific.com, April 14.

15. W. (Stone) Shi, S. L. Sun, B. C. Pinkham, &
    M. W. Peng, 2014, Domestic alliance
    network to attract foreign partners:

    Evidence from international joint ventures
    in China, *Journal of International Business
    Studies*, 45: 338–362; L. Cui & F. Jiang, 2012,
    State ownership effect on firms' FDI
    ownership decisions under institutional
    pressure: A study of Chinese outward-
    investing firms, *Journal of International
    Business Studies*, 43: 264–284; J. Xia,
    J. Tan, & D. Tan, 2008, Mimetic entry and
    bandwagon effect: The rise and decline of
    international equity joint venture in China,
    Strategic Management Journal, 29: 195–217.

16. C. Dulaney, 2015, Johnson Controls
    auto-interiors spinoff expected to begin
    operations in July, *Wall Street Journal Online*,
    www.wsj.com, April 14.

17. J. Reuer & S. Devarakonda, 2015,
    Mechanisms of hybrid governance:
    Administrative committees in non-equity
    alliances, *Academy of Management Journal*,
    in press; A. Majocchi, U. Mayrhofer, &
    J. Camps, 2013, Joint ventures or non-equity
    alliances? Evidence from Italian firms,
    Management Decision, 51: 380–395.

18. B. T. McCann, J. J. Reuer, & N. Lahiri,
    2015, Agglomeration and the choice
    between acquisitions and alliances:
    An information economics perspective,
    Strategic Management Journal, in press;
    S. P. Gudergan, T. Devinney, N. Richter, &
    R. Ellis, 2012, Strategic implications for
    (non-equity) alliance performance, *Long
    Range Planning*, 45: 451–476.

19. F. J. Contractor & J. J. Reuer, 2014,
    Structuring and governing alliances: New
    directions for research, *Global Strategy
    Journal*, 4: 241–256; J. J. Reuer, E. Klijn, &
    C. S. Lioukas, 2014, Board involvement
    in international joint ventures, *Strategic
    Management Journal*, 35: 1626–1644;
    J. Schweitzer & S. P. Gudergan, 2011,
    Contractual complexity, governance
    and organisational form in alliances,
    *International Journal of Strategic Business
    Alliances*, 2: 26–40.

20. 2015, Will Tim Cook stop outsourcing
    the manufacture of Apple products to
    homophobic China? *Ricochet*, www.
    ricochet.com, March 31.

21. B. Shobert, 2015, Will Apple's business
    model work on pharmaceuticals? *Forbes
    Online*, www.forbes, March 11.

22. J. Righetti, 2014, 5 reasons why China will
    remain the world's factory, www.linkedin.
    com/pulse, August 21.

23. D. Aristie, M. Vecchi, & F. Venturini,
    2015, University and inter-firm R&D
    collaborations: Propensity and intensity
    of cooperation in Europe, *Journal of
    Technology Transfer*, in press; D. Mindruta,
    2013, Value creation in university-firm
    research collaborations: A matching
    approach, *Strategic Management Journal*,
    34: 644–665.

24. K. Lange, M. Geppert, A. Saka-Helmhout, & F. Becker-Ritterspach, 2015, Changing business models and employee representation in the airline industry: A comparison of British Airways and Deutsche Lufthansa, *British Journal of Management*, in press; X. Hu, R. Caldentey, & G. Vulcano, 2013, Revenue sharing in airline alliances, *Management Science*, 59: 1177–1195; U. Wassmer, 2010, Alliance portfolios: A review and research agenda, *Journal of Management*, 36: 141–171.

25. W. Yang & K. E. Meyer, 2015, Competitive dynamics in an emerging economy: Competitive pressures, resources, and the speed of action, *Journal of Business Research*, 68: 1176–1185; T. de Leeuw, B. Lokshin, & G. Duysters, 2014, Returns to alliance portfolio diversity: The relative effects of partner diversity on firm's innovative performance and productivity, *Journal of Business Research*, 67: 1839–1849.

26. J. Marshall, 2015, News publishers for programmatic advertising alliance, *CMO Today*, www.blogs.wsj.com/cmo, March 18.

27. Treflis team, 2015, Expedia seeks Latin American dominance: Strengthens partnership with Decolar.com, *Forbes Online*, www.forbes.com, March 12.

28. D. J. Teece, 2014, A dynamic capabilities-based entrepreneurial theory of the multinational enterprise, *Journal of International Business Studies*, 45: 8–37; J. R. Williams, 1998, *Renewable Advantage: Crafting Strategy Through Economic Time*, New York: Free Press.

29. L. Burkitt, 2015, Carnival in talks with China Merchants on cruise ports, ships, *Wall Street Journal Online*, www.wsj.com, January 26.

30. S. Artinger & T. C. Powell, 2015, Entrepreneurial failure: Statistical and psychological explanations, *Strategic Management Journal*, in press; H. Rahmandad & N. Repenning, 2015, Capability erosion dynamics, *Strategic Management Journal*, in press; A. Tafti, S. Mithas, & M. S. Krishnan, 2013, The effect of information technology-enabled flexibility on formation and market value of alliances, *Management Science*, 59: 207–225.

31. J. J. Reuer & R. Ragozzino, 2014, Signals and international alliance formation: The roles of affiliations and international activities, *Journal of International Business Studies*, 45: 321–337; H. K. Steensma, J. Q. Barden, C. Dhanaraj, M. Lyles, & L. Tihanyi, 2008, The evolution and internalization of international joint ventures in a transitioning economy, *Journal of International Business Studies*, 39: 491–507.

32. C. B. Bingham, K. H. Heimeriks, M. Schijven, & S. Gates, 2015, Concurrent learning: How firms develop multiple dynamic capabilities in parallel, *Strategic Management Journal*, in press; S. T. Cavusgil & G. Knight, 2014, The born global firm: An entrepreneurial and

capabilities perspective on early and rapid internationalization, *Journal of International Business Studies*, 46: 3–16; H. E. Posen & D. A. Levinthal, 2012, Chasing a moving target: Exploitation and exploration in dynamic environments, *Management Science*, 58: 587–601.

33. H. Milanov & S. A. Fernhaber, 2014, When do domestic alliances help ventures abroad? Direct and moderating effects from a learning perspective, *Journal of Business Venturing*, 29: 377–391; X. Yin, J. Wu, & W. Tsai, 2012, When unconnected others connect: Does degree of brokerage persist after the formation of a multipartner alliance? *Organization Science*, 23: 1682–1699.

34. 2015, Micron, Seagate announce strategic alliance, Micron Home Page, www.micron.com, February 12.

35. H. M. Khamesh & M. Nasiriyar, 2014, Avoiding alliance myopia: Forging learning outcomes for long-term success, *Journal of Business Strategy*, 35: 37–44; A.-P. de Man, N. Roijakkers, & H. de Graauw, 2010, Managing dynamics through robust alliance governance structures: The case of KLM and Northwest Airlines, *European Management Journal*, 28: 171–181.

36. Airline alliances, 2015, *Maps of the World*, www.mapsoftheworld.com, April 22.

37. Q. Gu & X. Lu, 2014, Unraveling the mechanisms of reputation and alliance formation: A study of venture capital syndication in China, *Strategic Management Journal*, 35: 739–750; G. Vasudeva, J. W. Spencer, & H. J. Teegen, 2013, Bringing the institutional context back in: A cross-national comparison of alliance partner selection and knowledge acquisition, *Organization Science*, 24: 319–338; W. Shi & J. E. Prescott, 2011, Sequence patterns of firms' acquisition and alliance behavior and their performance implications, *Journal of Management Studies*, 48: 1044–1070.

38. U. Stettner & D. Lavie, 2014, Ambidexterity under scrutiny: Exploration and exploitation via internal organization, alliances, and acquisitions, *Strategic Management Journal*, 35: 1903–1929; N. Lahiri & S. Narayanan, 2013, Vertical integration, innovation and alliance portfolio size: Implications for firm performance, *Strategic Management Journal*, 34: 1042–1064; S. M. Mudambi & S. Tallman, 2010, Make, buy or ally? Theoretical perspectives on knowledge process outsourcing through alliances, *Journal of Management Studies*, 47: 1434–1456.

39. R. Kapoor & P. J. McGrath, 2014, Unmasking the interplay between technology evolution and R&D collaboration: Evidence from the global semiconductor manufacturing industry, 1990–2010, *Research Policy*, 43: 555–569; J. Hagedoorn & N. Wang, 2012, Is there complementarity or substitutability between internal and

external R&D strategies? *Research Policy*, 41: 1072–1083; M. Meuleman, A. Lockett, S. Manigart, & M. Wright, 2010, Partner selection decisions in interfirm collaborations: The paradox of relational embeddedness, *Journal of Management Studies*, 47: 995–1019.

40. E. Revilla, M. Sáenz, & D. Knoppen, 2013, Towards an empirical typology of buyer–supplier relationships based on absorptive capacity, *International Journal of Production Research*, 51: 2935–2951; J. Zhang & C. Baden-Fuller, 2010, The influence of technological knowledge base and organizational structure on technology collaboration, *Journal of Management Studies*, 47: 679–704; J. Wiklund & D. A. Shepherd, 2009, The effectiveness of alliances and acquisitions: The role of resource combination activities, *Entrepreneurship Theory and Practice*, 33: 193–212.

41. 2015, GE intelligent lighting to transform retail experience through Qualcomm collaboration, GE Home Page, www.ge.com, May 4.

42. T. Stynes, 2015, Sorrento reaches collaboration deal valued at $110 million, *Wall Street Journal Online*, www.wsj.com, March 16.

43. J. Wieczner, 2014, Can drugmakers find profit in collaboration? *Fortune Online*, www.fortune.com, February 11.

44. H. Parker & Z. Brey, 2015, Collaboration costs and new product development performance, *Journal of Business Research*, 68: 1653–1656; C. Häeussler, H. Patzelt, & S. A. Zahra, 2012, Strategic alliances and product development in high technology new firms: The moderating effect of technological capabilities, *Journal of Business Venturing*, 27: 217–233; M. Makri, M. A. Hitt, & P. J. Lane, 2010, Complementary technologies, knowledge relatedness, and invention outcomes in high technology mergers and acquisitions, *Strategic Management Journal*, 31: 602–628.

45. D. Cameron, 2015, Boeing-Lockheed venture plans new rocket with reusable engine, *Wall Street Journal Online*, www.wsj.com, April 13.

46. A. Martin, 2007, Merger for SABMiller and Molson Coors, *New York Times Online*, www.nytimes.com, October 10.

47. T. Mickle, 2015, Molson Coors, U.S. joint venture MillerCoors facing stiff challenges, *Wall Street Journal Online*, www.wsj.com, May 7.

48. H. Yang & H. K. Steensma, 2014, When do firms rely on their knowledge spillover recipients for guidance in exploring unfamiliar knowledge? *Research Policy*, 43: 1496–1507; N. Mouri, M. B. Sarkar, & M. Frye, 2012, Alliance portfolios and shareholder value in post-IPO firms: The moderating roles of portfolio structure and firm-level uncertainty, *Journal of Business Venturing*, 27: 355–371; J. J. Reuer & T. W. Tong, 2005, Real options in international joint ventures, *Journal of Management*, 31: 403–423.

49. 2014, Tesla Motors in talks with BMW, possible alliance in batteries, carbon fiber body parts, Tesla Home Page, www.myteslamotors.com, November 23.

50. H.-T. Normann, J. Rosch, & L. M. Schultz, 2015, Do buyer groups facilitate collusion? *Journal of Economic Behavior & Organization*, 109: 72–84; M. A. Fonseca & H. Normann, 2012, Explicit vs. tacit collusion—The impact of communication in oligopoly experiments, *European Economic Review*, 56: 1759–1772; M. Escrihuela-Villar & J. Guillén, 2011, On collusion and industry size, *Annals of Economics and Finance*, 12: 31–40.

51. J. Boone & K. Zigic, 2015, Trade policy in markets with collusion: The case of North-South R&D spillovers, *Research in Economics*, in press; M. Van Essen & W. B. Hankins, 2013, Tacit collusion in price-setting oligopoly: A puzzle redux, *Southern Economic Journal*, 79: 703–726; Y. Lu & J. Wright, 2010, Tacit collusion with price-matching punishments, *International Journal of Industrial Organization*, 28: 298–306.

52. J. Handy, 2014, Can a DRAM oligopoly really work? *Forbes Online*, www.forbes.com, May 30.

53. F. J. Mas-Ruiz, F. Ruiz-Moreno, & A. L. de Guevara Martinez, 2014, Asymmetric rivalry within and between strategic groups, *Strategic Management Journal*, 35: 419–439; R. W. Cooper & T. W. Ross, 2009, Sustaining cooperation with joint ventures, *Journal of Law, Economics, and Organization*, 25: 31–54.

54. M. T. Gustafson, I. T. Ivanov, & J. Ritter, 2015, Financial condition and product market cooperation, *Journal of Corporate Finance*, 31: 1–16; L. Zou, C. Yu, & M. Dresner, 2012, Multimarket contact, alliance membership, and prices in international airline markets, *Transportation Research Part E: Logistics and Transportation Review*, 48: 555–565; J. T. Prince & D. H. Simon, 2009, Multi-market contact and service quality: Evidence from on-time performance in the U.S. airline industry, *Academy of Management Journal*, 52: 336–354.

55. B. Chidmi, 2012, Vertical relationships in the ready-to-eat breakfast cereal industry in Boston, *Agribusiness*, 28: 241–259; N. Panteva, 2011, IBISWorld Industry Report 31123: Cereal production in the U.S., January.

56. E. Shroeder, 2014, Global breakfast cereal market to reach $43.2 billion by 2019, *Food Business News Online*, www.foodbusinessnews.com, February 14.

57. P. F. Skilton & E. Bernardes, 2015, Competition network structure and product market entry, *Strategic Management Journal*, in press; R. M. Bakker & J. Knoben, 2014, Built to last or meant to end: Intertemporal choice in strategic alliance portfolios, *Organization Science*, 26: 256–276; Z. Guedri & J. McGuire, 2011, Multimarket competition, mobility barriers, and firm performance, *Journal of Management Studies*, 48: 857–890.

58. I. K. Wang, H.-S. Yang, & D. J. Miller, 2015, Collaboration in the shadow of the technology frontier: Evidence from the flat panel display industry, *Managerial and Decision Economics*, in press; P. Massey & M. McDowell, 2010, Joint dominance and tacit collusion: Some implications for competition and regulatory policy, *European Competition Journal*, 6: 427–444.

59. A.H. Bowers, H. R. Greve, H. Mitsuhashi, & J. A. C. Baum, 2014, Competitive parity, status disparity, and mutual forbearance: Securities analysts' competition for investor attention, *Academy of Management Journal*, 57: 38–62.

60. Y. Liu & T. Ravichandran, 2015, Alliance experience, IT-enabled knowledge integration, and ex-ante value gains, *Organization Science*, 26: 511–530; P. Dussauge, B. Garrette, & W. Mitchell, 2004, Asymmetric performances: The market share impact of scale and link alliances in the global auto industry, *Strategic Management Journal*, 25: 701–711.

61. M. Rogan & H. R. Greve, 2014, Resource dependence dynamics: Partner reactions to mergers, *Organization Science*, 26: 239–255; L. Capron & W. Mitchell, 2012, *Build, Borrow or Buy: Solving the Growth Dilemma*, Cambridge: Harvard Business Review Press; C. Häussler, 2011, The determinants of commercialization strategy: Idiosyncrasies in British and German biotechnology, *Entrepreneurship Theory and Practice*, 35: 653–681.

62. F. Castellaneta & M. Zollo, 2014, The dimensions of experiential learning in the management of activity load, *Organization Science*, 26: 140–157; Y. Lew & R. R. Sinkovics, 2013, Crossing borders and industry sectors: Behavioral governance in strategic alliances and product innovation for competitive advantage, *Long Range Planning*, 46: 13–38; P. Ritala & H.-K. Ellonen, 2010, Competitive advantage in interfirm cooperation: Old and new explanations, *Competitiveness Review*, 20: 367–383.

63. H. M. Khamesh & M. Nasiriyar, 2014, Avoiding alliance myopia: Forging learning outcomes for long-term success, *Journal of Business Strategy*, 35(4): 37–44; H. Liu, X. Jiang, J. Zhang, & X. Zhao, 2013, Strategic flexibility and international venturing by emerging market firms: The moderating effects of institutional and relational factors, *Journal of International Marketing*, 21: 79–98; J. Anand, R. Oriani, & R. S. Vassolo, 2010, Alliance activity as a dynamic capability in the face of a discontinuous technological change, *Organization Science*, 21: 1213–1232.

64. B. T. McCann, J. J. Reuer, & N. Lahiri, 2015, Agglomeration and the choice between acquisitions and alliances: An information economics perspective, *Strategic Management Journal*, in press; S. Chang & M. Tsai, 2013, The effect of prior alliance experience on acquisition performance, *Applied Economics*, 45: 765–773.

65. 2013, TATA Sikorsky JV delivers first fully indigenous S-92 helicopter cabin, United Technologies Home Page, www.utc.com, October 24.

66. 2014, BMW expands joint venture with Chinese carmaker Brilliance, *DW*, www.dw.de, December 14.

67. I. Ater & O. Rigbi, 2015, Price control and advertising in franchising chains, *Strategic Management Journal*, in press; V. K. Garg, R. L. Priem, & A. A. Rasheed, 2013, A theoretical explanation of the cost advantages of multi-unit franchising, *Journal of Marketing Channels*, 20: 52–72; J. G. Combs, D. J. Ketchen, Jr., C. L. Shook, & J. C. Short, 2011, Antecedents and consequences of franchising: Past accomplishments and future challenges, *Journal of Management*, 37: 99–126.

68. B. R. Barringer & R. D. Ireland, 2016, *Entrepreneurship: Successfully Launching New Ventures*, 5th ed., Prentice-Hall, 510.

69. C.-W. Wu, 2015, Antecedents of franchise strategy and performance, *Journal of Business Research*, 68: 1581–1588; W. E. Gillis, J. G. Combs, & D. J. Ketchen, Jr., 2014, Using resource-based theory to help explain plural form franchising, *Entrepreneurship Theory and Practice*, 38: 449–472; D. Grewal, G. R. Iyer, R. G. Javalgi, & L. Radulovich, 2011, Franchise partnership and international expansion: A conceptual framework and research propositions, *Entrepreneurship Theory and Practice*, 35: 533–557.

70. J.-S. Chiou & C. Droge, 2015, The effects of standardization and trust on franchisee's performance and satisfaction: A study on franchise systems in the growth stage, *Journal of Small Business Management*, 53: 129–144; N. Mumdziev & J. Windsperger, 2013, An extended transaction cost model of decision rights allocation in franchising: The moderating role of trust, *Managerial and Decision Economics*, 34: 170–182; J. McDonnell, A. Beatson & C.-H. Huang, 2011, Investigating relationships between relationship quality, customer loyalty and cooperation: An empirical study of convenience stores' franchise chain systems, *Asia Pacific Journal of Marketing and Logistics*, 23: 367–385.

71. A. El Akremi, R. Perrigot, & I. Piot-Lepetit, 2015, Examining the drivers for franchised chains performance through the lens of the dynamic capabilities approach, *Journal of Small Business Management*, 53: 145–165; B. Merrilees & L. Frazer, 2013, Internal branding: Franchisor leadership as a critical determinant, *Journal of Business Research*, 66: 158–164; T. M. Nisar, 2011, Intellectual property securitization and growth capital in retail franchising, *Journal of Retailing*, 87: 393–405.

72. I. Alon, M. Boulanger, E. Misati, & M. Madanoglu, 2015, Are the parents to blame? Predicting franchisee failure, *Competitiveness Review*, 25: 205–217; D. Grace, S. Weaven, L. Frazer, & J. Giddings, 2013,

Examining the role of franchisee normative expectations in relationship evaluation, *Journal of Retailing*, 89: 219–230; W. R. Meek, B. Davis-Sramek, M. S. Baucus, & R. N. Germain, 2011, Commitment in franchising: The role of collaborative communication and a franchisee's propensity to leave, *Entrepreneurship Theory and Practice*, 35: 559–581.

73. M. W. Nyadzayo, M. J. Matanda, & M. T. Ewing, 2015, The impact of franchisor support, brand commitment, brand citizenship behavior, and franchisee experience on franchisee-perceived brand image, *Journal of Business Research*, in press; N. Gorovaia & J. Windsperger, 2013, Real options, intangible resources and performance of franchise networks, *Managerial and Decision Economics*, 34: 183–194; T. W. K. Leslie & L. S. McNeill, 2010, Towards a conceptual model for franchise perceptual equity, *Journal of Brand Management*, 18: 21–33.

74. H. Parker & Z. Brey, 2015, Collaboration costs and new product development performance, *Journal of Business Research*, 68: 1653–1656; S. Demirkan & I. Demirkan, 2014, Implications of strategic alliances for earnings quality and capital market investors, *Journal of Business Research*, 67: 1806–1816; M. Onal Vural, L. Dahlander, & G. George, 2013, Collaborative benefits and coordination costs: Learning and capability development in science, *Strategic Entrepreneurship Journal*, 7: 122–137.

75. C. E. Eesley, D. H. Hsu, & E. B. Roberts, 2014, The contingent effects of top management teams on venture performance: Aligning founding team composition with innovation strategy and commercialization environment, *Strategic Management Journal*, 35: 1798–1817; G. Ahuja, C. M. Lampert, & E. Novelli, 2013, The second face of appropriability: Generative appropriability and its determinants, *Academy of Management Review*, 38: 248–269; C. Choi & P. Beamish, 2013, Resource complementarity and international joint venture performance in Korea, *Asia Pacific Journal of Management*, 30: 561–576.

76. Z. Khan, O. Shenkar, & Y. K. Lew, 2015, Knowledge transfer from international joint ventures to local suppliers in a developing economy, *Journal of International Business Studies*, in press; R. Belderbos, T. W. Tong, & S. Wu, 2014, Multinationality and downside risk: The roles of option portfolio and organization, *Strategic Management Journal*, 35: 88–106; S. Veilleux, N. Haskell, & F. Pons, 2012, Going global: How smaller enterprises benefit from strategic alliances, *Journal of Business Strategy*, 33(5): 22–31;

77. A. Dechezlepretre, E. Neumayer, & R. Perekins, 2015, Environmental regulation and the cross-border diffusion of new technology: Evidence from automobile patents, *Research Policy*, 44: 244–257;

I. Arikan & O. Shenkar, 2013, National animosity and cross-border alliances, *Academy of Management Journal*, 56: 1516–1544.

78. Y. Kubota & J. Chow, 2015, French clout at Renault roils Nissan deal, *Wall Street Journal Online*, www.wsj.com, April 20.

79. Q. Gu & X. Lu, 2014, Unraveling the mechanisms of reputation and alliance formation: A study of venture capital syndication in China, *Strategic Management Journal*, 35: 739–750; L. Li, G. Qian, & Z. Qian, 2013, Do partners in international strategic alliances share resources, costs, and risks? *Journal of Business Research*, 66: 489–498; A. Zaheer & E. Hernandez, 2011, The geographic scope of the MNC and its alliance portfolio: Resolving the paradox of distance, *Global Strategy Journal*, 1: 109–126.

80. Z. Khan, Y. K. Lew, & R. R. Sinkovics, 2015, International joint ventures as boundary spanners: Technological knowledge transfer in an emerging economy, *Global Strategy Journal*, 5: 48–68; M. Meuleman & M. Wright, 2011, Cross-border private equity syndication: Institutional context and learning, *Journal of Business Venturing*, 26: 35–48.

81. J. J. Hotho, M. A. Lyles, & M. Easterby-Smith, 2015, The mutual impact of global strategy and organizational learning: Current themes and future directions, *Global Strategy Journal*, 5: 85–112; B. B. Nielsen & S. Gudergan, 2012, Exploration and exploitation fit and performance in international strategic alliances, *International Business Review*, 21: 558–574; D. Kronborg & S. Thomsen, 2009, Foreign ownership and long-term survival, *Strategic Management Journal*, 30: 207–219.

82. I.-S. Nam & R. Wall, 2015, Airbus, Korea Aerospace sign helicopter deal, *Wall Street Journal Online*, www.wsj.com, March 16.

83. S. Xu, A. P. Fenik, & M. B. Shaner, 2014, Multilateral alliances and innovation output: The importance of equity and technological scope, *Journal of Business Research*, 67: 2403–2410; D. Lavie, C. Lechner, & H. Singh, 2007, The performance implications of timing of entry and involvement in multipartner alliances, *Academy of Management Journal*, 50: 578–604.

84. 2015, Cisco Partner Summit, Cisco homepage, www.cisco.com, May 7.

85. 2015, Strategic alliances—IBM, Cisco Home Page, www.cisco.com, May 7.

86. C. Geldes, C. Felzensztein, E. Turkina, & A. Durand, 2015, How does proximity affect interfirm marketing cooperation? A study of an agribusiness cluster, *Journal of Business Research*, 68: 263–272; W. Fu, J. Revilla Diez, & D. Schiller, 2013, Interactive learning, informal networks and innovation: Evidence from electronics firm survey in the Pearl River Delta, China, *Research Policy*, 42: 635–646; A. T. Ankan & M. A. Schilling, 2011,

Structure and governance in industrial districts: Implications for competitive advantage, *Journal of Management Studies*, 48: 772–803.

87. A. Phene & S. Tallman, 2014, Knowledge spillovers and alliance formation, *Journal of Management Studies*, 51: 1058–1090; C. Casanueva, I. Castro, & J. L. Galán, 2013, Informational networks and innovation in mature industrial clusters, *Journal of Business Research*, 66: 603–613; J. Wincent, S. Anokhin, D. Örtqvist, & E. Autio, 2010, Quality meets structure: Generalized reciprocity and firm-level advantage in strategic networks, *Journal of Management Studies*, 47: 597–624; D. Lavie, 2007, Alliance portfolios and firm performance: A study of value creation and appropriation in the U.S. software industry, *Strategic Management Journal*, 28: 1187–1212.

88. Y. Zheng & H. Yang, 2015, Does familiarity foster innovation? The impact of alliance partner repeatedness on breakthrough innovations, *Journal of Management Studies*, 52: 213–230; L. Dobusch & E. Schübler, 2013, Theorizing path dependence: A review of positive feedback mechanisms in technology markets, regional clusters, and organizations, *Industrial & Corporate Change*, 22: 617–647; A. M. Joshi & A. Nerkar, 2011, When do strategic alliances inhibit innovation by firms? Evidence from patent pools in the global optical disc industry, *Strategic Management Journal*, 32: 1139–1160.

89. S. Perkins, R. Morck, & B. Yeung, 2014, Innocents abroad: The hazards of international joint ventures with pyramidal group firms, *Global Strategy Journal*, 4: 310–330; J. P. MacDuffie, 2011, Inter-organizational trust and the dynamics of distrust, *Journal of International Business Studies*, 42: 35–47; H. Kim, R. E. Hoskisson, & W. P. Wan, 2004, Power, dependence, diversification strategy and performance in keiretsu member firms, *Strategic Management Journal*, 25: 613–636.

90. B. Kang & K. Motohashi, 2015, Essential intellectual property rights and inventors' involvement in standardization, *Research Policy*, 44: 483–492; V. Van de Vrande, 2013, Balancing your technology-sourcing portfolio: How sourcing mode diversity enhances innovative performance, *Strategic Management Journal*, 34: 610–621; A. V. Shipilov, 2009, Firm scope experience, historic multimarket contact with partners, centrality, and the relationship between structural holes and performance, *Organization Science*, 20: 85–106.

91. K.-H. Huarng & A. Mas-Tur, 2015, Sprit of strategy (S.O.S.): The new S.O.S. for competitive business, *Journal of Business Research*, 68: 1383–1387; S. Gupta & M. Polonsky, 2014, Inter-firm learning and knowledge-sharing in multinational networks: An outsourced organization's perspective, *Journal of Business Research*,

67: 615–622; A. S. Cui & G. O'Connor, 2012, Alliance portfolio resource diversity and firm innovation, *Journal of Marketing*, 76: 24–43.

92. F. Collet & D. Philippe, 2014, From hot cakes to cold feet: A contingent perspective on the relationship between market uncertainty and status homophily in the formation of alliances, *Journal of Management Studies*, 51: 406–432; G. Cuevas-Rodriguez, C. Cabello-Medina, & A. Carmona-Lavado, 2014, Internal and external social capital for radical product innovation: Do they always work well together? *British Journal of Management*, 25: 266–284; G. Soda, 2011, The management of firms' alliance network positioning: Implications for innovation, *European Management Journal*, 29: 377–388.

93. E. Lam & C. Pellegrini, 2014, Apple-IBM deal snaps Blackberry rally on turnaround doubt, *BloombergBusiness*, www.bloomberg.com, July 17.

94. I. Castro & J. L. Roldan, 2015, Alliance portfolio management: Dimensions and performance, *European Management Review*, in press; C. Martin-Rios, 2014, Why do firms seek to share human resource management knowledge? The importance of inter-firm networks, *Journal of Business Research*, 67: 190–199.

95. A. Gambardella, C. Panico, & G. Valentini, 2015, Strategic incentives to human capital, *Strategic Management Journal*, 36: 37–52; A. G. Karamanos, 2012, Leveraging micro- and macro-structures of embeddedness in alliance networks for exploratory innovation in biotechnology, *R&D Management*, 42: 71–89; D. Somaya, Y. Kim, & N. S. Vonortas, 2011, Exclusivity in licensing alliances: Using hostages to support technology commercialization, *Strategic Management Journal*, 32: 159–186.

96. U. Ozmel & I. Guler, 2015, Small fish, big fish: The performance effects of the relative standing in partners' affiliate portfolios, *Strategic Management Journal*, in press; M. J. Nieto & L. Santamaría, 2010, Technological collaboration: Bridging the innovation gap between small and large firms, *Journal of Small Business Management*, 48: 44–69; P. Ozcan & K. M. Eisenhardt, 2009, Origin of alliance portfolios: Entrepreneurs, network strategies, and firm performance, *Academy of Management Journal*, 52: 246–279.

97. L.-Y. Wu, P.-Y. Chen, & K.-Y. Chen, 2015, Why does loyalty-cooperation behavior vary over buyer-seller relationship? *Journal of Business Research*, in press; H. R. Greve, H. Mitsuhashi, & J. A. C. Baum, 2013, Greener pastures: Outside options and strategic alliance withdrawal, *Organization Science*, 24: 79–98; H. R. Greve, J. A. C. Baum, H. Mitsuhashi, & T. J. Rowley, 2010, Built to last but falling apart: Cohesion, friction, and withdrawal from interfirm alliances,

Academy of Management Journal, 53: 302–322.

98. S. Dasi-Rodriguez & M. Pardo-del-Val, 2015, Seeking partners in international alliances: The influence of cultural factors, *Journal of Business Research*, 68: 1522–1526; G. Vasudeva & J. Anand, 2011, Unpacking absorptive capacity: A study of knowledge utilization from alliance portfolios, *Academy of Management Journal*, 54: 611–623; J.-Y. Kim & A. S. Miner, 2007, Vicarious learning from the failures and near-failures of others: Evidence from the U.S. commercial banking industry, *Academy of Management Journal*, 50: 687–714.

99. J. Marson, 2013, TNK-BP investors appeal to Rosneft's chief over shares, *Wall Street Journal Online*, www.wsj.com, April 17.

100. B. Kang & R. P. Jindal, 2015, Opportunism in buyer-seller relationships: Some unexplored antecedents, *Journal of Business Research*, 68: 735–742; L.-Y. Wu, P.-Y. Chen, & K.-Y. Chen, 2015, Why does loyalty-cooperation behavior vary over buyer-seller relationship? *Journal of Business Research*, in press; K. Zhou & D. Xu, 2012, How foreign firms curtail local supplier opportunism in China: Detailed contracts, centralized control, and relational governance, *Journal of International Business Studies*, 43: 677–692.

101. A. Spithoven & P. Teirlinck, 2015, Internal capabilities, network resources and appropriate mechanisms as determinants of R&D outsourcing, *Research Policy*, 44: 711–725; A. V. Werder, 2011, Corporate governance and stakeholder opportunism, *Organization Science*, 22: 1345–1358; T. K. Das & R. Kumar, 2011, Regulatory focus and opportunism in the alliance development process, *Journal of Management*, 37: 682–708.

102. I. Stern, J. M. Dukerich, & E. Zajac, 2014, Unmixed signals: How reputation and status affect alliance formation, *Strategic Management Journal*, 35: 512–531; A. S. Cui, 2013, Portfolio dynamics and alliance termination: The contingent role of resource dissimilarity, *Journal of Marketing*, 77: 15–32; M. B. Sarkar, P. S. Aulakh, & A. Madhok, 2009, Process capabilities and value generation in alliance portfolios, *Organization Science*, 20: 583–600.

103. S. McLain, 2015, New outsourcing frontier in India: Monitoring drug safety, *Wall Street Journal Online*, www.wsj.com, February 1.

104. M. Kafouros, C. Wang, P. Piiperopoulos, & M. Zhang, 2015, Academic collaborations and firm innovation performance in China: The role of region-specific institutions, *Research Policy*, 44: 803–817; S. Kraus, T. C. Ambos, F. Eggers, & B. Cesinger, 2015, Distance and perceptions of risk in internationalization decisions, *Journal of Business Research*, 68: 1501–1505; M. Nippa & S. Beechler, 2013, What do we know about the success and failure of international joint ventures? In search of relevance and

holism, in T. M. Devinney, T. Pedersen, & L. Tihanyi (eds.), *Philosophy of Science and Meta-knowledge in International Business and Management*, 26: 363–396

105. M. Menz & C. Scheef, 2014, Chief strategy officers: Contingency analysis of their presence in top management teams, *Strategic Management Journal*, 35: 461–471; I. Neyens & D. Faems, 2013, Exploring the impact of alliance portfolio management design on alliance portfolio performance, *Managerial & Decision Economics*, 34: 347–361; D. G. Sirmon, M. A. Hitt, R. D. Ireland, & B. A. Gilbert, 2011, Resource orchestration to create competitive advantage: Breadth, depth, and life cycle effects, *Journal of Management*, 37: 1390–1412; M. H. Hansen, R. E. Hoskisson, & J. B. Barney, 2008, Competitive advantage in alliance governance: Resolving the opportunism minimization-gain maximization paradox, *Managerial and Decision Economics*, 29: 191–208.

106. G. Speckbacher, K. Neumann, & W. H. Hoffmann, 2015, Resource relatedness and the mode of entry into new businesses: Internal resource accumulation vs. access by collaborative arrangement, *Strategic Management Journal*, in press; C. C. Chung & P. W. Beamish, 2010, The trap of continual ownership change in international equity joint ventures, *Organization Science*, 21: 995–1015.

107. D. J. Harmon, P. H. Kim, & K. J. Mayer, 2015, Breaking the letter vs. spirit of the law: How the interpretation of contract violations affects trust and the management of relationships, *Strategic Management Journal*, 36: 497–517; M. H. Hansen, R. E. Hoskisson, & J. B. Barney, 2008, Competitive advantage in alliance governance: Resolving the opportunism minimization-gain maximization paradox, *Managerial and Decision Economics*, 29: 191–208.

108. J. Marshall, 2015, News publishers for programmatic advertising alliance, *Wall Street Journal Online*, ww.wsj.com, March 18.

109. T. Felin & T. R. Zenger, 2014, Closed or open innovation? Problem solving and the governance choice, *Research Policy*, 43: 914–925; N. N. Arranz & J. C. F. de Arroyabe, 2012, Effect of formal contracts, relational norms and trust on performance of joint research and development projects, *British Journal of Management*, 23: 575–588.

110. B. S. Vanneste, P. Puranam, & T. Kretschmer, 2014, Trust over time in exchange relationships: Meta-analysis and theory, *Strategic Management Journal*, 35: 1891–1902; G. Ertug, I. Cuypers, N. Noorderhaven, & B. Bensaou, 2013, Trust between international joint venture partners: Effects of home countries, *Journal of International Business Studies*, 44: 263–282; J. J. Li, L. Poppo, & K. Z. Zhou, 2010, Relational mechanisms, formal contracts, and local knowledge acquisition by international subsidiaries, *Strategic Management Journal*, 31: 349–370.

111. H. Yang, Y. Zheng, & X. Zhao, 2014, Exploration or exploitation? Small firms' alliance strategies with large firms, *Strategic Management Journal*, 35: 146–157; S. E. Fawcett, S. L. Jones, & A. M. Fawcett, 2012, Supply chain trust: The catalyst for collaborative innovation, *Business Horizons*, 55: 163–178; H. C. Dekker & A. Van den Abbeele, 2010, Organizational learning and interfirm control: The effects of partner search and prior exchange experience, *Organization Science*, 21: 1233–1250.

112. A. Shipilov, R. Gulati, M. Kilduff, S. Li, & W. Tsai, 2014, Relational pluralism within and between organizations, *Academy of Management Journal*, 57: 449–459; R. Kumar & A. Nathwani, 2012, Business alliances: Why managerial thinking and biases determine success, *Journal of Business Strategy*, 33(5): 44–50; C. C. Phelps, 2010, A longitudinal study of the influence of alliance network structure and composition on firm exploratory innovation, *Academy of Management Journal*, 53: 890–913.

10

Corporate Governance

Studying this chapter should provide you with the strategic management knowledge needed to:

10-1   Define corporate governance and explain why it is used to monitor and control top-level managers' decisions.

10-2   Explain why ownership is largely separated from managerial control in organizations.

10-3   Define an agency relationship and managerial opportunism and describe their strategic implications.

10-4   Explain the use of three internal governance mechanisms to monitor and control managers' decisions.

10-5   Discuss the types of compensation top-level managers receive and their effects on managerial decisions.

10-6   Describe how the external corporate governance mechanism—the market for corporate control—restrains top-level managers' decisions.

10-7   Discuss the nature and use of corporate governance in international settings, especially in Germany, Japan, and China.

10-8   Describe how corporate governance fosters ethical decisions by a firm's top-level managers.

THE CORPORATE RAIDERS OF THE 1980S HAVE BECOME THE ACTIVIST SHAREHOLDERS OF TODAY

In the 1980s, large activist shareholders would buy significant stakes in companies and often seek to increase the debt load, sell off business units reducing diversification, and downsize by laying off many workers. If the firms did not respond as the activist shareholders required, they would make the company pay a premium on the shares they bought, often called "greenmail." Today activist investors are doing many of the same things, but it seems that they are being supported by institutional investors who often follow the activist investors' lead or support them in their activities. Interestingly, the number of activist funds have grown from just 76 in 2010 to 203 in 2014. Their activities have increased as well with 136 firms targeted in 2010 rising to 344 in 2014. One Citigroup analyst, Tobias Levkovich, suggested that "we suspect there is a limited universe for the activists, and eventually the arbitrage opportunity will be exhausted."

One of the strategies these activist investors pursue is to pressure firms to allow representatives to stand for election to the targeted company's board. Another strategy gaining momentum is the access to the proxy process to include shareholder resolutions for shareholder votes. This access has been allowed by the courts and the U.S. Securities and Exchange Commission's (SEC) efforts to require more proxy voting action opportunities to shareholders. However, the U.S. Chamber of Commerce and Society of Corporate Secretaries & Governance Professionals are worried that "the proliferation of the proxy access will lead to the nomination of 'special interest' directors harming long-term shareholders." Nonetheless, regulators'

Heidi Gutman/CNBC/NBCU Photo Bank/Getty Images

decisions have seemed to open the flood gates to firms allowing more proxy access. As such, firm shareholders will be able to vote on strategic issues presented by activist shareholders as well as lead activist shareholders by directly nominating board members who represent their interests.

Some of these firms are quite large and visible, such as DuPont, Vivendi, and QUALCOMM. For example, DuPont's CEO Ellen Kullman has fought a proxy battle in media outlets. Trian Fund Management L.P. representatives, headed by CEO Nelson Peltz, have criss-crossed the country as has CEO Kullman's team, seeking to persuade shareholders about their opposing positions regarding access to board seats. Trian wants four board seats, most importantly for Mr. Peltz, and is "seeking to oust the heads of several key board committees." Kullman has responded, "Mr. Peltz wants to establish a 'shadow management' team dedicated to pushing a short-term agenda." She argues that DuPont has cut $1 billion in cost and pursued other efficiencies and that Trian wants to nominate directors that lack the expertise and patience needed to steer an agricultural and chemical company that often requires decades to create innovation and launch products. Kullman argues, "can you cut costs and create a bump short-term? Yes, but where are you going to be in 2 years, in 5 years? Do you exist in 10?" Often these activist investors seek stock buybacks and increases in dividends as well as selling off "non-performing businesses." Over time, in part due to such activism, objections to corporate governance arrangements have become more strident and monitoring of top executives more intense.

However, there are risks to activist approaches, as evidenced in the Herbalife conflict. William Ackman's Pershing Square Capital Management L.P. has been alleging that nutritional-products company Herbalife is "an illegal pyramid scheme." Although typically activist investors push companies to improve short-term value through leadership changes, stock buybacks, and break-ups, others want the opposite to happen; they "short" the stock and make arguments that create turmoil and perceived weakness that result in the lowering of the company share price increasing the value of a short position. Such negative commentary has brought Herbalife under investigation by the SEC and the Federal Trade Commission (FTC). Of course, Herbalife's stock price has come down. Most short-sellers don't broadcast their position because it might cause a government backlash and investigation focused on them. Nonetheless, some such as Mr. Ackman's attacks on Herbalife, have brought this controversy into focus.

Although all of this activism has caused some chaos in the board room, it has made for overall better, albeit more intense, governance and has given more voice for shareholders into strategy issues which are pertinent to the topic of our book. As you go through this chapter, these issues will become clearer as the various governance devices are defined and their purpose explained to foster better understanding.

Sources: A. Ackerman & J. S. Lublin, 2015, Activists win ground in major boardrooms, *Wall Street Journal*, March 17, 215 B1, B2; R. Bender, 2015, Shareholder presses Vivendi further, *Wall Street Journal*, March 15, B3; D. Benoit, 2015, Herbalife fracas puts activist risk right in the spotlight, *Wall Street Journal*, March 17, C3; D. Benoit & D. Clark, 2015, Activists puts pressure on Qualcomm, *Wall Street Journal*, April 13, B1, B2; J. Bunge & C. Dulaney, 2015, DuPont posts declines ahead of vote, *Wall Street Journal*, April 22, b4; S. Gandel, 2015, In DuPont fight, Nelson Peltz pushes for open proxy, *Fortune*, www.fortune.com, March 13; A. Gara, 2015, DuPont spinoff fans flames in Trian Management's scorched earth fight. *Forbes*, www.forbes.com, March 30; L. Hoffman & D. Benoit, 2015, Activist investors ramp up, and boardroom rifts ensue, *Wall Street Journal*, April 17, C1, C2; B. Levisohn, 2015, Activism's Dark Side, *Barron's*, March 2, 11; A. VanderMey, 2015, Actively mediocre: Activist investors scold CEOs over stock prices, but their returns are just so-so, *Fortune*, May 1, 12.

As the Opening Case suggests, corporate governance is complex and designed to provide oversight of how firms operate. At a broader level, it reflects the type of infrastructure provided by individual nations as the framework within which companies compete. Given that we are concerned with the strategic management process firms use, our focus in this chapter is on corporate governance in companies (although we do also address governance at the level of nations). The complexity and the potential problems with corporate governance, such as having true checks and balances in the system of governance, are shown by the example of activist shareholders in the Opening Case.

Comprehensive in scope and complex in nature, corporate governance is a responsibility that challenges firms and their leaders. Evidence suggests that corporate governance is critical to firms' success and dealing appropriately with this challenge is important. Because of this, governance is an increasingly important part of the strategic management process.[1] For example, if the board makes the wrong decisions in selecting, governing, and compensating the firm's CEO as its strategic leader, the shareholders and the firm suffer. When CEOs are motivated to act in the best interests of the firm—in particular, the shareholders—the company's value is more likely to increase. Additionally, effective leadership succession plans and appropriate monitoring and direction-setting efforts by the board of directors contribute positively to a firm's performance.

Corporate governance is the set of mechanisms used to manage the relationships among stakeholders and to determine and control the strategic direction and performance of organizations.[2] At its core, corporate governance is concerned with identifying ways to ensure that decisions (especially strategic decisions) are made effectively and that they facilitate a firm's efforts to achieve strategic competitiveness.[3] Governance can also be thought of as a means to establish and maintain harmony between parties (the firm's owners and its top-level managers) whose interests may conflict.

In modern corporations—especially those in nations with "Westernized" infrastructures and business practices such as in the United States and the United Kingdom—ensuring that top-level managers' interests are aligned with other stakeholders' interests,

Corporate governance is the set of mechanisms used to manage the relationships among stakeholders and to determine and control the strategic direction and performance of organizations.

particularly those of shareholders, is a primary objective of corporate governance. Thus, corporate governance involves oversight in areas where owners, managers, and members of boards of directors may have conflicts of interest. Processes used to elect members of the firm's board of directors, the general management of CEO pay and more focused supervision of director pay, and the corporation's overall strategic direction are examples of areas in which oversight is sought.[4] Because corporate governance is an ongoing process concerned with how a firm is to be managed, its nature evolves in light of the types of never-ending changes in a firm's external environment that we discussed in Chapter 2.

The recent global emphasis on corporate governance stems mainly from the apparent failure of corporate governance mechanisms to adequately monitor and control top-level managers' decisions (as exemplified by the growing focus on governance issues among activist investors in the Opening Case). In turn, undesired or unacceptable consequences resulting from using corporate governance mechanisms cause changes such as electing new members to the board of directors with the hope of providing more effective governance. A second and more positive reason for this interest comes from evidence that a well-functioning corporate governance system can create a competitive advantage for an individual firm.[5]

As noted earlier, corporate governance is of concern to nations as well as to individual firms.[6] Although corporate governance reflects company standards, it also collectively reflects the societal standards of nations.[7] For example, the independence of board members and practices a board should follow to exercise effective oversight of a firm's internal control efforts are changes to governance standards that have been fostered in Singapore.[8] Efforts such as these are important because research shows that firms seek to invest in nations with national governance standards that are acceptable to them.[9] This is particularly the case when firms consider the possibility of expanding geographically into emerging markets.

In the chapter's first section, we describe the relationship on which the modern corporation is built—namely, the relationship between owners and managers. We use the majority of the chapter to explain various mechanisms owners use to govern managers and to ensure that they comply with their responsibility to satisfy stakeholders' needs, especially those of shareholders.

Three internal governance mechanisms and a single external one are used in the modern corporation. The three internal governance mechanisms described in this chapter are

1. ownership concentration, represented by types of shareholders and their different incentives to monitor managers;
2. the board of directors; and
3. executive compensation.

We then consider the market for corporate control, an external corporate governance mechanism. Essentially, this market is a set of potential owners seeking to acquire undervalued firms and earn above-average returns on their investments by replacing ineffective top-level management teams.[10] The chapter's focus then shifts to the issue of international corporate governance. We briefly describe governance approaches used in several countries outside of the United States and United Kingdom. In part, this discussion suggests that the structures used to govern global companies competing in both developed and emerging economies are becoming more, rather than less, similar. Closing our analysis of corporate governance is a consideration of the need for these control mechanisms to encourage and support ethical and socially responsible behavior in organizations.

10-1 Separation of Ownership and Managerial Control

Historically, U.S. firms were managed by founder-owners and their descendants. In these cases, corporate ownership and control resided with the same group of people. As firms grew larger, "the managerial revolution led to a separation of ownership and control in most large corporations, where control of the firm shifted from entrepreneurs to professional managers while ownership became dispersed among thousands of unorganized stockholders who were removed from the day-to-day management of the firm."[11] These changes created the modern public corporation, which is based on the efficient separation of ownership and managerial control. Supporting the separation is a basic legal premise suggesting that the primary objective of a firm's activities is to increase the corporation's profit and, thereby, the owners' (shareholders') financial gains.[12]

The separation of ownership and managerial control allows shareholders to purchase stock, which entitles them to income (residual returns) from the firm's operations after paying expenses. This right, however, requires that shareholders take a risk that the firm's expenses may exceed its revenues. To manage this investment risk, shareholders maintain a diversified portfolio by investing in several companies to reduce their overall risk.[13] The poor performance or failure of any one firm in which they invest has less overall effect on the value of the entire portfolio of investments. Thus, shareholders specialize in managing their investment risk.

Commonly, those managing small firms also own a significant percentage of the firm. In such instances, there is less separation between ownership and managerial control. Moreover, in a large number of family-owned firms, ownership and managerial control are not separated to any significant extent. Research shows that family-owned firms perform better when a member of the family is the CEO rather than when the CEO is an outsider.[14]

In many regions outside the United States, such as in Latin America, Asia, and some European countries, family-owned firms dominate the competitive landscape.[15] The primary purpose of most of these firms is to increase the family's wealth, which explains why a family CEO often is better than an outside CEO. Family ownership is also significant in U.S. companies in that at least one-third of the S&P 500 firms have substantial family ownership, holding on average about 18 percent of a firm's equity.[16]

Family-controlled firms face at least two critical issues related to corporate governance. First, as they grow, they may not have access to all of the skills needed to effectively manage the firm and maximize returns for the family. Thus, outsiders may be required to facilitate growth. Second, as they grow, they may need to seek outside capital and thus give up some of the ownership. In these cases, protecting the minority owners' rights becomes important.[17] To avoid these potential problems, when family firms grow and become more complex, their owner-managers may contract with managerial specialists. These managers make major decisions in the owners' firm and are compensated on the basis of their decision-making skills. Research suggests that firms in which families own enough equity to have influence without major control tend to make the best strategic decisions.[18]

Without owner (shareholder) specialization in risk bearing and management specialization in decision making, a firm may be limited by its owners' abilities to simultaneously manage it and make effective strategic decisions relative to risk. Thus, the separation and specialization of ownership (risk bearing) and managerial control (decision making) should produce the highest returns for the firm's owners.

10-1a Agency Relationships

The separation between owners and managers creates an agency relationship. An agency relationship exists when one or more persons (the principal or principals) hire another person or persons (the agent or agents) as decision-making specialists to perform a service.[19] Thus, an **agency relationship** exists when one party delegates decision-making responsibility to a second party for compensation (see Figure 10.1).

In addition to shareholders and top-level managers, other examples of agency relationships are top managers who hire subsidiary managers, client firms engaging consultants and the insured contracting with an insurer. Moreover, within organizations, an agency relationship exists between managers and their employees, as well as between top-level managers and the firm's owners.[20] However, in this chapter we focus on the agency relationship between the firm's owners (the principals) and top-level managers (the principals' agents) because these managers are responsible for formulating and implementing the firm's strategies, which have major effects on firm performance.[21]

The separation between ownership and managerial control can be problematic. Research evidence documents a variety of agency problems in the modern corporation.[22] Problems can surface because the principal and the agent have different interests and goals or because shareholders lack direct control of large publicly traded corporations. Problems also surface when an agent makes decisions that result in pursuing goals that conflict with those of the principals. Thus, the separation of ownership and control potentially allows divergent interests (between principals and agents) to occur, which can lead to managerial opportunism.

An **agency relationship** exists when one party delegates decision-making responsibility to a second party for compensation.

Figure 10.1 An Agency Relationship

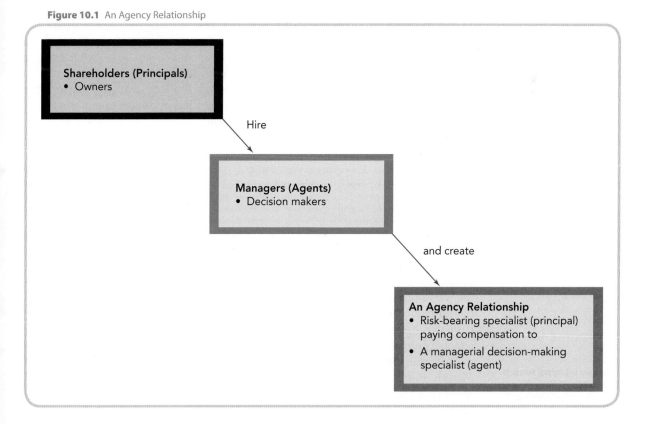

Shareholders (Principals)
• Owners

Hire

Managers (Agents)
• Decision makers

and create

An Agency Relationship
• Risk-bearing specialist (principal) paying compensation to
• A managerial decision-making specialist (agent)

Managerial opportunism is the seeking of self-interest with guile (i.e., cunning or deceit).[23] Opportunism is both an attitude (i.e., an inclination) and a set of behaviors (i.e., specific acts of self-interest).[24] Principals do not know beforehand which agents will or will not act opportunistically. A top-level manager's reputation is an imperfect predictor; moreover, opportunistic behavior cannot be observed until it has occurred. Thus, principals establish governance and control mechanisms to prevent agents from acting opportunistically, even though only a few are likely to do so. Interestingly, research suggests that when CEOs feel constrained by governance mechanisms, they are more likely to seek external advice that, in turn, helps them make better strategic decisions.[25]

The agency relationship suggests that any time principals delegate decision-making responsibilities to agents, the opportunity for conflicts of interest exists. Top-level managers, for example, may make strategic decisions that maximize their personal welfare and minimize their personal risk.[26] Decisions such as these prevent maximizing shareholder wealth. Decisions regarding product diversification demonstrate this situation.

10-1b Product Diversification as an Example of an Agency Problem

As explained in Chapter 6, a corporate-level strategy to diversify the firm's product lines can enhance a firm's strategic competitiveness and increase its returns, both of which serve the interests of all stakeholders and certainly shareholders and top-level managers. However, product diversification can create two benefits for top-level managers that shareholders do not enjoy, meaning that they may prefer product diversification more than shareholders do.[27]

One reason managers prefer more diversification compared to shareholders is the fact that it usually increases the size of a firm and size is positively related to executive compensation. Diversification also increases the complexity of managing a firm and its network of businesses, possibly requiring additional managerial pay because of this complexity.[28] Thus, increased product diversification provides an opportunity for top-level managers to increase their compensation.[29]

The second potential benefit is that product diversification and the resulting diversification of the firm's portfolio of businesses can reduce top-level managers' employment risk. *Managerial employment risk* is the risk of job loss, loss of compensation, and loss of managerial reputation.[30] These risks are reduced with increased diversification because a firm and its upper-level managers are less vulnerable to the reduction in demand associated with a single or limited number of product lines or businesses. Events that occurred at Lockheed Martin demonstrate these issues.

For a number of years, Lockheed Martin has been a major defense contractor with the United States federal government as its primary customer. Although it provides a variety of products and services (processes U.S. census forms, handles $600 billion of U.S. Social Security benefits each year, and manages over 50 percent of global air traffic), 79 percent of its revenue came from the U.S. government with 59 percent from the U.S. Department of Defense alone. This dependence on a single customer is risky, as shown by the U.S. government's recent attempts to reduce overall spending and to wind down the wars in Iraq and Afghanistan. Therefore, there are strong incentives for Lockheed Martin to diversify. Their earlier attempts to diversify into products that targeted other customer markets were largely unsuccessful. For example, it acquired Comcast with the intent of diversifying into the telecommunications industry. However, the acquisition was unsuccessful and Lockheed Martin eventually sold the business. Essentially, Lockheed Martin's organization and operations have been structured to serve the government, and specifically the military. Indeed, existing weapons systems compose a large portion of Lockheed Martin's current $45.6 billion in annual revenue.

Managerial opportunism is the seeking of self-interest with guile (i.e., cunning or deceit).

Lockheed Martin's new CEO in 2013, Marillyn Hewson, is tasked with charting a future for the company that likely includes diversification. The firm's Center for Innovation is working on several potential products and services in the health care and cybersecurity industries. So, it appears that it will try to diversify organically by developing innovations internally (using its current capabilities) rather than acquiring other firms as it did in the past. In fact, Hewson describes Lockheed Martin as a global security enterprise, suggesting its new focus and vision. While previous diversification efforts were unsuccessful, Lockheed Martin is trying again with a new CEO and emphasis on internal innovation and international expansion.[31]

Free cash flow is the source of another potential agency problem. Calculated as operating cash flow minus capital expenditures, free cash flow represents the cash remaining after the firm has invested in all projects that have positive net present value within its current businesses.[32] Top-level managers may decide to invest free cash flow in product lines that are not associated with the firm's current lines of business to increase the firm's degree of diversification (as is currently being done at Lockheed Martin). However, when managers use free cash flow to diversify the firm in ways that do not have a strong possibility of creating additional value for stakeholders and certainly for shareholders, the firm is overdiversified. Overdiversification is an example of self-serving and opportunistic managerial behavior. In contrast to managers, shareholders may prefer that free cash flow be distributed to them as dividends, so they can control how the cash is invested.[33]

In Figure 10.2, Curve S shows shareholders' optimal level of diversification. As the firm's owners, shareholders seek the level of diversification that reduces the risk of the firm's total failure while simultaneously increasing its value by developing economies of scale and scope (see Chapter 6). Of the four corporate-level diversification strategies shown in Figure 10.2, shareholders likely prefer the diversified position noted by point A on Curve S—a position that is located between the dominant business and related-constrained diversification strategies. Of course, the optimum level of diversification

Figure 10.2 Manager and Shareholder Risk and Diversification

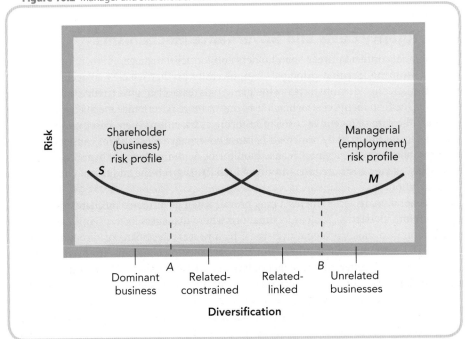

owners seek varies from firm to firm.[34] Factors that affect shareholders' preferences include the firm's primary industry, the intensity of rivalry among competitors in that industry, the top management team's experience with implementing diversification strategies, and the firm's perceived expertise in the new business and its effects on other firm strategies, such as its entry into international markets.[35]

As is the case for principals, top-level managers—as agents—also seek an optimal level of diversification. Declining performance resulting from too much diversification increases the probability that external investors (representing the market for corporate control) will purchase a substantial percentage of or the entire firm for the purpose of controlling it. If a firm is acquired, the employment risk for its top-level managers increases significantly. Furthermore, these managers' employment opportunities in the external managerial labor market (discussed in Chapter 12) are affected negatively by a firm's poor performance. Therefore, top-level managers prefer that the firms they lead be diversified. However, their preference is that the firm's diversification falls short of the point at which it increases their employment risk and reduces their employment opportunities.[36] Curve *M* in Figure 10.2 shows that top-level managers prefer higher levels of product diversification than do shareholders. Top-level managers might find the optimal level of diversification as shown by point *B* on Curve *M*.

In general, shareholders prefer riskier strategies and more focused diversification. Shareholders reduce their risk by holding a diversified portfolio of investments. Alternatively, managers cannot balance their employment risk by working for a diverse portfolio of firms; therefore, managers may prefer a level of diversification that maximizes firm size and their compensation while also reducing their employment risk. Finding the appropriate level of diversification is difficult for managers. Research has shown that too much diversification can have negative effects on the firm's ability to create innovation (managers' unwillingness to take on higher risks). Alternatively, diversification that strategically fits the firm's capabilities can enhance its innovation output.[37] However, too much or inappropriate diversification can also divert managerial attention from other important firm activities such as corporate social responsibility.[38] Product diversification, therefore, is a potential agency problem that could result in principals incurring costs to control their agents' behaviors.

10-1c Agency Costs and Governance Mechanisms

The potential conflict between shareholders and top-level managers shown in Figure 10.2, coupled with the fact that principals cannot easily predict which managers might act opportunistically, demonstrates why principals establish governance mechanisms. However, the firm incurs costs when it uses one or more governance mechanisms. **Agency costs** are the sum of incentive costs, monitoring costs, enforcement costs, and individual financial losses incurred by principals because governance mechanisms cannot guarantee total compliance by the agent. Because monitoring activities within a firm is difficult, the principals' agency costs are larger in diversified firms given the additional complexity of diversification.[39]

In general, managerial interests may prevail when governance mechanisms are weak and therefore ineffective, such as in situations where managers have a significant amount of autonomy to make strategic decisions. If, however, the board of directors controls managerial autonomy, or if other strong governance mechanisms are used, the firm's strategies should better reflect stakeholders and certainly shareholders' interests.[40] For example, effective corporate governance may encourage managers to develop strategies that demonstrate a concern for the environment (i.e., "green strategies").[41]

More recently, observers of firms' governance practices have been concerned about more egregious behavior beyond mere ineffective corporate strategies, such as that discovered at

Agency costs are the sum of incentive costs, monitoring costs, enforcement costs, and individual financial losses incurred by principals because governance mechanisms cannot guarantee total compliance by the agent.

Enron and WorldCom, and the more recent actions by major financial institutions. Partly in response to these behaviors, the U.S. Congress enacted the Sarbanes-Oxley Act (SOX) in 2002 and passed the Dodd-Frank Wall Street Reform and Consumer Protection Act (Dodd-Frank) in mid-2010.

Because of these two acts, corporate governance mechanisms should receive greater scrutiny.[42] While the implementation of SOX has been controversial to some, most believe that its use has led to generally positive outcomes in terms of protecting stakeholders and certainly shareholders' interests. For example, Section 404 of SOX, which prescribes significant transparency improvement on internal controls associated with accounting and auditing, has arguably improved the internal auditing scrutiny (and thereby trust) in firms' financial reporting. Moreover, research suggests that internal controls associated with Section 404 increase shareholder value.[43] Nonetheless, some argue that the Act, especially Section 404, creates excessive costs for firms. In addition, a decrease in foreign firms listing on U.S. stock exchanges occurred at the same time as listing on foreign exchanges increased. In part, this shift may be because of the costs SOX generates for firms seeking to list on U.S. exchanges.

Dodd-Frank is recognized as the most sweeping set of financial regulatory reforms in the United States since the Great Depression. The Act is intended to align financial institutions' actions with society's interests. Dodd-Frank includes provisions related to the categories of consumer protection, systemic risk oversight, executive compensation, and capital requirements for banks. Some legal analysts offer the following description of the Act's provisions: "(Dodd-Frank) creates a Financial Stability Oversight Council headed by the Treasury Secretary, establishes a new system for liquidation of certain financial companies, provides for a new framework to regulate derivatives, establishes new corporate governance requirements, and regulates credit rating agencies and securitizations. The Act also establishes a new consumer protection bureau and provides for extensive consumer protection in financial services."[44]

More intensive application of governance mechanisms as mandated by legislation such as SOX and Dodd-Frank affects firms' choice of strategies. For example, more intense governance might find firms choosing to pursue fewer risky projects, possibly decreasing shareholder wealth as a result. In considering how some provisions associated with Dodd-Frank dealing with banks might be put into practice, a U.S. federal regulator said, "To put it plainly, my view is that we are in danger of trying to squeeze too much risk and complexity out of banking."[45] As this comment suggests, determining governance practices that strike an appropriate balance between protecting stakeholders' interests and allowing firms to implement strategies with some degree of risk is difficult.

Next, we explain the effects of the three internal governance mechanisms on managerial decisions regarding the firm's strategies.

10-2 Ownership Concentration

Ownership concentration is defined by the number of large-block shareholders and the total percentage of the firm's shares they own. **Large-block shareholders** typically own at least 5 percent of a company's issued shares. Ownership concentration as a governance mechanism has received considerable interest because large-block shareholders are increasingly active in their demands that firms adopt effective governance mechanisms to control managerial decisions so that they will best represent owners' interests.[46] In recent years, the number of individuals who are large-block shareholders has declined. Institutional owners have replaced individuals as large-block shareholders.

Ownership concentration is defined by the number of large-block shareholders and the total percentage of the firm's shares they own.

Large-block shareholders typically own at least 5 percent of a company's issued shares.

In general, diffuse ownership (a large number of shareholders with small holdings and few, if any, large-block shareholders) produces weak monitoring of managers' decisions. One reason for this is that diffuse ownership makes it difficult for owners to effectively coordinate their actions. As noted earlier, diversification beyond the shareholders' optimum level can result from ineffective monitoring of managers' decisions. Higher levels of monitoring could encourage managers to avoid strategic decisions that harm shareholder value, such as too much diversification. Research evidence suggests that ownership concentration is associated with lower levels of firm product diversification.[47] Thus, with high degrees of ownership concentration, the probability is greater that managers' decisions will be designed to maximize shareholder value.[48] However, the influence of large-block shareholders is mitigated to a degree in Europe by strong labor representation on boards of directors.[49]

As noted, ownership concentration influences decisions made about the strategies a firm will use and the value created by their use. In general, ownership concentration's influence on strategies and firm performance is positive. For example, when large-block shareholders have a high degree of wealth, they have power relative to minority shareholders to appropriate the firm's wealth; this is particularly the case when they are in managerial positions. Excessive appropriation at the expense of minority shareholders is somewhat common in emerging economy countries where minority shareholder rights often are not as protected as they are in the United States. In fact, in some of these countries, state ownership of an equity stake (even minority ownership) can be used to control these potential problems.[50] The importance of boards of directors to mitigate excessive appropriation of minority shareholder value has been found in firms with strong family ownership where family members have incentives to appropriate shareholder wealth, especially in the second generation after the founder has departed.[51] In general, family-controlled businesses will outperform nonfamily controlled businesses, especially smaller and private firms because of the importance of enhancing the family's wealth and maintaining the family business.[52] However, families often try to balance the pursuit of economic and noneconomic objectives such that they sometimes may be moderately risk averse (thereby influencing their innovative output).[53]

10-2a The Increasing Influence of Institutional Owners

A classic work published in the 1930s argued that a separation of ownership and control had come to characterize the "modern" corporation.[54] This change occurred primarily because growth prevented founders-owners from maintaining their dual positions in what were increasingly complex companies. More recently, another shift has occurred: Ownership of many modern corporations is now concentrated in the hands of institutional investors rather than individual shareholders.[55]

Institutional owners are financial institutions, such as mutual funds and pension funds, that control large-block shareholder positions. Because of their prominent ownership positions, institutional owners, as large-block shareholders, have the potential to be a powerful governance mechanism. Estimates of the amount of equity in U.S. firms held by institutional owners range from 60 to 75 percent. Recent commentary suggests the importance of pension funds to an entire economy: "Pension funds are critical drivers of growth and economic activity in the United States because they are one of the only significant sources of long-term, patient capital."[56]

These percentages suggest that as investors, institutional owners have both the size and the incentive to discipline ineffective top-level managers and that they can significantly influence a firm's choice of strategies and strategic decisions.[57] As the Opening Case indicates, institutional and other large-block shareholders are becoming more active in their efforts to influence a corporation's strategic decisions, unless they have a

Institutional owners are financial institutions, such as mutual funds and pension funds, that control large-block shareholder positions.

business relationship with the firm. Initially, these shareholder activists and institutional investors concentrated on the performance and accountability of CEOs and contributed to the dismissal of a number of them. More recently, activists target the actions of boards more directly via proxy vote proposals that are intended to give shareholders more decision rights because they believe board processes have been ineffective.[58] A rule approved by the SEC allowing large shareholders (owning 1 to 5 percent of a company's stock) to nominate up to 25 percent of a company's board of directors enhances shareholders' decision rights.[59]

The institutional investor BlackRock, Inc., is the largest manager of financial assets in the world, with just under $4 trillion invested and holdings in most of the largest global corporations. Interestingly, it was once described as a "silent giant" because it did not engage in activism. However, recently the silent giant has been awakened, as it has begun asking more questions of the firms in which it holds significant investments. Most of its actions are "behind the scenes," only voting against a director or a company proposal when its unobtrusive actions have failed to change the firm's behavior. BlackRock has become more "confrontational" in order to ensure the value of its investments, and some wish that it would become even more active because of the power of its large equity holdings.[60] BlackRock's CEO, Larry Fink, recently sent a letter to S&P 500 listed firms suggesting that they focus on the long-term: "It is critical … to understand that corporate leaders' duty of care and loyalty is not to every investor or trader who owns their companies' shares at any moment in time, but to the company and its long-term owners,"[61] To date, research suggests that institutional activism may not have a strong direct effect on firm performance, but it may indirectly influence a targeted firm's strategic decisions, including those concerned with international diversification and innovation. Thus, to some degree at least, institutional activism has the potential to discipline managers and to enhance the likelihood of a firm taking future actions that are in shareholders' best interests such as investing in human capital.[62]

Board of directors is a group of elected individuals whose primary responsibility is to act in the owners' best interests by formally monitoring and controlling the firm's top level managers.

10-3 Board of Directors

Shareholders elect the members of a firm's board of directors. The **board of directors** is a group of elected individuals whose primary responsibility is to act in the owners' best interests by formally monitoring and controlling the firm's top-level managers.[63] Those elected to a firm's board of directors are expected to oversee managers and to ensure that the corporation operates in ways that will best serve stakeholders' interests, and particularly the owners' interests. Helping board members reach their expected objectives are their powers to direct the affairs of the organization and reward and discipline top-level managers.

Though important to all shareholders, a firm's individual shareholders with small ownership percentages are very dependent on the board of directors to represent their interests. Unfortunately, evidence suggests that boards have not been highly effective

Larry Fink, CEO of BlackRock, the largest mutual fund provider, has suggested that managers need to focus on long-term strategy rather than responding to short-term trader proposals.

Bloomberg/Getty Images

in monitoring and controlling top-level managers' decisions and subsequent actions.[64] Because of their relatively ineffective performance and in light of the recent financial crisis, boards are experiencing increasing pressure from shareholders, lawmakers, and regulators to become more forceful in their oversight role to prevent top-level managers from acting in their own best interests. Moreover, in addition to their monitoring role, board members increasingly are expected to provide resources to the firms they serve. These resources include their personal knowledge and expertise and their relationships with a wide variety of organizations.[65]

Generally, board members (often called directors) are classified into one of three groups (see Table 10.1). *Insiders* are active top-level managers in the company who are elected to the board because they are a source of information about the firm's day-to-day operations.[66] *Related outsiders* have some relationship with the firm, contractual or otherwise, that may create questions about their independence, but these individuals are not involved with the corporation's day-to-day activities. *Outsiders* provide independent counsel to the firm and may hold top-level managerial positions in other companies or may have been elected to the board prior to the beginning of the current CEO's tenure.[67]

Historically, inside managers dominated a firm's board of directors. A widely accepted view is that a board with a significant percentage of its membership from the firm's top-level managers provides relatively weak monitoring and control of managerial decisions.[68] With weak board monitoring, managers sometimes use their power to select and compensate directors and exploit their personal ties with them. In response to the SEC's proposal to require audit committees to be composed of outside directors, in 1984 the New York Stock Exchange (NYSE) implemented a rule requiring outside directors to head the audit committee. Subsequently, other rules required that independent outsider directors lead important committees such as the audit, compensation, and nomination committees.[69] These other requirements were instituted after SOX was passed, and policies of the NYSE now require companies to maintain boards of directors that are composed of a majority of outside independent directors and to maintain full independent audit committees. Thus, additional scrutiny of corporate governance practices is resulting in a significant amount of attention being devoted to finding ways to recruit quality independent directors and to encourage boards to take actions that fully represent shareholders' best interests.[70]

Critics advocate reforms to ensure that independent outside directors are a significant majority of a board's total membership; research suggests this has been accomplished.[71] However, others argue that having outside directors is not enough to resolve the problems in that CEO power can strongly influence a board's decision. One proposal to reduce the power of the CEO is to separate the chair's role and the CEO's role on the board so

Table 10.1 Classification of Board of Directors' Members

Insiders
• The firm's CEO and other top-level managers
Related outsiders
• Individuals not involved with the firm's day-to-day operations, but who have a relationship with the company
Outsiders
• Individuals who are independent of the firm in terms of day-to-day operations and other relationships

that the same person does not hold both positions.[72] A situation in which an individual holds both the CEO and chair of the board title is called *CEO duality*. As is shown in the CEO duality at JPMorgan Chase with Jamie Dimon, it is often very difficult to separate the CEO and chair positions after they have been given to one person.[73] Unfortunately, having a board that actively monitors top-level managers' decisions and actions does not ensure high performance. The value that the directors bring to the company also influences the outcomes. For example, boards with members having significant relevant experience and knowledge are the most likely to help the firm formulate and implement effective strategies.[74]

Alternatively, having a large number of outside board members can also create some problems. For example, because outsiders typically do not have contact with the firm's day-to-day operations and do not have ready access to detailed information about managers and their skills, they lack the insights required to fully and effectively evaluate their decisions and initiatives.[75] Outsiders can, however, obtain valuable information through frequent interactions with inside board members and during board meetings to enhance their understanding of managers and their decisions.

Because they work with and lead the firm daily, insiders have access to information that facilitates forming and implementing appropriate strategies. Accordingly, some evidence suggests that boards with a critical mass of insiders typically are better informed about intended strategic initiatives, the reasons for the initiatives, and the outcomes expected from pursuing them.[76] Without this type of information, outsider-dominated boards may emphasize financial, as opposed to strategic, controls to gather performance information to evaluate managers' and business units' performances. A virtually exclusive reliance on financial evaluations shifts risk to top-level managers who, in turn, may make decisions to maximize their interests and reduce their employment risk. Reducing investments in R&D, further diversifying the firm, and pursuing higher levels of compensation are some of the results of managers' actions to reach the financial goals set by outsider-dominated boards.[77] Additionally, boards can make mistakes in strategic decisions because of poor decision processes, and in CEO succession decisions because of the lack of important information about candidates as well as the firm's specific needs. Overall, knowledgeable and balanced boards are likely to be the most effective over time.[78]

10-3a Enhancing the Effectiveness of the Board of Directors

Because of the importance of boards of directors in corporate governance and as a result of increased scrutiny from shareholders—in particular, large institutional investors—the performances of individual board members and of entire boards are being evaluated more formally and with greater intensity.[79] The demand for greater accountability and improved performance is stimulating many boards to voluntarily make changes. Among these changes are:

1. increases in the diversity of the backgrounds of board members (e.g., a greater number of directors from public service, academic, and scientific settings; a greater percentage of ethnic minorities and women; and members from different countries on boards of U.S. firms);
2. the strengthening of internal management and accounting control systems;
3. establishing and consistently using formal processes to evaluate board member's performance;
4. modifying the compensation of directors, especially reducing or eliminating stock options as a part of their package; and
5. creating the "lead director" role[80] that has strong powers with regard to the board agenda and oversight of non-management board member activities.

An increase in the board's involvement with a firm's strategic decision-making processes creates the need for effective collaboration between board members and top-level managers. Some argue that improving the processes used by boards to make decisions and monitor managers and firm outcomes is important for board effectiveness.[81] Moreover, because of the increased pressure from owners and the potential conflict among board members, procedures are necessary to help boards function effectively while seeking to discharge their responsibilities.

Increasingly, outside directors are being required to own significant equity stakes as a prerequisite to holding a board seat. In fact, some research suggests that firms perform better if outside directors have such a stake; the trend is toward higher pay for directors with more stock ownership, but with fewer stock options.[82] However, other research suggests that too much ownership can lead to lower independence for board members.[83] In addition, other research suggests that diverse boards help firms make more effective strategic decisions and perform better over time.[84] Although questions remain about whether more independent and diverse boards enhance board effectiveness, the trends for greater independence and increasing diversity among board members are likely to continue.

10-3b Executive Compensation

The compensation of top-level managers, and especially of CEOs, generates a great deal of interest and strongly held opinions. Some believe that top-management team members, and certainly CEOs, have a great deal of responsibility for a firm's performance and that they should be rewarded accordingly.[85] Others conclude that these individuals (and again, especially CEOs) are greatly overpaid and that their compensation is not as strongly related to firm performance as should be the case.[86] One of the three internal governance mechanisms attempts to deal with these issues. Specifically, **executive compensation** is a governance mechanism that seeks to align the interests of managers and owners through salaries, bonuses, and long-term incentives such as stock awards and options.[87]

Long-term incentive plans (typically involving stock options and stock awards) are an increasingly important part of compensation packages for top-level managers, especially those leading U.S. firms. Theoretically, using long-term incentives facilitates the firm's efforts (through the board of directors' pay-related decisions) to avoid potential agency problems by linking managerial compensation to the wealth of common shareholders.[88] Effectively designed long-term incentive plans have the potential to prevent large-block stockholders (e.g., institutional investors) from pressing for changes in the composition of the board of directors and the top-management team because they assume that, when exercised, the plans will ensure that top-level managers will act in shareholders' best interests. Additionally, shareholders typically assume that top-level managers' pay and the firm's performance are more properly aligned when outsiders are the dominant block of a board's membership. Research results suggesting that fraudulent behavior can be associated with stock option incentives, such as earnings manipulation,[89] demonstrate the importance of the firm's board of directors (as a governance mechanism) actively monitoring the use of executive compensation as a governance mechanism.

Effectively using executive compensation as a governance mechanism is particularly challenging for firms implementing international strategies. For example, the interests of the owners of multinational corporations may be best served by less uniformity in the firm's foreign subsidiaries' compensation plans.[90] Developing an array of unique compensation plans requires additional monitoring, potentially increasing the firm's agency costs. Importantly, pay levels vary by regions of the world. For example, managerial pay is highest in the U.S. and much lower in Asia. Historically, compensation for top-level managers has been lower in India partly because many of the largest firms have strong family ownership and control.[91] Also, acquiring firms and participating in joint ventures

Executive compensation is a governance mechanism that seeks to align the interests of managers and owners through salaries, bonuses, and long-term incentives such as stock awards and options.

in other countries increases the complexity associated with a board of directors' efforts to use executive compensation as an effective internal corporate governance mechanism.[92]

10-3c The Effectiveness of Executive Compensation

As an internal governance mechanism, executive compensation—especially long-term incentive compensation—is complicated, for several reasons. First, the strategic decisions top-level managers make are complex and nonroutine, meaning that direct supervision (even by the firm's board of directors) is likely to be ineffective as a means of judging the quality of their decisions. The result is a tendency to link top-level managers' compensation to outcomes the board can easily evaluate, such as the firm's financial performance. This leads to a second issue in that, typically, the effects of top-level managers' decisions are stronger on the firm's long-term performance than its short-term performance. This reality makes it difficult to assess the effects of their decisions on a regular basis (e.g., annually). Third, a number of other factors affect a firm's performance besides top-level managerial decisions and behavior. Unpredictable changes in segments (economic, demographic, political/legal, etc.) in the firm's general environment (see Chapter 2) make it difficult to separate the effects of top-level managers' decisions and the effects (both positive and negative) of changes in the firm's external environment on the firm's performance.

Properly designed and used incentive compensation plans for top-level managers may increase the value of a firm in line with shareholder expectations, but such plans are subject to managerial manipulation.[93] Additionally, annual bonuses may provide incentives to pursue short-run objectives at the expense of the firm's long-term interests. Although long-term, performance-based incentives may reduce the temptation to underinvest in the short run, they increase executive exposure to risks associated with uncontrollable events, such as market fluctuations and industry decline. The longer term the focus of incentive compensation, the greater are the long-term risks top-level managers bear. Also, because long-term incentives tie a manager's overall wealth to the firm in a way that is inflexible, such incentives and ownership may not be valued as highly by a manager as by outside investors who have the opportunity to diversify their wealth in a number of other financial investments.[94] Thus, firms may have to overcompensate for managers using long-term incentives.[95] The Strategic Focus provides an examination of some of the issues that confront boards of directors with regard to how much to pay the CEO. The media often focuses on the size of the CEO compensation package, especially if it is exceptionally large and compares it to the pay of the average worker.

Much of the size of CEO pay has been driven by stock options and long-term incentives. Even though some stock option-based compensation plans are well designed with option strike prices substantially higher than current stock prices, some have been developed for the primary purpose of giving executives more compensation. Research of stock option repricing, where the strike price value of the option has been lowered from its original position, suggests that action is taken more frequently in high-risk situations.[96] However, repricing also happens when firm performance is poor, to restore the incentive effect for the option. Evidence also suggests that politics are often involved, which has resulted in "option backdating."[97] While this evidence shows that no internal governance mechanism is perfect, some compensation plans accomplish their purpose. For example, recent research suggests that long-term pay designed to encourage managers to be environmentally friendly has been linked to higher success in preventing pollution.[98]

As the Strategic Focus suggests, this internal governance mechanism is likely to continue receiving a great deal of scrutiny in the years to come. When designed properly and used effectively, each of the three internal governance mechanisms can contribute positively to the firm operating in ways that best serve stakeholders and especially shareholders' interests.

Strategic Focus

Do CEOs Deserve the Large Compensation Packages They Receive?

This question often circulates in the media regarding the large compensation packages that CEOs receive as leaders of large publically traded firms. The negative aspect played up in the media often pertains to the growing inequality between the top executives' pay and the average wages of U.S. workers. In 1983, average pay for leaders of the six largest banks was 40 times the average of all U.S. workers, while the average pay for leaders of the largest Fortune 500 companies was less than 38 times. However, since then large bank CEO compensation has grown exponentially compared to the average worker and now stands at 208 times, while non-bank workers average 224 times. In other words, large industrial companies' top executive compensation has grown even more than the bank executive compensation. Although average worker pay has grown 2.9 times over the last 30 years, bank executives pay has grown 15.4 times, while non-bank executives pay has grown 17.4 times.

Large oversized compensation packages, such as that awarded for 2014 by Discovery Communications CEO, David Zaslav at $156.1 million, add to the media fervor relative to executive compensation. Discovery Communications has primarily focused on developing cable channels, such as Discovery, Animal Planet, and TLC. However, in 2014, while the CEO's pay increased, the adjusted value of Discovery's stock fell 25 percent. The media focused on this discrepancy. However, CEO compensation is more complex than might be explored in the media headlines. Although the stock value was down in 2014, the company's revenue rose 13 percent while its income increased 5.6 percent. Parts of Zaslav's contract were attached to increases in revenue and net income. His package was also facilitated because he has grown market capitalization from $5 billion to $20 billion under his leadership. Some of the awards in the current year were because of value creation in previous years and value associated with future restricted stock option grants. Notwithstanding the complexities, CEO compensation continues to rise although not as much as in the pre-financial crisis period.

Interestingly, among the large diversified financial banks, such as JPMorgan Chase, Citigroup, Morgan Stanley, Goldman Sachs, and Wells Fargo, the CEOs average pay was around $18 million. In 2014, the average pay was 121 times that of the average worker at these large diversified banks, down 55 percent from 273 times in 2006 near the end of the pre-financial crisis period. This is obviously due to closer regulation of these large banks because of legislation such as the Dodd-Frank Act. Furthermore the Securities and Exchange Commission

is working to finalize rules requiring all public companies to report how much the CEO makes more than the firm's typical employee. This will give fodder to media outlets to dampen the oversized pay packages that CEOs have increasingly received over the last 30 years. In part, research from the field of sociology shows that these large pay packages have not always been due to performance increases, but due to the tight networks of managers who sit on executive compensation committees and boards of directors and do comparisons between firms. These inter-board networks have been associated with increases in compensation to help firms keep up with the trends at other firms. Also, because of large mergers and acquisitions such as those that have taken place among the large diversified banks, firms are much larger and executive compensation is associated with size and complexity of the operations top-level executives manage.

Frederick M. Brown/Getty Images

President and CEO of Discovery Communications, David Zaslav, presenting at a conference in this photo, has had his 2014 pay package scrutized heavily by the media.

Research from the finance discipline (versus sociology) finds that the mix of the pay package that most top executives receive has been changing. Instead of an over emphasis on stock options, top executives have been receiving compensation that is based on restricted stock ownership, which cannot be realized unless they meet significant performance targets over time. As such, there is less oversized risk taking that can result in disastrous consequences for these large firms. Accordingly, research finds that managers are taking more measured risks due to the compensation packages that they are receiving.

In summary, executive compensation is a complex issue that cannot be simply determined by the overall size of the package. Although executive compensation has grown dramatically, there are both legitimate and illegitimate reasons for such huge pay packages. Each case needs to be examined closely for possible problems of excess versus appropriateness. However, there is likely to be social problems due to the perception that top management executive compensation relative to the average worker has added to the inequality in our society. As such, care should be taken to manage this issue from a policy point-of-view. Managerial human capital should be rewarded for its capability and the value it creates, but lower levels workers and their human capital should also have opportunities to make progress.

Sources: D. Fitzgerald, 2015, Staples CEO Sargent's pay grew 15% to $12.4 million last year; Chief executive earned $2.6 million in non-equity incentive compensation in 2014, *Wall Street Journal*, www.wsj.com, April 13; K. Hagey, 2015, Discovery Communications CEO gets 2014 compensation of $1.561 million, *Wall Street Journal*, www.wsj.com, April 6; J. W. Kim, B. Kogut, & J.-S. Yang, 2015, Executive compensation, fat cats and best athletes, *American Sociological Review*, 80: 299–328; E. K. Lim, 2015, The role of reference point in CEO restricted stock and its impact on R&D intensity in high-technology firms, *Strategic Management Journal*, 36: 872–889; P. Rudegear, 2015, Wall Street's pay gap slims, *Wall Street Journal*, April 6, A1, A4; E. M. Fich, L. T. Starks, & A. S. Yore, 2014, CEO deal-making activities and compensation, *Journal of Financial Economics*, 114: 471–492; S. Williams, 2014, BG Group draws more heat over CEO compensations; one of the biggest revolts against executive pay in the U.K. in recent years, *Wall Street Journal*, www.wsj.com, November 28; R. Wilmers, 2014, Why excessive CEO pay is bad for the economy, *American Banker*, www.americanbanker.com, March 14.

By the same token, because none of the three mechanisms are perfect in design or execution, the market for corporate control, an external governance mechanism, is sometimes needed.

10-4 Market for Corporate Control

The **market for corporate control** is an external governance mechanism that is active when a firm's internal governance mechanisms fail.[99] The market for corporate control is composed of individuals and firms that buy ownership positions in or purchase all of potentially undervalued corporations typically for the purpose of forming new divisions in established companies or merging two previously separate firms. Because the top-level managers are assumed to be responsible for the undervalued firm's poor performance, they are usually replaced. An effective market for corporate control ensures that ineffective and/or opportunistic top-level managers are disciplined.[100]

Commonly, target firm managers and board members are sensitive about takeover bids emanating from the market for corporate control since being a target suggests that they have been ineffective in fulfilling their responsibilities. For top-level managers, a board's decision to accept an acquiring firm's offer typically finds them losing their jobs because the acquirer usually wants different people to lead the firm. At the same time, rejection of an offer also increases the risk of job loss for top-level managers because the pressure from the board and shareholders for them to improve the firm's performance becomes substantial.[101]

A hedge fund is an investment fund that can pursue many different investment strategies, such as taking long and short positions, using arbitrage, and buying and selling undervalued securities for the purpose of maximizing investors' returns. Growing rapidly, in 2014 hedge fund assets topped $3 trillion and are expected to exceed $5 trillion by 2018. It is expected that up to 65 percent of their funding comes from institutional investors.[102] Given investors' increasing desire to hold underperforming funds and their managers accountable, hedge funds have become increasingly active in the market for corporate control.[103] For example, "Some of the most complex deals in the current market, including Baker Hughes and Halliburton, Allergan and Actavis, Staples and Office Depot, and Time Warner Cable and Comcast, count prominent hedge funds as major stockholders" who are working to close these deals suggesting positive prospects for the combined firms.[104]

The **market for corporate control** is an external governance mechanism that is active when a firm's internal governance mechanisms fail.

In general, activist pension funds (as institutional investors and as an internal governance mechanism) are reactive in nature, taking actions when they conclude that a firm is underperforming. In contrast, activist hedge funds (as part of the market for corporate control) are proactive, "identifying a firm whose performance could be improved and then investing in it."[105] An example is found in the Opening Case with Trian Fund Management, L.P., headed by CEO Nelson Peltz, seeking to change the strategy at DuPont by replacing four board members favorable to Peltz's activist hedge fund. However, the activist fund, Trian, lost the shareholder vote to replace the directors, and DuPont was not forced to breakup into several separate businesses.[106] Interestingly, given the need to search for new opportunities, hedge funds have been pursuing more technology firm deals. In fact, in 2014, 20 percent of such investments were in the technology sector, the highest percentage for any sector. Hedge funds have traditionally avoided technology firms because they change rapidly, and, as such, their future success is difficult to forecast. Overall, activists have been winning more board seats, forcing mergers and divestitures, and winning stock buyback programs, such as the stock buyback program at Apple fostered by Carl Icahn.[107]

However, another possibility is suggested by research results—namely, that as a governance mechanism, investors sometimes use the market for corporate control to take an ownership position in firms that are performing well.[108] A study of active corporate raiders in the 1980s showed that takeover attempts often were focused on above-average performance firms in an industry.[109] This work and other recent research suggest that the market for corporate control is an imperfect governance mechanism.[110] Actually, mergers and acquisitions are highly complex strategic actions with many purposes and potential outcomes. As discussed in Chapter 7, some are successful and many are not—even when they have potential to do well—because implementation challenges when integrating two diverse firms can limit their ability to realize their potential.[111]

In summary, the market for corporate control is a blunt instrument for corporate governance; nonetheless, this governance mechanism does have the potential to represent shareholders' best interests. Accordingly, top-level managers want to lead their firms in ways that make disciplining by activists outside the company unnecessary and/or inappropriate.

There are a number of defense tactics top-level managers can use to fend off a takeover attempt. Managers leading a target firm that is performing well are almost certain to try to thwart the takeover attempt. Even in instances when the target firm is underperforming its peers, managers might use defense tactics to protect their own interests. In general, managers' use of defense tactics is considered to be self-serving in nature.

10-4a Managerial Defense Tactics

In the majority of cases, hostile takeovers are the principal means by which the market for corporate control is activated. A *hostile takeover* is an acquisition of a target company by an acquiring firm that is accomplished "not by coming to an agreement with the target company's management but by going directly to the company's shareholders or fighting to replace management in order to get the acquisition approved."[112]

Firms targeted for a hostile takeover may use multiple defense tactics to fend off the takeover attempt. Increased use of the market for corporate control has enhanced the sophistication and variety of managerial defense tactics that are used in takeovers.

Because the market for corporate control tends to increase risk for managers, managerial pay may be augmented indirectly through golden parachutes (where a CEO can receive up to three years' salary if his or her firm is taken over). Golden parachutes, similar to most other defense tactics, are controversial. Another takeover defense strategy is traditionally known as a "poison pill." This strategy usually allows shareholders (other than the acquirer) to convert "shareholders' rights" into a large number of common shares if an individual or company acquires more than a set amount of the target firm's stock (typically 10 to 20 percent). Increasing the total number of outstanding shares dilutes the potential acquirer's existing stake. This means that, to maintain or expand its ownership position, the potential acquirer must buy additional shares at premium prices. The additional purchases increase the potential acquirer's costs. Some firms amend the corporate charter so board member elections are staggered, resulting in only one third of members being up for reelection each year. Research shows that this results in managerial entrenchment and reduced vulnerability to hostile takeovers.[113] Additional takeover defense strategies are presented in Table 10.2.

Most institutional investors oppose the use of defense tactics. TIAA-CREF and CalPERS have taken actions to have several firms' poison pills eliminated. Many institutional investors also oppose severance packages (golden parachutes), and the opposition is increasing significantly in Europe as well.[114] However, an advantage to severance packages is that they may encourage top-level managers to accept takeover bids with the potential to best serve shareholders' interest.[115] Alternatively, research results show that

Table 10.2 Hostile Takeover Defense Strategies

Defense strategy	Success as a strategy	Effects on shareholder wealth
Capital structure change: Dilution of the target firm's stock, making it more costly for an acquiring firm to continue purchasing the target's shares. Employee stock option plans (ESOPs), recapitalization, issuance of additional debt, and share buybacks are actions associated with this strategy.	Medium	Inconclusive
Corporate charter amendment: An amendment to the target firm's charter for the purpose of staggering the elections of members to its board of directors so that all are not elected during the same year. This change to the firm's charter prevents a potential acquirer from installing a completely new board in a single year.	Very low	Negative
Golden parachute: A lump-sum payment of cash that is given to one or more top-level managers when the firm is acquired in a takeover bid.	Low	Negligible
Greenmail: The repurchase of the target firm's shares of stock that were obtained by the acquiring firm at a premium in exchange for an agreement that the acquirer will no longer target the company for takeover.	Medium	Negative
Litigation Lawsuits that help the target firm stall hostile takeover attempts: Antitrust charges and inadequate disclosure are examples of the grounds on which the target firm could file.	Low	Positive
Poison pill: An action the target firm takes to make its stock less attractive to a potential acquirer.	High	Positive
Standstill agreement: A contract between the target firm and the potential acquirer specifying that the acquirer will not purchase additional shares of the target firm for a specified period of time in exchange for a fee paid by the target firm.	Low	Negative

Sources: L. Guo, P. Lach, & S. Mobbs, 2015, Tradeoffs between internal and external governance: Evidence from exogenous regulatory shocks. *Financial Management*, 44: 81–114; H. Sapra, A. Subramanian, & K. V. Subramanian, 2014, Corporate governance and innovation: Theory and evidence, *Journal of Financial & Quantitative Analysis*, 49: 957–1003; M. Straska & G. Waller, 2014, Antitakeover provisions and shareholder wealth: A survey of the literature, *Journal of Financial & Quantitative Analysis*, 49: 1–32; R. Campbell, C. Ghosh, M. Petrova, & C. F. Sirmans, 2011, Corporate governance and performance in the market for corporate control: The case of REITS, *Journal of Real Estate Finance & Economics*, 42: 451–480; M. Ryngaert & R. Schlten, 2010, Have changing takeover defense rules and strategies entrenched management and damaged shareholders? The case of defeated takeover bids, *Journal of Corporate Finance*, 16: 16–37; N. Ruiz-Mallorqui & D. J. Santana-Martin, 2009, Ultimate institutional owner and takeover defenses in the controlling versus minority shareholders context, *Corporate Governance: An International Review*, 17: 238–254; J. A. Pearce II & R. B. Robinson, Jr., 2004, Hostile takeover defenses that maximize shareholder wealth, *Business Horizons*, 47(5): 15–24.

using takeover defenses reduces the amount of pressure managers feel to seek short-term performance gains, resulting in them concentrating on developing strategies with a longer time horizon and a high probability of serving stakeholders' interests. Such firms are more likely to invest in and develop innovation; when they do so, the firm's market value increases, thereby rewarding shareholders.[116]

An awareness on the part of top-level managers about the existence of external investors in the form of individuals (e.g., Carl Icahn) and groups (e.g., hedge funds) often positively influences them to align their interests with those of the firm's stakeholders, especially the shareholders. Moreover, when active as an external governance mechanism, the market for corporate control has brought about significant changes in many firms' strategies and, when used appropriately, has served shareholders' interests. Of course, the goal is to have the managers develop the psychological ownership of principals.[117] However, such sense of ownership can be taken too far such that narcissistic (i.e., egotistical) top executives can feel that they are personally central to the identity of the firm.[118]

10-5 International Corporate Governance

Corporate governance is an increasingly important issue in economies around the world, including emerging economies. Globalization in trade, investments, and equity markets increases the potential value of firms throughout the world using similar mechanisms to govern corporate activities. Moreover, because of globalization, major companies want to attract foreign investment. For this to happen, foreign investors must be confident that adequate corporate governance mechanisms are in place to protect their investments.

Although globalization is stimulating an increase in the intensity of efforts to improve corporate governance and potentially to reduce the variation in regions and nations' governance systems,[119] the reality remains that different nations do have different governance systems in place. Recognizing and understanding differences in various countries' governance systems, as well as changes taking place within those systems, improves the likelihood a firm will be able to compete successfully in the international markets it chooses to enter. Next, to highlight the general issues of differences and changes taking place in governance systems, we discuss corporate governance practices in two developed economies (Germany and Japan) and in the emerging economy of China.

10-5a Corporate Governance in Germany and Japan

In many private German firms, the owner and manager may be the same individual. In these instances, agency problems are not present.[120] Even in publicly traded German corporations, a single shareholder is often dominant. Thus, the concentration of ownership is an important means of corporate governance in Germany, as it is in the United States.[121]

Historically, banks occupied the center of the German corporate governance system. This is the case in other European countries as well, such as Italy and France. As lenders, banks become major shareholders when companies they financed seek funding on the stock market or default on loans. Although the stakes are usually less than 10 percent, banks can hold a single ownership position up to, but not exceeding 15 percent of the bank's capital. Although shareholders can tell banks how to vote their ownership position, they generally do not do so. The banks monitor and control managers, both as lenders and as shareholders, by electing representatives to supervisory boards.

German firms with more than 2,000 employees are required to have a two-tiered board structure that places the responsibility for monitoring and controlling managerial (or supervisory) decisions and actions in the hands of a separate group.[122] All the functions of strategy and management are the responsibility of the management board (the Vorstand); however, appointment to the Vorstand is the responsibility of the supervisory tier (the Aufsichtsrat). Employees, union members, and shareholders appoint members to the Aufsichtsrat. Proponents of the German structure suggest that it helps prevent corporate wrongdoing and rash decisions by "dictatorial CEOs." However, critics maintain that it slows decision making and often ties a CEO's hands. The corporate governance practices in Germany make it difficult to restructure companies as quickly as can be done in the United States. Because of the role of local government (through the board structure) and the power of banks in Germany's corporate governance structure, private shareholders rarely have major ownership positions in German firms. Additionally, there is a significant amount of cross-shareholdings among firms.[123] However, large institutional investors, such as pension funds (outside of banks and insurance companies), are also relatively insignificant owners of corporate stock. Thus, at least historically, German executives generally have not been dedicated to maximizing shareholder wealth to the degree that is the case for top-level managers in the United States and United Kingdom.[124]

However, corporate governance practices used in Germany have been changing in recent years. A manifestation of these changes is that a number of German firms are gravitating toward U.S. governance mechanisms. Recent research suggests that the traditional system in Germany produced some agency costs because of a lack of external ownership power. Interestingly, German firms with listings on U.S. stock exchanges have increasingly adopted executive stock option compensation as a long-term incentive pay policy.[125] Also, as the Strategic Focus illustrates, activist shareholders are entering Germany and Japan, although the strategy is more engagement with managers rather that confrontation as can be found in the United States and the United Kingdom.

The concepts of obligation, family, and consensus affect attitudes toward corporate governance in Japan. As part of a company family, individuals are members of a unit that envelops their lives; families command the attention and allegiance of parties throughout corporations. In addition, Japanese firms are concerned with a broader set of stakeholders than are firms in the United States, including employees, suppliers, and customers.[126] Moreover, a *keiretsu* (a group of firms tied together by cross-shareholdings) is more than an economic concept—it, too, is a family. Some believe, though, that extensive cross-shareholdings impede the type of structural change that is needed to improve the nation's corporate governance practices. However, recent changes in the governance code in Japan has been fostering better opportunities from improved corporate governance.[127] Consensus, another important influence in Japanese corporate governance, calls for the expenditure of significant amounts of energy to win the hearts and minds of people whenever possible, as opposed to top-level managers issuing edicts.[128] Consensus is highly valued, even when it results in a slow and cumbersome decision-making process.

As in Germany, banks in Japan have an important role in financing and monitoring large public firms.[129] Because the main bank in the keiretsu owns the largest share of stocks and holds the largest amount of debt, it has the closest relationship with a firm's top-level managers. The main bank provides financial advice to the firm and also closely monitors managers. Thus, although it is changing, Japan has traditionally had a bank-based financial and corporate governance structure, whereas the United States has a market-based financial and governance structure.[130] Commercial banks in the United States by regulation are not allowed to own shares of publicly traded firms.

Aside from lending money, a Japanese bank can hold up to 5 percent of a firm's total stock; a group of related financial institutions can hold up to 40 percent. In many cases, main-bank relationships are part of a horizontal keiretsu. A keiretsu firm usually owns less than 2 percent of any other member firm; however, each company typically has a stake of that size in every firm in the keiretsu. As a result, 30 to 90 percent of a firm is owned by other members of the keiretsu. Thus, a keiretsu is a system of relationship investments.

Strategic Focus

"Engagement" versus "Activist" Shareholders in Japan, Germany, and China

Activist shareholders and a strong market for corporate control have traditionally been absent in Japan. More recently, shareholders have been more active and the most successful ones have been labeled "engagement" funds. The change is signaled, for example, by the Japanese Government Pension Investment Fund choosing an activist investor, the Taiyo Pacific Partners LP, an U.S. based engagement fund, to manage some of its $1 trillion in assets. The CEO of Taiyo Pacific, Brian Heywood, suggested that "Japanese executives have become more open to outside perspectives as they have developed offshore operations and received more training abroad." Furthermore, the Japanese Financial Services Agency has introduced a "stewardship code" that calls on investors to "press for greater returns." As such, the Japanese environment is becoming more oriented towards "shareholder rights," although the approach is definitely engagement versus activist.

Besides a new brand of activism in Japan, activism is spreading around the globe including Germany. Cevian Capital, an activist fund, is involved in ownership with ThyssenKrupp and Bilfinder. Likewise, Elliott Management, another activist fund, is involved with Celesio and Kabel Deutschland. Although management teams are quite suspicious of activists in Germany and other continental European countries, "Germany is an area where activists may look because of its protections for minority investors in takeover deals."

Although some activism has taken place in mainland China, firms in Hong Kong has been targeted more by activist funds. Hong Kong listed companies have been loosening rules for foreign ownership and thereby companies have been paying more attention to what investors think in regard to governance and transparency. In mainland China, however, often shares are mostly owned by parent business group firms as well as the government or, because they are often younger, they are still owned by the firm's founders. As such, there is less potential influence for investors on company decisions. However the Shanghai-Hong Kong Stock Connect program has accelerated opportunities for activists on the mainland. Through the Connect program, foreign financial institutions can have direct access to mainland China's capital markets. This means that the foreign ownership will have more activist influence because of shareholder voting rights in local mainland China listed firms.

But how do owners from emerging market country and countries with significant government ownership influence the firms they invest in overseas? Interestingly, sovereign wealth funds, many from emerging economies, are playing a dominant role by investing in developed economies as well as other emerging economies. In their own way, they are playing an activist role. For example, since the global financial crisis, many German firms have sought investment from sovereign wealth firms from Gulf States in the Mideast. In particular, many German major automobile firms have recruited Gulf Cooperation Council (GCC) sovereign wealth fund investment during the stresses of financial restructuring spurred by the financial crisis. These sovereign wealth funds are long term investors and reduce the possibility of a hostile takeover which has become a more prominent feature in the German corporate governance landscape.

Sovereign wealth funds are also taking active roles in climate change. For instance, the Norwegian sovereign wealth fund is divesting its assets in coal. Their strategy is to focus their wealth to have an influence on salient sustainability issues, such as climate change.

Courtesy of The Hedgefund Journal.com

(L-R) Lars Förberg, Christer Gardell

Cevian Capital Founders Lars Forberg and Christer Gardell are engaged actively in fostering more shareholder value creation through their fund.

Another example is the acquisition activity of Brazilian multinationals, which have been supported by its sovereign wealth fund, the Brazilian Development Bank (BNDES). BNDES has been "involved in several large-scale operations and helped orchestrate mergers and acquisitions to build large 'national champions' in several industries." For example, "BNDES helped rescue Brazilian meatpacker JBS-Friboi, which aggressively expanded internationally by acquiring large U.S. producers, Swift and Pilgrim's Pride, among others. In summary, shareholder activism has been spreading globally throughout the world, and there are owners in emerging economies participating in the market for corporate control and in restructuring investments, especially sovereign wealth funds that also have influence in developed as well as developing countries by their large ownership positions. These funds often focus to support government strategies, such as in China's energy sector, where the Chinese government is seeking to acquire more energy assets and natural resources to support its economy. Sometimes these sovereign funds also support government positions such as the example provided from Norway fund divesting coal assets in order to increasing its emphasis on sustainability, an important social and political movement.

Sources: B. Alhashel, 2015, Sovereign wealth funds: A literature review, *Journal of Economics & Business*, 78: 1–13; L. Havelock, 2015, New battlegrounds: A global activism update, IR Magazine, www.irmagazine.com, March 10; K. M. Howl, 2015, Norway oil fund sheds more coal assets, *Wall Street Journal*, www.wsj.com, May 5; K. Narioka, 2015, Activist investors in Japan find some doors cracking open, *Wall Street Journal*, www.wsj.com, January 29; M. Goranova & L. V. Ryan, 2014, Shareholder activism: A multidisciplinary review, *Journal of Management*, 40: 1230–1268; D. Haberly, 2014, White knights from the Gulf: Sovereign wealth fund investment and the evolution of German industrial finance, *Economic Geography*, 90: 293–320; S. G. Lazzarini, A. Musacchio, R. Bandeira-de-Mello, & R. Marcon, R. 2015, What do state-owned development banks do? Evidence from BNDES, 2002–09 *World Development*, 66: 237–253; A. Musacchio & S. G. Lazzarini, 2014, *Reinventing State Capitalism: Leviathan in Business, Brazil and Beyond*, Cambridge: Harvard University Press; X. Sun, J. Li, Y. Wang, & W. Clark, 2014, China's sovereign wealth fund investments in overseas energy: the energy security perspective, *Energy Policy*, 65: 654–661.

Japan's corporate governance practices have been changing in recent years. For example, because of Japanese banks' continuing development as economic organizations, their role in the monitoring and control of managerial behavior and firm outcomes is less significant than in the past.[131] Also, deregulation in the financial sector has reduced the cost of mounting hostile takeovers.[132] As such, deregulation facilitated additional activity in Japan's market for corporate control, which was nonexistent in past years. And there are pressures for more changes because of weak performance by many Japanese companies. In fact, there has been significant criticism of the corporate governance practices of the Tokyo Electric Power Company after the severe problems at the Fukushima Daiichi nuclear power plant following the earthquake and tsunami in 2011. Most Japanese firms have boards that are largely composed of internal management, so they reflect the upper echelon of management. However, independent, nonexecutive board members are increasingly important in Japanese firms because they have adopted a new corporate governance code.[133] As the Strategic Focus illustrates, engagement funds are helping to change the landscape as well, given they have become more active in Japan.

10-5b Corporate Governance in China

China has a unique and large, socialist mixed with a market-oriented, economy. Over time, the government has done much to improve the corporate governance of listed companies.[134] These comments suggest that corporate governance practices in China have been changing with increasing privatization of businesses and the development of equity markets. However, the stock markets in China remain young and are continuing to develop. In their early years, these markets were weak because of significant insider trading, but with stronger governance these markets have improved.[135]

There has been a gradual decline in China in the equity held in state-owned enterprises and the number and percentage of private firms have grown, but the state still relies on direct and/or indirect controls to influence the strategies firms use. Even private firms try to develop political ties with the government because of their role in providing access to resources and to the economy.[136] In terms of long-term success, these conditions may affect firms' performance because research shows that firms with higher state ownership tend to have lower market value and more volatility in that value across time. This is because of agency conflicts in the firms and because the executives do not seek to maximize shareholder returns, given that they must also seek to satisfy social goals placed on them by the government.[137] This suggests a potential conflict between the principals, particularly the state owner and the private equity owners of the state-owned enterprises.[138]

Some evidence suggests that corporate governance in China may be tilting toward the Western model. For example, recent research shows that with increasing frequency, the compensation of top-level executives in Chinese companies is closely related to prior and current financial performance of their firm.[139] Research also shows that, due to the weaker institutions, firms with family CEOs experience more positive financial performance than others without the family influence.[140]

Changing a nation's governance systems is a complicated task that will encounter problems as well as successes while seeking progress. Thus, corporate governance in Chinese companies continues to evolve and likely will continue to evolve for some time to come as parties (e.g., the Chinese government and those seeking further movement toward free-market economies) interact to form governance mechanisms that are best for their nation, business firms, and citizens. However, along with changes in the governance systems of specific countries, multinational companies' boards and managers are also evolving. For example, firms that have entered more international markets are likely to have more top executives with greater international experience and to have a larger proportion of foreign owners and foreign directors on their boards.[141]

10-6 Governance Mechanisms and Ethical Behavior

The three internal and one external governance mechanisms are designed to ensure that the agents of the firm's owners—the corporation's top-level managers—make strategic decisions that best serve the interests of all stakeholders. In the United States, shareholders are commonly recognized as the company's most significant stakeholders. Increasingly though, top-level managers are expected to lead their firms in ways that will also serve the needs of product market stakeholders (e.g., customers, suppliers, and host communities) and organizational stakeholders (e.g., managerial and non-managerial employees).[142] Therefore, the firm's actions and the outcomes flowing from them should result in, at least, minimal satisfaction of the interests of all stakeholders. Without at least minimal satisfaction of its interests, a dissatisfied stakeholder will withdraw its support from the firm and provide it to another (e.g., customers will purchase products from a supplier offering an acceptable substitute).

Some believe that the internal corporate governance mechanisms designed and used by ethically responsible leaders and companies increase the likelihood the firm will be able to, at least, minimally satisfy all stakeholders' interests.[143] Scandals at companies such as Enron, WorldCom, HealthSouth, and Satyam (a large information technology company based in India), among others, illustrate the negative effects of poor ethical behavior on a firm's efforts to satisfy stakeholders. The issue of ethical behavior by top-level managers as a foundation for best serving stakeholders' interests is being taken seriously in countries throughout the world.[144]

The decisions and actions of the board of directors can be an effective deterrent to unethical behaviors by top-level managers. Indeed, evidence suggests that the most effective boards set boundaries for their firms' business ethics and values.[145] After the boundaries for ethical behavior are determined, and likely formalized in a code of ethics, the board's ethics-based expectations must be clearly communicated to the firm's top-level managers and to other stakeholders (e.g., customers and suppliers) with whom interactions are necessary for the firm to produce and sell its products. Moreover, as agents of the firm's owners, top-level managers must understand that the board, acting as an internal governance mechanism, will hold them fully accountable for developing and supporting an organizational culture in which only ethical behaviors are permitted. As explained in Chapter 12, CEOs can be positive role models for improved ethical behavior.[146]

A major issue confronted by multinational companies operating in international markets is that of bribery.[147] As a whole, countries with weak institutions that have greater bribery activity tend to have fewer exports as a result. In addition, small- and medium-sized firms are the most harmed by bribery. Thus, bribery tends to limit entrepreneurial activity that can help a country's economy grow. While larger multinational firms tend to experience fewer negative outcomes, their power to exercise more ethical leadership allows them greater flexibility in selecting which markets they will enter and how they will do so.[148]

Through effective governance that results from well-designed governance mechanisms and the appropriate country institutions, top-level managers, working with others, are able to select and use strategies that result in strategic competitiveness and earning above-average returns. While some firms' governance mechanisms are ineffective, other companies are recognized for the quality of their governance activities.

World Finance evaluates the corporate governance practices of companies throughout the world. For 2015, a sampling of this group's "Best Corporate Governance Awards" by country were given to Magna International (Canada), China Communications Services Corporation (China), BASF (Germany), Prosafe (Norway), British Telecom (United Kingdom), and Intel (United States). These awards are determined by analyzing a number of issues concerned with corporate governance, such as board accountability and financial disclosure, executive compensation, shareholder rights, ownership base, takeover provisions, corporate behavior, and overall responsibility exhibited by the company.[149]

SUMMARY

- Corporate governance is a relationship among stakeholders that is used to determine a firm's direction and control its performance. How firms monitor and control top-level managers' decisions and actions affects the implementation of strategies. Effective governance that aligns managers' decisions with shareholders' interests can help produce a competitive advantage for the firm.

- Three internal governance mechanisms are used in the modern corporation:

    - ownership concentration

    - the board of directors

    - executive compensation

    The market for corporate control is an external governance mechanism influencing managers' decisions and the outcomes resulting from them.

- Ownership is separated from control in the modern corporation. Owners (principals) hire managers (agents) to make decisions that maximize the firm's value. As risk-bearing specialists, owners diversify their risk by investing in multiple corporations with different risk profiles. Owners expect their agents (the firm's top-level managers, who are decision-making specialists) to

make decisions that will help to maximize the value of their firm. Thus, modern corporations are characterized by an agency relationship that is created when one party (the firm's owners) hires and pays another party (top-level managers) to use its decision-making skills.

- Separation of ownership and control creates an agency problem when an agent pursues goals that conflict with the principals' goals. Principals establish and use governance mechanisms to control this problem.

- Ownership concentration is based on the number of large-block shareholders and the percentage of shares they own. With significant ownership percentages, such as those held by large mutual funds and pension funds, institutional investors often are able to influence top-level managers' strategic decisions and actions. Thus, unlike diffuse ownership which tends to result in relatively weak monitoring and control of managerial decisions, concentrated ownership produces more active and effective monitoring. Institutional investors are a powerful force in corporate America and actively use their positions of concentrated ownership to force managers and boards of directors to make decisions that best serve shareholders' interests.

■ In the United States and the United Kingdom, a firm's board of directors, composed of insiders, related outsiders, and outsiders, is a governance mechanism expected to represent shareholders' interests. The percentage of outside directors on many boards now exceeds the percentage of inside directors. Through implementation of the SOX Act, outsiders are expected to be more independent of a firm's top-level managers compared with directors selected from inside the firm. Relatively recent rules formulated and implemented by the SEC to allow owners with large stakes to propose new directors are beginning to change the balance even more in favor of outside and independent directors. Additional governance-related regulations have resulted from the Dodd-Frank Act.

■ Executive compensation is a highly visible and often criticized governance mechanism. Salary, bonuses, and long-term incentives are used for the purpose of aligning managers' and shareholders' interests. A firm's board of directors is responsible for determining the effectiveness of the firm's executive compensation system. An effective system results in managerial decisions that are in shareholders' best interests.

■ In general, evidence suggests that shareholders and boards of directors have become more vigilant in controlling managerial decisions. Nonetheless, these mechanisms are imperfect and sometimes insufficient. When the internal mechanisms fail, the market for corporate control—as an external governance mechanism—becomes relevant. Although it, too, is imperfect, the market for corporate control has been effective resulting in corporations reducing inefficient diversification and implementing more effective strategic decisions.

■ Corporate governance structures used in Germany, Japan, and China differ from each other and from the structure used in the United States. Historically, the U.S. governance structure focused on maximizing shareholder value. In Germany, employees, as a stakeholder group, take a more prominent role in governance. By contrast, until recently, Japanese shareholders played virtually no role in monitoring and controlling top-level managers. However, Japanese firms are now being challenged by "activist" shareholders. In China, the central government still plays a major role in corporate governance practices. Internationally, all these systems are becoming increasingly similar, as are many governance systems both in developed countries, such as France and Spain, and in transitional economies, such as Brazil and India.

■ Effective governance mechanisms ensure that the interests of all stakeholders are served. Thus, strategic competitiveness results when firms are governed in ways that permit, at least, minimal satisfaction of capital market stakeholders (e.g., shareholders), product market stakeholders (e.g., customers and suppliers), and organizational stakeholders (e.g., managerial and non-managerial employees; see Chapter 2). Moreover, effective governance produces ethical behavior in the formulation and implementation of strategies.

KEY TERMS

agency costs 316
agency relationship 313
board of directors 319
corporate governance 310
executive compensation 322

institutional owners 318
large-block shareholders 317
managerial opportunism 314
market for corporate control 325
ownership concentration 317

REVIEW QUESTIONS

1. What is corporate governance? What factors account for the considerable amount of attention corporate governance receives from several parties, including shareholder activists, business press writers, and academic scholars? Why is governance necessary to control managers' decisions?

2. What is meant by the statement that ownership is separated from managerial control in the corporation? Why does this separation exist?

3. What is an agency relationship? What is managerial opportunism? What assumptions do owners of corporations make about managers as agents?

4. How is each of the three internal governance mechanisms—ownership concentration, boards of directors, and executive compensation—used to align the interests of managerial agents with those of the firm's owners?

5. What trends exist regarding executive compensation? What is the effect of the increased use of long-term incentives on top-level managers' strategic decisions?

6. What is the market for corporate control? What conditions generally cause this external governance mechanism to become active? How does this mechanism constrain top-level managers' decisions and actions?

7. What is the nature of corporate governance in Germany, Japan, and China?

8. How can corporate governance foster ethical decisions and behaviors on the part of managers as agents?

Mini-Case

The Imperial CEO, JPMorgan Chase's Jamie Dimon

Jamie Dimon, CEO of JPMorgan Chase & Co., is one of the very few top executives at large banks or major financial services firms who was unscathed by the substantial economic recession which began in 2008—a recession largely caused by those firms taking inappropriate risks. He is described as charismatic and an excellent leader. Yet, in 2012, JPMorgan Chase experienced its own scandal caused by exceptional risk taking. Traders in its London operations were allowed to build a huge exposure in credit derivatives that breached the acceptable risk limits of most analytical models. As a result, the bank suffered losses of more than $6 billion. It is referred to as the London Whale trading debacle. In 2013 and 2014, there were large regulatory and legal settlements. Most significant was a $13 billion settlement with regulators over mortgage bond sales in 2013. In addition, to this record settlement, "the bank paid $2.6 billion to resolve allegations that it didn't stop Bernie Madoff's Ponzi scheme and two fines of about $1 billion each stemming from currency rate manipulation and the London Whale trading loss." It may need an additional $20 billion in additional capital to satisfy regulatory bank safety rules. One Democratic Senator from Delaware, Ted Kaufman, noted: "I think Jamie Dimon is Teflon-coated."

Because of the huge loss and concerns about the lack of oversight that led to these fines and settlement, there was a move by shareholder activists to separate the CEO and chair of the board positions, requiring Dimon to hold only the CEO title. Playing key roles were the American Federation of State, County and Municipal Employees (AFSCME) and the Institutional Shareholder Services (ISS). The AFSCME was pushing to separate the holders of the CEO and chair positions at JPMorgan Chase. The ISS was pushing for shareholders to withhold the votes for three directors currently on the Morgan's board policy committee.

Dimon described the London Whale debacle as an anomaly caused by the inappropriate behavior of a few bad employees. However, this debacle plus the huge fines and settlements seems to suggest serious weaknesses in the bank's oversight of activities involving significant risk and compliance with regulatory rules.

Executives and board members of JPMorgan Chase worked hard to thwart these efforts. Lee Raymond, the former CEO of ExxonMobil who has been on the JPMorgan board for 28 years, played a key role in these efforts to support Dimon and avoid a negative vote. This group lobbied major institutional shareholders and even asked (though he declined) former U.S. President Bill Clinton to help work out a compromise with the AFSCME. They even suggested that Dimon would quit if he had to give up one of the roles and it would harm the stock price. In the end, Dimon and the bank won the vote with a two-thirds majority for Dimon to retain both positions.

Several analysts decried the vote and suggested that having a third of the shareholders vote against Dimon is not a major vote of confidence. One even suggested that the vote is not surprising because of the 10 largest institutional owners of the bank's stock, seven have CEOs who also hold the chair position. So, how could they openly argue that this is bad for JPMorgan when they do it in their organizations? Furthermore, these major institutional investors want the banks to engage in high-risk activities with the potential to produce high returns. This is especially true because the downside risk of losses is low as the government cannot afford to allow the big banks to fail.

One analyst suggested that the shareholders voted out of fear (potential loss of Dimon) and for personality instead of good corporate governance. Analysts for the *Financial Times* argued that the outcome of this vote demonstrates how weak shareholder rights are in the United States. Finally, another analyst noted that while splitting the CEO and chair positions does not guarantee good governance, it is a prerequisite for it. Lee Raymond suggested that the board would take action. Several speculate that such actions will not relate to Dimon duel positions, but rather to a reconfiguration of the board members on the risk and audit committees. Some have argued that certain members of these committees have little knowledge of their function and/or have financial ties to the bank, thereby creating a potential conflict of interest. One protection for Dimon is that the JPMorgan Chase continues to perform well, even with poor ratings from governance evaluators.

Sources: E. Bloxham, 2015, J.P. Morgan: Taking on more risk than it can handle?. *Fortune*, www.fortune.com, May 14; S. Gandel, 2015, After complaining about regulations, JPMorgan Chase beats estimates—again. *Fortune*, www.fortune.com, April 29; E. Glazer, 2014, J.P. Morgan's decade of Dimon, *Wall Street Journal*, June 30, C1; J. Eisinger, 2013, Flawed system suits the shareholders just fine, *New York Times DealBook*, http://dealbook.nytimes.com, May 29; J. Plender, 2013, The divine right of the imperial CEO, *Financial Times*, www.ft.com, May 26; J. Sommer, 2013, The CEO triumphant (at least at Apple and Chase), *New York Times*, www.nytimes.com, May 25; H. Moore, 2013, JP Morgan CEO Jamie Dimon remains the Indiana Jones of corporate America, *The Guardian*, www.guardian.com, May 21; J. Silver-Greenberg & S. Craig, 2013, Strong lobbying helps Dimon thwart a shareholder challenge, *New York Times DealBook*, http://dealbook.nytimes.com, May 21; D. Fitzpatrick, J. S. Lublin, & J. Steinberg, 2013, Vote strengthens Dimon's grip, *Wall Street Journal*, www.wsj.com, May 21; A. T. Crane & A. Currie, 2013, Dimon's Pyrrhic victory, *New York Times DealBook*, http://dealbook.nytimes.com, May 21; D. Benoit, 2013, J.P. Morgan's powerful board members, *Wall Street Journal*, www.wsj.com, May 20; M. Egan, 2013, Top J.P. Morgan directors back Dimon as CEO, Chair, *Fox Business*, www.foxbusiness.com, May 10.

Case Discussion Questions

1. How well do you think the governance system of JPMorgan Chase is working in protecting shareholder interests?

2. What particular governance devices are helping or hindering good governance in the JPMorgan Chase situation?

3. What do you recommend to improve the governance system specifically for JPMorgan Chase but also overall relative to the system of governance devices described in Chapter 10?

NOTES

1. G. Subramanian, 2015, Corporate governance 2.0. *Harvard Business Review*, 93(3): 96–105; X. Castaner & N. Kavadis, 2013, Does good governance prevent bad strategy? A study of corporate governance, financial diversification, and value creation by French corporations, 2000–2006, *Strategic Management Journal*, 34: 863–876.

2. I. Filatotchev & C. Nakajima, C. 2014, Corporate governance, responsible managerial behavior, and corporate social responsibility: Organizational efficiency versus organizational legitimacy? *Academy of Management Perspectives*, 28: 289–306; A. P. Cowen & J. J. Marcel, 2011, Damaged goods: Board decisions to dismiss reputationally compromised directors, *Academy of Management Journal*, 54: 509–527.

3. J. Joseph, W. Ocasio, & M. McDonnell, 2014, The structural elaboration of board independence: Executive power, institutional logics, and the adoption of CEO-only board structures in U.S. corporate governance, *Academy of Management Journal*, 57: 1834–1858; P. J. Davis, 2013, Senior executives and their boards: Toward a more involved director, *Journal of Business Strategy*, 34(1): 3–40.

4. S. Ayuso, M. A. Rodríguez, R. García-Castro, & M. A. Ariño, 2014, Maximizing stakeholders' interests: An empirical analysis of the stakeholder approach to corporate governance, *Business & Society*, 53: 414–439; D. R. Dalton, M. A. Hitt, S. T. Certo, & C. M. Dalton, 2008, The fundamental agency problem and its mitigation: Independence, equity and the market for corporate control, in J. P. Walsh and A. P. Brief (eds.), *The Academy of Management Annals*, NY: Lawrence Erlbaum Associates, 1–64; E. F. Fama & M. C. Jensen, 1983, Separation of ownership and control, *Journal of Law and Economics*, 26: 301–325.

5. H. Zeitoun, M. Osterloh, & B. S. Frey, 2014, Learning from ancient Athens: Demarchy and corporate governance, *Academy of Management Perspectives*, 28: 1–14; J. S. Harrison, D. A. Bosse, & R. A. Phillips, 2010, Managing for stakeholders, stakeholder utility functions, and competitive advantage, *Strategic Management Journal*, 31: 58–74.

6. B. Soltani & C. Maupetit, 2015, Importance of core values of ethics, integrity and accountability in the European corporate governance codes, *Journal of Management & Governance*, 19: 259–284; T. J. Boulton, S. B. Smart, & C. J. Zutter, 2010, IPO underpricing and international corporate governance, *Journal of International Business Studies*, 41: 206–222.

7. A. Capasso, G. Dagnino, & W. Shen, 2014, Special issue on 'corporate governance and strategic management in different contexts: Fostering interchange of a crucial relationship', *Journal of Management & Governance*, 18: 921–927; E. Vaara, R. Sarala, G. K. Stahl, & I. Bjorkman, 2012, The impact of organizational and national cultural differences on social conflict and knowledge transfer in international acquisitions, *Journal of Management Studies*, 49: 1–27; W. Judge, 2010, Corporate governance mechanisms throughout the world, *Corporate Governance: An International Review*, 18: 159–160.

8. L. S. Tsui-Auch & T. Yoshikawa, 2015, Institutional change versus resilience: A study of incorporation of independent directors in Singapore banks, *Asian Business & Management*, 14: 91–115.

9. G. Bell, I. Filatotchev, & R. Aguilera, 2014, Corporate governance and investors' perceptions of foreign IPO value: An institutional perspective, *Academy of Management Journal*, 57: 301–320; W. Kim, T. Sung, & S.-J. Wei, 2011, Does corporate governance risk at home affect investment choice abroad? *Journal of International Economics*, 85: 25–41.

10. H. Servaes & A. Tamayo, 2014, How do industry peers respond to control threats?. *Management Science*, 60: 380–399; J. Lee, 2013, Dancing with the enemy? Relational hazards and the contingent value of repeat exchanges in M&A markets, *Organization Science*, 24: 1237–1256; M. A. Hitt, R. E. Hoskisson, R. A. Johnson, & D. D. Moesel, 1996, The market for corporate control and firm innovation, *Academy of Management Journal*, 45: 697–716.

11. G. E. Davis & T. A. Thompson, 1994, A social movement perspective on corporate control, *Administrative Science Quarterly*, 39: 141–173.

12. F. Bertoni, M. Meoli, & S. Vismara, 2014, Board Independence, Ownership structure and the valuation of IPOs in Continental Europe, *Corporate Governance:*

An International Review, 22:116–131; V. V. Acharya, S. C. Myers, & R. G. Rajan, 2011, The internal governance of firms, *Journal of Finance*, 66: 689–720; R. Bricker & N. Chandar, 2000, Where Berle and Means went wrong: A reassessment of capital market agency and financial reporting, *Accounting, Organizations, and Society*, 25: 529–554.

13. T. M. Alessandri & A. Seth, 2014, The effects of managerial ownership on international and business diversification: Balancing incentives and risks, *Strategic Management Journal*, 35: 2064–2075; A. M. Colpan, T. Yoshikawa, T. Hikino, & E. G. Del Brio, 2011, Shareholder heterogeneity and conflicting goals: Strategic investments in the Japanese electronics industry, *Journal of Management Studies*, 48: 591–618; R. M. Wiseman & L. R. Gomez-Mejia, 1999, A behavioral agency model of managerial risk taking, *Academy of Management Review*, 23: 133–153.

14. M. Essen, M. Carney, E. R. Gedajlovic, & P. R. Heugens, 2015, How does family control influence firm strategy and performance? A meta-analysis of US publicly listed firms, *Corporate Governance: An International Review*, 23: 3–24; D. L. Deephouse & P. Jaskiewicz, 2013, Do family firms have better reputations than non-family firms? An integration of socioecomotional wealth and social identity theory, *Journal of Management Studies*, 50: 337–360; A. Minichilli, G. Corbetta, & I. C. MacMillan, 2010, Top management teams in family-controlled companies: 'Familiness', 'faultlines', and their impact on financial performance, *Journal of Management Studies*, 47: 205–222.

15. D. Miller, I. Le Breton-Miller, & R. Lester, 2013, Family firm governance, strategic conformity and performance: Institutional vs. strategic perspectives, *Organization Science*, in press; M. W. Peng & Y. Jiang, 2010, Institutions behind family ownership and control in large firms, *Journal of Management Studies*, 47: 253–273.

16. Essen, Carney, Gedajlovic, & Heugens, How does family control influence firm strategy and performance? A. meta-analysis of US publicly listed firms; E. Gedajlovic, M. Carney, J. J. Chrisman, & F. W. Kellermans, 2012, The adolescence of family firm research: Taking stock and planning for the future, *Journal of Management*, 38: 1010–1037; R. C. Anderson & D. M. Reeb, 2004, Board composition: Balancing family influence in S&P 500 firms, *Administrative Science Quarterly*, 49: 209–237.

17. Y. Cheung, I. Haw, W. Tan, & W. Wang, 2014, Board Structure and intragroup propping: Evidence from family business groups in Hong Kong. *Financial* Management, 43: 569–601; E. Lutz & S. Schrami, 2012, Family firms: Should they hire an outside CFO? *Journal of Business Strategy*, 33(1): 39–44; E.-T. Chen & J. Nowland, 2010, Optimal board monitoring in family-owned companies: Evidence from Asia, *Corporate Governance: An International Review*, 18: 3–17.

18. J. L. Arregle, L. Naldi, M. Nordquvist, & M. A. Hitt, 2012, Internationalization of family controlled firm: A study of the effects of external involvement in governance, *Entrepreneurship Theory and Practice*, 36: 1115–1143; D. G. Sirmon, J.-L. Arregle, M. A. Hitt, & J. W. Webb, 2008, Strategic responses to the threat of imitation, *Entrepreneurship Theory and Practice*, 32: 979–998.

19. R. M. Wiseman, G. Cuevas-Rodriguez, & L. R. Gomez-Mejia, 2012, Towards a social theory of agency, *Journal of Management Studies*, 49: 202–222; G. Dushnitsky & Z. Shapira, 2010, Entrepreneurial finance meets organizational reality: Comparing investment practices and performance of corporate and independent venture capitalists, *Strategic Management Journal*, 31: 990–1017.

20. A. K. Hoenen & T. Kostova, 2014, Utilizing the broader agency perspective for studying headquarters-subsidiary relations in multinational companies, *Journal of International Business Studies*, 46: 104–113; T. J. Quigley & D. C. Hambrick, 2012, When the former CEO stays on as board chair: Effects on successor discretion, strategic change and performance, *Strategic Management Journal*, 33: 834–859.

21. R. Krause, M. Semadeni, & A. A. Cannella, 2013, External COO/presidents as expert directors: A new look at the service role of boards, *Strategic Management Journal*, 34: 1628–1641; A. Mackey, 2008, The effects of CEOs on firm performance, *Strategic Management Journal*, 29: 1357–1367.

22. W. Li & Y. Lu, 2012, CEO dismissal, institutional development and environmental dynamism, *Asia Pacific Journal of Management*, 29: 1007–1026; L. L. Lan & L. Heracleous, 2010, Rethinking agency theory: The view from law, *Academy of Management Review*, 35: 294–314; Dalton, Hitt, Certo, & Dalton, 2008, The fundamental agency problem and its mitigation: Independence, equity and the market for corporate control.

23. B. Kang & R. P Jindal, 2015, Opportunism in buyer-seller relationships: Some unexplored antecedents, *Journal of Business Research*, 68: 735–742; K. Vafai, 2010, Opportunism in organizations, *Journal of Law, Economics, and Organization*, 26: 158–181; O. E. Williamson, 1996, *The Mechanisms of Governance*, NY: Oxford University Press, 6.

24. Y. Luo, Y. Liu, Q. Yang, V. Maksimov, & J. Hou, 2015, Improving performance and reducing cost in buyer-supplier relationships: The role of justice in curtailing opportunism, *Journal of Business Research*, 68: 607–615; F. Lumineau & D. Malhotra, 2011, Shadow of the contract: How contract structure shapes interfirm dispute resolution, *Strategic Management Journal*, 32: 532–555.

25. B. Balsmeier, A. Buchwald, & J. Stiebale, 2014, Outside directors on the board and innovative firm performance, *Research Policy*, 43: 1800–1815; M. L. McDonald, P. Khanna, & J. D. Westphal, 2008, Getting them to think outside the circle: Corporate governance CEOs' external advice networks, and firm performance, *Academy of Management Journal*, 51: 453–475.

26. Y. Ning, X. Hu, & X. Garza-Gomez, 2015, An empirical analysis of the impact of large changes in institutional ownership on CEO compensation risk, *Journal of Economics & Finance*, 39: 23–47; J. Harris, S. Johnson, & D. Souder, 2013, Model theoretic knowledge accumulation: The case of agency theory and incentive alignment, *Academy of Management Review*, 38: 442–454; L. Weber & K. J. Mayer, 2011, Designing effective contracts: Exploring the influence of framing and expectations, *Academy of Management Review*, 36: 53–75.

27. T. J. Boulton, M. V. Braga-Alves, & F. P. Schlingemann, 2014, Does equity-based compensation make CEOs more acquisitive?, *Journal of Financial Research*, 37: 267–294; T. Hutzschenreuter & J. Horstkotte, 2013, Performance effects of top management team demographic faultlines in the process of product diversification, *Strategic Management Journal*, 34: 704–726; E. Levitas, V. L. Barker, III, & M. Ahsan, 2011, Top manager ownership levels and incentive alignment in inventively active firms, *Journal of Strategy and Management*, 4: 116–135.

28. D. E. Black, S. S. Dikolli, & S. D. Dyreng, 2014, CEO pay-for-complexity and the risk of managerial diversion from multinational diversification, *Contemporary Accounting Research*, 31: 103–135 P. David, J. P. O'Brien, T. Yoshikawa, & A. Delios, 2010, Do shareholders or stakeholders appropriate the rents from corporate diversification? The influence of ownership structure, *Academy of Management Journal*, 53: 636–654; G. P. Baker & B. J. Hall, 2004, CEO incentives and firm size, *Journal of Labor Economics*, 22: 767–798.

29. A. S. Hornstein & Z. Nguyen, 2014, Is more less? Propensity to diversify via M&A and market reaction, *International Review of Financial Analysis*, 34: 76–88; S. W. Geiger & L. H. Cashen, 2007, Organizational size and CEO compensation: The moderating effect of diversification in downscoping organizations, *Journal of Managerial Issues*, 9: 233–252.

30. B. W. Benson, J. C. Park, & W. N. Davidson, 2014, Equity-based incentives, risk aversion, and merger-related risk-taking behavior, *Financial Review*, 49: 117–148; M. Larraza-Kintana, L. R. Gomez-Mejia, & R. M. Wiseman, 2011, Compensation framing and the risk-taking behavior of the CEO: Testing the influence of alternative

reference points, *Management Research: The Journal of the Iberoamerican Academy of Management*, 9: 32–55.

31. 2014, Lockheed Martin, Annual Report, www.lockheedmartin.com, May 20; B. Kowitt, 2013, Lockheed's secret weapon, *Fortune*, May 20, 196–204.

32. M. S. Jensen, 1986, Agency costs of free cash flow, corporate finance, and takeovers, *American Economic Review*, 76: 323–329.

33. J. P. O'Brien, P. David, T. Yoshikawa, & A. Delios, 2014, How capital structure influences diversification performance: A transaction cost perspective, *Strategic Management Journal*, 35: 1013–1031; R. E. Meyer & M. A. Hollerer, 2010, Meaning structures in a contested issue field: A topographic map of shareholder value in Austria, *Academy of Management Journal*, 53: 1241–1262; M. Jensen & E. Zajac, 2004, Corporate elites and corporate strategy: How demographic preferences and structural position shape the scope of the firm, *Strategic Management Journal*, 25: 507–524.

34. T. B. Mackey & J. B. Barney, 2013, Incorporating opportunity costs in strategic management research: The value of diversification and payout as opportunities forgone when reinvesting in the firm. *Strategic Organization*, 11: 347–363; S. F. Matusik & M. A. Fitza, 2012, Diversification in the venture capital industry: Leveraging knowledge under uncertainty, *Strategic Management Journal*, 33: 407–426; G. Kenny, 2012, Diversification: Best practices of the leading companies, *Journal of Business Strategy*, 33(1): 12–20.

35. T. M. Alessandri & A. Seth, 2014, The effects of managerial ownership on international and business diversification: Balancing incentives and risks, *Strategic Management Journal*, 35: 2064–2075; M. V. S. Kumar, 2013, The costs of related diversification: The impact of the core business on the productivity of related segments, *Organization Science*, 24: 1827–1846; F. Neffke & M. Henning, Skill relatedness and firm diversification, *Strategic Management Journal*, 34: 297–316.

36. S. Pathak, R. E. Hoskisson, & R. A. Johnson, 2014, Settling up in CEO compensation: The impact of divestiture intensity and contextual factors in refocusing firms, *Strategic Management Journal*, 35: 1124–1143; D. D. Bergh, R. A. Johnson, & R.-L. Dewitt, 2008, Restructuring through spin-off or sell-off: Transforming information asymmetries into financial gain, *Strategic Management Journal*, 29: 133–148.

37. S. K. Kim, J. D. Arthurs, A. Sahaym, & J. B. Cullen, 2013, Search behavior of the diversified firm: The impact of fit on innovation, *Strategic Management Journal*, 34: 999–1009.

38. J. Kang, 2013, The relationship between corporate diversification and corporate social performance, *Strategic Management Journal*, 34: 94–109.

39. K Kong-Hee & A. A. Rasheed, 2014, board heterogeneity, corporate diversification and firm performance, *Journal of Management Research*: 14: 121–139; E. Rawley, 2010, Diversification, coordination costs, and organizational rigidity: Evidence from microdata, *Strategic Management Journal*, 31: 873–891; T. K. Berry, J. M. Bizjak, M. L. Lemmon, & L. Naveen, 2006, Organizational complexity and CEO labor markets: Evidence from diversified firms, *Journal of Corporate Finance*, 12: 797–817.

40. U. V. Lilienfeld-Toal & S. Ruenzi, 2014, CEO ownership, stock market performance, and managerial discretion, *Journal of Finance*, 69: 1013–1050; R. Krause & M. Semadeni, 2013, Apprentice, departure and demotion: An examination of the three types of CEO-board chair separation, *Academy of Management Journal*, 56: 805–826.

41. W. Rees & T. Rodionova, 2015, The Influence of family ownership on corporate social responsibility: An international analysis of publicly listed companies, *Corporate Governance: An International Review*, 23: 184–202; J. L. Walls, P. Berrone, & P. H. Phan, 2012, Corporate governance and environmental performance: Is there really a link? *Strategic Management Journal*, 33: 885–913; C. J. Kock, J. Santalo, & L. Diestre, 2012, Corporate governance and the environment: What type of governance creates greener companies? *Journal of Management Studies*, 49: 492–514.

42. J. C. Coates & S. Srinivasan, 2014, SOX after ten years: A multidisciplinary review, *Accounting Horizons*, 28: 627–671; M. Hossain, S. Mitra, Z. Rezaee, & B. Sarath, 2011, Corporate governance and earnings management in the pre- and post-Sarbanes-Oxley act regimes: Evidence from implicated option backdating firms, *Journal of Accounting Auditing & Finance*, 28: 279–315; V. Chhaochharia & Y. Grinstein, 2007, Corporate governance and firm value: The impact of the 2002 governance rules, *Journal of Finance*, 62: 1789–1825.

43. S. C. Rice, D. P. Weber, & W. Biyu, 2015, Does SOX 404 have teeth? Consequences of the failure to report existing internal control weaknesses, *Accounting Review*, 90: 1169–1200; Z. Singer & H. You, 2011, The effect of Section 404 of the Sarbanes-Oxley Act on earnings quality, *Journal of Accounting and Finance*, 26: 556–589.

44. 2010, The Dodd-Frank Act: Financial reform update index, Faegre & Benson, www.faegre.com, September 7.

45. B. Appelmaum, 2011, Dodd-Frank supporters clash with currency chief, *New York Times*, www.nytimes.com, July 23.

46. B. J. Bushee, M. E. Carter, & J. Gerakos, 2014, Institutional investor preferences for corporate governance mechanisms, *Journal of Management Accounting Research*, 26: 123–149; M. Goranova, R. Dhanwadkar, & P. Brandes, 2010, Owners on both sides of the deal: Mergers and acquisitions

and overlapping institutional ownership, *Strategic Management Journal*, 31: 1114–1135; F. Navissi & V. Naiker, 2006, Institutional ownership and corporate value, *Managerial Finance*, 32: 247–256.

47. J. C. Hartzell, L Sun, & S. Titman, S. 2014, Institutional investors as monitors of corporate diversification decisions: Evidence from real estate investment trusts, *Journal of Corporate Finance*, 25: 61–72; B. L. Connelly, R. E. Hoskisson, L. Tihanyi, & S. T. Certo, 2010, Ownership as a form of corporate governance, *Journal of Management Studies*, 47: 1561–1589; M. Singh, I. Mathur, & K. C. Gleason, 2004, Governance and performance implications of diversification strategies: Evidence from large U.S. firms, *Financial Review*, 39: 489–526.

48. I. Busta, E. Sinani, & S. Thomsen, 2014, Ownership concentration and market value of European banks, *Journal of Management & Governance*, 18: 159–183; K. A. Desender, R. A. Aguilera, R. Crespi, & M. Garcia-Cestona, 2013, When does ownership matter? Board characteristics and behavior, *Strategic Management Journal*, 34: 823–842; J. Wu, D. Xu, & P. H. Phan, 2011, The effects of ownership concentration and corporate debt on corporate divestitures in Chinese listed firms, *Asia Pacific Journal of Management*, 28: 95–114.

49. M. van Essen, J. van Oosterhout, & P. Heugens, 2013, Competition and cooperation in corporate governance: The effects of labor institutions on blockholder effectiveness in 23 European countries, *Organization Science*, 24: 530–551.

50. C. Inoue, S. Lazzarni, & A. Musacchio, 2013, Leviathan as a minority shareholder: Firm-level implications of equity purchases by the state, *Academy of Management Journal*, 56: 1775–1801.

51. C. Singla, R. Veliyath, & R. George, 2014, Family firms and internationalization-governance relationships: Evidence of secondary agency issues, *Strategic Management Journal*, 35: 606–616; S.-Y. Collin & J. Ahlberg, 2012, Blood in the boardroom: Family relationships influencing the functions of the board, *Journal of Family Business Strategy*, 3: 207–219.

52. A. Zattoni, L. Gnan, & M. Huse, 2015, Does family involvement influence firm performance? Exploring the mediating effects of board processes and tasks, *Journal of Management*, 41: 1214–1243; D. Miller, A. Minichilli, & G. Corbetta, 2013, Is family leadership always beneficial? *Strategic Management Journal*, 34: 553–571; J. J. Chrisman, J. H. Chua, A. W. Pearson, & T. Barnett, 2012, Family involvement, family influence and family-centered non-economic goals in small firms, *Entrepreneurship Theory and Practice*, 36: 1103–1113.

53. L. R. Gomez-Mejia, J. T. Campbell, G. Martin, R. E. Hoskisson, M. Makri, & D. G. Sirmon, 2014, Socioemotional wealth as a mixed gamble: Revisiting family firm R&D investments with the behavioral agency model, *Entrepreneurship: Theory & Practice*, 38: 1351–1374; A. Konig, N. Kammerlander, & A. Enders, 2013, The family innovator's dilemma: How family influence affects the adoption of discontinuous technologies by incumbent firms, *Academy of Management Review*, 38: 418–441; J. J. Chrisman & P. C. Patel, 2012, Variations in R&D investments of family and nonfamily firms: Behavioral agency and myopic loss aversion perspectives, *Academy of Management Journal*, 55: 976–997.

54. A. Berle & G. Means, 1932, *The Modern Corporation and Private Property*, NY: Macmillan.

55. M. Wang, 2014, Which types of institutional investors constrain abnormal accruals?, *Corporate Governance: An International Review*, 22: 43–67; R. A. Johnson, K. Schnatterly, S. G. Johnson, & S.-C. Chiu, 2010, Institutional investors and institutional environment: A comparative analysis and review, *Journal of Management Studies*, 47: 1590–1613; M. Gietzmann, 2006, Disclosure of timely and forward-looking statements and strategic management of major institutional ownership, *Long Range Planning*, 39: 409–427.

56. D. Marchick, 2011, Testimony of David Marchick—The power of pensions: Building a strong middle class and a strong economy, The Carlyle Group homepage, www.carlyle.com, July 12.

57. J. Chou, L. Ng, V. Sibilkov, & Q. Wang, 2011, Product market competition and corporate governance, *Review of Development Finance*, 1: 114–130; S. D. Chowdhury & E. Z. Wang, 2009, Institutional activism types and CEO compensation: A time-series analysis of large Canadian corporations, *Journal of Management*, 35: 5–36.

58. R. Krause, K. A. Whitler, & M. Semadeni, 2014, Power to the principals! An experimental look at shareholder say-on-pay voting, *Academy of Management Journal*, 57: 94–115; Y. Ertimur, F. Ferri, & S. R. Stubben, 2010, Board of directors' responsiveness to shareholders: Evidence from shareholder proposals, *Journal of Corporate Finance*, 16: 53–72.

59. C. Mallin, 2012, Institutional investors: the vote as a tool of governance, *Journal of Management & Governance*, 16: 177–196; D. Brewster, 2009, U.S. investors get to nominate boards, *Financial Times*, www.ft.com, May 20.

60. S. Craig, 2013, The giant of shareholders, quietly stirring, *New York Times*, www.nytimes.com, May 18.

61. 2015, BlackRock's Fink tells S&P 500 firms to think long-term, *Fortune*, www.fortune.com, April 29

62. X. Liu, D. D. van Jaarsveld, R. Batt, & A. C. Frost, 2014, The influence of capital structure on strategic human capital: Evidence from U.S. And Canadian firms. *Journal of Management*, 40: 422–448; M. Hadani, M. Goranova, & R. Khan, 2011, Institutional investors, shareholder activism, and earnings management, *Journal of Business Research*, 64: 1352–1360; L. Tihanyi, R. A. Johnson, R. E. Hoskisson, & M. A. Hitt, 2003, Institutional ownership differences and international diversification: The effects of boards of directors and technological opportunity, *Academy of Management Journal*, 46: 195–211.

63. M. L. Heyden, J. Oehmichen, S. Nichting, & H. W. Volberda, 2015, Board background heterogeneity and exploration-exploitation: The role of the institutionally adopted board model, *Global Strategy Journal*, 5: 154–176; S. Garg, 2013, Venture boards: Differences with public boards and implications for monitoring and firm performance, *Academy of Management Review*, 38: 90–108; O. Faleye, R. Hoitash, & U. Hoitash, 2011, The costs of intense board monitoring, *Journal of Financial Economics*, 101: 160–181.

64. D. Barton & M. Wiseman, 2015, Where boards fall short, *Harvard Business Review*, 93(1/2): 98–104; J. T. Campbell, T. C. Campbell, D. G. Sirmon, L. Bierman, & C. S. Tuggle, 2012, Shareholder influence over director nomination via proxy access: Implications for agency conflict and stakeholder value, *Strategic Management Journal*, 33: 1431–1451; C. M. Dalton & D. R. Dalton 2006, Corporate governance best practices: The proof is in the process, *Journal of Business Strategy*, 27(4): 5–7.

65. A. Tushke, W. G. Sanders, & E. Hernandez, 2014, Whose experience matters in the boardroom? The effects of experiential and vicarious learning on emerging market entry, *Strategic Management Journal*, 35: 398–418; T. Dalziel, R. J. Gentry, & M. Bowerman, 2011, An integrated agency-resource dependence view of the influence of directors' human and relational capital on firms' R&D spending, *Journal of Management Studies*, 48: 1217–1242.

66. P. Khanna, C. D. Jones, & S. Boivie, 2014, Director human capital, information processing demands, and board effectiveness, *Journal of Management*, 40: 557–585; O. Faleye, 2011, CEO directors, executive incentives, and corporate strategic initiatives, *Journal of Financial Research*, 34: 241–277; C. S. Tuggle, D. G. Sirmon, C. R. Reutzel, & L. Bierman, 2010, Commanding board of director attention: Investigating how organizational performance and CEO duality affect board members' attention to monitoring, *Strategic Management Journal*, 31: 946–968.

67. C. Sundaramurthy, K. Pukthuanthong, & Y. Kor, 2014, Positive and negative synergies between the CEO's and the corporate board's human and social capital: A study of biotechnology firms, *Strategic Management Journal*, 35: 845–868; S. Chahine, I. Filatotchev, & S. A. Zahra, 2011, Building perceived quality of founder-involved IPO firms: Founders' effects on board selection and stock market performance, *Entrepreneurship Theory and Practice*, 35: 319–335; Y. Ertimur, F. Ferri, & S. R. Stubben, 2010, Board of directors' responsiveness to shareholders: Evidence from shareholder proposals, *Journal of Corporate Finance*, 16: 53–72.

68. E. Peni, 2014, CEO and Chairperson characteristics and firm performance, *Journal of Management & Governance*, 18: 185–205; M. A. Valenti, R. Luce, & C. Mayfield, 2011, The effects of firm performance on corporate governance, *Management Research Review*, 34: 266–283; D. Reeb & A. Upadhyay, 2010, Subordinate board structures, *Journal of Corporate Finance*, 16: 469–486.

69. A. D. Upadhyay, R. Bhargava, & S. D. Faircloth, 2014, Board structure and role of monitoring committees, *Journal of Business Research*, 67: 1486–1492; B. Bolton, 2014, Audit committee performance: ownership vs. independence—Did SOX get it wrong?, *Accounting & Finance*, 54: 83–112.

70. D. H. Zhu, W. Shen, & A. J. Hillman, 2014, Recategorization into the in-group: The appointment of demographically different new directors and their subsequent positions on corporate boards, *Administrative Science Quarterly*, 59: 240–270; A. Holehonnur & T. Pollock, 2013, Shoot for the stars? Predicting the recruitment of prestigious directors at newly public firms, *Academy of Management Journal*, 56: 1396–1419; M. McDonald & J. Westphal, 2013, Access denied: Low mentoring of women and minority first-time directors and its negative effects on appointments to additional boards, *Academy of Management Journal*, 56: 1169–1198.

71. Joseph, Ocasio, & McDonnell, The structural elaboration of board independence: Executive power, institutional logics, and the adoption of CEO-only board structures in U.S. corporate governance; R. C. Anderson, D. M. Reeb, A. Upadhyay, & W. Zhao, 2011, The economics of director heterogeneity, *Financial Management*, 40: 5–38; S. K. Lee & L. R. Carlson, 2007, The changing board of directors: Board independence in S&P 500 firms, *Journal of Organizational Culture, Communication and Conflict*, 11: 31–41.

72. R. Krause, M. Semadeni, & A. A. Cannella, 2014, CEO Duality: A review and research agenda, *Journal of Management*, 40: 256–286; S. Crainer, 2011, Changing direction: One person can make a difference, *Business Strategy Review*, 22: 10–16; R. C. Pozen, 2006, Before you split that CEO/chair, *Harvard Business Review* 84(4): 26–28.

73. E. Glazer, 2014, J.P. Morgan's decade of Dimon, *Wall Street Journal*, June 30, C1.

74. Barton & Wiseman, Where boards fall short; M. Huse, R. E. Hoskisson, A. Zattoni, & R. Vigano, 2011, New perspectives on board research: Changing the research agenda, *Journal of Management and Governance*, 15: 5–28; M. Kroll, B. A. Walters, & P. Wright, 2008, Board vigilance, director experience and corporate outcomes, *Strategic Management Journal*, 29: 363–382.

75. J. L. Coles, N. D. Daniel, & L. Naveen, 2014, Co-opted boards, *Review of Financial Studies*, 27: 1751–1796; S. Boivie, S. D. Graffin, & T. G. Pollock, 2012, Time for me to fly: Predicting director exit at large firms, *Academy of Management Journal*, 55: 1334–1359; A. Agrawal & M. A. Chen, 2011, Boardroom brawls: An empirical analysis of disputes involving directors, http://ssrn.com/abstracts=1362143.

76. J. C. Bedard, R. Hoitash, & U. Hoitash, 2014, Chief financial officers as inside directors, *Contemporary Accounting Research*, 31: 787–817; S. Muthusamy, P. A. Bobinski, & D. Jawahar, 2011, Toward a strategic role for employees in corporate governance, *Strategic Change*, 20: 127–138; Y. Zhang & N. Rajagopalan, 2010, Once an outsider, always an outsider? CEO origin, strategic change, and firm performance, *Strategic Management Journal*, 31: 334–346.

77. R. Krause & G. Bruton, 2014, Agency and monitoring clarity on venture boards of directors, *Academy of Management Review*, 39: 111–114; B. Baysinger & R. E. Hoskisson, 1990, The composition of boards of directors and strategic control: Effects on corporate strategy, *Academy of Management Review*, 15: 72–87.

78. B. Balsmeier, A. Buchwald, & J. Stiebale, 2014, Outside directors on the board and innovative firm performance, *Research Policy*, 43: 1800–1815; D. H. Zhu, 2013, Group polarization on corporate boards: Theory and evidence on board decisions about acquisition premiums, *Strategic Management Journal*, 800–822; G. A. Ballinger & J. J. Marcel, 2010, The use of an interim CEO during succession episodes and firm performance, *Strategic Management Journal*, 31: 262–283.

79. 2014, Low director turnover draws investor scrutiny, *Directors & Boards*, 38: 61; Boivie, Graffin, & Pollock, Time for me to fly; C. Shropshire, 2010, The role of the interlocking director and board receptivity in the diffusion of practices, *Academy of Management Review*, 35: 246–264.

80. 2015, Lead director charter, www.franklinresources.com, accessed on June 6; D. Carey, J. J. Keller, & M. Patsalos-Fox, 2010, How to choose the right nonexecutive board leader, *McKinsey Quarterly*, May.

81. A. J. Hillman, 2015, Board diversity: Beginning to unpeel the onion, *Corporate Governance: An International Review*, 23: 104–107; M. K. Bednar, 2012, Watchdog or lapdog? A behavioral role view of the media as a corporate governance mechanism, *Academy of Management Journal*, 55: 131–150; D. Northcott & J. Smith, 2011, Managing performance at the top: A balanced scorecard for boards of directors, *Journal of Accounting & Organizational Change*, 7: 33–56.

82. E. K. Lim & B. T. Mccann, 2013, The influence of relative values of outside director stock options on firm strategic risk from a multiagent perspective, *Strategic Management Journal*, 34: 1568–1590; I. Okhmatovskiy & R. J. David, 2011, Setting your own standards: Internal corporate governance codes as a response to institutional pressure, *Organization Science*, 1–22; J. L. Koors, 2006, Director pay: A work in progress, *The Corporate Governance Advisor*, 14: 14–31.

83. Y. Deutsch & M. Valente, 2013, The trouble with stock compensation, *MIT Sloan Management Review*, 54: 19–20; Y. Deutsch, T. Keil, & T. Laamanen, 2007, Decision making in acquisitions: The effect of outside directors' compensation on acquisition patterns, *Journal of Management*, 33: 30–56.

84. C. Post & K Byron, 2015, Women on boards and firm financial performance: A metaanalysis, *Academy of Management Journal*, in press; D. Cumming, T. Y. Leung, & O. Rui, 2015, Gender diversity and securities fraud, *Academy of Management Journal*, in press; A. J. Hillman, C. Shropshire, & A. A. Cannella, Jr., 2007, Organizational predictors of women on corporate boards, *Academy of Management Journal*, 50: 941–952.

85. E. A. Fong, X. Xing, W. H. Orman, & W. I. Mackenzie, 2015, Consequences of deviating from predicted CEO labor market compensation on long-term firm value, *Journal of Business Research*, 68: 299–305; M. van Essen, P. Heugens, J. Otten, & J. van Oosterhout, 2012, An institution-based view of executive compensation: A multilevel meta-analytic test, *Journal of International Business Studies*, 43: 396–423; M. J. Conyon, J. E. Core, & W. R. Guay, 2011, Are U.S. CEOs paid more than U.K. CEOs? Inferences from risk-adjusted pay, *Review of Financial Studies*, 24: 402–438.

86. M. van Essen, J. Otten, & E. J. Carberry, 2015, Assessing managerial power theory: a meta-analytic approach to understanding the determinants of CEO compensation, *Journal of Management*, 41: 164–202; C. Mangen & M. Magnan, 2012, "Say on pay": A wolf in sheep's clothing? *Academy of Management Perspectives*, 26: 86–104; E. A. Fong, V. F. Misangyi, Jr., & H. L. Tosi, 2010, The effect of CEO pay deviations on CEO withdrawal, firm size, and firm profits, *Strategic Management Journal*, 31: 629–651; J. P. Walsh, 2009, Are U.S. CEOs overpaid? A partial response to Kaplan, *Academy of Management Perspectives*, 23: 73–75.

87. A. Pepper & J. Gore, 2015, Behavioral agency theory: New foundations for theorizing about executive compensation, *Journal of Management*, 41: 1045–1068; G. P. Martin, L. R. Gomez-Mejia, & R. M. Wiseman, 2013, Executive stock options as mixed gambles: Revisiting the behavioral agency model, *Academy of Management Journal*, 56: 451–472; K. Rehbein, 2007, Explaining CEO compensation: How do talent, governance, and markets fit in? *Academy of Management Perspectives*, 21: 75–77.

88. E. Croci & D. Petmezas, 2015, Do risk-taking incentives induce CEOs to invest? Evidence from acquisitions, *Journal of Corporate Finance*, 32: 1–23; T. M. Alessandri, T. W. Tong, & J. J. Reuer, 2012, Firm heterogeneity in growth option value: The role of managerial incentives, *Strategic Management Journal*, 33: 1557–1566; D. H. M. Chng, M. S. Rodgers, E. Shih, & X.-B. Song, 2012, When does incentive compensation motivate managerial behaviors? An experimental investigation of the fit between compensation, executive core self-evaluation, and firm performance, *Strategic Management Journal*, 33: 1343–1362.

89. S. Jayaraman & T. Milbourn, 2015, CEO equity incentives and financial misreporting: The role of auditor expertise, *Accounting Review*, 90: 321–350; E. A. Fong, 2010, Relative CEO underpayment and CEO behavior towards R&D spending, *Journal of Management Studies*, 47: 1095–1122; X. Zhang, K. M. Bartol, K. G. Smith, M. D. Pfarrer, & D. M. Khanin, 2008, CEOs on the edge: Earnings manipulations and stock-based incentive misalignment, *Academy of Management Journal*, 51: 241–258; J. P. O'Connor, R. L. Priem, J. E. Coombs, & K. M. Gilley, 2006, Do CEO stock options prevent or promote fraudulent financial reporting? *Academy of Management Journal*, 49: 483–500.

90. J. J. Gerakos, J. D. Piotroski, & S. Srinivasan, 2013, Which U.S. market interactions affect CEO pay? Evidence from UK companies, *Management Science*, 59: 2413–2434; Y. Du, M. Deloof, & A Jorissen, 2011, Active boards of directors in foreign subsidiaries, *Corporate Governance: An International Review*, 19: 153–168; J. J. Reuer, E. Klijn, F. A. J. van den Bosch, & H. W. Volberda, 2011, Bringing corporate governance to international joint ventures, *Global Strategy Journal*, 1: 54–66.

91. S. Tsao, C. Lin, & V. Y. Chen, V. Y. 2015, Family ownership as a moderator between R&D investments and CEO compensation, *Journal of Business Research*, 68: 599–606; A. Ghosh, 2006, Determination of executive compensation in an emerging economy: Evidence from India, *Emerging Markets, Finance & Trade*, 42: 66–90.

92. J. J. Reuer, E. Klijn, & C. S. Lioukas, 2014, Board involvement in international joint ventures, *Strategic Management Journal*,

35: 1626–1644; M. Ederhof, 2011, Incentive compensation and promotion-based incentives of mid-level managers: Evidence from a multinational corporation, *The Accounting Review*, 86: 131–154; C. L. Staples, 2007, Board globalization in the world's largest TNCs 1993–2005, *Corporate Governance*, 15: 311–332.

93. G. Pandher & R. Currie, 2013, CEO compensation: A resource advantage and stakeholder-bargaining perspective, *Strategic Management Journal*, 34: 22–41; Y. Deutsch, T. Keil, & T. Laamanen, 2011, A dual agency view of board compensation: The joint effects of outside director and CEO stock options on firm risk, *Strategic Management Journal*, 32: 212–227.

94. Krause, Whitler, & Semadeni, Power to the principals! An experimental look at shareholder say-on-pay voting; L. K. Meulbroek, 2001, The efficiency of equity-linked compensation: Understanding the full cost of awarding executive stock options, *Financial Management*, 30: 5–44.

95. L H. Chan, K. W. Chen, C. Tai Yuan, & Y. Yangxin, 2015, Substitution between real and accruals-based earnings management after voluntary adoption of compensation clawback provisions, *Accounting Review*, 90: 147–174; 2013, The experts: Do companies spend too much on 'superstar' CEOs? *Wall Street Journal*, www.wsj.com, March 14.

96. E. K. Lim, 2015, The role of reference point in CEO restricted stock and its impact on R&D intensity in high-technology firms, *Strategic Management Journal*, 36: 872–889; Z. Dong, C. Wang, & F. Xie, 2010, Do executive stock options induce excessive risk taking? *Journal of Banking & Finance*, 34: 2518–2529; C. E. Devers, R. M. Wiseman, & R. M. Holmes, Jr., 2007, The effects of endowment and loss aversion in managerial stock option valuation, *Academy of Management Journal*, 50: 191–208.

97. C. Veld & B. H. Wu, 2014, What drives executive stock option backdating?, *Journal of Business Finance & Accounting*, 41: 1042–1070; T. G. Pollock, H. M. Fischer, & J. B. Wade, 2002, The role of politics in reprising executive options, *Academy of Management Journal*, 45: 1172–1182.

98. P. Berrone & L. R. Gomez-Mejia, 2009, Environmental performance and executive compensation: An integrated agency-institutional perspective, *Academy of Management Journal*, 52: 103–126.

99. R. V. Aguilera, K. Desender, M. K. Bednar, & J. H. Lee, 2015, Connecting the dots: Bringing external corporate governance into the corporate governance puzzle, *Academy of Management Annals*, 9:483–573; V. V. Acharya, S. C. Myers, & R. G. Rajan, 2011, The internal governance of firms, *Journal of Finance*, 66: 689–720; R. Sinha, 2006, Regulation: The market for corporate control and corporate governance, *Global Finance Journal*, 16: 264–282.

100. T. Laamanen, M. Brauer, & O. Junna, 2014, Performance of divested assets: Evidence from the U.S. software industry, *Strategic Management Journal*, 35: 914–925; T. Yoshikawa & A. A. Rasheed, 2010, Family control and ownership monitoring in family-controlled firms in Japan, *Journal of Management Studies*, 47: 274–295; R. W. Masulis, C. Wang, & F. Xie, 2007, Corporate governance and acquirer returns, *Journal of Finance*, 62: 1851–1889.

101. A. Macias & C. Pirinsky, C. 2015, Employees and the market for corporate control, *Journal of Corporate Finance*, 31: 33–53; C. Devers, G. McNamara, J. Haleblian, & M. Yoder, 2013, Do they walk the talk? Gauging acquiring CEO and director confidence in the value-creation potential of announced acquisitions, *Academy of Management Journal*, 56: 1679–1702; P.-X. Meschi & E. Metais, 2013, Do firms forget about their past acquisitions? Evidence from French acquisitions in the United States (1988–2006), *Journal of Management*, 39: 469–495; J. A. Krug & W. Shill, 2008, The big exit: Executive churn in the wake of M&As, *Journal of Business Strategy*, 29(4): 15–21.

102. H. Touryalai, 2014, Everybody loves hedge funds, assets hit record $3 trillion, *Forbes*, www.forbes.com, March 25.

103. M. Hitoshi, 2014, Hedge Fund activism in Japan: The limits of shareholder primacy, *Administrative Science Quarterly*, 59: 366–369; N. M. Boyson & R. M. Mooradian, 2011, Corporate governance and hedge fund activism, *Review of Derivatives Research*, 169–204; L. A. Bebchuk & M. S. Weisbach, 2010, The state of corporate governance research, *Review of Financial Studies*, 23: 939–961.

104. A. Gara, 2015, Breakup artist hedge funds betting billions on corporate marriages, Forbes, February 18, 6.

105. S. Bainbridge, 2011, Hedge funds as activist investors, *ProfessorBainbridge.com*, www.professorbainbridge.com, March 21.

106. D. Benoit & J. Bear, 2015, Goldman Sachs recaptures mojo with DuPont win, *Wall Street Journal*, www.wsj.com, May 22.

107. S. Ovide & D. Clark, 2015, Silicon Valley grits teeth over activist investors, *Wall Street Journal*, May 27, B1.

108. M. Cremers & A. Ferrell, 2014, Thirty years of shareholder rights and firm value, *Journal of Finance*, 69: 1167–1196; M. L. Humphery-Jenner & R. G. Powell, 2011, Firm size, takeover profitability, and the effectiveness of the market for corporate control: Does the absence of anti-takeover provisions make a difference? *Journal of Corporate Finance*, 17: 418–437.

109. J. P. Walsh & R. Kosnik, 1993, Corporate raiders and their disciplinary role in the market for corporate control, *Academy of Management Journal*, 36: 671–700.

110. K. Amess, S. Girma, & M. Wright, 2014, The wage and employment consequences of ownership change, *Managerial & Decision Economics*, 35: 161–171; M. Schijven & M. A. Hitt, 2012, The vicarious wisdom of crowds: Toward a behavioral perspective on investor reactions to acquisition announcements, *Strategic Management Journal*, 33: 1247–1268; J. Haleblian, C. E. Devers, G. McNamara, M. A. Carpenter, & R. B. Davison, 2009, Taking stock of what we know about mergers and acquisitions: A review and research agenda, *Journal of Management*, 35: 469–502.

111. F. Bauer & K. Matzler, 2014, Antecedents of M&A success: The role of strategic complementarity, cultural fit and degree and speed of integration, *Strategic Management Journal*, 35: 269–291; S. Mingo, 2013, The impact of acquisitions on the performance of existing organizational units In the acquiring firm: The case of the agribusiness company, *Management Science*, 59: 2687–2701; A. Sleptsov, J. Anand, & G. Vasudeva, 2013, Relational configurations with information intermediaries: The effect of firm-investment bank ties on expected acquisition performance, *Strategic Management Journal*, 34: 957–977.

112. 2014, Hostile takeover, *Investopedia*, www.investopedia.com, accessed on June 8.

113. M. Straska & G. Waller, 2014, Antitakeover provisions and shareholder wealth: A survey of the literature, *Journal of Financial & Quantitative Analysis*, 49: 1–32; P. Jiraporn & Y. Liu, 2011, Staggered boards, accounting discretion and firm value, *Applied Financial Economics*, 21: 271–285; O. Faleye, 2007, Classified boards, firm value, and managerial entrenchment, *Journal of Financial Economics*, 83: 501–529.

114. M. Holmén, E. Nivorozhkin, & R. Rana, 2014, Do anti-takeover devices affect the takeover likelihood or the takeover premium? *European Journal of Finance*, 20: 319–340; T. Sokoly, 2011, The effects of antitakeover provisions on acquisition targets, *Journal of Corporate Finance*, 17: 612–627; 2007, Leaders: Pay slips; management in Europe, *Economist*, June 23, 14.

115. J. A. Pearce II & R. B. Robinson, Jr., 2004, Hostile takeover defenses that maximize shareholder wealth, *Business Horizons* 47: 15–24.

116. M. Humphery-Jenner, 2014, Takeover defenses, innovation and value creation: Evidence from acquisition decisions, *Strategic Management Journal*, 35: 668–690; A. Kacperzyk, 2009, With greater power comes greater responsibility? Takeover protection and corporate attention to stakeholders, *Strategic Management Journal*, 30: 261–285.

117. P. Sieger, T. Zellweger, & K. Aquino, 2013, Turning agents into psychological principals: Aligning interests of non-owners through psychological ownership, *Journal of Management Studies*, 50: 361–388.

118. B. M. Galvin, D. Lange, & B. E. Ashforth, 2015, Narcissistic organizational identification: Seeing oneself as central to the organization's identity, *Academy of Management Review*, 40: 163–181.

119. E. Schiehll, C. Ahmadjian, & I. Filatotchev, 2014, National governance bundles perspective: Understanding the diversity of corporate governance practices at the firm and country levels, *Corporate Governance: An International Review*, 22: 179–184; A. Rasheed & T. Yoshikawa, 2012, *The convergence of corporate governance: Promise and prospects*, Basingstoke: Palgrave Macmillan; I. Haxhi & H. Ees, 2010, Explaining diversity in the worldwide diffusion of codes of good governance, *Journal of International Business Studies*, 41: 710–726.

120. M. P. Leitterstorf & S. B. Rau, 2014, Socioemotional wealth and IPO underpricing of family firms, *Strategic Management Journal*, 35: 751–760; P. C. Patel & J. J. Chrisman, 2014, Risk abatement as a strategy for R&D investments in family firms, *Strategic Management Journal*, 35: 617–627.

121. A. Haller, 2013, German corporate governance in international and European context, *International Journal of Accounting*, 48: 420–423; P. Witt, 2004, The competition of international corporate governance systems—a German perspective, *Management International Review*, 44: 309–333; A. Tuschke & W. G. Sanders, 2003, Antecedents and consequences of corporate governance reform: The case of Germany, *Strategic Management Journal*, 24: 631–649.

122. Tuschke, Sanders, & Hernandez, Whose experience matters in the boardroom?; D. Hillier, J. Pinadado, V. de Queiroz, & C. de la Torre, 2010, The impact of country-level corporate governance on research and development, *Journal of International Business Studies*, 42: 76–98.

123. Tuschke, Sanders, & Hernandez, Whose experience matters in the boardroom?

124. T. Duc Hung, 2014, Multiple corporate governance attributes and the cost of capital—Evidence from Germany, *British Accounting Review*, 46: 179–197; J. T. Addison & C. Schnabel, 2011, Worker directors: A German product that did not export? *Industrial Relations: A Journal of Economy and Society*, 50: 354–374; P. C. Fiss & E. J. Zajac, 2004, The diffusion of ideas over contested terrain: The (non)adoption of a shareholder value orientation among German firms, *Administrative Science Quarterly*, 49: 501–534.

125. M. Roth, 2013, Independent directors, shareholder empowerment and long-termism: The transatlantic perspective, *Fordham Journal of Corporate & Financial Law*, 18: 751–820; A. Chizema, 2010, Early and late adoption of American-style executive pay in Germany: Governance

and institutions, *Journal of World Business*, 45: 9–18; W. G. Sanders & A. C. Tuschke, 2007, The adoption of the institutionally contested organizational practices: The emergence of stock option pay in Germany, *Academy of Management Journal*, 50: 33–56.

126. J. P. O'Brien & P. David, 2014, Reciprocity and R&D search: Applying the behavioral theory of the firm to a communitarian context, *Strategic Management Journal*, 35: 550–565.

127. N. Kosaku, 2014, Japan seeks to lure investors with improved corporate governance, *Wall Street Journal*, www.wsj.com, June 28.

128. S. Varma, R. Awasthy, K. Narain, & R. Nayyar, 2015, Cultural determinants of alliance management capability—an analysis of Japanese MNCs in India, *Asia Pacific Business Review*, 21: 424–448; D. R. Adhikari & K. Hirasawa, 2010, Emerging scenarios of Japanese corporate management, *Asia-Pacific Journal of Business Administration*, 2: 114–132; M. A. Hitt, H. Lee, & E. Yucel, 2002, The importance of social capital to the management of multinational enterprises: Relational networks among Asian and Western firms, *Asia Pacific Journal of Management*, 19: 353–372.

129. T. Yeh, 2014, Large shareholders, shareholder proposals, and firm performance: Evidence from Japan, *Corporate Governance: An International Review*, 22: 312–329; W. P. Wan, D. W. Yiu, R. E. Hoskisson, & H. Kim, 2008, The performance implications of relationship banking during macroeconomic expansion and contraction: A study of Japanese banks' social relationships and overseas expansion, *Journal of International Business Studies*, 39: 406–427.

130. H. Aslan & P. Kumar, P. 2014, National governance bundles and corporate agency costs: A cross-country analysis, *Corporate Governance: An International Review*, 22: 230–251; P. M. Lee & H. M. O'Neill, 2003, Ownership structures and R&D investments of U.S. and Japanese firms: Agency and stewardship perspectives, *Academy of Management Journal*, 46: 212–225.

131. H. Sakawa, M. Ubukata, & N. Watanabel, 2014, Market liquidity and bank-dominated corporate governance: Evidence from Japan, *International Review of Economics & Finance*, 31: 1–11; X. Wu & J. Yao, 2012, Understanding the rise and decline of the Japanese main bank system: The changing effects of bank rent extraction, *Journal of Banking & Finance*, 36: 36–50.

132. K. Harrigan, 2014, Comparing corporate governance practices and exit decisions between US and Japanese firms, *Journal of Management & Governance*, 18: 975–988; K. Kubo & T. Saito, 2012, The effect of mergers on employment and wages: Evidence from Japan, *Journal of the Japanese and International Economics*, 26: 263–284;

N. Isagawa, 2007, A theory of unwinding of cross-shareholding under managerial entrenchment, *Journal of Financial Research*, 30: 163–179.

133. D. G. Litt, 2015, Japan's new corporate governance code: Outside directors find a role under 'Abenomics,' *Corporate Governance Advisor*, 23: 19–23.

134. F. Jiang & K. A. Kim, 2015, Corporate governance in China: A modern perspective, *Journal of Corporate Finance*, 32: 190–216; J. Yang, J. Chi, & M. Young, 2011, A review of corporate governance in China, *Asian-Pacific Economic Literature*, 25: 15–28.

135. R. Morck & B. Yeung, 2014, Corporate governance in China, *Journal of Applied Corporate Finance*, 26: 20–41; H. Berkman, R. A. Cole, & L. J. Fu, 2010, Political connections and minority-shareholder protection: Evidence from securities-market regulation in China, *Journal of Financial and Quantitative Analysis*, 45: 1391–1417; S. R. Miller, D. Li, E. Eden, & M. A. Hitt, 2008, Insider trading and the valuation of international strategic alliances in emerging stock markets, *Journal of International Business Studies*, 39: 102–117.

136. X. Yu, P. Zhang, & Y. Zheng, 2015, Corporate governance, political connections, and intra-industry effects: Evidence from corporate scandals in China, *Financial Management*, 44: 49–80; W. A. Li & D. T. Yan, 2013, Transition from administrative to economic model of corporate governance, *Nankai Business Review International*, 4: 4–8.

137. T. M. Rooker, 2015, Corporate governance or governance by corporates? Testing governmentality in the context of China's national oil and petrochemical business groups, *Asia Pacific Business Review*, 21: 60–76; J. Chi, Q. Sun, & M. Young, 2011, Performance and characteristics of acquiring firms in the Chinese stock markets, *Emerging Markets Review*, 12: 152–170; Y.-L. Cheung, P. Jiang, P. Limpaphayom, & T. Lu, 2010, Corporate governance in China: A step forward, *European Financial Management*, 16: 94–123.

138. G. Jiang, P. Rao, & H. Yue, 2015, Tunneling through non-operational fund occupancy: An investigation based on officially identified activities, *Journal of Corporate Finance*, 32: 295–311; J. Li & C. Qian, 2013, Principal-principal conflicts under weak institutions: A study of corporate takeovers in China, *Strategic Management Journal*, 34: 498–508; S. Globerman, M. W. Peng, & D. M. Shapiro, 2011, Corporate governance and Asian companies, *Asia Pacific Journal of Management*, 28: 1–14.

139. W. M Peng, S. L. Sun, & L. Markóczy, 2015, Human capital and CEO compensation during institutional transitions, *Journal of Management Studies*, 52: 117–147; P. Adithipyangkul, I. Alon, & T. Zhang, 2011, Executive perks: Compensation and corporate performance in China, *Asia*

Pacific Journal of Management, 28: 401–425; T. Buck, X. Lui, & R. Skovoroda, 2008, Top executives' pay and firm performance in China, *Journal of International Business Studies*, 39: 833–850.

140. R. Amit, Y. Ding, B Villalonga, & H. Zhang, H. 2015, The role of institutional development in the prevalence and performance of entrepreneur and family-controlled firms, *Journal of Corporate Finance*, 31: 284–305; A. Cai, J.-H. Luo, & D.-F. Wan, 2012, Family CEOs: Do they benefit firm governance In China? *Asia Pacific Journal of Management*, 29: 923–947.

141. H. Berkman, R. A. Cole, & L. J. Fu, 2014, Improving corporate governance where the state is the controlling block holder: Evidence from China, *European Journal of Finance*, 20: 752–777; L. Oxelheim, A. Gregoric, T. Randoy, & S. Thomsen, 2013, On the internationalization of corporate boards: The case of Nordic firms, *Journal of International Business Studies*, 44: 173–194.

142. S. Young & V. Thyil, 2014, Corporate social responsibility and corporate governance: Role of context in international settings, *Journal of Business Ethics*, 122: 1–24; S. Muthusamy, P. A. Bobinski, & D. Jawahar, 2011, Toward a strategic role for employees in corporate governance, *Strategic Change*, 20: 127–138; C. Shropshire & A. J. Hillman, 2007, A longitudinal study of significant change in stakeholder management, *Business & Society*, 46: 63–87.

143. G. K. Stahl & M. S. De Luque, 2014, Antecedents of responsible leader behavior: A research synthesis, conceptual framework, and agenda for future research, *Academy of Management Perspectives*, 28: 235–254; J. M. Schaubroeck, S. T. Hannah, B. J. Avolio, S. W. J. Kozlowski, R. G. Lord, L. K. Trevino, N. Dimotakis, & A. C. Peng, 2012, Embedding ethical leadership within and across organizational levels, *Academy of Management Journal*, 55: 1053–1078; R. A. G. Monks & N. Minow, 2011, *Corporate governance*, 5th ed., NY: John Wiley & Sons.

144. A. Soleimani, W. D. Schneper, & W. Newbury, 2014, The impact of stakeholder power on corporate reputation: A cross-country corporate governance perspective, *Organization Science*, 25: 991–1008; J. S. Chun, Y. Shin, J. N. Choi, & M. S. Kim, 2013, How does corporate ethics contribute to firm financial performance? The mediating role of collective organizational commitment and organizational citizenship behavior, *Journal of Management*, 39: 853–877; S. P. Deshpande, J. Joseph, & X. Shu, 2011, Ethical climate and managerial success in China, *Journal of Business Ethics*, 99: 527–534.

145. S. Kaplan, J. Samuels, & J. Cohen, 2015, An examination of the effect of CEO social ties and CEO reputation on nonprofessional investors' say-on-pay judgments, *Journal of Business Ethics*, 126: 103–117; A. P. Cowan &

J. J. Marcel, 2011, Damaged goods: Board decisions to dismiss reputationally compromised directors, *Academy of Management Journal*, 54: 509–527; J. R. Knapp, T. Dalziel, & M. W. Lewis, 2011, Governing top managers: Board control, social categorization, and their unintended influence on discretionary behaviors, *Corporate Governance: An International Review* 19: 295–310.

146. D. Gomulya & W. Boeker, 2014, How firms respond to financial restatement: CEO successors and external reactions, *Academy of Management Journal*, 57: 1579–1785.

147. Y. Li, F. Yao, & D. Ahlstrom, 2015, The social dilemma of bribery in emerging economies: A dynamic model of emotion, social value, and institutional uncertainty, *Asia Pacific Journal of Management*, 32: 311–334; Y. Jeong & R. J. Weiner, 2012, Who bribes? Evidence from the United Nations' oil-for-food program, *Strategic Management Journal*, 33: 1363–1383.

148. S.-H. Lee & D. H. Weng, 2013, Does bribery in the home country promote or dampen firm exports? *Strategic Management Journal*, 34: 1472–1487; J. O. Zhou & M. W. Peng, 2012, Does bribery help or hurt firm growth around the world? *Asia Pacific Journal of Management*, 29: 907–921.

149. 2015, Corporate governance awards 2015, *World Finance*, www.worldfinance.com/awards, March 4.

11

Organizational Structure and Controls

Studying this chapter should provide you with the strategic management knowledge needed to:

11-1   Define organizational structure and controls and discuss the difference between strategic and financial controls.

11-2   Describe the relationship between strategy and structure.

11-3   Discuss the different functional structures used to implement business-level strategies.

11-4   Explain the use of three versions of the multidivisional (M-form) structure to implement different diversification strategies.

11-5   Discuss the organizational structures used to implement three international strategies.

11-6   Define strategic networks and discuss how strategic center firms implement such networks at the business, corporate, and international levels.

LUXOTTICA'S DUAL CEO STRUCTURE: A KEY TO LONG-TERM SUCCESS OR A CAUSE FOR CONCERN?

Founded in Italy in 1961, Luxottica is the world's largest eyewear company, controlling over 80 percent of major eyewear brands. Alain Mikli, Arnette, Oakley, and Persol are some of the company's proprietary brands. Luxottica also makes products under license for a large number of well-known companies such as Armani, Bulgari, Burberry, Coach, Tiffany & Co., Tory Burch, and Versace, to name only a few. Additionally, Luxottica owns and operates a large number of eyewear storefront brands including LensCrafters, Pearle Vision, Laubman & Pank, and Sears Optical. Another measure of the scope of the firm's positions within the eyewear industry is its operations of "one of the largest managed vision care networks in the United States through EyeMed and the second largest lens finishing network, with three central laboratories, over 900 on-site labs at LensCrafters stores, a fully dedicated Oakley lab, and an additional facility based in China dedicated to North America optical retail."

As these product offerings and market positions show, Luxottica dominates all phases of the eyewear industry. One reason for this dominance is that the firm is vertically integrated in that it designs its own products, produces them through manufacturing facilities located throughout the world, and sells them in outlets such as those mentioned above. In the view of those leading the firm, Luxottica's extensive degree of vertical integration is a competitive advantage. The company says that its products are distinguished from competitors' offerings by their excellent design and the quality with which they are manufactured.

Late in 2014, Luxottica changed its organizational structure in a major way, as demonstrated by the fact that co-CEOs were appointed. Long-term Procter & Gamble executive Adil Mehboob-Khan accepted the responsibility for *distribution* in the firm's markets, while long-time Luxottica manager Massimo Vian was appointed as co-CEO with the responsibility for *products and operations*. Wholesale, retail optical, marketing, go-to-market, and e-commerce are examples of the units that comprise the distribution part of the new structure. Style & design, R&D and engineering, quality assurance, and purchasing are some of the units in the products and operations side of the structure. Each co-CEO holds a seat as a member of the firm's board of directors.

A dual CEO structure is unusual; many observers believe that this type of leadership structure cannot lead to long-term firm success. According to an observer of organizational structures, "the adoption of a co-CEO model is often a symptom of weakness. Having two people at the same level shows that the company is undecided about its leadership and it invites too much confusion." Another way of thinking about this some say, is that a ship with two captains is essentially a ship without a captain.

Although used infrequently in many countries, Italy is a nation in which a dual CEO structure is popular, particularly among family controlled/owned firms such as Luxottica. In fact, evidence indicates that more than one-third of "Italian family-owned businesses with annual revenue of more than 50 million euros have at least two bosses."

The critical issue when considering a dual CEO structure is the reason for choosing to use it. If there is a strong strategic rationale for the co-CEO structure, then arguably, a firm for which this is the case should organize itself in such a manner. Luxottica officials claim this is the case, saying that "this new organizational structure will support a new phase of development for

Courtesy of Luxottica

Luxottica that is consistent with its strategic vision and will allow it to take advantage of opportunities in a competitive global market of growing complexity and changing competitive dynamics." A current market opportunity for Luxottica is its collaboration with Google to work on the next version of Google Glass, the firm's futuristic eyewear product. Google's partnership with Luxottica is a result of Google's dissatisfaction with the results of its initial version of the product.

With respect to competitive dynamics, perhaps the co-CEO structure will help Luxottica compete against Warby Parker, the online eyeglass retailer that continues growing and that recently raised a round of capital that valued the firm at roughly $1.2 billion. The low price of Warby Parker's products is thought to be a competitive challenge for Luxottica given the higher costs of its differentiated eyewear.

Although unusual, the co-CEO structure may work for Luxottica. In the final analysis though, Luxottica's board must carefully monitor the firm's performance under a dual CEO structure and be prepared to make a change to that structure if evidence suggests that such an action would be in the firm's best interest.

Sources: 2015, Company profiles, Luxottica Home Page, www.luxottica.com, May 12; 2015, Our business model, Luxottica Home Page, www.luxottica.com, May 12; D. Macmillan, 2015, Eyeglass retailer Warby Parker is valued at $1.2 billion, *Wall Street Journal Online*, www.wsj.com, April 30; M. Mesco, 2015, Luxottica's profit surges as sales rise in North America, *Wall Street Journal Online*, www.wsj.com, May 4; M. Mesco, 2015, Italian eyewear maker Luxottica working on new version of Google Glass, CEO says, *Wall Street Journal Digits*, www.blogs.wsj.com, April 24; M. Mesco, 2015, Luxottica reports profit but looks for areas of growth, *Wall Street Journal Online*, www.wsj.com, March 2; 2014, Luxottica announces the implementation of a new governance structure based on a co-CEO model, Luxottica Home Page, www.luxottica, September 1.

As we explained in Chapter 4, all firms use one or more business-level strategies. Luxottica uses the differentiation strategy for its eyewear that is differentiated on the competitive dimensions of design, manufacturing, and brand name. In Chapters 6 through 9, we discussed other strategies that firms may choose to use (corporate-level, merger and acquisition, international, and cooperative), depending on the decisions made by those leading individual organizations. After being selected, strategies must be implemented effectively for organizations to achieve intended outcomes.

Organizational structure and controls, this chapter's topic, provide the framework within which strategies are implemented and used in both for-profit organizations and not-for-profit agencies.[1] However, as we explain, separate structures and controls are required to successfully implement different strategies. In all organizations, top-level managers have the final responsibility for ensuring that the firm has matched each of its strategies with the appropriate organizational structure and that both change when necessary. The match or degree of fit between strategy and structure influences the firm's attempts to earn above-average returns.[2] Thus, the ability to select an appropriate strategy and match it with the appropriate structure is an important characteristic of effective strategic leadership.[3] In this sense, it will be interesting to see if the co-CEO structure Luxottica recently put into place will prove to be an effective match with the firm's strategies.

This chapter opens with an introduction to organizational structure and controls. We then provide more details about the need for the firm's strategy and structure to be properly matched. The influence of strategy and structure on each other affects firms' efforts to match individual strategies with their appropriate structure.[4] As we discuss, strategy has a more important influence on structure, although once in place, structure influences strategy.[5] Next, we describe the relationship between growth and structural change successful firms experience. We then discuss the different organizational structures firms use to implement separate business-level, corporate-level, international, and cooperative strategies. We present a series of figures to highlight the different structures firms match with different strategies. Across time and based on their experiences, organizations, especially large and complex ones, customize these general structures to meet their unique needs.[6] Typically, firms try to form a structure that is complex enough to facilitate use of their strategies but simple enough for all parties to understand and use.[7]

11-1   Organizational Structure and Controls

Research shows that organizational structure and the controls that are a part of the structure affect firm performance.[8] In particular, evidence suggests that performance declines when the firm's strategy is not matched with the most appropriate structure and controls.[9] Even though mismatches between strategy and structure do occur, research indicates that managers try to act rationally when forming or changing their firm's structure.[10]

In Chapter 2's Opening Case, we talked about problems McDonald's is encountering when trying to cope effectively with changes that are taking place in the external environment. As we noted then, the firm is changing its menu to better accommodate some consumers' preferences for healthier food. Additionally though and more broadly, changes are being made to McDonald's organizational structure with the expectation that doing so will lead to enhanced firm performance. Defined comprehensively below, organizational structure essentially specifies the work that must be completed so the firm can implement its strategy.

McDonald's leaders, including new CEO Steve Easterbrook, believe that changes being made to the firm's structure will increase its efficiency (that is, its daily operations will improve) and its effectiveness (that is, it will better serve customers' needs). We discuss changes that have been made to McDonald's organizational structure in the Strategic Focus.

11-1a Organizational Structure

Organizational structure specifies the firm's formal reporting relationships, procedures, controls, and authority and decision-making processes.[11] A firm's structure determines and specifies the decisions that are to be made and the work that is to be completed by everyone within an organization as a result of those decisions.[12] Organizational routines serve as processes that are used to complete the work required by individual strategies.[13]

Developing an organizational structure that effectively supports the firm's strategy is difficult, especially because of the uncertainty (or unpredictable variation) about cause-effect relationships in the global economy's rapidly changing competitive environments.[14] When a structure's elements (e.g., reporting relationships, procedures, etc.) are properly aligned with one another, the structure increases the likelihood that the firm will operate in ways that allow it to better understand the challenging cause/effect relationships it encounters when competing against its rivals. Thus, helping the firm effectively cope with environmental uncertainty is an important contribution organizational structure makes to a firm as it seeks to successfully implement its strategy or strategies as a means of outperforming competitors.[15]

Appropriately designed organizational structures provide the stability a firm needs to successfully implement its strategies and maintain its current competitive advantages while simultaneously providing the flexibility to develop advantages it will need in the future.[16] More specifically, *structural stability* provides the capacity the firm requires to consistently and predictably manage its daily work routines,[17] while *structural flexibility* makes it possible for the firm to identify opportunities and then allocate resources to pursue them as a way of being prepared to succeed in the future.[18] Thus, an effectively

Organizational structure specifies the firm's formal reporting relationships, procedures, controls, and authority and decision-making processes.

Strategic Focus

Changing McDonald's Organizational Structure: A Path to Improved Performance?

Operating close to 37,000 restaurants worldwide and with annual sales closing in on $90 billion, McDonald's is huge. In fact, it is several times larger than Burger King and Wendy's, its closest competitors. In addition to the United States and Canada, McDonald's has a significant presence in France, German, Russia, and the United Kingdom.

But all is not well at McDonald's. Almost immediately upon being appointed as CEO, Steve Easterbrook said that "the reality is our recent performance has been poor. The numbers don't lie." Supporting Easterbrook's position is the fact that 2014 was one of the firm's worst financial performances in its 60-year history. Thus, changes are necessary. In response to this reality, and viewing himself as an internal activist, Easterbrook announced within 33 days of becoming CEO that he wants McDonald's to become a "progressive burger company." Changing the firm's organizational structure is critical to reaching this objective. Saying that he will not shy away "from the urgent need to reset this business" demonstrates the intensity with which Easterbrook is approaching McDonald's challenges.

For a number of years, McDonald's was structured around geographic segments including the United States, Europe, Asia/Pacific, Middle East, and Africa (APMEA). Over time though, this structural configuration became cumbersome, making McDonald's "too slow to effectively respond to the needs of its 69 million daily customers." The way this geography-based structure was being used resulted in "cumbersome" managerial practices and operational inefficiencies. Franchisees were reporting structural problems such as operational inefficiencies to McDonald's officials. In response to the franchisees' complaints, a McDonald's leader said the following: "You've told us that there are too many layers, redundancies in planning and communication, competing priorities, barriers to efficient decision making, and too much talking to ourselves instead of to and about our customers." Overall then, the need for changes to the firm's organizational structure was obvious to virtually everyone associated with the company.

Changes have indeed been made to McDonald's structure. Wanting to simplify, simplify, simplify, at the core of these changes is Easterbrook's desire to strip away the bureaucracy at McDonald's so the firm can anticipate trends as a foundation for moving nimbly and to fully understand and appropriately respond to customers' interests. Additionally, Easterbrook specified that the new structure should be built on "commercial logic" rather than simply geography.

With all of this as a background, a decision was made to restructure McDonald's into "four segments that combine markets with similar needs, challenges, and opportunities for growth." As of July 2015, McDonald's organizational structure found the firm organized into the following market segments:

1. *United States* (the largest market that accounts for over 40 percent of total firm revenue)
2. *International lead markets* (Australia, Canada, France, Germany, and the United Kingdom—markets with similar economic conditions and competitive dynamics that yield similar growth opportunities)
3. *High-growth markets* ("markets with relatively higher restaurant expansion and franchising potential including China, Italy, Poland, Russia, South Korea, Spain, Switzerland, and the Netherlands")
4. *Foundational markets* (all remaining markets in McDonald's system with each market having the potential to operate largely as a franchised model)

The countries shown in the color red are ones in which McDonald's has locations.

Courtesy of AG's Globalization

Will this new organizational structure contribute to McDonald's effort to increase revenues and profitability? Corporate officials are optimistic that this will prove to be the case. More specifically, the firm's leaders are confident the new structure will enable individual segments to identify and successfully address what are common needs of their markets and flexible organizational structure allows the firm to *exploit* current competitive advantages while *developing* new advantages that can be used in the future.[19] Alternatively, an ineffective structure that is inflexible may drive productive employees away because of frustration and an inability to create value while completing their work. Losing productive employees can result in a loss of knowledge within a firm. This is an especially damaging outcome when a departing employee, who may accept employment with a competitor, possesses a significant amount of tacit knowledge.

Modifications to the firm's current strategy or selection of a new strategy call for changes to its organizational structure. However, research shows that once in place, organizational inertia often inhibits efforts to change structure, even when the firm's performance suggests that it is time to do so.[20] In his pioneering work, Alfred Chandler found that organizations change their structures when inefficiencies force them to do so.[21] Chandler's contributions to our understanding of organizational structure and its relationship to strategies and performance are significant. Indeed, some believe that Chandler's emphasis on "organizational structure so transformed the field of business history that some call the period before Chandler's work was published 'B.C.,' meaning 'before Chandler.'"[22]

Firms seem to prefer the structural status quo and its familiar working relationships until their performance declines to the point where change is absolutely necessary.[23] Moreover, top-level managers often hesitate to conclude that the firm's structure or its strategy are the problem because doing so suggests that their previous choices were not the best ones. Because of these inertial tendencies, structural change is often induced instead by actions from stakeholders (e.g., those from the capital market and customers) who are no longer willing to tolerate the firm's performance. For example, this happened at large department store operator J. C. Penney, as the former CEO, Myron Ullman, replaced a relatively new CEO, Ron Johnson, whose turnaround strategy failed.[24] Additionally, some believe that Penney has yet to recover from the effects of the decisions Johnson made during his short 18-month tenure as the retailer's CEO.[25] Evidence shows that appropriate timing of structural change happens when top-level managers recognize that a current organizational structure

The New York times

Pictured here is Alfred Chandler, a scholar whose work enhanced our understanding of organizational structure and strategy.

no longer provides the coordination and direction needed for the firm to successfully implement its strategies.[26] Interestingly, many organizational changes take place in economic downturns because poor performance reveals organizational weaknesses. As we discuss next, effective organizational controls help managers recognize when it is time to adjust the firm's structure.

11-1b Organizational Controls

Organizational controls are an important aspect of structure.[27] **Organizational controls** guide the use of strategy, indicate how to compare actual results with expected results, and suggest corrective actions to take when the difference is unacceptable. It is difficult for a firm to successfully exploit its competitive advantages without effective organizational controls. Properly designed organizational controls provide clear insights regarding behaviors that enhance firm performance.[28] Firms use both strategic controls and financial controls to support implementation of their strategies.

Strategic controls are largely subjective criteria intended to verify that the firm is using appropriate strategies for the conditions in the external environment and the company's competitive advantages. Thus, strategic controls are concerned with examining the fit between what the firm *might do* (as suggested by opportunities in its external environment) and what it *can do* (as indicated by its internal organization in the form of its resources, capabilities, and core competencies). Effective strategic controls help the firm understand what it takes to be successful, especially where significant strategic change is needed.[29] Strategic controls demand rich communications between managers responsible for using them to judge the firm's performance and those with primary responsibility for implementing the firm's strategies (such as middle- and first-level managers). These frequent exchanges between managers are both formal and informal in nature.[30]

Strategic controls are also used to evaluate the degree to which the firm focuses on the requirements to implement its strategies. For a business-level strategy, for example, the strategic controls are used to study value chain activities and support functions (see Figures 3.3, 3.4, and 3.5, in Chapter 3) to verify that the critical activities and functions are being emphasized and properly executed. When implementing related diversification strategies at the corporate level, strategic controls are used to verify the sharing of activities (in the case of the related-constrained strategy) or the transferring of core competencies (in the case of the related-linked strategy) across businesses. To effectively use strategic controls when evaluating either of these related diversification strategies, headquarter executives must have a deep understanding of the business-level strategies being implemented within individual strategic business units.[31]

Financial controls are largely objective criteria used to measure the firm's performance against previously established quantitative standards. When using financial controls, firms evaluate their current performance against previous outcomes as well as against competitors' performance and industry averages. Accounting-based measures, such as return on investment (ROI) and return on assets (ROA), as well as market-based measures, such as economic value added, are examples of financial controls. Partly because strategic controls are difficult to use with extensive diversification,[32] financial controls are emphasized to evaluate the performance of the firm using the unrelated diversification strategy. The unrelated diversification strategy's focus on financial outcomes (see Chapter 6) requires using standardized financial controls to compare performances between business units and those responsible for leading them.[33]

Both strategic and financial controls are important aspects of a firm's structure; as noted previously, any structure's effectiveness is determined using a "balanced" combination of strategic and financial controls. But, determining the most appropriate balance

Organizational controls guide the use of strategy, indicate how to compare actual results with expected results, and suggest corrective actions to take when the difference is unacceptable.

Strategic controls are largely subjective criteria intended to verify that the firm is using appropriate strategies for the conditions in the external environment and the company's competitive advantages.

Financial controls are largely objective criteria used to measure the firm's performance against previously established quantitative standards.

to have in place between strategic and financial controls at specific points in time is challenging, partly because the relative use of controls varies by type of strategy. For example, companies and business units of large diversified firms using the cost leadership strategy emphasize financial controls (such as quantitative cost goals), while companies and business units using the differentiation strategy emphasize strategic controls (such as subjective measures of the effectiveness of product development teams).[34] As previously explained, a corporation-wide emphasis on sharing among business units (as called for by related diversification strategies) results in an emphasis on strategic controls, while financial controls are emphasized for strategies in which activities or capabilities are not shared (e.g., in an unrelated diversification strategy). Those determining how strategies are to be implemented must keep these relative degrees of balance between controls by type of strategy in mind when making implementation-related decisions.

11-2 Relationships between Strategy and Structure

Strategy and structure have a reciprocal relationship, and if aligned properly, performance improves.[35] This relationship highlights the interconnectedness between strategy formulation (Chapters 4, 6–9) and strategy implementation (Chapters 10–13). In general, this reciprocal relationship finds structure flowing from or following selection of the firm's strategy. Once in place though, structure can influence current strategic actions as well as choices about future strategies. The new structure in place at McDonald's that we mentioned earlier has the potential to influence implementation of strategies that are, in part, aimed to better identify and satisfy customers' changing needs.[36] Overall, those involved with a firm's strategic management process should understand that the general nature of the strategy/structure relationship means that changes to the firm's strategy create the need to change how the organization completes its work.

Moreover, because structure can influence strategy by constraining the potential alternatives considered, firms must be vigilant in their efforts to verify how their structure not only affects implementation of chosen strategies, but also the limits the structure placed on possible future strategies. Overall though, the effect of strategy on structure is stronger than is the effect of structure on strategy.

Regardless of the strength of the reciprocal relationships between strategy and structure, those choosing the firm's strategy and structure should be committed to matching each strategy with a structure that provides the stability needed to use current competitive advantages as well as the flexibility required to develop future advantages. Therefore, when changing strategies, the firm should simultaneously consider the structure that will be needed to support use of the new strategy; properly matching strategy and structure can create a competitive advantage. This process can be influenced by outside forces, such as significant media attention, which may either hinder the change or foster it.[37]

11-3 Evolutionary Patterns of Strategy and Organizational Structure

Research suggests that most firms experience a certain pattern of relationships between strategy and structure. Chandler[38] found that firms tend to grow in somewhat predictable patterns: "first by volume, then by geography, then integration (vertical, horizontal), and finally through product/business diversification"[39] (see Figure 11.1). Chandler interpreted his findings as an indication that firms' growth patterns determine their structural form.

Figure 11.1 Strategy and Structure Growth Pattern

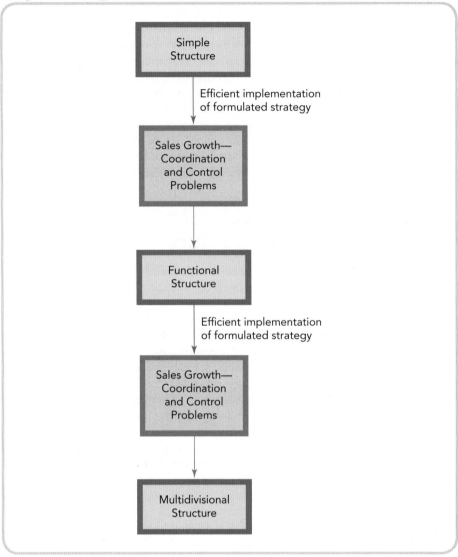

As shown in Figure 11.1, sales growth creates coordination and control problems the existing organizational structure cannot efficiently handle. Organizational growth creates the opportunity for the firm to change its strategy to try to become even more successful. However, the existing structure's formal reporting relationships, procedures, controls, and authority and decision-making processes lack the sophistication required to support using the new strategy,[40] meaning that a new organizational structure is needed.[41]

Firms choose from among three major types of organizational structures—simple, functional, and multidivisional—to implement strategies. Across time, successful firms move from the simple, to the functional, to the multidivisional structure to support changes in their growth strategies.

11-3a Simple Structure

The **simple structure** is a structure in which the owner-manager makes all major decisions and monitors all activities, while the staff serves as an extension of the manager's

The **simple structure** is a structure in which the owner-manager makes all major decisions and monitors all activities, while the staff serves as an extension of the manager's supervisory authority.

supervisory authority.[42] Typically, the owner-manager actively works in the business on a daily basis. Informal relationships, few rules, limited task specialization, and unsophisticated information systems characterize this structure. Frequent and informal communications between the owner-manager and employees make coordinating the work to be completed relatively easy. The simple structure is matched with focus strategies and business-level strategies, as firms implementing these strategies commonly compete by offering a single product line in a single geographic market. Local restaurants, repair businesses, and other specialized enterprises are examples of firms using the simple structure.

As the small firm grows larger and becomes more complex, managerial and structural challenges emerge. For example, the amount of competitively relevant information requiring analysis substantially increases, placing significant pressure on the owner-manager. Additional growth and success may cause the firm to change its strategy. Even if the strategy remains the same, the firm's larger size dictates the need for more sophisticated workflows and integrating mechanisms. At this evolutionary point, firms tend to move from the simple structure to a functional organizational structure.[43]

11-3b Functional Structure

The **functional structure** consists of a chief executive officer and a limited corporate staff, with functional line managers in dominant organizational areas such as production, accounting, marketing, R&D, engineering, and human resources.[44] This structure allows for functional specialization,[45] thereby facilitating active sharing of knowledge within each functional area. Knowledge sharing facilitates career paths as well as professional development of functional specialists. However, a functional orientation can negatively affect communication and coordination among those representing different organizational functions. For this reason, the CEO must verify that the decisions and actions of individual business functions promote the entire firm rather than a single function. The functional structure supports implementing business-level strategies and some corporate-level strategies (e.g., single or dominant business) with low levels of diversification. However, when changing from a simple to a functional structure, firms want to avoid introducing value-destroying bureaucratic procedures since such procedures typically have the potential to damage individuals' efforts to innovate as a means of supporting strategy implementation activities.

11-3c Multidivisional Structure

With continuing growth and success, firms often consider greater levels of diversification. Successfully using a diversification strategy requires analyzing substantially greater amounts of data and information when the firm offers the same products in different markets (market or geographic diversification) or offers different products in several markets (product diversification). In addition, trying to manage high levels of diversification through functional structures creates serious coordination and control problems,[46] a fact that commonly leads to a new structural form.[47]

The **multidivisional (M-form) structure** consists of a corporate office and operating divisions, each operating division representing a separate business or profit center in which the top corporate officer delegates responsibilities for day-to-day operations and business-unit strategy to division managers. Each division represents a distinct, self-contained business with its own functional hierarchy.[48] As initially designed, the M-form was thought to have three major benefits: "(1) it enabled corporate officers to more accurately monitor the performance of each business, which simplified the problem of control; (2) it facilitated comparisons between divisions, which improved the resource allocation process; and (3) it stimulated managers of poorly performing divisions to look for ways of improving performance."[49] Active monitoring of performance through the M-form increases the likelihood that decisions made

The **functional structure** consists of a chief executive officer and a limited corporate staff, with functional line managers in dominant organizational areas such as production, accounting, marketing, R&D, engineering, and human resources.

The **multidivisional (M-form) structure** consists of a corporate office and operating divisions, each operating division representing a separate business or profit center in which the top corporate officer delegates responsibilities for day-to-day operations and business-unit strategy to division managers.

by managers heading individual units will be in stakeholders' best interests. Because diversification is a dominant corporate-level strategy used in the global economy, the M-form is a widely adopted organizational structure.[50]

Used to support implementation of related and unrelated diversification strategies, the M-form helps firms successfully manage diversification's many demands.[51] Chandler viewed the M-form as an innovative response to coordination and control problems that surfaced during the 1920s in the functional structures then used by large firms such as DuPont and General Motors.[52] Research shows that the M-form is appropriate when the firm grows through diversification.[53] Partly because of its value to diversified corporations, some consider the multidivisional structure to be one of the twentieth century's most significant organizational innovations.[54]

No single organizational structure (simple, functional, or multidivisional) is inherently superior to the others. Peter Drucker says the following about this matter:

"There is no one right organization…. Rather the task … is to select the organization for the particular task and mission at hand."[55]

This statement suggests that the firm must select a structure that is "right" for successfully using the chosen strategy. Because no single structure is optimal in all instances, managers concentrate on developing proper matches between strategies and organizational structures rather than searching for an "optimal" structure. We now describe the strategy/structure matches that contribute positively to firm performance.

11-3d Matches between Business-Level Strategies and the Functional Structure

Firms use different forms of the functional organizational structure to support implementing the cost leadership, differentiation, and integrated cost leadership/differentiation strategies. The differences in these forms are accounted for primarily by different uses of three important structural characteristics: *specialization* (concerned with the type and number of jobs required to complete work[56]), *centralization* (the degree to which decision-making authority is retained at higher managerial levels[57]), and *formalization* (the degree to which formal rules and procedures govern work[58]).

Using the Functional Structure to Implement the Cost Leadership Strategy

Firms using the cost leadership strategy sell large quantities of standardized products to an industry's typical customer. Firms using this strategy need a structure that allows them to achieve efficiencies and produce their products at costs lower than those of competitors.[59] Simple reporting relationships, a few layers in the decision-making and authority structure, a centralized corporate staff, and a strong focus on process improvements through the manufacturing function rather than the development of new products by emphasizing product R&D help to achieve the needed efficiencies and thus characterize the cost leadership form of the functional structure[60] (see Figure 11.2). This structure contributes to the emergence of a low-cost culture—a culture in which employees constantly try to find ways to reduce the costs incurred to complete their work.[61] They can do this through the development of a product design that is simple and easy to manufacture, as well as through the development of efficient processes to produce the goods.[62]

In terms of centralization, decision-making authority is centralized in a staff function to maintain a cost-reducing emphasis within each organizational function (engineering, marketing, etc.). While encouraging continuous cost reductions, the centralized staff also verifies that further cuts in costs in one function won't adversely affect the productivity levels in other functions.[63]

Figure 11.2 Functional Structure for Implementing a Cost Leadership Strategy

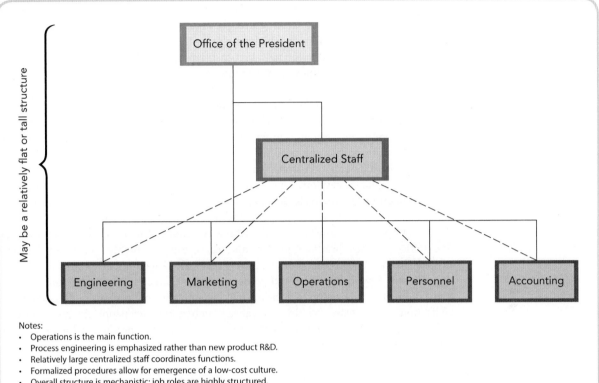

Notes:
- Operations is the main function.
- Process engineering is emphasized rather than new product R&D.
- Relatively large centralized staff coordinates functions.
- Formalized procedures allow for emergence of a low-cost culture.
- Overall structure is mechanistic; job roles are highly structured.

Jobs are highly specialized in the cost leadership functional structure; work is divided into homogeneous subgroups. Organizational functions are the most common subgroup, although work is sometimes batched on the basis of products produced or clients served. Specializing in their work allows employees to increase their efficiency, resulting in reduced costs. Guiding individuals' work in this structure are highly formalized rules and procedures, which often emanate from the centralized staff.

Walmart Stores, Inc. uses the functional structure to implement cost leadership strategies in each of its three operating segments (Walmart U.S., Sam's Clubs, and Walmart International). In the Walmart U.S. segment (which generates the largest share of the firm's total sales), the cost leadership strategy is used in the firm's Supercenter, Discount, Neighborhood Market, and digital retail formats.[64] For the entire corporation, the firm says that it is committed to "saving people money so they can live better."[65] Over the years, competitors' efforts to duplicate the success Walmart has achieved by implementing its cost leadership strategies have generally failed, partly because of the effective strategy/structure matches the firm has formed between the cost leadership strategy and the functional structure that is specific to the mandates of that strategy.

Using the Functional Structure to Implement the Differentiation Strategy

Firms using the differentiation strategy seek to produce products that customers perceive as being different in ways that create value for them. With this strategy, the firm sells nonstandardized products to customers with unique needs. Relatively complex and flexible reporting relationships, frequent use of cross-functional product development teams, and a strong focus on marketing and product R&D rather than manufacturing and process R&D (as with the cost leadership form of the functional structure) characterize the differentiation form of the functional structure (see Figure 11.3). From this structure emerges a development-oriented culture in which employees try to find ways to further differentiate current products and to develop new, highly differentiated products.[66]

Continuous product innovation demands that people throughout the firm interpret and take action based on information that is often ambiguous, incomplete, and uncertain. Following a strong focus on the external environment to identify new opportunities, employees often gather this information from people outside the firm (e.g., customers and suppliers). Commonly, rapid responses to the possibilities indicated by the collected information are necessary, suggesting the need for decentralized decision-making responsibility and authority. The differentiation strategy also needs a structure through which a strong technological capability is developed and strategic flexibility characterizes how the firm operates while competing against rivals. A strong technological capability and strategic flexibility enhance the firm's ability to take advantage of opportunities that changes in markets create.[67]

To support the creativity needed and the continuous pursuit of new sources of differentiation and new products, jobs in this structure are not highly specialized. This lack of specialization means that workers have a relatively large number of tasks in their job descriptions. Few formal rules and procedures also characterize this structure. Low formalization, decentralization of decision-making authority and responsibility, and low specialization of work tasks combine to create a structure in which people interact frequently to exchange ideas about how to further differentiate current products while developing ideas for new products that can be crisply differentiated at a point in the future.

Under Armour uses a differentiation strategy and matching structure to achieve success in the sports apparel market. Under Armour's objective is to create improved athletic

Figure 11.3 Functional Structure for Implementing a Differentiation Strategy

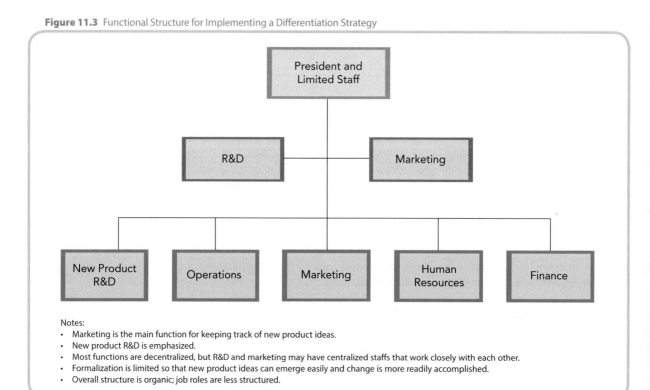

Notes:
- Marketing is the main function for keeping track of new product ideas.
- New product R&D is emphasized.
- Most functions are decentralized, but R&D and marketing may have centralized staffs that work closely with each other.
- Formalization is limited so that new product ideas can emerge easily and change is more readily accomplished.
- Overall structure is organic; job roles are less structured.

performance for customers through innovative design, testing, and marketing. The firm targets its products to athletes at all skill levels, from the novice to the professional. For each customer, the firm intends for its products to help that person improve her/his performance by using Under Armour's products. Calling it a "Universal Guarantee of Performance" (or UGOP), the firm says that its guarantee "means that every Under Armour product is doing something for you: it's making you better."[68]

Syda Productions/Shutterstock.com

When exercising, as is the case for this person, individuals wearing Under Armour gear and equipment may believe that the firm's products will "make them better."

Using the Functional Structure to Implement the Integrated Cost Leadership/Differentiation Strategy

Firms using the integrated cost leadership/differentiation strategy sell products that create value because of their relatively low cost and reasonable sources of differentiation. The cost of these products is low "relative" to the cost leader's prices, while their differentiation is "reasonable" when compared to the clearly unique features of the differentiator's products.

Although challenging to implement, the integrated cost leadership/differentiation strategy is used frequently in the global economy. The challenge of using this strategy is due largely to the fact that different value chain and support activities (see Chapter 3) are emphasized when using the cost leadership and differentiation strategies. To achieve the cost leadership position, production and process engineering need to be emphasized, with infrequent product changes. To achieve a differentiated position, marketing and new product R&D need to be emphasized while production and process engineering are not. Thus, effective use of the integrated strategy depends on the firm's successful combination of activities intended to reduce costs with activities intended to create differentiated features for a product. As a result, the integrated form of the functional structure must have decision-making patterns that are partially centralized and partially decentralized. Additionally, jobs are semispecialized, and rules and procedures call for some formal and some informal job behavior. All of this requires a measure of flexibility to emphasize one or the other set of functions at any given time.[69]

11-3e Matches between Corporate-Level Strategies and the Multidivisional Structure

As explained earlier, Chandler's research shows that the firm's continuing success leads to product or market diversification or both.[70] The firm's level of diversification is a function of decisions about the number and type of businesses in which it will compete as well as how it will manage those businesses (see Chapter 6). Geared to managing individual organizational functions, increasing diversification eventually creates information processing, coordination, and control problems that the functional structure cannot handle. Thus, using a diversification strategy requires the firm to change from the functional structure to the multidivisional structure to form an appropriate strategy/structure match.

As defined in Figure 6.1, corporate-level strategies have different degrees of product and market diversification. The demands created by different levels of diversification highlight the need for a unique organizational structure to effectively implement each

Figure 11.4 Three Variations of the Multidivisional Structure

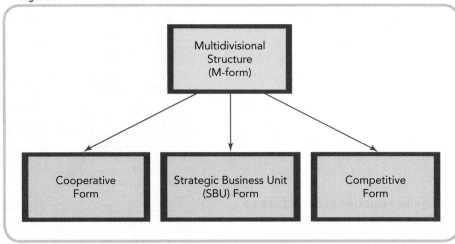

strategy (see Figure 11.4). We discuss the relationships between three diversification strategies and the unique organizational structure that should be matched with each one in the next three sections.

Using the Cooperative Form of the Multidivisional Structure to Implement the Related Constrained Strategy

The **cooperative form** is an M-form structure in which horizontal integration is used to bring about interdivisional cooperation. Divisions in a firm using the related constrained diversification strategy commonly are formed around products, markets, or both. In Figure 11.5, we use product divisions as part of the representation of the cooperative form of the multidivisional structure, although market divisions could be used instead of or in addition to product divisions to develop the figure.

We mentioned in Chapter 6 that Procter & Gamble (P&G) uses a related constrained strategy. We note here that the firm matches the cooperative form of the multidivisional structure to this strategy in order to effectively implement it.

As explained in Chapter 6, the related constrained strategy finds a firm sharing resources and activities across its businesses. Consumer understanding, scale, innovation, go-to-market capabilities, and brand-building are what P&G has identified as its five "core strengths" (or core resources). These strengths are shared across the four industry-based sectors that form the core of P&G's cooperative multidivisional organizational structure. These sectors are Baby, Feminine and Family Care; Beauty, Hair and Personal Care; Fabric and Home Care; and Health and Grooming. The reason P&G shares its five core strengths across the four industry-based sectors is that, according to the firm, these sectors are all "focused on common consumer benefits, share common technologies, and face common competitors."[71] Thus, through its organizational structure, P&G integrates its operations horizontally for the purpose of developing cooperation across the four sectors in which it competes.

Sharing divisional competencies facilitates a firm's efforts to develop economies of scope. As explained in Chapter 6, economies of scope (cost savings resulting from the sharing of competencies developed in one division with another division) are linked with successful use of the related constrained strategy. Interdivisional sharing of competencies, such as takes place within P&G, depends on cooperation, suggesting the use of the cooperative form of the multidivisional structure.[72]

The cooperative structure uses different characteristics of structure (centralization, standardization, and formalization) as integrating mechanisms to facilitate interdivisional cooperation. Frequent, direct contact between division managers, another

The **cooperative form** is an M-form structure in which horizontal integration is used to bring about interdivisional cooperation.

Figure 11.5 Cooperative Form of the Multidivisional Structure for Implementing a Related Constrained Strategy

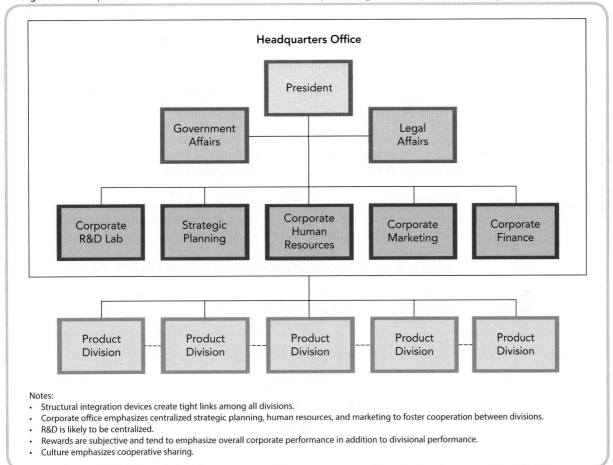

Notes:
- Structural integration devices create tight links among all divisions.
- Corporate office emphasizes centralized strategic planning, human resources, and marketing to foster cooperation between divisions.
- R&D is likely to be centralized.
- Rewards are subjective and tend to emphasize overall corporate performance in addition to divisional performance.
- Culture emphasizes cooperative sharing.

integrating mechanism, encourages and supports cooperation and the sharing of knowledge, capabilities, or other resources that could be used to create new advantages.[73] Sometimes, liaison roles are established in each division to reduce the time division managers spend integrating and coordinating their unit's work with the work occurring in other divisions. Temporary teams or task forces may be formed around projects whose success depends on sharing resources that are embedded within several divisions. Formal integration departments might be established in firms frequently using temporary teams or task forces.

Ultimately, a matrix organization may evolve in firms implementing the related constrained strategy. A *matrix organization* is an organizational structure in which there is a dual structure combining both functional specialization and business product or project specialization.[74] Although complicated, an effective matrix structure can lead to improved coordination among a firm's divisions.[75]

The success of the cooperative multidivisional structure is significantly affected by how well divisions process information. However, because cooperation among divisions implies a loss of managerial autonomy, division managers may not readily commit themselves to the type of integrative information-processing activities that this structure demands. Moreover, coordination among divisions sometimes results in an unequal flow of positive outcomes to divisional managers. In other words, when managerial rewards are based at least in part on the performance of individual divisions, the manager of the division that is able to benefit the most by the sharing of corporate competencies might be viewed as receiving relative gains at others' expense. Strategic controls are important in these instances, as divisional managers' performances can be evaluated, at least partly, on the basis of how well they have facilitated interdivisional cooperative efforts. In addition, using reward systems that emphasize overall company performance, besides outcomes achieved by individual divisions, helps overcome problems associated with the cooperative form. Still, the costs of coordination and inertia in organizations limit the amount of related diversification attempted (i.e., they constrain the economies of scope that can be created).[76]

Using the Strategic Business Unit Form of the Multidivisional Structure to Implement the Related Linked Strategy

The **strategic business unit (SBU) form** is an M-form consisting of three levels: corporate headquarters, strategic business units (SBUs), and SBU divisions.

Firms with fewer links or less constrained links among their divisions use the related linked diversification strategy. The strategic business unit form of the multidivisional structure supports implementation of this strategy. The **strategic business unit (SBU) form** is an M-form consisting of three levels: corporate headquarters, strategic business units (SBUs), and SBU divisions (see Figure 11.6). The SBU structure is used by large firms and can be complex, given associated organization size and product and market diversity.

Figure 11.6 SBU Form of the Multidivisional Structure for Implementing a Related Linked Strategy

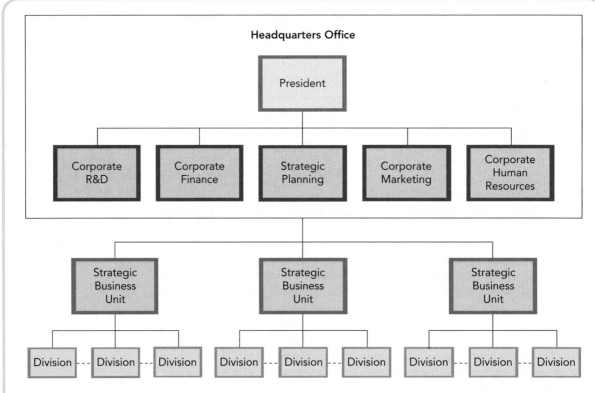

Notes:
- Structural integration among divisions within SBUs, but independence across SBUs.
- Strategic planning may be the most prominent function in headquarters for managing the strategic planning approval process of SBUs for the president.
- Each SBU may have its own budget for staff to foster integration.
- Corporate headquarters staff members serve as consultants to SBUs and divisions, rather than having direct input to product strategy, as in the cooperative form.

The divisions within each SBU are related in terms of shared products or markets or both, but the divisions of one SBU have little in common with the divisions of the other SBUs. Divisions within each SBU share product or market competencies to develop economies of scope and possibly economies of scale. The integrating mechanisms used by the divisions in this structure can be equally well used by the divisions within the individual strategic business units that are part of the SBU form of the multidivisional structure. In this structure, each SBU is a profit center that is controlled and evaluated by the headquarters office. Although both financial and strategic controls are important, on a relative basis, financial controls are vital to headquarters' evaluation of each SBU; strategic controls are critical when the heads of SBUs evaluate their divisions' performances. Strategic controls are also critical to the headquarters' efforts to evaluate the quality of the portfolio of businesses that has been formed and to determine if those businesses are being successfully managed. Sharing competencies among units within individual SBUs is an important characteristic of the SBU form of the multidivisional structure (see the notes to Figure 11.6).

A disadvantage associated with the related linked diversification strategy is that, even when efforts to implement it are being properly supported by use of the SBU form of the multidivisional structure, firms using this strategy and structure combination find it challenging to effectively communicate the value of their operations to shareholders and to other investors.[77] Furthermore, if coordination between SBUs is required, problems can surface because the SBU structure, similar to the competitive form discussed next, does not readily foster cooperation across SBUs. Accordingly, those responsible for implementing the related linked strategy must focus on successfully creating and using the types of integrating mechanisms we discussed earlier.

For many years, Sony Corporation used the related constrained strategy and the cooperative form of the multidivisional structure to implement it. Today though, and in response to declining firm performance, Sony appears to be using the related linked strategy and the SBU form of the multidivisional structure to implement what is a new strategy for the firm. As we discuss in the Strategic Focus, changes to the firm's strategy and organizational structure have occurred recently in order to increase Sony's efficiency (essentially, doing things *right*) and effectiveness (essentially, doing the *right* things).

Using the Competitive Form of the Multidivisional Structure to Implement the Unrelated Diversification Strategy

Firms using the unrelated diversification strategy want to create value through efficient internal capital allocations or by restructuring, buying, and selling businesses.[78] The competitive form of the multidivisional structure supports implementation of this strategy.

The **competitive form** is an M-form structure characterized by complete independence among the firm's divisions that compete for corporate resources (see Figure 11.7). Unlike the divisions included in the cooperative structure, divisions that are part of the competitive structure do not share common corporate strengths. Accordingly, integrating mechanisms are not part of the competitive form of the multidivisional structure.

The efficient internal capital market that is the foundation for using the unrelated diversification strategy requires organizational arrangements emphasizing divisional competition rather than cooperation.[79] Three benefits are expected from the internal competition. First, internal competition creates flexibility (e.g., corporate headquarters can have divisions working on different technologies and projects to identify those with the greatest potential). Resources can then be allocated to the division appearing to have the most potential to drive the entire firm's success. Second, internal competition challenges the status quo and inertia because division heads know that future resource allocations are a product of excellent current performance as well as superior positioning in terms of future performance. Third, internal competition motivates effort in that the challenge of

The **competitive form** is an M-form structure characterized by complete independence among the firm's divisions that compete for corporate resources.

Strategic **Focus**

Sony Corporation's New Organizational Structure: Greater Financial Accountability and Focused Allocations of Resources

Launched in 1946 in Japan, Sony gained a reputation for producing innovative products that were sold throughout the world. In fact, the firm's success was instrumental to Japan's development as a powerful exporter during the 1960s, 1970s, and 1980s. Sony was sometimes "first to market" with an innovative product, while sometimes being able to rapidly enhance a product's capabilities by innovating. Introduced in 1979, the Sony Walkman, which was a personal stereo tape deck, is an example of a "first to market" product from Sony. The transistor radio is a product that Sony innovated in a way that made the product, which was initially developed through a joint venture between Regency Electronics and Texas Instruments, commercially viable. Regardless of the type, innovation has been critical to how Sony competes in multiple product areas.

Realizing the value that could be gained by sharing resources, capabilities, and core competencies across types of businesses, Sony's success for many decades was a product of its commitment to "convergence," which the firm operationalized by linking its activities across businesses such as film, music, and digital electronics. In essence, Sony was successful for many years as a result of being able to effectively implement the related constrained strategy. But as we mentioned earlier when discussing the related constrained strategy and the structure needed to implement it, an inability to efficiently process information and coordinate an array of integrated activities between units are problems that may surface when using the cooperative form of the multidivisional structure. This appears to be the case for Sony. In response to performance problems that have plagued the firm for over a decade, Sony's CEO recently announced significant changes to the company's organizational structure. Put into place in October 2015, these structural changes are thought to be the foundation for improvements to Sony's ability to create value for customers and enhance wealth for shareholders.

At the core of the structural changes are efforts to group the firm's businesses in ways that allow Sony's upper-level leaders to more effectively allocate financial capital. A key objective is to allocate capital to the businesses with the strongest potential not just to grow, but to grow profitably.

Sony is now structured into three core sectors or business units—*growth drivers, stable profit generators,* and *volatility management.* In essence, the new structure is an example of the SBU form of the multidivisional structure. According to the CEO, these units have been formed to "emphasize profitability over volume, secure business unit autonomy with a focus on shareholder value, and provide a clearer definition of each business unit's position within Sony's overall business." Devices, Game & Network Services, Pictures, and Music comprise the growth drivers unit. Viewed as potentially profitable areas of growth, Sony intends to invest aggressively to support these businesses. Imaging Products & Solutions and Video and Sound are the business areas forming the stable profit generators unit. These businesses are expected to yield steady profits and positive cash flows. Finally, TV and Mobile Communications formed the volatility management unit. Operating in markets with high volatility and challenging competitive conditions, the intention with this unit is to find ways to generate stable profits. For all three units, Return on Equity (ROE) is the performance criterion being used to judge the success of each business that is included in one of the units. Each business is expected to achieve an annual ROE of 10 percent.

Pictured here is Sony's PS Vita as it was introduced during a shown in San Francisco, CA.

Three goals are being sought by using the SBU form of the multidivisional structure. First, Sony's CEO wants the organizational structure to be one that clearly promotes accountability and responsibility for each unit. The second goal "is to foster management policies and direction that place an emphasis on sustainable profit generation and the continuity of each business unit." The third goal revolves around the intention of continuing to eliminate unnecessary managerial layers as a means of enhancing innovation on the part of everyone involved with each business in each unit.

Sony's CEO is confident that the firm's commitment to implementing the SBU form of the multidivisional structure as a foundation for using the related linked strategy will yield positive outcomes. Time will tell if this is the case or not. But, the new organizational structure that has been created at Sony Corporation does appear to be one with the potential to support efforts to successfully use the related linked strategy.

Sources: 2015, Corporate Information, Sony Home Page, www.sony.com, May 17; 2015, Here's Sony's new business strategy, *Business Insider*, www.businessinsider.com, February 21; T. Mochizuki & E. Pfanner, 2015, Sony expects profits to surge this fiscal year, *Wall Street Journal Online*, www.wsj.com, April 30; T. Mochizuki & E. Pfanner, How Sony makes money off Apple's iPhone, *Wall Street Journal Online*, www.wsj.com, April 28; E. Pfanner & T. Mochizuki, 2015, Sony's mobile unit seeks profit, innovation, *Wall Street Journal Online*, www.wsj.com, March 2; M. Schilling, 2015, Sony strategy centers on splitting businesses, not selling—for now, *Variety*, www.variety.com, February 26.

Figure 11.7 Competitive Form of the Multidivisional Structure for Implementing an Unrelated Strategy

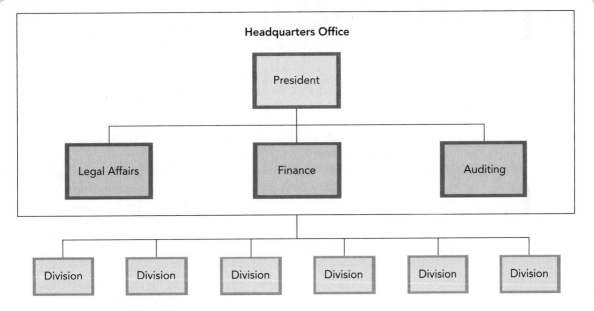

Notes:
- Corporate headquarters has a small staff.
- Finance and auditing are the most prominent functions in the headquarters office to manage cash flow and assure the accuracy of performance data coming from divisions.
- The legal affairs function becomes important when the firm acquires or divests assets.
- Divisions are independent and separate for financial evaluation purposes.
- Divisions retain strategic control, but cash is managed by the corporate office.
- Divisions compete for corporate resources.

competing against internal peers can be as great as the challenge of competing against external rivals.[80] In this structure, organizational controls (primarily financial controls) are used to emphasize and support internal competition among separate divisions and as the basis for allocating corporate capital based on divisions' performances.

Textron Inc., a large "multi-industry" company, seeks to identify, research, select, acquire, and integrate companies and has developed a set of rigorous criteria to guide decision making. Textron continuously looks to enhance and reshape its portfolio by divesting noncore

Pictured here is a Bell Helicopter, a product manufactured by one of Textron's business units.

assets and acquiring branded businesses in attractive industries with substantial long-term growth potential. Textron operates a number of independent businesses including Bell Helicopter, Textron Aviation, Textron Specialized Vehicles, and Textron Finance. Leaders of these businesses are responsible for effectively guiding the day-to-day competitive actions of their units. Consistent with the mandates of the competitive form of the multidivisional structure, "Textron's Corporate Office provides oversight, direction, and assistance to its businesses."[81] The profit earned by individual business units within Textron is an important measure the firm uses to decide future capital allocations.[82]

To emphasize competitiveness among divisions, the headquarters office maintains an arm's-length relationship with them, intervening in divisional affairs only to audit operations and discipline managers whose divisions perform poorly. In emphasizing competition between divisions, the headquarters office relies on strategic controls to set rate-of-return targets and financial controls to monitor divisional performance relative to those targets. The headquarters office then allocates cash flow on a competitive basis, rather than automatically returning cash to the division that produced it. Thus, the focus of the headquarters' work is on performance appraisal, resource allocation, and long-range planning to verify that the firm's portfolio of businesses will lead to financial success.

As is the case with the related linked diversification strategy, investors and shareholders find it challenging to understand the underlying value of the set of business units associated with a firm implementing the unrelated diversification strategy.[83] Because of this, upper-level managers must find effective ways of communicating their firm's underlying value to those investing capital in the firm.

The three major forms of the multidivisional structure should each be paired with a particular corporate-level strategy. Table 11.1 shows these structures' characteristics.

Table 11.1 Characteristics of the Structures Necessary to Implement the Related Constrained, Related Linked, and Unrelated Diversification Strategies

Structural Characteristics	Overall Structural Form		
	Cooperative M-Form (Related Constrained Strategy)	SBU M-Form (Related Linked Strategy)	Competitive M-Form (Unrelated Diversification Strategy)
Centralization of operations	Centralized at corporate office	Partially centralized (in SBUs)	Decentralized to divisions
Use of integration mechanisms	Extensive	Moderate	Nonexistent
Divisional performance evaluation	Emphasizes subjective (strategic) criteria	Uses a mixture of subjective (strategic) and objective (financial) criteria	Emphasizes objective (financial) criteria
Divisional incentive compensation	Linked to overall corporate performance	Mixed linkage to corporate, SBU, and divisional performance	Linked to divisional performance

Differences exist in the degree of centralization, the focus of the performance evaluation, the horizontal structures (integrating mechanisms), and the incentive compensation schemes. The most centralized and most costly structural form is the cooperative structure. The least centralized, with the lowest bureaucratic costs, is the competitive structure. The SBU structure requires partial centralization and involves some of the mechanisms necessary to implement the relatedness between divisions. Also, the divisional incentive compensation awards are allocated according to both SBUs and corporate performance.

11-3f Matches between International Strategies and Worldwide Structure

In Chapter 8 we explained that international strategies are increasingly important for companies' long-term competitive success in what is today virtually a borderless global economy.[84] Among other benefits, firms are able to search for new markets and then form the competencies necessary to serve them when implementing an international strategy.[85]

As with business-level and corporate-level strategies, unique organizational structures are necessary to successfully implement individual international strategies, given the different cultural, institutional, and legal environments around the world.[86] Forming proper matches between international strategies and organizational structures facilitates the firm's efforts to effectively coordinate and control its global operations. More importantly, research findings confirm the validity of the international strategy/structure matches we discuss here.[87]

Using the Worldwide Geographic Area Structure to Implement the Multidomestic Strategy

The *multidomestic strategy* decentralizes the firm's strategic and operating decisions to business units in each country so that product characteristics can be tailored to local preferences. Firms using this strategy try to isolate themselves from global competitive forces by establishing protected market positions or by competing in industry segments that are most affected by differences among local countries. The worldwide geographic area structure is used to implement this strategy. The **worldwide geographic area structure** emphasizes national interests and facilitates the firm's efforts to satisfy local differences (see Figure 11.8).

Using the multidomestic strategy requires little coordination between different country markets, meaning that formal integrating mechanisms among divisions around the world are not needed. Indeed, the coordination among units in a firm's worldwide geographic area structure that does take place is informal in nature.

From a historical perspective, we note that the multidomestic strategy/worldwide geographic area structure match evolved as a natural outgrowth of the multicultural European marketplace. Friends and family members of the main business who were sent as expatriates to foreign countries to develop the independent country subsidiary often adopted the worldwide geographic area structure. The relationship to corporate headquarters by divisions took place through informal communication.

Founded in San Francisco, CA, in 2009, Uber Technologies, Inc. claims that it is "evolving the way the world moves by seamlessly connecting riders to drivers through more possibilities for riders and more business for drivers."[88] Now growing rapidly outside its U.S. home market, Asia is the target of Uber's most recent international growth ambitions. Early evidence from the firm's entry into China, obviously a key market in Asia, is encouraging. In fact, the firm's China expansion manager recently said that "China has exceeded our wildest dreams."[89] Seemingly critical to this success is Uber's decision to "go local" in serving Chinese customers. Technology used to track its services, payment systems in place, and the marketing of its operations were all localized in the first 13 Chinese cities in which Uber chose to operate. Indeed, the firm decided to treat each city

The **worldwide geographic area structure** emphasizes national interests and facilitates the firm's efforts to satisfy local differences.

Figure 11.8 Worldwide Geographic Area Structure for Implementing a Multidomestic Strategy

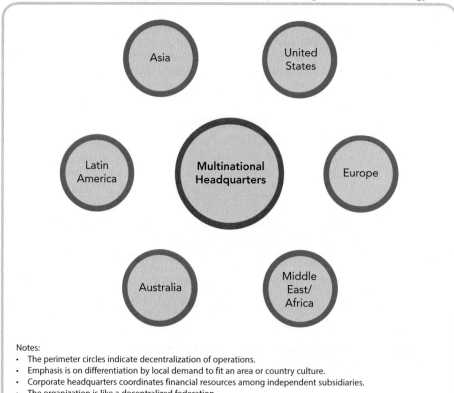

Notes:
- The perimeter circles indicate decentralization of operations.
- Emphasis is on differentiation by local demand to fit an area or country culture.
- Corporate headquarters coordinates financial resources among independent subsidiaries.
- The organization is like a decentralized federation.

as though it was a stand-alone country (facilitating this choice is the fact that each of the 13 cities had a population of 10 million or more).

There is a key challenge associated with effectively using the multidomestic strategy/ worldwide geographic area structure match—namely, the inability to create global efficiencies. This inability is a product of companies' focus on serving unique customer needs particularly well. The inability to create global efficiencies in this match challenges firms to find ways to control costs while trying to serve local customers' unique needs.

Will not being able to create global efficiencies be a problem for Uber? Perhaps. By the same token, as long as the firm can continue to identify and serve the unique needs of customers in different markets in ways that create value for them, being able to develop scale economies will not be a fatal blow to Uber's efforts to succeed in international markets.

In other instances, the nature of products companies seek to sell in international markets and market conditions themselves demand that a firm be able to develop economies of scale on a worldwide basis. This need calls for firms to use the global strategy and its structural match, the worldwide product divisional structure.

Using the Worldwide Product Divisional Structure to Implement the Global Strategy

With the corporation's home office dictating competitive strategy, the *global strategy* is one through which the firm offers standardized products across country markets. The firm's success depends principally on its ability to develop economies of scale while competing on a global basis and while serving customers without specific and unique needs relative to the firm's standardized product.

Figure 11.9 Worldwide Product Divisional Structure for Implementing a Global Strategy

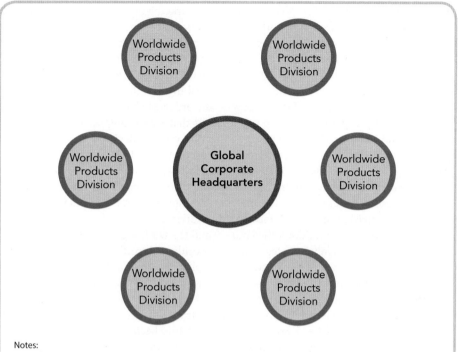

Notes:
- The "headquarters" circle indicates centralization to coordinate information flow among worldwide products.
- Corporate headquarters uses many intercoordination devices to facilitate global economies of scale and scope.
- Corporate headquarters also allocates financial resources in a cooperative way.
- The organization is like a centralized federation.

The worldwide product divisional structure supports use of the global strategy. In the **worldwide product divisional structure**, decision-making authority is centralized in the worldwide division headquarters to coordinate and integrate decisions and actions among divisional business units (see Figure 11.9).

Integrating mechanisms are important to the effective use of the worldwide product divisional structure. Direct contact between managers, liaison roles between departments, and both temporary task forces and permanent teams are examples of these mechanisms. The disadvantages of the global strategy/worldwide structure combination are the difficulties involved with coordinating decisions and actions across country borders and the inability to quickly respond to local needs and preferences. To deal with these types of disadvantages, firms sometimes choose to try to somewhat simultaneously focus on geography and products. This simultaneous focus is similar to the combination structure that we discuss next.

Using the Combination Structure to Implement the Transnational Strategy

The *transnational strategy* calls for the firm to combine the multidomestic strategy's local responsiveness with the global strategy's efficiency. Firms using this strategy are trying to gain the advantages of both local responsiveness and global efficiency.[90] The combination structure is used to implement the transnational strategy. The **combination structure** is a structure drawing characteristics and mechanisms from both the worldwide geographic area structure and the worldwide product divisional structure. The transnational strategy is often implemented through two possible combination structures: a global matrix structure and a hybrid global design.[91]

In the **worldwide product divisional structure**, decision-making authority is centralized in the worldwide division headquarters to coordinate and integrate decisions and actions among divisional business units.

The **combination structure** is a structure drawing characteristics and mechanisms from both the worldwide geographic area structure and the worldwide product divisional structure.

The global matrix design brings together both local market and product expertise into teams that develop and respond to the global marketplace. The global matrix design promotes flexibility in designing products in response to customer needs. However, it has severe limitations in that it places employees in a position of being accountable to more than one manager. At any given time, an employee may be a member of several functional or product group teams. Relationships that evolve from multiple memberships can make it difficult for employees to be simultaneously loyal to all of them. Although the matrix places authority in the hands of the managers who are most able to use it, it creates problems in regard to corporate reporting relationships that are so complex and vague that it is difficult and time-consuming to receive approval for major decisions.

We illustrate the hybrid structure in Figure 11.10. In this design, some divisions are oriented toward products while others are oriented toward market areas. Thus, in cases when the geographic area is more important, the division managers are area-oriented. In other divisions where worldwide product coordination and efficiencies are more important, the division manager is more product-oriented.

The fit between the multidomestic strategy and the worldwide geographic area structure and between the global strategy and the worldwide product divisional structure is apparent. However, when a firm wants to implement the multidomestic and global strategies simultaneously through a combination structure, the appropriate integrating mechanisms are less obvious. The structure used to implement the transnational strategy must be simultaneously centralized and decentralized, integrated and nonintegrated, formalized and nonformalized. Sometimes the structure becomes extremely complex, a reality that challenges managers to remain vigilant in efforts to verify that the hybrid structure is effectively supporting use of their firm's transnational strategy.

When Panasonic Corporation (a Japanese company formally named Matsushita) started selling home appliances in the Chinese market several decades ago, its only attempt at localization was to offer less expensive versions of its developed market standard offerings. Japanese firms often sold standard products across the world, implementing the global strategy using the worldwide product divisional structure. However, they found that local competitors such as Haier were quickly outpacing their appliance sales in China, Haier's home market. Through this experience, Panasonic learned to engage more deeply within a country or regional market to adapt its appliances more closely to the local customer's demands.[92] As a result, the firm is using the transnational strategy and may be using the hybrid form of the combination structure to implement it.[93] (Recently Panasonic's portfolio

Figure 11.10 Hybrid Form of the Combination Structure for Implementing a Transnational Strategy

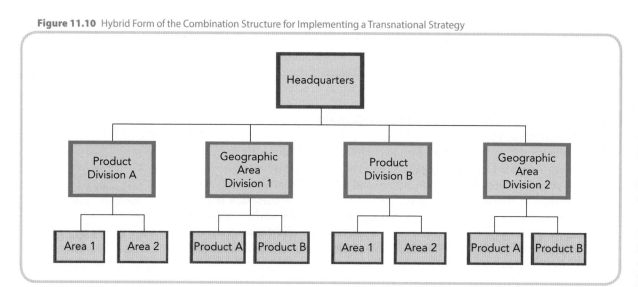

included 473 companies housed in multiple business units. This demonstrates the challenge a firm of this size and complexity faces when determining the optimal structure to match with individual strategies being used as a foundation for hopefully outperform rivals in regions and countries throughout the world.[94])

11-3g Matches between Cooperative Strategies and Network Structures

As discussed in Chapter 9, a network strategy exists when partners form several alliances in order to improve the performance of the alliance network itself through cooperative endeavors.[95] The greater levels of environmental complexity and uncertainty facing companies in today's competitive environment are causing more firms to use cooperative strategies such as strategic alliances.[96] Firms can form cooperative relationships with many of their stakeholders, including customers, suppliers, and competitors. When a firm becomes involved with combinations of cooperative relationships, it is part of a strategic network, or what others call an alliance constellation or portfolio.[97]

A *strategic network* is a group of firms that has been formed to create value by participating in multiple cooperative arrangements. An effective strategic network facilitates discovering opportunities beyond those identified by individual network participants. A strategic network can be a source of competitive advantage for its members when its operations create value that is difficult for competitors to duplicate and that network members can't create by themselves.[98] Strategic networks are used to implement business-level, corporate-level, and international cooperative strategies.

The typical strategic network is a loose federation of partners participating in the network's operations on a flexible basis. At the core or center of the strategic network, the *strategic center firm* is the one around which the network's cooperative relationships revolve (see Figure 11.11).

Figure 11.11 A Strategic Network

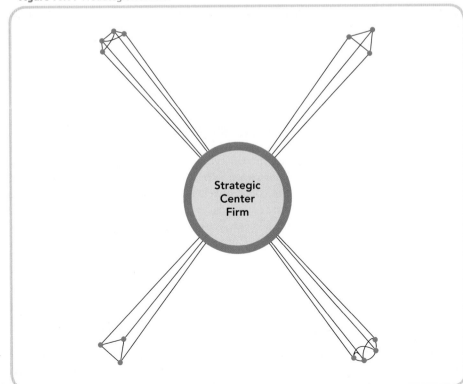

Because of its central position, the strategic center firm is the foundation for the strategic network's structure. Concerned with various aspects of organizational structure, such as formally reporting relationships and procedures, the strategic center firm manages what are often complex, cooperative interactions among network partners. To perform the tasks discussed next, the strategic center firm must make sure that incentives for participating in the network are aligned so that network firms continue to have a reason to remain connected.[99] The strategic center firm is engaged in four primary tasks as it manages the strategic network and controls its operations:[100]

Strategic Outsourcing. The strategic center firm outsources and partners with more firms than other network members. At the same time, the strategic center firm requires network partners to be more than contractors. Members are expected to find opportunities for the network to create value through its cooperative work.[101]

Competencies. To increase network effectiveness, the strategic center firm seeks ways to support each member's efforts to develop core competencies with the potential of benefiting the network.

Technology. The strategic center firm is responsible for managing the development and sharing of technology-based ideas among network members. The structural requirement that members submit formal reports detailing the technology-oriented outcomes of their efforts to the strategic center firm facilitates this activity.

Race to Learn. The strategic center firm emphasizes that the principal dimensions of competition are between value chains and between networks of value chains. Because of these interconnections, an individual strategic network is only as strong as its weakest value-chain link. With its centralized decision-making authority and responsibility, the strategic center firm guides participants in efforts to form network-specific competitive advantages. The need for each participant to have capabilities that can be the foundation for the network's competitive advantages encourages friendly rivalry among participants seeking to develop the skills needed to quickly form new capabilities that create value for the network.[102]

Interestingly, strategic networks are being used more frequently, partly because of the ability of a strategic center firm to execute a strategy that effectively and efficiently links partner firms. Improved information systems and communication capabilities (e.g., the Internet) facilitate effective organization and use of strategic networks.

11-4 Implementing Business-Level Cooperative Strategies

As explained in Chapter 9, there are two types of business-level complementary alliances—vertical and horizontal. Firms with competencies in different stages of the value chain form a vertical alliance to cooperatively integrate their different, but complementary, skills. Firms combining their competencies to create value in the same stage of the value chain are using a horizontal alliance. Vertical complementary strategic alliances such as those developed by Toyota Motor Corporation are formed more frequently than horizontal alliances.[103]

A strategic network of vertical relationships, such as the network in Japan between Toyota and its suppliers, often involves a number of implementation issues.[104] First, the strategic center firm encourages subcontractors to modernize their facilities and provides them with technical and financial assistance to do so, if necessary. Second, the strategic center firm reduces its transaction costs by promoting longer-term contracts with subcontractors, so that supplier-partners increase their long-term productivity. This approach differs from that of continually negotiating short-term contracts based on unit pricing. Third, the strategic center firm enables engineers in upstream companies (suppliers) to have better communications with those companies with whom it has contracts for services. As a result, suppliers and the strategic center firm become more interdependent and less independent.

The lean production system (a vertical complementary strategic alliance) pioneered by Toyota and others has been diffused throughout many industries.[105] In vertical complementary strategic alliances, such as the one between Toyota and its suppliers, the strategic center firm is obvious, as is the structure that firm establishes. However, the same is not always true with horizontal complementary strategic alliances where firms try to create value in the same part of the value chain. For example, airline alliances are commonly formed to create value in the marketing and sales primary activity segment of the value chain. Because air carriers commonly participate in multiple horizontal complementary alliances, such as the Oneworld alliance among American Airlines, British Airways, Iberia, Japan Airlines, TAM Airlines, and others, it is difficult to determine the strategic center firm. Moreover, participating in several alliances can cause firms to question partners' true loyalties and intentions. Also, if rivals band together in too many collaborative activities, one or more governments may suspect the possibility of explicit collusion among partnering firms (see Chapter 9). For these reasons, horizontal complementary alliances are used less often and less successfully than their vertical counterpart, although there are examples of success, such as some of the collaborations among automobile and aircraft manufacturers.

11-5 Implementing Corporate-Level Cooperative Strategies

Some corporate-level strategies are used to reduce costs. This was the objective with the collaboration that was formed initially between Walgreens and Swiss-based Alliance Boots, a pharmacy-led health and beauty group. This partnership helped the firms negotiate lower prices with drug suppliers, reducing their overall costs as a result of doing so.[106]

Unilever is partnering with some firms to reach a different objective. Committed to decoupling its growth from negative environmental and social effects from its operations, Unilever formed an alliance with Jacobs Engineering Group Inc. in 2010 to reduce the company's carbon, water, and waste footprint across its manufacturing locations throughout the world. Through a partnership with NGO Rainforest Alliance, Unilever was able to source "100 percent of all tea for its Lipton and PG Tips products from certified growers."[107] (Additional information about Unilever and its commitment to sustainability is provided in this chapter's Mini-Case.) Still other corporate-level cooperative strategies (such as franchising) are used to facilitate product and market diversification. As a cooperative strategy, franchising allows the firm to use its competencies to extend or diversify its product or market reach without completing a merger or acquisition.[108]

The potential to create synergy is a key reason corporate-level cooperative strategies, such as those involving Walgreens, Unilever, and active franchisers including McDonald's, are formed.[109] Historically, McDonald's approach to franchising as a corporate-level cooperative strategy found the firm emphasizing a limited value-priced menu. However, as mentioned in an earlier Strategic Focus, the firm's structure is being changed. One objective of these structural changes is to strip over $300 million from the firm's costs by the end of 2017. Selling 3,500 company-owned restaurants to franchisees by 2018 is an action being taken to help reduce costs. With these sales, global franchise ownership of McDonald's restaurants will reach 90 percent.[110] McDonald's' franchising system is a strategic network. Overall, McDonald's headquarters serves as the strategic center firm for the network's franchisees. The headquarters office uses strategic and financial controls to verify that the franchisees' operations create the greatest value for the entire network.

11-6 Implementing International Cooperative Strategies

Strategic networks formed to implement international cooperative strategies result in firms competing in several countries.[111] Differences among countries' regulatory environments increase the challenge of managing international networks and verifying that, at a minimum, a network's operations comply with all legal requirements.[112]

Distributed strategic networks are the organizational structure used to manage international cooperative strategies. As shown in Figure 11.12, several regional strategic center firms are included in the distributed network to manage partner firms' multiple cooperative arrangements.[113] The structure used to implement the international cooperative strategy is complex and demands careful attention to be used successfully.

Figure 11.12 A Distributed Strategic Network

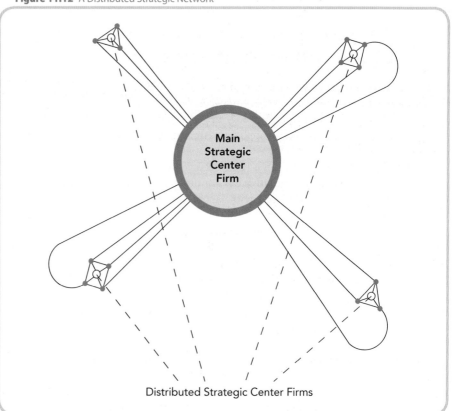

Distributed Strategic Center Firms

SUMMARY

■ Organizational structure specifies the firm's formal reporting relationships, procedures, controls, and authority and decision-making processes. Essentially, organizational structure details the work to be done in a firm and how that work is to be accomplished. Organizational controls guide the use of strategy, indicate how to compare actual and expected results, and suggest actions to take to improve performance when it falls below expectations. A proper match between strategy and structure can lead to a competitive advantage.

■ Strategic controls (largely subjective criteria) and financial controls (largely objective criteria) are the two types of organizational controls used to support the implementation of a strategy. Both controls are critical, although their degree of emphasis varies based on individual matches between strategy and structure.

■ Strategy and structure influence each other; overall though, strategy has a stronger influence on structure. Research indicates that firms tend to change structure when declining performance forces them to do so. Effective managers anticipate the need for structural change and quickly modify structure to better accommodate the firm's strategy when evidence calls for that action.

■ The functional structure is used to implement business-level strategies. The cost leadership strategy requires a centralized functional structure—one in which manufacturing efficiency and process engineering are emphasized. The differentiation strategy's functional structure decentralizes implementation-related decisions, especially those concerned with marketing, to those involved with individual organizational functions. Focus strategies, often used in small firms, require a simple structure until such time that the firm diversifies in terms of products and/or markets.

■ Unique combinations of different forms of the multidivisional structure are matched with different corporate-level diversification strategies to properly implement these strategies. The cooperative M-form, used to implement the related constrained corporate-level strategy, has a centralized corporate office and extensive integrating mechanisms. Divisional incentives are linked to overall corporate performance to foster cooperation among divisions. The related linked SBU M-form structure establishes separate profit centers within the diversified firm. Each profit center or SBU may have divisions offering similar products, but the SBUs are often unrelated to each other. The competitive M-form structure, used to implement the unrelated diversification strategy, is highly decentralized, lacks integrating mechanisms, and utilizes objective financial criteria to evaluate each unit's performance.

■ The multidomestic strategy, implemented through the worldwide geographic area structure, emphasizes decentralization and locates all functional activities in the host country or geographic area. The worldwide product divisional structure is used to implement the global strategy. This structure is centralized in order to coordinate and integrate different functions' activities to gain global economies of scope and economies of scale. Decision-making authority is centralized in the firm's worldwide division headquarters.

■ The transnational strategy—a strategy through which the firm seeks the local responsiveness of the multidomestic strategy and the global efficiency of the global strategy—is implemented through the combination structure. Because it must be simultaneously centralized and decentralized, integrated and nonintegrated, and formalized and nonformalized, the combination structure is difficult to organize and successfully manage. Two structures can be used to implement the transnational strategy: the matrix and the hybrid structure with both geographic and product-oriented divisions.

■ Increasingly important to competitive success, cooperative strategies are implemented through organizational structures framed around strategic networks. Strategic center firms play a critical role in managing strategic networks. Business-level strategies are often employed in vertical and horizontal alliance networks. Corporate-level cooperative strategies are used to pursue product and market diversification. Franchising is one type of corporate strategy that uses a strategic network to implement this strategy. This is also true for international cooperative strategies, where distributed networks are often used.

KEY TERMS

combination structure 367
competitive form 361
cooperative form 358
financial controls 350
functional structure 353
multidivisional (M-form) structure 353
organizational controls 350

organizational structure 347
simple structure 352
strategic business unit (SBU) form 360
strategic controls 350
worldwide geographic area structure 365
worldwide product divisional structure 367

REVIEW QUESTIONS

1. What is organizational structure and what are organizational controls? What are the differences between strategic controls and financial controls? What is the importance of these differences?

2. What does it mean to say that strategy and structure have a reciprocal relationship?

3. What are the characteristics of the different functional structures used to implement the cost leadership, differentiation, integrated cost leadership/differentiation, and focused business-level strategies?

4. What are the differences among the three versions of the multidivisional (M-form) organizational structures that are used to implement the related constrained, the related linked, and the unrelated corporate-level diversification strategies?

5. What organizational structures are used to implement the multidomestic, global, and transnational international strategies?

6. What is a strategic network? What is a strategic center firm? How is a strategic center firm used in business-level, corporate-level, and international cooperative strategies?

Mini-Case

Unilever Cooperates with Many Firms and Nonprofit Organizations to Implement Its Strategy While Creating a More Sustainable Environment

Unilever, a European-headquartered (in both the Netherlands and the United Kingdom) consumer products company, is committed to using a sustainable environment strategy while manufacturing its large array of food and beverage products. Historically, consumer products companies, especially those from Europe, have pursued the multidomestic strategy, needing to adapt their products to each country or region market. Accordingly, most have implemented their strategy using the worldwide geographic area structure. Many consumer product companies, such as Avon, have begun to use aspects of the worldwide product structure to become more efficient. This is also the case with Unilever. However, Unilever has continued to emphasize geographic areas, but it has done so using the transnational strategy while implementing the combination structure to meet local market responsiveness as well as global efficiency objectives. Moreover, its CEO, Paul Pullman, who took the job in 2009, has also suggested, "our purpose is to have a sustainable business model that is put at the service of the greater good."

Accordingly, Unilever created a manifesto in 2010 called the Sustainable Living Plan. This plan calls for Unilever to double its sales at the same time that it cuts its environmental footprint in half by 2020. One goal embedded in this plan is to source all of the firm's agricultural products in ways that "don't degrade the Earth." Unilver also has a campaign promising to improve the well-being of one billion people by "persuading them to wash their hands or brush their teeth, or by selling them food with less salt or fat." It seeks to realize many of these goals through cooperative strategies with other profit-seeking organizations as well as nonprofit entities.

In 2010, for instance, Unilever signed a contract with Jacobs Engineering Group Inc. forming a global (overall corporate) alliance to facilitate the efficiency of Unilever's capital improvement projects around the world. Unilever has 250 manufacturing sites and is expanding aggressively, especially in developing and emerging economies, to support its ambitious growth goals. Unilever expects emerging economies to drive 75 percent of its growth in the long term. The alliance with Jacobs Engineering will be managed out of Singapore and will provide engineering services for Unilever's manufacturing facilities around the world. Both companies will "work as a team to insure their sustainable growth model," implement cost reductions, and "drive co-innovation and implement the harmonization and cross-category standardization of designs." The alliance will also work with supply chain team members to increase speed to market with designs that "reduce carbon, water, and waste footprints across its manufacturing sites."

In alignment with marketing growth goals, Unilever has initiated the Unilever Nutrition Network. This organization has divided the world into six regions and focused on providing world-class nutrition and health innovation. Its goal is to generate ideas to facilitate sustainable product launches and improve existing products while strengthening their brand value. As part of this overall strategy, Unilever has used Salesforce's Chatter technology in the implementation of its new social marketing platform. This technology allows local markets and distributors of Unilever products to share insights and best practices with the marketing team from Unilever to help drive its "crafting brands for life" strategy.

In a recent Sustainable Living Plan report, Unilver described how it is working with a number of nonprofit, nongovernment organizations (NGOs) to help address real issues, facilitate solutions for suppliers for improving sustainable living, and reach customers in society at large who need information to improve their sustainability approaches to life with better food security and poverty alleviation. Initiatives include partnering with the following NGOs: the Consumer Goods Forum; the World Business Council for Sustainable Development; the World Economic Forum; the Tropical Forest Alliance 2020; Refrigerants, Naturally; the Global Green

Foundation Forum; and Zero Hunger Challenge and Scale-Up Nutrition initiatives supported by the United Nations.

Interestingly, Unilever no longer provides quarterly earnings guidance reports and suggests that this has allowed it to focus shareholders on its longer-term goals. Furthermore, since Pullman took over in 2009, Unilever has sustained its positive growth trajectory with better income performance and associated stock market performance. As can be seen, it is accomplishing these things through better organizational design, lofty objectives, but also by using a number of cooperative strategies with many organizations outside the organization, such as Jacobs Engineering and many NGOs.

Sources: 2013, In the green corner: How IBM, Unilever and P&G started winning again: Why big business is wising up to sustainability, *Strategic Direction*, 29(5): 19–22; 2013, Our nutrition network, www.unilever.com, accessed June 17; 2013, Unilever drives efficiency in capital investment program, www.unilever.com, accessed June 17; 2013, Unilever Sustainable Living Plan, www.unilever.com, accessed June 17; 2013, Unilever Annual Report 2012, www.unilever.com, accessed June 17; S. Anand & N. Gopalan, 2013, Consumers in India are an M&A target, *Wall Street Journal Online*, www.wsj.com, May 1; M. Gunther, 2013, Unilever's CEO has a green thumb, *Fortune*, June 10, 124–128; R. Shields, 2013, Unilever boosts international collaboration with social rollout, *Marketing Week*, www.marketingweek.com, May 2; A. Ignatius, 2012, Captain planet, *Harvard Business Review*, 90(6): 112–118.

Case Discussion Questions

1. Why have consumer product companies headquartered in Europe historically used the multidomestic strategy? In your view, is this an effective choice of international strategy for these firms? Why or why not?

2. To implement its "sustainable business model," what types of strategies is Unilever considering for use and why?

3. What organizational structure will Unilever need to use to reach its sustainability objectives?

4. What issues about organizational structure surface as a result of Unilever's proposed strategies and objectives regarding sustainability?

NOTES

1. A. Arora, S. Belenzon, & L. A. Rios, 2014, Make, buy, organize: The interplay between research, external knowledge, and firm structure, *Strategic Management Journal*, 35: 317–337; T. Felin, N. J. Foss, K. H. Heimeriks, & T. L. Madsen, 2012, Microfoundations of routines and capabilities: Individuals, processes, and structure, *Journal of Management Studies*, 49: 1351–1374; K. M. Eisenhardt, N. R. Furr, & C. B. Bingham, 2010, Microfoundations of performance: Balancing efficiency and flexibility in dynamic environments, *Organization Science*, 21: 1263–1273.

2. D. A. Levinthal & A. Marino, 2015, Three facets of organizational adaptation: Selection, variety, and plasticity, *Organization Science*, in press; R. Wilden, S. P. Gudergan, B. Nielsen, & I. Lings, 2013, Dynamic capabilities and performance: Strategy, structure and environment, *Long Range Planning*, 46: 72–96; R. E. Miles & C. C. Snow, 1978, *Organizational Strategy, Structure and Process*, NY: McGraw-Hill.

3. C. Heavey & Z. Simsek, 2015, Transactive memory systems and firm performance: An upper echelons perspective, *Organization Science*, in press; M. A. Valentine & A. C. Edmondson, 2015, Team scaffolds: How mesolevel structures enable role-based coordination in temporary groups, *Organization Science*, in press; Y. Y. Kor & A. Mesko, 2013, Dynamic managerial capabilities: Configuration and orchestration of top executives' capabilities and the firm's dominant logic, *Strategic Management Journal*, 34: 233–244; E. M. Olson, S. F. Slater, & G. T. M. Hult, 2007, The importance of structure and process to strategy implementation, *Business Horizons*, 48: 47–54.

4. M. Josefy, S. Kuban, R. D. Ireland, &
    M. A. Hitt, 2015, All things great and
    small: Organizational size, boundaries of
    the firm, and a changing environment,
    Academy of Management Annals, 9: 715–802;
    P. Boumgarden, J. Nickerson, & T. R. Zenger,
    2012, Sailing into the wind: Exploring
    the relationships among ambidexterity,
    vacillation, and organizational performance,
    Strategic Management Journal, 33: 587–610;
    T. Amburgey & T. Dacin, 1994, As the left
    foot follows the right? The dynamics of
    strategic and structural change, *Academy of
    Management Journal*, 37: 1427–1452.

5. M. Menz, S. Kunisch, & D. J. Collis, 2015,
    The corporate headquarters in the
    contemporary corporation: Advancing a
    multimarket firm perspective, *Academy
    of Management Annals*, 9: 633–714;
    L. F. Monteiro, N. Arvidsson, & J. Birkinshaw,
    2008, Knowledge flows within
    multinational corporations: Explaining
    subsidiary isolation and its performance
    implications, *Organization Science*, 19:
    90–107; B. Keats & H. O'Neill, 2001,
    Organizational structure: Looking through
    a strategy lens, in M. A. Hitt, R. E. Freeman, &
    J. S. Harrison (eds.), *Handbook of Strategic
    Management*, Oxford, U.K.: Blackwell
    Publishers, 520–542.

6. A. Shipilov, R. Gulati, M. Kilduff, S. Li, &
    W. Tsai, 2014, Relational pluralism within
    and between organizations, *Academy
    of Management Journal*, 57: 449–459;
    R. E. Hoskisson, C. W. L. Hill, & H. Kim,
    1993, The multidivisional structure:
    Organizational fossil or source of value?
    Journal of Management, 19: 269–298.

7. B. Grøgaard, 2012, Alignment of strategy
    and structure in international firms: An
    empirical examination, *International
    Business Review*, 21: 397–407; E. M. Olson,
    S. F. Slater, & G. T. M. Hult, 2005, The
    performance implications of fit among
    business strategy, marketing organization
    structure, and strategic behavior, *Journal of
    Marketing*, 69: 49–65.

8. M. Ahearne, S. K. Lam, & F. Kraus, 2014,
    Performance impact of middle managers'
    adaptive strategy implementation: The
    role of social capital, *Strategic Management
    Journal*, 35: 68–87; F. A. Csaszar, 2012,
    Organizational structure as a determinant
    of performance: Evidence from mutual
    funds, *Strategic Management Journal*, 33:
    611–632; T. Burns & G. M. Stalker, 1961,
    The Management of Innovation, London:
    Tavistok; P. R. Lawrence & J. W. Lorsch, 1967,
    Organization and Environment, Homewood,
    IL: Richard D. Irwin; J. Woodward, 1965,
    Industrial Organization: Theory and Practice,
    London: Oxford University Press.

9. A. K. Hoenen & T. Kostova, 2014, Utilizing
    the broader agency perspective for
    studying headquarters-subsidiary relations
    in multinational companies, *Journal of
    International Business Studies*, 46: 104–113;
    A. M. Rugman & A. Verbeke, 2008,

    A regional solution to the strategy and
    structure of multinationals, *European
    Management Journal*, 26: 305–313; H. Kim,
    R. E. Hoskisson, L. Tihanyi, & J. Hong, 2004,
    Evolution and restructuring of diversified
    business groups in emerging markets: The
    lessons from chaebols in Korea, *Asia Pacific
    Journal of Management*, 21: 25–48.

10. B. McEvily, G. Soda, & M. Tortoriello,
    2014, More formally: Rediscovering the
    missing link between formal organization
    and informal social structure, *Academy
    of Management Annals*, 8: 299–345;
    M. Reilly, P. Scott, & V. Mangematin, 2012,
    Alignment or independence? Multinational
    subsidiaries and parent relations, *Journal of
    Business Strategy*, 33(2): 4–11.

11. T. Felin, N. J. Foss, & R. E. Ployhart, 2015, The
    microfoundations movement in strategy
    and organization theory, *Academy of
    Management Annals*, 9: 575–632; J. Qiu,
    L. Donaldson, & B. Luo, 2012, The benefits of
    persisting with paradigms in organizational
    research, *Academy of Management
    Perspectives*, 26: 93–104; R. Greenwood &
    D. Miller, 2010, Tackling design anew:
    Getting back to the heart of organization
    theory, *Academy of Management Perspectives*,
    24: 78–88.

12. M. Dobrajska, S. Billinger, & S. Karim,
    2015, Delegation within hierarchies: How
    information processing and knowledge
    characteristics influence the allocation
    of formal and real decision authority,
    Organization Science, in press; D. Laureiro-
    Martinez, 2014, Cognitive control
    capabilities, routinization propensity, and
    decision-making authority, *Organization
    Science*, 25: 1111–1133.

13. M. Loock & G. Hinnen, 2015, Heuristics in
    organizations: A review and a research
    agenda, *Journal of Business Research*, in
    press; S. E. Perkins, 2014, When does prior
    experience pay? Institutional experience
    and the multinational corporation,
    Administrative Science Quarterly, 59: 145–181.

14. J. Reuer & S. Devarakonda, 2015,
    Mechanisms of hybrid governance:
    Administrative committees in non-equity
    alliances, *Academy of Management
    Journal*, in press; C. Cella, A. Ellul, &
    M. Giannetti, 2013, Investors' horizons and
    the amplification of market shocks, *Review
    of Financial Studies*, 26: 1607–1648; T. Yu,
    M. Sengul, & R. H. Lester, 2008, Misery
    loves company: The spread of negative
    impacts resulting from an organizational
    crisis, *Academy of Management Review*,
    33: 452–472; R. L. Priem, L. G. Love, &
    M. A. Shaffer, 2002, Executives' perceptions
    of uncertainty sources: A numerical
    taxonomy and underlying dimensions,
    Journal of Management, 28: 725–746.

15. A. Engelen, H. Kube, S. Schmidt, &
    T. C. Flatten, 2014, Entrepreneurial
    orientation in turbulent environments:
    The moderating role of absorptive
    capacity, *Research Policy*, 43: 1353–1369;

    E. Claver-Cortés, E. M. Pertusa-Ortega, &
    J. F. Molina-Azorín, 2012, Characteristics of
    organizational structure relating to hybrid
    competitive strategy: Implications for
    performance, *Journal of Business Research*,
    65: 993–1002.

16. J. B. Craig, C. Dibrell, & R. Garrett, 2014,
    Examining relationships among family
    influence, family culture, flexible planning
    systems, innovativeness and firm
    performance, *Journal of Family Business
    Strategy*, 5: 229–238; R. Kapoor & J. Lee,
    2013, Coordinating and competing in
    ecosystems: How organizational forms
    shape new technology investments,
    Strategic Management Journal, 34: 274–296.

17. H. Merchant, 2014, Configurations of
    governance structure, generic strategy,
    and firm size: Opening the black box
    of value creation in international joint
    ventures, *Global Strategy Journal*, 4:
    292–309; M. S. Feldman & W. J. Orlikowski,
    2011, Theorizing practice and practicing
    theory, *Organization Science*, 22: 1240–1253;
    J. Rivkin & N. Siggelkow, 2003, Balancing
    search and stability: Interdependencies
    among elements of organizational design,
    Management Science, 49: 290–311.

18. A. N. Kiss & P. S. Barr, 2015, New venture
    strategic adaptation: The interplay of belief
    structures and industry context, *Strategic
    Management Journal*, in press; A. J. Bock,
    T. Opsahl, G. George, & D. M. Gann, 2012,
    The effects of culture and structure on
    strategic flexibility during business model
    innovation, *Journal of Management Studies*,
    49: 279–305; S. Nadkarni & V. K. Narayanan,
    2007, Strategic schemas, strategic flexibility,
    and firm performance: The moderating
    role of industry clockspeed, *Strategic
    Management Journal*, 28: 243–270.

19. V. Gerasymenko, D. De Clercq, &
    H. J. Sapienza, 2015, Changing the business
    model: Effects of venture capital firms
    and outside CEOs on portfolio company
    performance, *Strategic Entrepreneurship
    Journal*, 9: 79–98; S. A. Fernhaber &
    P. C. Patel, 2012, How do young firms
    manage product portfolio complexity?
    The role of absorptive capacity and
    ambidexterity, *Strategic Management
    Journal*, 33: 1516–1539; S. Raisch &
    J. Birkinshaw, 2008, Organizational
    ambidexterity: Antecedents, outcomes,
    and moderators, *Journal of Management*,
    34: 375–409.

20. C.-A. Chen, 2014, Revisiting organizational
    age, inertia, and adaptability: Developing
    and testing a multi-stage model in the
    nonprofit sector, *Journal of Organizational
    Change Management*, 27: 251–272;
    M. Zhao, S. H. Park, & N. Zhour, 2014,
    MNC strategy and social adaptation in
    emerging markets, *Journal of International
    Business Studies*, 45: 842–861; B. W. Keats &
    M. A. Hitt, 1988, A causal model of linkages
    among environmental dimensions,
    macroorganizational characteristics, and

performance, *Academy of Management Journal*, 31: 570–598.

21. A. Chandler, 1962, *Strategy and Structure*, Cambridge, MA: MIT Press.

22. D. Martin, 2007, Alfred D. Chandler, Jr., a business historian, dies at 88, *New York Times*, www.nytimes.com, May 12.

23. D. Albert, M. Kreutzer, & C. Lechner, 2015, Resolving the paradox of interdependency and strategic renewal in activity systems, *Academy of Management Review*, 40: 210–234; B. T. Pentland, M. S. Feldman, M. C. Becker, & P. Liu, 2012, Dynamics of organizational routines: A generative model, *Journal of Management Studies*, 49: 1484–1508; R. E. Hoskisson, R. A. Johnson, L. Tihanyi, & R. E. White, 2005, Diversified business groups and corporate refocusing in emerging economies, *Journal of Management*, 31: 941–965.

24. P. Wahba, 2015, J.C. Penney still blaming Ron Johnson-era for flow profit, growth, *Fortune*, www.fortune.com, February 26; D. Moin & E. Clark, 2013, Ullman returns as Johnson exits, *WWD: Women's Wear Daily*, April 9, 1.

25. M. Townsend, 2015, J.C. Penney marks two years since Johnson nearly ruined it, *Bloomberg*, www.bloombergnews.com, April 8.

26. R. V. D. Jordao, A. A. Souza, & E. A. Avelar, 2014, Organizational culture and post-acquisition changes in management control systems: An analysis of a successful Brazilian case, *Journal of Business Research*, 67: 542–549; S. Sonenshein, 2014, How organizations foster the creative use of resources, *Academy of Management Journal*, 57: 814–848.

27. M. R. Allen, G. K. Adomdza, & M. H. Meyer, 2015, Managing for innovation: Managerial control and employee level outcomes, *Journal of Business Research*, 68: 371–379; G. Valentini, 2015, The impact of M&A on rivals' innovation strategy, *Long Range Planning*, in press; L. Marengo & C. Pasquali, 2012, How to get what you want when you do not know what you want: A model of incentives, organizational structure, and learning, *Organization Science*, 23: 1298–1310;

28. D. F. Kuratko, J. G. Covin, & J. S. Hornsby, 2014, Why implementing corporate innovation is so difficult, *Business Horizons*, 57: 647–655; D. W. Lehman & J. Hahn, 2013, Momentum and organizational risk taking: Evidence from the National Football League, *Management Science*, 59: 852–868; M. A. Hitt, K. T. Haynes, & R. Serpa, 2010, Strategic leadership for the 21st century, *Business Horizons*, 53: 437–444.

29. L. Thomas & V. Ambrosini, 2015, Materializing strategy: The role of comprehensiveness and management controls in strategy formation in volatile environments, *British Journal of Management*, 26: S105–S124; R. MacKay & R. Chia, 2013, Choice, chance, and

unintended consequences in strategic change: A process understanding of the rise and fall of Northco Automotive, *Academy of Management Journal*, 56: 208–230; I. Filatotchev, J. Stephan, & B. Jindra, 2008, Ownership structure, strategic controls and export intensity of foreign-invested firms in transition economies, *Journal of International Business Studies*, 39: 1133–1148.

30. S. Groda., A. J. Nelson, & R. M. Slino, 2015, Help-seeking and help-giving as an organizational routine: Continual engagement in innovative work, *Academy of Management Journal*, 58: 136–168; D. Minbaeva, T. Pedersen, I. Bjorkman, C. F. Fey, & H. J. Park, 2014, MNC knowledge transfer, subsidiary absorptive capacity and HRM, *Journal of International Business Studies*, 45: 38–51; D. M. Cable, F. Gino, & B. R. Staats, 2013, Breaking them in or eliciting their best? Reframing socialization around newcomers' authentic self-expression, *Administrative Science Quarterly*, 58: 1–36.

31. M. Menz & C. Scheef, 2014, Chief strategy officers: Contingency analysis of their presence in top management teams, *Strategic Management Journal*, 35: 461–471; K. Favaro, 2013, We're from corporate and we are here to help: Understanding the real value of corporate strategy and the head office, *Strategy+Business Online*, www.strategy-business.com, April 8; M. A. Hitt, R. E. Hoskisson, R. A. Johnson, & D. D. Moesel, 1996, The market for corporate control and firm innovation, *Academy of Management Journal*, 39: 1084–1119.

32. S. Karim & A. Kaul, 2015, Structural recombination and innovation: Unlocking intraorganizational knowledge synergy through structural change, *Organization Science*, 26: 439–455; W. P. Wan, R. E. Hoskisson, J. C. Short, & D. W. Yiu, 2011, Resource-based theory and corporate diversification: Accomplishments and opportunities, *Journal of Management*, 37: 1335–1368; M. A. Hitt, L. Tihanyi, T. Miller, & B. Connelly, 2006, International diversification: Antecedents, outcomes, and moderators, *Journal of Management*, 32: 831–867; R. E. Hoskisson & M. A. Hitt, 1988, Strategic control and relative R&D investment in multiproduct firms, *Strategic Management Journal*, 9: 605–621.

33. W. Su & E. Tsang, 2015, Product diversification and financial performance: The moderating role of secondary stakeholders, *Academy of Management Journal*, in press; I. Clark, 2013, Templates for financial control? Management and employees under the private equity business model, *Human Resource Management Journal*, 23: 144–159; D. Collis, D. Young, & M. Goold, 2007, The size, structure, and performance of corporate

headquarters, *Strategic Management Journal*, 28: 383–405.

34. R. Amit & C. Zott, 2015, Crafting business architecture: The antecedents of business model design, *Strategic Entrepreneurship Journal*, in press; X. S. Y. Spencer, T. A. Joiner, & S. Salmon, 2009, Differentiation strategy, performance measurement systems and organizational performance: Evidence from Australia, *International Journal of Business*, 14: 83–103.

35. P. Almodovar & A. M. Rugman, 2014, The M curve and the performance of Spanish international new ventures, *British Journal of Management*, 25: S6–S23; M. Dass & S. Kumar, 2014, Bringing product and consumer ecosystems to the strategic forefront, *Business Horizons*, 57: 225–234; X. Yin & E. J. Zajac, 2004, The strategy/governance structure fit relationship: Theory and evidence in franchising arrangements, *Strategic Management Journal*, 25: 365–383.

36. A. Gasparro, 2015, McDonald's puts its plan on display, *Morningstar*, www.morningstar.com, May 3.

37. G. Shani & J. Westphal, 2015, Persona non grata? Determinants and consequences of social distancing from journalists who engage in negative coverage of firm leadership, *Academy of Management Journal*, in press; E. Kulchina, 2014, Media coverage and location choice, *Strategic Management Journal*, 35: 596–605; M. K. Bednar, S. Boivie, & N. R. Prince, 2013, Burr under the saddle: How media coverage influences strategic change, *Organization Science*, 24: 910–925.

38. D. C. Mowery, 2010, Alfred Chandler and knowledge management within the firm, *Industrial & Corporate Change*, 19: 483–507; Chandler, *Strategy and Structure*.

39. Keats & O'Neill, Organizational structure, 524.

40. K. Srikanth & P. Puranam, 2014, The firm as a coordination system: Evidence from software services offshoring, *Organization Science*, 25: 1253–1271; E. Rawley, 2010, Diversification, coordination costs and organizational rigidity: Evidence from microdata, *Strategic Management Journal*, 31: 873–891.

41. S. M. Wagner, K. K. R. Ullrich, & S. Transchel, 2014, The game plan for aligning the organization, *Business Horizons*, 57: 189–201; A. Campbell & H. Strikwerda, 2013, The power of one: Towards the new integrated organization, *Journal of Business Strategy*, 34: 4–12.

42. S. Amdouni & S. Boubaker, 2015, Multiple large shareholders and owner-manager compensation: Evidence from French listed firms, *Journal of Applied Business Research*, 31: 1111–1129; C. Levicki, 1999, *The Interactive Strategy Workout*, 2nd ed., London: Prentice Hall.

43. M. Perkmann & A. Spicer, 2014, How emerging organizations take form: The role

of imprinting and values in organizational
bricolage, *Organization Science*, 25:
1785–1806; P. L. Drnevich & D. C. Croson,
2013, Information technology and business-
level strategy: Toward an integrated
theoretical perspective, *MIS Quarterly*,
37: 483–509; H. M. O'Neill, R. W. Pouder, &
A. K. Buchholtz, 1998, Patterns in the
diffusion of strategies across organizations:
Insights from the innovation diffusion
literature, *Academy of Management Review*,
23: 98–114.

44. J. Davoren, 2015, Functional structure
organization strength & weaknesses, *Small
Business*, http://smallbusiness.chron.com,
May 10.

45. D. Antons & F. Piller, 2015, Opening the
black box of 'not-invented-here': *Academy
of Management Perspectives*, in press;
P. Leinwand & C. Mainardi, 2013, Beyond
functions, *Strategy+Business*, www.
strategy-business.com, Spring, 1–5.

46. O. E. Williamson, 1975, *Markets and
Hierarchies: Analysis and Anti-Trust
Implications*, NY: The Free Press.

47. M. J. Sanchez-Bueno & B. Usero, 2014, How
may the nature of family firms explain
the decisions concerning international
diversification? *Journal of Business Research*,
67: 1311–1320; T. Hutzschenreuter &
J. Horstkotte, 2013, Performance effects
of top management team demographic
faultlines in the process of product
diversification, *Strategic Management
Journal*, 34: 704–726; Chandler, *Strategy and
Structure*.

48. Y. M. Zhou, 2015, Supervising across
borders: The case of multinational
hierarchies, *Organization Science*, 26:
277–292; J. Joseph & W. Ocasio, 2012,
Architecture, attention, and adaptation
in the multibusiness firm: General Electric
from 1951 to 2001, *Strategic Management
Journal*, 33: 633–660; J. Greco, 1999, Alfred
P. Sloan, Jr. (1875–1966): The original
"organization" man, *Journal of Business
Strategy*, 20(5): 30–31.

49. R. E. Hoskisson, C. E. Hill, & H. Kim, 1993, The
multidivisional structure: Organizational
fossil or source of value? *Journal of
Management*, 19: 269–298.

50. A. Zimmermann, S. Raisch, & J. Birkinshaw,
2015, How is ambidexterity initiated?
The emergent charter definition process,
Organization Science, in press; V. Binda,
2012, Strategy and structure in large Italian
and Spanish firms, 1950–2002, *Business
History Review*, 86: 503–525.

51. J. Hautz, M. Mayer, & C. Stadler, 2014, Macro-
competitive context and diversification:
The impact of macroeconomic growth and
foreign competition, *Long Range Planning*,
47: 337–352; C. E. Helfat & K. M. Eisenhardt,
2004, Inter-temporal economies of
scope, organizational modularity, and
the dynamics of diversification, *Strategic
Management Journal*, 25: 1217–1232;
A. D. Chandler, 1994, The functions of

the HQ unit in the multibusiness firm, in
R. P. Rumelt, D. E. Schendel, & D. J. Teece
(eds.), *Fundamental Issues in Strategy*,
Cambridge, MA: Harvard Business School
Press, 327.

52. O. E. Williamson, 1994, Strategizing,
economizing, and economic organization,
in R. P. Rumelt, D. E. Schendel, & D. J. Teece
(eds.), *Fundamental Issues in Strategy*,
Cambridge, MA: Harvard Business School
Press, 361–401.

53. V. A. Aggarwal & B. Wu, 2014,
Organizational constraints to adaptation:
Intrafirm asymmetry in the locus of
coordination, *Organization Science*, 26:
218–238; Hoskisson, Hill, & Kim, The
multidivisional structure: Organizational
fossil or source of value?

54. D. J. Teece, 2014, A dynamic capabilities-
based entrepreneurial theory of the
multinational enterprise, *Journal of
International Business Studies*, 45: 8–37;
R. Duchin & D. Sosyura, 2013, Divisional
managers and internal capital markets,
Journal of Finance, 68: 387–429;
O. E. Williamson, 1985, *The Economic
Institutions of Capitalism: Firms, Markets,
and Relational Contracting*, New York:
Macmillan.

55. M. F. Wolff, 1999, In the organization of the
future, competitive advantage will lie with
inspired employees, *Research Technology
Management*, 42(4): 2–4.

56. S. Y. Lee, M. Pitesa, S. Thau, & M. Pillutla,
2015, Discrimination in selection
decisions: Integrating stereotype fit and
interdependence theories, *Academy of
Management Journal*, in press; E. Schulz,
S. Chowdhury, & D. Van de Voort, 2013,
Firm productivity moderated link between
human capital and compensation: The
significance of task-specific human capital,
Human Resource Management, 52: 423–439.

57. N. Malhotra, C. R. (Bob) Hinings, 2015,
Unpacking continuity and change as a
process of organizational transformation,
Long Range Planning, 48: 1–22; L. G. Love,
R. L. Priem, & G. T. Lumpkin, 2002, Explicitly
articulated strategy and firm performance
under alternative levels of centralization,
Journal of Management, 28: 611–627.

58. S. Biancani, D. A. McFarland, & L. Dahlander,
2014, The semiformal organizational,
Organization Science, 25: 1306–1324;
T. F. Gonzalez-Cruz, A. Huguet-Roig, &
S. Cruz-Ros, 2012, Organizational
technology as a mediating variable
in centralization-formalization fit,
Management Decision, 50: 1527–1548.

59. D. G. Sirmon, M. A. Hitt, R. D. Ireland, &
B. A. Gilbert, 2011, Resource orchestration
to create competitive advantage: Breadth,
depth and life cycle effects, *Journal of
Management*, 37: 1390–1412.

60. N. J. Foss, J. Lyngsie, & S. A. Zahra,
2015, Organizational design correlates
of entrepreneurship: The roles of
decentralization and formalization for

opportunity discovery and realization,
Strategic Organization, in press. J. B. Barney,
2001, *Gaining and Sustaining Competitive
Advantage*, 2nd ed., Upper Saddle River, NJ:
Prentice Hall, 257.

61. H. Brea-Solis, R. Casadesus-Masanell, &
E. Grifell-Tatje, 2015, Business model
evaluation: Unifying Walmart's sources
of advantage, *Strategic Entrepreneurship
Journal*, 9: 12–33.

62. D. Martinez-Simarro, C. Devece, & C. Liopis-
Albert, 2015, How information systems
strategy moderates the relationship
between business strategy and
performance, *Journal of Business Research*,
68: 1592–1594; V. K. Garg, R. L. Priem, &
A. A. Rasheed, 2013, A theoretical
explanation of the cost advantages of
multi-unit franchising, *Journal of Marketing
Channels*, 20: 52–72; H. Wang & C. Kimble,
2010, Low-cost strategy through product
architecture: Lessons from China, *Journal of
Business Strategy*, 31: 12–20.

63. M. Dobrajska, S. Billinger, & S. Karim,
2015, Delegation within hierarchies: How
information processing and knowledge
characteristics influence the allocation
of formal and real decision authority,
Organization Science, in press.

64. P. Soni, 2015, What investors need to know
about Walmart's US segment, *Finance.
yahoo*, www.finance.yahoo.com, May 14.

65. 2015, Our story, Walmart Corporate, www.
walmartstores.com, May 13.

66. J. Schmidt, R. Makadok, & T. Keil, 2015,
Customer-specific synergies and market
convergence, *Strategic Management
Journal*, in press; A. Ma, Z. Yang, &
M. Mourali, 2014, Consumer adoption
of new products: Independent versus
interdependent self-perspectives, *Journal
of Marketing*, 78: 101–117; N. Takagoshi &
N. Matsubayashi, 2013, Customization
competition between branded firms:
Continuous extension of product line
from core product, *European Journal of
Operational Research*, 225: 337–352.

67. P. C. Patel, S. Thorgren, & J. Wincent, 2015,
Leadership, passion, and performance: A
study of job creation projects during the
recession, *British Journal of Management*,
26: 211–224; D. Singh & J. S. Oberoi, 2014,
A rule-based fuzzy-logic approach for
evaluating the strategic flexibility in
manufacturing organizations, *International
Journal of Strategic Change Management*,
5: 281–296; K. Z. Zhou & F. Wu, 2010,
Technological capability, strategic
flexibility and product innovation, *Strategic
Management Journal*, 31: 547–561.

68. 2015, About Under Armour, www.
underarmour.com, May 15.

69. J. H. Burgers & J. G. Covin, 2015, The
contingent effects of differentiation and
integration on corporate entrepreneurship,
Strategic Management Journal, in press;
L. Mirabeau & S. Maguire, 2014, From
autonomous strategic behavior to

emergent strategy, *Strategic Management Journal*, 35: 1202–1229; E. Claver-Cortés, E. M. Pertusa-Ortega, & J. F. Molina-Azorín, 2012, Characteristics of organizational structure relating to hybrid competitive strategy: Implications for performance, *Journal of Business Research*, 65: 993–1002.

70. Chandler, *Strategy and Structure*.

71. 2015, Strength in structure, Procter & Gamble Home Page, www.pg.com, May 9.

72. D. Maslach, 2015, Change and persistence with failed technological innovation, *Strategic Management Journal*, in press; S. Wagner, K. Hoisl, & G. Thoma, 2014, Overcoming localization of knowledge—the role of professional service firms, *Strategic Management Journal*, 35: 1671–1688; Y. M. Zhou, 2011, Synergy, coordination costs, and diversification choices, *Strategic Management Journal*, 32: 624–639; C. W. L. Hill, M. A. Hitt, & R. E. Hoskisson, 1992, Cooperative versus competitive structures in related and unrelated diversified firms, *Organization Science*, 3: 501–521.

73. M. Tortoriello, 2015, The social underpinnings of absorptive capacity: The moderating effects of structural holes on innovation generation based on external knowledge, *Strategic Management Journal*, 36: 586–597; M. Makri, M. A. Hitt, & P. J. Lane, 2010, Complementary technologies, knowledge relatedness and invention outcomes in high technology mergers and acquisitions, *Strategic Management Journal*, 31: 602–628.

74. M. Palmie, M. M. Keupp, & O. Gassmann, 2014, Pull the right levers: Creating internationally "useful" subsidiary competence by organizational architecture, *Long Range Planning*, 47: 32–48; J. Wolf & W. G. Egelhoff, 2013, An empirical evaluation of conflict in MNC matrix structure firms, *International Business Review*, 22: 591–601; S. H. Appelbaum, D. Nadeau, & M. Cyr, 2008, Performance evaluation in a matrix organization: A case study (part two), *Industrial and Commercial Training*, 40: 295–299.

75. T. W. Tong, J. J. Reuer, B. B. Tyler, & S. Zhang, 2015, Host country executives' assessments of international joint ventures and divestitures: An experimental approach, *Strategic Management Journal*, 36: 254–275; S. H. Appelbaum, D. Nadeau, & M. Cyr, 2009, Performance evaluation in a matrix organization: A case study (part three), *Industrial and Commercial Training*, 41: 9–14.

76. A. V. Sakhartov & T. B. Folta, 2014, Resource relatedness, redeployability, and firm value, *Strategic Management Journal*, 35: 1781–1797; O. Alexy, G. George, & A. J. Salter, 2013, Cui bono? The selective revealing of knowledge and its implications for innovative activity, *Academy of Management Review*, 38: 270–291; E. Rawley, 2010, Diversification, coordination costs, and organizational rigidity: Evidence from microdata, *Strategic Management Journal*, 31: 873–891.

77. E. R. Feldman, S. C. Gilson, & B. Villalonga, 2014, Do analysts add value when they most can? Evidence from corporate spin-offs, *Strategic Management Journal*, 35: 1446–1463; M. Kruehler, U. Pidun, & H. Rubner, 2012, How to assess the corporate parenting strategy? A conceptual answer, *Journal of Business Strategy*, 33(4): 4–17; M. M. Schmid & I. Walter, 2009, Do financial conglomerates create or destroy economic value? *Journal of Financial Intermediation*, 18: 193–216.

78. T. M. Alessandri & A. Seth, 2014, The effects of managerial ownership on international and business diversification: Balancing incentives and risks, *Strategic Management Journal*, 35: 2064–2075; N. T. Dorata, 2012, Determinants of the strengths and weaknesses of acquiring firms in mergers and acquisitions: A stakeholder perspective, *International Journal of Management*, 29: 578–590; R. E. Hoskisson & M. A. Hitt, 1990, Antecedents and performance outcomes of diversification: A review and critique of theoretical perspectives, *Journal of Management*, 16: 461–509.

79. Y. Yang, V. K. Narayanan, & D. M. De Carolis, 2014, The relationship between portfolio diversification and firm value: The evidence from corporate venture capital activity, *Strategic Management Journal*, 35: 1993–2011; A. Varmaz, A. Varwig, & T. Poddig, 2013, Centralized resource planning and yardstick competition, *Omega*, 41: 112–118; Hill, Hitt, & Hoskisson, Cooperative versus competitive structures, 512.

80. M. Arrfelt, R. M. Wiseman, G. McNamara, & G. T. M. Hult, 2015, Examining a key corporate role: The influence of capital allocation competency on business unit performance, *Strategic Management Journal*, in press; D. Holod, 2012, Agency and internal capital market inefficiency: Evidence from banking organizations, *Financial Management*, 41: 35–53.

81. 2015, How is Textron organized? Textron Home Page, www.textron.com, May 15.

82. 2015, Our company, Textron Home Page, www.textron.com, May 15

83. C. Custodio, 2014, Mergers and acquisitions accounting and the diversification discount, *Journal of Finance*, 69: 219–240.

84. R. Belderbos, T. W. Tong, & S. Wu, 2014, Multinationality and downside risk: The roles of option portfolio and organization, *Strategic Management Journal*, 35: 88–106; R. M. Holmes, Jr., T. Miller, M. A. Hitt, & M. P. Salmador, 2013, The interrelationships among informal institutions, formal institutions and inward foreign direct investment, *Journal of Management*, 39: 531–566; T. Yu & A. A. Cannella, Jr., 2007, Rivalry between multinational enterprises: An event history approach, *Academy of Management Journal*, 50: 665–686.

85. T. Huang, F. Wu, J. Yu, & B. Zhang, 2015, Political risk and dividend policy: Evidence from international political crises, *Journal of International Business Studies*, in press; A. H. Kirca, G. T. M. Hult, S. Deligonul, M. Z. Perryy, & S. T. Cavusgil, 2012, A multilevel examination of the drivers of firm multinationality: A meta-analysis, *Journal of Management*, 38: 502–530.

86. G. Vasudeva, E. A. Alexander, & S. L. Jones, 2015, Institutional logics and interorganizational learning in technological arenas: Evidence from standard-setting organizations in the mobile handset industry, *Organization Science*, in press; J.-L. Arregle, T. Miller, M. A. Hitt, & P. W. Beamish, 2013, Do regions matter? An integrated institutional and semiglobalization perspective on the internationalization of MNEs, *Strategic Management Journal*, 34: 910–934.

87. L. Li, G. Qian, & Z. lan, 2014, Inconsistencies in international product strategies and performance of high-tech firms, *Journal of International Marketing*, 22: 94–113; P. Almodóvar, 2012, The international performance of standardizing and customizing Spanish firms: The M curve relationships, *Multinational Business Review*, 20: 306–330; G. R. G. Benito, R. Lunnan, & S. Tomassen, 2011, Distant encounters of the third kind: Multinational companies locating divisional headquarters abroad, *Journal of Management Studies*, 48: 373–394.

88. 2015, Our company, Uber Home Page, www.uber.com, May 15.

89. R. Fannin, 2015, Uber proves going local and partnering works in China, *Forbes*, www.forbes.com, April 30.

90. H. Merchant, 2014, Configurations of governance structure, generic strategy, and firms size: Opening the black box of value creation in international joint ventures, *Global Strategy Journal*, 4: 292–309; B. Brenner & B. Ambos, 2013, A question of legitimacy? A dynamic perspective on multinational firm control, *Organization Science*, 24: 773–795; M. P. Koza, S. Tallman, & A. Ataay, 2011, The strategic assembly of global firms: A microstructural analysis of local learning and global adaptation, *Global Strategy Journal*, 1: 27–46.

91. K. Bondy & K. Starkey, 2014, The dilemmas of internationalization: Corporate social responsibility in the multinational corporation, *British Journal of Management*, 25: 4–22; J. Qiu & L. Donaldson, 2012, Stopford and Wells were right! MNC matrix structures do fit a "high-high" strategy, *Management International Review*, 52: 671–689; B. Connelly, M. A. Hitt, A. DeNisi, & R. D. Ireland, 2007, Expatriates and corporate-level international strategy: Governing with the knowledge contract, *Management Decision*, 45: 564–581.

92. T. Wakayama, J. Shintaku, & A. Tomofumi, 2012, What Panasonic learned in China, *Harvard Business Review*, 90(12): 109–113.

93. Wakayama, Shintaku, & Tomofumi, What Panasonic learned in China.

94. 2015, A better life, a better world, Panasonic Home Page, www.panasonic.com, May 15.

95. Y. Lku & T. Ravichandran, 2015, Alliance experience, IT-enable knowledge integration, and ex-ante value gains, *Organization Science*, 26: 511–530; I. Neyens & D. Faems, 2013, Exploring the impact of alliance portfolio management design on alliance portfolio performance, *Managerial & Decision Economics*, 34: 347–361.

96. D. Filiou & S. Golesorkhi, 2015, Influence of institutional differences on firm innovation from international alliances, *Long Range Planning*, in press; V. A. Aggarwal, N. Siggelkow, & H. Singh, 2011, Governing collaborative activity: Interdependence and the impact of coordination and exploration, *Strategic Management Journal*, 32: 705–730; J. Li, C. Zhou, & E. J. Zajac, 2009, Control, collaboration, and productivity in international joint ventures: Theory and evidence, *Strategic Management Journal*, 30: 865–884.

97. W. (Stone) Shi, S. L. Sun, B. C. Pinkham, & M. W. Peng, 2014, Domestic alliance network to attract foreign partners: Evidence from international joint ventures in China, *Journal of International Business Studies*, 45: 338–362; R. Gulati, P. Puranam, & M. Tushman, 2012, Meta-organization design: Rethinking design in interorganizational and community context, *Strategic Management Journal*, 33: 571–586; J. Wincent, S. Anokhin, D. Örtqvist, & E. Autio, 2010, Quality meets structure: Generalized reciprocity and firm-level advantage in strategic networks, *Journal of Management Studies*, 47: 597–624.

98. P. C. Patel, S. A. Fernhaber, P. P. McDougall-Covin, & R. P. van der Have, 2014, Beating competitors to international markets: The value of geographically balanced networks for innovation, *Strategic Management Journal*, 35: 691–711; V. Van de Vrande, 2013, Balancing your technology-sourcing portfolio: How sourcing mode diversity enhances innovative performance, *Strategic Management Journal*, 34: 610–621; T. P. Moliterno & D. M. Mahony, 2011, Network theory of organization: A multilevel approach, *Journal of Management*, 37: 443–467.

99. F. J. Contractor & J. J. Reuer, 2014, Structuring and governing alliances: New directions for research, *Global Strategy Journal*, 4: 241–256; L. Dooley, D. Kirk, & K. Philpott, 2013, Nurturing life-science knowledge discovery: Managing multi-organisation networks, *Production Planning & Control*, 24: 195–207; A. T. Arikan & M. A. Schilling, 2011, Structure and governance of industrial districts: Implications for competitive advantage, *Journal of Management Studies*, 48: 772–803.

100. C. Bellavitis, I. Filatotchev, & D. S. Kamuriwo, 2014, The effects of intra-industry and extra-industry networks on performance: A case of venture capital portfolio firms, *Managerial and Decision Economics*, 35: 129–144; R. Vandaie & A. Zaheer, 2014, Alliance partners and firm capability: Evidence from the motion picture industry, *Organization Science*, 26: 22–36.

101. M. A. O. Dos Santos, G. Svensson, & C. Padin, 2014, Implementation, monitoring and evaluation of sustainable business practices: Framework and empirical illustration, *Corporate Governance*, 14: 515–530; B. Baudry & V. Chassagnon, 2012, The vertical network organization as a specific governance structure: What are the challenges for incomplete contracts theories and what are the theoretical implications for the boundaries of the (hub-) firm? *Journal of Management & Governance*, 16: 285–303.

102. Z. Kahn, Y. K. Lew, & R. R. Sinkovics, 2015, International joint ventures as boundary spanners: Technological knowledge transfer in an emerging economy, *Global Strategy Journal*, 5: 48–68; R. Gulati, F. Wohlgezogen, & P. Zhelyazkov, 2012, The two facets of collaboration: Cooperation and coordination in strategic alliances, *Academy of Management Annals*, 6: 531–583; M. H. Hansen, R. E. Hoskisson, & J. B. Barney, 2008, Competitive advantage in alliance governance: Resolving the opportunism minimization-gain maximization paradox, *Managerial and Decision Economics*, 29: 191–208; G. Lorenzoni & C. Baden-Fuller, 1995, Creating a strategic center to manage a web of partners, *California Management Review*, 37: 146–163.

103. F. Zambuto, G. L. Nigro, & J. P. O'Brien, 2015, The importance of alliances in firm capital structure decisions: Evidence from biotechnology firms, *Managerial and Decision Economics*, in press; A. C. Inkpen, 2008, Knowledge transfer and international joint ventures: The case of NUMMI and General Motors, *Strategic Management Journal*, 29: 447–453; J. H. Dyer & K. Nobeoka, 2000, Creating and managing a high-performance knowledge-sharing network: The Toyota case, *Strategic Management Journal*, 21: 345–367.

104. A. Lipparini, G. Lorenzoni, & S. Ferriani, 2014, From core to periphery and back: A study on the deliberate shaping of knowledge flows in interfirm dyads and networks, *Strategic Management Journal*, 35: 578–595; N. Lahiri & S. Narayanan, 2013, Vertical integration, innovation and alliance portfolio size: Implications for firm performance, *Strategic Management Journal*, 34: 1042–1064; L. F. Mesquita, J. Anand, & J. H. Brush, 2008, Comparing the resource-based and relational views: Knowledge transfer and spillover in vertical alliances, *Strategic Management Journal*, 29: 913–941; M. Kotabe, X. Martin, & H. Domoto, 2003, Gaining from vertical partnerships: Knowledge transfer, relationship duration and supplier performance improvement in the U.S. and Japanese automotive industries, *Strategic Management Journal*, 24: 293–316.

105. Y. Luo, Y. Liu, Q. Yang, V. Maksimov, & J. Hou, 2015, Improving performance and reducing cost in buyer-supplier relationships: The role of justice in curtailing opportunism, *Journal of Business Research*, 68: 607–615; S. G. Lazzarini, D. P. Claro, & L. F. Mesquita, 2008, Buyer-supplier and supplier-supplier alliances: Do they reinforce or undermine one another? *Journal of Management Studies*, 45: 561–584; P. Dussauge, B. Garrette, & W. Mitchell, 2004, Asymmetric performance: The market share impact of scale and link alliances in the global auto industry, *Strategic Management Journal*, 25: 701–711.

106. Treflis team, 2015, Walgreens reports a strong Q2 driven by growth in holiday sales and Medicare Part D scripts, *Forbes*, www.forbes.com, April 10.

107. 2015, Strategic alliances: Not so niche anymore, *Coherence*, www.coherence360.com, May 10.

108. W. E. Gillis, J. G. Combs, & D. J. Ketchen, Jr., 2014, Using resource-based theory to help explain plural form franchising, *Entrepreneurship Theory and Practice*, 38: 449–472; A. M. Hayashi, 2008, How to replicate success, *MIT Sloan Management Review*, 49: 6–7; M. Tuunanen & F. Hoy, 2007, Franchising: Multifaceted form of entrepreneurship, *International Journal of Entrepreneurship and Small Business*, 4: 52–67.

109. R. Hahn & S. Gold, 2014, Resources and governance in "base of the pyramid"-partnerships: Assessing collaborations between businesses and non-business actors, *Journal of Business Research*, 67: 1321–1333; W. Vanhaverbeke, V. Gilsing, & G. Duysters, 2012, Competence and governance in strategic collaboration: The differential effect of network structure on the creation of core and noncore technology, *Journal of Product Innovation Management*, 29: 784–802; A. Zaheer, R. Gözübüyük, & H. Milanov, 2010, It's the connections: The network perspective in interorganizational research, *Academy of Management Perspectives*, 24: 62–77.

110. L. Baertlein, 2015, McDonald's reset to change structure, cut costs, boost franchises, *Reuters*, www.reuters.com, May 4.

111. C. Lioukas & J. Reuer, 2015, Isolating trust outcomes from exchange relationships: Social exchange and learning benefits of prior ties in alliances, *Academy of Management Journal*, in press; Y. Lew & R. R. Sinkovics, 2013, Crossing borders and industry sectors: Behavioral governance in strategic alliances and product innovation for competitive advantage, *Long Range Planning*, 46: 13–38; T. W. Tong, J. J. Reuer, & M. W. Peng, 2008, International joint

ventures and the value of growth options, *Academy of Management Journal*, 51: 1014–1029.

112. A. Peterman, A. Kourula, & R. Levitt, 2014, Balancing act: Government roles in an energy conservation network, *Research Policy*, 43: 1067–1082; H. Liu, X. Jiang, J. Zhang, & X. Zhao, 2013, Strategic flexibility and international venturing by emerging market firms: The moderating effects of institutional and relational factors, *Journal of International Marketing*, 21(2): 79–98; M. W. Hansen, T. Pedersen, & B. Petersen, 2009, MNC strategies and linkage effects in developing countries, *Journal of World Business*, 44: 121–130; A. Goerzen, 2005, Managing alliance networks: Emerging practices of multinational corporations, *Academy of Management Executive*, 19(2): 94–107.

113. M. de Vaan, 2014, Interfirm networks in periods of technological turbulence and stability, *Research Policy*, 43: 1666–1680; C. C. Phelps, 2010, A longitudinal study of the influence of alliance network structure and composition on firm exploratory innovation, *Academy of Management Journal*, 53: 890–913; L. H. Lin, 2009, Mergers and acquisitions, alliances and technology development: An empirical study of the global auto industry, *International Journal of Technology Management*, 48: 295–307.

12

Strategic Leadership

Studying this chapter should provide you with the strategic management knowledge needed to:

12-1 Define strategic leadership and describe top-level managers' importance.

12-2 Explain what top management teams are and how they affect firm performance.

12-3 Describe the managerial succession process using internal and external managerial labor markets.

12-4 Discuss the value of strategic leadership in determining the firm's strategic direction.

12-5 Describe the importance of strategic leaders in managing the firm's resources.

12-6 Explain what must be done for a firm to sustain an effective culture.

12-7 Describe what strategic leaders can do to establish and emphasize ethical practices.

12-8 Discuss the importance and use of organizational controls.

© RomanOkopny/Getty Images

CAN YOU FOLLOW AN ICON AND SUCCEED?
APPLE AND TIM COOK AFTER STEVE JOBS

Steve Jobs was Apple's founder and icon CEO. Much of Apple's phenomenal success, especially after 2000, was attributed to Steve Job's "genius" and leadership. Because of this and Tim Cook having a significantly different style from Jobs, he was given little chance for success. Yet, in 2014, several years after Cook assumed the CEO position, Apple had what Tim Cook referred to as an unbelievable year. Apple sold 200 million iPhones and had $200 billion in revenue. Apple's stock price increased by 65 percent, and the company's market value reached more than $700 billion, the largest ever of any U.S. firm. The $700 billion in market value is more than twice as much as either Microsoft or Exxon Mobil. Cook's primary experience has been as manager of operations; he was Apple's COO prior to assuming the CEO role. And, much of Apple's sales are based on products developed and introduced to the market under Job's leadership. So, the jury is still out on Cook, especially with regard to developing new products and making them a success in the marketplace. Steve Jobs was a master at this process.

Cook's style of leadership is much different from the approach used by Jobs. Some considered Jobs to be ruthless and impulsive and almost maniacal in developing new products and ensuring a high quality product desirable in the market. Cook's knowledge and skills do not make him an expert in product development, design, or marketing. So, he delegates those responsibilities but remains as the leader and decision maker. Cook tries to buffer and maintain Apple's corporate culture developed largely by Jobs.

Bloomberg/Getty Images

Thus, the emphasis remains on innovation that is valued in the marketplace. Cook has learned the importance of hiring other top managers with talent but who also fit into Apple's culture. He has made some very good hires, such as Angela Ahrendts who now heads Apple's very important retail stores. Cook takes a much less emotional approach than Jobs. Some refer to it as a "measured emotional approach to leadership." He empowers his team to manage their functional areas and emphasizes the need to take a long-run perspective.

Observers have been able to highlight other differences between Cook's and Job's strategic leadership approaches. Cook shares the limelight with his leadership team, whereas Jobs kept the light on himself. In fact, one analyst suggested that Cook is a good leader who builds an effective team around him. Cook is leading Apple to be more philanthropic than in the past. His strategy has entailed a major acquisition (an audio company for $3 billion) and developing enterprise solutions for corporate IT units, both strategic actions that Jobs eschewed. Apple has formed an alliance with IBM to develop enterprise applications many of which will be designed for the iPad, especially the new and larger versions.

Innovations developed during Cook's leadership include the Apple watch, introduced to the market in April 2015. Many are waiting to learn its rate of success. Initial reports suggest that demand is exceeding supply, causing Apple to increase production. In addition, hints provided by Cook suggest that Apple may be planning to enter the television market. Most importantly, Cook claims that Apple's goal is to change the way people work and will target the development of future products for that purpose.

Sources: T. Loftus, 2015, The morning download: Apple will 'change the way people work,' CEO Tim Cook says, *CIO Journal*, blogs.wsj.com, January 28: 2015, Apple's Tim Cook cites record sales and 'unbelievable' year, *New York Times*, www.nytimes.com, March 10; A. Chang, 2015, Apple CEO Tim Cook is forging an unusual path as a social activist, *Los Angeles Times*, www.latimes.com, March 31, A. Lashinsky, 2015, Becoming *Tim* Cook, *Fortune*, April 1, 60–72; T. Higgins, 2015, Apple iPhones sales in China outsell the U.S. for first time, *BloombergBusiness*, www.bloomberg.com, April 27; J. Lewis, 2015, Tim Cook: A courageous innovator, *Time*, April 27, 26; J. D'Onfro, 2015, Tim Cook dropped a major clue about Apple's next big product, *Yahoo Finance*, finance.yahoo.com, April 28.

As the Opening Case suggests, strategic leaders' work is demanding, challenging, and requires balancing short-term performance outcomes with long-term performance goals. Regardless of how long (or short) they remain in their positions, strategic leaders (and most prominently CEOs) affect a firm's performance.[1] Obviously, Steve Jobs was well known as a highly successful CEO who led Apple to achieve very high performance. There were questions about whether anyone could follow him as CEO and be successful. Those questions dogged Tim Cook, who became Apple's CEO after Jobs passed away. Yet, three and a half years into his tenure as CEO, Apple had an incredibly successful year and became the first company to achieve a market value of $700 billion.

A major message in this chapter is that effective strategic leadership is the foundation for successfully using the strategic management process. As implied in Figure 1.1 in Chapter 1 and through the Analysis-Strategy-Performance model, strategic leaders guide the firm in ways that result in forming a vision and mission. Often, this guidance involves leaders creating goals that stretch everyone in the organization as a foundation for enhancing firm performance. A positive outcome of stretch goals is their ability to provoke breakthrough thinking—thinking that often leads to innovation.[2] Additionally, strategic leaders work with others to verify that the analysis and strategy parts of the A-S-P model are completed effectively in order to increase the likelihood the firm will achieve strategic competitiveness and earn above-average returns. We show how effective strategic leadership makes all of this possible in Figure 12.1.[3]

To begin this chapter, we define strategic leadership and discuss its importance and the possibility of strategic leaders as a source of competitive advantage for a firm. These introductory comments include a brief consideration of different styles strategic leaders may use. We then examine the role of top-level managers and top management teams and their effects on innovation, strategic change, and firm performance. Following this discussion is an analysis of managerial succession, particularly in the context of the internal and external managerial labor markets from which strategic leaders are selected. Closing the chapter are descriptions of five key leadership actions that contribute to effective strategic leadership: determining strategic direction, effectively managing the firm's resource portfolio, sustaining an effective organizational culture, emphasizing ethical practices, and establishing balanced organizational controls.

12-1 Strategic Leadership and Style

Strategic leadership is the ability to anticipate, envision, maintain flexibility, and empower others to create strategic change as necessary.

Strategic change is change brought about as a result of selecting and implementing a firm's strategies.

Strategic leadership is the ability to anticipate, envision, maintain flexibility, and empower others to create strategic change as necessary. **Strategic change** is change brought about as a result of selecting and implementing a firm's strategies. Multifunctional in nature, strategic leadership involves managing through others, managing an entire organization rather than a functional subunit, and coping with change that continues to increase in the global economy. Because of the global economy's complexity, strategic leaders must learn how to effectively influence human behavior, often in uncertain environments.[4]

Figure 12.1 Strategic Leadership and the Strategic Management Process

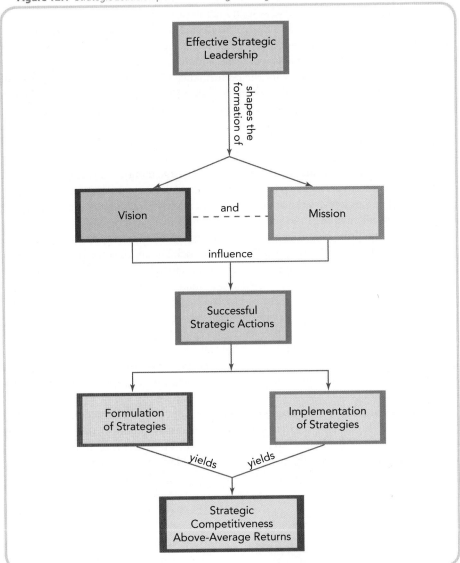

By word or by personal example, and through their ability to envision the future, effective strategic leaders meaningfully influence the behaviors, thoughts, and feelings of those with whom they work.[5]

The ability to attract and then manage human capital may be the most critical of the strategic leader's skills,[6] especially because the lack of talented human capital constrains firm growth. Indeed, in the twenty-first century, intellectual capital that the firm's human capital possesses, including the ability to manage knowledge and produce innovations, affects a strategic leader's success.[7]

Effective strategic leaders also create and then support the context or environment through which stakeholders (such as employees, customers, and suppliers) can perform at peak efficiency.[8] Being able to demonstrate the skills of attracting and managing human capital and establishing and nurturing an appropriate context for that capital to flourish is important, especially given that the crux of strategic leadership is the ability to manage the firm's operations effectively and sustain high performance over time.[9]

The primary responsibility for effective strategic leadership rests at the top, in particular with the CEO. Other commonly recognized strategic leaders include members of the board of directors, the top management team, and divisional general managers. In truth, any individual with responsibility for the performance of human capital and/or a part of the firm (e.g., a production unit) is a strategic leader. Regardless of their title and organizational function, strategic leaders have substantial decision-making responsibilities that cannot be delegated.[10] Strategic leadership is a complex but critical form of leadership. Strategies cannot be formulated and implemented for the purpose of achieving above-average returns without effective strategic leaders.

As a strategic leader, a firm's CEO is involved with a large number and variety of tasks, all of which, in some form or fashion, relate to effective use of the strategic management process.[11] ThyssenKrupp is the largest steel manufacturer in Germany with a long and successful tenure. However, ThyssenKrupp began to suffer financial problems, and a new CEO was recruited to turnaround the firm's performance. Accepting responsibility for reshaping the firm and handling the controversies facing it was Dr.-Ing. Heinrich Hiesinger. Formerly affiliated with another large German firm—Siemens—Hiesinger became chair of the executive board of ThyssenKrupp in January 2011. Hiesinger faced a number of issues. For example, the firm reported heavy losses during 2011 and 2012 and another smaller loss in 2013. The resignation, in March 2013, of ThyssenKrupp's supervisory chair and various scandals that emerged during the chair's service were additional problems requiring Hiesinger's attention. The range of issues with which Hiesinger had to deal highlights the complexity of a strategic leader's work as well as the influence of that work on a firm's shape and scope. He obviously dealt with the problems effectively because the firm returned to profitability in 2014 and continued on a positive path in 2015.[12]

A leader's style and the organizational culture in which it is displayed often affect the productivity of those being led. ThyssenKrupp's Heinrich Hiesinger has spoken about these realities, saying that in the past at the firm he is leading there was an "understanding of leadership in which 'old boys' networks' and blind loyalty were more important than business success."[13] Hiesinger worked hard to earn both trust and credibility with the firm's stakeholders.

PATRIK STOLLARZ/Getty Images

Heinrich Hiesler, Chairman of the Board for ThyssenKrupp, is addressing the shareholders as a part of his effort to maintain their trust.

The style of leadership used by those in top management positions is important. Likely, the leader's style will be based, at least partially, on his or her personal ideology and experience.[14] For example, based on his personal ideology, Tim Cook, CEO of Apple, initiated more philanthropic activities for the firm, and he spoke out on important social issues, such as treating all people equally regardless of ethnicity, gender, or sexual orientation. He also delegated responsibility and authority to other members of the Apple leadership team and empowered them to act. In this way, Cook displayed forms of what are referred to as responsible leadership (demonstrating concern for the firm's stakeholders and society at large).[15] Although Cook has tried to guard the Apple corporate culture, he has obviously made changes in the way people are managed and in the broader corporate focus. Thus, his style has been transformational as well.

Transformational leadership is considered to be one of the most effective strategic leadership styles. This style entails motivating followers to exceed the expectations others have of them, to continuously enrich their capabilities, and to place the interests of the organization above their own.[16] Transformational leaders develop and communicate a vision for the organization and formulate a strategy to achieve that vision. They make followers aware of the need to achieve valued organizational outcomes and encourage them to continuously strive for higher levels of achievement.

Transformational leaders have a high degree of integrity and character. Speaking about character, one CEO said the following:

"Leaders are shaped and defined by character. Leaders inspire and enable others to do excellent work and realize their potential. As a result, they build successful, enduring organizations."[17]

Additionally, transformational leaders have emotional intelligence. Emotionally intelligent leaders understand themselves well, have strong motivation, are empathetic with others, and have effective interpersonal skills.[18] As a result of these characteristics, transformational leaders are especially effective in promoting and nurturing innovation in firms.[19]

12-2 The Role of Top-Level Managers

To exercise the duties of their role, top-level managers make many decisions, such as the strategic actions and responses that are part of the competitive rivalry with which the firm is involved at a point in time (see Chapter 5). More broadly, they are involved with making many decisions associated with first selecting and then implementing the firm's strategies.

When making decisions related to using the strategic management process, managers (certainly top-level ones) often use their discretion (or latitude for action).[20] Managerial discretion differs significantly across industries. The primary factors that determine the amount of decision-making discretion held by a manager (especially a top-level manager) are

1. external environmental sources such as the industry structure, the rate of market growth in the firm's primary industry, and the degree to which products can be differentiated
2. characteristics of the organization, including its size, age, resources, and culture
3. characteristics of the manager, including commitment to the firm and its strategic outcomes, tolerance for ambiguity, skills in working with different people, and aspiration levels (see Figure 12.2)

Because strategic leaders' decisions are intended to help the firm outperform competitors, how managers exercise discretion when making decisions is critical to the firm's success[21] and affects or shapes the firm's culture.

Top-level managers' roles in verifying that their firm effectively uses the strategic management process are complex and challenging. Because of this, top management teams, rather than a single top-level manager, typically make these types of decisions.[22]

12-2a Top Management Teams

The **top management team** is composed of the individuals who are responsible for making certain the firm uses the strategic management process, especially for the purpose of

A **top management team** is composed of the individuals who are responsible for making certain the firm uses the strategic management process, especially for the purpose of selecting and implementing strategies.

Figure 12.2 Factors Affecting Managerial Discretion

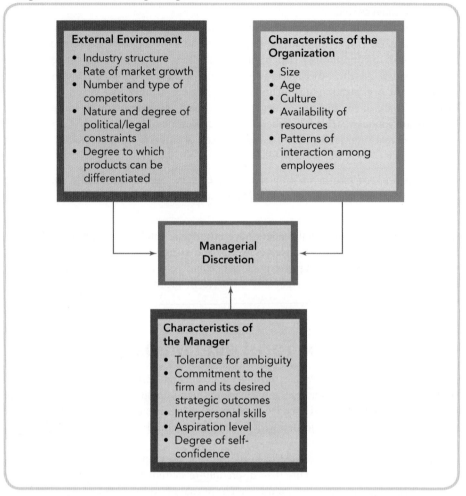

Source: Adapted from S. Finkelstein & D C. Hambrick, 1996, *Strategic Leadership: Top Executives and Their Effects on Organizations*, St. Paul, MN: West Publishing Company.

selecting and implementing strategies. Typically, the top management team includes the officers of the corporation, defined by the title of vice president and above or by service as a member of the board of directors.[23] Among other outcomes, the quality of a top management team's decisions affects the firm's ability to innovate and change in ways that contribute to its efforts to earn above-average returns.[24]

As previously noted, the complex challenges facing most organizations require the exercise of strategic leadership by a team of executives rather than by a single individual. Using a team to make decisions about how the firm will compete also helps to avoid another potential problem when these decisions are made by the CEO alone: managerial hubris. Research shows that when CEOs begin to believe glowing press accounts and to feel that they are unlikely to make errors, the quality of their decisions suffers.[25] Top-level managers need to have self-confidence but must guard against allowing it to become arrogance and a false belief in their own invincibility.[26] To guard against CEO overconfidence and the making of poor decisions, firms often use a top management *team* to make decisions required by the strategic management process.

Top Management Teams, Firm Performance, and Strategic Change

The job of top-level managers is complex and requires a broad knowledge of the firm's internal organization (see Chapter 3) as well as the three key parts of its external environment—the general, industry, and competitor environments (see Chapter 2). Therefore, firms try to form a top management team with the knowledge and expertise needed to operate the internal organization and who can deal with the firm's stakeholders as well as its competitors.[27] Firms also need to structure the top management team in a way to best utilize the members' expertise (e.g., create structural interdependence to make the best decisions).[28] To have these characteristics normally requires a heterogeneous top management team. A **heterogeneous top management team** is composed of individuals with different functional backgrounds, experience, and education. Increasingly, having international experience is a critical aspect of the heterogeneity that is desirable in top management teams, given the globalized nature of the markets in which most firms now compete.[29]

Research evidence indicates that members of a heterogeneous top management team benefit from discussing their different perspectives.[30] In many cases, these discussions, and the debates they often engender, increase the quality of the team's decisions, especially when a synthesis emerges within the team after evaluating different perspectives.[31] In effect, top management team members learn from each other and thereby develop a better decision.[32] In turn, higher-quality decisions lead to stronger firm performance.[33]

In addition to their heterogeneity, the effectiveness of top management teams is also influenced by the value gained when members of these teams work together cohesively. In general, the more heterogeneous and larger the top management team, the more difficult it is for the team to cohesively implement strategies effectively.[34] Noteworthy is the finding that communication difficulties among top-level managers with different backgrounds and cognitive skills can negatively affect strategy implementation efforts.[35] As a result, a group of top executives with diverse backgrounds may inhibit the process of decision making if it is not effectively managed. In these cases, top management teams may fail to comprehensively examine threats and opportunities, leading to suboptimal decisions. Thus, the CEO must attempt to achieve behavioral integration among the team members.[36]

Having members with substantive expertise in the firm's core businesses is also important to a top management team's effectiveness.[37] In a high-technology industry, for example, it may be critical for a firm's top management team members to have R&D expertise, particularly when growth strategies are being implemented. However, their eventual effect on decisions depends not only on their expertise and the way the team is managed but also on the context in which they make the decisions (the governance structure, incentive compensation, etc.).[38]

The characteristics of top management teams, and even the personalities of the CEO and other team members, are related to innovation and strategic change.[39] For example, more heterogeneous top management teams are positively associated with innovation and strategic change, perhaps in part because heterogeneity may influence the team, or at least some of its members, to think more creatively when making decisions and taking actions.[40]

Therefore, firms that could benefit by changing their strategies are more likely to make those changes if they have top management teams with diverse backgrounds and expertise. In this regard, evidence suggests that when a new CEO is hired from outside the industry, the probability of strategic change is greater than if the new CEO is from inside the firm or inside the industry.[41] Although hiring a new CEO from outside the industry adds diversity to the team, such a change can affect the firm's relationships with important stakeholders, especially the customers and employees.[42] Consistent with

A **heterogeneous top management team** is composed of individuals with different functional backgrounds, experience, and education.

earlier comments, we highlight here the value of transformational leadership to strategic change as the CEO helps the firm match environmental opportunities with its strengths, as indicated by its capabilities and core competencies, as a foundation for selecting and/ or implementing new strategies.[43]

The CEO and Top Management Team Power

We noted in Chapter 10 that the board of directors is an important governance mechanism for monitoring a firm's strategic direction and for representing stakeholders' interests, especially shareholders. In fact, higher performance normally is achieved when the board of directors is more directly involved in helping to shape the firm's strategic direction.[44]

Boards of directors, however, may find it difficult to direct the decisions and resulting actions of powerful CEOs and top management teams.[45] Often, a powerful CEO appoints a number of sympathetic outside members to the board or may have inside board members who are also on the top management team and report to her or him.[46] In either case, the CEO may significantly influence actions such as appointments to the board. Thus, the amount of discretion a CEO has in making decisions is related to the board of directors and the decision latitude it provides to the CEO and the remainder of the top management team.[47]

CEOs and top management team members can also achieve power in other ways. For example, a CEO who also holds the position of chair of the board usually has more power than the CEO who does not.[48] Some analysts and corporate "watchdogs" criticize the practice of *CEO duality* (when the positions of CEO and the chair of the board are held by the same person) because it can lead to poor performance and slow responses to change, partly because the board often reduces its efforts to monitor the CEO and other top management team members when CEO duality exists.[49]

Although it varies across industries, CEO duality occurs most commonly in larger firms. Increased shareholder activism has brought CEO duality under scrutiny and attack in both U.S. and European firms. In this regard, we noted in Chapter 10 that a number of analysts, regulators, and corporate directors believe that an independent board leadership structure without CEO duality has a net positive effect on the board's efforts to monitor top-level managers' decisions and actions, particularly with respect to financial performance. However, CEO duality's actual effects on firm performance (and particularly financial performance) remain inconclusive.[50] Moreover, recent evidence suggests that, at least in a sample of firms in European countries, CEO duality can have a positive effect on performance when a firm encounters a crisis.[51] Yet, recent evidence suggests that some firms have begun to separate the CEO and board chair positions. Some of the separations occur because of poor performance but not all. In other cases, the separation is created to allow an experienced board chair to mentor a new CEO (new CEO serves as an apprentice for a period of time).[52] Thus, it seems that nuances or situational conditions must be considered when analyzing the outcomes of CEO duality on firm performance. For example, power differentials can occur among top management team members when a family holds an important ownership position even in large public firms. Typically, top managers who are also members of the family may have a special form of power which can cause conflict unless the power can be balanced across the top management team.[53]

Top management team members and CEOs who have long tenure—on the team and in the organization—have a greater influence on board decisions. In general, long tenure may constrain the breadth of an executive's knowledge base. Some evidence suggests that with the limited perspectives associated with a restricted knowledge base, long-tenured top executives typically develop fewer alternatives to evaluate when making strategic decisions.[54] However, long-tenured managers also may be able to exercise more effective strategic control, thereby obviating the need for board members' involvement because effective strategic control generally leads to higher performance.[55] Intriguingly, it may be that "the liabilities of short tenure … appear to exceed the advantages, while the advantages of long tenure—firm-specific human and social capital, knowledge, and power—seem to outweigh the disadvantages of rigidity and maintaining the status quo."[56] Overall then, the relationship between CEO tenure and firm performance is complex and nuanced,[57] indicating that a board of directors should develop an effective working relationship with the top management team as part of its efforts to enhance firm performance.

Another nuance or situational condition to consider is the case in which a CEO acts as a *steward* of the firm's assets. In this instance, holding the dual roles of CEO and board chair facilitates the making of decisions and the taking of actions that benefit stakeholders. The logic here is that the CEO, desiring to be the best possible steward of the firm's assets, gains efficiency through CEO duality.[58] Additionally, because of this person's positive orientation and actions, extra governance and the coordination costs resulting from an independent board leadership structure become unnecessary.[59]

In summary, the relative degrees of power held by the board and top management team members should be examined in light of an individual firm's situation. For example, the abundance of resources in a firm's external environment and the volatility of that environment may affect the ideal balance of power between the board and the top management team. Moreover, a volatile and uncertain environment may create a situation where a powerful CEO is needed to move quickly. In such an instance, a diverse top management team may create less cohesion among team members, perhaps stalling or even preventing appropriate decisions from being made in a timely manner. In the final analysis, an effective working relationship between the board and the CEO and other top management team members is the foundation through which decisions are made that have the highest probability of best serving stakeholders' interests.[60]

12-3 Managerial Succession

The choice of top-level managers—particularly CEOs—is a critical decision with important implications for the firm's performance.[61] As discussed in Chapter 10, selecting the CEO is one of the boards of directors' most important responsibilities as it seeks to represent the best interests of a firm's stakeholders. Many companies use leadership screening systems to identify individuals with strategic leadership potential as well as to determine the criteria individuals should satisfy to be a candidate for the CEO position.

The most effective of these screening systems assesses people within the firm and gains valuable information about the capabilities of other companies' strategic leaders.[62] Based on the results of these assessments, training and development programs are provided to various individuals in an attempt to preselect and shape the skills of people with strategic leadership potential.

A number of firms have high-quality leadership programs in place, including Procter & Gamble (P&G), GE, IBM, and Dow Chemical. For example, P&G is thought to have talent throughout the organization

© Corepics VOF/Shutterstock.com

Managers participating in a leadership training program.

who are trained to accept the next level of leadership responsibility when the time comes. Managing talent on a global basis, P&G seeks to consistently provide leaders at all levels in the firm with meaningful work and significant responsibilities as a means of simultaneously challenging and developing them. The value created by GE's leadership training programs is suggested by the fact that many companies recruit leadership talent from this firm.[63]

In spite of the value high-quality leadership training programs can create, there are many companies that have not established training and succession plans for their top-level managers or for others holding key leadership positions (e.g., department heads, sections heads). With respect to family-owned firms operating in the United States, a recent survey found that only 41 percent of those surveyed have established leadership contingency plans while 49 percent indicated that they "review succession plans (only) when a change in management requires it."[64] The results are similar for family firms on a global basis as a broader survey of family firms in Asia, Europe, and Latin America found that only the most successful companies have a clear understanding of the party responsible for managing the CEO succession process. In 44 percent of the firms surveyed, the board of directors had that responsibility.[65] On a global scale, recent evidence suggests that "only 45 percent of executives from 34 countries around the world say their companies have a process for conducting CEO succession planning."[66] Unfortunately, the need for continuity in the use of a firm's strategic management process is difficult to attain without an effective succession plan and process in place.

Organizations select managers and strategic leaders from two types of managerial labor markets—internal and external.[67] An **internal managerial labor market** consists of a firm's opportunities for managerial positions and the qualified employees within that firm. An **external managerial labor market** is the collection of managerial career opportunities and the qualified people who are external to the organization in which the opportunities exist.

Employees commonly prefer that the internal managerial labor market be used for selection purposes, particularly when the firm is choosing members for its top management team and a new CEO. Evidence suggests that these preferences are often fulfilled. For example, about 66 percent of new CEOs selected in *Fortune 500* companies were promoted from within. And, the new CEOs chosen had worked at the firm and average of 12.8 years.[68] In the replacement for Steve Jobs at Apple, Tim Cook represents an internal promotion, as discussed in the Opening Case.

With respect to the CEO position, several benefits are thought to accrue to a firm using the internal labor market to select a new CEO, one of which is the continuing commitment to the existing vision, mission, and strategies for the firm. Also, because of their experience with the firm and the industry in which it competes, inside CEOs are familiar with company products, markets, technologies, and operating procedures. Another benefit is that choosing a new CEO from within usually results in lower turnover among existing personnel, many of whom possess valuable firm-specific knowledge and skills. In summary, CEOs selected from inside the firm tend to benefit from their

1. clear understanding of the firm's personnel and their capabilities
2. appreciation of the company's culture and its associated core values
3. deep knowledge of the firm's core competencies as well as abilities to develop new ones as appropriate
4. "feel" for what will and will not "work" in the firm[69]

In spite of the understandable and legitimate reasons to select CEOs from inside the firm, boards of directors sometimes prefer to choose a new CEO from the external

An **internal managerial labor market** consists of a firm's opportunities for managerial positions and the qualified employees within that firm.

An **external managerial labor market** is the collection of managerial career opportunities and the qualified people who are external to the organization in which the opportunities exist.

managerial labor market. Conditions suggesting a potentially appropriate preference to hire from outside include

1. the firm's need to enhance its ability to innovate
2. the firm's need to reverse its recent poor performance
3. the fact that the industry in which the firm competes is experiencing rapid growth
4. the need for strategic change[70]

Overall, the decision to use either the internal or the external managerial labor market to select a firm's new CEO is one that should be based on expectations; in other words, what does the board of directors want the new CEO and top management team to accomplish? We address this issue in Figure 12.3 by showing how the composition of the top management team and the CEO succession source (managerial labor market) interact to affect strategy. For example, when the top management team is homogeneous (its members have similar functional experiences and educational backgrounds) and a new CEO is selected from inside the firm, the firm's current strategy is unlikely to change. If the firm is performing well, absolutely and relative to peers, continuing to implement the current strategy may be precisely what the board of directors wants to happen. Alternatively, when a new CEO is selected from outside the firm and the top management team is heterogeneous, the probability is high that strategy will change. This, of course, would be a board's preference when the firm's performance is declining, both in absolute terms and relative to rivals. When the new CEO is from inside the firm and a heterogeneous top management team is in place, the strategy may not change, but innovation is likely to continue. An external CEO succession with a homogeneous team creates a more ambiguous situation. Furthermore, outside CEOs who lead moderate change often achieve increases in performance, but high strategic change by outsiders frequently leads to declines in performance.[71] In summary, a firm's board of directors should use the insights shown in Figure 12.3 to inform its decision about which of the two managerial labor markets to use when selecting a new CEO.

An interim CEO is commonly appointed when a firm lacks a succession plan or when an emergency occurs requiring an immediate appointment of a new CEO. Companies throughout the world use this approach.[72] Interim CEOs are almost always from inside the firm.

Figure 12.3 Effects of CEO Succession and Top Management Team Composition on Strategy

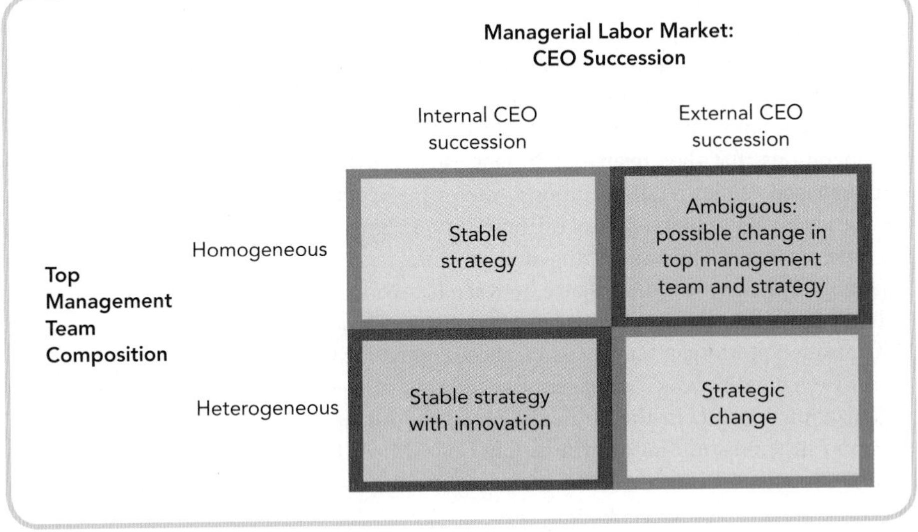

Sir Howard Stringer, the first foreign CEO of Sony in Japan.

Helga Esteb/Shutterstock.com

Their familiarity with the company's operations supports their efforts to "maintain order" for a period of time. Indeed, a primary advantage of appointing an interim CEO is that doing so can generate the amount of time the board of directors requires to conduct a thorough search to find the best candidate from the external and internal markets.

Not all changes in CEOs are successful. For example, some Japanese firms have experimented with foreign CEOs. The intent is to encourage strategic changes, but foreign-born CEOs must have the capability to gain acceptance from other managers and employees in the firm, or their changes are unlikely to be implemented effectively. Thus, most Japanese firms that hire foreign CEOs search for one who has work experience in Japan so that he or she understands the culture and the typical styles used in Japanese firms.[73] Additionally, firms have learned that it is generally important to retain target company executives after the firm is acquired. Without them, integration of the newly acquired firm into the acquiring firm is commonly more difficult. Moreover, the executives often have valuable knowledge and capabilities that are lost to the acquirer if they depart. Thus, turnover among these executives makes the acquisition less valuable to the acquiring firm.[74]

Changes in top management positions other than the CEO are also important. These changes often occur because a promising manager is recruited for a better position at another company, as Apple did with Angela Ahrendt who was recruited to manage its retail operations. She received a highly attractive compensation package to join the Apple top management team, as explained in the Opening Case. Adding high performing managers in key positions can help the firm build its capabilities, as Apple has done with Ahrendt. Yet, some managers are asked to depart because of the poor performance of the operations that they oversee.[75] In fact, this was the case for Ahrendt's predecessor who managed Apple's retail operations. Interestingly, performance was not an issue when Google changed its chief financial officer (CFO) in 2015. Patrick Pichette, Google's CFO at the time, announced he was retiring after seven years. He wanted to spend more time with his family and achieve more balance between his work and family. He was encouraged to retire by his wife and travel more with her. His replacement was Ruth Porat, who held the CFO position at Morgan Stanley when she accepted the CFO position at Google.[76]

As we have discussed, managerial succession in the CEO position is an important organizational event. In the Strategic Focus, we further describe the importance of a selection in choosing Mary Barra as CEO of GM. Although an insider, she has made several changes to increase efficiency (e.g., reducing the number of lead engineers

Strategic **Focus**

Trial by Fire: CEO Succession at General Motors

Late in 2013, Dan Akerson, the CEO of General Motors (GM) during a time of intense scrutiny and criticism of the firm, announced that he was accelerating his retirement. He had planned to retire at the end of 2014, but he learned that his wife had a severe illness, so he decided to retire early. To succeed Akerson, Mary Barra was chosen. She became the first woman CEO of a major automaker in the world. Her selection to become the new CEO for GM was a major celebration for breaking the "glass ceiling" in a formerly male-dominated industry. Her choice represented an inside succession, as she had spent her entire career at GM.

Barra had her hands full trying to create change in an archaic structure and corporate governance system. For example, for years GM used three lead engineers for every new product, requiring more time, extra coordination and often significant inefficiencies. Barra announced changes that resulted in only one lead engineer for every new vehicle. As it turned out the inefficient structure was a minor problem relative to what she soon encountered. She learned about a substantial problem with an ignition switch on GM vehicles that evidently caused wrecks, major injuries, and even death. Worse, the company had known about the problem for years but took no action to fix the problem or to acknowledge it. When she learned of the problem, Barra acted swiftly (although not quick enough for some). GM acknowledged the problem and made compensation offers to families of people who were killed in accidents because of the defective ignition switch. Additionally, GM recalled almost 30 million vehicles to fix the problem. But, this was a public relations disaster, and she was called to testify before Congress about the problem.

Beyond these actions, Barra is trying to change the culture at the company so that such problems do not occur in the future. Her "trial by fire" has been recognized by GM's board of directors because she earned $16.2 million in 2014, which is 80 percent more than her predecessor received. Her challenges continue. Barra is trying to increase capital spending by 20 percent to improve existing product lines and to continue developing an enhanced electric vehicle. However, she also has to deal with declining profits in GM's European and Latin American markets.

Regardless, Barra paid blue collar workers a larger bonus in 2015 than required by the union contract showing her commitment to GM employees. She also announced plans to distribute about $5 billion in dividends to shareholders by the end of 2016. She also hopes to bolster GM's stock price by buying back about $5 billion in stock in the same time period. Thus, Mary Barra made history being named as CEO of GM. She came up through the ranks and knew the firm but still faced substantial challenges during her first year in the position. She has weathered the trial by fire and has a vision for the future.

JEWEL SAMAD/AFP/Getty Images

Mary Barra, CEO of General Motors, introduces the new Chevrolet Volt.

Sources: G. Gardner, 2013, Dan Akerson leaves GM stronger than he found it, *Detroit Free Press*, www.freep.com, December 10; J. Jusko, 2014, CEO Mary Barra is driving culture change at General Motors, *IndustryWeek*, www.industryweek. com; 2014, Mary Barra General Motors, *European CEO*, www.europeanceo.com, November 27; B. Vlasic, 2015, General Motors chief pledges to move beyond recalls, *New York Times*, www.nytimes.com, January 8; C. M. Portillo, 2015, Let's take a peek at Mary Barra's 2015 to-do list at General Motors, *bizwomen*, www. bizjournals.com/bizwomen, January 14; B. Vlasic, 2015, Despite recalls, GM pays workers a big bonus, *New York Times*, www.nytimes.com, February 4; M. Lewis, 2015, GM's Barra bets she can deliver where predecessors fell short, *New York Times*, www.nytimes.com, March 9; R. Wright, 2015, GM disappoints as Europe and South America reverse, *Financial Times*, www.ft.com, April 23; J. D. Stoll, 2015, GM chief executive Mary Barra earned $16.2 million in 2014, *Wall Street Journal*, www.wsj. com, April 24.

on a new product from three to one) trying to change the culture. Changing the culture is very important to avoid future problems similar to the ignition switch malfunction. Barra is trying to resolve the ignition switch problem and increase the company's transparency on such problems. She appears to have been a very good choice as the new CEO of General Motors. Next, we discuss key actions that effective strategic leaders demonstrate while helping their firm use the strategic management process.

12-4 Key Strategic Leadership Actions

Certain actions characterize effective strategic leadership; we present the most important ones in Figure 12.4. Many of the actions interact with each other. For example, managing the firm's resources effectively includes developing human capital and contributes to establishing a strategic direction, fostering an effective culture, exploiting core competencies, using effective and balanced organizational control systems, and establishing ethical practices. The most effective strategic leaders create viable options in making decisions regarding each of the key strategic leadership actions.[77]

12-4a Determining Strategic Direction

Determining strategic direction involves specifying the vision and the strategy or strategies to achieve this vision over time.[78] The strategic direction is framed within the context of the conditions (i.e., opportunities and threats) that strategic leaders expect their firm to face in roughly the next three to five years.

The ideal long-term strategic direction has two parts: a core ideology and an envisioned future. The core ideology motivates employees through the company's heritage while the envisioned future encourages them to stretch beyond their expectations of accomplishment and requires significant change and progress to be realized.[79] The envisioned future serves as a guide to many aspects of a firm's strategy implementation process, including motivation, leadership, employee empowerment, and organizational design.

Determining strategic direction involves specifying the vision and the strategy or strategies to achieve this vision over time.

Figure 12.4 Exercise of Effective Strategic Leadership

The strategic direction could include a host of actions such as entering new international markets and developing a set of new suppliers to add to the firm's value chain.[80]

Sometimes though, the work of strategic leaders does not result in selecting a strategy that helps a firm reach the vision. This can happen when top management team members and, certainly, the CEO are too committed to the status quo. While the firm's strategic direction remains rather stable across time, actions taken to implement strategies to achieve the vision should be somewhat fluid, largely so the firm can deal with unexpected opportunities and threats that surface in the external environment. An inability to adjust strategies as appropriate is often caused by an aversion to what decision makers conclude are risky actions. An aversion to risky actions is common in firms that have performed well in the past and for CEOs who have been in their jobs for extended periods of time.[81] Research also suggests that some CEOs are erratic or even ambivalent in their choices of strategic direction, especially when their competitive environment is turbulent and it is difficult to identify the best strategy.[82] Of course, these erratic or ambivalent behaviors are unlikely to produce high performance and may lead to CEO turnover. Interestingly, research has found that incentive compensation in the form of stock options encourages talented executives to select the best strategies and thus achieve the highest performance. However, the same incentives used with less talented executives produce lower performance.[83]

In contrast to risk-averse CEOs, charismatic ones may foster stakeholders' commitment to a new vision and strategic direction. Nonetheless, even when being guided by a charismatic CEO, it is important for the firm not to lose sight of its strengths and weaknesses when making changes required by a new strategic direction. The most effective charismatic CEO leads a firm in ways that are consistent with its culture and with the actions permitted by its capabilities and core competencies.[84]

Finally, being ambicultural can facilitate efforts to determine the firm's strategic direction and select and use strategies to reach it. Being ambicultural means that strategic leaders are committed to identifying the best organizational activities to take particularly when implementing strategies, regardless of their cultural origin.[85] Ambicultural actions help the firm succeed in the short term as a foundation for reaching its vision in the longer term.[86]

12-4b Effectively Managing the Firm's Resource Portfolio

Effectively managing the firm's portfolio of resources is another critical strategic leadership action. The firm's resources are categorized as financial capital, human capital, social capital, and organizational capital (including organizational culture).[87]

Clearly, financial capital is critical to organizational success; strategic leaders understand this reality.[88] However, the most effective strategic leaders recognize the equivalent importance of managing each remaining type of resource as well as managing the integration of resources (e.g., using financial capital to provide training opportunities to the firm's human capital). Most importantly, effective strategic leaders manage the firm's resource portfolio by organizing the resources into capabilities, structuring the firm to facilitate using those capabilities, and choosing strategies through which the capabilities can be successfully leveraged to create value for customers.[89] Exploiting and maintaining core competencies and developing and retaining the firm's human and social capital are actions taken to reach these important objectives.

Exploiting and Maintaining Core Competencies

Examined in Chapters 1 and 3, *core competencies* are capabilities that serve as a source of competitive advantage for a firm over its rivals. Typically, core competencies relate to skills within organizational functions, such as manufacturing, finance, marketing, and research and development. Strategic leaders must verify that the firm's core competencies are understood when selecting strategies and then emphasized when implementing those strategies. This suggests, for example, that with respect to their strategies, Apple emphasizes its design competence, while Netflix recognizes and concentrates on its competence of being able to deliver physical, digital, and original content.[90]

Core competencies are developed over time as firms learn from the results of the competitive actions and responses taken during the course of competing with rivals. On the basis of what they learn, firms continuously reshape their capabilities for the purpose of verifying that they are, indeed, the path through which core competencies are being developed and used to establish one or more competitive advantages.

Dan Akerson became CEO of GM in July 2009, a time when the firm required a transformation in order to survive as the foundation for then being able to compete successfully against its global rivals. One of the first decisions Akerson made was to allocate resources for the purpose of building new capabilities in technology development and in marketing, especially in customer service. Akerson helped to turnaround the company, bringing it out of bankruptcy and trying to enrich its core competencies. Now, as explained in the Strategic Focus, Mary Barra is changing the culture and trying to increase the efficiency of GM. In addition, she is trying to gain the trust of human capital (e.g., by paying special bonuses to blue collar workers) thereby building her internal social capital. Strong human capital and social capital are critical for GM to develop and maintain strong core competencies. As we discuss next, human capital and social capital are critical to a firm's success. This is the case for GM as the firm strives to continuously improve its performance. One reason for human capital's importance is that it is the resource through which core competencies are developed and used.

Developing Human Capital and Social Capital

Human capital refers to the knowledge and skills of a firm's entire workforce. From the perspective of human capital, employees are viewed as a capital resource requiring continuous investment.[91]

Bringing talented human capital into the firm and then developing that capital has the potential to yield positive outcomes. A key reason for this is that individuals' knowledge and skills are proving to be critical to the success of many global industries (e.g., automobile manufacturing) as well as industries within countries (e.g., leather and shoe manufacturing in Italy). This fact suggests that "as the dynamics of competition accelerate, people are perhaps the only truly sustainable source of competitive advantage."[92] In all types of organizations—large and small, new and established, and so forth—human capital's increasing importance suggests a significant role for the firm's human resource management function.[93] As one of a firm's support functions on which firms rely to create value (see Chapter 3), human resource management practices facilitate selecting and especially implementing the firm's strategies.[94]

Effective training and development programs increase the probability that some of the firm's human capital will become effective strategic leaders. Increasingly, the link between effective programs and firm success is becoming stronger because the knowledge gained by participating in these programs is integral to forming and then sustaining a firm's competitive advantage.[95] In addition to building human capital's knowledge and skills, these programs inculcate a common set of core values and present a systematic view of the organization, thus promoting its vision and helping form an effective organizational culture.

Effective training and development programs also contribute positively to the firm's efforts to form core competencies.[96] Furthermore, the programs help strategic leaders improve skills that are critical to completing other tasks associated with effective strategic leadership, such as determining the firm's strategic direction, exploiting and maintaining

Human capital refers to the knowledge and skills of a firm's entire workforce. From the perspective of human capital, employees are viewed as a capital resource requiring continuous investment.

the firm's core competencies, and developing an organizational culture that supports ethical practices. Thus, building human capital is vital to the effective execution of strategic leadership.

When investments in human capital (such as providing high-quality training and development programs) are successful, the outcome is a workforce capable of learning continuously. This is an important outcome in that continuous learning and leveraging the firm's expanding knowledge base are linked with strategic success.[97]

Learning also can preclude errors. Strategic leaders may learn more from failure than success because they sometimes make the wrong attributions for the successes.[98] For example, the effectiveness of certain approaches and knowledge can be context specific. Thus, some "best practices" may not work well in all situations. We know that using teams to make decisions can be effective, but sometimes it is better for leaders to make decisions alone, especially when the decisions must be made and implemented quickly (e.g., in crisis situations).[99] As such, effective strategic leaders recognize the importance of learning from success *and* from failure when helping their firm use the strategic management process. To ensure more effective use of the strategic management process, firms have begun to create more diversity among top management team leaders.[100]

When facing challenging conditions, firms may decide to lay off some of their human capital, a decision that can result in a significant loss of knowledge. Research shows that moderate-sized layoffs may improve firm performance primarily in the short run, but large layoffs produce stronger performance downturns in firms because of the loss of human capital.[101] Although it is also not uncommon for restructuring firms to reduce their investments in training and development programs, restructuring may actually be an important time to increase investments in these programs. The reason for this is that restructuring firms have less slack and cannot absorb as many errors; moreover, the employees who remain after layoffs may find themselves in positions without all the skills or knowledge they need to create value through their work.

Viewing employees as a resource to be maximized rather than as a cost to be minimized facilitates successful implementation of a firm's strategies, as does the strategic leader's ability to approach layoffs in a manner that employees believe is fair and equitable. A critical issue for employees is the fairness in the layoffs and how they are treated in their jobs, especially relative to their peers.[102]

Social capital involves relationships inside and outside the firm that help in efforts to accomplish tasks and create value for stakeholders.[103] Social capital is a critical asset given that employees must cooperate with one another and others, including suppliers and customers, in order to complete their work. In multinational organizations, employees often must cooperate across country boundaries on activities such as R&D to achieve performance objectives (e.g., developing new products).[104]

External social capital is increasingly critical to firm success in that few if any companies possess all of the resources needed to successfully compete against their rivals. Firms can use cooperative strategies, such as strategic alliances (see Chapter 9), to develop social capital. Social capital can be built in strategic alliances as firms share complementary resources. Resource sharing must be effectively managed to ensure that the partner trusts the firm and is willing to share its resources.[105] Social capital created this way yields many benefits. For example, firms with strong social capital are able to be more ambidextrous; that is, they can develop or have access to multiple capabilities, providing them with the flexibility to take advantage of opportunities and to respond to threats.[106]

Research evidence suggests that the success of many types of firms may partially depend on social capital. Large multinational firms often must establish alliances in order to enter new foreign markets; entrepreneurial firms often must establish alliances to gain access to resources, venture capital, or other types of resources (e.g., special expertise

Social capital involves relationships inside and outside the firm that help in efforts to accomplish tasks and create value for stakeholders.

Strategic **Focus**

All the Ways You Can Fail!

NBC News experienced several major problems in 2014. Likely, the biggest problem was the suspension of popular nightly news anchor, Brian Williams, for embellishing his role in several past news stories. When this came to light, concerns about his credibility and thus NBC News credibility caused the top executives to take action. In addition, NBC's former top morning show, the Today Show, fell in the ratings. Because of this, Jamie Horowitz was hired from ESPN to make major changes. However, Horowitz and the staff on the show had major differences of opinion, especially with the manner in which Horowitz dealt with staff. These high profile clashes led top executives to let Horowitz go. As a result, Andrew Lack, former president of NBC News, was hired to replace Patricia Fili-Krushel as chair of the NBC Universal News Group. Time will tell if Lack can restore stability, credibility, and high ratings to NBC.

Nokia is an almost textbook case on how to fail. In 2009, Nokia was the market leader in the global smartphone market, but by 2014 it was not listed as a rival in the market. The Nokia brand had disappeared. Before the launch of the Apple iPhone, Nokia had access to the touch screen technology, and Nokia technology specialists recommended integrating it into its smartphones. But, the top leadership at Nokia rejected this idea because Nokia was doing well and using this technology entailed risk. Of course, rivals Samsung and Apple implemented the technology, and those two firms along with others took the smartphone market from Nokia. Nokia's leaders made absolutely horrible decisions and failed because of it.

The Standard Charter bank's profits declined in 2014 by 37 percent relative to the profit achieved in 2013. Most people attribute the bank's performance problems to its weak capital position and its major exposures to risk in Asian markets. The CEO, Peter Sands, was asked to resign. Investors and others had lost confidence in his ability to manage the bank effectively. Essentially, he made minor changes (e.g., reducing costs) but avoided large changes likely needed to turn around the performance of the bank. To replace Sands as CEO, the bank chose William T. Winters, a former head of JPMorgan Chase's investment bank. Standard Charter has experienced many problems in recent years. For example, it has experienced losses on bad loans in increasing amounts. In 2012, it paid fines of $667 million because of charges that it had transferred billions of dollars to Iran and other such countries in violation of the OFAC sanctions. In 2014, it paid $300 million to settle claims that its computer system failed to identify suspicious transactions with high-risk clients. Winters is said to be a very savvy manager

of risk. Investors at Standard Charter should hope it is true, as they now need that expertise and a leader who makes good decisions.

The problems experienced by each of the firms were due to poor executive decisions. In the case of NBC, top managers failed to provide appropriate oversight to ensure the credibility of its news. Also, poor personnel decisions were made. In the case of Nokia, substantial conservatism led to a very poor product decision. In that case, the company fell from market leader to no longer being in existence. Finally, Standard Charter leaders made poor decisions, failing to manage its risks. Additionally, it made perhaps unethical decisions for which the firm was fined. Finally, inadequate technologies led to additional failures.

Andrew Lack hired to become the chair of the NBC Universal News Group.

Bobby Bank/Getty Images

Sources: J. Bean, 2014, Bye Nokia—A failure of management over leadership, *Jonobean*, jonobean.com, November 12; P. J. Davies, 2015, How to give Standard Chartered breathing room it needs, *Wall Street Journal*, www.wsj.com, February 26; J. Anderson & C. Bray, 2015, Standard Charter overhauls leadership, *New York Times*, www.nytimes.com, February 26; J. Flint, 2015, NBC News bringing in new leadership, after high-profile stumbles, *Wall Street Journal*, www.wsj.com, March 3; C. Bray, 2015, Standard Charter profit fell 37% in 2014, *New York Times*, www.nytimes.com, March 4.

that the entrepreneurial firm cannot afford to maintain in-house).[107] However, a firm's culture affects its ability to retain quality human capital and maintain strong internal social capital.

As explained in the Strategic Focus, NBC News, Nokia, and Standard Charter all experienced failures because of poor top managers' decisions. NBC News made poor decisions in the way it managed its human capital, and because of this, it lost the confidence of its audience (loss of social capital). Nokia was overly conservative. Its top executives made monumental mistakes. Standard Charter was losing the confidence of its investors with very poor decisions (including perhaps some unethical ones).

12-4c Sustaining an Effective Organizational Culture

In Chapter 1, we defined *organizational culture* as the complex set of ideologies, symbols, and core values that are shared throughout the firm and that influence how the firm conducts business. Because organizational culture influences how the firm conducts its business and helps regulate and control employees' behavior, it can be a source of competitive advantage.[108] Given that each firm's culture is unique, it is possible that a vibrant organizational culture is an increasingly important source of differentiation for firms to emphasize when pursuing strategic competitiveness and above-average returns. Thus, shaping the context within which the firm formulates and implements its strategies—that is, shaping the organizational culture—is another key strategic leadership action.[109]

Entrepreneurial Mind-Set

Especially in large organizations, an organizational culture often encourages (or discourages) strategic leaders and those with whom they work from pursuing (or not pursuing) entrepreneurial opportunities. (We define and discuss entrepreneurial opportunities in Chapter 13.) This is the case in both for-profit and not-for-profit organizations.[110] This issue is important because entrepreneurial opportunities are a vital source of growth and innovation.[111] Therefore, a key action for strategic leaders to take is to encourage and promote innovation by pursuing entrepreneurial opportunities.[112]

One way to encourage innovation is to invest in opportunities as real options—that is, invest in an opportunity in order to provide the potential option of taking advantage of the opportunity at some point in the future.[113] For example, a firm might buy a piece of land to have the option to build on it at some time in the future should the company need more space and should that location increase in value to the company. Oil companies acquire land leases with an option to drill for oil. Firms might enter strategic alliances for similar reasons. In this instance, a firm might form an alliance to have the option of acquiring the partner later or of building a stronger relationship with it (e.g., developing a new joint venture).[114]

In Chapter 13, we describe how firms of all sizes use strategic entrepreneurship to pursue entrepreneurial opportunities as a means of earning above-average returns. Companies are more likely to achieve the success they desire by using strategic entrepreneurship when their employees have an entrepreneurial mind-set.[115]

Five dimensions characterize a firm's entrepreneurial mind-set: autonomy, innovativeness, risk taking, proactiveness, and competitive aggressiveness.[116] In combination, these dimensions influence the actions a firm takes to be innovative when using the strategic management process.

Autonomy, the first of an entrepreneurial orientation's five dimensions, allows employees to take actions that are free of organizational constraints and encourages them to do so. The second dimension, *innovativeness*, "reflects a firm's tendency to engage in and support new ideas, novelty, experimentation, and creative processes that may result in new products, services, or technological processes."[117] Cultures with a tendency toward innovativeness encourage employees to think beyond existing knowledge, technologies, and parameters to find creative ways to add value. *Risk taking* reflects a willingness by employees and their firm to accept measured levels of risks when pursuing entrepreneurial opportunities. The fourth dimension of an entrepreneurial orientation, *proactiveness*, describes a firm's ability to be a market leader rather than a follower. Proactive organizational cultures constantly use processes to anticipate future market needs and to satisfy them before competitors learn how to do so. Finally, *competitive aggressiveness* is a firm's propensity to take actions that allow it to consistently and substantially outperform its rivals.[118]

Changing the Organizational Culture and Restructuring

Changing a firm's organizational culture is more difficult than maintaining it; however, effective strategic leaders recognize when change is needed. Incremental changes to the firm's culture typically are used to implement strategies.[119] More significant and sometimes even radical changes to organizational culture support selecting strategies that differ from those the firm has implemented historically. Regardless of the reasons for change, shaping and reinforcing a new culture requires effective communication and problem solving, along with selecting the right people (those who have the values desired for the organization), engaging in effective performance appraisals (establishing goals that support the new core values and measuring individuals' progress toward reaching them), and using appropriate reward systems (rewarding the desired behaviors that reflect the new core values).[120]

Evidence suggests that cultural changes succeed only when the firm's CEO, other key top management team members, and middle-level managers actively support them.[121] To effect change, middle-level managers in particular need to be highly disciplined to energize the culture and foster alignment with the firm's vision and mission.[122] In addition, managers must be sensitive to the effects of other changes on organizational culture. For example, downsizings can negatively affect an organization's culture, especially if they are not implemented in accordance with the dominant organizational values.[123] Mary Barra is trying to change the General Motors corporate culture as explained in the earlier Strategic Focus. In so doing, she appears to be sensitive to having the right people in key managerial positions and in supporting the firm's employees as demonstrated by giving the blue collar employees bonuses even though the firm had to pay for injuries caused by the ignition switch failure and endure the high costs of a large recall of vehicles to fix the problem.

12-4d Emphasizing Ethical Practices

The effectiveness of processes used to implement the firm's strategies increases when they are based on ethical practices. Ethical companies encourage and enable people at all levels to act ethically when taking actions to implement strategies. In turn, ethical practices and the judgment on which they are based create "social capital" in the organization, increasing the "goodwill available to individuals and groups" in the organization.[124] Alternatively, when unethical practices evolve in an organization, they may become acceptable to many managers and employees.[125] Once deemed acceptable, individuals are more likely to engage in unethical practices to meet their goals when current efforts to meet them are insufficient.[126]

To properly influence employees' judgment and behavior, ethical practices must shape the firm's decision-making process and be an integral part of organizational culture. In fact, a values-based culture is the most effective means of ensuring that employees comply with the firm's ethical standards. However, developing such a culture requires constant nurturing and support in corporations located in countries throughout the world.[127]

As explained in Chapter 10, some strategic leaders and managers may occasionally act opportunistically, making decisions that are in their own best interests.

This tends to happen when firms have lax expectations in place for individuals to follow regarding ethical behavior. In other words, individuals acting opportunistically take advantage of their positions, making decisions that benefit themselves to the detriment of the firm's stakeholders.[128] Sometimes executives take such actions due to their own greed and hubris.[129] However, when there is evidence of executive wrongdoing, such as having to restate the financial earnings, stockholders and other investors often react very negatively. In fact, it is not uncommon for new CEOs to be hired when wrongdoing comes to light.[130]

Strategic leaders as well as others in the organization are most likely to integrate ethical values into their decisions when the company has explicit ethics codes, the codes are integrated into the business through extensive ethics training, and shareholders expect ethical behavior.[131] Thus, establishing and enforcing a meaningful code of ethics is an important action to take to encourage ethical decision making as a foundation for using the strategic management process.

Strategic leaders can take several actions to develop and support an ethical organizational culture. Examples of these actions include

1. establishing and communicating specific goals to describe the firm's ethical standards (e.g., developing and disseminating a code of conduct)
2. continuously revising and updating the code of conduct, based on inputs from people throughout the firm and from other stakeholders
3. disseminating the code of conduct to all stakeholders to inform them of the firm's ethical standards and practices
4. developing and implementing methods and procedures to use in achieving the firm's ethical standards (e.g., using internal auditing practices that are consistent with the standards)
5. creating and using explicit reward systems that recognize acts of courage (e.g., rewarding those who use proper channels and procedures to report observed wrongdoings)
6. creating a work environment in which all people are treated with dignity[132]

The effectiveness of these actions increases when they are taken simultaneously and thereby are mutually supportive. When strategic leaders and others throughout the firm fail to take actions such as these—perhaps because an ethical culture has not been created—problems are likely to occur.

12-4e Establishing Balanced Organizational Controls

Organizational controls (discussed in Chapter 11) have long been viewed as an important part of the strategic management process particularly the parts related to implementation (see Figure 1.1). Controls are necessary to help ensure that firms achieve their desired outcomes. Defined as the "formal, information-based … procedures used by managers to maintain or alter patterns in organizational activities," controls help strategic leaders build credibility, demonstrate the value of strategies to the firm's stakeholders, and promote and support strategic change.[133] Most critically, controls provide the parameters for implementing strategies as well as the corrective actions to be taken when implementation-related adjustments are required. For example, in light of an insider-trading scandal, KPMG LLP reviewed its training and monitoring programs. The firm's existing safeguards "include training for employees, a whistleblower system, and monitoring of the personal investments of partners and managers." KPMG also moved to safeguard its reputation, even though it was not implicated in the scandal.[134]

In this chapter, we focus on two organizational controls—strategic and financial—that were introduced in Chapter 11. Strategic leaders are responsible for helping the firm develop and properly use these two types of controls.

As we explained in Chapter 11, financial control focuses on short-term financial outcomes. In contrast, strategic control focuses on the *content* of strategic actions rather than their *outcomes*. Some strategic actions can be correct but still result in poor financial outcomes because of external conditions, such as an economic recession, unexpected domestic or foreign government actions, or natural disasters. Therefore, emphasizing financial controls often produces more short-term and risk-averse decisions because financial outcomes may be caused by events beyond leaders and managers' direct control. Alternatively, strategic control encourages lower-level managers to make decisions that incorporate moderate and acceptable levels of risk because leaders and managers throughout the firm share the responsibility for the outcomes of those decisions and actions resulting from them.

The challenge for strategic leaders is to balance the use of strategic and financial controls for the purpose of supporting efforts to improve the firm's performance. The balanced scorecard is a tool strategic leaders use to achieve the sought after balance.

The Balanced Scorecard

The **balanced scorecard** is a tool firms use to determine if they are achieving an appropriate balance when using strategic and financial controls as a means of positively influencing performance.[135] This tool is most appropriate to use when evaluating business-level strategies; however, it can also be used with the other strategies firms implement (e.g., corporate, international, and cooperative).

The underlying premise of the balanced scorecard is that firms jeopardize their future performance when financial controls are emphasized at the expense of strategic controls.[136] This occurs because financial controls provide feedback about outcomes achieved from past actions but do not communicate the drivers of future performance. Thus, an overemphasis on financial controls may promote behavior that sacrifices the firm's long-term, value-creating potential for short-term performance gains. In effect, managers can make self-serving decisions when they focus on the shortterm. Research shows that decisions balancing short-term goals with long-term goals generally lead to higher performance.[137] An appropriate balance of strategic controls and financial controls, rather than an overemphasis on either, allows firms to achieve higher levels of performance.

Four perspectives are integrated to form the balanced scorecard:

- *financial* (concerned with growth, profitability, and risk from the shareholders' perspective)
- *customer* (concerned with the amount of value customers perceive was created by the firm's products)
- *internal business processes* (with a focus on the priorities for various business processes that create customer and shareholder satisfaction)
- *learning and growth* (concerned with the firm's effort to create a climate that supports change, innovation, and growth)

Thus, using the balanced scorecard finds the firm seeking to understand how it responds to shareholders (financial perspective), how customers view it (customer perspective), what processes to emphasize to successfully use its competitive advantage (internal perspective), and what it can do to improve its performance in order to grow (learning and growth perspective).[138] Generally speaking, firms tend to emphasize strategic controls when assessing their performance relative to the learning and growth perspective, whereas the tendency is to emphasize financial controls when assessing performance in terms of the financial perspective.

Firms use different criteria to measure their standing relative to the balanced scorecard's four perspectives. We show sample criteria in Figure 12.5. The firm should select the

The **balanced scorecard** is a tool firms use to determine if they are achieving an appropriate balance when using strategic and financial controls as a means of positively influencing performance.

Figure 12.5 Strategic Controls and Financial Controls in a Balanced Scorecard Framework

Perspectives	Criteria
Financial	• Cash flow • Return on equity • Return on assets
Customer	• Assessment of ability to anticipate customers' needs • Effectiveness of customer service practices • Percentage of repeat business • Quality of communications with customers
Internal Business Processes	• Asset utilization improvements • Improvements in employee morale • Changes in turnover rates
Learning and Growth	• Improvements in innovation ability • Number of new products compared to competitors • Increases in employees' skills

number of criteria that will allow it to have both a strategic and financial understanding of its performance without becoming immersed in too many details.[139]

Strategic leaders play an important role in determining a proper balance between strategic and financial controls, whether they are in single-business firms or large diversified firms. A proper balance between controls is important, in that "wealth creation for organizations where strategic leadership is exercised is possible because these leaders make appropriate investments for future viability (through strategic control), while maintaining an appropriate level of financial stability in the present (through financial control)."[140] In fact, most corporate restructuring is designed to refocus the firm on its core businesses, thereby allowing top executives to reestablish strategic control of their separate business units.[141]

Successfully using strategic control frequently is integrated with appropriate autonomy for the various subunits so that they can gain a competitive advantage in their respective markets.[142] Strategic control can be used to promote the sharing of both tangible and intangible resources among interdependent businesses within a firm's portfolio. In addition, the autonomy provided allows the flexibility necessary to take advantage of specific marketplace opportunities. As a result, strategic leadership promotes simultaneous use of strategic control and autonomy.

As we have explained in this chapter, strategic leaders are critical to a firm's ability to successfully use all parts of the strategic management process, including strategic entrepreneurship, which is the final topic included in the "strategy" part of this text's Analysis-Strategy-Performance model. We turn our attention to this topic in Chapter 13.

SUMMARY

- Effective strategic leadership is a prerequisite to successfully using the strategic management process. Strategic leadership entails the ability to anticipate events, envision possibilities, maintain flexibility, and empower others to create strategic change.

- Top-level managers are an important resource for firms to develop and exploit competitive advantages. In addition, when they and their work are valuable, rare, imperfectly imitable, and nonsubstitutable, strategic leaders are also a source of competitive advantage.

- The top management team is composed of key managers who play a critical role in selecting and implementing the firm's strategies. Generally, they are officers of the corporation and/or members of the board of directors.

- The top management team's characteristics, a firm's strategies, and the firm's performance are all interrelated. For example, a top management team with significant marketing and research and development (R&D) knowledge positively contributes to the firm's use of a growth strategy. Overall, having diverse skills increases the effectiveness of most management teams.

- Typically, performance improves when the board of directors and the CEO are involved in shaping a firm's strategic direction. However, when the CEO has a great deal of power, the board may be less involved in decisions about strategy formulation and implementation. By appointing people to the board and simultaneously serving as CEO and chair of the board, CEOs have increased power.

- In managerial succession, strategic leaders are selected from either the internal or the external managerial labor market. Because of their effect on firm performance, the selection of strategic leaders has implications for a firm's effectiveness. There are a variety of reasons that companies select the firm's strategic leaders from either internal or external sources. In most instances, the internal market is used to select the CEO, but the number of outsiders chosen is increasing. Outsiders often are selected to initiate major changes in strategy.

- Effective strategic leadership has five key leadership actions: determining the firm's strategic direction, effectively managing the firm's resource portfolio (including exploiting and maintaining core competencies and managing human capital and social capital), sustaining an effective organizational culture, emphasizing ethical practices, and establishing balanced organizational controls.

- Strategic leaders must develop the firm's strategic direction, typically working with the board of directors to do so. The strategic direction specifies the image and character the firm

wants to develop over time. To form the strategic direction, strategic leaders evaluate the conditions (e.g., opportunities and threats in the external environment) they expect their firm to face over the next three to five years.

- Strategic leaders must ensure that their firm exploits its core competencies, which are used to produce and deliver products that create value for customers, when implementing its strategies. In related diversified and large firms in particular, core competencies are exploited by sharing them across units and products.

- The ability to manage the firm's resource portfolio and the processes used to effectively implement its strategy are critical elements of strategic leadership. Managing the resource portfolio includes integrating resources to create capabilities and leveraging those capabilities through strategies to build competitive advantages. Human capital and social capital are perhaps the most important resources.

- As a part of managing resources, strategic leaders must develop a firm's human capital. Effective strategic leaders view human capital as a resource to be maximized—not as a cost to be minimized. Such leaders develop and use programs designed to train current and future strategic leaders to build the skills needed to nurture the rest of the firm's human capital.

- Effective strategic leaders build and maintain internal and external social capital. Internal social capital promotes cooperation and coordination within and across units in the firm. External social capital provides access to resources from external parties that the firm needs to compete effectively.

- Shaping the firm's culture is a central task of effective strategic leadership. An appropriate organizational culture encourages the development of an entrepreneurial mind-set among employees and an ability to change the culture as necessary.

- In ethical organizations, employees are encouraged to exercise ethical judgment and to always act ethically. Improved ethical practices foster social capital. Setting specific goals to meet the firm's ethical standards, using a code of conduct, rewarding ethical behaviors, and creating a work environment where all people are treated with dignity are actions that facilitate and support ethical behavior.

- Developing and using balanced organizational controls is the final key leadership action associated with effective strategic leadership. The balanced scorecard is a tool that measures the effectiveness of the firm's strategic and financial controls. An effective balance between these two controls allows for flexible use of core competencies, but within the parameters of the firm's financial position.

KEY TERMS

balanced scorecard 404
determining strategic direction 396
external managerial labor market 392
heterogeneous top management team 389
human capital 398

internal managerial labor market 392
strategic leadership 384
social capital 399
strategic change 384
top management team 387

REVIEW QUESTIONS

1. What is strategic leadership? Why are top-level managers considered to be important resources for an organization?

2. What is a top management team, and how does it affect a firm's performance and its abilities to innovate and design and bring about effective strategic change?

3. What is the managerial succession process? How important are the internal and external managerial labor markets to this process?

4. What is the effect of strategic leadership on determining the firm's strategic direction?

5. How do strategic leaders effectively manage their firm's resource portfolio to exploit its core competencies and

leverage the human capital and social capital to achieve a competitive advantage?

6. What must strategic leaders do to develop and sustain an effective organizational culture?

7. As a strategic leader, what actions could you take to establish and emphasize ethical practices in your firm?

8. Why are strategic controls and financial controls important aspects of strategic leadership and the firm's strategic management process?

Mini-Case

A Change at the Top at Procter & Gamble: An Indication of How Much the CEO Matters?

A. G. Lafley joined Procter & Gamble (P&G) in 1977 as brand assistant for Joy dishwashing liquid. From this beginning, he worked his way through the firm's laundry division, becoming highly visible due to a number of successes including the launching of liquid Tide. A string of continuing accomplishments throughout the firm resulted in Lafley's appointment as P&G's CEO in June 2000, a post he held until retiring in mid-2009. Bob McDonald, who joined P&G in 1980, was Lafley's handpicked successor. McDonald took the top position at P&G in July 2009, but resigned under pressure in May 2013. Lafley, revered by many, was asked to come out of retirement and return to P&G as president, CEO, and chair of the board of directors. Lafley said that when

contacted to return to P&G, he agreed immediately to do so, committing to remain "as long as needed to improve the company's performance." However, speculation is that Lafley likely would not remain beyond three years.

What went wrong for McDonald, a long-time P&G employee who seemed to know the firm well and who received Lafley's support? Not surprisingly, a number of possibilities have been mentioned in response to this question. Some concluded that, under McDonald's leadership, P&G suffered from "poor execution globally," an outcome created in part by P&G's seemingly ineffective responses to aggressive competition in emerging markets. Other apparent problems were a failure to control the firm's costs and employees' loss of confidence in

McDonald's leadership. Still others argued that McDonald did not fully understand the effects on U.S. consumers of the recession in place when he took over, and that, during that time period, P&G "was selling BMWs when cash-tight consumers were looking for Kias." The net result of these types of problems included P&G "losing a step to rivals like Unilever." In turn, this caused investors to become frustrated by "P&G's inability to consistently keep up with its rivals' sales growth and share price gains."

But why bring Lafley back? In a few words, because of his previous success. Among other achievements during his first stint as P&G's main strategic leader were building up the firm's beauty business, acquiring Gillette, expanding the firm's presence in emerging markets, and launching hit products such as Swiffer and Febreze. An overall measure of P&G's success during Lafley's initial tenure as CEO is the fact that the firm's shares increased 63 percent in value while the S&P fell 37 percent in value. Thus, multiple stakeholders, including investors and employees, may believe that Lafley can return the firm to the "glory days" it experienced from 2000 to 2009.

Product innovations are a core concern and an area receiving a significant amount of attention. Analysts suggest that P&G needs to move beyond incremental innovations, seeking to again create entirely new product categories as it did with Swiffer and Febreze. This will be challenging, at least in the short run, given recent declines in allocations to the firm's research and development programs. These reductions have resulted in a product pipeline focused mainly on "reformulating rather than inventing." Additionally, efforts are underway to continue McDonald's strong, recent commitments to reduce the firm's "bloated" cost structure and reenergize the competitive actions it will take in global markets.

Restructuring P&G's multiple brands and products into four sectors, each of which will be headed by a president, is a major change Lafley is initiating. Currently, the firm has two global business divisions—beauty and grooming and household care. Final decisions about the precise compositions of the four sectors were not announced by mid-2013. Speculation, though, was that each sector would be formed "to reflect synergies between various businesses." For example, one expectation was that paper-based products such as "Bounty paper towels, Charmin toilet paper, Pampers diapers and Always feminine care products" would be combined to form a sector. Moreover, Lafley's replacement was expected to be selected from among the four presidents who would be chosen to lead the new sectors.

Sources: D. Benoit, 2013, Critical P&G analysts still waiting on results, *Wall Street Journal*, www.wsj.com, May 24; D. Benoit, 2013, Procter & Gamble gets an upgrade, *Wall Street Journal*, www.wsj.com, May 24; J. Bogaisky, 2013, Congrats, Bill Ackman: Bob McDonald out at P&G; A. G. Lafley returning as CEO, *Forbes*, www.forbes.com, May 23; E. Byron & J. S. Lublin, 2013, Embattled P&G chief replaced by old boss, *Wall Street Journal*, www.wsj.com, May 23; L. Coleman-Lochner & C. Hymowitz, 2013, Lafley's CEO encore at P&G puts rock star legacy at risk: Retail, *Bloomberg*, www.bloomberg.com, May 28; J. S. Lublin & S. Ng, 2013, P&G lines up executives in race for CEO Lafley's successor, *Wall Street Journal*, www.wsj.com, May 30; J. Ritchie, 2013, P&G's hiring of Lafley may buy time for innovation, *Business Courier*, www.bizjournals.com/cincinnati, May 31.

Case Discussion Questions

1. What makes a CEO's job so complex? Use the mini-case to provide examples that help support your answer.

2. Is it a good practice to rehire a former CEO who has retired? Please explain the potential advantages and disadvantages of doing so.

3. What should P&G do to replace Lafley when he retires for a second time? What actions should they take to prepare for the succession?

NOTES

1. M. C. Diaz-Fernandez, M. R. Gonzales-Rodriguez, & B. Simonetti, 2015, Top Management team's intellectual capital and firm performance *European Management Journal*, in press; D. C. Hambrick & T. J. Quigley, 2014, Toward more accurate contextualization of the CEO effect on firm performance, *Strategic Management Journal*, 35: 473–491; A. Mackey, 2008, The effect of CEOs on firm performance, *Strategic Management Journal*, 29: 1357–1367.

2. V. Govindarajan, 2012, The timeless strategic value of unrealistic goals, *HBR Blog Network*, www.hbr.org, October 22.

3. D. Martin, 2014, Thinking about thinking, *Journal of Business Strategy*, 35(5): 49–54; B.-J. Moon, 2013, Antecedents and outcomes of strategic thinking, *Journal of Business Research*, 66: 1698–1708; M. A. Hitt, K. T. Haynes, & R. Serpa, 2010, Strategic leadership for the 21st century, *Business Horizons*, 53: 437–444; R. D. Ireland & M. A. Hitt, 2005, Achieving and maintaining strategic competitiveness in the 21st century: The role of strategic leadership, *Academy of Management Executive*, 19: 63–77.

4. D. Cooper, P. C. Patel, & S. M. B, Thatcher, 2014, It depends: Environmental context and the effects of faultlines on top management team performance, *Organization Science*, 25: 633–652.

5. T. von den Driesch, M. E. S. da Costa, T. C. Flatten, & M. Brettel, 2015, How CEO experience, personality, and network affect firms' dynamic capabilities, *European Management Journal*, in press: M. T. Hansen, H. Ibarra, & U. Peyer, 2013, The best-performing CEOs in the world, *Harvard Business Review*, 91(1): 81–95.

6. M. A. Hitt, C. Miller, & A. Colella, 2015, *Organizational Behavior*, 4th ed., Hoboken, NJ: John Wiley & Sons; D. Frank & T. Obloj, 2014, Firm-specific human capital, organizational incentives, and agency costs: Evidence from retail banking, *Strategic Management Journal*, 35: 1279–1301; B. A. Campbell, R. Coff, & D. Kryscynski, 2012, Rethinking sustained competitive advantage from human capital, *Academy of Management Review*, 37: 376–395.

7. M. A. Axtle-Ortiz, 2013, Perceiving the value of intangible assets in context, *Journal of Business Research*, 56: 417–424.

8. P. J. H. Schoemaker, S. Krupp, & S. Howland, 2013, Strategic leadership: The essential skills, *Harvard Business Review*, 91(1-2): 131–134.

9. C. Chadwick, J. F. Super, & K. Kwon, 2015, Resource orchestration in Practice: CEO emphasis on shrm, commitment-based hr systems and firm performance, *Strategic Management Journal*, 36: 360–376; J. J. Sosik,

10. W. A. Gentry, & J. U. Chun, 2012, The value of virtue in the upper echelons: A multisource examination of executive character strengths and performance, *Leadership Quarterly*, 23: 367–382.

10. D. M. Cable, F. Gino, & B. R. Staats, 2013, Breaking them in or eliciting their best? Reframing socialization and newcomers' authentic self-expression, *Administrative Science Quarterly*, 58: 1–36; T. Hulzschenreuter, I. Kleindienst, & C. Greger, 2012, How new leaders affect strategic change following a succession event: A critical review of the literature, *The Leadership Quarterly*, 23: 729–755.

11. C. Crossland, J. Zyung, N. J. Hiller, & D. C. Hambrick, 2014, CEO career variety: Effects on firm-level strategic and social novelty, *Academy of Management Journal*, 57: 652–674.

12. C. Alessi, 2015, ThyssenKrup swings to profit on cost-cutting, weaker euro, *Wall Street Journal*, www.wsj.com, February 13; S. Reed, 2014, ThyssenKrup post first annual profit in 3 years, *New York Times*, www.nytimes.com, November 20; T. Andresen, 2013, Thyssen woes tarnish 99-year-old steel baron's legacy, *Bloomberg*, www.bloomberg.com, May 21; J. Hromadko, 2013, ThyssenKrupp offers workers amnesty to resolve corruption case, *Wall Street Journal*, www.wsj.com, April 16.

13. J. Ewing, 2012, Embattled German steel maker reports a huge loss, *New York Times*, www.nytimes.com, December 11.

14. F. Briscoe, M. K. Chin, & D. C. Hambrick, 2014, CEO ideology as an element of the corporate opportunity structure for social activists, *Academy of Management Journal*, 57: 1786–1809.

15. J. P. Doe & N. R. Quigley, 2014, Responsible leadership and stakeholder management: Influence pathways and organizational outcomes, *Academy of Management Perspectives*, 28: 255–274.

16. X. Zhang, N. Li, J Ulrich, & R. von Dick, 2015, Getting everyone on board: The effect of differentiated transformational leadership by CEOs on top management team effectiveness and leader-rated firm performance, *Journal of Management*, in press; J. C. Ryan & S. A. A. Tipu, 2013, Leadership effects on innovation propensity: A two-factor full range of leadership model, *Journal of Business Research*, 66: 2116–2129; A. E. Colbert, A. L. Kristof-Brown, B. H. Bradley, & M. R. Barrick, 2008, CEO transformational leadership: The role of goal importance congruence in top management teams, *Academy of Management Journal*, 51: 81–96.

17. H. S. Givray, 2007, When CEOs aren't leaders, *BusinessWeek*, September 3, 102.

18. Y. Dong, M.-G. Seo, & K. Bartol, 2014, No pain, no gain: An affect-based model of developmental job experience and the buffering effects of emotional intelligence, *Academy of Management Journal*, 57: 1056–1077; D. Goleman, 2004, What makes a leader? *Harvard Business Review*, 82(1): 82–91.

19. C. M. Leitch, C. McMullan, & R. T. Harrison, 2013, The development of entrepreneurial leadership: The role of human, social and institutional capital, *British Journal of Management*, 24: 347–366; Y. Ling, Z. Simsek, M. H. Lubatkin, & J. F. Veiga, 2008, Transformational leadership's role in promoting corporate entrepreneurship: Examining the CEO-TMT interface, *Academy of Management Journal*, 51: 557–576.

20. T. Hutzschenreuter & I. Kleindienst, 2013, (How) does discretion change over time? A contribution toward a dynamic view of managerial discretion, *Scandinavian Journal of Management*, 29: 264–281; T. L. Waldron, S. D. Graffin, J. F. Porac, & J. B. Wade, 2013, Third-party endorsements of CEO quality, managerial discretion, and stakeholder reactions, *Journal of Business Research*, 66: 2592–2599.

21. B. E. Lewis, J. L. Walls, & G. W. S. Dowell, 2014, Difference in degrees: CEO characteristics and firm environmental disclosure, *Strategic Management Journal*, 35: 712–722; R. Klingebiel, 2012, Options in the implementation plan of entrepreneurial initiatives: Examining firms' attainment of flexibility benefit, *Strategic Entrepreneurship Journal*, 6: 307–334; D. G. Sirmon, J.-L. Arregle, M. A. Hitt, & J. W. Webb, 2008, The role of family influence in firms' strategic responses to threat of imitation, *Entrepreneurship Theory and Practice*, 32: 979–998.

22. O. R. Mihalache, J. J. P. Jansen, F. A. J. van den Bosch, & H. W. Volberda, 2014, Top management team shared leadership and organizational ambidexterity: A moderated mediation framework, *Strategic Entrepreneurship Journal*, 8: 128–148.

23. M. Menz, 2012, Functional top management team members: A review, synthesis, and research agenda, *Journal of Management*, 38: 45–80; A. M. L. Raes, U. Glunk, M. G. Heijitjes, & R. A. Roe, 2007, Top management team and middle managers, *Small Group Research*, 38: 360–386.

24. A. Ganter & A. Hecker, 2014, Configurational paths to organizational innovation: Qualitative comparative analyses of antecedents and contingencies, *Journal of Business Research*, 67:1285–1292; O. R. Mihalach, J. J. P. Jansen,

F. A. J. Van Den Bosch, & H. W. Volberda, 2012, Offshoring and firm innovation: The moderating role of top management team attributes, *Strategic Management Journal*, 33: 1480–1498.

25. K. T. Haynes, M. A. Hitt, & J. T. Campbell, 2015, The dark side of leadership: Toward a mid-range theory of hubris and greed in entrepreneurial contexts, *Journal of Management Studies*, 52: 479–505; J. Li & Y. Tang, 2010, CEO hubris and firm risk taking in China: The moderating role of managerial discretion, *Academy of Management Journal*, 53: 45–68; M. L. A. Hayward, V. P. Rindova, & T. G. Pollock, 2004, Believing one's own press: The causes and consequences of CEO celebrity, *Strategic Management Journal*, 25: 637–653.

26. A. Y. Ou, A. S Tsui, A. J. Kinicki, D. A. Waldman, Z. Xiao, & L. J. Song, 2014, Humble chief executive officers' connections to top management team integration and middle manager response, *Administrative Science Quarterly*, 59: 34–72; P. J. C. Patel & D. Cooper, 2014, The harder they fall, the faster they rise: Approach avoidance focus in Narcissistic CEOs, *Strategic Management Journal*, 35: 1528–1540.

27. A. Carmeli, A. Tishler, & A. C. Edmondson, 2012, CEO relational leadership and strategic decision quality in top management teams: The role of team trust and learning from failure, *Strategic Organization*, 10: 31–54; V. Souitaris & B. M. M. Maestro, 2010, Polychronicity in top management teams: The impact on strategic decision processes and performance in new technology ventures, *Strategic Management Journal*, 31: 652–678.

28. D. C. Hambrick, S. E. Humphrey, & A. Gupta, 2015, Structural interdependence, within top management teams: A key moderator of upper echelon predictions, *Strategic Management Journal*, 36: 449–461.

29. O. Levy, S. Taylor, N. A. Boyacigiller, T. E. Bodner, M. A. Peiperl, & S. Beechler, 2015, Perceived senior leadership opportunities in MNCs: The effect of social hierarchy and capital, *Journal of International Business Studies*, 46: 285–307.

30. R. Olie, A. van Iteraon, & Z. Simsek, 2012–13, When do CEOs versus top management teams matter in explaining strategic decision-making processes? Toward an institutional view of strategic leadership effects, *International Studies of Management and Organization*, 42(4): 86–105; Y. Ling & F. W. Kellermans, 2010, The effects of family firm specific sources of TMT diversity: The moderating role of information exchange frequency, *Journal of Management Studies*, 47: 322–344.

31. R. Klingebiel & A. De Meyer, 2013, Becoming aware of the unknown: Decision making during the implementation of a strategic initiative, *Organization Science*, 24: 133–153;

A. Srivastava, K. M. Bartol, & E. A. Locke, 2006, Empowering leadership in management teams: Effects on knowledge sharing, efficacy, and performance, *Academy of Management Journal*, 49: 1239–1251; D. Knight, C. L. Pearce, K. G. Smith, J. D. Olian, H. P. Sims, K. A. Smith, & P. Flood, 1999, Top management team diversity, group process, and strategic consensus, *Strategic Management Journal*, 20: 446–465.

32. A. Nadolska & H. G. Barkema, 2014, Good learners: How top management teams affect the success and frequency of acquisitions, *Strategic Management Journal*, 35: 1483–1507.

33. T. Buyl, C. Boone, W. Hendricks, & P. Matthyssens, 2011, Top management team functional diversity and firm performance: The moderating role of CEO characteristics, *Journal of Management Studies*, 48: 151–177; B. J. Olson, S. Parayitam, & Y. Bao, 2007, Strategic decision making: The effects of cognitive diversity, conflict, and trust on decision outcomes, *Journal of Management*, 33: 196–222.

34. S. Finkelstein, D. C. Hambrick, & A. A. Cannella, Jr., 2008, *Strategic Leadership: Top Executives and Their Effects on Organizations*, NY: Oxford University Press.

35. A Minichilli, G. Corbetta, & I. C. Macmillan, 2010, Top management teams in family-controlled companies: 'Familiness', 'faultlines', and their impact on financial performance, *Journal of Management Studies*, 47: 205–222; J. J. Marcel, 2009, Why top management team characteristics matter when employing a chief operating officer: A strategic contingency perspective, *Strategic Management Journal*, 30: 647–658.

36. T. Buyl, C. Boone, & W. Hendriks, 2014, Top management team members' decision influence and cooperative behavior: An empirical study in the information technology industry, *British Journal of Management*, 25: 285–304; Z. Simsek, J. F. Veiga, M. L. Lubatkin, & R. H. Dino, 2005, Modeling the multilevel determinants of top management team behavioral integration, *Academy of Management Journal*, 48: 69–84.

37. A. A. Cannella, J. H. Park, & H. U. Lee, 2008, Top management team functional background diversity and firm performance: Examining the roles of team member collocation and environmental uncertainty, *Academy of Management Journal*, 51: 768–784.

38. J. W. Ridge, F. Aime, & M. A. White, 2015, When much more of a difference makes a difference: Social comparison and tournaments in the CEO's top team, *Strategic Management Journal*, 36: 618–636; A. S. Cui, R. J. Calantone, & D. A. Griffith, 2011, Strategic change and termination of interfirm partnerships, *Strategic Management Journal*, 32: 402–423.

39. P. Herrmann & S. Nadkarni, 2014, Managing strategic change: The duality of CEO personality, *Strategic Management Journal*, 35: 1318–1342; A. E. Colbert, M. R. Barrick, & B. H. Bradley, 2014, Personality and leadership composition in top management teams: Implications for organizational effectiveness, *Personnel Psychology*, 67: 351–387.

40. C. Shalley, M. A. Hitt, & J. Zhou, 2015, Integrating creativity, innovation and entrepreneurship to successfully navigate in the new competitive landscape, in C. Shalley, M. A. Hitt, & J. Zhou (eds.) *Handbook of Creativity, Innovation and Entrepreneurship*, NY: Oxford University Press, pp. 1–14; K. Liu, J. Li, W. Hesterly, & A. A. Cannella, Jr., 2012, Top management team tenure and technological inventions at post-IPO biotechnology firms, *Journal of Business Research*, 65: 1349–1356.

41. J. Tian, J. Haleblian, & N. Rajagopalan, 2011, The effects of board human and social capital on investor reactions to new CEO selection, *Strategic Management Journal*, 32: 731–747; Y. Zhang & N. Rajagopalan, 2003, Explaining the new CEO origin: Firm versus industry antecedents, *Academy of Management Journal*, 46: 327–338.

42. X. Luo, V. K. Kanuri, & M. Andrews, 2014, How does CEO tenure matter? The mediating role of firm-employee and firm-customer relationships, *Strategic Management Journal*, 35: 492–511.

43. P. Y. T. Sun & M. H. Anderson, 2012, Civic capacity: Building on transformational leadership to explain successful integrative public leadership, *The Leadership Quarterly*, 23: 309–323; I. Barreto, 2010, Dynamic capabilities: A review of the past research and an agenda for the future, *Journal of Management*, 36: 256–280.

44. D. H. Zhu & G. Chen, 2015, CEO narcissism and the impact of prior board experience on firm strategy, *Administrative Science Quarterly*, 60: 31–65; M. L. McDonald & J. D. Westphal, 2010, A little help here? Board control, CEO identification with the corporate elite, and strategic help provided to CEOs at other firms, *Academy of Management Journal*, 53: 343–370; L. Tihanyi, R. A. Johnson, R. E. Hoskisson, & M. A. Hitt, 2003, Institutional ownership and international diversification: The effects of boards of directors and technological opportunity, *Academy of Management Journal*, 46: 195–211.

45. K. B. Lewellyn & M. I. Muller-Kahle, 2012, CEO power and risk taking: Evidence from the subprime lending industry, *Corporate Governance: An International Review*, 20: 289–307; S. Wu, X. Quan, & L. Xu, 2011, CEO power, disclosure quality and the variability in firm performance, *Nankai Business Review International*, 2: 79–97.

46. J. Joseph, W. Ocasio, & M.-H. McDonnell, 2014, The structural elaboration of board independence: Executive power,

institutional logics, and the adoption of CEO-only board structures in U.S. corporate governance, *Academy of Management Journal*, 57: 1834–1858; S. Kaczmarek, S. Kimino, & A. Pye, 2012, Antecedents of board composition: The role of nomination committees, *Corporate Governance: An International Review*, 20: 474–489.

47. M. van Essen, P.-J. Engelen, & M. Carney, 2013, Does 'good' corporate governance help in a crisis? The impact of country- and firm-level governance mechanisms in the European financial crisis, *Corporate Governance: An International Review*, 21: 201–224; M. A. Abebe, A. Angriawan, & Y. Lui, 2011, CEO power and organizational turnaround in declining firms: Does environment play a role? *Journal of Leadership and Organizational Studies*, 18: 260–273.

48. C.-H. Liao & A. W.-H. Hsu, 2013, Common membership and effective corporate governance: Evidence from audit and compensation committees, *Corporate Governance: An International Review*, 21: 79–92.

49. P. Cullinan, P. B. Roush, & X. Zheng, 2012, CEO/Chair duality in the Sarbanes-Oxley era; Board independence versus unity of command, *Research on Professional Responsibility and Ethics in Accounting*, 16: 167–183; C. S. Tuggle, D. G. Sirmon, C. R. Reutzel, & L. Bierman, 2010, Commanding board of director attention: Investigating how organizational performance and CEO duality affect board members' attention to monitoring, *Strategic Management Journal*, 32: 640–657; J. Coles & W. Hesterly, 2000, Independence of the chairman and board composition: Firm choices and shareholder value, *Journal of Management*, 26: 195–214.

50. R. Krause & M. Semadeni, 2013, Apprentice, departure, and demotion: An examination of the three types of CEO-board chair separation, *Academy of Management Journal*, 56: 805–826.

51. M. van Essen, P.-J. Engelen, & M. Carney, 2013, Does "good" corporate governance help in a crisis? The impact of country- and firm-level governance mechanisms in the European financial crisis, *Corporate Governance: An International Review*, 21: 201–224.

52. R. Krause & M. Semadeni, 2014, Last dance or second chance? Firm performance, CEO career horizon, and the separation of board leadership roles, *Strategic Management Journal*, 35: 808–825.

53. P. C. Patel & D. Cooper, 2014, Structural power equality between family and non-family TMT members and the performance of family firms, *Academy of Management Journal*, 57: 1624–1649.

54. E. Matta & P. W. Beamish, 2008, The accentuated CEO career horizon problem: Evidence from international acquisitions, *Strategic Management Journal*, 29: 683–700;

N. Rajagopalan & D. Datta, 1996, CEO characteristics: Does industry matter? *Academy of Management Journal*, 39: 197–215.

55. W. Lewis, J. L. Walls, & G. W. S. Dowell, 2014, Difference in degrees: CEO characteristics and firm environmental disclosure, *Strategic Management Journal*, 35: 712–722; R. A. Johnson, R. E. Hoskisson, & M. A. Hitt, 1993, Board involvement in restructuring: The effect of board versus managerial controls and characteristics, *Strategic Management Journal*, 14 (Special Issue): 33–50.

56. Z. Simsek, 2007, CEO tenure and organizational performance: An intervening model, *Strategic Management Journal*, 28: 653–662.

57. M. A. Fitza, 2014, The use of variance decomposition in the investigation of CEO effects: How large must the CEO effect be to rule out chance? *Strategic Management Journal*, 35: 1839–1852; X. Luo, V. K. Kanuri, & M. Andrews, 2014, How does CEO tenure matter? The mediating role of firm-employee and firm-customer relationships, *Strategic Management Journal*, 35: 492–511.

58. M. Hernandez, 2012, Toward an understanding of the psychology of stewardship, *Academy of Management Review*, 37: 172–193.

59. J. W. Ridge & A. Ingram, 2015, Modesty in the top management team: Investor reaction and performance implications, *Journal of Management*, in press; K. Boyd, D. Miller, I. LeBreton-Miller, & B. Scholnick, 2008, Stewardship vs. stagnation: An empirical comparison of small family and non-family businesses, *Journal of Management Studies*, 51: 51–78; J. H. Davis, F. D. Schoorman, & L. Donaldson, 1997, Toward a stewardship theory of management, *Academy of Management Review*, 22: 20–47.

60. M. Menz & C. Scheef, 2014, Chief strategy officers: Contingency analysis of their presence in top management teams, *Strategic Management Journal*, 35: 461–471; A. Holehonnur & T. Pollock, 2013, Shoot for the stars? Predicting the recruitment of prestigious directors at newly public firms, *Academy of Management Journal*, 56: 1396–1419; B. Espedal, O. Kvitastein, & K. Gronhaug, 2012, When cooperation is the norm of appropriateness: How does CEO cooperative behavior affect organizational performance? *British Journal of Management*, 23: 257–271.

61. X. Zhang, N. Li, J. Ullrich, & R. van Dick, 2015, Getting everyone on board: The effect of differentiated transformational leadership by CEOs on top management team effectiveness and leader-related firm performance, *Journal of Management*, in press; J. G. Messersmith, J.-Y. Lee, J P. Guthrie, & Y.-Y Ji, 2014, Turnover at the top: Executive team departures and firm performance, *Organization Science*, 25: 776–793.

62. C. H. Mooney, M. Semadeni, & I. F. Kesner, 2015, The selection of an interim CEO: Boundary conditions and the pursuit of temporary leadership, *Journal of Management*, in press; S. D. Graffin, S. Boivie, & M. A. Carpenter, 2013, Examining CEO succession and the role of heuristics in early-stage CEO evaluation, *Strategic Management Journal*, 34: 383–403.

63. J. P. Donlon, 2013, 40 best companies for leaders 2013, *Chief Executive*, www.chiefexecutive.net, January 12.

64. 2013, Deloitte, Perspectives on family-owned businesses: Governance and succession planning, www.deloitte.com, January.

65. C. Peterson-Withorn, 2015, new survey pinpoints what keeps family businesses going for generations, *Forbes*, www.forbes.com, April 23.

66. 2013, Intersearch survey reveals status of CEO succession plans in companies around the world, Intersearch, www.pendlpiswanger.at/images/content/file/Artikel/CEOsuccession, February.

67. S. Mobbs & C. G. Raheja, 2012, Internal managerial promotions: Insider incentives and CEO succession, *Journal of Corporate Finance*, 18: 1337–1353; S. Rajgopal, D. Taylor, & M. Venkatachalam, 2012, Frictions in the CEO labor market: The role of talent agents in CEO compensation, *Contemporary Accounting Research*, 29: 119–151.

68. 2015, CEO Statistics, Statistic Brain Research Institute, www.statisticbrain.com, March 11.

69. M. Nakauchi & M. F. Wiersema, 2015, Executive succession and strategic change, *Strategic Management Journal*, 36: 298–306; M. Elson & C. K. Ferrere, 2012, When searching for a CEO, there's no place like home, *Wall Street Journal*, www.wsj.com, October 29.

70. W. Li & J. Lu, 2014, Board independence, CEO succession and the scope of strategic change, *Nankai Business Review International*, 5: 309–325.

71. J. J. Marcel, A. P. Cowen, & G. A. Ballinger, 2015, Are disruptive CEO successions viewed as a governance lapse? Evidence from board turnover, *Journal of Management*, in press; Y. Zhang & N. Rajagopalan, 2010, Once an outsider, always an outsider? CEO origin, strategic change and firm performance, *Strategic Management Journal*, 31: 334–346.

72. V. Mehrotra, R. Morck, J. Shim, & Y. Wiwattanakantang, 2013, Adoptive expectations: Rising sons in Japanese family firms, *Journal of Financial Economics*, 108: 840–854; G. A. Ballinger & J. J. Marcel, 2010, The use of an interim CEO during succession episodes and firm performance, *Strategic Management Journal*, 31: 262–283.

73. S. Pandey & S. Rhee, 2015, An inductive study of foreign CEOs of Japanese firms, *Journal of Leadership and Organizational Studies*, 22: 202–216.

74. J. A. Krug, P. Wright, & M. J. Kroll, 2014, Top management turnover following mergers

and acquisitions; Solid research to date but still much to be learned, *Academy of Management Journal*, 28: 147–163.

75. T. Buyl, C. Boone, & J. B. Wade, 2015, non-CEO executive mobility: The impact of poor firm performance and TMT attention, *European Management Review*, in press.

76. J. Baer, 2015, Google hires Morgan Stanley's Porat as finance chief, *Wall Street Journal*, www.wsj.com, March 24; C. Dougherty, 2015, Google CFO is retiring to spend more time with family (No, really), *New York Times*, bits.blogs.nytimes.com, March 10.

77. D. H. Weng & Z. Lin, 2014, Beyond CEO tenure: The effect of CEO newness on strategic changes, *Journal of Management*, 40: 2009–2032; T. Hutzschenreuter, I. Kleindienst, & C. Greger, 2012, How new leaders affect strategic change following a succession event: A critical review of the literature, *The Leadership Quarterly*, 23: 729–755; J. Kotter, 2012, Accelerate! *Harvard Business Review*, 90(11): 45–58.

78. F. F. Jing, G. C. Avery, & H. Bergsteiner, 2014, Enhancing performance in small professional firms through vision communication and sharing, *Asia Pacific Journal of Management*, 31: 599–620; L. Mirabeau & S. Maguire, 2014, From autonomous strategic behavior to emergent strategy, *Strategic Management Journal*, 35: 1202–1229; G. A. Shinkle, A. P. Kriauciunas, & G. Hundley, 2013, Why pure strategies may be wrong for transition economy firms, *Strategic Management Journal*, 34: 1244–1254.

79. Herrmann & Nadkarni, 2014, Managing strategic change; T. Barnett, R. G. Long, & L. E. Marler, 2012, Vision and exchange in intra-family succession: Effects on procedural justice climate among nonfamily managers, *Entrepreneurship Theory and Practice*, 36: 1207–1225.

80. S. Mantere, H. A. Schildt, & J. A. A. Sillince, 2012, Reversal of strategic change, *Academy of Management Journal*, 55: 172–196; S. Sonenshein, 2012, Explaining employee engagement with strategic change implementation: A meaning-making approach, *Organization Science*, 23: 1–23.

81. P. Chaigneau, 2013, Explaining the structure of CEO incentive pay with decreasing relative risk aversion, *Journal of Economics and Business*, 67: 4–23; G. Chen & D. C. Hambrick, 2012, CEO replacement in turnaround situations: Executive (mis)fit and its performance implications, *Organization Science*, 23: 225–243; P. L. McClelland, X. Ling, & V. L. Barker, 2010, CEO commitment to the status quo: Replication and extension using content analysis, *Journal of Management*, 36: 1251–1277.

82. S. Nankarni & J. Chen, 2014, Bridging yesterday, today and tomorrow: CEO temporal focus, environmental dynamism and rate of new product introduction, *Academy of Management Journal*, 57:

1810–1833; J. R. Mitchell, D. A. Shepherd, & M. P. Sharfman, 2011, Erratic strategic decisions: When and why managers are inconsistent in strategic decision making, *Strategic Management Journal*, 32: 683–704.

83. R. Mudambi & T. Swift, 2014, Knowing when to leap: Transitioning between exploitative and explorative R&D, *Strategic Management Journal*, 35: 126–145; J. Wowak & D. C. Hambrick, 2010, A model of person-pay interaction: How executives vary in their response to compensation arrangements, *Strategic Management Journal*, 31: 803–821.

84. G. A. Shinkle & B. T. McCann, 2014, New product deployment: The moderating influence of economic institutional context, *Strategic Management Journal*, 35: 1090–1101; P. M. Wilderom, P. T. van den Berg, & U. J. Wiersma, 2012, A longitudinal study of the effects of charismatic leadership and organizational culture on objective and perceived corporate performance, *The Leadership Quarterly*, 23: 835–848.

85. M.-J. Chen & D. Miller, 2012, West meets east: Toward an ambicultural approach to management, *Academy of Management Perspectives*, 24: 17–24; M.-J. Chen & D. Miller, 2011, The relational perspective as a business mindset: Managerial implications for East and West, *Academy of Management Perspectives*, 25: 6–18.

86. U. Stettner & D. Lavie, 2014, Ambidexterity under scrutiny: Exploration and exploitation via internal organization, alliances and acquisitions, *Strategic Management Journal*, 35: 1903–1925; M. Y. C. Chen, C. Y. Y. Lin, H.-E. Lin, & E. F. McDonough, III, 2012, Does transformational leadership facilitate technological innovation? The moderating roles of innovative culture and incentive compensation, *Asia Pacific Journal of Management*, 29: 239–264.

87. A. Gambardella, C. Panico, & G. Valentini, 2015, Strategic incentives to human capital, *Strategic Management Journal*, 36: 37–52; M. D. Huesch, 2013, Are there always synergies between productive resources and resource deployment capabilities? *Strategic Management Journal*, 34: 1288–1313; J. Kraaijenbrink, J.-C. Spender, & A. J. Groen, 2010, The resource-based view: A review and assessment of its critiques, *Journal of Management*, 36: 349–372.

88. S. D. Julian & J. C. Ofori-dankwa, 2013, Financial resource availability and corporate social responsibility expenditures in a sub-Saharan economy: The institutional difference hypothesis, *Strategic Management Journal*, 34: 1314–1330; T. Vanacker, V. Collewaert, & I. Paeleman, 2013, The relationship between slack resources and the performance of entrepreneurial firms: The role of venture capital and angel investors, *Journal of Management Studies*, 50: 1070–1096.

89. Y. Li, H. Chen, Y. Liu, & M. W. Peng, 2014, Managerial ties, organizational learning, and opportunity capture: A social capital perspective, *Asia Pacific Journal of Management*, 31: 271–291; E. A. Clinton, S. Sciascia, R. Yadav, & F. Roche, 2013, Resource acquisition in family firms: The role of family-influenced human and social capital, *Entrepreneurship Research Journal*, 3: 44–61; H. A. Ndofor, D. G. Sirmon, & X. He, 2011, Firm resources, competitive actions and performance: Investigating a mediated model with evidence from the in-vitro diagnostics industry, *Strategic Management Journal*, 32: 640–657.

90. A. Carr, 2013, Death to core competency: Lessons from Nike, Apple, Netflix, *Fast Company*, www.fastcompany.com, February 14.

91. P. M. Wright, R. Coff, & T. P. Moliterno, 2014, Strategic human capital: Crossing the great divide, *Journal of Management*, 40: 353–370; R. E. Ployhart, C. H. Van Idderkinge, & W. J. MacKenzie, 2011, Acquiring and developing human capital in service contexts: The interconnectedness of human capital resources, *Academy of Management Journal*, 54: 353–368.

92. M. A. Hitt, L. Bierman, K. Uhlenbruck, & K. Shimizu, 2006, The importance of resources in the internationalization of professional service firms: The good, the bad and the ugly, *Academy of Management Journal*, 49: 1137–1157; M. A. Hitt, L. Bierman, K. Shimizu, & R. Kochhar, 2001, Direct and moderating effects of human capital on strategy and performance in professional service firms: A resource-based perspective, *Academy of Management Journal*, 44: 13–28.

93. A. Mackey, J. C. Molloy, & S. S. Morris, 2014, Scarce human capital in managerial labor markets, *Journal of Management*, 40: 399–421; H. Aquinis, H. Joo, & R. K. Gottfredson, 2013, What monetary rewards can and cannot do: How to show employees the money, *Business Horizons*, 56: 241–249.

94. A. Chatterji & A. Patro, 2014, Dynamic capabilities and managing human capital, *Academy of Management Perspectives*, 28: 395–408; R. R. Kehoe & P. M. Wright, 2013, The impact of high-performance human resource practices on employees' attitudes and behaviors, *Journal of Management*, 39: 366–391.

95. Z. J. Zhao & J. Anand, 2013, Beyond boundary spanners: The 'collective bridge' as an efficient interunit structure for transferring collective knowledge, *Strategic Management Journal*, 34: 1513–1530; J. Pfeffer, 2010, Building sustainable organizations: The human factor, *Academy of Management Perspectives*, 24(1): 34–45.

96. K. Z. Zhou & C. B. Li, 2012, How knowledge affects radical innovation: Knowledge base, market knowledge acquisition, and internal knowledge sharing, *Strategic Management Journal*, 33: 1090–1102.

97. J. R. Lecuona & M. Reitzig, 2014, Knowledge worth having in 'excess': The value of tacit and firm-specific human resource slack, *Strategic Management Journal*, 35: 954–973; T. R. Holcomb, R. D. Ireland, R. M. Holmes, & M. A. Hitt, 2009, Architecture of entrepreneurial learning: Exploring the link among heuristics, knowledge, and action, *Entrepreneurship, Theory & Practice*, 33: 173–198.

98. Y. Zheng, A. S. Miner, & G. George, 2013, Does the learning value of individual failure experience depend on group-level success? Insights from a university technology transfer office, *Industrial and Corporate Change*, 22: 1557–1586; R. Hirak, A. C. Peng, A. Carmeli, & J. M. Schaubroeck, 2012, Linking leader inclusiveness to work unit performance: The importance of psychological safety and learning from failure, *The Leadership Quarterly*, 23: 107–117.

99. Hitt, Miller, & Colella, *Organizational Behavior*.

100. A. Cook & C. Glass, 2014, Above the glass ceiling: When are women and racial/ethnic minorities promoted to CEO? *Academy of Management Journal*, 35: 1080–1089.

101. R. Hoskisson, W. Shi, H. Yi, & J. Jin, 2013, The evolution and strategic positioning of private equity firms, *Academy of Management Perspectives*, 27: 22–38; P. M. Norman, F. C. Butler, & A. L. Ranft, 2013, Resources matter: Examining the effects of resources on the state of firms following downsizing, *Journal of Management*, 39: 2009–2038; R. D. Nixon, M. A. Hitt, H. Lee, & E. Jeong, 2004, Market reactions to corporate announcements of downsizing actions and implementation strategies, *Strategic Management Journal*, 25: 1121–1129.

102. R. J. Bies, 2013, The delivery of bad news in organizations: A framework for analysis, *Journal of Management*, 39: 136–162; B. C. Holtz, 2013, Trust primacy: A model of the reciprocal relations between trust and perceived justice, *Journal of Management*, 39: 1891–1923.

103. C. Galunic, G. Krtug, & M. Gargiulo, 2012, The positive externalities of social capital: Benefiting from senior brokers, *Academy of Management Journal*, 55: 1213–1231; P. S. Adler & S. W. Kwon, 2002, Social capital: Prospects for a new concept, *Academy of Management Review*, 27: 17–40.

104. M. Ahearne, S. K. Lam, & F. Krause, 2014, Performance impact of middle managers' adaptive strategy implementation: The role of social capital, *Strategic Management Journal*, 35: 68–87; Y.-Y. Chang, Y. Gong, & M. W. Peng, 2012, Expatriate knowledge transfer, subsidiary absorptive capacity, and subsidiary performance, *Academy of Management Journal*, 55: 927–948; S. Gao, K. Xu, & J. Yang, 2008, Managerial ties, Absorptive capacity & innovation, *Asia Pacific Journal of Management*, 25: 395–412.

105. K. H. Heimeriks, M. Schijven, & S. Gates, 2012, Manifestations of higher-order routines: The underlying mechanisms of deliberate learning in the context of postacquisition integration, *Academy of Management Journal*, 55: 703–726; P. Ozcan & K. M. Eisenhardt, 2009, Origin of alliance portfolios: Entrepreneurs, network strategies, and firm performance, *Academy of Management Journal*, 52: 246–279; W. H. Hoffmann, 2007, Strategies for managing a portfolio of alliances, *Strategic Management Journal*, 28: 827–856.

106. A. M. Kleinbaum & T. E. Stuart, 2014, Inside the black box of the corporate staff: Social networks and the implementation of corporate strategy, *Strategic Management Journal*, 35: 24–47.

107. D. K. Panda, 2014, Managerial networks and strategic orientation in SMEs: Experience from a transition economy, *Journal of Strategy and Management*, 7: 376–397; B. J. Hallen & K. M. Eisenhardt, 2012, Catalyzing strategies and efficient tie formation: How entrepreneurial firms obtain investment ties, *Academy of Management Journal*, 55: 35–70.

108. A. Klein, 2011, Corporate culture: Its value as a resource for competitive advantage, *Journal of Business Strategy*, 32(2): 21–28; J. B. Barney, 1986, Organizational culture: Can it be a source of sustained competitive advantage? *Academy of Management Review*, 11: 656–665.

109. B. Schneider, M. G. Ehrhart, & W. H. Macey, 2013, Organizational climate and culture, *Annual Review of Psychology*, 64: 361–388; E. F. Goldman & A. Casey, 2010, Building a culture that encourages strategic thinking, *Journal of Leadership and Organizational Studies*, 17: 119–128.

110. C. B. Dobni, M. Klassen, & W. T. Nelson, 2015, Innovation strategy in the US: Top executives offer their views, *Journal of Business Strategy*, 36(1): 3–13; P. G. Klein, J. T. Mahoney, A. M. McGahan, & C. N. Pitelis, 2013, Capabilities and strategic entrepreneurship in public organizations, *Strategic Entrepreneurship Journal*, 7: 70–91; R. D. Ireland, J. G. Covin, & D. F. Kuratko, 2009, Conceptualizing corporate entrepreneurship strategy, *Entrepreneurship Theory and Practice*, 33: 19–46.

111. M. S. Wood, A. McKelvie, & J. M. Haynie, 2014, Making it personal: Opportunity individuation and the shaping of opportunity beliefs, *Journal of Business Venturing*, 29: 252–272; R. D. Ireland & J. W. Webb, 2007, Strategic entrepreneurship: Creating competitive advantage through streams of innovation, *Business Horizons*, 50: 49–59.

112. P. L. Schultz, A. Marin, & K. B. Boal, 2014, The impact of media on the legitimacy of new market categories: The case of broadband internet, *Journal of Business Venturing*, 29: 34–54; S. A. Alvarez & J. B. Barney, 2008, Opportunities, organizations and entrepreneurship, *Strategic Entrepreneurship Journal*, 2: 171–174.

113. Y. Tang, J. Li, & H. Yang, 2015, What I see, what I do: How executive hubris affects firm innovation, *Journal of Management*, in press; R. E. Hoskisson, M. A. Hitt, R. D. Ireland, & J. S. Harrison, 2013, *Competing for Advantage*, 3rd ed., Mason, OH: Thomson Publishing.

114. G. Cao, Z. Simsek, & J. J. P. Jansen, 2105, CEO social capital and entrepreneurial orientation of the firm: Bonding and bridging effects, *Journal of Management*, in press; T. W. Tong & S. Li, 2013, The assignment of call option rights between partners in international joint ventures, *Strategic Management Journal*, 34: 1232–1243.

115. C. Bjornskov & N. Foss, 2013, How strategic entrepreneurship and the institutional context drive economic growth, *Strategic Entrepreneurship Journal*, 7: 50–69; M. A. Hitt, R. D. Ireland, D. G. Sirmon, & C. A. Trahms, 2011, Strategic entrepreneurship: Creating value for individuals, organizations and society, *Academy of Management Perspectives*, 25: 57–75; P. G. Kein, 2008, Opportunity discovery, entrepreneurial action and economic organization, *Strategic Entrepreneurship Journal*, 2: 175–190.

116. A. Engelen, C. Neumann, & S. Schmidt, 2015, Should entrepreneurially oriented firms have narcissistic CEOs? *Journal of Management*, in press; G. T. Lumpkin & G. G. Dess, 1996, Clarifying the entrepreneurial orientation construct and linking it to performance, *Academy of Management Review*, 21: 135–172.

117. Lumpkin & Dess, Clarifying the entrepreneurial orientation construct, 142.

118. Ibid., 137.

119. C. L. Wang & M. Rafiq, 2014, Ambidextrous organizational culture, contextual ambidexterity and new product innovation: A comparative study of UK and Chinese high-tech firms, *British Journal of Management*, 25: 58–76; P. Pyoria, 2007, Informal organizational culture: The foundation of knowledge workers' performance, *Journal of Knowledge Management*, 11: 16–30.

120. C. Kane & J. Cunningham, 2014, Turnaround leadership core tensions during the company turnaround process, *European Management Review*, 32: 968–980; W. Langvardt, 2012, Ethical leadership and the dual roles of examples, *Business Horizons*, 55: 373–384.

121. M. N. Kastanakis & B. G. Voyer, 2014, The effect of culture on perception and cognition: A conceptual framework, *Journal of Business Research*, 67: 425–433; J. Kotter, 2011, Corporate culture: Whose job is it? *Forbes*, http://blog.forbes.com/johnkotter, February 17.

122. M. I. Garces & P. Morcillo, 2012, The role of organizational culture in the resource-based view: An empirical study of the Spanish nuclear industry, *International*

Journal of Strategic Change Management,
4: 356–378; E. Mollick, 2012, People and
process, suits and innovators: the role of
individuals in firm performance, *Strategic
Management Journal*, 33: 1001–1015.

123. W. McKinley, S. Latham, & M. Braun, 2014,
Organizational decline and innovation:
Turnarounds and downward spirals,
Academy of Management Review, 39:
88–110; R. Fehr & M. J. Gelfand, 2012, The
forgiving organization: A multilevel
model of forgiveness at work, *Academy
of Management Review*, 37: 664–688;
E. G. Love & M. Kraatz, 2009, Character,
conformity, or the bottom line? How
and why downsizing affected corporate
reputation, *Academy of Management
Journal*, 52: 314–335.

124. Adler & Kwon, Social capital.

125. J. L. Campbell & A. S. Goritz, 2014,
Culture corrupts! A qualitative study
of organizational culture in corrupt
organizations, *Journal of Business Ethics*,
120: 291–311; J. Pinto, C. R. Leana, &
F. K. Pil, 2008, Corrupt organizations or
organizations of corrupt individuals? Two
types of organization-level corruption,
Academy of Management Review, 33:
685–709.

126. A. Arnaud & M. Schminke, 2012, The ethical
climate and context of organizations:
A comprehensive model, *Organization
Science*, 23: 1767–1780; M. E. Scheitzer,
L. Ordonez, & M. Hoegl, 2004, Goal setting
as a motivator of unethical behavior,
Academy of Management Journal, 47:
422–432.

127. J. A. Pearce, 2013, Using social identity
theory to predict managers' emphases on
ethical and legal values in judging business
issues, *Journal of Business Ethics*, 112:
497–514; M. Zhao, 2013, Beyond cops and
robbers: The contextual challenge driving
the multinational corporation public crisis
in China and Russia, *Business Horizons*, 56:
491–501.

128. H. A. Ndofor, C. Wesley, & R. L. Priem, 2015,
Providing CEOs with opportunities to
cheat: The effects of complexity based
information asymmetries on financial
reporting fraud, *Journal of Management*,
in press; I. Okhmaztovksiy & R. J. David,
2012, Setting your own standards: Internal
corporate governance codes as a response
to institutional pressure, *Organization

Science*, 23: 155–176; X. Zhang, K. M. Bartol,
K. G. Smith, M. D. Pfaffer, & D. M. Khanin,
2008, CEOs on the edge: Earnings
manipulation and stock-based incentive
misalignment, *Academy of Management
Journal*, 51: 241–258.

129. K. T. Haynes, J. T. Campbell, & M. A. Hitt,
2015, When more is not enough: Executive
greed and its influence on shareholder
wealth. *Journal of Management*, in press;
Haynes, Hitt, & Campbell, The Dark Side of
Leadership; P. M. Picone, G. B. Dagnino, &
A. Mina, 2014, The origin of failure:
A multidisciplinary appraisal of the hubris
hypothesis and proposed research agenda,
Academy of Management Perspectives, 28(4):
447–468.

130. K. A, Gangloff, B. L. Connelly, & C. L. Shook,
2015, Of scapegoats and signals: Investor
reactions to CEO succession in the
aftermath of wrongdoing, *Journal of
Management*, in press; D. Gomulya &
W. Boeker, 2014, How firms respond to
financial restatement: CEO successors
and external reactions, *Academy of
Management Journal*, 57: 1759–1785.

131. M. S. Schwartz, 2013, Developing and
sustaining an ethical corporate culture: The
core elements, *Business Horizons*, 56: 39–50;
J. M. Stevens, H. K. Steensma, D. A. Harrison,
& P. L. Cochran, 2005, Symbolic or
substantive document? Influence of ethics
codes on financial executives' decisions,
Strategic Management Journal, 26: 181–195.

132. W. H. Bishop, 2013, The role of ethics in
21st century organizations, *Journal of
Business Ethics*, 118: 635–637; B. E. Ashforth,
D. A. Gioia, S. L. Robinson, & L. K. Trevino,
2008, Re-viewing organizational corruption,
Academy of Management Review, 33:
670–684.

133. Control (management), 2015, *Wikipedia*,
http://en.wikipedia.org/wiki/control, May
18; M. D. Shields, F. J. Deng, & Y. Kato, 2000,
The design and effects of control systems:
Tests of direct- and indirect-effects models,
Accounting, Organizations and Society, 25:
185–202.

134. M. Rapoport, 2013, KPMG finds its
safeguards 'sound and effective,' *Wall Street
Journal*, www.wsj.com, June 4.

135. Balanced scorecard, 2015, *Wikipedia*, en.
wikipedia.org/wiki/Balanced_scorecard,
May 18; M. Friesl & R. Silberzahn, 2012,
Challenges in establishing global

collaboration: Temporal, strategic and
operational decoupling, *Long Range
Planning*, 45: 160–181; R. S. Kaplan &
D. P. Norton, 2009, The balanced scorecard:
Measures that drive performance (HBR
OnPoint Enhanced Edition), *Harvard
Business Review*, March.

136. B. E. Becker, M. A. Huselid, & D. Ulrich, 2001,
*The HR Scorecard: Linking People, Strategy,
and Performance*, Boston, MA: Harvard
Business School Press, 21.

137. K. T. Haynes, M. A. Josefy, & M. A. Hitt,
2015, Tipping point: Managers' self-
interest, greed, and altruism, *Journal of
Leadership & Organizational Studies*, 22:
265–279; R. S. Kaplan & D. P. Norton, 2001,
Transforming the balanced scorecard from
performance measurement to strategic
management: Part I, *Accounting Horizons*,
15 (1): 87–104.

138. R. S. Kaplan, 2012, The balanced scorecard:
Comments on balanced scorecard
commentaries, *Journal of Accounting
and Organizational Change*, 8: 539–545;
R. S. Kaplan & D. P. Norton, 1992, The
balanced scorecard—measures that drive
performance, *Harvard Business Review*,
70(1): 71–79.

139. A. Danaei & A. Hosseini, 2013, Performance
measurement using balanced scorecard: A
case study of pipe industry, *Management
Science Letters*, 3: 1433–1438; M. A. Mische,
2001, *Strategic Renewal: Becoming a High-
Performance Organization*, Upper Saddle
River, NJ: Prentice Hall, 181.

140. G. Rowe, 2001, Creating wealth in
organizations: The role of strategic
leadership, *Academy of Management
Executive*, 15: 81–94.

141. J. Xia & S. Li, 2013, The divestiture of
acquired subunits: A resource dependence
approach, *Strategic Management Journal*,
34: 131–148; R. E. Hoskisson, R. A. Johnson,
D. Yiu, & W. P. Wan, 2001, Restructuring
strategies of diversified business groups:
Differences associated with country
institutional environments, in M. A. Hitt,
R. E. Freeman, & J. S. Harrison (eds.),
Handbook of Strategic Management, Oxford,
UK: Blackwell Publishers, 433–463.

142. J. Wincent, S. Thorgren, & S. Anokhin,
2013, Managing maturing government-
supported networks: The shift from
monitoring to embeddedness controls,
British Journal of Management, 24: 480–497.

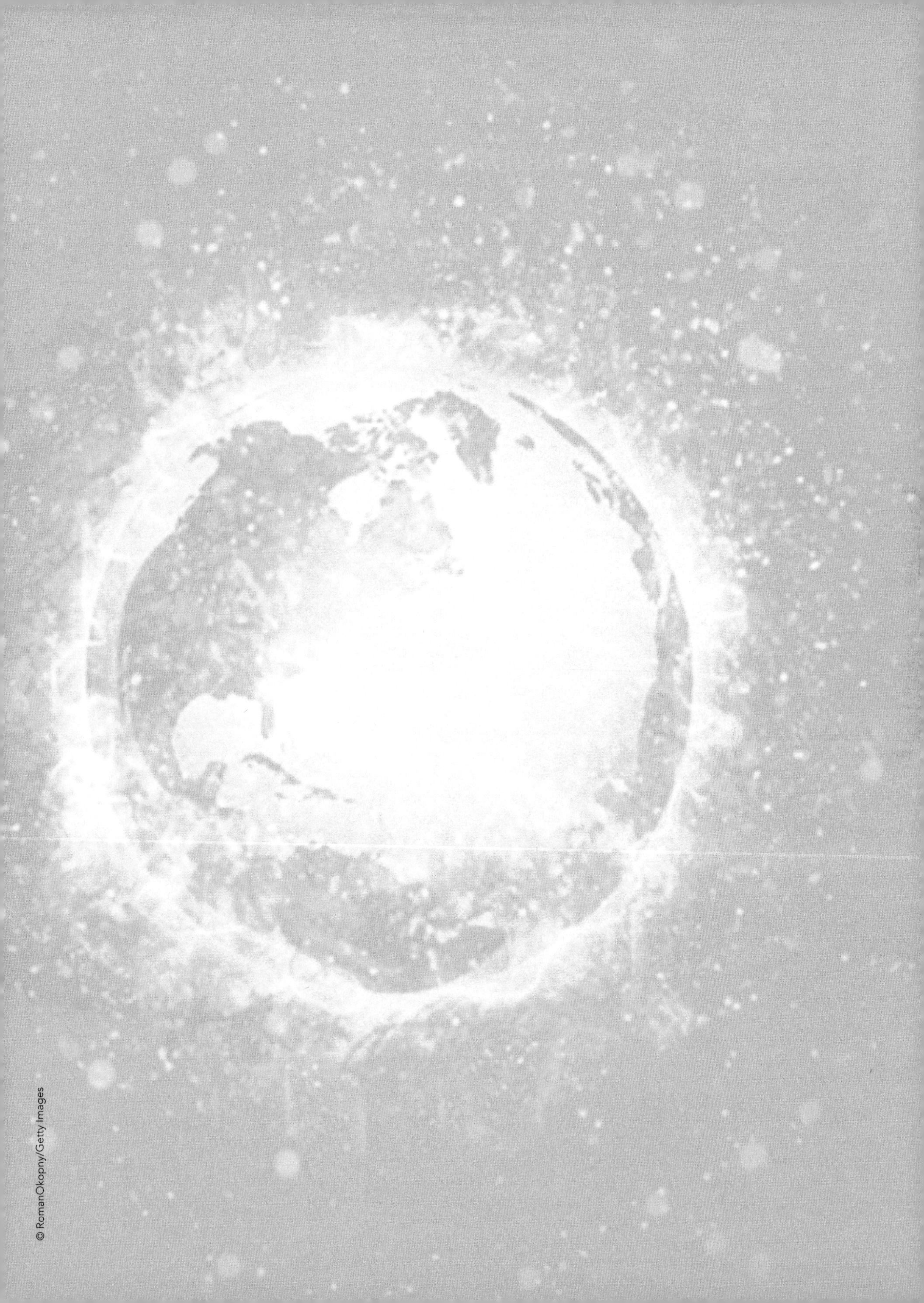

13

Strategic Entrepreneurship

Studying this chapter should provide you with the strategic management knowledge needed to:

13-1   Define strategic entrepreneurship and corporate entrepreneurship.

13-2   Define entrepreneurship and entrepreneurial opportunities and explain their importance.

13-3   Define invention, innovation, and imitation, and describe the relationship among them.

13-4   Describe entrepreneurs and the entrepreneurial mind-set.

13-5   Explain international entrepreneurship and its importance.

13-6   Describe how firms internally develop innovations.

13-7   Explain how firms use cooperative strategies to innovate.

13-8   Describe how firms use acquisitions as a means of innovation.

13-9   Explain how strategic entrepreneurship helps firms create value.

ENTREPRENEURIAL FERVOR AND INNOVATION DRIVE DISNEY'S SUCCESS

The founder, Walt Disney, once said that as long as there is imagination, Disneyland would never be finished. Likewise, one could say that as long as there is an entrepreneurial spirit and innovation, the Disney Company will never be complete. Sheryl Sandberg, COO of Facebook and a Disney board member suggested that some companies focus on technology and others focus on content, but Disney focuses on and integrates them both. Disney is perhaps best known for its cartoon characters (e.g., Mickey Mouse) and its theme parks (e.g., Disneyland and Disney World). But today, it is much more. For example, during the tenure of the current CEO, Bob Iger, Disney has acquired Pixar (major animation studio), Marvel entertainment (super heroes), Lucasfilm (*Star Wars*) and Magic Bands, among others. And, the company integrates and builds on the innovative capabilities of all of these highly creative operations.

All of these units and others within Disney are being shaped (or strongly influenced) by novel technologies. At one of Disney's five research divisions, Imagineering, new innovations are being developed and previewed by Iger and others to select the ones that are the most economically viable. Interestingly, 84 percent of Disney's active patents have been filed since 2005. The novel technologies are evident in Disney' various divisions but most certainly in its cinematic units (Pixar, Marvel, and Lucasfilm). Disney works to "cross pollinate its films to create a cinematic universe. For example, characters from one film are used to create another film that is related but unique as well. Marvel's cinematic universe includes films which have produced total revenues of $7.2 billion and include two of the top ten all-time highest gross revenue producing films.

Disney is continuing to create. As an example, its Lucasfilm division, which Disney bought in 2012, released its new Star Wars epic, *Star Wars: Episode VII—The Force Awakens* in December 2015. And it has produced *Star Wars Rebels*, an animated series aimed at boys, for Disney's cable network. Long before it was acquired by Disney, Lucasfilm worked hard to build and maintain its 'fan communities.' For example, it had a head of fan relations holding biennial meetings, referred to as the 'Star Wars Celebration,' that drew as

Frazer Harrison/Getty Images

many as 45,000 people interested in the *Star Wars* stories and characters. Disney learns from the businesses it acquires. As an example, Disney now has a head of fan relations for the company.

Pixar has developed several animated movies to be released in 2015 and 2016. Among them are *The Good Dinosaur*, *Finding Dory* (a character from *Finding Nemo*), *Zootopia* (an animal tale), and *Moana* (a musical set in Polynesia). Each of these stories is unique, creative, and likely will be highly successful, based on the overwhelmingly successful *Frozen*, the highest grossing animated movie of all time, and the also highly successful *Big Hero 6*. And, Disney not only makes money from box office sales; it also receives returns from consumer products (e.g., based on characters from the movies) and related themes and products will be incorporated in attractions at Disney theme parks.

In 2015, Disney signed a contract with IMAX Corporation to show Disney's animated and live-action movies in the IMAX theaters. The initial agreement runs for three years and provides another and a different outlet for Disney entertainment. In this way, the Disney brand receives greater visibility with the public and continues to increase in value.

Interestingly, Disney's largest profits come from its media division, which includes ABC television network and ESPN. ESPN is a highly valuable unit, with the main ESPN channel being received in 95 million homes. Although it has been primarily sold in packages and on cable, Disney will soon introduce an unbundled subscription to ESPN. Thus, Disney has many ways to create profits, but most of them come from innovations and being creative in the way it deals with and reaches the consuming public.

Sources: M. Lev-Ram, 2015, Empire of Tech, *Fortune*, January 1, 48–56; A. Chen, 2015, Disney, IMAX sign three-year agreement, *Wall Street Journal*, www.wsj.com, April 8; B. Barnes, 2015, For Lucasfilm, the way of its force lies in its 'Star War's fans, *New York Times*, www.nytimes.com, April 17; A. Sakoui & C. Palmeri, 2015, My universe is bigger than your universe, *BloombergBusiness*, www.bloomberg.com, April 23; A. Sakoui, 2015, Disney boosts 'Avengers' U.S. sales total to $191.3 million, *BloombergBusiness*, www.bloomberg.com, May 4; N. Tartaglione, 2015, Disney/Pixar spotlight on 'Finding Dory', 'Good Dinosaur' & more charms Cannes, *Deadline Breaking News*, www.deadline.com, May 20.

In Chapter 6, we explained that Disney had diversified its operations. One of the reasons to diversify is to spread the risk, and it appears that Disney's strategic decisions have been effective. For example, in the second fiscal quarter of 2015, Disney reported that its profits increased by 10 percent, which was well beyond what analysts forecasted. There were declines in profits from the movie and cable businesses, as expected, but Disney had significant increases in profits from its theme parks, cruise line, media and network businesses, and consumer products. Although the movie business was doing well, its revenues did not equal the phenomenal success of its animated movie *Frozen* in the previous year. Income from its other businesses more than offset the decline in movies. Interestingly, Disney's most profitable division focuses on media and networks (ESPN and ABC). However, as explained in the Opening Case, Disney's innovations (creativity and technology) in studio entertainment and interactive businesses are likely to drive future revenues and profits. Of course, successful innovations in its movie entertainment spill over to consumer products and theme parks, suggesting the synergy that Disney creates using its related diversified businesses (see Chapter 6 for more detail).[1] As noted in the Opening Case, Disney is a highly creative company, but its success in innovation has been driven in recent years through acquisitions of innovative businesses such as Pixar, Marvel, and Lucasfilm. These acquisitions have been successful partly because the firm gained access to knowledge that has the potential to meaningfully contribute to enhanced innovative outputs in other operations held by Disney. Disney learned from its acquired businesses. It learned the importance of and how to build and maintain a strong and loyal fan base (as done by Lucasfilm).[2] Building knowledge from external sources by making acquisitions of businesses with valuable knowledge or through networks of relationships contributes to innovation, and helps firms compete both domestically and internationally.[3] Moreover, these sources of information and knowledge help firms identify opportunities to pursue and strategies to implement and exploit today's opportunities while simultaneously trying to find opportunities to exploit in the future.[4]

The focus of this chapter is on strategic entrepreneurship, which is a framework firms use to effectively integrate their entrepreneurial and strategic actions. More formally, **strategic entrepreneurship** involves taking entrepreneurial actions using a strategic perspective. In this process, the firm tries to find opportunities in its external environment that it can exploit through innovations. Identifying opportunities to exploit through innovations is the *entrepreneurship* dimension of strategic entrepreneurship. Determining the best way to competitively manage the firm's innovation efforts is the *strategic* dimension.[5]

Strategic entrepreneurship involves taking entrepreneurial actions using a strategic perspective.

Thus, firms using strategic entrepreneurship integrate their actions to find opportunities, innovate, and then implement strategies for the purpose of appropriating value from the innovations they have developed to pursue identified opportunities.[6]

We consider several topics to explain strategic entrepreneurship. First, we examine entrepreneurship and innovation in a strategic context. Definitions of entrepreneurship, entrepreneurial opportunities, and entrepreneurs (those who engage in entrepreneurship to pursue entrepreneurial opportunities) are presented. We then describe international entrepreneurship, a process through which firms take entrepreneurial actions outside of their home market. After this discussion, the chapter shifts to descriptions of the three ways firms innovate—internally, through cooperative strategies, and by acquiring other companies.[7] We discuss these methods separately. Not surprisingly, most large firms use all three methods to innovate. The chapter closes with summary comments about how firms use strategic entrepreneurship to create value.

Before turning to the chapter's topics, we note that a major portion of the material in this chapter deals with entrepreneurship and innovation that takes place in established organizations. This phenomenon is called **corporate entrepreneurship**, and it is the use or application of entrepreneurship within an established firm.[8] Corporate entrepreneurship is critical to the survival and success of for-profit organizations[9] as well as public agencies.[10] Of course, innovation and entrepreneurship play a critical role in the degree of success achieved by startup entrepreneurial ventures as well. Because of this, a significant portion of the content examined in this chapter is equally important in both entrepreneurial ventures and established organizations.

13-1 Entrepreneurship and Entrepreneurial Opportunities

Entrepreneurship is the process by which individuals, teams, or organizations identify and pursue entrepreneurial opportunities without being immediately constrained by the resources they currently control.[11] **Entrepreneurial opportunities** are conditions in which new goods or services can satisfy a need in the market. These opportunities exist because of competitive imperfections in markets and among the factors of production used to produce them or because they were independently developed by entrepreneurs.[12] Entrepreneurial opportunities come in many forms, such as the chance to develop and sell a new product and the chance to sell an existing product in a new market.[13] Firms should be receptive to pursuing entrepreneurial opportunities whenever and wherever they may surface.

As these two definitions suggest, the essence of entrepreneurship is to identify and exploit entrepreneurial opportunities—that is, opportunities others do not see or for which they do not recognize the commercial potential—and manage risks appropriately as they arise.[14] As a process, entrepreneurship results in the "creative destruction" of existing products (goods or services) or methods of producing them and replaces them with new products and production methods.[15] Thus, firms committed to entrepreneurship place high value on individual innovations as well as the ability to continuously innovate across time.[16]

We study entrepreneurship at the level of the individual firm. However, evidence suggests that entrepreneurship is the economic engine driving many nations' economies in the global competitive landscape.[17] Thus, entrepreneurship and the innovation it spawns are important for companies competing in the global economy and for countries seeking to stimulate economic climates with the potential to enhance the living standard of their citizens.

Corporate entrepreneurship is the use or application of entrepreneurship within an established firm.

Entrepreneurship is the process by which individuals, teams, or organizations identify and pursue entrepreneurial opportunities without being immediately constrained by the resources they currently control.

Entrepreneurial opportunities are conditions in which new goods or services can satisfy a need in the market.

13-2 Innovation

In his classic work, *The Theory of Economic Development*, Joseph Schumpeter argued that firms engage in three types of innovative activities.[18] **Invention** is the act of creating or developing a new product or process. **Innovation** is a process used to create a commercial product from an invention. Thus, innovation follows invention[19] in that invention brings something new into being while innovation brings something new into use. Accordingly, technical criteria are used to determine the success of an invention whereas commercial criteria are used to determine the success of an innovation.[20] Finally, **imitation** is the adoption of a similar innovation by different firms. Imitation usually leads to product standardization, and imitative products often are offered at lower prices but without as many features. Entrepreneurship is critical to innovative activity because it acts as the linchpin between invention and innovation.[21]

For most companies, innovation is the most critical of the three types of innovative activities. The reason for this is that while many companies are able to create ideas that lead to inventions, commercializing those inventions sometimes proves to be difficult.[22] Patents are a strategic asset, and the ability to regularly produce them can be an important source of competitive advantage, especially when a firm intends to commercialize an invention and when a firm competes in a knowledge-intensive industry (e.g., pharmaceuticals).[23] In a competitive sense, patents create entry barriers for a firm's potential competitors.[24]

Peter Drucker argued that "innovation is the specific function of entrepreneurship, whether in an existing business, a public service institution, or a new venture started by a lone individual."[25] Moreover, Drucker suggested that innovation is "the means by which the entrepreneur either creates new wealth-producing resources or endows existing resources with enhanced potential for creating wealth."[26] Thus, entrepreneurship and the innovation resulting from it are critically important for all firms seeking strategic competitiveness and above-average returns.

The realities of global competition suggest that, to be market leaders, companies must regularly innovate. This means that innovation should be an intrinsic part of virtually all of a firm's activities. Recent work found that the word 'innovation' appeared 33,000 times in U.S. firms' quarterly and annual reports suggesting the importance of innovation to firms' success.[27] Moreover, firms should recognize the importance of their human capital to efforts to innovate.[28] Thus, as this discussion suggests, innovation is a key outcome firms seek through entrepreneurship, and it is often the source of competitive success, especially for companies competing in highly competitive and turbulent environments.[29]

13-3 Entrepreneurs

Entrepreneurs are individuals, acting independently or as part of an organization, who perceive an entrepreneurial opportunity and then take risks to develop an innovation and exploit it. Entrepreneurs can be found throughout different parts of organizations—from top-level managers to those working to produce a firm's products.

Entrepreneurs tend to demonstrate several characteristics: they are highly motivated, willing to take responsibility for their projects, self-confident, and often optimistic.[30] In addition, entrepreneurs tend to be passionate and emotional about the value and importance of their innovation-based ideas.[31] They are able to deal with uncertainty and are more alert to opportunities than others.[32] To be successful, entrepreneurs often need to have good social skills and to plan exceptionally well (e.g., to obtain venture capital).[33] Entrepreneurship entails much hard work if it is to be successful, but it can

Invention is the act of creating or developing a new product or process.

Innovation is a process used to create a commercial product from an invention. Thus, innovation follows invention in that invention brings something new into being while innovation brings something new into use.

Imitation is the adoption of a similar innovation by different firms.

Entrepreneurs are individuals, acting independently or as part of an organization, who perceive an entrepreneurial opportunity and then take risks to develop an innovation and exploit it.

also be highly satisfying—particularly when entrepreneurs recognize and follow their passions. According to Jeff Bezos, Amazon.com's founder:

"One of the huge mistakes people make is that they try to force an interest on themselves. You don't choose your passions; your passions choose you."[34]

Evidence suggests that successful entrepreneurs have an entrepreneurial mind-set that includes recognition of the importance of competing internationally as well as domestically.[35] The person with an **entrepreneurial mind-set** values uncertainty in markets and seeks to continuously identify opportunities in those markets that can be pursued through innovation.[36] Those without an entrepreneurial mind-set tend to view opportunities to innovate as threats.

Display of Warby Parker's popular eyewear, the product of Fast Company's most innovative company in 2015.

Because it has the potential to lead to continuous innovations, an individual's entrepreneurial mind-set can be a source of competitive advantage for a firm. Entrepreneurial mind-sets are fostered and supported when knowledge is readily available throughout a firm. Indeed, research shows that units within firms are more innovative when people have access to new knowledge.[37] Transferring knowledge, however, can be difficult, often because the receiving party must have adequate absorptive capacity (or the ability) to understand the knowledge and how to productively use it.[38] Learning requires that the new knowledge be linked to the existing knowledge. Thus, managers need to develop the capabilities of their human capital to build on their current knowledge base while incrementally expanding it.[39]

Some companies are known to be highly committed to entrepreneurship, suggesting that many working within them have an entrepreneurial mind-set. In 2015, *Fast Company* identified Warby Parker as the most innovative company, with Apple, Alibaba, Google, and Instagram rounding out the top five most innovative firms.[40] Warby Parker was chosen as the most innovative company in 2015 for developing the first top 'made-on-the-Internet brand of popular eyewear. After only five years, its annual revenue exceeds $100 million. Over time, the cofounders believe that their brand can be used for other products in addition to eyewear.[41].

13-4 International Entrepreneurship

International entrepreneurship is a process in which firms creatively discover and exploit opportunities that are outside their domestic markets.[42] Thus, entrepreneurship is a process that many firms exercise at both the domestic and international levels.[43] This is true for entrepreneurial ventures as suggested by the fact that an increasing number of them (perhaps as much as 50 percent) move into international markets early in their life cycle. Large, established companies commonly have significant foreign operations and often start new ventures in international markets, too.[44]

A key reason that firms choose to engage in international entrepreneurship is that, in general, doing so enhances their performance.[45] Nonetheless, those leading firms generally understand that taking entrepreneurial actions in markets outside the firm's home

Entrepreneurial mind-set values uncertainty in markets and seeks to continuously identify opportunities in those markets that can be pursued through innovation.

International entrepreneurship is a process in which firms creatively discover and exploit opportunities that are outside their domestic markets.

setting is challenging and not without risks, including risks of unstable foreign currencies, market inefficiencies, insufficient infrastructures to support businesses, and limitations on market size.[46] Thus, the decision to engage in international entrepreneurship needs to be a product of careful analysis.

Even though entrepreneurship is a global phenomenon, meaning that it is practiced throughout the world, its rate of use differs within individual countries. For example, a new report ranking the most entrepreneurial countries showed that the 10 most entrepreneurial countries in 2014 were (from the most to the least entrepreneurial): India, Turkey, United States, Brazil, China, Iceland, Ireland, Russia, Estonia, and Austria. The report showed that many of the most entrepreneurial countries were emerging economies. It also showed that personal and national wealth experienced the highest rates of growth in the most entrepreneurial countries.[47] Thus, as argued by others, there is a strong positive relationship between the rate of entrepreneurship and economic development within a country.

Culture is one reason for the different rates of entrepreneurship among countries across the globe. Research suggests that a balance between individual initiative and a spirit of cooperation and group ownership of innovation is needed to encourage entrepreneurial behavior. This means that for firms to be entrepreneurial, they must provide appropriate autonomy and incentives for individual initiative to surface while simultaneously promoting cooperation and group ownership of an innovation as a foundation for successfully exploiting it. Thus, international entrepreneurship often requires teams of people with unique skills and resources, especially in cultures that place high value on either individualism or collectivism. In addition to a balance of values for individual initiative and cooperative behaviors, firms engaging in international entrepreneurship must concentrate more than companies engaging in domestic entrepreneurship on building the capabilities needed to innovate and on acquiring the resources needed to make strategic decisions through which innovations can be successfully exploited.[48]

The level of investment outside of the home country made by young ventures is also an important dimension of international entrepreneurship. In fact, with increasing globalization, a larger number of new ventures have been "born global."[49] One reason for this is likely because new ventures that enter international markets increase their learning of new technological knowledge and thereby enhance their performance.[50] They increase their knowledge through the external networks (e.g., suppliers, customers) that they establish in the new foreign markets including strategic alliances in which they participate.[51]

The probability of entering and successfully competing in international markets increases when the firm's strategic leaders, and especially its top-level managers, have international experience.[52] Because of the learning and economies of scale and scope afforded by operating in international markets, both young and established internationally diversified firms often are stronger competitors in their domestic market as well. Additionally, as research has shown, internationally diversified firms are generally more innovative.[53]

The ability of a firm to develop and sustain a competitive advantage may be based partly or largely on its ability to innovate. This is true for firms engaging in international entrepreneurship as well as those that have yet to do so. As we discuss next, firms can follow different paths to innovate internally. Internal innovation is the first of three approaches firms use to innovate.

13-5 Internal Innovation

Efforts in firms' research and development (R&D) function are one primary source of internal innovations. Through effective R&D, firms are able to generate patentable processes and goods that are innovative in nature. Increasingly, successful R&D results from integrating the skills available in the global workforce. Thus, the ability to have a competitive advantage based on innovation is more likely to accrue to firms capable of integrating the talent of human capital from countries around the world.[54]

R&D and the new products and processes it can spawn affect a firm's efforts to earn above-average returns while competing in today's global environment. Because of this, firms try to use their R&D labs to create disruptive technologies and products. Although critical to long-term competitive success, the outcomes of R&D investments are uncertain and often not achieved in the short term, meaning that patience is required as firms evaluate the outcomes of their R&D efforts.[55]

As noted earlier, successful R&D programs must have high quality human capital—star scientists. Yet, not all ideas begin in the laboratory. For example, firms have learned that customers are often good sources for new products that will satisfy their needs.[56] They also use external networks such as other scientists, published research, and even alliance partners (discussed later in this chapter).[57] They may even be able to use public knowledge, such as that on a current technology, that can be combined to create an improved technology or perhaps even a new technology.[58]

Companies have created several means of obtaining employees' ideas for new products and other types of innovation. At LinkedIn, employees are encouraged to come up with ideas for innovations, develop a team to work on it and to make a pitch for the innovation to an executive team. Whirlpool uses structured ideation sessions with employees to identify new ideas for innovations. At Ericsson, employees are encouraged to participate in 'ideaboxes.' After employees submit an idea, they are matched with 'idea-to-innovation' managers to develop it further and determine if it is feasible and valuable. Ericsson then has an internal venture funding group that provides startup capital to the best ideas.[59]

13-5a Incremental and Novel Innovation

Firms invest in R&D to produce two types of innovations—incremental and novel. Most innovations are *incremental*—that is, they build on existing knowledge bases and provide small improvements in current products. Incremental innovations are evolutionary and linear in nature.[60] In general, incremental innovations tend to be introduced into established markets where customers understand and accept a product's characteristics. Basically, incremental innovations exploit an existing technology to provide an improvement over a current product. From the firm's perspective, incremental innovations tend to yield lower profit margins compared to those associated with the outcomes of novel or breakthrough innovations, largely because competition among firms offering products to customers that have incremental innovations is primarily on the price variable.[61] Adding a different kind of whitening agent to a soap detergent is an example of an incremental innovation, as are minor improvements in the functionality in televisions (e.g., slightly better picture quality). Companies introduce more incremental than novel innovations to markets, largely because they are cheaper, easier, and faster to produce, and involve less risk. Yet, firms normally cannot rely solely on incremental innovations. If they do so, they move from being market leaders to market laggards.[62] However, incremental innovation can be risky for firms if its frequency of introduction creates more change than can be appropriately absorbed.[63]

In contrast to incremental innovations, *novel* or *breakthrough innovations* usually provide significant technological changes (breakthroughs) and create new knowledge.[64] Revolutionary and nonlinear in nature, novel innovations typically use new technologies to serve newly created markets. The development of the original personal computer was a breakthrough innovation.

Google's new self-driving car is an example of a novel innovation. Under development for several years, Google announced in 2015 that several prototype vehicles were being

Google's self-driving car is an example of a novel innovation.

David Paul Morris/Bloomberg/Getty Images

tested on city streets. The company also noted that the cars are very safe. At present, one of the biggest obstacles to introducing the vehicles to the consumer market is convincing regulators on their safety and ability to adhere to the rules and laws of operating automobiles on public streets and highways.[65] Because they establish new functionalities for users, novel or breakthrough innovations have strong potential to lead to significant growth in revenue and profits. For example, Toyota's innovation, embodied in the Prius, "the first mass-produced hybrid-electric car," changed this segment of the automobile industry.[66] Developing new processes is a critical part of producing novel innovations. Both types of innovations can create value, meaning that firms should determine when it is appropriate to emphasize either incremental or novel innovation. However, novel innovations have the potential to contribute more significantly to a firm's efforts to earn above-average returns, although they also are more risky.

Novel or breakthrough innovations are rare because of the difficulty and risk involved in their development. The value of the technology and the market opportunities are highly uncertain.[67] Because novel innovation creates new knowledge and uses only some or little of a firm's current product or technological knowledge, creativity is required; creativity is as important to efforts to innovate in not-for-profit organizations as it is in for-profit firms.[68] Creativity is an outcome of using one's imagination. In the words of Jay Walker, founder of Priceline.com, "Imagination is the fuel. You're not going to get innovation if you don't have imagination." Imagination finds firms thinking about what customers will want in a changing world. For example, Walker says, those seeking to innovate within a firm could try to imagine "what the customer is going to want in a world where, for instance, their cellphone is in their glasses."[69] Imagination is more critical to novel than incremental innovations.

Creativity alone does not directly lead to innovation. Rather, creativity as generated through imagination discovers, combines, or synthesizes current knowledge, often from diverse areas.[70] Increasingly, when trying to innovate, firms seek knowledge from current users to understand their perspective about what could be beneficial innovations to the firm's products.[71] Collectively, the gathered knowledge is then applied to develop new products that can be used in an entrepreneurial manner to move into new markets, capture new customers, and gain access to new resources.[72] Such innovations are often developed in separate business units that start internal ventures.[73]

Strong, supportive leadership is required for the type of creativity and imagination needed to develop novel innovations. The fact that creativity is "messy, chaotic, sometimes even disgusting, and reeks of failure, experimentation, and disorganization"[74] is one set of reasons why leadership is so critical to its success.

This discussion highlights the fact that internally developed incremental and novel innovations result from deliberate efforts. These deliberate efforts are called *internal corporate venturing*, which is the set of activities firms use to develop internal inventions and especially innovations.[75]

Strategic **Focus**

Innovation Can Be Quirky

Quirky is a unique new venture founded in 2009 that combines the opportunities provided by the Internet of everything with the more physical world of business (e.g., industrial design, manufacturing, and marketing) to produce innovations. Some have referred to the company as an innovation machine—the mission is to commercialize new product ideas. Ben Kaufman, founder and CEO of the company, suggests that the goal is "to create an engine that accelerates the process of identifying and developing ideas for all kinds of products."

Quirky has built a social network of inventors and others, some of whom submit ideas for new products, who are used to evaluate new product ideas (for marketability and manufacturing feasibility). The approximately one million people involved in this network also offer ideas on how to refine and improve the product ideas. Quirky receives around 4,000 product ideas each week and brought 400 Quirky-generated products to the market by 2015. It has received funding from some large venture capital firms and by one major corporate partner, GE (invested $30 million).

After a product idea is evaluated, refined, and sometimes improved, Quirky uses large 3-D printers to create prototypes. The firm also begins searching for a manufacturer and simultaneously seeking a market for the products through retailers (such as Home Depot, Target, Walmart, etc.). Given the promise of this company to commercialize inventions (create innovation), it raised $185 million in venture capital and grew to 300 employees, opening new offices in California to complement its New York headquarters.

Although there was much excitement, Quirky experienced problems. Some of its products failed to achieve a following in the marketplace (the social network evaluations were not adequate for marketing research), and other products had quality problems (due to inadequate quality control). Quirky tried to move products to the market too quickly. As a result it lost $120 million dollars and had to reduce operations to avoid having a cash shortage. As such, Quirky laid off about 20 percent of its staff and made some other changes to focus its activities.

Quirky decided to focus its efforts to sign up more corporate partners in addition to GE. It is trying to focus more of its efforts on products for the smart home, products that communicate with a smartphone or home Wi-Fi network. Quirky's Wink smartphone and tablet app provides a digital dashboard to link and control smart-home devices (e.g., lights, lawn sprinklers, garage doors, air conditioning, etc.). Quirky now has 15 companies that will offer about 60 Wink-enabled products. Among them are GE, Honeywell, and Philips. The products are sold under the company's own brand but will carry a tagline: "Powered by Quirky."

Courtesy of Innovation excellence

Innovative products developed by Quirky through its partnership with GE.

Sources: S. Lohr, 2014, Quirky to create a smart-home products company, *New York Times*, www.nytimes.com, June 22; G. Karol, 2014, NYC startup Quirky launches platform for Internet of things, *FOXBusiness*, www.foxbusiness.com, June 24; M. Baratz, 2014, Counting down with…Ben Kaufman, *Fortune*, fortune.com, July 21; S. Lohr, 2015, The invention mob, brought to you by Quirky, *New York Times*, www.nytimes.com, February 14; B. Popper, 2015, How the invention factory at Quirky almost imagined its way out of business, The Verge, www.theverge.com, April 24; J. D'Onfro, 2015, How a Quirky 28-year-old plowed through $15 million and almost destroyed his startup, Business Insider, www.businessinsider.com, April 29.

The example of Quirky in the Strategic Focus demonstrates the creative potential of innovation and simultaneously the risk and uncertainty involved in creating and trying to commercialize inventions (particularly novel ones). Quirky is a unique and potentially valuable company that takes new product ideas offered by inventors and evaluates them. For the ones deemed to have potential value, Quirky then develops prototypes, finds a

Figure 13.1 Model of Internal Corporate Venturing

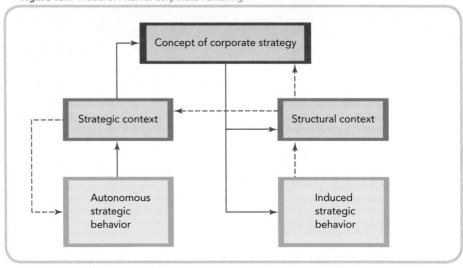

Source: Adapted from R. A. Burgelman, 1983, A model of the interactions of strategic behavior, corporate context, and the concept of strategy, *Academy of Management Review*, 8:65.

manufacturer, and markets the products. In this way, it facilitates many innovations from inventive new ideas that would be unlikely to find a market without such help. Yet, it, too, takes much risk and found that it had to do better market research on the ideas and ensure high quality control of the products produced and marketed. It also has become more focused, which should allow it to be more efficient and to gain some economies of scale, which it badly needed.

As shown in Figure 13.1, autonomous and induced strategic behaviors are the two types of internal corporate venturing. Each venturing type facilitates development of both incremental and novel innovations. However, a larger number of novel innovations spring from autonomous strategic behavior, while a larger number of incremental innovations come from induced strategic behavior.

In essence, autonomous strategic behavior results in influences to change aspects of the firm's strategy and the structure in place to support its implementation. In contrast, induced strategic behavior results from the influences of the strategy and structure the firm currently has in place to support efforts to innovate (see Figure 13.1). These points are emphasized in the discussions below of the two types of internal corporate venturing.

13-5b Autonomous Strategic Behavior

Autonomous strategic behavior is a bottom-up process in which product champions pursue new ideas, often through a political process, by means of which they develop and coordinate the actions required to innovate and to bring the innovation to the market.[76] Actually, the process used by Quirky, as explained in the Strategic Focus, is an example of autonomous strategic behavior. A *product champion* is an individual with an entrepreneurial mind-set who seeks to create support for developing an innovation. Product champions play critical roles in moving innovations forward.[77] Commonly, product champions use their social capital to develop informal networks within the firm. As progress is made, these networks become more formal as a means of pushing an innovation to marketplace success.[78] Quirky plays the role of the product champion outside the bounds of an individual organization. Internal innovations springing from autonomous strategic behavior differ from the firm's current strategy and structure, taking it into new markets and perhaps new ways of creating value.

As a means of innovating, autonomous strategic behavior is more effective when new knowledge, especially tacit knowledge, is diffused continuously throughout the firm.[79]

13-5c Induced Strategic Behavior

Induced strategic behavior, the second form of corporate venturing through which innovations are developed internally, is a top-down process whereby the firm's current strategy and structure foster innovations that are closely associated with that strategy and structure.[80] In this form of venturing, the strategy in place is filtered through a matching structural hierarchy. In essence, induced strategic behavior results in internal innovations that are consistent with the firm's current strategy. Thus, the firm's CEO and its top management team play an active and key role in induced strategic behavior.[81] This is the case at IBM, where CEO Virginia Rometty challenged the firm's employees "to move faster and respond more quickly to customers" as a foundation for developing innovations that will facilitate the firm's efforts to "shift to new computing models."[82]

Induced innovation allows the firm and its managers to determine the type and amount of innovation desired.[83] For example, the firm could develop an intense innovation process in order to be the industry leader by regularly introducing new products even if they cannibalize currently successful products.[84] This has been the approach employed by Intel for many years. An induced approach to innovation is used by a firm to determine if it wishes to create open innovation, where innovation is used to establish industry standards, or closed innovation, which the firm uses to generate returns disallowing others to use it.[85] The majority of innovation is closed innovation, but open innovation has become more common, especially in some industries. Often, firms engage in evolutionary, path dependent R&D, which over time becomes more incremental (because of the path dependence in the knowledge based used).[86]

13-6 Implementing Internal Innovations

An entrepreneurial mind-set is critical to firms' efforts to innovate internally, partly because such a mind-set helps them deal with the environmental and market uncertainty that are associated with efforts taken to commercialize inventions.[87] When facing uncertainty, firms try to continuously identify the most attractive opportunities to pursue strategically. Thus firms use an entrepreneurial mind-set to simultaneously identify opportunities, develop innovations to meet those opportunities, and execute strategies to successfully exploit the opportunities identified in the marketplace.[88] Often, firms provide incentives to individuals to be more entrepreneurial as a foundation for successfully developing internal innovations, sometimes encouraging work teams to specify what they believe are the most appropriate incentives for the firm to use.[89]

Having processes and structures in place through which a firm can successfully exploit developed innovations is critical. In the context of internal corporate ventures, managers must allocate resources, coordinate activities, communicate with many different parties in the organization, and make a series of decisions to convert the innovations resulting from either autonomous or induced strategic behaviors into successful market entries.[90] As we describe in Chapter 11, organizational structures are the sets of formal relationships that support processes managers use to exploit the firm's innovations.

Effective integration of the functions involved in internal innovation efforts—from engineering to manufacturing and distribution—is required to implement the incremental and novel innovations resulting from internal corporate ventures.[91] Increasingly, product development teams are being used to achieve the desired integration across organizational functions. Such integration involves coordinating and applying the knowledge and skills of different functional areas to maximize innovation.[92] Teams must help to make decisions about which projects to continue supporting and which to terminate. Emotional commitments sometimes increase the difficulty of deciding to terminate an innovation-based project.

13-6a Cross-Functional Product Development Teams

Cross-functional product development teams facilitate efforts to integrate activities associated with different organizational functions, such as design, manufacturing, and marketing. Among the team members are research scientists who have the technological content knowledge to bring to the group development decisions.[93] These teams may also include people from major suppliers because they have knowledge that can meaningfully inform a firm's innovation processes.[94] In addition, new product development processes can be completed more quickly and the products can be more easily commercialized when cross-functional teams work collaboratively.[95] Using cross-functional teams, product development stages are grouped into parallel processes so that the firm can tailor its product development efforts to its unique core competencies and to the needs of the market.

Horizontal organizational structures support cross-functional teams in their efforts to integrate innovation-based activities across organizational functions.[96] Therefore, instead of being designed around vertical hierarchical functions or departments, the organization is built around core horizontal processes that are used to produce and manage innovations. Some of the horizontal processes that are critical to innovation efforts are formal and are defined and documented as procedures and practices. More commonly, however, these important processes are informal and are supported properly through horizontal organizational structures—structures that typically find individuals communicating frequently on a face-to-face basis.

Team members' independent frames of reference and organizational politics are two barriers with the potential to prevent effective use of cross-functional teams to integrate the activities of different organizational functions.[97] Team members working within a distinct specialization (e.g., a particular organizational function) may have an independent frame of reference typically based on common backgrounds and experiences. They are likely to use the same decision criteria to evaluate issues, such as product development efforts, when making decisions within their functional units.

Research suggests that functional departments vary along four dimensions: time orientation, interpersonal orientation, goal orientation, and formality of structure.[98] Thus, individuals from different functional departments having different orientations in terms of these dimensions can be expected to perceive innovation-related activities differently. For example, a design engineer may consider the characteristics that make a product functional and workable to be the most important of its characteristics. Alternatively, a person from the marketing function may judge characteristics that satisfy customer needs to be most important. These different orientations can create barriers to effective communication across functions and may even generate intra-team conflict as different parts of the firm try to work together to innovate.[99]

Some organizations experience a considerable amount of political activity (called organizational politics). How resources will be allocated to different functions is a key source of such activity. This means that inter-unit conflict may result from aggressive competition for resources among those representing different organizational functions. This type of conflict between functions creates a barrier to cross-functional integration efforts. Those trying to form effective cross-functional product development teams seek ways to mitigate the damaging effects of organizational politics. Emphasizing the critical role each function plays in the firm's overall efforts to innovate is a method used in many firms to help individuals see the value of inter-unit collaborations.

13-6b Facilitating Integration and Innovation

Shared values and effective leadership are important for achieving cross-functional integration and implementing internal innovations.[100] As part of culture, shared values are framed around the firm's vision and mission and become the glue that promotes integration between functional units.

Strategic leadership is also important to efforts to achieve cross-functional integration and promote internal innovation. Working with others, leaders are responsible for setting goals and allocating resources needed to achieve them. The goals include integrated development and commercialization of new products. Effective strategic leaders also ensure a high-quality communication system to facilitate cross-functional integration. A critical benefit of effective communication is the sharing of knowledge among team members, who in turn are then able to communicate an innovation's existence and importance to others in the organization. Shared values and leadership practices shape the communication routines that make it possible to share innovation-related knowledge throughout the firm.[101]

13-6c Creating Value from Internal Innovation

The model in Figure 13.2 shows how firms seek to create value through internal innovation processes (autonomous strategic behavior and induced strategic behavior). As shown, an entrepreneurial mind-set is foundational to the firm's efforts to consistently identify entrepreneurial opportunities that it can pursue strategically with and through innovations. Cross-functional teams are important for promoting integrated new product design ideas and gaining commitment to their subsequent implementation. Effective leadership and shared values promote integration and vision for innovation and commitment to it. The end result of successful innovations is the creation of value for stakeholders such as customers and shareholders.[102] However, competitive rivalry (see Chapter 5) affects the degree of success a firm achieves through its innovations. Thus, firms must carefully

Figure 13.2 Creating Value through Internal Innovation Processes

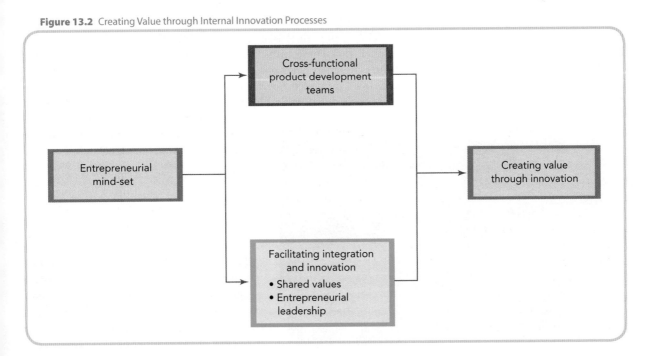

study competitors' responses to their innovations to have the knowledge required to know how to adjust their innovation-based efforts, and even when to abandon those efforts if market conditions indicate the need to do so.[103]

In the next two sections, we discuss the other approaches firms use to innovate—cooperative strategies and acquisitions.

13-7 Innovation through Cooperative Strategies

Alliances with other firms can contribute to innovations in several ways. First, they provide information on new business opportunities and the innovations that might be developed to exploit them.[104] In other instances, firms use cooperative strategies to align what they believe are complementary assets with the potential to lead to future innovations. Compared to other approaches to innovation, combining complementary assets through alliances has the potential to more frequently result in "breakthrough" innovations.[105]

Rapidly changing technologies, globalization, and the need to innovate at world-class levels are primary influences on firms' decisions to innovate by cooperating with other companies. Indeed, some believe that, because of these conditions, firms are becoming increasingly dependent on cooperative strategies as a path to innovation and, ultimately, to competitive success in the global economy.[106] Both entrepreneurial ventures and established firms use cooperative strategies to innovate. An entrepreneurial venture, for example, may seek investment capital as well as established firms' distribution capabilities to successfully introduce one of its innovative products to the market.[107] Alternatively, more-established companies may need new technological knowledge and can gain access to it by forming a cooperative strategy with entrepreneurial ventures.[108] Alliances between large pharmaceutical firms and biotechnology companies increasingly have been formed to integrate the knowledge and resources of both to develop new products and bring them to market.

In some instances, large established firms form an alliance to innovate. This is the case for Inter IKEA Group, the parent company of the IKEA furniture brand, and Marriott International, Inc. These firms formed an alliance to develop Moxy, a new hotel brand that the companies believe is innovative in its design and the value it creates for customers. IKEA provided novel and innovative construction techniques to keep manufacturing costs down while Marriott provided the value in unique design..

Thus, the Moxy brand was developed to innovatively combine value with style. In the words of Marriott's CEO:

"This is a fresh new take on the economy segment. I think it benefits from being new and combining value with style. Too much of the value product you see in Europe is devoid of style."

The hotel was designed to serve the millennials with moderate prices and an open lobby/restaurant/bar with music at one end and space where guests can work on their devises at the other. The first Moxy Hotel opened in the summer of 2014.[109]

Courtesy of Marriott

The first Moxy Hotel that is innovative in both its design and the value it creates for customers.

However, alliances formed to foster innovation are not without risks. In addition to conflict that is natural when firms try to work together to reach a mutual goal, the members of an alliance also take a risk that a partner will appropriate their technology or knowledge and use it for its own benefit.[110] Carefully selecting partner firms mitigates this risk. The ideal partnership is one in which the firms have complementary skills as well as compatible strategic goals.[111] When this is the case, firms encounter fewer challenges and risks as they try to effectively manage the partnership they formed to develop innovations. Companies also want to constrain the number of cooperative arrangements they form to innovate in that becoming involved in too many alliances puts them at risk of losing the ability to successfully manage each of them.[112]

13-8 Innovation through Acquisitions

Firms sometimes acquire companies to gain access to their innovations and to their innovative capabilities.[113] One reason companies do this is that capital markets value growth; acquisitions provide a means to rapidly extend one or more product lines and increase the firm's revenues.[114] In spite of this fact, a firm should have a strategic rationale for a decision to acquire a company. Typically, the rationale is to gain ownership of an acquired company's innovations and access to its innovative capabilities. A number of large technology-based companies have acquired firms largely for these purposes. For example, Microsoft acquired Mojang AB in 2014 to gain access to the technological capabilities of Minecraft. Minecraft is a videogame but different from the norm. It does not provide the context; it allows the players to construct it themselves. So, they get what they want. In other words, they create their own (and desired) innovation. So, Minecraft is a game that is determined by the players not a design team working for the company providing the game. Mojang was highly profitable because of the high demand for Minecraft. In 2013, it made a profit of $115 million on $291 million in sales for a return of almost 40 percent (incredibly high). Microsoft paid about $2.5 billion to acquire Mojang.[115]

Similar to internal corporate venturing and strategic alliances, acquisitions are not a risk free approach to innovation. A key risk of acquisitions is that a firm may substitute an ability to buy innovations for an ability to develop them internally. This may result when a firm concentrates on financial controls to identify, evaluate, and then manage acquisitions. Of course, strategic controls are the ones through which a firm identifies a strategic rationale to acquire another company as a means of developing innovations. Thus, the likelihood a firm will be successful in its efforts to innovate increases by developing an appropriate balance between financial and strategic controls. In spite of the risks though, choosing to acquire companies with complementary capabilities and knowledge sets can support a firm's efforts to innovate successfully when the acquisitions are made for strategic purposes and are then properly integrated into the acquired firm's strategies.[116] Firms that have not been as successful at producing innovation as needed are more likely to acquire firms with technological capabilities, or that have new, potentially valuable innovations, if they have enough financial capital to do so.[117] For example, in recent years some large pharmaceutical firms that have been unsuccessful at producing new blockbuster drugs have resorted to acquisitions in order to gain access to new valuable drugs held by the acquired firm.

The ability to learn new capabilities that can facilitate innovation-related activities from acquired companies is an important benefit that can accrue to an acquiring firm. Additionally, firms that emphasize innovation and carefully select companies to acquire that also emphasize innovation and the technological capabilities on which innovations are often based are likely to remain innovative.[118] Thus, some firms produce innovations internally. Others use external knowledge and external sources for innovations.

Strategic Focus

What Explains the Lack of Innovation at American Express? Is It Hubris, Inertia, or Lack of Capability?

The lack of innovation and entrepreneurial focus at American Express may be becauseof hubris, inertia, *and* lack of capability. American Express (AmEx) had a terrible year in 2014. It lost two major partnerships, and lost a major court case, all of which are likely to have negative effects on its revenues. The executives at AmEx must think so as well because they are cutting costs and plan to layoff as many as 4,000 employees.

AmEx lost its partnership as the exclusive co-branded credit card with the major retailer Costco in 2014. This represents a major problem for AmEx as that business generated approximately eight percent of AmEx's total revenues in 2014. Interestingly, card holders used the AmEx card for many other purchases outside of Costco, as about 70 percent of the revenue generated by the card came from its use in other venues. AmEx also lost its partnership with Jet Blue in the same year.

In addition, AmEx lost a major court case. AmEx charges each merchant higher fees when a customer uses its card to make a purchase than do other major credit card companies such as Visa and MasterCard. AmEx has a contract with each merchant using its card that does not allow the merchant to recommend to the customer to use a different card or to offer discounts favoring other cards. A federal judge ruled that this requirement by AmEx was in 'restraint of trade' and, therefore, violated antitrust laws. This is important because AmEx may have to reduce its fees charged to merchants, and if so, it may have to decrease the rewards paid back to customers. In turn, it could lose some customers if the rewards become equal to or less than competitors' cards.

AmEx has not advanced its purchasing technology in some time, advances such as facilitating customers' car rentals or restaurant reservations. It has been considered to be the "most prestigious" card and thus built a brand image. It also has been respected because it captured and held the most wealthy clientele. However, it has begun to lose some of its wealthiest clients. One such client has been a long-time user of the AmEx card. However, he recently changed because the

"rewards" received with other cards are better. In fact, because he uses the cards for almost all of his purchases, he stands to receive thousands of dollars more in rewards with the other cards.

AmEx recently announced a renewed focus on affluent customers and more benefits for those holding (and using) the 'Gold Card.' It will offer double points for restaurant purchases and a personalized travel service. The annual fee for the 'Premier Gold Card' also increased by a little more than 11 percent. The fee increase for the regular Gold Card was about 28 percent. Although, AmEx executives stated that they continue to target growth goals, most analysts believe that AmEx revenues are likely to fall over the next year or two. Innovation and a new strategy are needed.

Will the new American Express Gold Rewards Card help the firm to regain its competitive position in tthe industry?

Sources: E. Dexheimer, 2015, AmEx is losing its millionaires, *BloombergBusiness*, www.bloomberg.com, February 12; J. Davidson, 2015, Why American Express users should be worried about their rewards, *Money*, www.money.com, February 20; H. Stout, 2015, With revamped gold cards, bruised American Express returns focus to affluent, *New York Times*, www.nytimes.com, February 26; J. Kell, 2015, Visa replaces American Express as Costco's credit card, *Fortune*, www.fortune.com, March 2; H. Tabuchi, 2015, Amex to ask for stay of ruling prohibiting merchants from promoting other cards, *New York Times*, www.nytimes.com, March 25; J. Carney, 2015, American Express struggles to keep up, *Wall Street Journal*, www.wsj.com, April 6; 2015, Stronger dollar drives revenue down at American Express, *New York Times*, www.nytimes.com, April 16.

Both strategies can be successful if implemented effectively.[119] Yet, some mergers can insulate firms, especially large ones with significant market power, because an acquisition may provide an almost monopoly on a particular type of technology. This type of acquisition may focus the firm on path-dependent knowledge development and incremental innovations. It may also discourage new firms from entering the market, thereby reducing entrepreneurial activity in the industry.[120]

American Express has some significant problems, as explained in the Strategic Focus. It has lost two major corporate partners that account for perhaps as much as 10 percent of its annual revenue, In addition, it lost a major court case that may also reduce its revenues or increase its costs. These concerns, when coupled with the fact that the firm has not been innovative (while its rivals have been introducing innovative new services and taking market share), suggest a rather bleak future. It seems that, due to inertia and possibly hubris, AmEx has maintained its strategy and is losing its competitive advantage. AmEx executives need to be entrepreneurial and strategic. In other words, they need to engage in strategic entrepreneurship. To close this chapter, we describe how strategic entrepreneurship helps firms create value for stakeholders.

13-9 Creating Value through Strategic Entrepreneurship

Entrepreneurial ventures and younger firms often are more effective at identifying opportunities than are larger established companies.[121] As a consequence, entrepreneurial ventures often produce more breakthrough innovations than do larger, more established organizations. Entrepreneurial ventures' strategic flexibility and willingness to take risks, at least partially, account for their ability to identify opportunities and then develop breakthrough innovations. Yet, because these innovations are often quite novel, they are also risky. Thus, they sometimes fail which frequently means that the new venture fails because such firms have little slack.[122] Alternatively, larger, well-established firms often have more resources and capabilities to manage their resources for the purpose of exploiting identified opportunities, but these efforts by large firms generally result in more incremental than breakthrough innovations. For example, in recent times, Boeing has focused on developing incremental innovations to build on and improve the successful new aircraft such as the 787 Dreamliner. Currently, Boeing is developing seven new models that will upgrade its existing fleet, largely taking advantage of the technologies already in use.[123]

Thus, younger, entrepreneurial ventures generally excel in the *taking of entrepreneurial actions* part of strategic entrepreneurship, while larger, more established firms generally excel at the *using a strategic perspective* part of strategic entrepreneurship. Another way of thinking about this is to say that entrepreneurial ventures excel at opportunity-seeking (that is, entrepreneurial) behavior, while larger firms excel at advantage-seeking (that is, strategic) behavior. However, competitive success and superior performance relative to competitors accrues to firms that are able to identify and exploit opportunities and establish a competitive advantage as a result of doing so.[124] On a relative basis then, entrepreneurial ventures are challenged to become more strategic, while older, more established firms are challenged to become more entrepreneurial.

Firms trying to learn how to simultaneously be more entrepreneurial and strategic (that is, firms trying to use strategic entrepreneurship) recognize that, after identifying opportunities, entrepreneurs within entrepreneurial ventures and established organizations must develop capabilities that will become the basis of their firm's core competencies and competitive advantages. The process of identifying opportunities is entrepreneurial, but this activity alone is not sufficient to create maximum value, or even to survive over time. In fact, the early goals for entrepreneurial firms are to survive and grow, allowing them to accumulate resources to finance additional innovation and growth.[125] As we learned in Chapter 3, to successfully exploit opportunities, a firm must develop capabilities that are valuable, rare, difficult to imitate, and nonsubstitutable. When capabilities satisfy these four criteria, the firm has one or more competitive advantages to use in efforts to exploit the identified opportunities. Without a competitive advantage, the firm's success will be only temporary (as explained in Chapter 1). An innovation may be valuable and rare early in its life, if a market perspective is used in its development. However, competitive actions must be taken to introduce the new product to the market and protect its position in the market against competitors in order to gain a competitive advantage.[126] In combination, these actions constitute strategic entrepreneurship.

Some large organizations are trying to become more capable of effectively using strategic entrepreneurship. For example, an increasing number of large, widely known firms, including Wendy's International, Gucci Group, Starbucks, and Perry Ellis International, have established a top-level managerial position commonly called president or executive vice president of emerging brands. Other companies such as Coca-Cola, GE, Whirlpool, and Humana have established a position within their top management teams to focus on innovation.[127] These individuals are often known as chief innovation officers.

The essential responsibility of top-level managers focusing on emerging brands or innovation is to verify that their firm is consistently finding entrepreneurial opportunities. They must effectively manage the firm's portfolio of innovation projects, deciding which ones require more investment and which ones should be terminated.[128] These people know that some innovation projects fail but, they also try to learn from those failures to make future ones more successful.[129] The chief innovation officers must then work collaboratively with the firm's chief strategy officer to coordinate the new products with the firm's strategic approach and to implement them. In this sense, those responsible for identifying opportunities the firm might want to pursue and those responsible for selecting and implementing the strategies the company would use to pursue those opportunities share responsibility for verifying that the firm is taking entrepreneurial actions using a strategic perspective. These individuals also help the firm determine the innovations necessary to pursue an opportunity, and if those innovations should be developed internally, through a cooperative strategy, or by completing an acquisition. In the final analysis, the objective of these top-level managers is to help firms identify opportunities and then develop successful incremental and breakthrough innovations and strategies to exploit them.

Firms must carefully analyze their portfolio of innovations and decide which existing products or technologies it should exploit with incremental innovations to improve them and when they need to develop more novel products or technologies. As noted, Boeing invested heavily to develop a new aircraft with breakthrough technologies in the 787 Dreamliner. Now, it is trying to exploit those innovations with incremental innovations. Yet, it must be careful because the emphasis on the innovative technologies can become path-dependent, making it difficult to then break away from them to develop a novel innovation when needed.[130] Interestingly, Honda has recently broken from its conservative innovative tradition to deliver a new personal jet called the HondaJet. It is a seven-passenger jet that is priced at about $4.5 million. In addition to autos, Honda also makes robots, boats, and lawn mowers. With this new product, it enters a new industry. Michimasa Fujino, the CEO of Honda Aircraft Co, suggests that Honda is looking to the future and providing for its longevity.[131]

The Asahi Shimbun/Getty Images

Honda's new focus on the innovative frontier produced its new personal jet, the HondaJet. It carries seven passengers and is priced at $4.5 million.

Many analysts believe that innovation is required to be competitive in global markets over time. Earlier, we listed the top ten countries for entrepreneurial activity. The United States was ranked third, but it was among mostly emerging-economy countries trying to encourage more entrepreneurial activities. The list of the top countries that invest in and produce the most innovation is different, primarily established countries. And the United States is number six in this ranking. The top ten innovative countries are: South Korea, Japan, Germany, Finland, Israel, United States, Sweden, Singapore, France, and United Kingdom.[132] Thus, the competition is significant, requiring even well-known and respected firms such as American Express to be innovative if they wish to compete effectively and survive over time. They must practice strategic entrepreneurship.

SUMMARY

- Strategic entrepreneurship involves taking entrepreneurial actions using a strategic perspective. Firms using strategic entrepreneurship simultaneously engage in opportunity-seeking and advantage-seeking behaviors. The purpose is to continuously find new opportunities and quickly develop innovations and exploit them.

- Entrepreneurship is a process used by individuals, teams, and organizations to identify entrepreneurial opportunities without being immediately constrained by the resources they control. Corporate entrepreneurship is the application of entrepreneurship (including the identification of entrepreneurial opportunities) within ongoing, established organizations. Entrepreneurial opportunities are conditions in which new goods or services can satisfy a need in the market. Entrepreneurship positively contributes to individual firms' performance and stimulates growth in countries' economies.

- Firms engage in three types of innovative activities:

  - invention, which is the act of creating a new good or process

  - innovation, or the process of creating a commercial product from an invention

  - imitation, which is the adoption of similar innovations by different firms.

Invention brings something new into being while innovation brings something new into use.

- Entrepreneurs see or envision entrepreneurial opportunities and then take actions to develop innovations and exploit them. The most successful entrepreneurs (whether they are establishing their own venture or are working in an established organization) have an entrepreneurial mind-set, which is an orientation that values the potential opportunities available because of marketplace uncertainties.

- International entrepreneurship, or the process of identifying and exploiting entrepreneurial opportunities outside the firm's domestic markets, is important to firms around the globe.

- Evidence suggests that firms capable of effectively engaging in international entrepreneurship generally outperform those competing only in their domestic markets.

- Three basic approaches are used to produce innovation:

  - internal innovation, which involves R&D and forming internal corporate ventures

  - cooperative strategies such as strategic alliances

  - acquisitions

Autonomous strategic behavior and induced strategic behavior are the two forms of internal corporate venturing. Autonomous strategic behavior is a bottom-up process through which a product champion facilitates the commercialization of an innovation. Induced strategic behavior is a top-down process in which a firm's current strategy and structure facilitate the development and implementation of product or process innovations. Thus, induced strategic behavior is driven by the organization's current corporate strategy and structure, while autonomous strategic behavior can result in a change to the firm's current strategy and structure arrangements.

- Firms create two types of innovations—incremental and novel—through internal innovation that takes place in the form of autonomous strategic behavior or induced strategic behavior. Overall, firms produce more incremental innovations, but novel innovations have a higher probability of significantly increasing sales revenue and profits. Cross-functional integration is often vital to a firm's efforts to develop and implement internal corporate venturing activities and to commercialize the resulting innovation. Cross-functional teams now commonly include representatives from external organizations, such as suppliers. Additionally, integration and innovation can be facilitated by developing shared values and effectively using strategic leadership.

- To gain access to the specialized knowledge required to innovate in the global economy, firms may form a cooperative relationship, such as a strategic alliance with other companies, some of which may be competitors.

■ Acquisitions are another means firms use to obtain innovation. Innovation can be acquired through direct acquisition, or firms can learn new capabilities from an acquisition, thereby enriching their internal innovation abilities.

■ The practice of strategic entrepreneurship by all types of firms, large and small, new and more established, creates value for all stakeholders, especially for shareholders and customers. Strategic entrepreneurship also contributes to the economic development of countries.

KEY TERMS

corporate entrepreneurship 419
entrepreneurship 419
entrepreneurial opportunities 419
entrepreneurs 420
entrepreneurial mind-set 421

invention 420
innovation 420
imitation 420
international entrepreneurship 421
strategic entrepreneurship 418

REVIEW QUESTIONS

1. What is strategic entrepreneurship? What is corporate entrepreneurship?

2. What is entrepreneurship, and what are entrepreneurial opportunities? Why are they important aspects of the strategic management process?

3. What are invention, innovation, and imitation? How are these concepts interrelated?

4. What is an entrepreneur, and what is an entrepreneurial mind-set?

5. What is international entrepreneurship? Why is it important?

6. How do firms develop innovations internally?

7. How do firms use cooperative strategies to innovate and to have access to innovative capabilities?

8. How does a firm acquire other companies to increase the number of innovations it produces and improve its capability to innovate?

9. How does strategic entrepreneurship help firms create value?

Mini-Case

An Innovation Failure at JCPenney: Its Causes and Consequences

Former CEO Ron Johnson designed and tried to implement a new strategy for JCPenney (JCP). However, the firm's target "middle market" customers did not respond well to the new strategy and the innovations associated with it. In fact, some say that Johnson's innovations and strategy alienated what had historically been the firm's target customers.

Johnson came to JCP after successful stints at Target and Apple. At Apple, he was admired for the major role he played in developing that firm's wildly successful Apple Stores, which a number of analysts say brought about "a new world order in retailing." It was Johnson's ability to establish what some viewed as path-breaking visions and to develop innovations to reach them that appealed to JCP's board when he was hired.

Comparing JCP to the Titanic, Johnson came to the CEO position believing that innovation was the key to

shaking up the firm. Moreover, he reminded analysts, employees, and others that he came to JCP to "transform" the firm, not to marginally improve its performance. Describing what he intended to do at JCP, Johnson said that "in the U.S., the department store has a chance to regain its status as the leader in style, the leader in excitement. It will be a period of true innovation for this company."

The essence of Johnson's vision for JCP was twofold. First, he eliminated the firm's practice of marking up prices on goods and then offering discounts, heavy promotions, and coupons to entice its bargain-hunting target customers. Instead, Johnson introduced a three-tiered pricing structure that focused on what were labelled "everyday low prices." To customers though, the pricing structure was confusing and failed to convince them that the "everyday low prices" were actually "low enough" compared to competitors' prices.

Innovation was at the core of the second part of the new CEO's vision, with one objective being to give JCP a more youthful image. The innovations Johnson implemented to create this image included establishing branded boutiques within JCP stores. To do this, JCP set up branded boutiques "along a wide aisle, or 'street' dotted with places to sit, grab a cup of coffee, or play with Lego blocks." With an initial intention of having 100 branded shops within JCP stores by 2015, Johnson asked people "to envision an entire store of shops with a street and square in the middle representing a new way to interface with the customer." Disney was one of the brands to be included as a shopping destination, as were Caribou Coffee, Dallas-based Paciugo Gelato & Café, and Giggle, a store dedicated to making "it a whole lot easier to become a parent" by offering innovative and stylish "must-have baby items." In addition, and as noted in Chapter 4's Opening Case, Levi's, IZOD, Liz Claiborne, and Martha Stewart branded items were to be included as part of the boutiques.

But, these innovations and the strategy used to exploit them did not work. So what went wrong? Considering the components of the model shown in Figure 13.2 yields a framework to answer this question. While it is true that Johnson had an entrepreneurial mind-set, cross-functional teams were not used to facilitate implementation of the desired innovations such as the boutique stores. In essence, it seems that Johnson himself, without the involvement of others throughout the firm, was instrumental in deciding that the boutiques were to be used as well as how they were to be established and operated within selected JCP stores. In addition, the values associated with efforts to change JCP from its historic roots of being a general merchant in the space between department stores and discounters to becoming a firm with a young, hip image were not shared among the firm's stakeholders. Finally, Johnson's work as an entrepreneurial leader was, seemingly, not as effective as should have been the case. Because of mistakes such as these, the level of success desired at JCP through internally developed innovations was not attained.

Sources: 2013, J.C. Penney ousts CEO Ron Johnson, *Wall Street Journal*, www.wsj.com, April 8; D. Benoit, 2013, J.C. Penney asks customers for second chance, *Wall Street Journal*, www.wsj.com, May 1; D. Benoit, 2013, Ackman thought Johnson could turn around 'Titanic' JCPenney, *Wall Street Journal*, www.wsj.com, April 8; S. Gerfield, 2013, J.C. Penney rehires Myron Ullman to clean up Ron Johnson's mess, *Bloomberg Businessweek*, www.businessweek.com, April 11; S. Clifford, 2013, J.C. Penney's new plan is to reuse its old plans, *New York Times*, www.nytimes.com, May 16; S. Denning, 2013, J.C. Penney: Was Ron Johnson's strategy wrong? *Forbes*, www.forbes.com, April 9; M. Halkias, 2012, J.C. Penney's Ron Johnson shows off his vision of future to 300 analysts, *Dallas News*, www.dallasnews.com, September 19.

Case Discussion Questions

1. The new CEO tried to be innovative. Were the innovations introduced, more incremental or more novel? Please explain.

2. Do the innovations implemented by JCP sound interesting to you? Would you shop at a store with these features? Why or why not?

3. What are the reasons that the innovations implemented by the new CEO failed?

4. What recommendations do you have for turning around the performance of JCP?

NOTES

1. B. Fritz, 2015, Disney unveils details on 'Star Wars: VIII' and 'Frozen' Sequel, *Wall Street Journal*, www.wsj.com, March 12; M. Lev-Ram, 2015, Empire of Tech, *Fortune*, January 1, 48–56.

2. B. Yu, S. Hao, D. Ahlstrom, S. Si, & D Liang, 2014, Entrepreneurial firms' network competence, technological capability, and new product development performance, *Asia Pacific journal of Management*, 31: 687–704; A. Lipparini, G. Lorenzoni, & S. Ferriani, 2014, From core to periphery and back: A study on the deliberate shaping of knowledge flows in interfirm dyads and networks, *Strategic Management Journal*, 35: 578–595.

3. L. Dai, V. Maksimov, B. A. Gilbert, & S. A. Fernhaber, 2014, Entrepreneurial orientation, and international scope: The differential roles of innovativeness, proactiveness and risk taking, *Journal of Business Venturing*, 29: 511–524; P. C. Patel, S. A. Fernhaber, P. P. McDougall-Covin, & R. P. van der Have, 2014, Beating competitors to international markets: The value of geographically balanced networks for innovation, *Strategic Management Journal*, 35: 691–711.

4. M. Gruber, S. M. Kim, & J. Brinckmann, 2015, What is an attractive business opportunity? An empirical study of opportunity evaluation decisions of technologists, managers and entrepreneurs, *Strategic Entrepreneurship Journal*, in press.

5. M. Wright, B. Clarysse, & S. Mosey, 2012, Strategic entrepreneurship, resource orchestration and growing spin-offs from universities, *Technology Analysis & Strategic Management*, 24: 911–927.

6. T. Felin, S. Kauffman, R. Koppl, & G. Longo, 2014, Economic opportunity and evolution: Beyond landscapes and bounded rationality, *Strategic Entrepreneurship Journal*, 8: 269–282; M. A. Hitt, R. D. Ireland, D. G. Sirmon, & C. A. Trahms, 2011, Strategic entrepreneurship: Creating value for individuals, organizations, and society. *Academy of Management Perspectives*, 25: 57–75.

7. H. Yang, Y. Zheng, & X. Zhao, 2014, Exploration or exploitation? Small firms' alliance strategies with large firms, *Strategic Management Journal*, 35: 146–157; J. Q. Barden, 2012, The influences of being acquired on subsidiary innovation adoption, *Strategic Management Journal*, 33: 1269–1285.

8. D. Kuratko, 2015, Corporate entrepreneurship: Accelerating creativity and innovation in organizations, in C. Shalley, M. A. Hitt, & J. Zhou (eds.), *The Oxford Handbook of Creativity, Innovation and Entrepreneurship*, NY: Oxford University Press, 477–488; D. F. Kuratko & D. B. Audretsch, 2013, Clarifying the domains of corporate entrepreneurship, *International Entrepreneurship and Management Journal*, 9: 323–335; K. Shimizu, 2012, Risks of corporate entrepreneurship: Autonomy and agency issues, *Organization Science*, 23: 194–206.

9. S. L. Sun, X. Yang, & W. Li, 2014, Variance-enhancing corporate entrepreneurship under deregulation: an option portfolio approach, *Asia Pacific Journal of Management*, 31: 733–761; D. Urbano & A. Turro, 2013, Conditioning factors for corporate entrepreneurship: An in(ex)ternal approach, *International Entrepreneurship and Management Journal*, 9: 379–396.

10. V. Hinz & S. Ingerfurth, 2013, Does ownership matter under challenging conditions? *Public Management Review*, 15: 969–991.

11. M. Keyhani, M. Levesque, & A. Madhok, 2015, Toward a theory of entrepreneurial rents: A simulation of the market process, *Strategic Management Journal*, 36: 76–96; P. M. Moroz & K. Hindle, 2012, Entrepreneurship as a process: Toward harmonizing multiple perspectives, *Entrepreneurship Theory and Practice*, 36: 781–818.

12. J. T. Perry, G. N. Chandler, & G. Markova, 2012, Entrepreneurial effectuation: A review and suggestions for future research, *Entrepreneurship Theory and Practice*, 36: 837–861; S. A. Alvarez & J. B. Barney, 2008, Opportunities, organizations and entrepreneurship, *Strategic Entrepreneurship Journal*, 2: 265–267.

13. N. J. Foss, J. Lyngsie, & S. A. Zahra, 2013, The role of external knowledge sources and organizational design in the process of opportunity exploitation, *Strategic Management Journal*, 34: 1453–1471; P. G. Klein, 2008, Opportunity discovery, entrepreneurial action and economic organization, *Strategic Entrepreneurship Journal*, 2: 175–190.

14. D. A. Shepherd, T. A. Williams, & H. Patselt, 2015, Thinking about entrepreneurial decision making: Review and research agenda, *Journal of Management*, 41: 11–46; J. Tang, K. M. Kacmar, & L. Busenitz, 2012, Entrepreneurial alertness in the pursuit of new opportunities, *Journal of Business Venturing*, 27: 77–94; S. A. Zahra, 2008, The virtuous cycle of discovery and creation of entrepreneurial opportunities, *Strategic Entrepreneurship Journal*, 2: 243–257.

15. J. Schumpeter, 1934, *The Theory of Economic Development*, Cambridge, MA: Harvard University Press.

16. E. E. Powell & T. Baker, 2014, It's what you make of it: Founder identity and enacting strategic responses to adversity, *Academy of Management Journal*, 57: 1406–1433; C. A. Siren, M. Kohtamaki, & A. Kuckertz, 2012, Exploration and exploitation strategies, profit performance, and the mediating role of strategic learning: Escaping the exploitation trap, *Strategic Entrepreneurship Journal*, 6: 18–41; J. H. Dyer, H. B. Gregersen, & C. Christensen, 2008, Entrepreneur behaviors and the origins of innovative ventures, *Strategic Entrepreneurship Journal*, 2: 317–338.

17. C. Bjornskov & N. Foss, 2013, How strategic entrepreneurship and the institutional context drive economic growth, *Strategic Entrepreneurship Journal*, 7: 50–69; W. J. Baumol, R. E. Litan, & C. J. Schramm, 2007, *Good Capitalism, Bad Capitalism, and the Economics of Growth and Prosperity*, New Haven, CT: Yale University Press.

18. Schumpeter, *The Theory of Economic Development*.

19. L. Aarikka-Stenroos & B. Sandberg, 2012, From new-product development to commercialization through networks, *Journal of Business Research*, 65: 198–206.

20. M. I. Leone & T. Reichstein, 2012, Licensing-in fosters rapid invention! The effect of the grant-back clause and technological unfamiliarity, *Strategic Management Journal*, 33: 965–985; R. A. Burgelman & L. R. Sayles, 1986, *Inside Corporate Innovation: Strategy, Structure, and Managerial Skills*, NY: Free Press.

21. K. R. Fabrizio & L. G. Thomas, 2012, The impact of local demand on innovation in a global industry, *Strategic Management Journal*, 33: 42–64; M. W. Johnson, 2011, Making innovation matter. *Bloomberg Businessweek*, www.businessweek.com, March 3.

22. R. Aalbers & W. Dolfsma, 2014, Innovation despite reorganization, *Journal of Business Strategy*, 35(3): 18–25; S. F. Latham & M. Braun, 2009, Managerial risk, innovation and organizational decline, *Journal of Management*, 35: 258–281.

23. L. Marengo, C. Pasquali, M. Valente, & G. Dosi, 2012, Appropriability, patents, and rates of innovation in complex products industries, *Economics of Innovation and New Technology*, 21: 753–773; S. Moon, 2011, How does the management of research impact the disclosure of knowledge? Evidence from scientific publications and patenting behavior, *Economics of Innovation & New Technology*, 20: 1–32.

24. M. Ridley, 2013, A welcome turn away from patents, *Wall Street Journal*, www.wsj.com, June 21.

25. P. F. Drucker, 1998, The discipline of innovation, *Harvard Business Review*, 76(6): 149–157.

26. Ibid.

27. C. B. Dobni, M. Klassen, & T. Nelson, 2015, Innovation strategy in the U.S.: Top executives share their views, *Journal of Business Strategy*, 36(1): 3–13; B. R. Bhardwaj, Sushil, & K. Momaya, 2011, Drivers and enablers of corporate entrepreneurship: Case of a software giant from India, *Journal of Management Development*, 30: 187–205.

28. J. Brinckmann & S. M. Kim, 2015, Why we plan: The impact of nascent entrepreneurs' cognitive characteristics and human capital on business planning, *Strategic Entrepreneurship Journal*, in press; Y. Yanadori & V. Cui, 2013, Creating incentives for innovation? The relationship between pay dispersion in R&D groups and firm innovation performance, *Strategic Management Journal*, 34: 1502–1511.

29. C. Shalley, M. A. Hitt, & J. Zhou, 2015, Introduction: Integrating creativity, innovation, and entrepreneurship to enhance the organizations capability to navigate in the new competitive landscape, in C. Shalley, M. A. Hitt, & J. Zhou (eds.), *The Oxford Handbook of Creativity, innovation and Entrepreneurship*, NY: Oxford University Press, 1–14; J. Lampel, P. P. Jha, & A. Bhalla, 2012, Test-driving the future: How design competitions are changing innovation, *Academy of Management Perspectives*, 26: 71–85.

30. J. Raffiee & J. Feng, 2014, Should I quit my day job?: A hybrid path to entrepreneurship, *Academy of Management Journal*, 57: 936–963; D. Ucbasaran, P. Westhead, M. Wright, & M. Flores, 2010, The nature of entrepreneurial experience, business failure and comparative optimism, *Journal of Business Venturing*, 25: 541–555; K. M. Hmielski & R. A. Baron, 2009, Entrepreneurs' optimism and new venture performance: A social cognitive perspective, *Academy of Management Journal*, 52: 473–488.

31. Y. Yamakawa, M. W. Peng, & D. L. Deeds, 2015, Rising from the ashes: Cognitive determinants of venture growth after entrepreneurial failure, *Entrepreneurship Theory and Practice*, 39: 209–236; M.-D. Foo, 2011, Emotions and entrepreneurial opportunity evaluation, *Entrepreneurship: Theory & Practice*, 35: 375–393; M. S. Cardon, J. Wincent, J. Singh, & M. Drovsek, 2009, The nature and experience of entrepreneurial passion, *Academy of Management Review*, 34: 511–532.

32. C. Schlaegel & M. Koenig, 2014, Determinants of entrepreneurial intent: A meta-analytic test and integration of competing models, *Entrepreneurship Theory and Practice*, 38: 291–332; M. McCaffrey, 2014, On the theory of entrepreneurial incentives and alertness, *Entrepreneurship Theory and Practice*, 38: 891–911; M. S. Wood, A. McKelvie, & J. M. Haynie, 2014, Making it personal: Opportunity individuation and the shaping of opportunity beliefs, *Journal of Business Venturing*, 29: 252–272.

33. Y. Bammens & V. Collewaert, 2014, Trust between entrepreneurs and angel investors: Exploring the positive and negative implications for venture performance assessments, *Journal of Management*, 40: 1980–2008; S. W. Smith & S. K. Shah, 2013, Do innovative users generate more useful insights? An analysis of corporate venture capital investments in the medical device industry, *Strategic Entrepreneurship Journal*, 7: 151–167; W. Stam, S. Arzlanian, & T. Elfring, 2014, Social capital of entrepreneurs and small firm performance: A meta-analysis of contextual and methodological moderators, *Journal of Business Venturing*, 29: 152–173.

34. T. Prive, 2013, Top 32 quotes every entrepreneur should live by, *Forbes*, www.forbes.com, May 2.

35. J. G. Covin & D. Miller, 2014, International entrepreneurial orientation: Conceptual considerations, research themes, measurement issues, and future research directions, *Entrepreneurship Theory and Practice*, 38: 11–44.

36. J. York, S. Sarasvathy, & A. Wicks, 2013, An entrepreneurial perspective on value creation in public-private ventures, *Academy of Management Review*, 28: 307–309; A. Chwolka & M. G. Raith, 2012, The value of business planning before start-up—A decision-theoretical perspective, *Journal of Business Venturing*, 27: 385–399.

37. W. Drechsler & M. Natter, 2012, Understanding a firm's openness decisions in innovation, *Journal of Business Research*, 65: 438–445; W. Tsai, 2001, Knowledge transfer in intraorganizational networks: Effects of network position and absorptive capacity on business unit innovation and performance, *Academy of Management Journal*, 44: 996–1004.

38. S. Artinger & T. C. Powell, 2015, Entrepreneurial failure: Statistical and psychological explanations, *Strategic Management Journal*, in press; M. Spraggon & V. Bodolica, 2012, A multidimensional taxonomy of intra-firm knowledge transfer processes, *Journal of Business Research*, 65: 1273–1282; S. A. Zahra & G. George, 2002, Absorptive capacity: A review, reconceptualization, and extension, *Academy of Management Review*, 27:185–203.

39. G. Cassar, 2014, Industry and startup experience on entrepreneur forecast performance in new firms, *Journal of Business Venturing*, 29: 137–151.

40. 2015, The world's 50 most innovative companies, *Fast Company*, March, 67–134.

41. M. Chafkin, 2015, #1—Warby Parker, *Fast Company*, March, 68–71.

42. S. Terjesen, J. Hessels, & D. Li, 2015, Comparative international entrepreneurship: A review and research agenda, *Journal of Management*, in press; P. McDougall-Covin, M. V. Jones, & M. G. Serapio, 2014, High-potential concepts, phenomena, and theories for the advancement of international entrepreneurship research, *Entrepreneurship Theory and Practice*, 38: 1–10.

43. A. Al-Aali & D. J. Teece, 2014, International entrepreneurship and the theory of the (long-lived) international firm: A capabilities perspective, *Entrepreneurship Theory and Practice*, 38: 95–116; A. N. Kiss, W. M. Davis, & S. T. Cavusgil, 2012, International entrepreneurship research in emerging economies: A critical review and research agenda, *Journal of Business Venturing*, 27: 266–290.

44. H. Berry, 2014, Global integration and innovation: Multicountry knowledge generation within MNCs, *Strategic Management Journal*, 35: 869–890.

45. L. Sleuwaegen & J. Onkelinx, 2014, International commitment, post-entry growth and survival of international new ventures, *Journal of Business Venturing*, 29: 106–120; P. Almodovar & A. M. Rugman, 2014, The M curve and the performance of Spanish international new ventures, *British Journal of Management*, 25: S6–S23.

46. K. D. Brouthers, G. Nakos, & P. Dimitratos, 2015, SME entrepreneurial orientation, international performance and the moderating role of strategic alliances, *Entrepreneurship Theory and Practice*, in press; T. A. Khoury, A. Cuervo-Cazurra, & L. A. Dau, 2014, Institutional outsiders and insiders: The response of foreign and domestic inventors to the quality of intellectual property rights protection, *Global Strategy Journal*, 4: 200–220; P. Stenholm, Z. J. Acs, & R. Wuebker, 2013, Exploring country-level institutional arrangements on the rate and type of entrepreneurial activity, *Journal of Business Venturing*, 28: 176–193.

47. 2014, New report ranks world's most entrepreneurial countries, Oracle Capital Group, orcap.co.uk, June 23.

48. W. Q. Judge, Y. Liu-Thompkins, J. L. Brown, & C. Pongpatipat, 2015, The impact of home country institutions on corporate technological entrepreneurship via R&D investments and virtual world presence, *Entrepreneurship Theory and Practice*, 39: 237–266; E. Autio, S. Pathak, & K. Wennberg, 2013, Consequences of cultural practices for entrepreneurial behaviors, *Journal of International Business Studies*, 44: 334–362; U. Stephan & L. M. Uhlaner,

2010, Performance-based vs. socially supportive culture: A cross-cultural study of descriptive norms and entrepreneurship, *Journal of International Business Studies*, 41: 1347–1364.

49. J.-F. Hennart, 2014, The accidental internationalists: A theory of born globals, *Entrepreneurship Theory and Practice*, 38: 117–135; T. K. Madsen, 2013, Early and rapidly internationalizing ventures: Similarities and differences between classifications based on the original international new venture and born global literatures, *Journal of International Entrepreneurship*, 11: 65–79.

50. S. T. Cavusgil & G. Knight, 2015, The born global firm: An entrepreneurial and capabilities perspective on early and rapid internationalization, *Journal of International Business Studies*, 46: 3–16; S. A. Fernhaber & D. Li, 2013, International exposure through network relationships: Implications for new venture internationalization, *Journal of Business Venturing*, 28: 316–334; S. A. Zahra, R. D. Ireland, & M. A. Hitt, 2000, International expansion by new venture firms: International diversity, mode of market entry, technological learning and performance, *Academy of Management Journal*, 43: 925–950.

51. M. Musteen, D. K. Datta, & M. M. Butts, 2014, Do international networks and foreign market knowledge facilitate SME internationalization? Evidence from the Czech Republic, *Entrepreneurship Theory and Practice*, 38: 749–774; G. Nakos, K. D. Brouthers, & P. Dimitratos, 2014, International alliances with competitors and non-competitors: The disparate impact on SME international performance, *Strategic Entrepreneurship Journal*, 8: 167–182.

52. D. J. McCarthy, S. M. Puffer, & S. V. Darda, 2010, Convergence in entrepreneurial leadership style: Evidence from Russia, *California Management Review*, 52(4): 48–72; H. U. Lee & J. H. Park, 2008, The influence of top management team international exposure on international alliance formation, *Journal of Management Studies*, 45: 961–981; H. G. Barkema & O. Chvyrkov, 2007, Does top management team diversity promote or hamper foreign expansion? *Strategic Management Journal*, 28: 663–680.

53. R. Belderbos, B. Lokshin, & B. Sadowski, 2015, The returns to foreign R&D, *Journal of International Business Studies*, 46: 491–504; S. Awate, M. M. Larsen, & R. Mudambi, 2015, Accessing vs sourcing knowledge: A comparative study of R&D internationalization between emerging and advanced economy firms, *Journal of International Business Studies*, 46: 63–86.

54. K. Grigoriou & F. T. Rothaermel, 2014, Structural microfoundations of innovation: The role of relational stars, *Journal of Management*, 40: 586–615; A. Teixeira & N. Fortuna, 2010, Human capital, R&D, trade, and long-run productivity: Testing

the technological absorption hypothesis for the Portuguese economy, 1960–2001, *Research Policy*, 39: 335–350.

55. R. J. Genry & W. Shen, 2013, The impacts of performance relative to analyst forecasts and analyst coverage on firm R&D intensity, *Strategic Management Journal*, 34: 121–130; L. A. Bettencourt & S. L. Bettencourt, 2011, Innovating on the cheap, *Harvard Business Review*, 89(6): 88–94.

56. A. K. Chatterji & K. R. Fabrizio, 2014, Using users: When does external knowledge enhance corporate product innovation? *Strategic Management Journal*, 35: 1427–1445.

57. R. Funk, 2014, Making the most of where you are: Geography, networks, and innovation in organizations, *Academy of Management Journal*, 57: 193–222; M. Sytch & A. Tatarynowicz, 2014, Exploring the locus of innovation: The dynamics of network communities and firms' invention productivity, *Academy of Management Journal*, 57: 249–279.

58. E. Operti & G. Carnabuci, 2014, Public knowledge, private gain: The effect of spillover networks on firms' innovation performance, *Journal of Management*, 40: 1042–1074.

59. J. Morgan, 2015, Five examples of companies with internal innovation programs, *Huffington Post*, www.huffingtonpost.com, April 9.

60. R. Mudambi & T. Swift, 2014, Knowing when to leap: Transitioning between exploitative and explorative R&D, *Strategic Management Journal*, 35: 126–145; P. Ritala & P. Hurmelinna-Laukkanen, 2013, Incremental and radical innovation in coopetition—The role of absorptive capacity and appropriability, *Journal of Product Innovation Management*, 30: 154–169; C. B. Bingham & J. P. Davis, 2012, Learning sequences: Their existence, effect, and evolution, *Academy of Management Journal*, 55: 611–641.

61. S. Roy & K. Sivakumar, 2012, Global outsourcing relationships and innovation: A conceptual framework and research propositions, *Journal of Product and Innovation Management*, 29: 513–530.

62. S. W. Smith, 2014, Follow me to the innovation frontier? Leaders, laggards and the differential effects of imports and exports on technological innovation, *Journal of International Business Studies*, 45: 248–274.

63. D. McKendrick & J. Wade, 2010, Frequent incremental change, organizational size, and mortality in high-technology competition, *Industrial and Corporate Change*, 19: 613–639.

64. N. Argyres, L. Bigelow, & J. A. Nickerson, 2015, Dominant designs, innovation shocks and the follower's dilemma, *Strategic Management Journal*, 36: 216–234.

65. B. R. Fitzgerald, 2015, Google taking its self-driving cars to the open road, *Wall Street Journal, www.wsj.com*, May 15.

66. T. Magnusson & C. Berggren, 2011, Entering an era of ferment—radical vs incrementalist strategies in automotive power train development, *Technology Analysis & Strategic Management*, 23: 313–330; 2005, Getting an edge on innovation, *BusinessWeek*, March 21, 124.

67. R. Roy & M. B. Sarkar, 2015, Knowledge, firm boundaries, and innovation: Mitigating the incumbent's curse during radical technological change, *Strategic Management Journal*, in press; B. Buisson & P. Silberzahn, 2010, Blue Ocean or fast-second innovation? A four-breakthrough model to explain successful market domination, *International Journal of Innovation Management*, 14: 359–378.

68. R. K. Mitchell, J. B. Smith, J. A. Stamp, & J. Carlson, 2015, Organizing creativity: Lessons from the *Eureka! Ranch* experience, in C. Shalley, M. A. Hitt, & J. Zhou (eds.), *The Oxford Handbook of Creativity, Innovation and Entrepreneurship*, NY: Oxford University Press, 301–337; Z. Lindgardt & B. Shaffer, 2012, Business model innovation in social-sector organizations, *bcg.perspectives*, bcgperspectives.com, November 7.

69. 2013, The power of imagination, *Wall Street Journal*, www.wsj.com, February 25.

70. S. Harvey, 2014, Creative synthesis: Exploring the process of extraordinary group creativity, *Academy of Management Review*, 39: 324–343; D. Lavie & I. Drori, 2012, Collaborating for knowledge creation and application: The case of nanotechnology research programs, *Organization Science*, 23: 704–724.

71. A. K. Chatterji & K. Fabrizio, 2012, How do product users influence corporate invention? *Organization Science*, 23: 971–987.

72. Kuratko, Corporate entrepreneurship; N. R. Furr, F. Cavarretta, & S. Garg, 2012, Who changes course? The role of domain knowledge and novel framing in making technology changes, *Strategic Entrepreneurship Journal*, 6: 236–256; J. M. Oldroyd & R. Gulati, 2010, A learning perspective on intraorganizational knowledge spill-ins, *Strategic Entrepreneurship Journal*, 4: 356–372.

73. M. L. Sosa, 2013, Decoupling market incumbency from organizational prehistory: Locating the real sources of competitive advantage in R&D for radical innovation, *Strategic Management Journal*, 34: 245–255; S. A. Hill, M. V. J. Maula, J. M. Birkinshaw, & G. C. Murray, 2009, Transferability of the venture capital model to the corporate context: Implications for the performance of corporate venture units, *Strategic Entrepreneurship Journal*, 3: 3–27.

74. J. Brady, 2013, Some companies foster creativity, others fake it, *Wall Street Journal*, www.wsj.com, May 21.

75. B. Wu, Z. Wan, & D. A. Levinthal, 2014, Complementary assets as pipes and prisms: Innovation incentives and trajectory choices, *Strategic Management Journal*, 35: 1257–1278; A. Sahaym, H. K. Steensma, & J. Q. Barden, 2010, The influence of R&D investment on the use of corporate venture capital: An industry-level analysis, *Journal of Business Venturing*, 25: 376–388; R. A. Burgelman, 1995, *Strategic Management of Technology and Innovation*, Boston, MA: Irwin.

76. D. Kandemir & N. Acur, 2012, Examining proactive strategic decision-making flexibility in new product development, *Journal of Product Innovation Management*, 29: 608–622.

77. K. B. Kahn, G. Barczak, J. Nicholas, A. Ledwith, & H. Perks, 2012, An examination of new product development best practice, *Journal of Product Innovation Management*, 29: 180–192.

78. S. S. Durmusoglu, 2013, Merits of task advice during new product development: Network centrality antecedents and new product outcomes of knowledge richness and knowledge quality, *Journal of Product Innovation Management*, 30: 487–499; D. Kelley & H. Lee, 2010, Managing innovation champions: The impact of project characteristics on the direct manager role, *Journal of Product Innovation Management*, 27: 1007–1019.

79. N. Kim, S. Im, & S. F. Slater, 2013, Impact of knowledge type and strategic orientation on new product creativity and advantage in high-technology firms, *Journal of Product Innovation Management*, 30: 136–153; U. de Brentani & S. E. Reid, 2012, The fuzzy front-end of discontinuous innovation: Insights for research and management, *Journal of Product Innovation Management*, 29: 70–87.

80. L. Mirabeau & S. Maguire, 2014, From autonomous strategic behavior to emergent strategy, *Strategic Management Journal*, 35: 1202–1229.

81. N. Anderson, K. Potocnik, & J. Zhou, 2014, Innovation and creativity in organizations: A state-of-the-science review, prospective commentary and guiding framework, *Journal of Management*, 40: 1297–1333; S. Im, M. M. Montoya, & J. P. Workman, Jr., 2013, Antecedents and consequences of creativity in product innovation teams, *Journal of Product Innovation Management*, 30: 170–185; S. Borjesson & M. Elmquist, 2012, Aiming at innovation: A case study of innovation capabilities in the Swedish defence industry, *International Journal of Business Innovation and Research*, 6: 188–201.

82. S. E. Ante, 2013, IBM's chief to employees: Think fast, move faster, *Wall Street Journal*, www.wsj.com, April 24.

83. A. Caldart, R. S. Vassolo, & L. Silvestri, 2014, Induced variation in administrative systems: Experimenting with contexts for innovation, *Management Research*, 12: 123–151.

84. S. B. Choi & C. Williams, 2014, The impact of innovation intensity, scope, and spillovers on sales growth in Chinese firms, *Asia Pacific Journal of Management*, 31: 25–46.

85. P. T. Gianidodis, J. E. Ettlie, & J. J. Urbana, 2014, Open service innovation in the global banking industry: Inside-out versus outside-in strategies, *Academy of Management Perspectives*, 28: 76–91.

86. A. Compagni, V. Mele, & D. Ravasi, 2015, How early implementations influence later adoptions of innovation: Social positioning and skill reproduction in the diffusion of robotic surgery, *Academy of Management Journal*, 58: 242–278; T. Vanacker, S. Manigart, & M. Meuleman, 2014, Path-dependent evolution versus intentional management of investment ties in science-based entrepreneurial firms, *Entrepreneurship Theory and Practice*, 38: 671–690.

87. J. Jia, G. Wang, X. Zhao, & X. Yu, 2014, Exploring the relationship between entrepreneurial orientation and corporate performance: The role of competency of executives in entrepreneurial-oriented corporations, *Nankai, Business Review*, 5: 326–344.

88. T. Kollmann & C. Stockmann, 2014, Filling the entrepreneurial orientation—performance gap: The mediating effects of exploratory and exploitative innovations, *Entrepreneurship Theory and Practice*, 38: 1001–1026.

89. P. Patanakul, J. Chen, & G. S. Lynn, 2012, Autonomous teams and new product development, *Journal of Product Innovation Management*, 29: 734–750.

90. S. Kuester, C. Homburg, & S. C. Hess, 2012, Externally directed and internally directed market launch management: The role of organizational factors in influencing new product success, *Journal of Product Innovation Management*, 29: 38–52.

91. G. Barcjak & K. B. Kah, 2012, Identifying new product development best practice, *Business Horizons*, 56: 291–305; C. Nakata & S. Im, 2010, Spurring cross-functional integration for higher new product performance: A group effectiveness perspective, *Journal of Product Innovation Management*, 27: 554–571.

92. J. P. Eggers, 2012, All experience is not created equal: Learning, adapting, and focusing in product portfolio management, *Strategic Management Journal*, 33: 315–335; R. Slotegraaf & K. Atuahene-Gima, 2011, Product development team stability and new product advantage: The role of decision-making processes, *Journal of Marketing*, 75: 96–108; R. Cowan & N. Jonard, 2009, Knowledge portfolios and the organization of innovation networks, *Academy of Management Review*, 34: 320–342.

93. P. R. Kehoe & D. Tzabbar, 2015, Lighting the way or stealing the shine? An examination of the duality in star scientists' effects on firm innovation performance, *Strategic Management Journal*, 36: 709–727.

94. M. Brettel, F. Heinemann, A. Engelen, & S. Neubauer, 2011, Cross-functional integration of R&D, marketing, and manufacturing in radical and incremental product innovations and its effects on project effectiveness and efficiency, *Journal of Product Innovation Management*, 28: 251–269.

95. D. De Clercq, N. Thongpapanl, & D. Dimov, 2013, Getting more from cross-functional fairness and product innovativeness: Contingency effects of internal resource and conflict management, *Journal of Product Innovation Management*, 30: 56–69; G. Gemser & M. M. Leenders, 2011, Managing cross-functional cooperation for new product development success, *Long Range Planning*, 44: 26–41.

96. F. Aime, S. Humphrey, D. DeRue, & J. Paul, 2014, The riddle of heterarchy: Power transitions in cross-functional teams, *Academy of Management Journal*, 57: 327–352

97. E. L. Anthony, S. G. Green, & S. A. McComb, 2014, Crossing functions above the cross-functional project team: The value of lateral coordination among functional department heads, *Journal of Engineering and Technology Management*, 31: 141–158; V. V. Baunsgaard & S. Clegg, 2013, 'Walls or boxes': The effects of professional identity, power and rationality on strategies for cross-functional integration, *Organization Studies*, 34: 1299–1325.

98. M. Baer, K. T. Dirks, & J. A. Nickerson, 2013, Microfoundations of strategic problem formulation, *Strategic Management Journal*, 34: 197–214; R. Oliva & N. Watson, 2011, Cross-functional alignment in supply chain planning: A case study of sales and operations planning, *Journal of Operations Management*, 29: 434–448; A. C. Amason, 1996, Distinguishing effects of functional and dysfunctional conflict on strategic decision making: Resolving a paradox for top management teams, *Academy of Management Journal*, 39: 123–148.

99. T. A. De Vries, F. Walter, G. S. van der Vegt, & P. J. M. D. Essens, 2014, Antecedents of individuals' inter-team coordination: Broad functional experiences as a mixed blessing, *Academy of Management Journal*, 57: 1334–1359; H. K. Gardner, 2012, Performance pressure as a double-edged sword: Enhancing team motivation while undermining the use of team knowledge, *Administrative Science Quarterly*, 57: 1–46; D. Clercq, B. Menguc, & S. Auh, 2009, Unpacking the relationship between an innovation strategy and firm performance: The role of task conflict and political activity, *Journal of Business Research*, 62: 1046–1053;.

100. V. Gupta & S. Singh, 2015, Leadership and creative performance behaviors in R&D laboratories: Examining the mediating role of justice perceptions, *Journal of Leadership and Organizational Studies*, 22: 21–36; Y. Chung & S. E. Jackson, 2013, The internal and external networks of knowledge-intensive teams: The role of task routineness, *Journal of Management*, 39: 442–468; J. Daspit, C. J. Tillman, N. G. Boyd, & V. McKee, 2013, Cross-functional team effectiveness: An examination of internal team environment, shared leadership, and cohesion influences, *Team Performance Management*, 19: 34–56.

101. W. Sun, A. Su, & Y. Shang, 2014, Transformational leadership, team climate, and team performance within the NPD team: Evidence from China, *Asia Pacific Journal of Management*, 31: 127–147; H. K. Gardner, F. Gino, & B. R. Staats, 2012, Dynamically integrating knowledge in teams: Transforming resources into performance, *Academy of Management Journal*, 55: 998–1022.

102. Q. Li, P. Maggitti, K. Smith, P. Tesluk, & R. Katila, 2013, Top management attention to innovation: The role of search selection and intensity in new product introductions, *Academy of Management Journal*, 56: 893–916; N. Stieglitz & L. Heine, 2007, Innovations and the role of complementarities in a strategic theory of the firm, *Strategic Management Journal*, 28: 1–15.

103. V. Gaba & S. Bhattacharya, 2012, Aspirations, innovation, and corporate venture capital: A behavioral perspective, *Strategic Entrepreneurship Journal*, 6: 178–199; K. Wennberg, J. Wiklund, D. R. DeTienne, & M. S. Cardon, 2010, Reconceptualizing entrepreneurial exit: Divergent exit routes and their drivers, *Journal of Business Venturing*, 25: 361–375.

104. U. Stettner & D. Lavie, 2014, Ambidexterity under scrutiny: Exploration and exploitation via internal organization, alliances and acquisitions, *Strategic Management Journal*, 35:1903–1929; H. Milanov & S. A. Fernhaber, 2014, When do domestic alliances help ventures abroad? Direct and moderating effects from a learning experience, *Journal of Business Venturing*, 29: 377–391; S. Terjesen, P. C. Patel, & J. G. Covin, 2011, Alliance diversity, environmental context and the value of manufacturing capabilities among new high technology ventures, *Journal of Operations Management*, 29: 105–115.

105. H. Kim, N. K. Park, & J. Lee, 2014, How does the second-order learning process moderate the relationship between innovation inputs and outputs of large Korean firms? *Asia Pacific Journal of Management*, 31: 69–103; S. Zu, F. Wu, & E. Cavusgil, 2013, Complements or substitutes? Internal technological strength, competitors alliance participation, and innovation development, *Journal of Product Innovation Management*, 30: 750–762.

106. J. West & M. Bogers, 2014, Leveraging external sources of innovation: A review of research on open innovation, *Journal of Product Innovation Management*, 31: 814–831; D. Li, 2013, Multilateral R&D alliances by new ventures, *Journal of Business Venturing*,

28: 241–260; D. Li, L. Eden, M. A. Hitt, & R. D. Ireland, 2008, Friends, acquaintances, or strangers? Partner selection in R&D alliances, *Academy of Management Journal*, 51: 315–334.

107. C. Shu, C. Liu, S. Gao, & M. Shanley, 2014, The knowledge spillover theory of entrepreneurship in alliances, *Entrepreneurship Theory and Practice*, 38: 913–940; C. Beckman, K. Eisenhardt, S. Kotha, A. Meyer, & N. Rajagopalan, 2012, Technology entrepreneurship, *Strategic Entrepreneurship Journal*, 6: 89–93.

108. Yang, Zheng & Zhao, Exploration or exploitation?; G. Dushnitsky & D. Lavie, 2010, How alliance formation shapes corporate venture capital investment in the software industry: A resource-based perspective, *Strategic Entrepreneurship Journal*, 4: 22–48.

109. G. Oates, 2014, Marriott wants Moxy to deliver the millennial customer with help from Ikea, *Skift*, skift.com, February 3; A. Berzon & K. Hudson, 2013, IKEA's parent plans a hotel brand, *Wall Street Journal*, www.wsj.com, March 5.

110. H. Van Kranenburg, J. Hagedoorn, & S. Lorenz-Orlean, 2014, *Global Strategy Journal*, 4: 280–291; X. Jiang, M. Li, S. Gao, Y. Bao, & F. Jiang, 2013, Managing knowledge leakage in strategic alliances: The effects of trust and formal contracts, *Industrial Marketing Management*, 42: 983–991; A. Kaul, 2013, Entrepreneurial action, unique assets, and appropriation risk: Firms as a means of appropriating profit from capability creation, *Organization Science*, 24: 1765–1781.

111. J. Partanen, S. K. Chetty, & A. Rajala, 2014, Innovation types and network relationships, *Entrepreneurship Theory and Practice*, 38: 1027–1055; G. Cuevas-Rodriguez, C. Cabello-Medina, & A. Carmona-Lavado, 2014, Internal and external social capital for radical product innovation: Do they always work well together? *British Journal of Management*, 25: 266–284; M. A. Hitt, M. T. Dacin, E. Levitas, J. L. Arregle, & A. Borza, 2000, Partner selection in emerging and developed market contexts: Resource-based and organizational learning perspectives, *Academy of Management Journal*, 43: 449–467.

112. B. B. Tyler & T. Caner, 2015, New product introductions below aspirations, slack and R&D alliances: A behavioral perspective, *Strategic Management Journal*, in press; R. Vandaie & A. Zaheer, 2014, Surviving bear hugs: Firm capability, large partner alliances, and growth, *Strategic Management Journal*, 35: 566–577.

113. J. Sears & G. Hoetker, 2014, Technological overlap, technological capabilities and resource recombinations by technological acquisitions, *Strategic Management Journal*, 35: 48–67; A. Madhok & M. Keyhani, 2012, Acquisitions as entrepreneurship: Asymmetries, opportunities, and the internationalization of multinationals

from emerging economies, *Global Strategy Journal*, 2: 26–40;

114. M. A. Hitt, D. King, H. Krishnan, M. Makri, M. Schijven, K. Shimizu, & H. Zhu, 2009, Mergers and acquisitions: Overcoming pitfalls, building synergy and creating value, *Business Horizons*, 52: 523–529; H. G. Barkema & M. Schijven, 2008, Toward unlocking the full potential of acquisitions: The role of organizational restructuring, *Academy of Management Journal*, 51: 696–722.

115. I. Mochari, 2014, Gaming DIY: How Minecraft became an innovation powerhouse, *Inc.*, www.inc.com, September 2.

116. C. Grimpe & K. Hussinger, 2014, Resource complementarity and value capture in firm acquisitions: The role of intellectual property rights, *Strategic Management Journal*, 35: 1762–1780; M. Humphrey-Jenner, 2014, Takeover defenses, innovation, and value creation: Evidence from acquisition decisions, *Strategic Management Journal*, 35: 668–690; M. Makri, M. A. Hitt, & P. J. Lane, 2010, Complementary technologies, knowledge relatedness, and invention outcomes in high technology M&As, *Strategic Management Journal*, 31: 602–628.

117. R. Lungeanu, I. Sgtern, & E. J. Zajac, 2015, When do firms change technology-sourcing vehicles? The role of poor innovative performance and financial slack, *Strategic Management Journal*, in press.

118. M. Wagner, 2013, Determinants of acquisition value: The role of target and acquirer characteristics, *International Journal of Technology Management*, 62: 56–74; M. E. Graebner, K. M. Eisenhardt, & P. T. Roundy, 2010, Success and failure in technology acquisitions: Lessons for buyers and sellers, *Academy of Management Perspectives*, 24: 73–92; M. A. Hitt, J. S. Harrison, & R. D. Ireland, 2001, *Mergers and Acquisitions: A Guide to Creating Value for Stakeholders*, NY: Oxford University Press.

119. A. Arora, S. Belenzon, & L. A. Rios, 2014, Make, buy, organize: The interplay between research, external knowledge and firm structure, *Strategic Management Journal*, 35: 317–337.

120. S. K. Majumdar, R. Moussawi, & U. Yaylacicegi, 2014, Do incumbents' mergers influence entrepreneurial entry? An evaluation, *Entrepreneurship Theory and Practice*, 38: 601–633.

121. R. Fini, R. Grimaldi, G. L. Marzocchi, & M. Sobrero, 2012, The determinants of corporate entrepreneurial intention within small and newly established firms, *Entrepreneurship Theory and Practice*, 36: 387–414; D. Elfenbein & B. Hamilton, 2010, The small firm effect and the entrepreneurial spawning of scientists and engineers, *Management Science*, 56: 659–681.

122. A. Hyytinen, M. Pajarinen, & P. Rouvinen, 2014, Does innovativeness reduce startup survival rates?, *Journal of Business Venturing*, 29: 564–581.

123. J. Ostrower, 2015, At Boeing, innovation means small steps, not giant leaps, *Wall Street Journal*, www.wsj.com, April 2.

124. B. Larraneta, S. A. Zahra, & J. L. G. Gonzalez, 2012, Enriching strategic variety in new ventures through external knowledge, *Journal of Business Venturing*, 27: 401–413; H. Greve, 2011, Positional rigidity: Low performance and resource acquisition in large and small firms, *Strategic Management Journal*, 32: 103–114.

125. L. Naldi & P. Davidsson, 2014, Entrepreneurial growth: The role of international knowledge acquisition as moderated by firm age, *Journal of Business Venturing*, 29: 687–703.

126. R, Klingbiel & C. Rammer, 2014, Resource allocation strategy for innovation portfolio management, *Strategic Management Journal*, 35: 246–268; G. Wu, 2012, The effect of going public on innovative productivity and exploratory search, *Organization Science*, 23: 928–950; D. G. Sirmon & M. A. Hitt, 2009, Contingencies within dynamic managerial capabilities: Interdependent effects of resource investment and deployment on firm performance, *Strategic Management Journal*, 30: 1375–1394.

127. R. B. Tucker, 2013, Are chief innovation officers delivering results? *Innovation Excellence*, www.innovationexcellence.com, March 22.

128. J. Behrens & H. Patzelt, 2015, Corporate entrepreneurship managers' project terminations: Integrating portfolio-level, individual-level and firm-level effects, *Entrepreneurship Theory and Practice*, in press; Y. Yang, V. K. Narayanan, & D. M. De Carolis, 2014, The relationship between portfolio diversification and firm value: The evidence from corporate venture capital activity, *Strategic Management Journal*, 35: 1993–2011.

129. J. P. Eggers, 2014, Competing technologies and industry evolution: The benefits of making mistakes in the flat panel display industry, *Strategic Management Journal*, 35: 159–178.

130. H. R. Greve & M.-D. Seidel, 2015, The thin red line between success and failure: Path dependence in the diffusion of innovative production technologies, *Strategic Management Journal*, 36: 475–496.

131. J. Ostrower, 2015, With jet, Honda enters new realm, *Wall Street Journal*, www.wsj. com, May 17.

132. P. Coy, 2015, What's in the innovation sandwich? *Bloomberg BusinessWeek*, January 19, 49–51.

Preparing an Effective Case Analysis

Preparing an Effective Case Analysis

What to Expect from In-Class Case Discussions

As you will learn, classroom discussions of cases differ significantly from lectures. The case method calls for your instructor to guide the discussion and to solicit alternative views as a way of encouraging your active participation when analyzing a case. When alternative views are not forthcoming, your instructor might take a position just to challenge you and your peers to respond thoughtfully as a way of generating still additional alternatives. Often, instructors will evaluate your work in terms of both the quantity and the quality of your contributions to in-class case discussions. The in-class discussions are important in that you can derive significant benefit by having your ideas and recommendations examined against those of your peers and by responding to thoughtful challenges by other class members and/or the instructor.

During case discussions, your instructor will likely listen, question, and probe to extend the analysis of case issues. In the course of these actions, your peers and/or your instructor may challenge an individual's views and the validity of alternative perspectives that have been expressed. These challenges are offered in a constructive manner; their intent is to help all parties involved with analyzing a case develop their analytical and communication skills. Developing these skills is important in that they will serve you well when working for all types of organizations. Commonly, instructors will encourage you and your peers to be innovative and original when developing and presenting ideas. Over the course of an individual discussion, you are likely to form a more complex view of the case as a result of listening to and thinking about the diverse inputs offered by your peers and instructor. Among other benefits, experience with multiple case discussions will increase your knowledge of the advantages and disadvantages of group decision-making processes.

Both your peers and instructor will value comments that contribute to identifying problems as well as solutions to them. To offer relevant contributions, you are encouraged to think independently and, through discussions with your peers outside of class, to refine your thinking. We also encourage you to avoid using "I think," "I believe," and "I feel" to discuss your inputs to a case analysis process. Instead, consider using a less emotion laden phrase, such as "My analysis shows…." This highlights the logical nature of the approach you have taken to analyze a case. When preparing for an in-class case discussion, you should plan to use the case data to explain your assessment of the situation. Assume that your peers and instructor are familiar with the basic facts included in the case. In addition, it is good practice to prepare notes regarding your analysis of case facts before class discussions and use them when explaining your perspectives. Effective notes signal to classmates and the instructor that you are prepared to engage in a thorough discussion of a case. Moreover, comprehensive and detailed notes eliminate the need for you to memorize the facts and figures needed to successfully discuss a case.

The case analysis process described above will help prepare you effectively to discuss a case during class meetings. Using this process results in consideration of the issues required to identify a focal firm's problems and to propose strategic actions through which the firm can increase the probability it will outperform its rivals. In some instances, your instructor may ask you to prepare either an oral or a written analysis of a particular case. Typically, such an assignment demands even more thorough study and analysis of the case contents. At your instructor's discretion, oral and written analyses may be completed by individuals or by groups of three or more people. The information and insights gained by completing the six steps shown in Table 1 often are of value when developing an oral or a written analysis. However, when preparing an oral or written presentation, you must consider the overall framework in which your information and inputs will be presented. Such a framework is the focus of the next section.

Preparing an Oral/Written Case Presentation

Experience shows that two types of thinking (analysis and synthesis) are necessary to develop an effective oral or written presentation (see Exhibit 1). In the analysis stage, you should first analyze the general external environmental issues affecting the firm. Next, your environmental analysis should focus on the particular industry (or industries, in the case of a diversified company) in which a firm operates. Finally, you should examine companies against which the focal firm competes. By studying the three levels of the external environment (general, industry, and competitor), you will be able to identify a firm's opportunities and threats. Following the external environmental analysis is the analysis of the firm's internal organization. This analysis provides the insights needed to identify the firm's strengths and weaknesses.

Table 1 An Effective Case Analysis Process

Step 1: Gaining Familiarity	a. In general—determine who, what, how, where, and when (the critical facts of the case). b. In detail—identify the places, persons, activities, and contexts of the situation. c. Recognize the degree of certainty/uncertainty of acquired information.
Step 2: Recognizing Symptoms	a. List all indicators (including stated "problems") that something is not as expected or as desired. b. Ensure that symptoms are not assumed to be the problem (symptoms should lead to identification of the problem).
Step 3: Identifying Goals	a. Identify critical statements by major parties (for example, people, groups, the work unit, and so on). b. List all goals of the major parties that exist or can be reasonably inferred.
Step 4: Conducting the Analysis	a. Decide which ideas, models, and theories seem useful. b. Apply these conceptual tools to the situation. c. As new information is revealed, cycle back to substeps a and b.
Step 5: Making the Diagnosis	a. Identify predicaments (goal inconsistencies). b. Identify problems (discrepancies between goals and performance). c. Prioritize predicaments/problems regarding timing, importance, and so on.
Step 6: Doing the Action Planning	a. Specify and prioritize the criteria used to choose action alternatives. b. Discover or invent feasible action alternatives. c. Examine the probable consequences of action alternatives. d. Select a course of action. e. Design an implementation plan/schedule. f. Create a plan for assessing the action to be implemented.

Source: C. C. Lundberg and C. Enz, 1993, A framework for student case preparation, *Case Research Journal*, 13 (Summer): 144, NACRA, North American Case Research Association.

As noted in Exhibit 1, you must then change the focus from analysis to synthesis. Specifically, you must synthesize information gained from your analysis of the firm's external environment and internal organization. Synthesizing information allows you to generate alternatives that can resolve the significant problems or challenges facing the focal firm. Once you identify a best alternative, from an evaluation based on predetermined criteria and goals, you must explore implementation actions.

In Table 2, we outline the sections that should be included in either an oral or a written presentation: strategic profile and case analysis purpose, situation analysis, statements of strengths/weaknesses and opportunities/threats, strategy formulation, and strategy implementation. These sections are described in the following discussion. Familiarity with the contents of your book's thirteen chapters is helpful because the general outline for an oral or a written presentation shown in Table 2 is based on an understanding of the strategic management process detailed in those chapters. We follow the discussions of the parts of Table 2 with a few comments about the "process" to use to present the results of your case analysis in either a written or oral format.

Strategic Profile and Case Analysis Purpose

You will use the strategic profile to briefly present the critical facts from the case that have affected the focal firm's historical strategic direction and performance. The case facts should not be restated in the profile; rather, these comments should show how the critical facts lead to a particular focus for your analysis. This primary focus should be emphasized in this section's conclusion. In addition, this section should state important assumptions about case facts on which your analyses are based.

Situation Analysis

As shown in Table 2, a general starting place for completing a situation analysis is the general environment.

General Environmental Analysis. Your analysis of the general environment should focus on trends in the seven segments of the general environment (see Table 3). Many of the segment issues shown in Table 3 for the seven segments are explained more fully in Chapter 2 of your book. The objective you should have in evaluating these trends is to be able to *predict* the segments that you expect

Exhibit 1 Types of Thinking in Case Preparation: Analysis and Synthesis

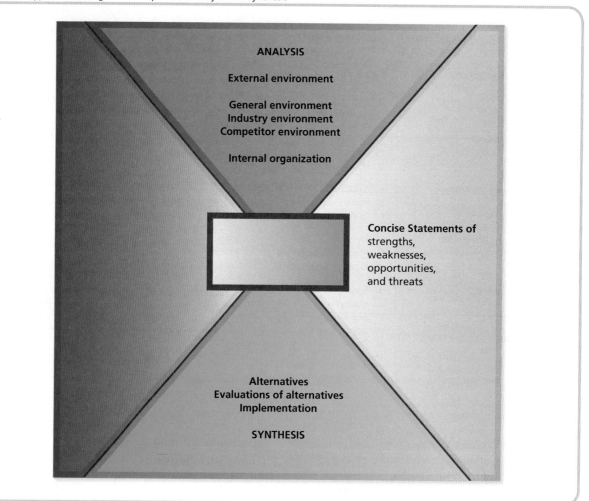

to have the most significant influence on your focal firm over the next several years (say three to five years) and to explain your reasoning for your predictions.

Industry Analysis. Porter's five force model is a useful tool for analyzing the industry (or industries) in which your firm competes. We explain how to use this tool in Chapter 2. In this part of your analysis, you want to determine the attractiveness of an industry (or a segment of an industry) in which your firm is competing. As attractiveness increases, so does the possibility your firm will be able to earn profits by using its chosen strategies. After evaluating the power of the five forces relative to your firm, you should make a judgment as to *how* attractive the industry is in which your firm is competing.

Table 2 General Outline for an Oral or Written Presentation

 I. Strategic Profile and Case Analysis Purpose
 II. Situation Analysis
    A. General environmental analysis
    B. Industry analysis
    C. Competitor analysis
    D. Internal analysis
 III. Identification of Environmental Opportunities and Threats and Firm Strengths and Weaknesses (SWOT Analysis)
 IV. Strategy Formulation
    A. Strategic alternatives
    B. Alternative evaluation
    C. Alternative choice
 v. Strategic Alternative Implementation
    A. Action items
    B. Action plan

Table 3 Sample General Environmental Categories

Technological Trends
- Information technology continues to become cheaper with more practical applications
- Database technology enables organization of complex data and distribution of information
- Telecommunications technology and networks increasingly provide fast transmission of all sources of data, including voice, written communications, and video information
- Computerized design and manufacturing technologies continue to facilitate quality and flexibility

Demographic Trends
- Regional changes in population due to migration
- Changing ethnic composition of the population
- Aging of the population
- Aging of the "baby boom" generation

Economic Trends
- Interest rates
- Inflation rates
- Savings rates
- Exchange rates
- Trade deficits
- Budget deficits

Political/Legal Trends
- Antitrust enforcement
- Tax policy changes
- Environmental protection laws
- Extent of regulation/deregulation
- Privatizing state monopolies
- State-owned industries

Sociocultural Trends
- Women in the workforce
- Awareness of health and fitness issues
- Concern for overcoming poverty
- Concern for customers

Global Trends
- Currency exchange rates
- Free-trade agreements
- Trade deficits

Physical Environment Trends
- Environmental sustainability
- Corporate social responsibility
- Renewable energy
- Goals of zero waste
- Ecosystem impact of food and energy production

Competitor Analysis. Firms also need to *analyze* each of their primary competitors. This analysis should identify competitors' current strategies, strategic intent, strategic mission, capabilities, core competencies, and a competitive response profile (see Chapter 2). This information is useful to the focal firm in formulating an appropriate strategy and in predicting competitors' probable responses. Sources that can be used to gather information about an industry and companies with whom the focal firm competes are listed in Appendix I. Included in this list is a wide range of publications, such as periodicals, newspapers, bibliographies, directories of companies, industry ratios, forecasts, rankings/ratings, and other valuable statistics.

Internal Analysis. Assessing a firm's strengths and weaknesses through a value chain analysis facilitates moving from the external environment to the internal organization. Analysis of the value chain activities and the support functions of the value chain provides opportunities to understand how external environmental trends affect the specific activities of a firm. Such analysis helps highlight strengths and weaknesses (see Chapter 3 for an explanation and use of the value chain).

For purposes of preparing an oral or a written presentation, it is important to note that strengths are internal resources and capabilities that have the potential to be core competencies. Weaknesses, on the other hand, are internal resources and capabilities that have the potential to place a firm at a competitive disadvantage relative to its rivals. Thus, some of a firm's resources and capabilities are strengths; others are weaknesses.

When evaluating the internal characteristics of the firm, your analysis of the functional activities emphasized is critical. For instance, if the strategy of the firm is primarily technology driven, it is important to evaluate the firm's R&D activities. If the strategy is market driven, marketing functional activities are of paramount importance. If a firm has financial difficulties, critical financial ratios would require careful evaluation. In fact, because of the importance of financial health, most cases require financial analyses. Appendix II lists and operationally defines several common financial ratios. Included are tables describing profitability, liquidity, leverage, activity, and shareholders' return ratios. Leadership, organizational culture, structure, and control systems are other characteristics of firms you should examine to fully understand the "internal" part of your firm.

Identification of Environmental Opportunities and Threats and Firm Strengths and Weaknesses (SWOT Analysis)

The outcome of the situation analysis is the identification of a firm's strengths and weaknesses and its environmental threats and opportunities. The next step requires that you *analyze* the strengths and weaknesses and the opportunities and threats for configurations that benefit or do not benefit your firm's efforts to perform well. Case analysts and organizational strategists as well seek to match a firm's strengths with its opportunities. In addition, strengths are chosen to prevent any serious environmental threat from negatively affecting the firm's performance. The key objective of conducting a SWOT analysis is to determine how to position the firm so it can take advantage of opportunities, while simultaneously avoiding or minimizing environmental threats. Results from a SWOT analysis yield valuable insights into the selection of a firm's strategies. The analysis of a case should not be overemphasized relative to the synthesis of results gained from your analytical efforts. There may be a temptation to spend most of your oral or written case analysis on results from the analysis. It is important, however, that you make an equal effort to develop and evaluate alternatives and to design implementation of the chosen strategy.

Strategy Formulation—Strategic Alternatives, Alternative Evaluation, and Alternative Choice

Developing alternatives is often one of the most difficult steps in preparing an oral or a written presentation. Developing three to four alternative strategies is common (see Chapter 4 for business-level strategy alternatives and Chapter 6 for corporate-level strategy alternatives). Each alternative should be feasible (i.e., it should match the firm's strengths, capabilities, and especially core competencies), and feasibility should be demonstrated. In addition, you should show how each alternative takes advantage of the environmental opportunity or avoids/buffers against environmental threats. Developing carefully thought out alternatives requires synthesis of your analyses' results and creates greater credibility in oral and written case presentations.

Once you develop strong alternatives, you must evaluate the set to choose the best one. Your choice should be defensible and provide benefits over the other alternatives. Thus, it is important that both alternative development and the evaluation of alternatives be thorough. The choice of the best alternative should be explained and defended.

Strategic Alternative Implementation-Action Items and Action Plan

After selecting the most appropriate strategy (that is, the strategy with the highest probability of helping your firm in its efforts to earn profits), implementation issues require attention. Effective synthesis is important to ensure that you have considered and evaluated all critical implementation issues. Issues you might consider include the structural changes necessary to implement the new strategy. In addition, leadership changes and new controls or incentives may be necessary to implement strategic actions. The implementation actions you recommend should be explicit and thoroughly explained. Occasionally, careful evaluation of implementation actions may show the strategy to be less favorable than you thought originally. A strategy is only as good as the firm's ability to implement it.

Process Issues

You should ensure that your presentation (either oral or written) has logical consistency throughout. For example, if your presentation identifies one purpose, but your analysis focuses on issues that differ from the stated purpose, the logical inconsistency will be apparent. Likewise, your alternatives should flow from the configuration of strengths, weaknesses, opportunities, and threats you identified by analyzing your firm's external environment and internal organization.

Thoroughness and clarity also are critical to an effective presentation. Thoroughness is represented by the comprehensiveness of the analysis and alternative generation. Furthermore, clarity in the results of the analyses, selection of the best alternative strategy, and design of implementation actions are important. For example, your statement of the strengths and weaknesses should flow clearly and logically from your analysis of your firm's internal organization.

Presentations (oral or written) that show logical consistency, thoroughness, and clarity of purpose, effective analyses, and feasible recommendations (strategy and implementation) are more effective and are likely to be more positively received by your instructor and peers. Furthermore, developing the skills necessary to make such presentations will enhance your future job performance and career success.

Appendix I Sources for Industry and Competitor Analyses

Abstracts and Indexes	
Periodicals	ABI/*Inform*
	Business Periodicals Index
	InfoTrac Custom Journals
	InfoTrac Custom Newspapers
	InfoTrac OneFile
	EBSCO Business Source Premiere
	Lexis/Nexis Academic
	Public Affairs Information Service Bulletin (PAIS)
	Reader's Guide to Periodical Literature
Newspapers	*NewsBank—Foreign Broadcast Information*
	NewsBank-Global NewsBank
	New York Times Index
	Wall Street Journal Index
	Wall Street Journal/Barron's Index
	Washington Post Index
Bibliographies	*Encyclopedia of Business Information Sources*
Directories	
Companies—General	*America's Corporate Families and International Affiliates*
	Hoover's Online: The Business Network www.hoovers.com/free
	D&B Million Dollar Directory (databases: http://www.dnbmdd.com)
	Standard & Poor's Corporation Records
	Standard & Poor's Register of Corporations, Directors, and Executives
	(http://www.netadvantage.standardandpoors.com for all of *Standard & Poor's*)
	Ward's Business Directory of Largest U.S. Companies
Companies—International	*America's Corporate Families and International Affiliates*
	Business Asia
	Business China
	Business Eastern Europe
	Business Europe
	Business International
	Business International Money Report
	Business Latin America

(Continued)

Appendix I (Continued) Sources for Industry and Competitor Analyses

Abstracts and Indexes	
	Directory of American Firms Operating in Foreign Countries
	Directory of Foreign Firms Operating in the United States
	Hoover's Handbook of World Business
	International Directory of Company Histories
	Mergent's International Manual
	Mergent Online (http://www.fisonline.com—for "Business and Financial Information Connection to the World")
	Who Owns Whom
Companies—Manufacturers	*Thomas Register of American Manufacturers*
	U.S. Office of Management and Budget, Executive Office of the President, *Standard Industrial Classification Manual*
	U.S. Manufacturer's Directory, Manufacturing & Distribution, USA
Companies—Private	*D&B Million Dollar Directory*
	Ward's Business Directory of Largest U.S. Companies
Companies—Public	Annual Reports and 10-K Reports
	Disclosure (corporate reports) *Q-File*
	Securities and Exchange Commission Filings & Forms (EDGAR) http://www.sec.gov/edgar.shtml
	Mergent's Manuals:
	▪ *Mergent's Bank and Finance Manual*
	▪ *Mergent's Industrial Manual*
	▪ *Mergent's International Manual*
	▪ *Mergent's Municipal and Government Manual*
	▪ *Mergent's OTC Industrial Manual*
	▪ *Mergent's OTC Unlisted Manual*
	▪ *Mergent's Public Utility Manual*
	▪ *Mergent's Transportation Manual*
	Standard & Poor's Corporation, *Standard Corporation Descriptions:* http://www.netadvantage.standardandpoors.com
	▪ *Standard & Poor's Analyst Handbook*
	▪ *Standard & Poor's Industry Surveys*
	▪ *Standard & Poor's Statistical Service*
Companies—Subsidiaries and Affiliates	*America's Corporate Families and International Affiliates*
	Ward's Directory
	Who Owns Whom
	Mergent's Industry Review
	Standard & Poor's Analyst's Handbook
	Standard & Poor's Industry Surveys (2 volumes)
	U.S. Department of Commerce, *U.S. Industrial Outlook*
Industry Ratios	Dun & Bradstreet, *Industry Norms and Key Business Ratios*
	RMA's Annual Statement Studies
	Troy Almanac of Business and Industrial Financial Ratios
Industry Forecasts	International Trade Administration, *U.S. Industry & Trade Outlook*
Rankings & Ratings	Annual Report on American Industry in *Forbes Business Rankings Annual*
	Mergent's Industry Review http://www.worldcatlibraries.org
	Standard & Poor's Industry Report Service http://www.netadvantage.standardandpoors.com
	Value Line Investment Survey
	Ward's Business Directory of Largest U.S. Companies
Statistics	*American Statistics Index (ASI)* Bureau of the Census, U.S. Department of Commerce, *Economic Census Publications*
	Bureau of the Census, U.S. Department of Commerce, *Statistical Abstract of the United States*
	Bureau of Economic Analysis, U.S. Department of Commerce, *Survey of Current Business*
	Internal Revenue Service, U.S. Treasury Department, *Statistics of Income: Corporation Income Tax Returns*
	Statistical Reference Index (SRI)

Appendix II Financial Analysis in Case Studies

Table A-1 Profitability Ratios

Ratio	Formula	What It Shows
1. Return on total assets	$\dfrac{\text{Profits after taxes}}{\text{Total assets}}$ or $\dfrac{\text{Profits after taxes} + \text{Interest}}{\text{Total assets}}$	The net return on total investments of the firm or The return on both creditors' and shareholders' investments
2. Return on stockholders' equity (or return on net worth)	$\dfrac{\text{Profits after taxes}}{\text{Total stockholders' equity}}$	How profitably the company is utilizing shareholders' funds
3. Return on common equity	$\dfrac{\text{Profits after taxes} - \text{Preferred stock dividends}}{\text{Total stockholders' equity} - \text{Par value of preferred stock}}$	The net return to common stockholders
4. Operating profit margin (or return on sales)	$\dfrac{\text{Profits before taxes and before interest}}{\text{Sales}}$	The firm's profitability from regular operations
5. Net profit margin (or net return on sales)	$\dfrac{\text{Profits after taxes}}{\text{Sales}}$	The firm's net profit as a percentage of total sales

Table A-2 Liquidity Ratios

Ratio	Formula	What It Shows
1. Current ratio	$\dfrac{\text{Current assets}}{\text{Current liabilities}}$	The firm's ability to meet its current financial liabilities
2. Quick ratio (or acid-test ratio)	$\dfrac{\text{Current assets} - \text{Inventory}}{\text{Current liabilities}}$	The firm's ability to pay off short-term obligations without relying on sales of inventory
3. Inventory to net working capital	$\dfrac{\text{Inventory}}{\text{Current assets} - \text{Current liabilities}}$	The extent to which the firm's working capital is tied up in inventory

Table A-3 Leverage Ratios

Ratio	Formula	What It Shows
1. Debt-to-assets	$\dfrac{\text{Total debt}}{\text{Total assets}}$	Total borrowed funds as a percentage of total assets
2. Debt-to-equity	$\dfrac{\text{Total debt}}{\text{Total shareholders' equity}}$	Borrowed funds versus the funds provided by shareholders
3. Long-term debt-to-equity	$\dfrac{\text{Long-term debt}}{\text{Total shareholders' equity}}$	Leverage used by the firm
4. Times-interest-earned (or coverage ratio)	$\dfrac{\text{Profits before interest and taxes}}{\text{Total interest charges}}$	The firm's ability to meet all interest payments
5. Fixed charge coverage	$\dfrac{\text{Profits before taxes and interest} + \text{Lease obligations}}{\text{Total interest charges} + \text{Lease obligations}}$	The firm's ability to meet all fixed-charge obligations including lease payments

Table A-4 Activity Ratios

Ratio	Formula	What It Shows
1. Inventory turnover	$$\frac{Sales}{Inventory\ of\ finished\ goods}$$	The effectiveness of the firm in employing inventory
2. Fixed-assets turnover	$$\frac{Sales}{Fixed\ assets}$$	The effectiveness of the firm in utilizing plant and equipment
3. Total assets turnover	$$\frac{Sales}{Total\ assets}$$	The effectiveness of the firm in utilizing total assets
4. Accounts receivable turnover	$$\frac{Annual\ credit\ sales}{Accounts\ receivable}$$	How many times the total receivables have been collected during the accounting period
5. Average collecting period	$$\frac{Accounts\ receivable}{Average\ daily\ sales}$$	The average length of time the firm waits to collect payment after sales

Table A-5 Shareholders' Return Ratios

Ratio	Formula	What It Shows
1. Dividend yield on common stock	$$\frac{Annual\ dividend\ per\ share}{Current\ market\ price\ per\ share}$$	A measure of return to common stockholders in the form of dividends
2. Price-earnings ratio	$$\frac{Current\ market\ price\ per\ share}{After\text{-}tax\ earnings\ per\ share}$$	An indication of market perception of the firm; usually, the faster-growing or less risky firms tend to have higher PE ratios than the slower-growing or more risky firms
3. Dividend payout ratio	$$\frac{Annual\ dividends\ per\ share}{After\text{-}tax\ earnings\ per\ share}$$	An indication of dividends paid out as a percentage of profits
4. Cash flow per share	$$\frac{After\text{-}tax\ profits + Depreciation}{Number\ of\ common\ shares\ outstanding}$$	A measure of total cash per share available for use by the firm

NAME INDEX

COMPANY INDEX

SUBJECT INDEX